Matthew Feldman

POLITICS, INTELLECTUALS, AND FAITH
Essays by Matthew Feldman

Edited and with an introduction by Archie Henderson

Matthew Feldman

POLITICS, INTELLECTUALS, AND FAITH

Essays by Matthew Feldman

Edited and with an introduction by Archie Henderson

Bibliografische Information der Deutschen Nationalbibliothek
Die Deutsche Nationalbibliothek verzeichnet diese Publikation in der Deutschen Nationalbibliografie; detaillierte bibliografische Daten sind im Internet über http://dnb.d-nb.de abrufbar.

Bibliographic information published by the Deutsche Nationalbibliothek
Die Deutsche Nationalbibliothek lists this publication in the Deutsche Nationalbibliografie; detailed bibliographic data are available in the Internet at http://dnb.d-nb.de.

ISBN-13: 978-3-8382-0986-9
© *ibidem*-Verlag, Stuttgart 2020
Alle Rechte vorbehalten

Das Werk einschließlich aller seiner Teile ist urheberrechtlich geschützt. Jede Verwertung außerhalb der engen Grenzen des Urheberrechtsgesetzes ist ohne Zustimmung des Verlages unzulässig und strafbar. Dies gilt insbesondere für Vervielfältigungen, Übersetzungen, Mikroverfilmungen und elektronische Speicherformen sowie die Einspeicherung und Verarbeitung in elektronischen Systemen.

All rights reserved. No part of this publication may be reproduced, stored in or introduced into a retrieval system, or transmitted, in any form, or by any means (electronical, mechanical, photocopying, recording or otherwise) without the prior written permission of the publisher. Any person who does any unauthorized act in relation to this publication may be liable to criminal prosecution and civil claims for damages.

Printed in the EU

Table of Contents

Acknowledgements 7

Introduction 9

Part 1: Ezra Pound, Modernist and Fascist

1. An Ideologue's Journey: Ezra Pound from Tradition in Italian Fascism to the Postwar Fascist Tradition 25

2. The 'Pound Case' in Historical Perspective: An Archival Overview 39

3. Ezra Pound and Ernst Kantorowicz: From Medieval to Modern Autocracies 55

4. Make it Crude: Ezra Pound's Antisemitic Propaganda for the BUF and PNF 73

5. Reappraising the 'Pound Case', 1940–45 93

6. Ezra Pound's Political Faith from First to Second Generation; or, "It is 1956 Fascism" 111

7. 'Penny-wise…': Ezra Pound's Posthumous Legacy to Fascism 131

8. "Fascism for the Third Millennium": An Overview of Language and Ideology in Italy's CasaPound Movement 157

Part 2: War and Empire: The Fascist Way and the Liberal Way

9. The Holocaust in the NDH: Genocide between Political Religion and Religious Politics 181

10. Showing the 'Unshowable'?: A Generation of "Mainstream" Films on the Shoah 203

11. "Intellectual" Discourses on the Radical Right: From Double-Speak to Holocaust Denial 219

12. On Radical Right Mainstreaming in Europe and the US 235

13.	On 'Lone Wolf' Terrorism	257
14.	Terrorist 'Radicalising Networks': A Qualitative Case Study on Radical Right Lone-Wolf Terrorism	277
15.	Choose Definitively Between Hell and Reason	299
16.	'It became Necessary to Destroy the Town to Save it': The United States Between Liberalism and Warfare before Donald Trump	315
17.	A Failed Just War in Iraq	335

Part 3: Ends and Odds

18.	Between 'Geist' and 'Zeitgeist': Martin Heidegger as Ideologue of Metapolitical Fascism	351
19.	Hate Globally, Act Locally: A Case Study of Universal Nazism Online	381
20.	A Case Study in Soviet Political Religion: Modernism and the Construction of a Stalinist Utopia	397
21.	Samuel Beckett's Nominalist Politics and the Pitfalls of 'Presentism'	417
	Sources List	433

Acknowledgements

My thanks to Matthew Feldman for the opportunity to edit his stimulating and thoughtful collection of essays and for his timely responses to my numerous queries. I am most grateful to Valerie Lange, Jana Dävers, and Christian Schön of ***ibidem***-Verlag for their patience, dedication, and professionalism.

For Luisa

Introduction

Archie Henderson

Matthew Feldman is a noted scholar of twentieth century literature and history. His publications include three monographs and numerous volumes edited or co-edited by him. His first collection of essays was *Falsifying Beckett: Essays on Archives, Philosophy and Methodology in Beckett Studies* (Stuttgart: ***ibidem***-Verlag, 2015), containing pieces published over a dozen years. This collection, his second, covers a wider chronology and range of subject matter, but finds in its title, "Politics, Intellectuals, and Faith," a unifying theme. What is of overriding concern to Feldman in these essays, written for academic and general audiences between 2002 and 2020, is how, and why, intellectuals of the twentieth-century were drawn to extremism; how the kind of fervent devotion—akin to religious devotion—that they expressed was in fact essential in the construction of totalitarian rule; and how some legacies have influenced, above all, fascist and radical right movements to this day.

Part 1, "Ezra Pound, Modernist and Fascist," consists of a series of interrelated essays devoted to the American poet Ezra Pound (1885-1972), who was the subject of Feldman's compact monograph *Ezra Pound's Fascist Propaganda, 1935-45* (Basingstoke: Palgrave Macmillan, 2013). "Modernist" and "fascist," the two roles for which Pound is probably best known, are frequently considered to be the "two sides" of the poet, which are conveniently separated and compartmentalized in many discussions of his life and works. In this bifurcated formulation, the modernist half of the famous poet's life is the triumph, the fascist half is the tragedy. Feldman does not see it this way. For him, the two sides cannot be so neatly divided, at least during World War II. Just like a coin, one "side" cannot stand alone without the other. Feldman wants to understand how Pound's life—one of the most fascinating of the twentieth century—could have turned out the way it did. For this, he needs to ask and answer the question, "Just how deeply involved was Ezra Pound with fascism?" The question has been evaded by most (but not all) Pound scholars—presumably for fear of what would turn up by way of an answer.

Calling it "high time to start taking Ezra Pound's fascism seriously," Feldman frames his monograph's approach to Pound's last decade in Fascist Italy by arguing that "fascism's 'political faith', typically mapping onto traditional Christian practices, can be usefully understood as a defining feature of fascist ideology." In the words of historian Emilio Gentile, "the construction of a fascist religion, centred around the sacralization of the state, appears to be an attempt to evoke—in order to legitimize the fascist regime—the sacred nature of the Roman archetype as 'an expression of an ethical-religious concept, in which the essential reasons behind the state's existence and power are projected as symbols of faith.'" "It was necessary," said Mussolini (*My Autobiography*, p. 69), "to lay the foundation of a new civilization." As Gentile explains this notion, in the move away from "many centuries of decadence, the Italian people had the chance to create a new civilization; but only total subservience to the *duce*'s leadership, and belief in the fascist religion, would have given Italians the moral force necessary to rise to the challenge." Feldman sees Mussolini's foundation-laying—what Gentile terms, in an article of that title, the "Fascist anthropological revolution"—as "part of a socio-political, revolutionary attempt to overcome perceived decadence by seeking to create literally 'new men' of action and faith: warrior-priests with the will to turn myth into reality and establish a secular utopia; or in Pound's words, a 'paradiso terrestre.'" As applied to Pound—who also advocated for a "new civilization" in 1928—and in many instances before and since—this means that "Pound's veneration for Mussolini only starts to make sense, then, against the unmistakable backdrop of Fascism's 'political faith' [...] Even as an expatriate in Fascist Italy, Pound's commitment to the 'Fascist faith' was far from idiosyncratic; it was representative." Extending far beyond his delivery of antisemitic speeches over Rome Radio, Pound's transnational fascist commitments show a dimension of the poet that is not encapsulated in the standard picture of him as a hopeless idealist in wartime Italy: "For too long, Pound's fascist activism has simply been dismissed as either mad or bad, the product of political naiveté or misplaced economic idealism. Some or all of these factors may apply but, in short, this misses the wood for the trees. All too often lacking in supporting evidence, this tradition will be directly countered by the archivally driven view advanced here: Pound was a committed and significant English-language strategist and producer of fascist propaganda before, and during, Europe's most destructive war." Feldman's book stirred considerable controversy among Pound scholars, with its unflinching portrait of Pound as the committed fascist overshadowing his role as the "quintessential modernist and composer of some of the twentieth century's most admired verse."

In the eight essays that comprise Part 1, Feldman goes beyond the date range and topics covered in *Ezra Pound's Fascist Propaganda, 1935-1945* (while including one chapter from the latter). He identifies some key moments in the timeline leading to the poet's being "all in" with activism on behalf of Italian Fascism. These include, of course, his famous meeting with Mussolini in 1933, but also include his reading of a book by Kantorowicz; his print propaganda for the Italian invasion of Abyssinia in the mid-1930s and for the British Union of Fascists between 1936 and 1940, both of which coincided with and reflected his growing antisemitism; and his encounter with Hitler's *Mein Kampf* in 1942. During his postwar years of confinement at Saint Elizabeths Hospital in Washington, D.C., Pound attracted numerous neo-fascist visitors—with Eustace Mullins, John Kasper, and Matthias Koehl counted among the most notorious of them—and influenced likeminded devotees in the United Kingdom and Australia. Feldman concludes Part 1 with a look at Pound's influence on the Italian neo-Fascist group named after him.

Feldman starts off the first chapter in this volume with a striking quotation from Lawrence Rainey, who asserted in 1999 that it was "the allure, the thrill, the prospect of terror [...] that attracted Ezra Pound to Fascism," and not "the multiplicity of motives" that, as scholars have tried to argue, led Pound—and numerous other European intellectuals—"towards the totalitarian temptation." Feldman, however, rejects Rainey's notion of intellectuals as, in essence, bystanders standing agape before the spectacle of totalitarianism, seeing them instead as potentially "key cultural influencers" who were in a unique position to "lead the leaders" on matters of culture. In this connection, Pound's cultural influence has been a particular long-lasting one, extending beyond his work in Fascist Italy to the younger generation of fascists and radical right extremists who gathered around him on the grass at St Elizabeths, as well as contemporary neo-fascist groups such as CasaPound, explicitly named after the poet. In fact, Feldman focuses not on the spectacle of Fascist terror as a motivator for Pound, but on his hero worship of *Il Duce* and "key aspects of Fascism's cultural nationalism" as "essential drivers in his turn toward fascist ideology." Feldman sees Pound, though resident in Italy for nearly a decade, as having first been "radicalized" in 1932-33, followed by a second "radicalisation," or redoubling of his commitment to the Fascist cause, after another decade had elapsed (1942-43), which in turn brought him back to a reconsideration of historical figures representing older, pre-Fascist "Italian traditions to bolster his support for the wartime Axis." In December 1943, during this second radicalisation, Pound wrote a letter to regime functionary Alessandro Pavolini recommending a law mandating the showcasing of *The Protocols of the Elders by Zion*, among other books, by booksellers. Pound's rationale is as shocking today as it was when Feldman quoted it in *Ezra Pound's Fascist Propaganda, 1935-45*: "The arrest of Jews will create a wave of useless mercy; thus the need to disseminate the Protocols [of the Elders of Zion]. The intellectuals are capable of a passion more durable than the emotional, but they need to understand the reasons for a conflict." Feldman's concern is to understand how Pound's example could have helped build the foundations for the postwar "fascist traditions" that followed Mussolini; it is only through an understanding of high-profile cases such as Pound's that democratic societies can work toward their "wish to be inoculated from fascist ideology."

In the following chapter, Feldman summarizes the standard picture of Pound as a "naive modernist, swept along by the radical politics of his day," seeking through archival investigation to return the story to its "historical and political contexts." In answer to the question "Just how deeply involved was Ezra Pound with fascism?" Feldman finds that Pound was "far more of a committed political pugilist" than the standard account allows for. The FBI file on Pound suggests, for instance, even if it does not establish with certainty, that "Ezra Pound was a member of a committee in the Ministry of Popular Culture which met every morning to formulate anti-Allied propaganda and that Pound was the head of the United States Division of that committee." Those allegations remain to be investigated; in any event, the FBI file proves that Pound exchanged numerous letters with Gian Gaetano Cabella, a newspaper editor and important regime official—amongst scores of other Fascist apparatchiks—and wrote position papers on framing Axis propaganda.

In Chapter 3, Feldman argues that Pound's reading of Ernst Kantorowicz's idiosyncratic *Frederick The Second 1994-1250* in the early 1930s, probably between 1932 and 1933, may have been an essential way station for his "conversion" to Italian fascism, part of his first wave of ideological "radicalisation." His lionization of Mussolini led him to abandon his libertarian belief in the minimal state, a view which persisted until the mid-1920s at least, in favor of totalitarian government, modelled on Frederick II of Sicily, who, like Mussolini after him, attempted "to enlighten Europe both culturally and economically." Pound might have read Kantorowicz after his meeting with Mussolini in 1933, but he had certainly read Dante's *De Monarchia* beforehand. Dante's "manifesto for secular rule" can be read—and Pound probably did read it—as a justification of total rule in the Mussolinian vein. The difference between Dante's ideal ruler and Frederick II, at least as presented by Kantorowicz, is that "Dante provides the idea that the state is divinely sanctioned; Kantorowicz, by contrast, argues strenuously that the state is willed into being by the autocrat, and ordered by his temporal omniscience, which is numinous in and of itself." In Feldman's words, "Kantorowicz portrays the emperor as an artifex," making him a precursor to Mussolini, still another artifex in Pound's eyes.

The "Make it crude" of Chapter 4's title is explained by Feldman's thesis that, in delivering his propaganda broadcasts over Rome Radio, "[t]he prophet of modernism's quest to 'make it new' had descended, abruptly it seemed, into crude demagogy." Feldman goes on to explain that the "it" refers specifically to Pound's antisemitism, which turned overt around 1935, for reasons that Feldman tries to dissect. The descent into crudity spanned the years 1935-39, when he was writing propaganda for the *British-Italian Bulletin* and publications of Oswald Mosley's

British Union of Fascists (BUF). Pound's earliest antisemitic propaganda for the *British-Italian Bulletin* (1935-1936) was heavily encoded; but "by 1939, these were often less antisemitic codes than stock canards." By the period of his wartime broadcasts, Pound's antisemitic propaganda became "increasingly bound up with Pound's denunciation of usurers and conspirators." Feldman concludes that Pound's vituperative attacks on elites "got more extreme as he went along, from the 1920s to the 1930s to the 1940s." Feldman sees the poet's words delivered over the radio as "the best weapon in Pound's own armoury" to aid what the poet referred to in a letter to William Carlos Williams as "the Axis side of the line." Pound's fascist broadcasts were not delivered in a vacuum; rather, they operated as an eliminationist backdrop to the Holocaust. Close to home, "Jews trapped in the Salò Republic, like Primo Levi, were being rounded up and transported to Auschwitz-Birkenau." Feldman argues that, regardless of Pound's probable ignorance of "the greatest crime in history," "the parallel history of the Holocaust is nevertheless relevant, if only because words help to condition action; something poets appreciate far better than most."

Turning to archives at Yale's Beinecke Library, the FBI file on Pound, BBC's Written Archive Centre and The National Archives in London, in Chapter 5 Feldman draws a picture of Pound as "a committed, strategic and significant propagandist for Fascism's wartime Ministry of Popular Culture." Elaborating on his view that "Ezra Pound used his best weapons, his words, to fight the Allies as a radio propagandist for Fascist Italy," Feldman describes the poet's propaganda strategies as arguably extending beyond his self-appointed "duties as an American citizen," which Pound used to justify his broadcasts. Numbered among those strategies were "closer collaboration with Nazi Germany, especially in terms of anti-Semitic discourse; active participation in a 'New Europe'"; and Italian cultural leadership in radio, press, and music. Pound presented a "publications project" to the Ministry for Popular Culture in November 1939, and later even suggested compulsory reading for Allied prisoners of war: Volpe's *History of the Fascist Revolution*. He continued to discuss these and similar initiatives for much of the war with Camillo Pellizzi, rightly perceived by C. David Heymann to be "his tightest bond with a high-ranking Fascist official."

Chapter 6 holds that "Pound was far closer to interwar fascist theory and practice than has been previously maintained." Between 1936 and 1940, Feldman shows that Pound's chief journalistic outlet was Mosley's British Union of Fascists, to which he "contributed propaganda advice, corresponding regularly with the leadership; recommending potential authors; and subscribing to movement publications—in addition to acting as one of the leading contributors" to BUF publications. Pound's 1930s advocacy of a "United States of Europe" under fascist hegemony was nearly a generation ahead of its time; the cause was subsequently taken up by "second wave" British fascism following the war. In fact, Pound was one of the very few who supported both Mosley's "first wave" fascism for BUF as well as his post-war "second wave" fascism through the Union Movement's house journal *The European* in the 1950s.

The last two chapters on Pound address the poet's legacy among later generations of fascism. In Chapter 7, Feldman and his co-author Andrea Rinaldi argue that "Pound remains an important touchstone for different shades of extreme right thought—most notably in the US, Britain and Italy." They remind us that Pound was politically active on behalf of the fascist cause as late as 1961, or three years after his release from St. Elizabeths. In the spring of that year he attended a press conference in Rome held by Sir Oswald Mosley; on May 1, he walked in a parade sponsored by the neo-Fascist Movimento Sociale Italiano (MSI). The authors also see Pound's influence at work in contemporary neo-fascism—"Fascism of the Third Millennium"—which may be best observed in the case of the explicitly fascist movement CasaPound Italia and Britain's New Right. The influence extends from Pound's radical right circle on the grounds at St. Elizabeths and in correspondence during his residency there—a fascist echo chamber if there ever was one—to far-flung individuals and groups up to the present. The authors conclude that "activists from New Zealand to Italy, and Britain to the United States, testify to his continuing relevance in—at least—three 'faces' of the contemporary extreme right: white supremacism, neo-fascism, and New Right 'metapolitics'. In each, he is lauded as a political martyr and cultural icon."

In Chapter 8, Feldman and co-author Anna Castriota discuss the fascist movement CasaPound, which confusingly and contradictorily supports left-wing housing occupations, praises Mussolini, and names itself after an American fascist poet. The question the authors raise is: What does CasaPound see in Pound the poet that few others do, at least to the degree that justifies naming an entire group after him? Gianluca Iannone, CasaPound's founder, avers that "Ezra Pound had to suffer for his ideas"—those ideas being the views of the losing side in the Second World War: fascism and antisemitism (the latter of which, incidentally, Iannone denies on Pound's behalf and on behalf of CasaPound). Iannone's statement is another way of rendering Pound's famous line—made after his arrest, and repeatedly quoted to this day by Italian radical right or fascist figures: "If a man isn't willing to take some risk for his opinions, either his opinions are no good or he's no good." Indeed, it seems to be Pound's awareness that "words have consequences"—for both winners and losers, books are a weapon of war just as much as the rifle in the Fascist slogan "libro e moschetto"—and his willingness to speak out regardless of the cost, that inspired Iannone and CasaPound to honor the poet. Feldman and Castriota find

CasaPound's approach to social housing and poverty relief to be evidence of a "hybridization of 'neo-fascism and the third way' tradition of Italian Fascism." In this reading, it is in no way a contradiction in terms for fascists to be promoting social justice; attempts to "regenerate the 'national community' through voluntaristic social initiatives" has its roots in the Verona Manifesto of 1943.

Part 2 of this collection is entitled "War and Empire: the fascist way and the liberal way." "The fascist way" speaks for itself; yet Feldman also asks, is liberal democracy much better? Can there be liberalism without war? Can human rights be anything other than empty words? With its wholesale plundering of the earth, has liberalism helped to hasten the moment of eschatological collapse? These are profoundly disturbing questions that need to be asked, especially as we ask ourselves what kind of a world we want to see after the ongoing Coronavirus pandemic has run its course. Chapter 9 begins with an excerpt by a Holocaust survivor named Duro Schwartz, an improbable survivor of a Ustaša-run extermination centre—the only death camp run independently from Nazi Germany. The collective horrors of the camp would seem enough to bring on the day of judgment; and this was but one camp. Feldman calls wartime Croatia a "genocidal hybrid between crucifix and dagger." Wartime Catholicism has been subjected to vicious revisionist and often politically-charged attacks for its alleged complicity in Croatian brutality in particular and in the European genocide in general. Rejecting the most extreme of these attacks, Feldman points to the Vatican's wartime interventions on behalf of Jews. As to the Ustaša regime, Feldman sees wartime Croatia as a fascist state with a political religion directed to sacralizing the nation—not the God of the Catholic Church—while instrumentalizing Catholicism for its own ends. It was not Catholicism per se that "may be regarded as a fellow-traveler of fascism," but radical right "political Catholicism," the movement that arose in reaction to the perceived decadence of modernity in the early decades of the twentieth century. Yet this does not absolve the many Catholic perpetrators, whether in the Independent State of Croatia (NDN), or beyond it: "Clearly scores of Catholics, within and outside the Church alike, behaved devilishly."

Chapter 10 then takes up the question of the possibility or appropriateness of commercial films on the Holocaust. Could, for example, the harrowing memoir by Duro Schwartz, described in the previous chapter, be given its due in such a film, or filmed at all? Feldman examines how a "diverse range of international films have navigated this 'showing the unshowable' of the Shoah." The films he surveys keep their cinematic distance (in time or space or by the use of black humour or untranslated dialogue) from the worst of the horrors, tending "to circumvent, avoid and perhaps minimise those un-representable realities comprising the Final Solution." In the surveyed "mainstream" Holocaust films—*Schindler's List* (1993), *Life is Beautiful* [*La Vita è bella*] (1999), *Jakob the Liar* (1999), *The Pianist* (2003), and *Black Book* [*Zwartboek*] (2006)—the most graphic violence remains off-stage for the most part, and the stories they tell move towards the "trope of Hollywood-style positive endings," which, however, tend to be muted or ambiguous. Feldman finds that "for all of its seeming faults of sentimentality and representational evasion, this genre of Shoah film has been remarkably successful."

In Chapter 11, Feldman explores the use of "fifth column discourse" by postwar radical right groups, by means of which an attack on liberal democracy is waged from within a country through carefully chosen, sanitized rhetoric and institutional self-censorship. The latter, self-censorship, is required because of mainstream rejection and discrediting of fascist and antisemitic rhetoric in the wake of World War II. Not only did the colored shirts and rallies have to be abandoned, but the rhetoric had to change as well—as it began to at the end of the Cold War. In academic terminology, radical right groups developed an "exoteric," or "moderate 'front-stage'" intended for public consumption, and an "esoteric," or "radical 'back-stage'" aimed at an audience comprising activists and militants. In a Trojan Horse effect, the public-facing rhetoric uses seemingly inclusive and democratic language for exclusive and undemocratic ends, which only the radical-right initiated can discern. Feldman cites the example of Holocaust denial, which began during the war at the hands of the Axis perpetrators themselves. Today, this anti-Semitic conspiracy theory is dressed up as Holocaust "revisionism." As Feldman emphasizes, the LaRouche movement in the US—led by its cultic leader, Lyndon LaRouche, until his recent death—is one of the more sophisticated purveyors of "masked antisemitic theories."

With the *cordon sanitaire* broken down in parts of Europe, the goalposts of discourse have moved, with previously centre-right parties shifting further to the right and forming new alliances that were formerly unthinkable. In Chapter 12, Feldman terms this a movement toward a "near-right politics." These developments have stirred the embers of a long-dormant question: is the reformist radical right—or worse, revolutionary fascism itself—on its way back? Fascism stepped into the vacuum of leadership after World War I. History, however, does not repeat itself, and the same historical circumstances will not reassemble and give another opening to fascism. Feldman points out, though, that "many fascist tropes were dangerously mainstreamed in interwar Europe," citing as an example the infamous Nuremberg Laws, or Nazi race laws, followed by several radical right regimes thereafter. This technique has been repackaged by today's radical right in obviously successful ways. Among its other advantages, mainstreaming by the radical right disguises any links it may have to historical fascism. Vitally, contemporary neo-fascism is more than disguised historical fascism; it has introduced two new changes: ethno-pluralism, which is racism by another name, or "white separatism through the back door," allowing for the popular appeal of their message; and the stripping of overtly fascist trappings like coloured shirts and parades, to similar effect. In recent decades, radical right movements "have truly learnt to speak the language of reform rather than revolution." Besides mainstreaming their message for popular consumption, the radical right has also encoded the message to retain the loyalty and support of its most committed followers. The online mainstreaming of the radical right, furthermore, is "surely a challenge to liberal stability and legitimacy, and perhaps even a long-term threat to democratic security." Rather than an interwar assault on power, "it is an ideological assault on the liberal status quo in Europe": "That means extra susceptibility in a major crisis. And it also means the germs of a collective madness are again in the air." It is at the point that Feldman issues his rallying cry: "We need 'political immunologists' desperately today. For if liberalism fails over the next generation, it will be because we, its guardians, failed it. Let us demonstrate that liberal values include the protection of minority groups, equality of rights, and freedom from fear. This is the kernel of liberalism."

Feldman next turns his attention to the recent growth in so-called "lone wolf terrorism": "why has what is termed here 'self-activating terrorism' spiked so massively this century; and just as pressingly, how does lone wolf terrorism relate to radical right extremism?" In Chapter 13, Feldman traces the roots of lone wolf terrorism to nineteenth-century anarchism, whose self-declared war on their symbolic, often bourgeois targets waned between the world wars but has been revived by the radical right, especially the American radical right, beginning in the 1980s. Contemporary lone wolf terrorism, or what Feldman defines as self-directed terrorism, "is personally constructed and undertaken in terms of motivation, targets, and justification." Attacks on their symbolic targets—whether "the bourgeoisie or multiculturalism in Europe and the United States"—are seen by radical right actors as "strikes in a war against parts of their own society." The radical right's embrace of the internet and digital technologies has gone hand in hand with the rise in self-directed terrorism. For instance, the internet not only "provided motive, means, and opportunity" for Andres Breivik's terrorist attacks on 22 July 2011, but it also allowed him to post online his far-right manifesto *2083*—including its "step-by-step manual for lone wolf terrorism"—on the same date.

In Chapter 14, Feldman looks at the role played by "radicalising networks" in two prosecuted cases in which he was personally involved as an expert witness in court. Feldman locates a distinction between self-directed terrorists and accomplices on the ground, meaning that "having two or more co-conspirators in the conspiracy fundamentally changes terrorist dynamics." This does not mean that self-activating terrorists are complete loners; they may have an active support network in the form of friends or family, or indeed virtually; and they may have a passive, or indirect, radicalising network that they draw upon for reading material or inspiration. As an example of a passive self-radicalising extremist, Feldman points to the case of Neil Lewington, a would-be bomber who was apprehended in 2008. Among the material confiscated by the police were items linked to two post-war fascist movements: Combat 18/Blood & Honour and Christian Identity/KKK. These groups formed Lewington's indirect "community of support" online. The relationship to fascist ideology, detailed in Feldman's testimony, was noted by the sentencing judge in his address to Lewington. By contrast, Ian Davison was a would-be lone wolf who was passively preparing terrorist attacks online, while at the same time cultivating an active support network via the organisation he led for 18 months, the Aryan Strike Force (ASF). In addition to the 21 book-length texts that he had personally uploaded to the ASF website, including *Mein Kampf* and paramilitary manuals, Davison posted texts on the ASF forum about his neo-Nazi views and announced his germ warfare plans online. Davison's "active engagement with neo-Nazi fora clearly contributed to his 2010 sentencing."

Written in the aftermath of the 9/11 attacks and US military retaliation, Chapter 15 is perhaps Feldman's most anguished and angry essay. He takes a hard look at globalisation and its (neo-)liberal proponents. Globalisation is not just economic exploitation of the poor; it is also war on the poor, whether conceived in the wider sense (global unsustainability) or the narrower sense (5,000 Iraqi children dying monthly in the decade following the imposition of Western sanctions in 1990). "Standing on the side of Life" and "against the 'storm of death' threatening 'general destruction'" is art, which "weaves an intricate and vivid tapestry of human interactions." In fighting "openly against the instinct of death at work in our history," "art is not only a guide and a refuge, but an oracle as well." The American-led "War on Terror" presented parallels with Kafka's *The Trial*, as Feldman discusses. The character Block's case, "without promise of conclusion, echoes the ongoing crisis of Iraq following the 1991 Gulf War." As Feldman warns us, "the global threats created as a result of human factionalism simply cannot coexist with the parochialism which has thus far shaped so much of human history, and another sixty years similar to the last will assuredly realise the 'inverted utopia' we cannot imagine."

Chapter 16 bears the title "'it became necessary to destroy the town to save it': The United States Between Liberalism and Warfare before Donald Trump." This provocative title points to the absurdities engendered by the perennial conflict between the American ideal of enduring peace and the aggressive practices of American foreign policy. Feldman raises the question of how central political violence—which, in America's case, has long meant perpetual wars—is to liberalism. In view of contemporary political realities, Feldman defines warfare as "organised violence supported by an interested party with the intention of killing large numbers of people to achieve their political aims." This definition, which does not distinguish between combatants and civilians, broadens Clausewitz's traditional understanding of war to make it nearly synonymous with terrorism. Feldman goes a step further and argues that "the functioning of liberalism is predicated upon war and the institutions of war." This link between war and liberalism predates the end of the Cold War. Feldman concludes that "liberalism as we understand it today is inextricable from the 'massification of militarism' in the political, economic, and cultural spheres."

In Chapter 17, Feldman looks at the Iraq War from the viewpoint of its justness. A Just War in the Christian tradition consists of just cause and just conduct in conflict. Feldman contends that the 2003 US-led pre-emptive attack on Iraq failed on both counts: the cause lacked right authority and the right intention and failed the test of last resort; and the conduct clearly failed to ensure a just outcome. Lacking by all accounts were "credible evidence of Weapons of Mass Destruction in Iraq"; a "UN resolution backing an invasion"; and "independently-verified proof of Al-Qaida partnering with Saddam Hussein in Iraq." This raises an unusual question to consider: what would it take, or what would be just, to correct a failed just war? The unjustness of the invasion and occupation of Iraq was so great that, ironically, it might actually be more just (though not necessarily recommended) to reoccupy the country in order to restore the status quo ante (that is, an autocratic Iraq without Saddam). Feldman suggests that weight should be given, before war is declared, to the disparity of strength between the respective parties to a conflict. This disparity is not generally counted as a factor in the analysis of just war doctrine and is often ignored by the British and American press; but the 54 countries that protested against the Iraq invasion recognized it as an expression of European-American imperial hegemony.

In the chapter which opens Part 3, "Ends and Odds," Feldman returns full circle to a major intellectual figure of the 20th century who gravitated toward fascism between the wars: not Pound, in this case, but the German philosopher Martin Heidegger. Feldman sees the myth of socio-cultural decline and renewal to be the core of fascism; and here, he situates Heidegger in the context of non-Nazi strands of fascism prevalent in interwar Germany which supported the same myth. By this measure, Heidegger was hardly alone in his longing for an extensive spiritual renewal in Germany, but in his ultimate rejection of Nazi populism and the prospects of secular revolutionary change. Like them, his 'philosophical' acceptance of fascism culminated in disillusion with National Socialism—although for less ideological than personal reasons. In 1950, under the doctoral supervision of Heidegger's one-time ally, the existential philosopher, Karl Jaspers, *Die Konservative Revolution in Deutschland 1918-1932* by Armin Mohler presented metapolitical fascism as a unified and reasonable alternative to modernity; an alternative seeking to end the present "interregnum." This idea was picked up later by the French Nouvelle Droite, which emphasized the "right to difference" as a critique of modernity's egalitarianism, drawing for intellectual support from Heidegger among others of his ilk (such as the jurist Carl Schmitt or the poet Gottfried Benn). As with the ongoing "Pound case", contemporary fascists seem to understand the political undertones of Heidegger's works better than a fair few scholars.

The aforementioned British far-right extremist group, the Aryan Strike Force (ASF), is a representative case study in contemporary neo-Nazi activism. This is the theme of Chapter 19, which finds that the so-called "Aryan" community—perceived by the postwar radical right to need "saving" from "immigrants, multi-cultural society and non-whites more generally"—is geographically dispersed around the world. Postwar fascist movements therefore tend to be "international in scope, and racial in motivation." The ASF may be described as a neo-Nazi groupuscule whose impact and connections, especially its international links, are magnified by their use of the internet. ASF followed two extreme right-wing traditions: a longstanding Euro-American neo-Nazi movement, and an embrace of the internet to communicate, organise and propagate the message of Universal Nazism. Groups that follow the 1962 "Cotswold Declaration"—a collaboration by the extreme right wing in Britain and the USA—"advocate global Nazi ideology, biological anti-Semitism, paramilitary violence, and an unshakeable 'faith' in the existence and superiority of a worldwide 'Aryan' race." ASF used the internet to upload military manuals, racist books and extremist videos. ASF's adherence to a kind of neo-Nazi "special relationship" between the US and UK is demonstrated by the founding of a US Division.

In crossing the ideological Rubicon Feldman then turns to the Soviet Constructivists. Pioneers of the avant-garde, specifically photomontage, they flourished amidst the utopian aftermath of the Russian Revolution as a synthesis of communist politics and high modernism. Citing Kenneth Burridge's remark that "there is no human activity which cannot assume religious significance," Feldman argues in Chapter 20 that "a kind of ersatz faith underpinned much of Stalinism's transformative zeal in the 1930s." This application of "political religion" thus makes space for "totalitarian art." In line with James's and Durkheim's definitions of religion based on its functions, "secular faiths" may be seen in the same light: "if one's definition of religion stems from a functionalist perspective, then political religions may hold a potentially similar power over people as other religions." As a case study, Feldman turns to the 1930s monthly journal the *USSR in Construction*, whose "mixed-media presentation may be more effectively described as a cultural sermon from devotees of a seductive political religion: one making use of idiosyncratically Russian pictorial traditions, as well as cutting-edge Modernist genres like photomontage; the publication also uses Bolshevik propaganda techniques and of course, Marxist-Leninist ideology." Relevantly here, "propaganda" in its root meaning is the propagation of the faith.

In the book's concluding essay, Feldman argues for Samuel Beckett's political nominalism as a "third option [...] between an apolitical Beckett and a 'soft left' Beckett: humanistic but not partisan, engaged specifically and individually rather than identified with an 'ism.'" Beckett's politics, in Feldman's reading, "were shaped by the particular and the personal, and each political act or statement demands especial consideration in its own, socio-historical context." His politics, then, were "a succession of isolated engagements rather than overarching 'sides' or 'ideologies' or organisational strategies." In this view, it is a mistake to employ presentism "to describe Beckett's work as engaging with the Holocaust," for instance, as it took nearly a generation after the war for the notion of the Holocaust to be firmly established—the term only came into widespread use in early 1960s. Based on what Feldman has written in this chapter, it seems fair to say that, unlike Pound—with whom he is bookended in this collection—Beckett would not have entangled himself in activism in the name of an abstract ideal where real human beings could be hurt. Feldman's image of this "traumatised witness" of 20th century Europe, in the words of the 1969 Nobel Prize Award ceremony, "sounding liberation to the oppressed, and comfort to those in need"—which is all of us—is a fitting way with which to end his collection of essays.

This brief account does not do justice to the collection's richness of detail and intensity of argument. As it contains no throwaway lines and wastes no words, the book—unusually for such a collection, both scholarly and passionate—must be savored for its nuances. The running themes of the book can only be touched upon here: working paradoxes and boundaries of all kinds—linguistic, civic, political, and otherwise—and their breaches; the industrial-scale dehumanizing of human beings that must be called out and fought; the watershed moment of 1945—a date mentioned in every chapter—and the fact that we are still living in its shadow; and the use or misuse of language as a political weapon. Yet this is countersigned with the message of hope—in a world that sometimes seems devoid of it—for if words can be weaponized for war, they can also be instrumentalized for peace.

Part 1
Ezra Pound, Modernist and Fascist

1. An Ideologue's Journey: Ezra Pound from Tradition in Italian Fascism to the Postwar Fascist Tradition

> The solemn rhetoric of 'faith' could scarcely conceal the dynamic of terror. And it was terror—the allure, the thrill, the prospect of terror—that attracted Ezra Pound to Fascism. Yeats, Heidegger, Wyndham Lewis, Céline, Paul de Man, Gottfried Benn, Marinetti—the list of intellectuals who supported Fascism is all too familiar. Generations of scholars have tried to explain the multiplicity of motives that led them towards the totalitarian temptation. Yet it may have been wasted labour. Had we turned our attention to what was happening at ground level, to what took place on the streets almost daily under the culture of Fascism, we would have seen what contemporaries could not have failed to remark: the spectacle, at once riveting and terrifying, offered by the combination of violence and unbridled power.
>
> Lawrence Rainey[1]

In contemporary parlance Ezra Pound was 'radicalised' in Fascist Italy during wintertime 1932-1933, after living in Rapallo for nearly a decade. Granted, Pound's hero worship of *Il Duce* was a pivotal factor—one solidified by his only meeting with Mussolini on the ominous date of 30 January 1933, and oft-recounted in later prose and even poetry (as in Canto 41)—but at the same time, key aspects of Fascism's cultural nationalism were also essential drivers in his turn toward fascist ideology. The first part of this survey will gesture at extant historiography on this subject, ranging from Pound's work on Cavalcanti and Frederick II in the early 1930s, to encounters with Futurists like Marinetti and Libera in 1932; in fact, viewing the latter's exhibition at the Fascist Decennio in December 1932 was instrumental in Pound's decision to support the National Fascist Party (Partito Nazionale Fascista, or PNF).[2]

Pound's propaganda for Mussolini involved hundreds, perhaps even thousands, of radio items composed for the regime. This frenzy of activity commenced shortly after Italy's entry into World War Two in 1940, at the onset of the Axis 'new order' in Europe.[3] I have recently argued[4] that Pound was further radicalised in spring 1942 after reading *Mein Kampf*, especially Hitler's chapter "Propaganda and Organization". His engagement with the most destructive form of fascism, Nazism, helped Pound rededicate himself to the Axis cause during 1942-43, leading to his issuance of policy recommendations, extensive correspondence with PNF elites, and an offer to fight the USSR. Importantly, Pound was aware of the mass Jewish arrests in Italy in the final months of 1943, at which time he began correspondence with Julius Evola—a key fascist ideologue—then based in the Office of

Race.⁵ After this second period of radicalisation during the Holocaust, Pound again returned to older Italian traditions to bolster his support for the wartime Axis. This included lionisation of figures from the country's past like Sigismondo Malatesta and Antonio Vivaldi in his previously-unseen radio speeches of the period, also containing some of the most virulent antisemitism produced anywhere by the Axis.

These two periods, separated by a decade, hold key insights into the ways in which Pound drew upon mythic conceptions of the Italian nation in his propaganda for Fascism and later the Axis. Yet Italian Fascism was not the only fascist tradition to which Pound contributed. Set a decade later, the final part of this survey introduces still-neglected materials dating from Pound's postwar institutionalisation at St Elizabeths that reveal how his sanitisation of the Fascist regime inspired a new generation of fascists. Many neo-fascists made a pilgrimage to visit him in Washington, D.C., while his close circle advanced new conspiracy theories that have become staples of contemporary fascism: that a 'Jewish plot' was behind race-mixing and the Federal Reserve in the US, and that the Holocaust was fabricated. In these and other examples, the famous poet drew upon esoteric traditions to buttress his fascist beliefs and, after the war, contributed to a neo-fascist tradition of ideologues defending Axis horrors against a supposedly more corrupt liberal-socialist international order. As this suggests, in reply to Lawrence Rainey's striking conclusion in the *LRB* of fully 20 years ago in the epigraph above—and with fascism's stench hanging in the air more powerfully than at any time since the end of the Second World War—I start from the view that intellectuals, then as now, act as key cultural influencers. Understanding their siren call in studying fascist radicalisation and extremism is essential for societies that wish to be inoculated from fascist ideology.

While doubtless violence and terror were inscribed into the very DNA of fascism between the wars, for many intellectuals like Pound it was precisely the promise of the opposite that attracted them; in Heidegger's words, the promise of 'leading the leaders' on matters of culture.⁶ Put another way, cultural elites and intellectuals often thought fascism would improve their standing vis-à-vis 'the masses'— unless, of course, they were 'degenerate': Jewish, gay, or left-wing—in an invariably growing list. In this way, intellectual support for fascism was not wholly unlike 'occultism' in its etymological sense: something "hidden or secret in the sense of being mysterious to ordinary understanding or scientific reason".⁷ As it turns out, at least in Pound's case, esoteric insight led from the pursuit of an allegedly suppressed secret wisdom and obscured tradition to veneration of right authority as personified in the Italian dictator, Benito Mussolini, whom Pound called an 'artifex' in relation to the pivotal moment of his fascist radicalisation. In surveying Pound's trajectory from esotericism to neo-Nazism, this overview will look briefly at a selected year of Pound's socio-political undertakings over five decades: 1913; 1923; 1933; 1943; and 1953. Throughout this time, Pound may be understood as "a village explainer", in the words of Gertrude Stein (to which she continued, "excellent if you were a village, but if you were not, not").[8] Yet this sketch contends that, for more than a generation after his infamous Axis collaboration, Pound was also an important and influential fascist ideologue, attempting to explain Mussolini's 'new Italy'.

Even before commencing his opus, *The Cantos*—unfinished at his death in 1972, and published in instalments appearing between World War One and Woodstock—Pound took Europe by storm at the start of the 20th century. The 1908 collection of poems *A Lume Spento* put him on Europe's cultural map, while his efforts in London during the ensuing years often centred on esoteric figures like Cavalcanti and recovered obscured wisdom, such as his early translation of the "The Seafarer" from the 10th century Anglo-Saxon. Even Pound's later invocation to 'make it new'—often seen as shorthand for modernism—was taken from antiquity. These tendencies kicked into high gear from autumn 1913, when Pound received Ernest Fenollosa's notebooks on east Asian Noh drama, which he undertook to introduce and demystify. Pound's mentor in this work was the famed Irish poet and occultist, W.B. Yeats, with whom he spent three winters as a literary secretary in rural Sussex, England:

> the builders of literary modernism came to know one another during the Stone Cottage winters. Most important of all, Pound began to think of Yeats and himself as an artistic and social elite—a secret society—that excluded even some of their closest friends. Stone Cottage was a seedbed for *The Cantos* and for Yeats's later esoterica, but it was also a breeding ground for some of the unfortunate excesses of *Jefferson and/or Mussolini* and *On the Boiler*.

Yeats' and Pound's "self-consciousness as a member of a select few" was unshakeable, according to James Longenbach's masterful 1988 study, *Stone Cottage*; which continues: "it seems likely that part of Pound's attraction to the occult, and his desire to maintain an esoteric doctrine of the Image […] was another way to set himself apart from the mob [….] Everything Pound and Yeats studied at Stone Cottage was chosen for its esoteric value: Noh drama, Chinese poetry, western demonology, even Lady Gregory's folklore".[9]

While Pound fought shy of Yeats's more explicit occultism, including psychical experiments and practical magic, the years before the Great War nevertheless helped form what another critic termed "a view of European history which supposes that some individuals or groups—some 'conspiracy of intelligence'—maintained a special knowledge or wisdom in the face of official scorn, neglect, and persecution". In hindsight, this proved a short jump to antisemitic conspiracy theories. In the years to come, Pound pursued a "celestial" or esoteric tradition in *The Cantos,* in Leon Surette's estimation, "initially conceived as a kind of séance, whereby the dead souls pass on wisdom and experience".[10] In another scholar's words, the first version of *The Cantos*, published in *Poetry* in 1917, was "structured on the model of cultic initiation."[11] Whether or not these characterisations of his early work are far-fetched, much of Pound's poetry and prose was doubtless esoteric, in the sense familiar to avant-garde modernists of the time, as elitist and specialized. This contemptuous view of 'the masses' was present across all of Pound's writing, and was contrasted with a positive view of 'enlightened individuals'. Amongst the first such world-historical figure reanimated from the archives by Pound was the quintessential 'Renaissance man', Sigismondo Malatesta, in 1923.

Following Pound's recasting of *The Cantos* in the 1920s, his epic "poem containing history" would increasingly venerate individual leadership as an engine of history. Even if unconsciously, for Pound, wise leaders understood "European history as a story of an oppressed alternate culture", to use Surette's formulation.[12] In what would soon take shape as Pound's lifetime project, diverse figures like John Scotus Erigena, Malatesta, John Adams and Confucius were all pressganged into this insight role; indeed, writes Demetres Tryphonopoulos, this line of leadership figures represents "Pound's rediscovered, fictional 'tradition,' rising from the ancient rites of Delphi, Dodona, and Mithras through the Medieval manifestations of the tradition in the Albigenses, the Knights Templar, and Erigena to its later appearances in John Heydon and Swedenborg".[13] In a book dedicated to perhaps the most important of these esoteric figures for Pound, Erigena, Mark Byron has recently contended: "The commonality in all these figures is their attempt to formulate systems of human action and contemplation, whether by means of theophany, a total social and individual schema, or an access to the permanent world of the gods".[14]

Stephen Sicari stresses that the *Malatesta Cantos*, by mythicizing the historical figure of Sigismondo, "mark the beginning of Pound's extension of the wanderer's journey toward a political goal."[15] Already in 1923, this goal appeared to at least partly travel via fascism. Pound's research on Sigismondo in the Rimini archives in Spring 1923, moreover, was significant for another reason; it marked his first real engagement with blackshirts on the ground: Pound's growing interest in Italian Fascism [...] began to crystallise in 1923. By early 1924 Pound was writing letters to Mussolini through a mutual acquaintance, proposing that the new dictator take Pound on as an advisor who would direct a programme of Italian cultural renovation. In December 1924 Pound left Paris for Italy. As he later recalled [in an unpublished 1933 essay], 'I bet on Italian fascism years ago and came here to live in the middle of it.'[16]

After a favourable experience of Fascist officials helping him with the Malatesta papers in spring 1923, it took only five months for Pound, through the aforementioned mutual acquaintance named Nancy Cox-McCormack—who later sculpted the first bust of the Duce—to private press "Mussolini to adopt a program of cultural patronage outlined and to be directed by Pound himself"; for Rainey, it represented Pound's own "resolution to the question of art, authority and public consensus".[17] Cultural leaders needed to be intellectuals, not bureaucrats; especially if "cultural heritage" included the "transmission of secret knowledge from high antiquity".[18] From this perspective, where better than Fascist Italy, centred on Mussolini's 'Third Rome' after the civilizational feats of the ancient Roman Empire and Italian Renaissance?

In Pound's Mussolini, then, esotericism met authority, and his anti-democratic dreams of a cultural elite reshaping the masses held out the prospect of achievement. Yet it was Pound's one and only audience with Il Duce, on 30 January 1933, that cemented his conversion to what scholars term the "political faith" of fascism.[19] This short meeting with "the Boss" was quickly immortalized in "Canto 41". Yet perhaps more importantly, Pound spent the ensuing fortnight feverishly writing *Jefferson and/or Mussolini*—tellingly subtitled *L'Idea Statale Fascism as I Have Seen it*—which viewed Il Duce's political genius and will toward order as comparable to those of Thomas Jefferson. Thus, the distortions of ideological faith were already taking effect by 1933: for Jefferson, the exercise of liberty was a supreme political virtue; for Mussolini, the precise opposite obtained. For the latter's was clearly not extremism in the defense of liberty, but unprecedented political violence in Italy defending a violent dictatorship. When it came to liberty, in fact, in the two plus years from writing to publishing *Jefferson and/or Mussolini*, Pound made Mussolini's favoured slogan on the matter his own: "Liberty is a duty, not a right."[20] If that was scarcely a Jeffersonian sentiment, it was nothing compared what came next. Indeed, in Surette's words, it "is difficult to say which is more bizarre—Pound's appeal to an unbelievable secret history of Europe or his perception of Mussolini as a martyr in the struggle against arbitrary authority".[21] At least initially, it was precisely in seeing Mussolini as an "artifex" rather than martyr—a wise ruler in the tradition of Malatesta or Jefferson, rather than Nero or Caligula—that blinded Pound to the pitiless realities of fascist praxis.

By the time *Jefferson and/or Mussolini* finally appeared with Stanley Nott in 1935 Pound was all in for fascism. For example, following the Italian invasion of Abyssinia from late 1935, Pound contributed one gratis op-ed a fortnight to the *British-Italian Bulletin*, a propaganda paper published by the Italian Fascists in London. Once that outlet closed shop following Fascism's illegal occupation in East Africa in mid-1936, Pound switched venues to the British Union of Fascists, publishing nearly a text a month for more than three years, until that movement was proscribed by the British authorities in May 1940. By that time, Pound had become a hardened antisemite—one virtually indistinguishable from Nazi propagandists—and broadcast frequently between 1940 and 1945 on behalf of the Axis. He was paid handsomely for these, at more than $200,000 in today's currency, and interacted with virtually every Axis leader in Italy at the time—including, after 1943, the Nazi occupation authorities in the Salò Republic.[22]

By summer 1943, rightly concludes Vincent Arnold's *The War of Illusions*, "war propaganda ceased to be an Italian product. Propaganda, like everything else in the new Italian Social Republic was now under control of Nazi Germany. Indeed for Italy the war was over and nothing remained except to follow the lead of its Axis partner."[23] Likewise for Pound, in the chaotic days after Italy officially joined the Allies on 8 September 1943, the Nazis seem to have left a forged passport for him at the German Embassy in Rome. Instead of collecting it, he crossed enemy lines heading north and, in the words of Anne Conover, arrived to "be interviewed by the new minister of popular culture, Fernando Mezzasoma, hoping to broadcast again from Milan, the new center of radio propaganda".[24] In offering his services to the RSI fascists in the Salò Republic, Pound allegedly declared: "Give me a bed, a bowl of soup and a microphone."[25]

Things then went from bad to worse. Pound's first RSI typescript was, fittingly, in German only a fortnight later, 23 November 1943, with his views again in keeping with Axis propaganda. In urgent need of propagandists, Pavolini sent a letter three days later expressing "my deepest sympathy for your unchanging and fervent fascist faith." Following the RSI's belated "reconstruction" of radio propaganda at the end of 1943, Pound thus began his work as what he called "a foreign collaborator". During this time, there can be no doubt that Pound aligned himself with a pro-Nazi faction in the Salò Republic. This included correspondence with the Office of Race, where, as mentioned, Julius Evola was then based, with one letter opening: "The power of Jews comes from monopoly. The most dangerous monopoly is monetary", thus "everything that frees us from usury attacks Jewish power". Still another letter in Italian featured recommended slogans like "Berlin has noticed and approved our initiative"; and another warned against "efforts by Jews to destroy other nations". As Pound rightly discerned, these heretofore-extreme views were now RSI policy under Nazi occupation. The most notorious may be found in a letter to the fanatically antisemitic Secretary of the Fascist Party and head of Black Brigades. Writing to Alessandro Pavolini on 2 December 1943, Pound recommended "a law" be passed requiring booksellers to showcase the following books for at least three months, "since the bookstores largely in the hands of the Jews *were* rather a hindrance than a help in spreading useful books":

- The Protocols of Zion;
- The Duties of Man, of Mazzini;
- The Politics of Aristotle;
- The Testament of Confucius.

The arrest of Jews will create a wave of useless mercy; thus the need to disseminate the Protocols. The intellectuals are capable of a passion more durable than the emotional, but they need to understand the reasons for a conflict.[26]

This letter indicates that Pound knew the Italian Fascists had moved far beyond 'only' preaching anti-Semitism by this point. For centuries well-assimilated and statistically over-represented in membership ranks of the PNF itself, Italian Jewry found itself devastated by the 1938 Race Laws, facing persecution, dismissal from government posts, and sometimes worse. Unfathomably harsher were autumn 1943 arrests and deportations. Out of nearly 43,000 Jews in northern Italy in September 1943, at least 8,529 perished in the Holocaust. On 16 October in Rome, for instance, where Pound had been working only the month before—following SS "house to house searches, the lorries waiting along the streets, the mass of people detained for dozens of hours in some enclosed area"—more than 1,000 Roman Jews were deported to their deaths at Auschwitz-Birkenau. In Milan, where Pound started radio propaganda for the RSI that November, another 846 Jews were deported on the same day as those in Rome.[27]

Of course, the RSI had earlier codified these actions in point seven of the Veronese Charter: "Persons belonging to the Jewish race are aliens, and during this war belong to an enemy nationality."[28] In terms of local context, the third largest deportation of Jews from mainland Italy took place roughly 15 miles from Pound's Rapallo home. On 3 November 1943 in Genoa, up to 300 Jews were deported. Although sensing some late hesitancies, Redman nevertheless characterizes Pound's anti-Semitism as reaching "a new level of virulence in this period", in keeping with his "full support for the regime's anti-Semitic propaganda."[29] Even if he could not know the extent of suffering inflicted upon Italian Jewry during the Holocaust, Pound certainly knew of—and seems to have approved—Italian antisemitic persecution and mass arrests in autumn 1943. With Nazism and Fascist Republicanism now inseparable, it merits stressing that Pound's Axis propaganda commenced, and continued, at a time when Italian Jews were already marked for murder. Put another way, Pound would not have seen yellow-starred Jews in the Salò Republic because they were in hiding, or had already been killed. Following his indictment, arrest and abortive trial for treason—at which he was declared insane and remanded to St Elizabeths asylum in 1946, where he spent the next dozen years—Pound never retracted his veneration for Mussolini; his Axis collaboration; nor the antisemitic fuel he pitched onto the pyres of the contemporaneous Holocaust.

In fact, in the years after World War Two, Pound helped to launch a new fascist tradition of Holocaust denial and neo-Nazism. All of this was done from the grounds of St Elizabeths, where Pound was given a great deal of latitude in terms of visitors—unaccountably so in terms of his freedom to welcome fascists, and unaccountably in relation to the scant documentation of their visits to Pound, as only a fraction of the expected institutional Visitor's Log records relating to Pound have survived. Recorded on two of the five surviving pages from the logs are names which suggest the volume of fascist visitors to Pound—names such as the Britons Peter Whigham and Denis Goacher, who took a pilgrimage to visit Pound in St Elizabeths and who wrote for Oswald Mosley's postwar magazine, *The European*. They published numerous articles on Pound, as well as reviews of his work.

The precise kind of "awareness" may be seen in two of his closest and most influential ideological disciples, John Kasper and Eustace Mullins, who literally sat at Pound's feet for his esoteric 'wisdom' about Jews, fascism and postwar American politics. As Alec Marsh has impressively shown, Kasper headed the Seaboard White Citizens' Council in the 1950s, a more respectable face of the campaign against desegregation. So noxious was Kasper that, amongst his visits across the South, he needed only ten days in Clinton, Tennessee, to initiate race riots that led to the calling in of the National Guard.[30] This, in turn, led to Kasper's incarceration, and he was photographed entering prison with Hitler's *Mein Kampf* under his arm. For his part, Mullins penned the first biography of Pound, the 1961 *This Difficult Individual*, at a time when he also headed the Aryan League of America. Mullins was chiefly responsible for the antisemitic conspiracy theory about the American Federal Reserve, contained in his allegedly Pound-commissioned *Secrets of the Federal Reserve* from a decade earlier. This was far from the only conspiracy theory Mullins advanced; for instance, in keeping with his early and influential Holocaust Denial, here is how Mullins is described in the scholarly literature:

> Mullins directly blames international Jewish bankers for the world's evils and imputes all of America's troubles to the Jews, even such problems as rising medical costs and difficulties in the health care system. Mullins's beliefs came from Ezra Pound, a staunch anti-Semite who, according to a 1982 *Aryan Nations Newsletter*, was 'a great admirer of Adolf Hitler and Mussolini." Mullins boasts about visiting Pound 'every day for three years,' saying each day Pound lectured him on world history. Mullins admits, 'That's how I found out what I know.'[31]

These connections, in turn, might be more briefly exemplified by Matthias Koehl, another American neo-Nazi in Pound's orbit. Koehl visited Pound multiple times in the 1950s and went on to join the American Nazi Party, as well as later leading both the National Socialist White People's Party and the World Union of National Socialists. Fittingly, Koehl was known for his advocacy of so-called 'esoteric Nazism'. He recalled meeting Pound in the following terms:

> The Ezra Pound I knew was cheerfully unrepentant, firm in his beliefs, and staunchly true to those principles he had upheld throughout his life. Never once did he give so much as the slightest hint that he had any regret about anything he had ever done or spoken during the '30s and '40s—not excluding his celebrated views on the Jewish Question. In fact, his pointed references to any number of nefarious Jewish practices left no doubt as to where he stood on that particular issue.[32]

Their connection may be symbolised in Pound's 1953 inscription to Koehl, a sentiment long reciprocated by right-wing extremists, like him, drawing upon Pound's legacy:

Exactly 50 years later, to conclude, a movement explicitly touting "fascism for the third millennium" emerged, having "repurposed" a building in Rome as "CasaPound Italia" on 26 December 2003. It is a fitting tribute. For is the leader of those avowed fascist revolutionaries not correct in contending: "Ezra Pound was a poet, an economist and an artist. He was a revolutionary and a fascist".[33] The irony is that the fascist activists of CasaPound may well understand Pound's politics rather better than his indefatigable defenders in Pound Studies. And so, finally, in returning full circle to Lawrence Rainey's contention, it seems to me that connecting Pound's radicalisation and radical right advocacy to, say, the practices of a contemporary fascist movement bearing the canonical modernist's name—at a time when 'faith' in liberal democracy draining away year upon year—turns out to be scarcely "wasted labour" after all.

Endnotes

[1] Lawrence Rainey, "Between Mussolini and Me", *London Review of Books* 21/6 (March 1999), pp. 22-25, available online at: https://www.lrb.co.uk/the-paper/v21/n06/lawrence-rainey/between-mussolini-and-me (all websites last accessed 22 February 2020). This overview was originally provided as a presentation at the Hebrew University of Jerusalem's *"Tradition, Esoterism and Fascism: Then and Now"* workshop on 29-30. December 2019. I am grateful to the organisers of the event for hosting me, and to the ensuing discussions helping in the completion of this introduction.

[2] The first Anglophone book on the MRF decennio is Antonio Morena, *Mussolini's Decennale: Aura and Mythmaking in Fascist Italy* (London: University of Toronto Press, 2015), see especially pp. 47ff.

[3] An excellent cultural overview has been provided on this mercifully brief experiment; see Benjamin G. Martin, *The Nazi-Fascist New Order for European Culture* (London: Harvard University Press, 2016).

[4] Matthew Feldman, *Ezra Pound's Fascist Propaganda, 1935-45* (Basingstoke: Palgrave, 2013), Ch. 6, "Pound's Propaganda Themes and Strategies, 1940-43," pp. 114-142.

[5] See Feldman, *Ezra Pound's Fascist Propaganda, 1935-45*, pp. 117ff. and 153ff., respectively.

[6] Cited in Tom Rockmore, *On Heidegger's Nazism and Philosophy* (Oxford: University of California Press, 1992), p. 55.

[7] Demetres P. Tryphonopoulos, "Introduction" to Leon Surette and Demetres Tryphonopoulos, eds., *Literary Modernism and the Occult Tradition* (Orono, MA: University of Maine, 1996), which helpfully continues: "occultism makes a 'claim to knowledge of a scientific nature which is inaccessible to the accepted methods of positive, objective scientific research'", p. 20.

[8] Gertrude Stein, cited in David Wheatley, "The vain theories of a village explainer", *The Irish Times* (13 May 2006), online at: https://www.irishtimes.com/news/the-vain-theories-of-a-village-explainer-1.1002751.

[9] James Longenbach, *Stone Cottage: Pound, Yeats and Modernism* (Oxford: Oxford University Press, 1988), cited pp. xi-xii and 54

[10] Leon Surette, *The Birth of Modernism: Ezra Pound, T.S. Eliot, W.B. Yeats, and the Occult* (Quebec: McGill-Queen's University Press, 1994), pp. 122 and 124.

[11] Demetres Tryphonopoulos, *The Celestial Tradition: A Study of Ezra Pound's* The Cantos (Waterloo: Wilfrid Laurier University Press, 1992), p. 101.

[12] Surette, *The Birth of Modernism*, p. 98.

[13] Demetres Tryphonopoulos, "Ezra Pound's Occult Education", *Journal of Modern Literature* 17/1 (Summer 1990), p. 90.

[14] Mark Byron, *Ezra Pound's Eriugena* (London: Bloomsbury, 2016), p. 254.

[15] Stephen Sicari, *Pound's Epic Ambition: Dante and the Modern World* (Albany: State University of New York Press, 1991), p. 89.

[16] A. Walton Litz and Lawrence Rainey, "Ezra Pound", in *The Cambridge History of Literary Criticism*, Vol. 7 (Cambridge: Cambridge University Press, 2000), p. 87.

[17] Lawrence Rainey, *Institutions of Modernism: Literary Elites and Public Culture* (London: Yale University Press, 1998), p. 109.

[18] Surette, *The Birth of Modernism*, p. 123.

[19] See, for instance, Emilio Gentile has delimited these characteristics as the primacy of faith and myth in the political arena; guided by the "consecrated" figure of Mussolini; alongside *"ethical commandments"* and a *"political liturgy"*, extending to "a system of beliefs, myths, rituals, and symbols that deified the nation and state and celebrated the personality cult of 'Il Duce' as a living myth", "Political Religion: A Concept and its Critics", *Totalitarian Movements and Political Religions* 6/1 (2005), pp. 30ff. See also Piero Melograni, "The Cult of the Duce in Mussolini's Italy", *Journal of Contemporary History* 11/4 (1976), pp. 221-237, which adds: "Approval for the cult of the Duce came from all sorts of quarters, even from the least expected people. In 1933, Sigmund Freud sent the Duce a copy of one of his books, with the significant dedication: 'To Benito Mussolini, from an old man who greets in the Ruler the Hero of Culture'", p. 233.

[20] Cited in Tim Redman, *Ezra Pound and Italian Fascism* (Cambridge: Cambridge University Press, 1991), p. 114.

[21] Surette, *The Birth of Modernism*, p. 100.

[22] See Feldman, *Ezra Pound's Fascist Propaganda*, chs. 5 and 6.

[23] W. Vincent Arnold, *The Illusion of Victory: Fascist Propaganda and the Second World War* (New York: Peter Lang, 1998), p. 227.

[24] Anne Conover, *Olga Rudge and Ezra Pound: "What thou lovest well..."* (London: Yale University Press, 2001), p. 150. For detail on Pound's escape from Rome in September 1943, see David Bradshaw and James Smith, "Ezra Pound, James Strachey Barnes (The 'Italian Lord Haw-Haw') and Italian Fascism", *Review of English Studies* 64/266 (2013), pp. 672-693; and Claudia Baldoli and Brendan Fleming, eds., *A British Fascist in the Second World War: The Italian War Diary of James Strachey Barnes 1943-1945* (London: Bloomsbury, 2014), especially entries for 13 and 14 September 1943.

[25] Pound, cited in Mary de Rachewiltz, "Fragments of an Atmosphere", *Agenda* 17/3-4-18/1 (1979/80), pp. 157-170 (at 169).

[26] See Feldman, *Ezra Pound's Fascist Propaganda*, ch. 6, cited p. 154.

[27] Liliana Picciotto, "The Shoah in Italy: Its History and Characteristics", Joshua Zimmerman, ed., *Jews in Italy under Fascist and Nazi Rule* (Cambridge: Cambridge University Press, 2005), pp. 213, 215.

[28] *Ibid.* at 215. The complete Verona Charter, in another English translation, may be found online at https://www.politicsforum.org/forum/viewtopic.php?t=102658.

[29] Redman, *Ezra Pound and Italian Fascism*, pp. 243 and 268.

[30] See Alec Marsh, *John Kasper and Ezra Pound: Saving the Republic* (London: Bloomsbury, 2015), pp. 133ff.; and his forthcoming *Ezra Pound's "Washington Cantos" and the Struggle for Light* (London: Bloomsbury, 2020).

[31] See Richard Abanes, "America's Patriot Movement: Infiltrating the Church with a Gospel of Hate", Christian Research Institute, online at: http://www.equip.org/PDF/DP700.pdf; italics added.

[32] See https://nationalvanguard.org/2017/06/matt-koehl-and-ezra-pound-the-untold-story/.

[33] Cited in Colin Liddell, "In the House of Pound: An Interview with Gianluca Iannone" (2011), republished by Counter-Currents, online at: https://www.counter-currents.com/2015/03/in-the-house-of-pound/. For a recent analysis of CasaPound, see Elisabetta Cassina Wolff, "CasaPound Italia: 'Back to Believing. The Struggle Continues'", *Fascism* 8/1 (2019), pp. 61-88, available online at https://www.academia.edu/40112465/CasaPound_Italia_Back_to_Believing_The_Struggle_Continues.

2. The 'Pound Case' in Historical Perspective: An Archival Overview

> Of things ill done and done to others' harm
> Which once you took for exercise of virtue
>
> - 'Little Gidding', from the *Four Quartets* by T.S. Eliot

I.

The above epigraph from the wartime poem 'Little Gidding' by T.S. Eliot, a long-time collaborator and later defender of Ezra Pound, would appear to aptly characterise the latter's twelve-year activism for fascism... ending so ignominiously in May 1945. In one of the great ironies of modern history, the poet-turned-propagandist mistook fascism and anti-Semitism for political 'virtue'—in trying to create what he later called a 'paradiso terrestre'[1] via Italian Fascism. While his fellow Americans were celebrating V-E Day (Victory in Europe Day), Pound was being held for treason within eyeshot of the Leaning Tower of Pisa; that beautiful and poignant reminder of human imperfection. Initially detained at the US Army Disciplinary Training Centre in what he later called a "gorilla cage",[2] the tower must have been an imposing reminder of Pound's wartime hubris; of the impossibility of earthly paradise; and of the effects of serving Benito Mussolini's crumbling, crooked regime to the very last. How had it all come to this for one of the great patriarchs of modernism?

Today, Pound's story has become familiar enough to provide a domesticated answer; indeed, the generalist account is largely stripped of its contemporaneous ideological growl and intellectual rabidity.[3] So the story goes: frustrated with the United States and Britain, Pound moves to Rapallo in 1924 and slowly starts to both melt down and (perhaps as a result) support Italian Fascism—resulting in vituperative anti-Semitism and nearly-incomprehensible broadcasts for the propaganda arm of Radio Rome prior to his detention in Pisa, trial in Washington, D.C., and institutionalisation at St Elizabeths. A period of rehabilitation and reflection then finds Pound returning to award-winning poetry; leaving St Elizabeths after more than a dozen years, returning to Italy in 1958 to live out the rest of his days in the completion of his great epic, *The Cantos*: The End. While none of the above is inaccurate, strictly speaking, it paints an overly reassuring picture of the naive modernist, swept along by the radical politics of his day (maybe even suffering from a longstanding, delusional breakdown to boot[4]).

The following shall argue quite the opposite; namely, that Ezra Pound was far more an evangelist for fascist ideology, and far more of a committed political pugilist—if something of a ham-fisted one—than has been previously recognised. More to the point, much greater nuance can now attend the question 'What happened to Ezra Pound?'—if nevertheless still dimly—thanks to untapped archives, overlooked texts and letters, as well as recently-released documents pertaining to the course and consequences of Pound's propaganda for Fascist Italy. Collectively, these materials shed substantial new light on what was already being dubbed, in September 1945, by the American Federal Bureau of Investigation (FBI) 'the Pound case'. In returning to that case with an archival overview, this essay gestures toward several historical and political contexts, which are intended to complicate the seemingly comfortable questions around the breadth, depth, and lucidity of Pound's politics before, during, and after the Second World War in Europe.

II.

By the time Ezra Pound moved to the northern Italian town of Rapallo in 1924, he had already been a generation's *enfant terrible* for nearly a generation, authoring numerous books of poetry, articles and manifestos, and was widely regarded as the high priest of modernism, forever beseeching the faithful to 'make it new'. Yet the newness of Italy's ruling political ideology also led Pound to comment as early as 1926, in a letter to *Poetry* editor Harriet Monroe: 'I personally think extremely well of Mussolini. If one compares him to American presidents (the last three) or British premiers, etc., in fact one can NOT without insulting him. If the intelligentsia don't think well of him, it is because they know nothing about "the state," and government, and have no particularly large sense of values.'[5] As several critics have rightly noted, this was a relationship with fascist ideology that was only to deepen with time.[6]

A recent article by David Barnes[7] has helpfully squared up to Pound's engagement with Italian Fascism, arguing that it is not dichotomous from, but coterminous with, his poetry. Focussing on the 'propagandistic drive on the part of Pound' in Cantos 72 and 73, Barnes retraces some of the poet's correspondence with leading Futurist F.T. Marinetti in making clear that Pound was not the only idiosyncratic supporter in Mussolini's stable. For Barnes, this not only results in a 'pugilistic representation' (Barnes 21) of Marinetti in Canto 73, but also helps to clarify and contextualise the more general, and 'unique jumble that Pound's thinking consisted of in the late 1930s and the 1940s' (30). Yet if Barnes breaks new ground analysing the extent of Pound's 'blurred distinctions between aesthetic and political spheres'

(19), the perspective nonetheless covers familiar territory, leaving largely untouched the 'anti-Semitic, Nazi-Fascism' of Pound's wartime years (28). Building upon the insightful synthesis of Pound's art and politics in Barnes' article, however, the argument here seeks to go still further; that is, Pound may have been a strange bird to Italian Fascists given his poetry and background, but he was far more important to the regime's propaganda—and to evolving American policy on treason—than has been advanced to date. It is here that archives provide the greatest detail, and indeed, surprises, with respect to Pound's engagement with fascist ideology.

By way of providing an alternative approach to the 'Pound Case', the correspondence with a key artistic devotee, Archibald MacLeish, onetime lawyer and three-time Pulitzer Prize winner, is both highly underutilised and particularly insightful. For his part, MacLeish was an American establishment mover and shaker, and his is an equally fascinating story: moving from avowed pacifist as late as 1935 to Assistant Secretary of State and foremost cultural voice in the United States of the 1940s. In a sense, he was Pound's mirror image as a, perhaps *the*, leading propagandist for the Allied campaign during World War Two, heading the Office of Facts and Figures and helping to establish and direct the subsequent Office for War Information. And all this at the same time the energetic MacLeish was acting as the wartime Librarian of Congress, where his papers have long been on open access.

The MacLeish file in Washington, D.C. is enormous.[8] To date, only a fraction of the 61 boxes of files have been employed by scholars, despite the fact that MacLeish was in correspondence with everyone from President Truman to John Dos Passos.[9] In terms of Ezra Pound, for example, the two dozen letters by MacLeish included in the selected *Letters of Archibald MacLeish*—themselves covering fully 35 years—form less than half of the extant letters to Pound in the files (and include none of the literally dozens of letters from him). Still more relevantly, this voluminous correspondence effectively charts Pound's transition from purely aesthetic concerns across the 1920s, to politico-economic activism over the 1930s and beyond. Thus, the earliest letters ranging from 1926 to 1931 attack MacLeish's supposedly derivative modernist poetry, as contained in letters of 5 December 1926 and 24 January 1931:

> I gone an' worked out a mode, and if Mons. McL. can do it , then how many more will be doing it within 3 years.
>
> My criticism (or whatever) of you has never been malign. We all pass through (or else not through) the marsupial phase, no disgrace.

Yet after 30 January 1933—when Pound met Mussolini for the only time, ironically on the day Hitler took power in Germany—Pound's adherence to the Fascist 'faith' became emphatic, no less so than his ensuing conversion to economic conspiracy theories. Examples of Pound's ideological exhortations abound in the unpublished correspondence in MacLeish's file at the Library of Congress. Already on 3 October 1933, Pound declared that 'sane economics and the war problem do link up', while 15 months later, at the end of 1934, he asserted:

> As long as the N.Y Times is what it is / lies will float up ... however the drivveling idiocy of the bastards is such that their eulogies give the show away. Is the country still to any % inhabited by people who swallow this guff? [...] TIME to sweep out particular shit piles[10]

By this time Pound and MacLeish were on different sides of the ideological fence, with MacLeish working for *Fortune* magazine and later forming *Contemporary Historians Inc.* with John Dos Passos and Ernest Hemingway to make the propaganda film *The Spanish Earth,* prior to formally joining FDR's New Dealers at the very end of the 1930s. For his part, following the publication of his *Jefferson and/or Mussolini* in 1935, Pound's fascist publicism then extended to 29 editorials in the weekly, English-language insert for *L'Italia Nostra,* the *British-Italian Bulletin,* on behalf of the Italian invasion of Abyssinia in 1935. This was followed by no fewer than 40 texts for Oswald Mosley's British Union of Fascists, from various newspaper articles to longer journal pieces and a standalone pamphlet (and the only one of the BUF series to be republished after the war), *What Is Money For?*[11] Needless to say, long before the outbreak of war, Pound's battle lines were clearly drawn.

Whereas Pound advised MacLeish poetically before the war, MacLeish did much more for Pound after it, as a well-connected figure in the wartime US government—indeed, ultimately in 1945-6, the Assistant Secretary of State and head of the first American delegation to the United Nations. For instance, the very day after Pound's 26 July 1943 treason indictment *in absentia*—alongside those of other seven US citizens also broadcasting shortwave propaganda for the Axis—MacLeish sent some of the offending radio transcripts to Ernest Hemingway, leading the latter to seek clemency for his old friend: 'He deserves punishment and disgrace but what he really deserves most is ridicule'.[12] But the trained lawyer in MacLeish knew there was a still greater danger, leading him to liaise with the War Department, as he noted in response to Hemingway:

> I have had word from the War Department—informal it is true—to the effect that the Pound business will probably be alright. By which I understand that there will be no summary action. Which is about all we can ask for, as far as the military are concerned.[13]

MacLeish's intervention ensured that Pound was not shot or hanged outright as a traitor, for, as will be shown presently, there was ample evidence that the broadcasts were not the only instances of Pound's 'adhering to the enemy, giving them aid and comfort'—as treason is defined by the US Constitution.

Now, it is also true that, at the time, Pound had few options in northern Italy: looking after his aged mother (his father had died in 1942), as well as his wife and mistress; but also chronically short of money and even shorter of publishing outlets (even if the latter, given his increasingly shrill fascist rhetoric across the 1930s, was more of a self-inflicted injury than anything else). But at the same time—and arguably more important than all of the above considerations to him—Pound thought that virtuously struggling for, as he and other fascists had it, a 'new Europe' under Axis hegemony, would bring about the economic justice that he had been calling for since first meeting the famous Social Creditor, Major C.H. Douglas, in late 1919; indeed, that he had been screaming for since the onset of the World Economic Crisis in the 1930s. For it should also be recognized that Pound saw the closest approximation of his idiosyncratic brand of 'Volitionist Economics' in Benito Mussolini's conception of Corporatism, especially that launched (if largely in name only) in the short-lived Salò Republic between Autumn 1943 and Spring 1945—an under-reported period in Pound's life with which this article shall conclude.

Yet MacLeish, the modest protagonist of the 'Pound Case', only dedicated himself to Pound's freedom a decade later, after visiting the 'bedlam' of St. Elizabeths in 1955 and resolving to get him out—not just for Pound's benefit, but also to avoid further besmirching the US's reputation during the ongoing Cold War. As he wrote to Pound in Oct. 1957, 'I love this Republic and can't be quiet when it violates its own principles'—to which Pound replied, 'your administration and the foul press constantly suppressed and continue to suppress necessary data'.[14] Pound refused to recant; moreover, his letters continued to patronise MacLeish's patriotism. Given such continued hostility, it is not surprising to find that, as recorded by his official biographer, MacLeish felt that 'whoever offers [Pound] a hand will have his fingers broken'.[15]

Several of MacLeish's fingers were enough, it seems, for him to lead the charge to secure Pound's freedom, after more than a dozen years in St Elizabeths asylum, by having the indictment quashed. Facilitating this *volte-face* were three years of letters by MacLeish to the superintendent at St. Elizabeths, Dr Winfred Overholser; Pound's publisher at New Directions, James Laughlin; as well as an array of international figures including the UN Secretary General, the American Attorney General, the Under Secretary of State, and the President of the American Academy of Arts and Letters. In fact, MacLeish drafted the very letter sent to the

Attorney General, eventually signed by Hemingway, T.S. Eliot and Robert Frost, that formally instigated Pound's freedom. This bare sketch of events during the mid-1950s bears out what another intimate and minority voice at this time, Harry Meacham, had already argued more than forty years ago: 'it was all Archie' (Donaldson, 449). Indeed, MacLeish's help ultimately facilitated Pound's release into his wife's care, and they sailed for Italy in May 1958—with Pound offering a fascist salute upon disembarkation. After a quarter of a century, Ezra Pound's fascist faith had remained intact. That he could express it outside an asylum owed more to Archibald MacLeish than anyone else.

III.

But the MacLeish correspondence is only of assistance in respect of either side of the crucible of the 'Pound Case': Pound's actions during World War Two. For the war years, underused archives also offer new perspectives. It is clear, for instance, that the American government went to considerable lengths to gather evidence against Ezra Pound. One major indication is the 292-page Department of Justice report on Pound, covering fully a decade from 1942. As these recently-declassified DOJ files on Pound are now freely available online, it is hoped that research into the wartime government's own actions regarding the Pound Case may be more clearly understood. Few explicit references to this body of documentation have appeared in Pound criticism to date, despite the fact that valuable insights are contained over 6 .pdf documents available a few mouse-clicks away.[16] To cite just two points of interest; first, numerous excerpts from Pound's radio broadcasts do not appear to be available elsewhere, for instance:

> And every hour that you go on with this was is an hour lost to you and your children. And every sane act you commit is committed in homage to Mussolini and Hitler. Every reform, every lurch towards the just price toward the control of a market is an act of homage to Mussolini and Hitler. They are your leaders, however much you think you are conducted by Roosevelt or (told) up by Churchill. You follow Mussolini and Hitler in every constructive act of your government.[17]

This is but part of one of perhaps 300 speeches Pound broadcasted over shortwave radio for Fascist Italy during the war. Most remain undocumented; but then again, far more archival research is surely needed to test the depth of Pound's activities for Mussolini's Italy. Second, by way of demonstrating the energetic efforts of the American government in prosecuting history's first case of radio treason, no less a figure than President Roosevelt sent a memorandum on 1 October 1942 to the US Attorney General, Francis Biddle, advocating a treason indictment:

> There are a number of Americans in Europe who are aiding Hitler et al on the radio. Why should we not proceed to indict them for treason even though we might not be able to try them until after the war? I understand Ezra Pound, Best, Anderson and a few others are broadcasting for Axis microphones.[18]

As FDR's memo makes plain, Pound's indictment emanated from the very heart of the American government. In fact, the Department of Justice files also show that Pound's wartime defence, outlined in a letter to Attorney General Biddle a week after his late July 1943 indictment, was considered by the DOJ's legal team to be most sane—even politically cunning. This view was advanced long ago by C. David Heymann who, quoting the letter in full in *Ezra Pound: The Last Rower*, called Pound's missive 'lucid and reasonably temperate':

> I do not believe that the simple fact of speaking over the radio, wherever placed, can in itself constitute treason. I think that must depend on what is said, and on the motives for speaking. (qtd. 136-8)

But the DOJ was not buying the First Amendment defence, nor did they feel—especially during wartime—that only a conscious 'intent to betray' could constitute treason. It thus mattered little to US authorities that Pound prefaced many of his radio broadcasts by claiming he was only speaking his mind, rather than at the direction of the Italian Ministry of Popular Culture. As the government was to argue in the similar case of *US v. Chandler*—the trial of a pro-Nazi broadcaster indicted alongside Pound in 1943, who recorded under the pseudonym 'Paul Revere'—

> In the field of radio propaganda, "mere words" was no defense […] the mere utterance of disloyal statement is not treason; aid and comfort must be given to the enemy. But the communication of an idea, whether by speech or writing, is as much an act as throwing a brick… (Rushing 124)

In consequence, Douglas Chandler was given a life sentence, and was only pardoned in 1959, that is, after MacLeish had secured Pound's release as mentally unfit to stand trial.

To be sure, however, as far as the United States government archives are concerned, the most important repository of documents relating to the 'Pound Case' is the 1,513-page FBI file (now available for commercial purchase on microfilm), containing portions apparently declassified as long ago as 1982. Again surprisingly, the single article focussing solely on Pound's now-declassified FBI file was only published in 2009. Karen Leick's survey concentrates overwhelmingly on the question of Pound's sanity—as speculated in FBI interviews with the likes of William Carlos Williams, George Antheil, Kay Boyle, Hemingway, MacLeish and others. Quite apart from the missed opportunity to give an overview of this important new material, new contexts, and new considerations in the 'Pound Case', Leick seems to work backwards, teleologically, from Pound's 1945 insanity plea to mine quotations from old friends and contacts who thought he had 'gone crazy'. Yet in this respect, the most comprehensive account of this pivotal period in his life and work, Tim Redman's indispensable *Ezra Pound and Italian Fascism*, cites a letter by Pound's lawyer, Julien Cornell, which states: '"I discussed with him [Pound] the possibility of pleading insanity as a defense, and he has no objections. In fact, he told me that the idea had already occurred to him"'. This profoundly undercuts his mental incompetency plea for, as Redman rightly notes, 'if Pound knew enough to concur in the incapacity defence, he was not incapacitated'. (qtd. 224)

Furthermore, the FBI file shows that Pound was politically cannier; was more bureaucratically involved with Italian Fascism; and was more important to Mussolini's regime than has been posited, with very few exceptions,[19] in the secondary literature. By way of example, the FBI files show that Pound's famous Confucian translation, "The Unwobbling Pivot" of 1947, was originally published by the Salò Republic under the title *L'Asse che non vacilla* [*The Axis Which Will Not Waiver*]—referred to as 'The Axis' in Pound's captured correspondence with PNF officials—the double meaning in the title being the likely reason this version was pulped by advancing Allied armies with the seizure of Milan in February 1945.[20] Given the conditions of invasion and civil war in Italy at this time, of course, it is doubtless the case, as Redman has further noted, that the period 'between the formation of the Republic of Salò on 23 September 1943 and Pound's arrest in early May 1945, is the least documented of his adult years.' (Redman 233) Even so, there seems little doubt that the reference to the Axis in the title of Pound's translation was neither coincidental nor apolitical, as Pound wrote in letter on 2 November 1944, also included in the FBI file: 'The value of philosophy (or of a specific philosophy) is that it strengthens courage. Confucius is material which should be taken into the trenches'. (Redman 264)

IV.

By way of conclusion, it is worth further emphasising that the archives hold many more Pound texts; much more wartime context; and a great deal of unknown history, all bearing upon a case that has been widely discussed but less well understood. For the materials surveyed here suggest much deeper ideological activism on Pound's part, and with greater lucidity, than has been typically maintained by scholars. By way of challenging the critical frameworks alternatively debating Ezra

Pound's wartime insanity; political naïveté; or even First Amendment rights to *speech* (rather than seditious *actions* on behalf of the Fascist Axis), this article shall briefly highlight two additional considerations raised in Pound's expansive FBI file. In turn, like the archival perspective on offer for the 'Pound case' as a whole, these final two examples point toward a different set of responses to the question 'What happened?'—particularly in terms of Ezra Pound's political commitment and usefulness to Mussolini's Italy.[21] Perhaps, instead, a more fruitful question might be, 'Just how deeply involved was Ezra Pound with fascism?'

For their part, FBI investigators believed that 'Pound belonged to [...] an organisation dedicated to anti-Allied propaganda [...and] also advised that Ezra Pound was a member of a committee in the Ministry of Popular Culture which met every morning to formulate anti-Allied propaganda and that Pound was the head of the United States Division of that committee.' They further suspected that he was paid handsomely by the Ministry from a 'secret fund for foreign broadcasters' for work that also included, for instance, 'suggesting certain books for Allied prisoners of War. Pound suggests VOLPE'S HISTORY OF THE FASCIST REVOLUTION.'[22]

If this is indeed the case, Pound undertook a far more significant role than merely broadcasting Fascist propaganda to the United States. And not just to Americans: another document provides the translation of a radio broadcast in French, apparently written by Pound and clearly aimed at Vichy France.[23] Other materials in the FBI file include Pound's position papers on framing Axis propaganda; additional excerpts from undocumented radio broadcasts; records of payments and statements by eye-witnesses; Pound's correspondence with leading functionaries of Fascist regime/s, and a great deal more.

For example, consider the case of Gian Gaetano Cabella, Pound's editor for the newspaper *Il Popolo di Alessandria*, for whom he wrote more than 60 articles in the last 18 months of the war.[24] The two exchanged numerous letters,[25] although his name is unlikely to be recognised by Pound scholars. Cabella was, in fact, a long-time and important regime activist; it was he who recorded Mussolini's final political testament a week before his 28 April 1945 lynching: 'I was not bluffing when I declared that the Fascist idea will be the idea of the twentieth century [...] History will vindicate me.' (qtd in Griffin 88-9) As this suggests, Pound was in closer proximity to the Fascist regime, and taken more seriously by it, than has been accepted in the familiar narrative of the 'Pound Case'. For as the files FBI show, Pound was at work for the Fascist regime/s on a variety of fronts, to the bitter end.

A glance at Pound's Fascist-era poetry, finally, underscores this propagandistic range and tenacity. It also, in my view, suggests that a neat demarcation between propaganda, on the one hand, and poetry on the other, was not a distinction borne of the war itself, but of Pound criticism after it. In February 1942, for example, Pound read two Cantos over the air—the second specifically given as Canto 46, which includes some of Pound's anti-Semitic conspiracism:

> Mr Roth-schild, hell knows which Roth-schild
> 1861, '64 or there sometime, "very few people
> "will understand this. Those who do will be occupied
> "getting profits. The general public will probably not
> "see it's against their interest."[26]

After the fall of Mussolini some eighteen months later, Pound returned to composing Cantos for the first time since American entry into the war. In 1944, also for the first time, he completed two Cantos wholly in Italian: the infamous Cantos 72 and 73.[27] While the first commemorated the recent death of the Fascist icon and leading Futurist, F.T. Marinetti, the second tells the story of an Italian girl turned suicide-bomber, following her rape by a group of Canadian soldiers (of which there is no actual record). In Lawrence Rainey's authoritative summation, the poem simply reworks 'a tawdry fabrication issued by propaganda authorities […] in occupied Milan' (6).

Canto 73 can be ultimately understood as little more than 'black propaganda', and represents Pound's final artistic work before the "Pisan Cantos" sequence (covering Cantos 74 to 84), which received the first Bollingen Award in 1949. Moreover, the preceding two Cantos were initially published in the Fascist newspaper *Marina Repubblicana* (*Republican Navy*, on 15 January and 1 February 1945, respectively)—one of the final publications still appearing under the crumbling Salò Republic—with an initial preface announcing to readers, in part: 'Ezra Pound is American, but a friend, in the highest and purest sense of the word, to Fascist Italy."[28] Three months earlier, Pound had also sent Cantos 72 and 73 to Salò's Minister of Popular Culture, Fernando Mezzasoma, with the deferential covering note: 'I do not know where the enclosed Cantos are useful in any way. No doubt they are too crude for the refined and too complex for the simple-minded."[29] Around the time of their appearance in print in early 1945, moreover, Pound then took the liberty of sending Cantos 72 and 73 directly to *Il Duce* at Lake Garda.[30]

If only as a reminder of those with whom Pound was communicating in the dying days of the war, no less than the fact than he put his poetry directly in the service of wartime propaganda, it is worth ending here with Canto 73, subtitled 'Cavalcanti-Republican Correspondence'. By linking the Florentine Poet with the Salò Republic, it is Pound himself, by way of negative example, demonstrating the inextricability of art and politics at this time—at the very least in his own, rightly infamous instance—as well as, hopefully, the literary and historical relevance of archival research into this, and other, modernist 'cases':

> The enemy blown to hell,
>   twenty were dead,
> The girl also dead
>   among the rabble [...]
> To die for the fatherland
>   in the Romagna!
> Dead they are not dead,
> I have returned
> from the third heaven
> to see Romagna,
> To see the mountains
>   in the recovery,
> What a beautiful winter!
>   In the North the fatherland is reborn,
> But what girls![31]

Endnotes

[1] See Ezra Pound, "Notes for CXVII et seq.", in *The Cantos of Ezra Pound*:
'The dreams clash
    and are shattered –
and that I tried to make a paradiso
            terrestre', p. 816.

[2] For a good account of Pound's initial detention in the "gorilla cage" amongst "social misfits, soldiers who had turned their guns on their commanding officers, thieves, rapists and murderers", see E. Fuller Torrey, pp. 1-18, quoted p. 5.

[3] Older accounts tend to be more sympathetic, including Julien Cornell; Charles Norman; and Noel Stock. Subsequent works have tended to be more critical, including Robert Casillo; Leon Surette; and the most recent biography by A. David Moody.

[4] For this argument, see Wendy Flory's "Pound and antisemitism", pp. 284-300.

[5] Ezra Pound to Harriet Monroe, 30 Nov. 1926, cited in D. D. Paige ed., *The Letters of Ezra Pound, 1907-1941*, p. 205.

[6] See, for example, Burton Hatlen, "Ezra Pound and Fascism"; Marjorie Perloff, "Fascism, Anti-Semitism, Isolationism: Contextualizing the 'Case of EP'", pp. 145-69; and Bill Freind, "'Why do you want to put your ideas in order?': Re-thinking the Politics of Ezra Pound", pp. 545-563.

[7] David Barnes, "Fascist Aesthetics: Ezra Pound's Cultural Negotiations in 1930s Italy," p. 21.

[8] See the Library of Congress index for the papers of Archibald MacLeish at: lcweb2.loc.gov/cgibin/query/h?faid/faid:@field%28DOCID+ms997016%29 (all websites last accessed 26/9/2010).

[9] See Scott Donaldson, *Archibald MacLeish: An American Life*; and R.J. Winnick's edited *Letters of Archibald MacLeish, 1907 to 1982*.

[10] Library of Congress, Washington, D.C., Papers of Archibald MacLeish, Ezra Pound Correspondence.

[11] See Matthew Feldman, "Make it Crude: Ezra Pound's Antisemitic propaganda for the BUF and PNF".

[12] Letter, Ernest Hemingway to Archibald MacLeish discussing Ezra Pound's mental health and other literary matters, 10 August [1943] (Archibald MacLeish Papers), reproduced in facsimile online at http://memory.loc.gov/cgi-bin/ampage?collId=mcc&fileName=035/page.db&recNum=0&itemLink=r?ammem/mcc:@field(DOCID+@lit(mcc/035)).

[13] MacLeish Papers, Hemingway Correspondence.

[14] MacLeish Papers, Pound Correspondence.

[15] Cited in Donaldson, p. 446. In infamous radio broadcasts, Pound had occasionally attacked MacLeish personally, as with one manuscript from 23 April 1942, reprinted in Leonard Doob, ed., '*Ezra Pound Speaking*'. The address is simply titled "MacLEISH", and contains *ad hominem* attacks (like most of his broadcasts):

> 'I ask Archie to say OPENLY why handing out four billion in excess profits on the gold wheez, between 1932 and '40, handing it to a dirty gang of kike and hyper-kikes on the London gold exchange, six firms, is expected to HELP Americanism, or why it should be regarded as a model of devotion to the American spirit. Or why ANY hones American should vote for the continuance of that swindle, or for keepin' in office the men and kikes who were responsible for putting' it over the people.' (p. 105)

16 Available online, in six downloadable parts, at: justice.gov/criminal/foia/ezra-pound.html. For use of the DOJ files on the Pound Case, see the insightful article by Robert Corrigan, "Ezra Pound and the Italian Ministry of Popular Culture".
17 Ezra Pound, Department of Justice Files, Part 1, p. 24. This radio speech was delivered on 26 May 1942, and is cited in an essay by Charles Norman, "The Case For and Against Ezra Pound," p. [m14].
18 Ezra Pound, Department of Justice Files, Part 1, p. 3.
19 Good exceptions include Richard Sieburth and James Laughlin in *The Paris Review* 128 (Fall 1993), pp. 194-206 and 308-317, respectively; Tim Redman, "The Repatriation of Pound, 1939-1942: A View from the Archives", pp. 447-457; and Robert Omar Pound, Robert E. Spoo and Dorothy Pound, eds., *Ezra and Dorothy Pound: Letters in Captivity, 1945-46*.
20 The English translation is available in Ezra Pound's *Confucius* as "Chung Yung: The Unwobbling Pivot". See also Ezra Pound, FBI File, Section 13.
21 After the fall of Mussolini in July 1943, Pound apparently travelled by 'cattle truck' and even foot to the Fascists' radio station in northern Italy to continue his broadcasts for the newly-established Salò Republic. Upon his arrival in Milan, Pound evidently declared: 'Give me a bed, a bowl of soup and a microphone'; for further details of Pound in Salò, see Humphrey Carpenter, *A Serious Character: The Life of Ezra Pound*, pp. 632-642, quoted p. 633. Although it has not been established whether or not Pound actually made any broadcasts for the Salò Republic, it is clear he received payment from the German Occupation authorities (*ibid.*), and was believed by the FBI to have been 'submitting short news comments to the "Jerry's Front Calling" program at Milan' from Autumn 1943; Ezra Pound, FBI File, Section 10.
22 *Ibid.*, Sections 3 and 4.
23 *Ibid.*, Section 10.
24 A few of these articles from 1944 are reproduced and available online at: web.archive.org/web/20040606235016/http://www.antoniomaconi.it/libri/pound/index.htm.
25 Ezra Pound, FBI File, Section 11ff.
26 Pound, "Canto 46" in *The Cantos*, quoted p. 231. It is a safe bet that Canto 45, the infamous "Usura" jeremiad, was read the week before the interlinked Canto 46 was transmitted on 12 February 1942.
27 According to Ron Bush, these Cantos first appeared in the U.S. in 1987; see his excellent "Modernism, Fascism and the Composition of Ezra Pound's *Pisan Cantos*", pp. 69-87, cited p. 71. A strong analysis of these poems is undertaken in Patricia Cockram's "Collapse and Recall: Ezra Pound's Italian Cantos", pp. 535-544.
28 Cited in Massimo Bacigalupo, "Ezra Pound's Cantos 72 and 73: An Annotated Translation", pp. 9-41, cited p. 21. Bacigalupo's insightful text concludes: 'Far from being an irrelevant and embarrassing digressions, Cantos 72 and 73, we may safely conclude, are central' to *The Cantos*, p. 28.
29 Cited in Massimo Bacigalupo, *The Forméd Trace: The Later Poetry of Ezra Pound*, p. 53.
30 Pound's Cantos were evidently discovered amongst Mussolini's papers; see Barbara C. Eastman, "The Gap in *The Cantos*: 72 and 73", pp. 415-427.
31 Romagna is Mussolini's birthplace; see Bacigalupo, "Ezra Pound's Cantos 72 and 73", p. 18. The Italian originals for these Cantos are presented in Faber versions of the fourth collected edition from 1987 and its subsequent impressions, pp. 424-435.

Works Cited

Barnes, David. "Fascist Aesthetics: Ezra Pound's Cultural Negotiations in 1930s Italy." *Journal of Modern Literature* 34.1 (Fall 2010): 19-35. Available available online at http://www.academia.edu/2017676/Fascist_Aesthetics_Ezra_Pounds_Cultural_Negotiations_in_1930s_Italy.

Bacigalupo, Massimo. *The Forméd Trace: The Later Poetry of Ezra Pound*. New York: Columbia UP, 1980.

—. "Ezra Pound's Cantos 72 and 73: An Annotated Translation." *Paideuma* 20.1/2 (1991): 10-41.

Bush, Ronald. "Modernism, Fascism, and the Composition of Ezra Pound's *Pisan Cantos*." *Modernism/modernity* 2.3 (September 1995): 69-87.

Carpenter, Humphrey. *A Serious Character: The Life of Ezra Pound*. London: Faber, 1988.

Casillo, Robert. *The Genealogy of Demons: Fascism, Anti-Semitism and the Myths of Ezra Pound*. Evanston, IL: Northwestern UP, 1988.

Cockram, Patricia. "Collapse and Recall: Ezra Pound's Italian Cantos." *Journal of Modern Literature* 23.3/4 (Summer 2000): 535-544.

Cornell, Julien. *The Trial of Ezra Pound*. London: Faber, 1966.

Corrigan, Robert. "Ezra Pound and the Italian Ministry of Popular Culture." *The Journal of Popular Culture*, 5.4 (Spring 1972): 767-781.

Donaldson, Scott. *Archibald MacLeish: An American Life*. London: Houghton Mifflin, 1992.

Eastman, Barbara C. "The Gap in *The Cantos*: 72 and 73." *Paideuma* 8.3 (Winter 1979): 415-427.

Eliot, T.S. *Four Quartets*. London: Faber, 2000.

Feldman, Matthew. "Make it Crude: Ezra Pound's Antisemitic propaganda for the BUF and PNF." *Holocaust Studies* 15.1/2 (2010): 59-77.

Flory, Wendy. "Pound and anti-Semitism." *The Cambridge Companion to Ezra Pound*. Ed. Ira B. Nadel. Cambridge: Cambridge UP, 1999. 284-300.

Friend, Bill. "'Why do you want to put your ideas in order?': Re-thinking the Politics of Ezra Pound." *Journal of Modern Literature* 23.3/4 (Summer 2000): 545-563.

Gentile, Emilio. *Politics as Religion*. Trans. George Staunton. Princeton, NJ: Princeton UP, 2006.

Griffin, Roger, ed. *Fascism*. Oxford: Oxford UP, 1995.

Hatlen, Burton. "Ezra Pound and Fascism." *Ezra Pound and History*. Ed. Marianne Korn. Bangor: U of Maine P, 1985. 145-172.

Heymann, C. David. *Ezra Pound: The Last Rower*. New York: Seaver Books, 1976.

Leick, Karen. "Madness, Paranoia, and Ezra Pound's FBI File." *Modernism on File: Writers, Artists and the FBI, 1920-1956*. Eds. Claire A. Culleton and Karen Leick. Basingstoke: Palgrave, 2008. 105-126.

MacLeish, Archibald. Papers of Archibald MacLeish. Library of Congress, Washington, DC.

—. *Letters of Archibald MacLeish, 1907 to 1982*. Ed. Donald Winnick. Boston: Houghton Mifflin, 1983.

Moody, A. David. *Ezra Pound: Poet. Vol. I*. Oxford: Oxford UP, 2007.

Norman, Charles. "The Case For and Against Ezra Pound." *PM*, New York (25 Nov. 1945), pp. [m 12-m 14, m 16], m 17.

Norman, Charles. *The Case of Ezra Pound*. New York: Funk and Wagnalls, 1968.

Perloff, Marjorie. "Fascism, Anti-Semitism, Isolationism: Contextualizing the 'Case of EP.'" *Paideuma* 17.2/3 (Fall/Winter 1998): 7-21.

Pound, Ezra. Department of Justice, Pound Files. VI Parts. Web. 31 March 2011.

—. FBI File on Ezra Pound. Primary Source/Scholarly Resources. Microfilm.

—. *The Cantos of Ezra Pound*. London: Faber, 1998.

—. *Confucius*. New York: New Directions, 1969.

—. *Ezra and Dorothy Pound: Letters in Captivity, 1945-1946*. Eds. Omar Pound and Robert Spoo. Oxford: Oxford UP, 1999.

—. *"Ezra Pound Speaking": Radio Speeches of World War II*. Ed. Leonard Doob. Westport, CT: Greenwood P, 1978.

—. *The Letters of Ezra Pound, 1907-1941*. Ed. D. D. Paige. New York: Harcourt Brace and Company, 1950.

Rainey, Lawrence, ed. *A Poem Containing History: Textual Studies in the Cantos*. Lansing: U of Michigan P, 2000.

Redman, Tim. *Ezra Pound and Italian Fascism*. Cambridge: Cambridge UP, 1991.

—. "The Repatriation of Pound, 1939-1942: A View from the Archives." *Paideuma* 8.3 (Winter 1979): 447-457.

Rushing, Conrad L. "'Mere Words': The Trial of Ezra Pound." *Critical Inquiry* 14.1 (Autumn 1987): 111-133.

Surette, Leon. *Pound in Purgatory: From Economic Radicalism to Anti-Semitism.* Chicago: Chicago UP, 1998.

Stock, Noel. *The Life of Ezra Pound.* London: Routledge, 1970.

Torrey, E. Fuller. *The Roots of Treason: Ezra Pound and the Secrets of St Elizabeths.* London: Sidgwick and Jackson, 1984.

US Constitution. Art. III, Sec. 3. Web. 5 April 2011.

3. Ezra Pound and Ernst Kantorowicz: From Medieval to Modern Autocracies

Ezra Pound's extant World War Two radio scripts range from slogans and short, often anonymous, items to longer typescripts and roundtable interviews for the Axis. Their languages reflect the multiple audiences they were intended to address: primarily written in English, there are also texts in French, German and Italian. These extensive endeavours in the written word were accompanied by consistent and energetic propaganda strategies advanced by Pound throughout the war, which were, on the whole, taken seriously by several regime functionaries in fascist Italy. These activities led to Pound's arrest on charges of treason in 1945, which became a *cause célèbre* not only for mid-century intellectuals in the United States, but also for radical right-wing activists internationally. Following psychiatric examinations and an 'insanity hearing' which concluded that Pound was not mentally fit to stand trial for treason, he was incarcerated in St. Elizabeths asylum from 1945 until 1958. One of the great patriarchs of modernism was then released into the care of his wife, Dorothy Pound, and spent the remaining fourteen years of his life in Italy.

Pound's enthusiasm for Mussolini and Italian fascism scarcely abated while he was incarcerated; if anything, Pound's fascism grew more extreme, as evidenced by his relationship with such neo-Nazis as John Kasper (Marsh 2015) and Eustace Mullins—Pound's first biographer (Feldman 2014). While incarcerated, Pound continued to read (and translate) works by Mussolini, as well as other radical right books such as *Hitler's Table Talk* (Hitler 1953), which he would sometimes loan to friends. Likewise, from the 1950s and beyond he was working with various radical right organizations in the United States, Britain, Italy and elsewhere. Pound's *Cantos* even reference the infamous forgery *The Protocols of the Learned Elders of Zion*—for example, the use of the phrase 'historic blackout' ('Canto XCV')—which is a recurrent theme in his deeply anti-Semitic letters to Olivia Rossetti Agresti (see Henderson 2009: 514–16, 693, 747–48). This remains a subject that scholars of Pound have, on the whole, strenuously tried to avoid facing; this regrettable state of affairs was recently crowned by David Moody's lawyerly defence of Pound's politics in the third instalment of his otherwise-panoramic Pound biography (2015).

Given the sheer weight of evidence, the bill for these evasions will one day come due. Yet if the subject of Pound's wartime and post-war radical right activism has been poorly covered in Pound Studies, rather more attention has been paid to when he may have first crossed the Rubicon in his support for Italian fascism.

Lawrence Rainey (1998) sees Pound's initial turn towards fascism as early as his 1922 *Malatesta Cantos*, and certainly by 1923 through his connection to the Mussolini-supporting American sculptor, Nancy Cox-McCormack. In Miranda Hickman's excellent summation: 'Pound sought to collaborate with Cox-McCormack to present to Mussolini a program of cultural patronage that could transform Italy into an international cultural centre.' (2011: 283)

However, as late as January 1925 Pound's view of the state, as set forth in his short prose text 'Definitions', was far from the ideal adumbrated by Mussolini as 'our ferocious totalitarian will' that very year:

> 1. A good state is one which impinges least upon the peripheries of its citizens.
> 2. The function of the state is to facilitate the traffic, i. e. the circulation of goods, air, water, heat, coal (black or white), power, and even thought; and to prevent the citizens from impinging on each other. ([1925] 1981)

True, Pound had claimed on 30 November 1926 that 'I personally think extremely well of Mussolini' (Pound [1950] 1971: 205), but on the whole, the 1920s seems too early for Pound's—at least public—embrace of Il Duce and his totalitarian project.

Following the onset of the Great Depression at the end of the decade, Pound's admiration for the 'Italian awakening', as he put it in a 1931 *New Review* text (Baechler et al. 1991: 329), was becoming more enthusiastic and explicit. For the first time, in April 1932, he met Filippo Marinetti, the founder of Futurism and one of the earliest supporters of fascism, coming away with stacks of 'fascist licherachoor' in the process (Feldman 2013: 14). For Catherine Paul, this was a decisive spring; less so for his meeting with Marinetti than the appearance of *Guido Cavalcanti Rime*, a volume by Pound that contributed to Italy's 'looking to its cultural heritage as a means of enlivening its modernity': 'By diving into Italy's cultural heritage, and emerging with Cavalcanti in his teeth, Pound would offer to modern Italy pieces of its past that could well serve its present' (2016: 66, 65). Paul makes a convincing case that, in spring 1932, Pound's well-known engagement with medievalism was turned, with Cavalcanti (later the narrator of Pound's most Axis-friendly Canto from 1944, LXXIII, his final instalment before *The Pisan Cantos* sequence), into 'one of Pound's earliest contributions to the Fascist cultural projects in Italy' (Paul 2016: 80).

Paul's identification of medievalism, no doubt for long a fascination of Pound's (see Byron 2014), with Italian cultural reclamation is a tantalizing one in terms of his contemporaneous embrace of fascism. Yet it does not adequately account for Pound's hero worship of 'the Boss', which was scarcely present before his one and only meeting with Mussolini—an audience later immortalized in 'Canto XLI'—on the ominous date of 30 January 1933. After that fateful meeting,

Pound spent the ensuing fortnight feverishly writing the extraordinary *Jefferson and/or Mussolini* (1935), which notoriously dubbed the dictator an 'artifex' and called him both a genius and a great man. Although the volume was not published until 1935 (by Stanley Nott in London), by mid-February 1933—when the *c.* 140 page draft of *Jefferson and/or Mussolini* was allegedly completed—the pieces had fallen into place. Crucially, as will be shown below, his paean to Mussolini's allegedly artistic brilliance hinged upon what scholars now term 'political religion': 'Any thorough judgment of MUSSOLINI will be in a measure an act of faith, it will depend on what you *believe* the man means, what you believe that he wants to accomplish.' (Pound 1935: 33)

Between the publication of *Guido Cavalcanti Rime* in spring 1932 and his public declaration of loyalty in winter 1933, Pound had been 'primed' for Italian fascism by his attendance, in December 1932, of the *Decennio*, a decennial exhibition of the 1922 March on Rome. Jeffrey Schnapp has described the *Mostra della Rivoluzione Fascista* (*MRF*), seen by nearly four million visitors, in the following terms:

> The aim of the fifteen 'historical' rooms was to make palpable to visitors the emotions of awe and terror associated with the revolutionary violence of [F]ascism-as-movement so as to then perform a sort of 'return to order,' associated with [F]ascism-as-state, as the visitor left behind the building's periphery to march through four final spacious rooms aligned along the central axis: a Hall of Honor, containing a reconstruction of Mussolini's first Milanese office, the Gallery of the Fasces, featuring the banners of individual Fascist groups, the 'Mussolini room', containing a reconstruction of his second Milanese office, and a *Sacrarium,* celebrating the 'martyrs' of the revolution. This complex of nineteen rooms occupied the entirety of the ground floor of the Palazzo delle Esposizioni. The building's second floor was dedicated not to the past, but to the regime's present and future plans. It contained a room representing the activities of Fascist organizations abroad, a library with 5,000 volumes concerned with Fascism, and three small halls dedicated to the regime's achievements in the fields of labor, agriculture, transportation, industry, and commerce. (Schnapp 2007: 63, 65; original emphasis)

There can be no doubt this was a key moment of radicalization for Ezra Pound. In connecting history with the present, the *MRF* exhibition redoubled Pound's enthusiasm for fascist Italy, both through its sacralizing of Italian fascism's conquest of power, and by crowning Mussolini as the infallible head of the movement. The nexus of political faith and secular autocracy so powerfully evinced by the *Decennio* exhibition would be a palpable feature of Pound's thinking thereafter.

In keeping with Paul's insights about the importance of medievalism to Pound no less than Italian Fascism's approach to cultural heritage, there is an additional source, neglected by Pound Studies to date, which may have helped Pound to see in Mussolini's leadership a nexus of secular and sacral power. As will be argued over the remainder of this essay, Ernst Kantorowicz's *Frederick The Second 1994–1250* may well have been an essential way station on Pound's 'conversion' to Italian fascism. Just as Pound famously saw in Mussolini a constructive force that he contrasted with a decadent democratic capitalism, so too did Kantorowicz contrast Frederick II with his nemesis, Pope Gregory; as here, in a passage highlighted in Pound's copy with a pencil line down the left-hand margin, strongly suggestive of his interest:

> whereas Pope Gregory was solely negative and destructive, aiming at the annihilation of his foe, Frederick had a constructive aim. Without so expressing it, Frederick countered each negation of the Pope's by pointing to himself, the Emperor of *Justitia*, the Rescuer, the Bringer of Salvation in a day of chaos. ([1927]1931: 504)

There can be no doubt Pound read the 1931 English translation of this 1927 edition, for housed in Pound's personal library collection in the Harry Ransom Center at the University of Texas at Austin is his annotated copy. On the back flyleaf in pencil, for example, a minimum of 25 paginated entries are noted down (13, 25, 41, 53, 61, 62, 81, 80-88, 108, 130, 148, 157, 171, 274, 281, 286, 298, 308, 312, 339, 340, 354, 359, 362, 359). Many marginal annotations are also evident throughout the book, up to p. 677, as well as marks at the index (for example, under the entries Falcon Book and Falcons, p. 701).[1] This was clearly a book in which Pound took great interest, potential reasons for which are discussed below. Before addressing these reasons, however, it first merits stressing the centrality of 'political religion' to totalitarian rule—especially fascist totalitarian rule, above all, in Nazi Germany and fascist Italy—and within this operant secular faith, the role of 'charismatic leadership' in this febrile equation.[2]

Like many other 'charisma-hungry' intellectuals in Italy and across inter-war Europe, Pound's attraction to fascism's political religion had much to do with the 'cult of the leader'. Indeed, in the words of a key scholar in this field, Emilio Gentile, there was an inherent and necessary link in Italian Fascism between the totalitarian will to monopolize political power and the way in which it conceived its own ideology as a fundamentalist and dogmatic religion that could not tolerate the coexistence of other political convictions and demanded that Italians believe in its myths and celebrate its rituals. (Gentile 2006: 33) Gentile, a leading Italian historian, has further delimited these characteristics as the primacy of faith and myth in the political arena, guided by the 'consecrated' figure of Mussolini, alongside *ethical commandments* and a *political liturgy*, extending to 'a system of beliefs, myths, rituals, and symbols that deified the nation and state and celebrated the personality cult of "Il Duce" as a living myth' (Gentile 2000: 22, original emphasis)

Leader worship represented the absolute cornerstone of the fascist regime (Duggan 2013); so much so that the Italian foreign minister in the early 1930s,

Dino Grandi, referred to Mussolini as the 'Pope of Fascism'. Another snapshot of this devotion was provided some 40 years ago by Piero Melograni's 'The Cult of the Duce in Mussolini's Italy':

> Approval for the cult of the Duce came from all sorts of quarters, even from the least expected people. In 1933, Sigmund Freud sent the Duce a copy of one of his books, with the significant dedication: 'To Benito Mussolini, from an old man who greets in the Ruler the Hero of Culture'. (1976: 233)

Bearing his adherence to the 'Cult of the Duce', from the mid-1930s to the end of the Second World War Pound sent Mussolini more than 50 letters, as well as most of his published texts during this period. Pound even kept a personal scrapbook of Mussolini's activities. As this suggests, Pound's was a genuinely felt devotion to 'Mussolinism'; and again, for millions of others, this was an absolutely essential ingredient for fascism's political religion, a theory defined by Richard Shorten as 'pseudo religious modernisms' that are 'appropriations and imitations of religious beliefs and sentiments in secular outlooks' (2012: 61).

Roughly coterminous with his shift towards pro-fascist propaganda, the remaining two-thirds of Pound's epic poem, *The Cantos* (1999), had, by the middle 1930s, turned into a 'fascist epic', as John Lauber (1978) and others have argued. Massimo Bacigalupo has even gone so far as to describe Pound's *Cantos* as 'the sacred poem of the Nazi-Fascist millennium' (1980: x). For instance, this engagement with fascism is evident as late as 'Canto CV'—part of the final 'Thrones' sequence, which, as Pound explained late in life to Donald Hall, is 'dedicated to the spirits of the people who have been responsible for good government'; that is, 'an order possible or at any rate conceivable on earth' (Redman 1992: 200). At the opposite spectrum from his 1925 understanding of the state as limited in its intervention into individuals' lives, Pound advocated a very different idea three and a half decades later:

> And Muss saved, rem salvavit,
>   in Spain
>   il salvabile.
>   semina motuum
>   From Sulmona
>   the lion-fount—
>   must be Sulmona, Ovidio's
> Federico noted the hawk form. (Pound 1999: 760)

As will be suggested further below, this is in effect a fusion of Il Duce and Frederick Hohenstaufen (1194–1250), King of Sicily, Germany, Jerusalem and Holy Roman Emperor—given variously as Frederick II, Federico II or King Federigo, depending on the source. Like Mussolini's 'saving the salvageable' (a translation from the quotation above) by sending military forces to aid General Francisco Franco during the Spanish Civil War, so Frederick II, author of a celebrated treatise on Falconry, built a vital aqueduct in the town of Sulmona and made the latter the capital of the medieval Abruzzo. As for 'semina motuum', Pound unpacked this phrase in his translation of Confucius's *Ta Hio, The Great Learning*: 'One humane family can humanize a whole state; one courteous family can lift a whole state into courtesy; one grasping and perverse man can drive a nation to chaos' (Liebregts 2004: 295).

As a representative of one of those families putatively capable of humanizing an entire state, Frederick Hohenstaufen snakes through the entirety of Pound's *Thrones* (Pound 1999: 669–794), a sequence that simply defines the state as 'order, inside a boundary' (1990: 722). As for Frederick II's son-in-law, Ezzelino of Romano, it is hard not to see in the following description by Ernst Kantorowicz, Frederick's twentieth-century biographer, exactly why Pound might be so taken with Kantorowicz's book: 'The devil of Treviso, he became the ancestor of Sigismondo Malatesta and of Cesare Borgia'; meaning, in short, that he was a forerunner of Pound's beloved Renaissance. Found at the top of p. 612, this quotation has a marginal line in pencil, strongly suggestive of Pound's interest. Just as importantly, this view is contrasted with another book Pound knew well: Jacob Burckhardt's canonical 1860 study *Civilisation of the Renaissance in Italy*,

> which describes Frederick and his son-in-law Ezzelino as political models for the later Renaissance despots. While Burckhardt, however, had conceived this model as ultimately Eastern, Kantorowicz, in a highly evocative allegory, depicted the Trecento tyrants as bastard offspring from the rape of the 'maid Italy' by the German Kaiser Frederick. According to Burckhardt, the Renaissance was closely related to the "Italian genius"; Kantorowicz, by contrast, represented Italy less as the cradle than as the womb of modernity. (Ruehl 2015: 199)

Two general points need to be raised. The first of these is about sources, and the second point relates to the Zeitgeist, or better, perhaps, to the cultural backdrop of medieval Europe. First, it is well to remember that the historical and archival sources for medieval Europe are comparatively scarce. That is due in no small measure to the fact that literacy at the time meant literacy in Latin, and was mostly the preserve of a clerical (that is, religious) elite—and manuscript preservation, transmission and textual learning more generally were all in their infancy.[3] Consequently, far more than for scholars working with printed materials, the burden of interpretation for medievalists remains of cardinal importance. Put simply, one can more easily take liberties with sources and interpretations between roughly the fifth and fifteenth centuries AD than we can today with typeset or preserved archival materials from the last few centuries. This might be summarized by the title of

Norman Cantor's otherwise mischievous 1992 text, *Inventing the Middle Ages*, which describes Ernst Kantorowicz's seminal study, *Frederick The Second, 1194–1250*, in terms of its compositional context as 'constitut[ing] a tocsin for militant nationalism and faith in the great leader' (Cantor 1992: 96). In keeping with this sense here, the remainder of this essay is far less interested in the historical accuracy of Kantorowicz's biography than in what Pound, that self-conscious modern and proselytizer of the drive to 'make it new'—itself a phrase taken from a Chinese emperor's bathtub in the eighteenth century BC—might have appropriated from it.

Second, it is important to note that certain debates define—or at least colour— entire epochs. In the modern period one of these might be the role of technology in the transformation of daily life; some argue that it has had a fundamental, even revolutionary impact on human life—and even human nature—while others see in technological change little more than an outgrowth of pre-existing trends and civilizational mores. In the millennium of medieval Europe, there can be little doubt that one of the defining struggles was between spiritual and temporal power. It mattered a great deal, for instance, that what Kantorowicz aptly calls Frederick II's 'unclerical mind' ([1927] 1931: 213) meant that the emperor was excommunicated no fewer than four times by the Vatican. Pope Gregory IX—possibly following the mystic Joachim of Fiore—declared Frederick to be the precursor to the Antichrist.[4] This feud centred upon an issue essentially powering R. H. C. Davis's standard textbook *A History of Medieval Europe*, according to which 'the problem […] of the relationship between Church and State […] was to be fundamental for all medieval history' ([1957] 1972: 8). That claim is on the first page of his opening chapter, while the secular ascendancy of St. Louis over the Vatican closes his book. Other histories likewise understand the interactions between empire and papacy to be, as it were, of cardinal importance: 'After nine-and-a-half centuries, the problem posed by Constantine's conversion was still unsolved. The Empire had fallen and the Papacy had overstepped the pinnacle of its power.' (Davis [1957] 1972: 390)

These twin problematics of medievalism—first, the treatment of sources; and second, the struggle for primacy whereby 'under the empire of Frederick, Ghibelline became synonymous with the imperial, and Guelf with the papal party' (Davis [1957] 1972: 68)—are central to what ensues. These dual tropes connect to Ezra Pound in the early 1930s: his sacralization of Mussolini's dictatorship was to some degree shaped by his encounter with Ernst Kantorowicz's idiosyncratic *Frederick The Second, 1194–1250*—a text described only 25 years ago as a 'fascist classic' (Rowan 1994: 296). It was so received by the leadership of the Third Reich: 'The messianism of [Kantorowicz's] biography' from 1927—first translated into English in 1931—was received with 'enthusiasm […] by many officials of the Nazi party and the Wehrmacht'; in fact, Hermann Göring was so taken with the book that he even presented a copy to Mussolini. (Ruehl 2000: 188–189)

Furthermore, Kantorowicz's credentials were *nearly* perfect: he had served in the Great War, and then fought the Communists in Germany as a member of the radical right Freikorps in 1919. By the next year, he had moved into Stefan George's literary circle, which began to embrace an increasingly völkisch, or ethnic-based, nationalism. By the writing of *Frederick The Second* in the mid-1920s, it is no stretch to characterize Kantorowicz as a 'conservative revolutionary': a non-Nazi form of fascism in Weimar Germany that was in the pattern of Oswald Spengler, Ernst Jünger or Moeller van den Bruck. It was the latter, for example, who coined the phrase 'Third Reich', but who refused to endorse the Nazis on account of their *hoi polloi* violence and vulgar 'Aryanism'. The sad irony is that, despite holding similar values, Kantorowicz was a German Jew who was forced to emigrate to the United States in 1938 (Abulafia 1977: 204). Yet a decade earlier, with the NSDAP in the electoral wilderness and the revolutionary nationalism of fascist ideology not yet Nazism's sole preserve in Germany, Kantorowicz's 'völkisch nationalist ideas permeated his biography of Frederick II much more deeply than critics have hitherto allowed' (Ruehl 2000: 205–56).

With this context established, it is also clear that Pound first encountered Kantorowicz's *Frederick The Second* at a critical time: likely between October 1932—the month the *MRF* exhibition opened, as made clear by the inscription front flyleaf, 'D. Pound / Oct. 1932'—and 1934 at the latest. At the earlier date Pound was starting to praise Italian fascist rule and Mussolini's autocracy publicly, even if it would be another three years before he threw in his lot as a fascist propagandist. By the latter date, 1934, Pound had embraced anti-Semitism—to the extent that from the end of that year he had tasked one of his disciples, John Drummond, to act as a researcher for him on the 'Jew prob[lem]' (cited in Feldman 2013: 18).

Given Pound's nascent anti-Semitism, Kantorowicz's well-known Jewishness would likely have precluded Pound's reading him 'carefully' by the mid-1930s. At the very least, there can be no doubt that, by the end of 1937, Pound had read *Frederick The Second*—aptly described by R. H. C. Davis as 'learned and readable in spite of its extremist viewpoint' ([1957] 1972: 390) (Davis was describing Kantorowicz's study, not Pound's turn to fascist politics!). Pound, at that point finishing his last piece of extended cultural criticism, the *Guide to Kulchur*, exclaimed: 'The attempt of Frederic II of Sicily to enlighten Europe both culturally and economically was a MAJOR event' (Pound 1970: 261). Again, this contention depends upon how one interprets 'enlighten', let alone 'MAJOR event'. In order to grasp this nettle, we will now go on to argue that Pound's reading of this book was several years earlier, at a critical moment in the early 1930s. Crucially, it seems, the chiliasm suffusing Kantorowicz's biography helped prepare Ezra Pound for his sacralization of Mussolini's dictatorship.

The Italian dictator, in turn, was instrumental in Pound's 'conversion' to fascist ideology: 'Pound's admiration for Mussolini was a—perhaps *the*—key catalyst in his evolution toward a pro-Fascist position' (Dasenbrock 1990: 511; original emphasis). At the very least, this should make clear that Pound's embrace of fascist ideology was a high-stakes affair—both then, for him, but also now, for scholarship on this absurdly long-occluded relationship. As the literary scholar Reed Way Dasenbrock convincingly argues, Pound read Dante's *De Monarchia* (1904)—the principal political doctrine by another medieval titan—fully four times between the 1920s and early 1940s; that is, commencing just around the time Pound was becoming explicitly political in his writing and letters. To be sure, there is much in Dante's *De Monarchia* to intrigue Pound, a text that is, revealingly, in Dante's introductory words, 'primarily adapted for action rather than for speculation' (1904). (Almost uniquely, Pound marked this passage in both of his copies of Dante's collected works, referring to the Latin passages of *De Monarchia.*) Throughout, Dante argues at length that the Emperor receives the right to rule directly from God. The absolute ruler of the temporal sphere does not need the sanction of the spiritual sphere, the papacy, to sanction political rule: *natural order in things cannot come to pass without Right [i.e. political rule], since the foundation of Right is inseparably bound to the foundation of order. The preservation of this order is therefore necessarily Right* (Dante 1904, Introduction 2: 2).

Still later in his 75-page Ghibelline manifesto Dante becomes even more explicit: 'the Supreme Pontiff to lead the human race to life eternal by means of revelation, and the Emperor to guide it to temporal felicity by means of philosophic instruction'. Read with twenty-first-century eyes this justifies a kind of total rule evocative of the fascist *Führerprinzip*: 'The prerogative to grant authority to the temporal domain is contrary to the nature of the Church'; or again, 'there must be one king to direct and govern. If not, not only the inhabitants of the kingdom fail in their end, but the kingdom lapses into ruin'. In addition to autocracy and order, finally, is what Dante calls 'unity in wills'; a kind of medieval ubermensch that characterizes the Emperor:

> the human race for its best disposition is dependent on unity in wills. But this state of concord is impossible unless one will dominates and guides all others into unity [....] Nor is this directing will a possibility unless there is one common Prince whose will may dominate and guide the wills of all others. (Dante 1904: 58)

Albeit few and far between, other voices in Pound Studies have endorsed this reading. Tim Redman notes that *De Monarchia* and *Jefferson and/or Mussolini* 'parallel each other'; in a more general vein, Pound's current biographer, David

Moody, notes that Pound 'wanted to make the *virtu* of the past a force in the present [...] to refashion the mentality of his world' (both cited in Paden 2010: 194–95). Some of Pound's annotations of *De Monarchia* are telling examples of his use of Dante's ideas; for instance, in respect of the actual ruler, Pound annotates 'no bearing on monarchy', which Dasenbrock incisively understands to mean that 'Dante's focus to a large extent is simply on what makes for good government, not necessarily on monarchy' (1991: 175). These and other 'appropriations' from Dante led Dasenbrock to argue that 'many of the themes of Pound's politics, particularly his enthusiasm for the figure of Mussolini, can be made explicable by reference to the ideas of *De Monarchia*. Indeed, it is not too much to call Pound the last Ghibelline and to see in his idealization of Mussolini one final belated echo of Dante' (1991: 173).

However, this Dantesque echo is a necessary, but not sufficient, link to Pound's modern, sacralized conception of autocracy. For none of Dante's arguments amount to a deification of the leader—the pivot upon which Pound's devotion to fascism turns. Instead, Dante's tract argues quite the opposite: his is a manifesto for secular rule, separated from the Church. By contrast, according to David Abulafia, Kantorowicz pictures Frederic the Second as a 'hero [who] is both the object of prophecy and, on a quite different level, the embodiment of the Roman Empire' (1977: 196). Indeed, Federigo Segundo is mentioned in Chapter 12 of Pound's *Jefferson and/or Mussolini*, which takes a line much more similar to Kantorowicz than Dante vis-à-vis the state (Pound 1935: 128):

> THE fascist revolution was FOR the preservation of certain liberties and FOR the maintenance of a certain level of culture, certain standards of living, it was NOT a refusal to come down to a level of riches or poverty, but a refusal to surrender certain immaterial prerogatives, a refusal to surrender a great slice of the cultural heritage.
> I assert again my own firm belief that the Duce will stand not with despots and the lovers of power but with the lovers of *Order*.

Accordingly, I want to conclude by suggesting that the medieval 'X-factor' for Pound's embrace of fascist totalitarianism is more clearly heard in Kantorowicz's sacralized, modern(ist) mediation of authority, not Dante's contemporaneous, Ghibelline rendering. Or to put it in the terms of *Frederick The Second*, in a passage again containing a pencilled line in the margin: 'The feeling never arose that there was a discrepancy between the Empire as a divine world-embracing institution and the actual imperial territory of political realities' (Kantorowicz [1927] 1931: 563).

Kantorowicz clearly reinforces Dante's 'spheres of influence' argument in *De Monarchia*, declaring: 'Dante reconciled the Eagles and the Cross' ([1927] 1931: 611). But his presentation of leadership is, in contrast to Dante's, derived not from reason but a modern, political faith. Dante provides the idea that the state is divinely sanctioned but separate to the Church; Kantorowicz, by contrast, argues strenuously that the state is willed into being by the divinely-appointed autocrat, which then *becomes numinous in and of itself*. Kantorowicz thus speaks of an 'Imperial Church' ([1927] 1931: 234) and the 'Justice-God-Emperor's' 'sacred wishes'. Put simply, 'God had been forcefully brought down into the state':

> After the reign for over one thousand years of a God manifesting himself mainly in wonders and miracles, a God begins to appear in full daylight, outside and alongside the Church, a God who can only be recognised by wide-awake intelligence, as Law. Here the whole tension is expressed between Church and Empire, both immediately related to God, a tension which reaches its culmination in Dante. ([1927] 1931: 238)

Also in this chapter, which addresses the politics of Dante, 'Frederick evolves the importance of the State as an end in itself, attributes to the State a divine power of healing fully equal to the healing power of the Church'; and again, 'The State was in itself an end, a means of salvation, the needs of the State were therefore divine and necessary to salvation' ([1927] 1931: 241). This is significantly different from Dante's rendering of autocracy, and one far more in tune with post-First World War fascism. In Martin Ruehl's excellent summation, Kantorowicz proposes a 'deification of the state' and the 'notion of a national redeemer' (Ruehl 2000: 241–242): *Macht und Staat über alles.*

Still more explicitly, Kantorowicz insists in *Frederick The Second*:

> The Justice-God, conceived by the Emperor as a power working in accordance with law, is the characteristic symbol of the Sicilian State. Here is the answer to a riddle: Kaiser Frederick, in relation to the Empire, where his role like that of his predecessor remained pre-eminently that of the guardian and conserver of *Pax et Justitia*, appears 'medieval,' while in relation to his Sicilian State he is felt to be 'modern,' because he is a power at work [...] This new alertness, this conception of God as a constant force independent of the Church, links the new State with the Renaissance. ([1927]1931: 238–99)

Across these pages—in keeping with too many others to count in this 700-page tome (see additional examples provided in the appendix)—Kantorowicz even goes so far as to call Frederick 'an Apostle of Enlightenment' ([1927]1931: 247); 'the most many sided-man of his age and unquestionably also the most learned, a philosopher and dialectician', a ruler who elevated 'knowledge to the same plane as magic'. Thus was 'the whole magnificent structure of his State—like every work of art, a unity': 'one of those rare and priceless transition moments in which all and everything is valid simultaneously: myth and insight, faith and knowledge, miracle and law, corroborating yet belying each other, co-operating yet conflicting' ([1927]1931: 247–48).

For those with even a passing knowledge of Pound's interest, the attraction is unmistakable. For a man who declared the end of Christian Europe via advertising his *Blast* in the summer of 1914, Frederick's anti-Papalism would surely have been of interest, as would his founding of the first secular seat of learning for the training of bureaucrats at the University of Naples in 1224. But more importantly, throughout *Frederick The Second* Kantorowicz portrays the emperor as an artifex; a patron of eastern and western learning as well as a cultivator of vernacular Italian poetry; a gatekeeper of the renaissance; and vitally, a herald of the modern. Yet another marginal annotation appears, revealingly, on p. 604, describing 'the clearsighted fatalism of the man of action: a survival of the heroic age'.

All of this, surely, would have appealed to Pound. But in the context of the early 1930s, above all, it was the notion of sacralized autocracy that flipped Pound's switch in 1932/1933. For it was precisely these phrases towards which Pound gravitated, as shown by his copy of Kantorowicz's biography: 'The history of Frederick II demonstrates how much a law-giver can accomplish by force and compulsion, so long as he knows what his aims are, and so long as those aims are just'—itself a marginal annotation in Pound's copy of *Frederic The Second, 1194–1250* ([1927]1931: 292).

Appendix

Extracts from: Ernst Kantorowicz *FREDERICK II, 1194-1250* (London: Constable and Co., 1931)

Frederick II had wedded the God of the other world to the *Justitia* of this: *Dus et Justitia* is the recurrent formula; and thus, and thus alone, was it possible to comprehend the one universal God as a particular God of the state—to represent him, appeal to him, worship him—without the Church's aid. (234)

The State with its finite boundaries is no abstraction based on an idea but a living principle, active and potent to its uttermost boundary. (238)

At every stage of his career it was clear that Frederick was full of primeval hate for any disturber of his sacred order. (604)

He had taken on himself a new mission, the office of Hammer of the World and Scourge of God: not without the demonic joy of creative genius in being free to destroy: not without the pain and sorrow of preserving genius in being forced to destroy. Pope Gregory had once said that Frederick loved to hear himself called Antichrist; but Frederick had endured to the last limit of endurance before becoming Antichrist indeed. (607-8)

Thus under the figure of Caesar Augustus, Kaiser Frederick is reflected twofold in a double mirror as Antichrist and as the Messianic Judge. Caesar, Messiah, Antichrist: these are the three fundamentally identical manifestations of Frederick II since Cortenuova, since the beginning of his World Rule. He remained unchanged; only the fluctuations of circumstance show us his form lit with a different glow. The more he genuinely approximated to a Roman Augustus from whom salvation was to come the more he resembled the very antithesis. A genuine Roman Emperor reincarnate who erected statues to himself, inevitably appeared as Nero or as Antichrist beside the Galilean. The whole life of Frederick II could be interpreted either in the Messianic or the Anti-Christian spirit (608)

The conception of a Roman-Christian Caesar implied the fusion of two worlds; the tension of two extreme forces. Each perpetually denied the other, each owed the other the fullness of its vitality. A smaller man than Frederick II would have succumbed under the strain, but at such altitudes the same miracle is ever renewed and ever challenges man's admiration [....] Frederick summed up the situation in his fundamental dogma of the secular State: true freedom exists only under the yoke of the Imperium. For once these antitheses could co-exist in one form and shape without thus losing firmness of texture or of outline: Emperor and Galilean; Pagan and Christian; Saviour and Antichrist. (610-11)

Just because Frederick II had so nearly been the Saviour (and indeed in the eyes of the faithful still was) he had the opportunity to be the very Antichrist. Since as a priest he knew all mysteries no mystery was safe from his fearless mocking attack. (606)

Endnotes

[1] It bears noting that another two dozen pages are also noted, although these are likely in Dorothy Pound's hand.
[2] For a further discussion see Eatwell and Gentile's chapters in António Costa Pinto, Roger Eatwell and Stein Ugelvik Larsen, eds., *Charisma and Fascism* (2007).
[3] For a detailed analysis of medieval literacy, see Franz H. Bäuml (1980).
[4] Gregory IX anathematized Frederick in strikingly apocalyptic terms:

> A great beats has come out of the sea [...] this scorpion spewing passion from the sting in his tail [...] full of the names of blasphemy [...] raging with the claws of the bear and the mouth of the lion, and the limbs and likeness of the leopard [...] behold the head and tail and body of the beast, of this Frederick, this co-called emperor. (quoted in Wright 2011: 120)

References

Abulafia, David (1977), "Kantorowicz and Frederick II", *History*, 62:205, pp. 193–210. Rpt. in Abulafia, *Italy, Sicily, and the Mediterranean, 1100-1400* (London: Variorum Reprints, 1987), pp. 15–32.

Alighieri, Dante (1904), *The De Monarchia of Dante Alighieri* (ed. and trans. Aurelia Henry), Boston and New York: Houghton, Mifflin and Company.

Bacigalupo, Massimo (1980), *The Forméd Trace: The Later Poetry of Ezra Pound*, New York: Columbia University Press.

Baechler, Lea et al. (eds.) (1991), *Ezra Pound's Poetry and Prose: Volume*, London: Garland.

Bäuml, Franz H. (1980), "Varieties and consequences of medieval literacy and illiteracy", *Speculum*, 55:2, April, pp. 237–65.

Byron, Mark (2014), *Ezra Pound's Eriugena*, London: Bloomsbury.

Cantor, Norman (1992), *Inventing The Middle Ages Lives, Works and Ideas of the Great Medievalists of the 20th Century*, Cambridge: Lutterworth Press.

Costa Pinto, António, Roger Eatwell and Stein Ugelvik Larsen eds. (2007), *Charisma and Fascism*, Abingdon: Routledge

Dasenbrock, Reed W. (1990), "Ezra Pound, the Last Ghibelline", *Journal of Modern Literature*, Spring, 16:4, pp. 511–33.

—. (1991), *Imitating the Italians: Wyatt, Spenser, Synge, Pound, Joyce*, London: Johns Hopkins University Press.

Davis, R. H. C. ([1957] 1972), *A History of Medieval Europe: From Constantine to Saint Louis*, London: Longman.

Duggan, Christopher (2013), *Fascist Voices: An Intimate History of Mussolini's Italy*, Oxford: Oxford University Press.

Feldman, Matthew (2013), *Ezra Pound's Fascist Propaganda 1935-45*, Basingstoke: Palgrave Macmillan.

—. (2014), "Ezra Pound's political faith from first to second generation; or, 'It is 1956 Fascism'", in *Modernism, Christianity and Apocalypse*, Erik Tonning, Matthew Feldman and David Addyman (eds.), Leiden: Brill, pp. 277–301.

Gentile, Emilio (2000), "The sacralization of politics", *Totalitarian Movements and Political Religions*, 1:1, pp. 18–55.

—. (2006), *Politics as Religion* (trans. George Staunton), Princeton: Princeton University Press.

Henderson, Archie (2009), *'I Cease Not to Yowl' Reannotated: New Notes on the Pound/Agresti Correspondence*, North Charleston: CreateSpace.

Hickman, Miranda (ed.) (2011), *'One Must Not Go Altogether with the Tide': The Letters of Ezra Pound and Stanley Nott*, Kingston, CA: McGill-Queen's University Press.

Hitler, Adolf (1953) *Hitler's Table Talk 1941-44: His Private Conversations*, trans. Norman Cameron and R.H. Stevens. London: Weidenfeld and Nicolson.

Kantorowicz, Ernst ([1927] 1931), *Frederick the Second 1194-1250* (trans. E. O. Lorimer), London: Constable & Co.

Lauber, John (1978), "Pound's Cantos: A Fascist Epic", *Journal of American Studies*, 12: 1, April, pp. 3–21.

Liebregts, Peter (2004), *Ezra Pound and Neoplatonism*, Madison, NJ: Fairleigh Dickinson University Press.

Marsh, Alec (2015), *John Kasper and Ezra Pound: Saving the Republic*, London: Bloomsbury.

Melograni, Piero (1976), "The cult of the Duce in Mussolini's Italy", *Journal of Contemporary History*, Special Issue: Theories of Fascism, 11:4, October, pp. 221–37.

Moody, A. David (2015), *Ezra Pound, Poet: The Tragic Years, 1939–1972*, Oxford: Oxford University Press.

Paden, William D. (2010), "Provençal and the troubadours", in *Ezra Pound in Context*, Cambridge: Cambridge University Press, pp. 181–91.

Paul, Catherine (2016), *Fascist Directive: Ezra Pound and Italian Cultural Nationalism*, Clemson: Clemson University Press.

Pound, Ezra ([1925] 1981), 'Definitions', January. Rpt. in *Der Querschnitt: Das Magazin der aktuellen Ewigkeitswerte* (ed. Christian Ferber), Berlin: Ullstein.

—. (1935), *Jefferson and/or Mussolini*, London: Stanley Nott.

—. ([1950] 1971), *The Selected Letters of Ezra Pound* (ed. D. D. Paige), New York: New Directions.

—. (1970), *Guide To Kulchur*, New York: New Directions.

—. (1999), *The Cantos*, New York: New Directions.

Rainey, Lawrence (1998), *Institutions of Modernism: Literary Elites and Public Culture*, Yale: Yale University Press.

Redman, Tim (1992), *Ezra Pound and Italian Fascism*, Cambridge: Cambridge University Press.

Rowan, Steven (1994), "Comment: Otto Brunner", in Hartmut Lehmann and James Van Horn Melton (eds.), *Paths of Continuity: Central European Historiography from the 1930s to the 1950s*, Cambridge: Cambridge University Press, pp. 293–97.

Ruehl, Martin (2000), "'In This Time without Emperors': The politics of Ernst Kantorowicz's Kaiser Friedrich der Zweite Reconsidered", *Journal of the Warburg and Courtauld Institutes*, 63, pp. 187–242.

—. (2015) *The Italian Renaissance in the German Historical Imagination: 1860-1930*. Cambridge: Cambridge University Press.

Shorten, Richard (2012), *Modernism and Totalitarianism*, Basingstoke: Palgrave Macmillan.

Schnapp, Jeffrey T. (2007), "Mostre", http://www.jeffreyschnapp.com/wp-content/uploads/2011/07/Mostre.pdf. Accessed 14 June 2018.

Wright, Jonathan (2011), *Heretics: The Creation of Christianity from the Gnostics to the Modern Church*, Boston and New York: Houghton Mifflin, Harcourt.

4. Make it Crude:
Ezra Pound's Antisemitic Propaganda for the BUF and PNF

I.

In April 1942, the journal *Poetry*—a prestigious monthly he had done so much to establish exactly 30 years earlier, as part of the 'American Renaissance' in the humanities—carried an angry editorial entitled 'The End of Ezra Pound'. The famous American poet's 'enemy propaganda' for Fascist Italy had 'effectively written *finis* to his long career as inspired *enfant terrible'*. *Poetry*'s artistic indictment derived from his Radio Rome broadcasts for the Italian Ministry of Culture during the Second World War. Those of Pound's inflammatory speeches for Mussolini's National Fascist Party (PNF) which were delivered between America's entry into World War II and Mussolini's fall from power in late July 1943 were adjudged most harshly; indeed, they constituted the evidence for the first case of alleged 'radio treason' in American history.[1] More to the point, in the wake of the Japanese attack on Pearl Harbor, in the mind of *Poetry's* editorialist, Eunice Tietjens, Pound no longer evoked Emerson, Dickinson or Thoreau, but Benedict Arnold. 'That it should be one of the poets who is thus playing Lord Haw-Haw, no matter how ineffectually,' concluded this fellow poet, 'seems to cast a slur on the whole craft'.[2] Pound had, in fact, been exchanging letters with Lord Haw-Haw (the American-born German fascist propagandist and holder of a British passport, William Joyce), who was similarly broadcasting Anglophone radio propaganda from Nazi Germany). In an unusual display of humility, Pound sought his counterpart's 'guidance' on his move into radio broadcasting.[3] This advice never materialised, for Joyce stopped responding to Pound's 'effusive fan letters' after a while, finding him 'even odder' than he was.[4]

Contained here are three of the four elements considered in this article: Ezra Pound, fascism and propaganda—the latter extending to both the PNF and Oswald Mosley's British Union of Fascists (BUF). As for the fourth, and most important, issue, antisemitism, consider this: having just learned the extent of these withering American attacks on him, Pound directly addressed the 'Jewish Question' on 30 April 1942: 'Don't start a pogrom...not an old style killing of small Jews. That system is no good whatsoever. Of course if some man had a stroke of genius and could start a pogrom UP AT THE TOP, there might be something to say for it.'[5] Now, Pound could not have known that, at the time of his comments, Nazi Germany had opened the first purpose-built extermination centre in human history,

Belzec, as part of Operation Reinhard in Poland. Yet his antisemitic broadcasts for Fascist Italy are not historically significant for their effects—in the manner of, say, Julius Streicher's *Der Stürmer*—and, at any rate, Pound's propaganda was principally aimed southward, toward Allied forces then fighting in North Africa. Rather, what is so remarkable is that an American poet of such international standing should be propagating the fascist political faith so emphatically in the first place. Equally remarkable is that the antisemitic propaganda increasingly bound up with Pound's denunciation of usurers and conspirators on the radio became so coarse. Leonard Doob's excellent edition of Pound's radio speeches revealed in a quantitative appendix, for example, that fully 71 of Pound's 110 broadcasts reproduced in *Ezra Pound Speaking* criticised 'Powerful Jews'.[6] The prophet of modernism's quest to 'make it new' had descended, abruptly it seemed, into crude demagogy.

II.

'It took me, I think it was, TWO years, insistence and wangling etc to GET HOLD of their microphone,' wrote Pound in the final stage of his imprisonment in the US, during 1955-58.[7] For Pound, both at the time and since, the stakes of his engagement with Mussolini's Italy remained high, and they continue to be much-debated in Pound studies. For on the one hand, Pound remains the archetypal modernist, integral to the literary canon and frequently encountered on undergraduate English Studies courses—think of his WWI 'Imagist' programme and his Vorticist magazine with Wyndham Lewis, *Blast*, or his memorable indictment of the folly of that war and the ensuing disillusionment of the peace settlements and demobilisation in Part I of the 1920 *Hugh Selwyn Mauberley*:

> There died a myriad,
> And of the best, among them,
> For an old bitch gone in the teeth,
> For a botched civilization.[8]

Yet on the other hand, his fascist antisemitism has its plaudits as well. For Pound continues to be championed by neo-fascists, especially in the United States, as a leading fascist intellectual and antisemitic ideologue.[9] In sum, the Pound Case has not disappeared from view for any lack of interest from extremists, students, and scholars alike.

At least in terms of the latter, still another reason for attaching importance to Pound's activism on behalf of fascism, as Marjorie Perloff aptly noted in 1988, is that 'intellectuals have paid little attention to the actual political context in which the "the case of Ezra Pound" took place'.[10] Perloff's call was effectively answered in 1992, with the publication of Tim Redman's *Ezra Pound and Italian Fascism*, which echoes her plea for historical contextualisation: 'Pound's activity on behalf of Italian fascism needs to be understood historically and with a great deal of specificity'.[11] The generation since Perloff's groundbreaking article has seen a series of additional studies, in which Pound's association with Italian Fascism has been well documented. And while the extent of the greatest crime in history was a largely kept secret at the time of Pound's wartime broadcasts, the parallel history of the Holocaust is nevertheless relevant, if only because words help to condition action; something poets appreciate far better than most. Between his (qualified) endorsement of pogroms in April 1942 and his radio excerpt entitled 'Pogrom' from 21 March 1943, the Third Reich had moved well beyond Pound's satirical recommendation for Jewish emigration to Australia:

> Don't go out and die in the desert for the sake of high kikery. Don't die for Tel Aviv, and Goldsmid and Jerusalem...Sell 'em Australia. And SELECT the seed for the new penal settlement...The Jews have ruin'd every country they have got hold of. The Jews have worked out a system, very neat system, for the ruin of the rest of mankind, one nation after another.[12]

By this time, of course, the Nazis had moved beyond both 'encouraged' interwar emigration, and notions of forced emigration of Jews to Madagascar, fleetingly considered in 1940. Indeed, in the very months between Pound's two above-cited statements, the Holocaust was at its most murderous. Of 5.9 million Jews murdered in the Shoah, Christopher Browning highlights that roughly 75% were alive in Spring 1942; less than a year later, roughly 75% were dead: 'At the core of the Holocaust was a short, intense wave of mass murder. The center of gravity of this mass murder was Poland, where in March 1942, despite two and a half years of terrible hardship, deprivation, and persecution, every major Jewish community was still intact, and where eleven months later only the remnants of Polish Jewry survived in a few rump ghettos and labour camps.'[13]

When it came to antisemitism, Pound's wartime views therefore may be considered more radical than Italian policy, and less so than Nazi policy. And in-between the two, the targets of Pound's demonology were disappearing all around him under the Nazi occupation of northern Italy in late 1943 and 1944. At just this time, Jews trapped in the Salò Republic, like Primo Levi, were being rounded up and transported to Auschwitz-Birkenau. In this view, it is not that Pound's 'broadcasts were not treasonous simply because they were useless', as Eliot Weinberger avers, as 'Pound was indeed crying "Fire!" in a crowded theater, but he was crying "Fire!" in Bulgarian.'[14] But even if this metaphor effectively describes Pound's highly idiosyncratic radio addresses, he was nevertheless shouting at the top of his lungs as often as possible. And let us be clear: this was not a fire, but an inferno, as Levi, amongst so many others, suffered and, more rarely, also recounted:

> There is no rationality in the Nazi hatred: it is a hate that is not in us; it is outside man, it is a poison fruit sprung from the deadly trunk of fascism, but it is outside and beyond fascism itself. We cannot understand it, but we can and must understand from where it springs, and we must be on our guard. If understanding is impossible, knowing is imperative, because what happened could happen again. Conscience can be seduced and obscured again—even our consciences.
>
> For this reason, it is everyone's duty to reflect on what happened. Everybody must know, or remember, that when Hitler and Mussolini spoke in public, they were believed, applauded, admired, adored like gods. They were 'charismatic leaders'; they possessed a secret power of seduction that did not proceed from the credibility or the soundness of the things they said but from the suggestive way in which they said them...[15]

However, this article does not set out to analyse the effects of antisemitic propaganda on innocent victims of the Shoah like Levi. Nor recounted here is the equally revealing narrative following Ezra Pound's 26 July 1943 indictment for treason, his Kafkaesque trials in custody from May 1945, and twelve and a half years' subsequent institutionalisation at St. Elizabeths in the United States. Suffice it to say that Pound continued to work on behalf of Italy throughout the war; for example, on 31 March 1944, this indicative letter was sent to Fernando Mezzasoma, Salò's Minister of Popular Culture:

> Until recently, England was the main target of our radio propaganda campaign...[but] if you have transmitters powerful enough to reach...the JEWnited States...we could broadcast for ten minutes every other hour and repeat each broadcast a number of times. The purpose of the broadcasts seems obvious to me: 'London lies' (and is well aware of her lies). 'Do not believe the lies broadcast by the B.B.C.' My own voice should probably be used for this project...Something must also be done with the daily newspapers which are still in the hands of the reactionaries, anti-Fascists, anti-social-republicans...I would very much like to find a publication where a serious group of Fascist Republicans can collaborate—that is, work together with mutual understanding.[16]

And if similarly omitted by space, it is clear that Pound's poetry—during the war years at least, and arguably persisting into his postwar, award-winning *Pisan Cantos*[17]—was infected with much of the same antisemitic venom. By way of cursory glance, in the same year that a month-long visitor to Pound's adopted home later reported that Pound believed that Jews 'had organized a relentless conspiracy against mankind',[18] 1941, Pound drafted notes for the next stage of his mammoth poetic epic, *The Cantos,* beginning:

> The Evil is Usury, *neschek* [Hebrew for 'money-lending']
> the serpent
> *neschek* whose name is known, the defiler,
> beyond race and against race
> the defiler

Moreover, this intended addition to *The Cantos* later adds a point that shall be pursued further presently:

> "A pity that poets have used symbol and metaphor
> and no man learned anything from them
> for their speaking in figures."
>
> All other sins are open,
> Usura alone not understood.[19]

While this thinly-veiled attack on Jews needs little symbolic decoding, Pound's earlier antisemitic propaganda often does, even in his extensive prose texts (collected in 11 volumes by Garland Publishing under the title *Ezra Pound's Poetry and Prose* in 1991). Examination of these during the later 1930s, in fact, reveals a consistent pattern of antisemitic encoding, by recourse to literary tropes like metonymy, literary innuendo and conspiracist rhetoric. Yet many of these editorials and pamphlets have received virtually no scholarly comment in Pound Studies or elsewhere. This is surprising, for Pound's publicism for Britain's Blackshirts adds depth of evidence for his engagement with fascism, reveals an earlier and more nuanced form of antisemitic propaganda and, of course, took place during the precise period in which Pound was simultaneously making enquiries in Rome, trying to 'GET HOLD of their microphone'. In fact, Pound's writing for the BUF was only curtailed by the movement's demise in 1940, its leading figures interned under Defence Regulation 18(a). Moving back in time, as it were, thus helps to reveal the way in which Pound's antisemitic propaganda coevolved with his support for both Mussolini's PNF and Mosley's BUF.

If only impressionistically, then, this extended introduction has delineated the themes that form the nexus of this article: fascist ideology, increasingly vitriolic antisemitism, as well as modern propaganda. In the present context, 'modern' is intended both in terms of means—high-circulation publication in interwar 'little magazines', say, or radio broadcasts punctuated by thoroughly avant-garde stylistics—but also 'modern' in a wider, secular sense: modern propaganda was no longer the preserve of Catholic counter-revolutionaries, turning to the carrot rather than the stick through the Congregation for the Propagation of the Faith during the Thirty Years War in the seventeenth century.[20] And this is the underlying thesis put forward here: if totalitarian movements like Nazism, Stalinism and the Italian PNF can be usefully understood as 'political religions'—that is, as phenomenologically resembling a religion, but with what Pound called 'paradiso terrestre'[21] located in the class, race or nation, not in a supernatural deity—then correspondingly, the notion that such regimes' propaganda is simply brainwashing becomes untenable, or only partially satisfactory. Instead, as Pound, Haw-Haw, Axis Sally, and their fellow crusaders well appreciated, this was the propagation of an ideological faith. To be sure, such a job relied heavily upon the demonisation of enemies, systematic duplicity and demagogy. But this was also—indeed, was perhaps fundamentally—the annunciation of an expected new order, one which used the press as a pulpit from which to disseminate the faith of a political religion.

The opening for such a reading has been made by what Richard Shorten has called the 'revival' of political religion theory, placed alongside Roger Griffin's understanding of the 'new consensus' in research into fascist ideology.[22] Given the fruitful results of both, in fact, the latter may be read as a nationalistic manifestation of the former. For instance, Emilio Gentile has concisely defined political religions 'as the sacralization of a political system founded on an unchallengeable monopoly of power, ideological monism, and the obligatory and unconditional subordination of the individual and the collectivity to its code of commandments'.[23] While his recent *Politics as Religion* is only taken with political religions in power—meaning totalitarian movements like Mussolini's Italy or Maoist China—it is clear that Gentile's approach also embraces abortive, or 'mimetic', fascist movements like Mosley's British Union of Fascists.[24] When yoked to new readings of fascism as a revolutionary political ideology containing both 'positive' (in Griffin's phrase, 'palingenetic ultra-nationalism') and 'negative' (antisemitism, anti-communism, anti-liberalism and so on) ideological components, political religion emerges as a useful heuristic tool with which to consider the unmistakably 'sacred' dimensions of fascist ideology, which will be here understood as

> a specifically modern form of secular 'millenarianism' constructed culturally and politically, not religiously, as a revolutionary movement centring upon the 'renaissance' of a given people (whether perceived nationally, ethnically, culturally, or religiously) through the total reordering of all perceivedly 'pure' collective energies towards a realisable utopia; an ideological core implacably hostile to democratic representation and socialist materialism, equality and individualism, in addition to any specific enemies viewed as alien or oppositional to such a programme.[25]

For students of Griffin's approach to fascism and/or Gentile's approach to the 'sacralization of politics', the first sentence of Ezra Pound's essay, 'A Visiting Card', may be read as a succinct evocation of the fascist faith. The next two sentences, in the reading of fascist propaganda as the *secular propagation of faith on behalf of a political religion* proposed here, emerge as just as strongly as a form of artistic devotion to Pound's fascist ideal than as an outrageous judgement of wartime Italy in 1942:

> A thousand candles together blaze with intense brightness. No one candle's light damages another's. So is the liberty of the individual in the ideal and fascist state.[26]

III.

The looming significance of the second world war to break out in a generation—a consideration that should not be lost upon those of Pound's generation (he was born in 1885)—is, with respect to the so-called 'Pound Case' at least, still open to basic historiographical disagreements. In terms of the critical issue of Pound's antisemitism, the pivotal and persisting questions seem to be threefold: when did antisemitism manifest itself; what form did it take; and how did this impact upon his public writing, especially his poetry? While the latter question is better explored elsewhere, as early as 1955 Victor Ferkiss found that the 'basis of the alliance between poetry and politics' in Pound's thinking centred on Italian Fascism's perceived—to him at least—attack on capitalistic 'usury', thus placing it alongside Pound's valorised Social Credit macroeconomics: 'Pound saw in Mussolini an ally in the fight against the usurers and saw the Fascist economists as working toward an appreciation of economic realities and the destruction of the rule of the international banker.'[27] This view essentially approaches Pound's antisemitism through his relationship with Fascist Italy; and in particular, his admiration for Benito Mussolini. Here, the suggestion is that, as Italian policy on Jews radicalised in the later 1930s, so too did Pound's association of usury with a specifically Jewish conspiracy—a persuasive argument considering the belligerence of that wartime antisemitism, one that shall be developed presently. And as sketched above, even Pound's poetry, clearly, was not wholly immune from this infection during the Second World War, even if the extent and duration of his poetic racism remains an area of stringent dispute amongst literary critics.

Ferkiss's political-studies approach raises still another fruitful angle of consideration, namely Pound's American background. Although Pound essentially left the United States for good and moved to Europe in 1908—returning only on holiday or business thereafter, and eventually in chains in November 1945—Ferkiss argued that he was nonetheless rooted in a specifically American context of 'populist beliefs and attitudes [that] form the core of Pound's philosophy, just as they provide the basis of American fascism generally'. Tim Redman has also endorsed this view of populist influences as 'surprisingly accurate' in the influential *Cambridge Companion to Ezra Pound*, interestingly noting Pound's overly defensive reaction to Ferkiss's article, and concluding: 'Populist concerns do coincide with a great number of Pound's principal points, and give the best overall explanation of his positions'.[28] Further supporting this view, Pound was during the 1930s in correspondence with leading American far-rightists—if perhaps not fascists of Mussolini's stamp, as he clearly recognised—including Huey 'Kingfish' Long, Hugo R. Fack and Father Charles Coughlin. And to be sure, Pound consistently attempted to strike a populist tone in praising the latter, for instance, in the *New English Weekly* on 24 October 1935: 'If Father Coughlin's nine million adherents can turn from passive listening to active enquiry we can get the new economics into the next presidential campaign.'[29]

But if Pound's messianic allegiance to what he called the 'new economics'— essentially a version of Major C.H. Douglas's Social Credit, later influenced by Silvio Gesell's economic theory on the 'stamp scrip'[30]—has long been recognised[31], debates over the potentially earlier provenance of Pound's antisemitism only came to the fore in 1988 with publication of Robert Casillo's *The Genealogy of Demons*.[32] Casillo largely took populist readings of Pound's youthful milieu a step further, tagging Pound's upbringing with a 'suburban prejudice' against Jews that lasted until around 1910, when Pound moved into the second 'phase' of his antisemitism and 'at this point Pound's prejudice was not polite or suburban but considerably more ugly. Even so, antisemitism was not yet important in his thought'. And Pound's antisemitism, holds Casillo, took on a more codified and stereotypical form by a third 'phase', lasting for most of the interwar years. By this point, Pound's antisemitism begins to erupt publicly, which Casillo charts in both his prose and poetry, specifically the ongoing poetic epic Pound had started in 1917, *The Cantos*. Finally, Casillo discerns a fourth and final stage of Pound's antisemitism, which 'began in the 1940s' and which is only concludes by a famous, if overly stylised (for it was, in essence, a throwaway remark), retraction of Pound's antisemitism to Allen Ginsberg in 1967.[33] This final stage is heavily 'coloured by biological racism, and bearing an unmistakeable resemblance to the Nazi version, it now figured within a political ideology'. Even if Reed Way Dasenbrock's review rightly finds that Casillo's groundbreaking arguments represent a degree of 'overkill', the idea that Pound's antisemitism devolved between different types is nevertheless important:

> Another persistent idea is that Pound's anti-Semitism is only economic. It takes little trouble to show that his prejudice is essentialist, racial, and biological, these being fundamental aspects of modern anti-Semitism.[34]

Other explanations for Pound's antisemitism taking such a noxious turn include Wendy Flory's assertion that his 'mental condition deteriorated precipitously' in the mid-1930s, leading to a kind of 'paranoid psychosis', or 'Persecutory Delusion', that 'took the form of his long-standing campaigning for world-wide economic reform'. Such a psychological reading—difficult to substantiate as it is—also points to a radical break in Pound's outlook and writings during the 1930s, rather than an evolution from 'suburban', to cultural, to biological antisemitism. Although this account also comes across as overstated, Flory is certainly closer to the mark than Casillo in terms of Pound's outlook prior to the Great Depression, noting that the 'writings and behaviour in his youth provides no evidence of particular anti-Semitic animus'.[35] And while this need not preclude a dose of 'suburban prejudice' against Jews—regrettably all too common in interwar Europe and the United States in any case—Flory is right to suggest that the interwar period witnessed a new embrace of virulent antisemitism on Pound's part, rather than merely a stage that may be read backwards from the notorious radio broadcasts between 1941 and 1943.

Explaining Pound's turn toward overt antisemitism around 1935 by recourse to a psychological break, however, is both too convenient and ignores the context in which Pound wrote. In attending to the latter, Leon Surette's recent monograph offers the most nuanced account of Pound's antisemitism to date. He disagrees with Casillo's finding of eugenic racism in Pound's prejudice towards Jews (even if 'in his most virulent phases he adopts the rhetoric of the Nazis' biological racism'); and in terms of economic antisemitism, makes the important point that Pound 'was an economic radical for nearly twenty years before he became an anti-Semite and conspiracy theorist.' Instead, finds the 1998 *Pound in Purgatory*, Pound's descent toward becoming 'a full-fledged anti-Semite' can be traced to specific engagements with leading antisemites in late 1934 and early 1935.[36] This extends to Father Coughlin's antisemitic broadcasts and writings (such as *Money!*) from the United States; Pound's subscription to the American Silver Shirts' journal *Liberation* (particularly works by its antisemitic founder and editor, William Dudley Pelley); a visit to Rapallo by an Englishman named John Drummond in the second half of 1934, who acted as a 'research assistant' into questions of antisemitic conspiracy theories; and finally and most significantly, an exchange of letters with Hugo Fack over winter 1934/5.

For Surette, this helps to explain and contextualise Pound's hostility to Nazi Germany before 1938, as well as why he continued to have Jewish friends (such as Louis Zukofsky) before, during, and after World War II. In a word, he was converted to antisemitism in the mid-1930s. This allowed Pound to designate faceless Jews as the malicious and conspiratorial 'Other' with increasing venom over the next decade:

> Though Pound's activities and propaganda of the early thirties demonstrate a lack of political perspicacity and a misplaced confidence in his own economic wisdom, prior to 1934 he is free of conspiracy theory, and prior to 1938 there are no anti-Semitic slurs or suggestions of a Jewish conspiracy in his published economic evangelism.[37]

While Surette's empirical research convincingly locates a caesura in Pound's thinking about Jews around late 1934—one that is 'logical' rather than 'pathological' insofar as it was directed by a sequence of documented influences around this time—as will be shown, however, Pound's antisemitism needed a period of gestation far shorter than four years before spilling out into public propaganda on behalf of fascism.

As this suggests, Surette's intervention is also helpful for another reason. For in making at least *some* sense of Pound's propaganda on behalf of fascism, Surette also seems to follow Burton Hatlen's assessment that, by 1938 at the latest, 'his thinking falls into a distinctly fascist pattern'. That is to say, in a kind of personification of Italian Fascism, Pound got more extreme as he went along, from the 1920s to the 1930s to the 1940s, moving 'from an attempt to create/recover an experience of community to an all-consuming, paranoid fascination with the ENEMY'.[38] Whatever the accuracy of this view regarding Mussolini's political religion, it offers a good critical template with which to consider Pound's antisemitism in fascist publications in the period leading up to World War Two. But Pound's propaganda from the second half of the 1930s is critically important for another reason as well. As Ron Bush has importantly pointed out, one reason for Pound's propaganda work was straightforward: he needed money. At roughly $17 per broadcast, Pound could continue to support his extended family in Rapallo during the war years, where he had lived since 1924.[39] And with the British and American authorities systematically freezing his assets and royalties, as well as intercepting his post, Pound could no longer communicate with, let alone contribute to, the Anglo-American intellectual milieu as he had done in previous decades (a fact he often noted bitterly during the war).

Moreover, the scale of Pound's earlier fascist propaganda is immense, even considering his staggering output of texts between 1935 and 1940. As a result, the extent of Ezra Pound's activism for both Mosley's BUF and Mussolini's PNF is all the more noteworthy, especially when considering his letter to fellow BUF writer, Odon Por, at the beginning of his publicism for both fascist movements. 'British Ital Bulletin offered to pay me and of course I can NOT accept money for writing Ital propaganda/ and they officially possibly cant [sic] afford to offer me a proper SALARY'.[40] The same complaint was also directed to an American correspondent, Harold Thompson, professor of literature at Pound's 1905 college alma mater, Hamilton:

> The regeneration of Italy is very different from a Macbethian aim, which wd/ have been merely to get Giolitti's or the King's job.
>
> I suggest you write to Dott. C. Camagna,
> 15 Greek St. London W.
> British
> ask for the Italian Bulletin
>
> containing almost weekly essays. No I am not being paid, and I am not hired by Italy to write Italian propaganda.[41]

Yet what Pound lacked in remuneration he more than compensated for in terms of enthusiasm. Following publication of his *Jefferson and/or Mussolini* in 1935, Pound's fascist publicism then extended to 29 editorials in the weekly, English-language insert for *L'Italia Nostra*, the *British-Italian Bulletin*, and another 40 texts for the BUF. The latter included fully thirty articles for the movement's weekly 'highbrow' newspaper, *Action*, nine for the *British Union Quarterly* and one for *Fascist Week;* as well as a stand-alone pamphlet entitled *What is money for?*, containing the likes of:

> In the 1860s one of the Rothschilds was kind enough to admit that the banking system was contrary to public interest, and that was before the shadow of Hitler's jails had fallen ACROSS the family fortunes.
>
> It is this generation's job to do what was left undone by the early [American] democrats. The guild system, endowing the people by occupation and vocation with corporate powers, gives them the means to protect themselves for all time from the money power.
>
> If you don't like the guild idea, go get results with some other, but don't lose your head and forget what clean men are driving at.[42]

Now, the use of the Rothschilds as a metonymy for all Jews is a form of antisemitic conspiracism, and this 1939 text is wholly in keeping with the majority of accounts of Pound's antisemitism following the passage of the Italian Racial Laws in July 1938.[43] But Pound had already been employing antisemitic stereotypes through literary tropes like metonymy and allegory long before this. In a 1936 letter to Joseph Ibbotson, for example, Pound averred that 'Jews ought to be forced to do their OWN delousing. Wonder did you notice my paragraphs on Shylock[?]'.[44] Part of the text in question, taken from a pamphlet from May 1935 entitled *Social Credit: An Impact*, is cited by the editors of the Ibbotson/Pound correspondence:

> Usury and sodomy, the Church condemned as a pair, to one hell, the same for one reason, namely that they are both against natural increase.
>
> Dante knew this and said it. It is registered in the Merchant of Venice, where Shylock wants no mere shinbone or elbow, but wants to end Antonio's natural increase. You can find it in the Lombard chronicles, the laws against making eunuchs.

Crucially, however, the following line, only two sentences later, is omitted: 'It is our generation's job so to hammer a few simple truths into the human consciousness that no Meyer Anselm can efface them.'[45] Meyer Anselm was credited with founding both the Rothschild family and the international bank bearing their name in the late eighteenth century. And by the middle of 1935, he was already a leading antagonist in Pound's crusade.

IV.

Thus, in looking more closely at the years 1935-39, Pound's endeavour to 'make it crude'—the 'it' referring to his antisemitism—becomes distinctly visible as a pattern of progressively unveiled antisemitic references, codes, and stereotypes in the years before the Second World War. To explore this feature of Pound's propaganda, the final section of this article will consider his publicism in fascist journals from the later 1930s; at a period when he wilfully, and literally freely, supported both the BUF and PNF during critical points in their respective histories.

At this point wholly consumed by the eccentric financial ideas of Social Credit, the 'New Economics'—as advocated, in his eyes, by Mussolini, Mosley and Father Coughlin, as well as the rogue economists Silvio Gesell and Major C.H. Douglas—many of Pound's prose texts from these years contain similar antisemitic allusions to the above. That said, by 1939, these were often less antisemitic codes than stock canards: 'Usury is against nature's increase and Shylock was after Antonio's means of fecundity'.[46] The trope of nefarious Jewish financier is woven into virtually every text on economics that Pound wrote after 1935. Similarly, in another 1939 issue of the *British Union Quarterly*, in an essay ostensibly devoted to the termination of T.S. Eliot's review magazine, *The Criterion*, Pound rambled on to stock Jewish conspiracy theories—in this case, relating to supposed monopoly press ownership—in order to explain the 'mercantilist clutch' forcing the closure of the journal.[47] But if using the best weapon in Pound's own armoury, his words, to aid 'the Axis side of the line' was a course he had fully decided upon by this point, it need not mean that all Pound's propaganda weapons were pointed and referential before the outbreak of the war in Europe. For example, months prior to Italian Fascism's enactment of the Racial Laws, Pound was ahead of the antisemitic curve in both Britain and Italy; indeed, perhaps in terms of a public position, in early 1938, the following was as blunt as any Nazi propagation of racial antisemitism:

> The Semitic poison is in the Semite tempered by Semitic instability, by the Semite's wobble from one excess to another.

> This instability makes him a peril to static and paralytically-minded races...If you believe that a whole race should be punished for the sin of some of its members, I admit that the expulsion of the two million Jews in New York would not be an excessive punishment for the harm done by Jewish finance to the English race in America...
>
> A race may possibly be held responsible for its worst individuals. The Jewish race has not for ages taken the responsibility for the enforcement of its own law. In the Gospel story, whether you take it as fact or as illustrative fiction, the execution of Jesus was achieved by passing the buck. The law enforcement was up to the Romans. If a man is going to be anti-Semite, let him be objectively anti-Semite. Let him gather as many facts as he can, and not blink them.[48]

Like the previous two examples, 'The Revolution Betrayed' is taken from the *British Union Quarterly*, a journal in which Pound published more frequently than any other contributor—in nine of the first ten issues, in fact—more than runners-up Jorian Jenks, Arthur Reade, and Alexander Raven Thomson. Interestingly, during the wartime internment and interrogation of the latter, Ezra Pound was named as one of the principal suppliers of information for Thomson's editorial duties at the BUF's Greater Britain Publications, a fact highlighted in several Special Branch documents held at the British National Archives.[49] Pound's significance to BUF policy is also confirmed by his own voluminous correspondence. In April 1938, for example, Pound gave Thomson editorial advice on the *British Union Quarterly*, actually attempting to get his abovementioned pamphlet, *What is money for?*, adopted as BUF 'doctrine', for 'not anything of mine ... runs counter to B[ritish].U[nion]. Nothing CONSCIOUSLY does so.'[50]

But Raven Thomson was no doubt well aware of this convergence, for he had been publishing Pound for more than a year in his other editorship, which he later told interrogators had a peak circulation of 30,000 weekly copies, namely *Action*. Between 20 February 1937 and 25 April 1940, Pound published 30 texts in that BUF organ, including three notes 'From Ezra Pound' that have not been previously identified by bibliographers.[51] In the first, from 20 February 1937, Pound decried the 'stink and decay of demoliberal democracy', followed in the second, a fortnight later, with the assertion: 'Nothing but sheer bestial and craven ignorance of the nature of money upholds the present perverters. Naturally, the same applies to Blum's fogs and all other taxpayers.'[52]

Raymond Blum, the French Premier at the time, was both Jewish and a long-time Socialist—or a 'Jewish Ramsay McDonald', as Pound put it privately in a letter to US politician George Tinkham of 12 April 1937.[53] These associations were clearly intended, and were likely not missed by Pound's readership in *Action*, and ideological propagation from America's most famous, turned infamous, poet doubtless helped legitimate the BUF, and its antisemitism, at this time: a critical point in their brief history when, paradoxically, British fascism adopted a pacific position toward the virtually inevitable war with Nazi Germany and Fascist Italy. Despite the martial rhetoric from both Pound and the BUF, the latter's 'Mind Britain's Business' campaign, strangely enough, reflected Pound's own claim to be verbally assaulting Jews in order to actually be trying to prevent international conflict.

But this was nonsense, as Pound's first foray into fascist publicism demonstrates; and in a few instances, makes manifest:

> Italy does not need colonies 'to employ' her sons. Italy needs Abyssinia to attain ECONOMIC INDEPENDENCE, by which I do not mean written permission from the enemies of all mankind; I mean the MATERIAL WEALTH, the raw materials necessary to feed and clothe the people of Italy. And I hope Italy gets every last inch of it.

Significantly entitled 'The Fascist Ideal', this article on 'the New Italy' from 18 April 1936, concludes: 'The Fascist ideal of RESPONSIBILITY is vastly higher than the ideal of liberty, especially in the degraded form in which the latter has come to us.'[54] In short, Ezra Pound's earliest appearance in fascist journals was done willingly and *pro bono*; on behalf of a weekly insert explicitly designed to legitimate the Italian invasion of Abyssinia in October 1935. Before briefly considering Pound's role in the *British-Italian Bulletin*, intersecting historical events are critical to recall. In shattering the so-called Stresa Front against Nazi Germany formed earlier that year (in specific response to the 1934 assassination of Austrian Chancellor Dollfuss), Italy's invasion of Abyssinia on 3 October 1935 decisively shook the tottering European balance of power.[55] Twelve months later, Italy had been censured by the League of Nations and estranged from Britain and France, and had, ominously, formed the Rome-Berlin Axis with Nazi Germany. A propaganda offensive aimed at Britain was consequently undertaken by the Italian regime in response, as briefly discussed in Claudia Baldoli's account of British-Italian relations in the 1930s.[56]

During these months, however, Mussolini's Italy lobbied for support, or at least acquiescence, from countries like Britain; thus, even while the 'war crimes' were at their height in Ethiopia, *L'Italia Nostra* played its directed role. As part of the PNF's propaganda offensive, the *British-Italian Bulletin* published a total of fifty English language issues, collectively aimed at softening up British opinion over the Italo-Abyssinian War. And even in print, Pound was clearly aware that this was a propaganda exercise for Fascist Italy, as defensively addressed in 'For A Decent Europe':

> I am not writing Italian propaganda, any more than I am writing British propaganda. I am, if you like, writing European propaganda for the sake of a decent Europe, wherein the best people will not be murdered for the monetary profit of the lowest and rottenest, and wherein the divergent national component might collaborate for a sane unstarved civilisation.[57]

In the first ten months of 1936, Pound contributed 28 further articles to the *British-Italian Bulletin* regarding 'the regeneration of Italy' (29 February). This remit encompassed a wide range of subjects, such as a denunciation of League of Nations sanctions, entitled 'Italy's Frame-Up' (18 Feb. 1936); a defence of intellectual life under totalitarian rule called 'No Tame Robots In Fascist Italy' (25 Jan.); and another, 'The Italian Bank Act', that praised the Italian monetary system. The latter, one of Pound's earliest publications containing antisemitic rhetoric, damns the 'German jew [sic]' Karl Marx with faint praise before vilifying those objecting to science 'in the interest of age-old evil, of evil known for centuries to be evil. It is made in the cause of 60 per cent. usury...in the cause of blind greed that sees not its end.' As with a further article on the same subject a month later, Pound's earliest antisemitic propaganda is heavily encoded, drawing upon his literary abilities through the use of symbolism and allusion: 'I cannot conceive another little war for the benefit of Messieurs Rothschild as being really popular with the rank and file of the British People.'[58]

It is hard to overstate Pound's impact on the *British-Italian Bulletin*, and its explicit endeavour to propagate what one headline called 'An Unbiased Plea for Fair Play To Italy' over the Ethiopian invasion. Appearing in the eighth instalment of the *Bulletin*, a 10-page 'Christmas Special' from 27 December 1935 contained a colour map of occupied Abyssinia, as well as the first article by Ezra Pound. From this date, Pound contributed to two thirds (that is, 28 of the next 42) of the remaining issues, which thereafter doubled in size, from 2 to 4 pages. And that first article, 'A Keystone For Europe', was placed prominently on the front page. 'No man living', Pound initiated his fascist publicism by declaring, 'has preserved the Peace of Europe as has Benito Mussolini.'[59]

Moving backwards has taken us to 1935, and to the start of Ezra Pound's fascist publicism. The intersections of history, as have I hoped to show, certainly bore heavily on what posterity has dubbed 'The Pound Case'—as well as on the choices that uniquely talented, but also all too representative, propagandist made in support of fascist ideology. Pursuing the earlier impulses and writings that brought Pound to publicly support the PNF and BUF is the subject for another paper, but this one concludes with one of the more obvious causes lurking behind his fascist propagation: faith. For in his aforementioned *Jefferson and/or Mussolini*, also published in 1935, Pound asserted that 'Any judgment of MUSSOLINI will be in a measure an act of faith, it will depend on what you *believe* the man means, what you believe that he wants to accomplish.'[60] To Pound, Mussolini was the embodiment of the New Man, and the 'regeneration' of Italy was personified in his dictatorial 'will to order': 'the ideal state'.[61] Pound had written the manuscript—later to be 'rejected by 40 publishers'—in a manic three weeks during February 1933, following an event that may not be unfairly described as a conversion. For on 30 January 1933, or 'XI in our era'—as refashioned in Pound's stylized account of the meeting—the two had met for the only time, an experience later prompting Pound's poetic homage, excerpted below. In fact, this was only weeks after Mussolini had met the self-styled Duce of British fascism, Oswald Mosley, setting him up with 'subsidies of 60,000 pounds a year' for the newly-founded BUF.[62]

Given his subsequent faith in both of these 'bosses', as well as in 'the spread of fascism', from that point on, it is perhaps fitting that Ezra Pound was granted his interview with Il Duce in Rome at the precise hour that Adolf Hitler, the Nazis' Führer, first took his seat as German Chancellor—thus making the previously mythic Third Reich a progressively all-too-terrifying reality for Europe's Jews. Ezra Pound was moved enough by his meeting with Mussolini to subsequently compose these prose and poetic lines just after:

> I assert again my own first belief that the Duce will not stand with despots and the lovers of power but with the lovers of
>
> > *To kalon* [The Beautiful]
> > ORDER
>
> POSTSCRIPT OR VALEDICTION, on going to press over two years after writing. These things being so, is it to be supposed that Mussolini has regenerated Italy, merely for the sake of reinfecting her with the black death of the capitalist monetary system?[63]

'Ma questo,'
    said the Boss, 'divertente.'
Catching the point before the aesthetes had got there;
Having drained off the muck by Vada
From the marshes, by Circeo, where no one else wd. have drained it.
Waited 2000 years, ate grain from the marshes;
Water supply for ten million, another one million '*vani*'
That is rooms for people to live in.
XI of our era.[64]

Endnotes

[1] Tim Redman, "The Repatriation of Pound, 1939-1942: A View from the Archives", *Paideuma* 8/3 (1979), p. 455.
[2] Editorial [Eunice Tietjens], "The End of Ezra Pound", *Poetry*, April 1942, pp. 38-40 (at 40), available online at www.poetryfoundation.org/poetrymagazine/browse?contentId=59805 (all websites last accessed 21 February 2020).
[3] Humphrey Carpenter, *A Serious Character: The Life of Ezra Pound* (London: Faber, 1988), pp. 593-94.
[4] Mary Kenny, *Germany Calling: The Biography of William Joyce* (London: Penguin, 2008), p. 211.
[5] Leonard Doob (ed.), *'Ezra Pound Speaking': Radio Speeches of World War II* (Westport, CT: Greenwood Press, 1978), p. 115.
[6] *Ibid.*, p. 424. See also the useful review of Doob's edited book by Daniel Pearlman, "The Anti-Semitism of Ezra Pound", *Contemporary Literature*, 22/1 (1981), pp. 104-115.
[7] Pound to Harry Meacham, cited in Noel Stock, *The Life of Ezra Pound* (London: Routledge and Kegan Paul, 1970), p. 390.
[8] Ezra Pound, from "Part V", *Hugh Selwyn Mauberley* [1920], cited in George Perkins, Sculley Bradley, Richmond Croom Beatty and E. Hudson Long (eds.), *The American Tradition in Literature* (New York: McGraw Hill, 1990), p. 1314.
[9] The postwar championing of Ezra Pound by sectors of the American far-right is a story in and of itself, from leading US neo-fascist ideologue, Eustace Mullins's, claim that he was a protégé of Pound's at St Elizabeths, reproduced and available on David Duke's website (https://web.archive.org/web/20090205041419/http://davidduke.com/general/the-autobio graphical-reminiscences-of-eustace-mullins_2676.html), to Pound's influence on the far-right during years of direct contact in St Elizabeths. For brief discussion of the latter, see William McNaughton, "The Secret History of St. Elizabeths", *Paideuma*, 30/1-2 (2001), pp. 69-96. There are also numerous neo-fascist, antisemitic and racist websites bearing tribute to Ezra Pound, such as a dedicated 'Special Issue' of Willis Carto's *Barnes Review* dedicated to Pound in 1995, followed by an article by Michael Collins Piper in the same journal from 1997, entitled "What Did Ezra Pound Really Say?", available online at: https://web.archive.org/web/20010419011926/http://www.ety.com/HRP/rev/epound.htm. For details on the latter's background, see George Michael, "Michael Collins Piper: An American Far Right Emissary to the Islamic World", *Totalitarian Movements and Political Religions*, 9/1 (2008), pp. 61-78, available online at https://www.researchgate.net/publication/233199329_Michael_Collins_Piper_An_American_Far_Right_Emissary_to_the_Islamic_World. On this same website, hosting the *Historical Review Press*, one of Pound's antisemitic radio broadcasts, from 18 March 1942, has also been made available: https://web.archive.org/web/20100702144941/http://www.ety.com/HRP/jewishstudies/ezrapoundspeech.htm. For a good overview of Pound's influence on the American far right, see Carlo Pacelli's online article, "Ezra Skinhead: *The Cantos* as the Anthem of Fascism", available at: www.flashpointmag.com/skin.htm.
[10] Marjorie Perloff, "Fascism, Anti-Semitism, Isolationism: Contextualizing the 'Case of EP'", *Paideuma*, 17/2-3 (1988), p. 9.
[11] Tim Redman, *Ezra Pound and Italian Fascism* (Cambridge: Cambridge University Press, 1991), p. 10.
[12] Doob, *"Ezra Pound Speaking"*, pp. 255-56.

[13] Browning, Christopher (ed.), *The Path to Genocide: Essays on Launching the Final Solution* (Cambridge: Cambridge University Press, 1992), p. 169.
[14] Eliot Weinberger, cited in Perloff, "Fascism, Anti-Semitism, Isolationism", p. 16.
[15] Primo Levi, cited in Roger Griffin (ed.), *Fascism* (Oxford: Oxford University Press, 1995), p. 391.
[16] C. David Heymann, *Ezra Pound: The Last Rower* (London: Faber and Faber, 1976), pp. 333-34.
[17] For an excellent discussion of persisting fascist tropes in Ezra Pound's postwar work on *The Cantos*, see two recent article by Ron Bush, "Modernism, Fascism, and the Composition of Ezra Pound's *Pisan Cantos*", *Modernism/Modernity* 2/3 (1995), pp. 69-87; and "Art Versus the Descent of the Iconoclasts: Cultural Memory in Ezra Pound's *Pisan Cantos*", *Modernism/Modernity*, 14/1 (2007), pp. 71-95.
[18] Romano Bilenchi, "Rapallo 1941", *Paideuma*, 8/3 (1979), p. 440.
[19] Ezra Pound, "Addendum for C", in *The Cantos of Ezra Pound* (London: Faber and Faber, 1998), pp. 812-13.
[20] See Philip M. Taylor, *Munitions of the Mind: A history of propaganda from the ancient world to the present day* (Manchester: Manchester University Press, 2003), pp. 111ff. A good overview of recent literature on propaganda as it relates to totalitarian movements, albeit specifically in Germany, is provided in Christoph Classen's "Thoughts on the Significance of Mass-Media Communications in the Third Reich and the GDR", in *Totalitarian Movements and Political Religions*, 8/3-4 (2007), pp. 547-562.
[21] Pound, "Notes for CXVII et seq.", in *The Cantos*, p. 802
[22] Richard Shorten, "The status of ideology in the return of political religion theory", *Journal of Political Ideologies*, 12/2 (2007), p. 165; see also the editorial introduction to Roger Griffin (ed.), *International Fascism: Theories, Causes and the New Consensus* (London: Arnold, 1998).
[23] Emilio Gentile, *Politics as Religion* (Oxford: Princeton University Press, 2006), p. xi.
[24] For a good analysis of the BUF through the lens of Griffin's 'new consensus', see Gary Love's reading of the British Blackshirts as a partially 'mimetic' fascist movement in "'What's the big idea?' Oswald Mosley, the British Union of Fascists and Generic Fascism", *Journal of Contemporary History* 42/3 (2007), pp. 447-468.
[25] Matthew Feldman (ed.), *A Fascist Century: Essays by Roger Griffin* (Basingstoke: Palgrave, 2008), p. xviii.
[26] Ezra Pound,"A Visiting Card" in William Cookson (ed.) *Selected Prose: 1909-1965* (London: Faber and Faber, 1973), p. 276.
[27] Victor Ferkiss, "Ezra Pound and American Fascism", *The Journal of Politics*, 17/2 (1955), p. 178.
[28] *Ibid.*, p. 174; and Tim Redman, "Pound's Politics and Economics", *The Cambridge Companion to Ezra Pound* (Cambridge: Cambridge University Press, 2001), p. 262.
[29] Ezra Pound, cited in Lea Baechler, A. Walton Litz and James Longenbach (eds.), *Ezra Pound's Poetry and Prose: Contributions to Periodicals*, vol. VI [1933-1935] (London: Garland, 1991), p. 332.
[30] Pound's economics have been covered widely; for example, in the Pound Studies journal *Paideuma*, see Roxana Preda's "Social Credit in America: A view from Pound's Economic Correspondence, 1933-1940", 34/2-3 (2005), pp. 201-227; or Michael Coyle's "'A Profounder Didacticism': Ruskin, Orage and Pound's Reception of Social Credit", 17/1 (1988), pp. 7-28.
[31] For an insightful account of how Pound's economic ideas may have led to the 'association of usury and Jews' in the 1930s, see A. David Moody, "EP with Two Pronged Fork of Terror

and Cajolery': The Construction of His Anti-Semitism (up to 1939)", *Paideuma*, 29/3 (2000), p. 73.

[32] Robert Casillo, *The Genealogy of Demons: Fascism, Anti-Semitism and the Myths of Ezra Pound* (Evanston: Northwestern University Press, 1988), citations in this paragraph from pp. 4-7.

[33] Pound famously declared to Allen Ginsberg in 1967 that 'the worst mistake I made was that stupid, suburban prejudice of anti-Semitism. All along, that spoiled everything.' Cited in Heymann, Ezra Pound: The Last Rower, p. 298.

[34] Reed Way Dasenbrock, "Pound's Demonology" *American Literary History*, 1 (Spring 1989), p. 238; and Casillo, The Genealogy of Demons, p. 13. A good, recent survey of Pound's anti-semitism in terms of successive stages is also put forward by Ellen Cardona in the journal *Flashpoint*, available online at the following addresses: www.flashpointmag.com/card2.htm; www.flashpointmag.com/card.htm; www.flashpointmag.com/cardchap2.htm; and www.flashpointmag.com/cardchap3.htm.

[35] Wendy Flory, "Pound and antisemitism", *The Cambridge Companion to Ezra Pound*, pp. 287-8.

[36] Surette, *Pound in Purgatory: From Economic Radicalism to Anti-Semitism* (Chicago: University of Chicago Press, 1999), pp. 239-241.

[37] *Ibid.*, p. 254.

[38] Burton Hatlen, "Pound and Fascism", in Marianne Korn (ed.), *Ezra Pound and History* (Orono: National Poetry Foundation/University of Maine, 1985), pp. 157-58.

[39] See Stock, *The Life of Ezra Pound*, pp. 390-1 passim.

[40] Redman, Ezra Pound and Italian Fascism, p. 167.

[41] Pound to Harold W. Thompson (April 1936), cited in Cameron McWhirter, "'Dear Poet-General and Walloper': The Correspondence of Ezra Pound and Harold W. Thompson 1936-1939", in *Paideuma* 29/3-4 (2001), p. 116.

[42] Ezra Pound, *What Is Money For?* (London: Greater Britain Publications, 1939), p. 9.

[43] Paul Baxa also makes the important point that Hitler's week-long state visit to Fascist Italy in May 1938 substantially radicalised PNF policy months before the passage of the Racial Laws. See "Capturing the Fascist Moment: Hitler's Visit to Italy in 1938 and the Radicalization of Fascist Italy", in *The Journal of Contemporary History*, 42/2 (2007), pp. 227-242.

[44] Ezra Pound, cited in *Ezra Pound: Letters to Ibbotson, 1935-1952* (Orono: National Poetry Foundation/University of Maine Press, 1979), p. 47.

[45] Ezra Pound, "An Impact" [May 1935], reprinted in Noel Stock (ed.), *Impact: Essays on Ignorance and the Decline of American Civilization* (Chicago: Henry Regnery Company, 1960), p. 144.

[46] Ezra Pound, "Banks are a blessing", *British Union Quarterly*, 3/1 (1939) p. 51.

[47] Ezra Pound, "The *Criterion* Passes", *British Union Quarterly*, 3/2 (1939), p. 56.

[48] Ezra Pound, "The Revolution Betrayed", *British Union Quarterly*, 2/1 (1938), pp. 37-38.

[49] See the Pound Papers in the National Archives in Kew, listed under the heading KV2/875 [PF34.319/Ezra Pound].

[50] Pound, letter to Raven Thomson (April 1938), in Roxana Preda (ed.), *Ezra Pound's Economic Correspondence, 1933-1940* (Gainesville: University Press of Florida, 2007), p. 213.

[51] See the relevant portions of Donald Gallup's otherwise excellent *Ezra Pound: A Bibliography* (Charlottesville: Bibliographical Society of the University of Virginia and St. Paul's/University Press of Virginia, 1983). For Pound's journal publications during the critical years 1933-1940, see pp. 286-325.

[52] Ezra Pound, "From Ezra Pound", *Action* 20 Feb 1937 and 5 March 1937.

[53] Philip J. Burns (ed.), *'Dear Uncle George:' The Correspondence Between Ezra Pound and Congressman Tinkham of Massachusetts* (Orono: National Poetry Foundation/University of Maine Press, 1996), p. 119.
[54] Ezra Pound, *British Italian Bulletin*, 18 April 1936.
[55] See Richard Parkhurst, "Italian Fascist War Crimes in Ethiopia: A History of Their Discussion, from the League of Nations to the United Nations (1936–1949)", in *Northeast African Studies* 6/2 (1999), pp. 100ff.
[56] Claudia Baldoli, *Italian Fascism and Britain's Italians in the 1930s* (Oxford: Berg, 2003), pp. 106-112.
[57] *British-Italian Bulletin*, 14 March 1936.
[58] Ezra Pound, *British-Italian Bulletin*, 4 April 1936 and 23 May 1936.
[59] *Ibid.*, 27 December 1935.
[60] Ezra Pound, *Jefferson and/or Mussolini: L'Idea Statale, Fascism as I have seen it* (London: Stanley Nott, 1935), pp. 33-34.
[61] The argument that Pound's activism on behalf of Italian Fascism stemmed from his idolisation of Benito Mussolini can be found, for instance, in Thomas Cody, "Adams, Mussolini, and the Personality of Genius", *Paideuma* 3/4 (1989), pp. 77-103. Pound's more general tendency toward placing 'heroic' figures upon an artistic pedestal—like Confucius, Sigismondo Malatesta and even Filippo Marinetti—has been convincingly demonstrated in Lawrence Rainey's influential monograph, *Institutions of Modernism: Literary Elites and Public Culture* (London: Yale University Press, 1998), ch.1.
[62] Brian Sullivan and Philip Cannistraro, *Il Duce's Other Woman* (New York: Morrow, 1993), p. 341.
[63] Ezra Pound, *Jefferson and/or Mussolini*, pp. 127-8.
[64] Ezra Pound, "Canto XLI", in *The Cantos*, p. 202.

5. Reappraising the 'Pound Case', 1940–45

LIBERTY A DUTY

FASCIO
A thousand candles together blaze with intense brightness. No one's candle damages another's. So is the liberty of the individual in the ideal and fascist state.
Pound, "A Visiting Card" (1942)[1]

During World War II, Ezra Pound used his best weapons, his words, to fight the Allies as a radio propagandist for Fascist Italy. In the final days of war in Europe, he was arrested on charges of treason and imprisoned in an outdoor cage next to military rogues at the US Army Detention Training Center near Pisa. Following his FBI interrogation in early May 1945, Pound began drafting one of his most memorable poetic sequences, *The Pisan Cantos*—highly controversial recipient of the 1949 Bollingen Prize—while at the same time sparking a remarkable public discussion about exactly what should be done with him.[2] By 1945, what was already being called the 'Pound Case' was acting as a lightning rod for debate, seeming to bear out Pound's wartime view as expressed to his close collaborator, Adriano Ungaro—a University of Leeds lecturer of Italian from 1933 to 1940, and then chief Anglophone censor at Radio Rome during World War II[3]: "All the U.S. runs on 'poic'nality'/ they are MOSTLY below the level of ideas/ can['] t understand an idea/ all they can get is SO/ and SO SAID SO." Yet the full dimensions of Pound's wartime activities were largely unknown then, and little better understood today. As suggested in Part I, much of what is known owes to the groundbreaking scholarship of Tim Redman—even if his archival discoveries have not been meaningfully advanced to date. Moreover, the largest gap in the critical literature is indicated in Pound's letter to Ungaro, cited by Redman without full awareness of its implications. In the rest of the letter Pound implies a far more extensive role in Axis propaganda than his published wartime broadcasts and Italian texts: "I like Morelli's reading of my stuff. *The anonymous stuff is in some ways better than the personal*/When anonymous I can be omniscient/when I speak in my own voice I have to be modest and stick to what I have seen first hand."[4]

Even without access to exhaustive manuscript evidence now capable of painting a far clearer picture, some of Pound's less charitable detractors were already howling for blood in 1945. Did Pound deserve the same kind of public execution as Mussolini? A number of his contemporaries certainly thought so. One, contributing to *The New Masses*' 1945 Christmas Special, in a text entitled 'Should Ezra Pound Be Shot?', argued yes, for in "his wildest moments of human vilification Hitler never approached our Ezra [....] He knew all America's weaknesses and he played them as expertly as Goebbels ever did."[5] This advocate of frontier justice, ironically enough, was Arthur Miller, later the playwright of the celebrated anti-McCarthy allegory from 1952, *The Crucible*. His view was not to prevail for, on 21 December 1945, Pound was denied bail and transferred to St Elizabeths Asylum, where he would spend the next dozen years in captivity and a vexing legal limbo. In the decades since, debates over Pound's wartime actions and subsequent institutionalization have bitterly divided critics, often shedding more heat than light on pertinent issues of sanity, culpability and treason.[6] As evidenced by the letter to Ungaro above, one weakness shared by his defenders and critics alike is that none have been able to establish precisely what Pound did, and said, during World War II. Alongside Redman's work, Noel Stock's authorized biography remains the most reliable survey of this period. Nevertheless, gaps in the historical record impeded Stock's account—despite several tantalizing hints contained therein:

> Pound entered into his job as broadcaster with the same zeal he had always brought to any subject that claimed his attention. He wrote messages for others to read, slogans for a war of nerves against England, advised on how to present propaganda and even suggested that a chair be established to enable him to teach this art—but whether these things occurred after America had entered the war, I cannot be certain. Judging by the indictment drawn up against him by the American government in 1945, some at least of these activities took place after the country was at war. That he was useful to the Italian propagandists is borne out by the fact that they used him in chats with other speakers.[7]

Given this extraordinary set of circumstances—one of the US's leading 'personalities' on trial for allegedly (for he was never convicted) treasonous radio broadcasts—most would agree with Benjamin Friedlander's recent view that Pound's radio broadcasts were "one of the central facts of his life". Yet it is striking how little is actually known about them. In attempting an explanation, Friedlander considers that these scripts and recordings "have an aberrational status among Pound scholars, who for many decades received them with embarrassment and apologetics, segregating them from Pound's other prose and from his poetry".[8] This may well be the case, even if the present account emphasizes that no such distinction between Pound's prose and poetry—at least during World War II—remains tenable. In addition to the wealth of previously unexamined manuscripts at Yale's Beinecke Library archives employed here, what the FBI themselves referred to as Pound's "bulky file" will also be used, alongside supporting documentation from BBC's Written Archive Centre and The National Archives in London. These reveal a very different side of Pound as a committed, strategic and significant propagandist for Fascism's wartime Ministry of Popular Culture. The latter, in Guido Bonsaver's view, was "a well-oiled propaganda machine" and, especially in terms of censorship, "a careful arbitrator of Italy's cultural production."⁹ In approaching Pound's wartime propaganda efforts for the oft-shorthanded 'Minculpop', Part II necessarily commences with a lengthy discussion addressing persistent misunderstandings concerning Pound's fascist activism. Ensuing sections will then survey his propaganda strategies and techniques, followed by Pound's little-known activism for the Salò Republic.

Throughout, it will become clear that longstanding academic views on Pound's propaganda need substantial correction. His undertakings were born of far more than the significant, twin considerations of financial need and restricted travel; rather, he self-consciously toed the Party line out of loyalty to and belief in the Axis cause. In her comment upon this period, Frances Stonor Saunders's passing impression is much closer to the mark than wide swathes of Pound scholarship: "'There is too much future, and nobody but me and Muss and half a dozen others to attend to it,' Ezra Pound once declaimed. Mussolini had been Pound's idol for twenty years. He kept a scrapbook of his life and work" and, after meeting the Duce, "had been so pleased that he hung the official notice granting the interview on the wall of his apartment in Rapallo".¹⁰ Pound's propaganda activities also mirrored those of Fascist Italy at the time, itself increasingly indistinguishable from Nazi propaganda—especially with respect to anti-Semitic rhetoric.

A good indicator of Pound's commitment is provided by the above epigraph from "A Visiting Card", first published in English by Peter Russell in 1952, which continues: "In August, 1942, the following elucidatory statement was heard on the Berlin radio: the power of the state, whether it be Nazi, Fascist, or Democratic, is always the same, that is—absolute; the different forms of administration are merely a matter of the different activities which one agrees not to allow."¹¹ It scarcely needs stressing that the European 'New Order' under Nazi hegemony was long making a mockery of all such equivalences in practice; already by this time, and historically unprecedentedly, being Jewish, gay, disabled, a Roma and Sinti traveler or any other socio-political 'undesirable' meant mass murder through shooting, gassing or overwork in the thousands of concentration camps scarring wartime Europe. While it bears restating that this study is less concerned with what Pound did or did not know during this time, or with either damning or exculpating his fascist propaganda during these critical years—and even less so his mental health or guilt—the following sections attempt to put the record straight by charting his Anglophone wartime propaganda via the perspective of international fascism as a political religion.

First, however, it bears noting that the very term 'international fascism' seems oxymoronic given fascist ideology's well-known emphasis upon ultra-nationalism.

Nevertheless, as early as February 1923, the Fascist Grand Council in Italy endorsed the existence of the '*Fasci* Abroad'; intended "to 'remake' the Italians abroad and to expand Fascism in other countries". Unaffiliated branches appeared, in fact, as early as 1921—that is, fully a year before Mussolini's March on Rome—explicitly (self-)tasked with the 'fascistisation' of overseas Italians. From the very beginning, therefore, an important strand of Fascism looked beyond the confines of the nation in advancing this nascent ideological doctrine. Furthermore, as Claudia Baldoli's excellent study reveals, the "Italian *Fasci* Abroad were the most important means for the diffusion of this kind of 'spiritual' imperial dream". In turn, perhaps the most important of these Fasci were based in London—home to some 15,000 Italians between the wars—aided by weekly updates provided in the tellingly titled, London-based newspaper, *L'Italia Nostra* (*Our Italy*, published between 1928-1940).[12] The first head, or 'inspector' of the London Fasci was Camillo Pellizzi, a professor of Italian at King's College, London until 1943, "who promoted the idea of spiritual revolution in order to build a new civilisation based on the expansion of *italianità* in the world, had stated this in precise terms as early as 1924. Italian Fascists abroad were not to be merely propaganda agents but apostles of a new religion."[13] Like the all-encompassing civilizations of Catholicism and Ancient Rome before it, the secular faith represented by Mussolini's Fascism expanded far beyond Italy's traditional borders. National rebirth was but the herald of a larger, civilizational palingenesis across modern Europe:

> Pellizzi argued that the Rome of antiquity had not been a nation in the generally recognized sense. He proceeded to point out that the subsequent empire of the universal Church was not a nation either. The universal Church that arose out of dying Rome was born as a *faith*—*not* a nation. Out of its resurgent civilization and its rekindled faith, Fascism was destined to ultimately create not simply a nation animated by revolutionary impulse, but an empire.[14]

Well before Fascism's mercifully short-lived colonization of East Africa, Pellizzi and other 'universal fascists' thus viewed Italy's fundamental mission as no less than the construction of an 'empire of the spirit' in Europe. And like 'universal fascism' itself, such a view was not the sole preserve of Italian nationals; yet "wanted to extend Fascist ideas on a worldwide plane".[15] One important exemplar, later a close friend and collaborator of Pound's, James 'Giacomo' Barnes, had even directed the short-lived 'CINEF' [*Centre international d'études sur le fascisme*] in Switzerland between 1927 and 1929—the first institute to examine fascism as a discrete and generic ideology.[16] Alongside Pellizzi, Barnes was a long-term correspondent of Pound's (the former between 1935 and 1960, and exchanges with Barnes covering at least 1941 and 1955), who also would later also act as a pro-Axis broadcaster during WWII. In this capacity, it appears that Barnes hosted

Pound at his home in Rome when the latter travelled from Rapallo in order to record his propaganda broadcasts for EIAR; still later, according to the FBI, they worked together on "Jerry's Front Calling" for the Salò Republic.[17] Yet a generation beforehand, while still the 'non-aligned' director of CINEF in 1928, Barnes made precisely the same arguments as Pellizzi, the Fasci and many others over the 1920s. In his 1928 *The Universal Aspects of Fascism*, Barnes asserted that Fascism would create for Italy a new imperial idea, one advancing a "new universal message, a culture in the making":

> Empire, therefore, is indissolubly connected with a culture, an idea, a type of civilisation, a way of approaching the problems of life. Hence there is a sense in the word Empire which transcends its territorial sense; and this is its spiritual sense, its really more important sense, in that its territorial sense is but a ready-made receptacle to receive the spirit. But the spirit may, after filling the receptacle, be defused beyond it. A powerful national State, respected among other States, with a great civilisation, a great culture, will exercise inevitably a powerful attraction beyond its frontiers. It will influence the culture of other Nations. It will have an assimilating effect beyond what is strictly its own province; and this influence in itself is a kind of Empire-building. It is, in fact, the finest form of Empire-building, for it conquers without destroying life…[18]

As the 1920s gave way to the 1930s, even Mussolini — who had famously declared that "Fascism was not for export" in 1928[19]—flirted heavily with the idea of Fascism as a missionary doctrine: "'from 1929…, fascism has become a universal phenomenon... the new political and economic forms of the twentieth-century are fascist'".[20] After seeing the aforementioned MRF Decennio in 1932 (which, tellingly, had a room dedicated to the Fasci all'Estero), Mussolini was said to have remarked: "In ten years Europe will be fascist or fascistized".[21] From June of the very next year the most important, if short-lived, vehicle for the attempted Fascistization of Europe was launched: CAUR [*Comitato d'Azione per l'Universalità di Roma*]. Intended as a counterweight to the 'New Germany', at that time still a potentially-hostile rival, the "Action Committee for the Universality of Rome" formalized this Fascist 'universalism' via propaganda exchanges, subsidies and publications between 1933 and 1936 (part of a larger project attempting to counterbalance the influence of Nazism prior to the dramatic changes engendered by Italy's invasion of Abyssinia).[22] Reaching their apex at the Montreux Conference in December 1934, the centrality of racism and, in particular, anti-Semitism to the ideology and practice of fascism were debated in detail by leading fascist ideologues of the time—ranging from Catholic countries like Ireland (Eoin O'Duffy) and France (Marcel Bucard) to Orthodox ones like Romania (Ion Mota), right the way through to Nordic countries such as Norway (Vidkun Quisling) and, perhaps surprisingly, Switzerland (General Arthur Fonjallaz). Despite attempting to confederate hyper-nationalist movements "into a loose organization which paid fealty to the genius of Mussolini and the leadership of Italian fascism", notes Michael Ledeen, "tension between fascist Italy and Nazi Germany was clear from the beginning of the CAUR".[23] This was made explicit by Nazi Germany's notable absence from Montreux, though even earlier dissent had been raised by the leader of the Spanish Falange, Jose Antonio Primo de Rivera:

> In every country fascism assumes styles and characteristics of its own, which are the circumstantial and local element surrounding the permanent an unique essence of the movement... Hitlerism has some essential principles which coincide with our own, but it also has some Germanic and Lutheran characteristics which obviously do not fit in with the Roman idea of universality, nor the Spanish one, and these principles are summed up in the word "racism".[24]

In attempting to the square the circle of collaborative nationalism, the director of CAUR, Eugenio Coselschi (to whom Pound sent suggestions along with a record of his admiration for the Duce in 1934), insisted that a lowest common denominator could be found amongst those having "their spirit oriented towards the principles of a political, economic, and social renovation, based on the concepts of the hierarchy of the State and the principle of collaboration between the classes". Coselschi's statement is strikingly in keeping with recent scholarship on fascism as a revolutionary form of 'palingenesis'; again in the CAUR director's words, "a revolution inspired by a true mysticism and an elevated ideal, founded on Corporativism."[25]

Alongside the intellectual leadership provided by Coselschi and the editor of *Antieuropa*, Asvero Gravelli, the driving force of CAUR seems to have been Mussolini's son-in-law, Galeazzo Ciano, between 1933 and 1936 (precisely the years in which Pound corresponded with him).[26] Although largely ignored by Anglophone scholars, Michael Ledeen's 1972 study argues that this was indeed a "significant act" by Mussolini's Italy insofar as CAUR represented the "first institutionalization of the ideology of universal fascism".[27] Although both domestic Italian politics and the unchecked expansion of Nazi Germany ultimately put paid to the Corporatist-led ecumenicalism of CAUR, the short-lived organization serves as a reminder that, at least until the mid-1930s, non-biologically racist fascists, especially those from Catholic countries, were likely to look toward the Corporate State for inspiration and leadership. Under the direction of Fascist Italy—until the later 1930s, when the rearmament of Germany and invalidation of Treaty of Versailles provisions made Nazism *primus inter pares* of European fascism—revolutionary nationalisms were encouraged to take autochthonous decisions on racism and anti-Semitism, militarism and anti-Bolshevism; all within an 'internationalist' framework of parallel regenerative movements across Europe. "And so the 'supernational' idea harmonizes perfectly with the national idea", Coselschi proclaimed at Montreux:

> the reconstitutions of a State on new bases, of a unified, strong and disciplined State, the organization of labor; liberties contained within sane and honest limits; installation of order and justice; agreement between social classes; coordinated and solid collaboration between producers... [28]

Correspondingly, CAUR was instrumental in supporting European fascist movements like the Croatian Ustasha, Belgian Rexists and Mosley's BUF, the latter a consequent recipient of some £60,000 per annum prior to the launch of the Fascist-Nazi Axis in October 1936.[29] It was actually only the latter—namely, Mussolini's response to League of Nations sanctions resulting from the Abyssinian War—that broke the anti-German 'Stresa Front' of the preceding two years. As a result of these crucial shifts in the fragile European balance of powers, CAUR swiftly fell by the wayside, as did the increasingly marginalized Fasci Abroad. But not before ensnaring Ezra Pound in fascist universalism. With sentiments virtually indistinguishable to that of CAUR's chief ideologies, Pound was to advocate fascism on behalf of a 'decent' European civilization from December 1935. Unlike international communism, this "community of interests" would assume a "creative and reconstructive" form, for, in Coselschi's view, even corporatism expressed a spiritual nature under fascist ideology:

> Organising corporations according to the cycle of production means imparting to the new structure of the State the character of a higher rule and of a higher spirituality, namely an [sic] universal character that spreads as an example for all the people to follow and that is capable of giving to all the world the rule for a new life, for a new balance and for a perfect settlement.[30]

Pound's "A Visiting Card" is thus relevant not only as an expression of that very fascist creed, but also as evidence of Pound's continuing propaganda efforts for Fascist Italy. For "Carta da Visita" was originally published in Italian in December 1942 and was, along with Pound's Italian translation of the Confucian *Ta Hio*, sent to Mussolini personally, with a covering note explaining they were "expressions of fascist faith".[31] One of Pound's few published prose texts during World War II was written that autumn; during a period that, amongst others, E. Fuller Torrey's 1984 *The Roots of Treason* has asserted was a lull in Pound's broadcasting (which he dates between 26 July 1942 and 18 February 1943). Having apparently consulted neither Pound's extant texts at Yale nor the Foreign Broadcast Intelligence Service's 42 broadcasts recorded at this period of supposed "quiescence", Torrey seems to base his reading upon the large gap between scripts numbered 59 and 60 reproduced in *"Ezra Pound Speaking"*.[32] To date, this remains the most authoritative reproduction of speeches, containing 120 scripts transcribed by the Federal Communications Commission (FCC) between October 1941 and Pound's indictment for treason on 26 July 1943. Even so, Doob's 1978 work only scratches the surface of Pound's wartime propaganda.

Finally, as further stressed below, there was no clear distinction between Pound's wartime propaganda and his other contemporaneous writings—including the only Cantos written during the war, the long-unpublished and long-untranslated "Canto LXXII" and "Canto LXXIII". In the case of a six-page radio typescript from 20 August 1942, "Evidence", both the date given and the themes addressed correlate closely to "A Visiting Card":

> the fascist concept of individual glory is on the model of LIGHT/ put a thousand candles together and they give a considerable light/ NO single light in any way damagin[g] the light of the other candles [....] There is more scope for the individual in the corp/state than in any splay footed inorganic drivvlin democracy that the world has yet seen [....] Occupied fr/ would have been unoccupied before now; if left to the Axis decision/ The SANE world is copying fascism here there and everywhere / ALL that you do well inside Eng/ is part of Mosley's program/ "To morrow we live" [....] Have [you] YET read the Protocols [of the Elders of Zion]/? Have you ANY conception of what fascism IS?[33]

As this manuscript suggests, in terms of Pound's wartime propaganda for Fascist Italy, there is a great deal more to say.

Italy had remained on the sidelines in September 1939, only joining the "stab in the back of France" on 10 June 1940, with German victory already imminent and Churchill's defiant speech following the Dunkirk evacuation, "we shall not flag or fail [...] we shall never surrender", delivered the previous week.[34] As an outgrowth of Fascist Italy's unpreparedness for total war in 1940, writes Vincent Arnold, "the Ministry of Popular Culture lacked a comprehensive plan for wartime propaganda".[35] As noted above, there is some evidence that Pound started writing for the radio at just this time; that is, at the outset of Fascist Italy's disastrous participation in World War II. The earliest text seems to be an untitled, four-page typescript headed "1." with crayon in the top right margin. While Pound's wartime numbering system for his broadcasts is all but impossible to reconstruct, this text appears to date from the Italian entry into the war, opening: "It is my firm believe that this war was unnecessary. It need never have started. It was started by a small number of men; who need not have started it."[36] As with many of the literally thousands of radio texts, items and slogans contained in Pound's papers at the Beinecke archives, it is unclear whether this early text was ever transmitted; quite possibly, it was written in hopes of securing work with Minculpop. At any rate, as will be detailed below, Pound had been consistently espousing several propaganda strategies. The first of these was closer collaboration with Nazi Germany, especially in terms of anti-Semitic discourse and active participation in a 'New Europe'. Clearly a junior partner in the Axis by 1940, Pound's vision for Fascist Italy was to provide a cultural lead via radio, press, and music. These components will be briefly described below, prior to concluding this chapter with a look at Pound's specific views on producing effective propaganda for Radio Rome.

Even before the outbreak of war, Pound had gravitated toward the biological anti-Semitism and militaristic expansionism of Nazi Germany. To be sure, he was hardly alone in doing so in late 1930s Italy. As Paul Baxa has persuasively shown, Hitler's week-long state visit in early May 1938 provided a "triumphant fascist spectacle" whereby the "kindred spirit" of Nazism and Italian Fascism were "sacralized through a series of ceremonies". Less tangibly, if no less importantly, Hitler's visit "was designed to send a message to the rest of the world about the character and destiny of fascism. Coming as it did in a triumphant moment in fascist history [Germany's 11 March 1938 takeover of Austria], the visit reinforced the notion of fascism as the *avant-garde* of political movements."[37] Even the stridently anti-fascist journalist in exile, Max Ascoli, observed the same year that both fascist regimes "announced to the world that they are forerunners and the founders of a new civilization [.... fascism] can dare to be a religion, to invent new rituals, to deny the Jewish and the Christian heritage which is the basis of our civilization."[38] Within months, the "staunchly biological–deterministic" "Manifesto of Racial Scientists" was published by a leading newspaper, *Giornale d'Italia*—with the "spiritual racism" and anti-biologism guiding previous Fascist policy now "fiercely denied". This announced a "Nordicist" anti-Semitism under Mussolini's explicit direction.[39] Published on 14 July 1938, this terse declaration laid the groundwork for the Racial Laws that autumn, which were eugenically racist and quintessentially Nazi: "The population of Italy today is of Aryan origin and its civilization is Aryan [....] The Jews do not belong to the Italian race."[40]

Shortly afterwards, against the advice of military experts, Mussolini signed the aforementioned Pact of Steel on 22 May 1939, affirming "the inner affinity between their ideologies and the comprehensive solidarity of their interests [....] in the midst of a world of unrest and disintegration, to serve the task of safeguarding the foundations of European civilization."[41] In an historical irony worthy of fiction, *Il Duce*, who had launched Italian Fascism on the back of his interventionist journalism during World War I, now tried to fend off calls by radical Fascists to immediately join World War II—for he still needed to convince a more conservative establishment (primarily monarchy, church and military). As Elizabeth Wiskemann long ago claimed, as late as winter 1939, "scarcely any Fascist leader" was pro-Nazi; whereas with the latter's success in overrunning France and the Low Countries, regime functionaries "were all enthusiasm at least for intervention."

Apart from political elites, Paul Corner adds that this sentiment was anathema to the general populace, for whom the "prospect of fighting alongside the Nazis was almost universally unpopular."[42] Ultimately, it was only when "the Germans turned western Europe upside down" in spring 1940 that Mussolini decided to invade south-eastern France, thus "driv[ing] generals and king into war by telling them they need not fight." For one, given Britain's willingness to continue fighting—principally including, at least until D-Day in June 1944, the Mediterranean theatre of operations—and considering the Italian military's utter inadequacy at the time, as made plain by battlefield debacles in France (June 1940), Greece (October 1940) and North Africa (November 1940), Mussolini's "megalomaniacal" participation in World War II would quickly prove to be a fatal mistake.[43] Mere months into Italy's disastrous war, concludes another scholar of Fascism, "[o]nly Mussolini's personal prestige was still strong enough to hold the regime together."[44]

Correspondingly, Pound seems to have followed much the same path of radicalization vis-à-vis Nazi Germany as many other fascists. As recounted in Part I, his acceptance of biological anti-Semitism was first publicly announced around this time. In fact, a year to the day that the *Giornale d'Italia* published its "Manifesto degli scienziati razzisti," Pound concluded a letter to Joseph Ibbotson, college librarian of his Alma Mater in the US, Hamilton College, with a provocative swastika under his signature. That summer, he also attended the 1938 Venetian Biennale, where he later asserted "in the teeth of current snobbisms" that the Nazi-co-opted exhibition designed by Ernst Haider "was the best pavilion there".[45] Another snapshot of this turn is revealed in Pound's correspondence with the musician Gerhart Münch, with whom he worked on the 'Vivaldi Revival' in Fascist Italy during the 1930s. Their extant letters were strictly concerned with matters musical and artistic until 12 April 1938 when Münch, by then back in Germany, revealed that he was considering closer collaboration with the Nazi Party. "Do for God's sake work WITH THE PARTY, the party is right and is the future", Pound replied three days later—echoing Mussolini's well-known prophecy that the twentieth century was to be "a century of the right, a fascist century"—"And the future is RIGHT".[46] Commenting upon his contemporaneous essay for *Germany and You*, "European Paideuma", to Münch on 25 October 1939, Pound displayed a canniness quite at odds with prevailing notions of his political "naiveté":

> I have been tempted to come up to Berlin and write, I mean I have FELT the temptation to offer my services [....] The only trouble with my coming to Germany is that it wd. probably make it impossible for me to carry on any useful political work in the U.S. afterward, and the U.S. neutrality etc. is more use to Germany than my services. Still I am for being as useful as possible. Can you get in touch with H.R. Hoffmann Riedenerweg I. Starnberg. He gets out a mimeograph bulletin in English. Everyone needs MORE knowledge of jew finance and of the WAY it works.[47]

Six weeks earlier Pound had written to Rolf Hoffmann, "a German editor of propaganda magazines (for which he hoped to write) that 'this war is a war of jews against Hitler'."[48] By early December 1939, with his subscription to *Germany and You* delayed by the war—as Pound often lamented, especially as his family's much-needed income checks ceased arriving by mid-1940—he requested "special literature" from Hoffmann in order to "prove certain things about Germany instead of merely believing them". Pound then added: "I was solemnly told by a diplomat two months ago that I wd. be killed if I went to Berlin. I had told him I had a strong impulse to go there."[49] As with Ibbotson above, Pound's pro-Nazi views were not only expressed to German ultranationalists, but to American elites as well. Thus, the day after Germany's invasion of Poland, Pound wrote to Massachusetts Congressman George Tinkham: "UNTIL the present kike government of England is damn well licked the Aryan population/ especially rural population of Eng/ will never get a square deal".[50] More of the same followed in the closing months of 1939, reports John Tytell: "He wrote James Laughlin that in his view 'Roosevelt represents Jewry' and signed his letter 'Heil Hitler'. To Cummings he wrote that 'Germany is 90% right in the present show'. He wrote Congressman Horace 'Jerry' Voorhis that if war began it was the fault of 'international usury' ".[51] To the isolationist senator Burton K. Wheeler, Pound was similarly concise on 19 July 1940: "if Germany moves fast enough it may be postponed for 15 years"—the "it" referring to Americans being "slaughtered for Hazard, Hambro and Rothschild". (During World War II, an increasing number of Pound's letters would bear the 'Heil Hitler' salutation to known pro-Nazis like Rolf Hoffmann and William Joyce; to the latter, insightfully, Pound wrote: "A poem has to be good in 200 years/ or it is bad. Quite different technique for talk that has to take effect NOW or never [....] I think I was right to transmit from Rome/ I know this country and do not know Germany; and can not speak German well enough to make my ideas clear.")[52]

By summer 1940, at which point he seems to have been submitting radio typescripts to Radio Rome prospectively, Pound's anti-Semitism had become quite extreme:

> The MORE the material cost of the war falls on the men who started it, the better and the sooner we have a sane Europe [....] Letting the BIG JEWS into America is equivalent, as I see it to breaking a test tube full of typhus or plague germs. Turning it loose on territory not yet immunized. I shd/ like to prevent ANOTHER 20 years uneasiness.[53]

Fascist Italy was now at war, growing daily closer to Nazi Germany ideologically, militarily and 'racially' in the formation of the Axis 'New Order'. Pound was likewise discerning an increasing convergence between his long-held economic theories and fascist practice. In the same unpublished letter to Hoffmann cited above, Pound declared of the Third Reich's Minister for Economics: "FUNK'S declarations are absolute vindication of all the economics I have written during the past 20 years". Pound's belief that his economic theories had been adopted by fascist practice was equally emphatic in a penultimate letter to Congressman Tinkham on 7 November 1940—just as confirmation was hitting the newswires of Roosevelt's landslide re-election over Republican challenger Wendell Willkie for an unprecedented third term—"As you may have noticed both Funk and Riccardi are now quoting me without being aware of it [....] or at any rate I am orthodox for 1940 instead of being a lone voice."[54] At the end of October 1940 Pound made a similar declaration to the Japanese poet, Katue Kitasono, who had facilitated his occasional articles for the *Japan Times*.[55]

While Pound's 11 articles for the *Japan Times*, published between December 1939 and October 1940, are perhaps better understood as expressions of financial need rather than fascist propaganda, Pound's FBI file nevertheless reveals that he sent a prospective *Japan Times* article to Minculpop on 10 May 1940. In the same letter, the FBI translated a report from the hard-liner Alessandro Pavolini to his Ministry, noting that Pound "has been offered the position of correspondent in Italy for the 'Japan Times'. Before accepting this position he would like to know the political leanings of said newspaper, and who are the financial backers, and particularly if said newspaper is connected with Jewish elements."[56] While not his first for the *Japan Times*, the likely article in question, "Why there is a war in Europe", was far more political than those previously comprising his "Letter from Rappalo [sic]" series. Praising Mussolini's Italy as "the first occidental nation to believe that among the first rights of a man or a country is the right to keep out of debt", Pound continued: "This point of view both pained and shocked the international usurers. The tension became unbearable in 1938 when Dr. Schacht openly stated (during Hitler's visit to Rome) that 'money which is not issued against exchangeable goods is mere printed paper'".[57] Although beyond the scope of this study— for Imperial Japan was a reactionary autocracy, not a fascist state—similar Italian articles over 1940 repeated these sentiments. This is exemplified by Pound's text for the Fascist student newspaper, *Libro e Moschetto*, which Noel Stock summarized as expounding upon the "duty of the studious section of the population not only to obey but to savour the high intellectual value of Fascism in action and to analyse and respect the wisdom of the Duce". In light of his increasing financial concerns, Redman rightly notes that "a lot of Pound's correspondence during this period involves attempts, direct or indirect, to promote work for himself."[58] Yet it bears reiterating that this had to be work for the 'right' outlets (that is, free from "Jewish elements"). Financial strain and belief in the Axis cause were not mutually exclusive, of course; instead, they were twin drivers for Pound's increasingly significant fascist activism.

The wartime months preceding Pound's propaganda broadcasts for Fascist Italy also established key links with regime functionaries. In addition to reproducing letters to several of these—including Mussolini, Count Ciano, and other Fascist leaders—C. David Heymann reports that Pound presented a "publications project" to the Ministry for Popular Culture in November 1939. He continued to discuss the matter with Camillo Pellizzi, rightly perceived by Heymann to be "his tightest bond with a high-ranking Fascist official".[59] Their exchange over 1940 touched upon Pound's work on the *Ta Hio*, recommended translations of *Jefferson and/or Mussolini* and even revision of the Italian educational curriculum. Pellizzi, having been appointed by Mussolini as President of the Institute for Fascist Culture in April 1940, disarmingly wrote to Pound that "in the matter of books we must take some initiative: not only forbid certain books, but secure the publication in Italian of others." Several of Pound's works ultimately would be translated into Italian during the war—to some degree, at least, a further testament to his influence and acceptance amongst the Fascist regime.[60] Still more relevant here, moreover, was the gift of a radio by Pound's friend Natalie Barney at the end of March 1940, which he found a "devil of an invention. But got to be faced".

In terms of propaganda, it seems Pound attempted to collaborate on wartime radio as early as the next month. Relying upon Niccolò Zapponi's scholarship, Carpenter reports that Pound visited Minculpop on 25 April 1940, stressing that "'the absolute domination of the Jews in the North American press and publishing' made it quite impossible to have the Italian viewpoint aired there [... thus] 'those few Americans who see the truth'" needed to "'illuminate their own fellow-citizens'."[61] Pound may well have been initially turned down in his various attempts to directly collaborate with the regime, for the evidence here is inconclusive. He certainly persisted in his efforts: Pound's FBI file reports that he wrote to Pavolini on 11 November 1940, requesting a meeting to discuss "an improvement in the Italian propaganda against anti-Fascism. Pound states that more propaganda must be directed to the United States in order to combat the anti-Fascism there."[62] This approach appears to have been far more successful—registered by an ensuing flurry of correspondence with (and within) Minculpop in late 1940, also summarized by the FBI—yet supporting details for Pound's transition to full-time broadcasting over winter 1940–41 are, frankly, inadequate. This is but a symptom of the wider uncertainties over Pound's activities during World War II, which led his daughter, Mary de Rachewiltz, to complain as long ago as 1980: "Pound's radio broadcasts have never been faced squarely."[63] To which one can but answer: touché.

Endnotes

[1] Ezra Pound, the opening of "A Visiting Card", William Cookson, ed., *Ezra Pound: Selected Prose, 1909–1965* (London: Faber, 1973), 276. "LIBERTY A DUTY" was one of Mussolini's favored mottos.

[2] Amongst the many texts on this subject, Robert A. Corrigan's "Ezra Pound and the Bollingen Prize Controversy", *Midcontinent American Studies Journal* 8/2 (1967) provides a helpful bibliography of 1949 publications debating Pound's award, pp. 52ff. On the composition of *The Pisan Cantos* in 1945, see Ron Bush, "Modernism, Fascism and the Composition of Ezra Pound's *Pisan Cantos*", *Modernism/modernity* 2/3 (1995); and "Art Versus the Descent of the Iconoclasts: Cultural Memory in Ezra Pound's *Pisan Cantos*", *ibid.*, 14/1 (2007).

[3] According to Cecil Brown in 1942, Adriano Ungaro "hated England, and to him freedom was 'being told what to do.'" See "America's Fifth Column in Europe", *Liberty Magazine* (Rye, NY), 4 July 1942, p. 25; and *University of Leeds Calendar, 1967/68*, p. 112. I am grateful to Archie Henderson for this information.

[4] Pound to Ungaro, 27 June 1941, excerpted in Tim Redman, *Ezra Pound and Italian Fascism* (Cambridge: Cambridge University Press, 1992), p. 211; hereafter *Redman/EPIF*; italics added.

[5] Arthur Miller, cited in Wendy Flory, "Pound and Antisemitism", *The Cambridge Companion to Ezra Pound*, ed., Ira B. Nadel (Cambridge: Cambridge University Press, 1999), p. 285.

[6] The wide range of accounts covering these well-documented years include Julien Cornell, *The Trial of Ezra Pound* (London:Faber, 1966); Harry Meacham, *The Caged Panther, Ezra Pound at St Elizabeths* (New York: Twayne Publishers, 1967); Catherine Seelye, ed., *Charles Olson and Ezra Pound: An Encounter at St. Elizabeths* (New York: Grossmann Publishers, 1975); Conrad L. Rushing, "'Mere Words': The Trial of Ezra Pound", *Critical Inquiry* 14.1 (1987), pp. 111-133; Jerome Kavka, "Ezra Pound's Personal History: A Transcript, 1946", *Paideuma* 20/1–2 (1991), pp. 143-185; Donald W. Jackanicz, "Ezra Pound at St Elizabeths Hospital: The Case File of Patient 58,102", *Manuscripts* 43/3 (1991), pp. 193-206; William McNaughton, "The Secret History of St. Elizabeths", *Paideuma* 30/1-2 (2001), pp. 69-96; and most recently, Romolo Rossi, "A Psychiatrist's Recollections of Ezra Pound", *Ezra Pound, Language and Persona*, eds. Massimo Bacigalupo and William Pratt (Genova: Università degli studi di Genova, 2008).

[7] Noel Stock, *The Life of Ezra Pound* (London: Routledge and Kegan Paul, 1970), p. 396; hereafter Stock/LEP.

[8] Benjamin Friedlander, "Radio Broadcasts", *Ezra Pound in Context*, ed., Ira B. Nadel (Cambridge: Cambridge University Press, 2011), pp. 122–123; hereafter Nadel/EPIC.

[9] Guido Bonsaver, *Censorship and Literature in Fascist Italy* (London: University of Toronto Press, 2007), p. 192.

[10] Frances Stonor Saunders, *The Woman who Shot Mussolini* (London: Faber and Faber, 2010), p. 311.

[11] Pound, "A Visiting Card", p. 276.

[12] Baldoli, 2. According to a contemporaneous propaganda pamphlet, by 1934 there were "460 *Fasci*, 269 *Sezioni fasciste*, 22 *Fasci Femminili* and 74 *Case d'Italia* throughout the world with a total membership of 173,630", *ibid.*, p. 9.

[13] Baldoli, p. 26. For more on Camillo Pellizzi, a key "protagonist of the regime's cultural policies", see Cannistraro, *The Historical Dictionary of Fascist Italy*, p. 418. Praising Giovanni

Gentile's ethical system of actualism in a lecture to the Aristotelian Society on 17 March 1924, Pellizzi declared:

> For the idealists a positive religion is necessary; so, rather would they start one by themselves than be accused of having none. Once cannot be *moral* unless one is *social*; so, one cannot be religious without accepting a definite liturgy and a positive creed. [....] This is no longer the problem of finding out the purest and highest moral precepts; it is that of having some of them actually and constantly practised in a social milieu; of having them at work as the basis on which a nation can live, a state can be built, and a new system of laws can be developed.

"The Problems of Religion for the Modern Italian Idealists", pp. 164, 166; off-print available in the Foligno Collection 455, Taylorian Library Archives, University of Oxford. Pellizzi's tenure at UCL was apparently only terminated on 7 July 1943, following more than three years of war between Britain and Italy: bare details are available in Italian, online at: www.biografieonline.it/biografia.htm?BioID=1237&biografia=Camillo+Pellizzi (all websites last accessed 21 February 2020). I am very grateful to Clare Hills-Nova for her assistance with this information.

[14] See A. James Gregor, *Mussolini's Intellectuals: Fascist Social and Political Thought* (Oxford: Princeton University Press, 2005), ch. 8, cited p. 177.

[15] "Universal Fascism", cited in Cannistraro, *The Historical Dictionary of Fascist Italy*, p. 556.

[16] For CINEF's chief publication, see James Barnes, ed., *A Survey of Fascism: Year Book* (London: International Centre of Fascist Studies, 1928).

[17] Pound and James Strachey (Giacomo) Barnes, FBI File, Section 10. See also David Bradshaw and James Smith, "'What a Chap is Ezra!': Pound's Friendship and Collaboration with James Strachey Barnes, 'The Italian Lord Haw-Haw'", *The Review of English Studies* 64/266 (September 2013), pp. 622-693.

[18] James Strachey Barnes, *The Universal Aspects of Fascism* (London: Williams and Norgate, 1928), p. 160-62. His subsequent book, *Fascism* (London: Butterworth, 1931), was even more unequivocal on 'fascist universalism' (p. 232):

> Fascism itself is more universal than nationalist. It is nationalist only in the sense that it believes in patriotism as a force for good, and insists on the merging of individual interests in the general interests [...] it believes that the only right way of moving away from our present conditions of international chaos towards higher international unity, is by building upon the foundation of self-respecting, strong and highly organized national entities.

[19] Roger Griffin, "Europe for the Europeans: Fascist Myths of the European New Order, 1922-1992", in Matthew Feldman ed., *A Fascist Century* (Basingstoke: Palgrave, 2008), 138. It is important to note that one of Mussolini's principal reasons for his oft-cited 1928 declaration was the Fasci's notoriously thuggish behavior; for example, "between 1921 and 1932 a total of 45 militants abroad were killed and 283 wounded". In consequence, all Fasci Italiani all'Estero were subsumed under the direction of the Foreign Ministry and its various diplomatic corps from 1928; for further discussion, see Luca de Caprariis, "'Fascism for Export?' The Rise and Eclipse of the Fasci Italiani all'Estero", in the *Journal of Contemporary History* 35/2 (2000), cited p. 156.

[20] Philip Morgan, *Fascism in Europe, 1919-1945* (London: Routledge, 2003), p. 168.

[21] Fogu, p. 165.

22   For a brief overview of 'CAUR' (Comitato d'Azione per l'Universalità di Roma), see Philip Morgan, *Fascism in Europe, 1919-1945* (London: Routledge, 2003), pp. 168-171; and Baldoli, pp. 56-58. The most detailed account is available in Italian; see Marco Cuzzi, *L'Internazionale delle Camicie Nere: CAUR, 1933-1939* (Milan: Ugo Mursia Editore, 2005).

23   For the only extended Anglophone discussion of CAUR—only formally disbanded following the blitzkrieg against Poland in September 1939, if long dormant by then—see Michael Ledeen, *Universal Fascism: The Theory and Practice of the Fascist International* (New York: H. Fertig, 1972), esp. chs 3 and 4; cited 115, 109-110. A short English survey is also available in Arnd Bauerkämper, "Transnational Fascism: Cross-Border Relations between Regimes and Movements in Europe, 1922-1939", in *East Central Europe* 37 (2010), pp. 227-231.

24   José Antonio Primo de Rivera, cited in Ledeen, *Universal Fascism*, 110-111. For CAUR's account of the Montreux Conference, see the publication in French by Comitati d'Azione per la Universalità di Roma, *Réunion de Montreux: 16-17 Décembre 1934, XIII* (Rome: Bureau de Presse des Comités, 1935).

25   Pound to Eugenio Coselschi, undated letter [before 28 Mar. 1934], YBL 10/457; and Coselschi, cited in Ledeen, pp. 115, 122.

26   For Pound's correspondence with Eugenio Coselschi, see the "Guide to the Ezra Pound Papers", 68 (YBL Box 10, Folder 457); and for Pound's correspondence with Galeazzo Ciano, see *ibid.*, 66 (YBL Box 9, Folder 401).

27   Ledeen, pp. 104, 109.

28   Coselschi, cited in *ibid.*, 117; italics in original.

29   Sullivan and Cannistraro, 341.

30   Eugenio Coselschi, "A Roman Construction", preface to *The Organised Foundation of Corporations* (Rome: CAUR, n.d. [1934]); pamphlet available in the Foligno Collection 1296, Taylorian Library Archives, University of Oxford.

31   J.J. Wilhelm, *Ezra Pound: The Tragic Years, 1925-1972* (University Park: Pennsylvania State University Press, 1994), p. 194.

32   On the Foreign Broadcast Intelligence Service (FBIS Record Group 262.5) recordings of Pound's transmissions, totaling 170 between 2 October 1941 and 25 July 1943, see Friedlander, "Radio Broadcasts", *Nadel/EPIC*, 124 n.14. I am grateful to Archie Henderson for bringing this reference to my attention.

33   Pound, "No. 84, 'Evidence'", 20 August 1942, "Ezra Pound Papers", Beinecke Rare Book and Manuscript Library, YCAL MSS 43, 130/5473; hereafter YBL. Pound's reference is to British fascist leader Oswald Mosley's *Tomorrow We Live* from 1938, available online at https://ia801305.us.archive.org/22/items/BUFandOswaldMosley/Tomorrow%20We%20Live%20-%20Mosley%20Oswald.pdf.

34   Elizabeth Wiskemann, *The Rome-Berlin Axis* (London: Collins, 1966), 251; and Winston Churchill, "Wars Are Not Won by Evacuations", 4 June 1940, *The Speeches of Winston Churchill*, ed. David Cannadine (London: Penguin Books, 1990), p. 165.

35   W. Vincent Arnold, *The Illusion of Victory* (New York: Peter Lang, 1998), p. 11.

36   Pound, "'It is my belief that this war ...': typescript", [1940?], YBL 131/5539. I am grateful to Andrea Rinaldi for his assistance with this typescript.

37   Paul Baxa, "Capturing the Fascist Moment: Hitler's Visit to Italy in 1938 and the Radicalization of Fascist Italy", *Journal of Contemporary History* 42/2 (2007), pp. 239, 241.

38   Max Ascoli, *Fascism for Whom?* (New York: W.W. Norton, 1938), pp. 311, 316.

39   Aaron Gillette, *Racial Theories in Fascist Italy* (London: Routledge, 2002), pp. 70–71.

40   "Manifesto of Racial Scientists", 14 July 1938, trans. and reprinted in Giuseppe Finaldi, *Mussolini and Italian Fascism* (Harlow: Pearson, 2008), pp. 151–152.

41 "The Pact of Steel between Italy and Germany", 22 May 1939, *ibid.*, p. 154.
42 Wiskemann, *The Rome-Berlin Axis*, 250; and Paul Corner, "Fascist Italy in the 1930s: Popular Opinion in the Provinces", *Popular Opinion in Totalitarian Regimes*, Paul Corner, ed. (Oxford: Oxford University Press, 2009), p. 135.
43 MacGregor Knox, *Common Destiny: Dictatorship, Foreign Policy and War in Fascist Italy and Nazi Germany* (Cambridge: Cambridge University Press, 2000), pp. 145, 159.
44 Roland Sarti, *The Ax Within: Italian Fascism in Action* (New York: New Viewpoints, 1974), p. 210.
45 Pound to Joseph Ibbotson, 14 July 1939, *Letters to Ibbotson, 1935–1952*, eds. Vittoria I. Mondolfo and Margaret Hurley (Orono: National Poetry Foundation, University of Maine, 1979), 101, 105; and Pound, "European Paideuma", in *Machine Art and Other Writings: The Lost Thought of the Italian Years*, ed., Maria Luisa Ardizzone (London: Duke University Press, 1996), p. 134.
46 Gerhart Münch to Pound, 12 April 1938, YBL 36/1503; and Pound to Münch, 15 April 1938, YBL 36/1503. On the 'Vivaldi Revival', see "Books and Music", 26 October 1941, Leonard Doob, ed., *"Ezra Pound Speaking": Radio Speeches of WWII* (Westport, CT: Greenwood Press, 1978), #2; hereafter *Doob/EPS*; and Catherine Paul, "Ezra Pound, Alfredo Casella and the Fascist Cultural Nationalism of the Vivaldi Revival", *Quaderni di Palazzo Serra* 15 (2008).
47 Pound to Münch, 25 October 1939, YBL 36/1504. The view that Pound's political views betrayed a "Pollyanna attitude" (179) was recently advanced by Leon Surette in his *Dreams of a Totalitarian Utopia: Literary Modernism and Politics* (London: McGill-Queen's University Press, 2011), pp. 244ff.
48 Pound, cited in Alec Marsh, *Ezra Pound: Critical Lives* (London: Reaktion Books, 2011), p. 152.
49 Pound to Hoffmann, 6 December 1939, YBL 22/990. I am grateful to Alec Marsh for his assistance with this correspondence.
50 Pound to Tinkham, 2 September 1939, *"Dear Uncle George": The Correspondence between Ezra Pound and Congressman Tinkham of Massachusetts*, ed. Philip J. Burns (Orono: National Poetry Foundation, 1996), p. 176.
51 John Tytell, *Ezra Pound: The Solitary Volcano* (London: Bloomsbury, 1987), p. 254.
52 Pound to Burton K. Wheeler, 19 July 1940, YBL 55/2502; and Pound to William Joyce, 18 July 1941, YBL 26/1117; see also Mary Kenny, *Germany Calling: A Biography of William Joyce, Lord Haw-Haw* (Dublin: New Island, 2004), 211; and Horst J.P. Bergmeier and Rainer E. Lotz, *Hitler's Airwaves: The Inside Story of Nazi Radio Broadcasting and Propaganda Swing* (London: Yale University Press, 1997), pp. 75–79.
53 Pound to Hoffmann, 31 August 1940, YBL 22/990.
54 *Ibid.*; and Pound to Tinkham, 7 November 1940, *"Dear Uncle George"*, p. 214.
55 Pound to Katue Kitasono, 29 October 1940, *Ezra Pound and Japan: Letters and Essays*, ed., Sanehide Kodama (Redding Ridge, CT: Black Swan Books, 1987), p. 101.
56 Pound to the Ministry of Popular Culture, 10 May 1940 and 30 April 1940, Ezra Pound's FBI file, divided into 12 sections on microfilm, Section 7; hereafter *FBI/Pound*. The only text to date specifically covering Pound's FBI file is Karen Leick, "Madness, Paranoia and Ezra Pound's FBI file", *Modernism on File: Writers, Artists and the FBI, 1920–1950*, eds. Claire A. Culleton and Karen Leick (Basingstoke: Palgrave Macmillan, 2008).
57 Pound, "Why There Is a War in Europe", *Japan Times Weekly*, 13 June 1940, Lea Baechler et al., eds., *Ezra Pound's Poetry and Prose*, 11 volumes (London: Garland, 1991), *VIII*, pp. 43–44; hereafter *EPPP*.

58 Pound, cited in *Stock/LEP*, 385; and *Redman/EPIF*, p. 198.
59 David Heymann, *Ezra Pound, The Last Rower, A Political Profile* (New York: Seaver Books, 1976), pp. 101-102, 112.
60 Pound to Pellizzi, 4 May 1940, *ibid.*, 7 May 1940, *ibid.*; 9 May 1940, *ibid.*; and Pellizzi to Pound, 27 December 1940, YBL 40/1690. Pound's World War II publications are listed in Donald Gallup, *Ezra Pound: A Bibliography* (Charlottesville: Bibliographical Society of the University of Virginia and St. Paul's, 1983), pp. 66–73 and 321–333.
61 Pound to Ronald Duncan, 31 March 1940, *The Selected Letters of Ezra Pound*, ed. D.D. Paige (London: Faber and Faber, 1971), 441; and Humphrey Carpenter, *A Serious Character: The Life of Ezra Pound* (London: Faber, 1988), p. 579.
62 Frank L. Amprim, "Communication #482", 1 November 1944, *FBI/Pound*, Section p. 4.
63 Mary de Rachewiltz, "Fragments of an Atmosphere", *Agenda* 17/2–3-18/1 (1980), p. 157.

6. Ezra Pound's Political Faith from First to Second Generation; or, "It is 1956 Fascism"

In late November 2002, the National Archives in Kew, London, released several large MI-5 surveillance files, mostly covering leading British fascists interned under Defence Regulations 18a and 18b. Within this series are two surprising files from these "Right Wing Extremists" papers, KV/875 and KV/876. Surprising, that is, not because the subject under surveillance was considered—as he in fact was—a leading supplier of information to British fascism from abroad in autumn 1940; but rather, because he was not British, but American, and had not lived in the United Kingdom since 1920. In fact, just after the armistice concluding the Great War, the initial pages of this MI-5 file reported on 12 December 1918 that "there is no ground to regard the above with suspicion, and his sentiments are pro-ally".[1] Yet on V-E day, 8 May 1945, this long-term Italian resident could hardly be considered "pro-Ally," as this interrogation statement in Britain's War Office files from V-E day makes clear:

> I am not anti-Semitic, and I distinguish between the Jewish usurer and the Jew who does an honest day's work for a living.
>
> Hitler and Mussolini were simple men from the country. I think that Hitler was a Saint, and wanted nothing for himself. I think that he was fooled into anti-Semitism and it ruined him. That was his mistake. When you see the "mess" that Italy gets into by "bumping off" Mussolini, you will see why someone could believe in some of his efforts.[2]

Thereafter, this radical right ideologue—clearly identified as such by Britain's secret services from the middle 1930's onward—became the chief protagonist in one of the century's first "celebrity trials." He ultimately avoided treason charges through a deal; one whereby he pled insanity and was institutionalised in the U.S. for the next dozen years.

That ideologue, of course, is given away in this chapter's title: the famous modernist poet and patriarch Ezra Pound, pioneer of the avant-garde drive to, as he liked to put it, "make it new." As has been covered elsewhere by leading Pound scholars like Tim Redman, Miranda Hickman, and Leon Surette, Pound had embraced the revolutionary right in the 1930's, turning to Mussolini's Italy and other permutations of fascist ideology as a "political religion" capable of regenerating a perceivably decadent civilisation through the trifecta of will, belief and charismatic leadership; or in Mussolini's well-known slogan: "Believe, Obey, Fight" (see image 1).³ As there is little space to traverse the well-charted waters of "political religion" theory here, a few definitional asides must suffice. At the forefront of understanding this form of "secular faith" is Emilio Gentile, who detects this secular embrace of the sacred when

> a political movement confers a sacred status on an earthly entity (the nation, the country, the state, humanity, society, race, proletariat, history, liberty, or revolution) and renders it an absolute principle of collective existence, considers it the main source of values for individual and mass behaviour, and exalts it as the supreme ethical precept of public life. It thus becomes an object for veneration and dedication, even to the point of self-sacrifice.⁴

Correspondingly, in 1928—five years before his only meeting with Mussolini and immediate "conversion" to the PNF's operant "political religion"—Pound expressed his longing for no less than a "new civilization" in his short-lived "little magazine" *The Exile*.⁵ That same year, coincidentally, one of the first Anglophone studies of Mussolini's "New Italy" appeared, arguing that Italian Fascism represented a "religious revival": "The cult of the New Rome is admittedly a 'myth' in the Sorelian sense, whose value lies not in its literal truth, but in its power to command obedience, devotion and sacrifice." "Thus fascism represents a religious revival," continued the American academic, Herbert Schneider, based upon spiritual devotion to the nation and "in conceiving politics as creative action and will."⁶ And this view from a neutral observer! Characteristically, Mussolini was more direct and immodest on the Fascist revolution in his English autobiography, also published that year: "It was necessary to lay the foundation of a new civilization."⁷ This was no mere talk, but part of a socio-political attempt to overcome perceived national decadence through what scholars have called an "anthropological revolution"—one literally bent on creating "new men" of action and faith, warrior-priests with the will to turn myth into reality and to build a secular utopia. This "palingenetic" impulse, as Roger Griffin has noted, demarcates Italian Fascism as "*a modernist political movement for the age of the masses*." Still more concisely, Pound's most recent biographer, Alec Marsh, has asserted: "Fascism is, in fact, a modernist politics."⁸

In the five years prior to commencing his wartime propaganda for Radio Rome, Pound's chief journalistic outlet was provided by Oswald Mosley's British Union of Fascists and National Socialists (hereafter BUF), which aired Pound's ideas in no fewer than 39 articles written between 1936 and 1940; that is, just as western Europe was drifting to war against the Italo-German Axis, with Pound becoming an increasingly inflexible ideologue for fascism at this time. Put another way, one of modernism's leading figures shared Oswald Mosley and the BUF's political faith in fascist ideology and contributed propaganda advice, corresponding regularly with the leadership; recommending potential authors; and subscribing to movement publications—in addition to acting as one of the leading contributors for both the weekly middlebrow journal *Action* (29 articles) and the more highbrow journal the *British Union Quarterly* (8 articles in 13 issues; a standalone pamphlet called *What is Money For?* and an article in the BUF's short-lived *The Fascist Quarterly* rounded out this publicism). Moreover, Pound went so far as to offer his well-known Canto 45, "With Usura," to Oswald Mosley for free inclusion in the BUF press, surely bearing out Eric Bulson's recent contention that, though "it may be customary to distinguish between the two Pounds, one a journalist, the other a poet, he never did so himself. For Pound, there was a time and a place in his life for both." Such a "time and place," in turn, was nowhere more in evidence than in his activism for interwar fascism in Britain. While the inclusion of one of Pound's epic poetic sequences from *The Cantos* never came to pass in 1939, twenty years later things would be very different, and Mosley would include Canto 101 in the final issue of his postwar review, *The European*, as described below.[9]

Quite apart from his engagement with other far-right movements, dismissing Pound's relationship with the BUF in the second half of the 1930's, as his biographers have been wont to do, is far too hasty. Beyond close convergences on key policy issues, by contrast, Pound's propaganda for the BUF consistently mirrored the trajectory of interwar fascist ideology generally—increasingly sucked into the vortex of German Nazism in the 1930s progressed—as well as British permutations of fascism in particular. The latter, in fact, Pound dubbed the "local version" of totalitarianism in a 1939 BUF article, while an earlier text for *Action* advocated no less than a "United States of Europe" under fascist hegemony.[10] The latter point, as will become clear, was to be fervently taken up by "second wave" British fascism following the socio-political caesura of 1945. Yet there can be little doubt that, in these and other respects, Pound was far closer to interwar fascist theory and practice than has been previously maintained. In fact, as he wrote to Raven Thomson in 1939, "'Action' seems to be full of people saying what I would say, and having learned the main points I have been preaching (I mean me along with the others)."[11] In this highly charged atmosphere—of apparently invariable drift toward another "total war" in Europe—the BUF continued to publish its weekly "House Journal," *Action*, at this point extending to twenty pages and roughly 14,000 sales.[12] Pound was front and centre in many of the issues to which he contributed; and just as importantly, he was both highly informed and reasonably influential in the dissemination of the BUF's fascist propaganda during the later 1930's.

If the relationship between Pound and British fascism was both close and mutually beneficial before the war, that changed markedly during WWII with the start of his paid radio broadcasts for Fascist Italy, which continued until 1945 with some of the coarsest anti-Semitism yet heard in English. This is not the place to retrace the well-known "Pound Case"; suffice it to say that, fittingly for what was to ensue, no less a figure than President Roosevelt pressed for the initiation of treason proceedings.[13] After his arrest and detention, this led to Pound's drafting of the award-winning poetic sequence, *The Pisan Cantos*, contemporaneous with a legal declaration of insanity and a transfer, late in 1945, to St Elizabeths asylum—where he would spend the next dozen years before the US government released him into his wife's guardianship. Throughout this period, and indeed beyond—as suggested by his high level contacts with Italian neo-Fascists like Ugo Dadone, Valerio Borghese and Amalia Bacelli, after his return to Italy in the late 1950's—Pound remained a committed "believer" in fascist ideology, as the following excerpt from a Feb. 1951 letter to fellow poet Louis Dudek spells out:

> AS the fascists were partito unico, that is the WHOLE of the governing power in Italy, there were DIFFERENCES of view among them. Fascist militarists (very few) Cavourian fascists (i.e. liberals), royalists, republicans, left wingers, i.e. extreme socialists, and swine, namely capitalist corrupters, but also capitalist conservatives.
>
> when I say "militarist" even that needs qualification, there were men who reacted to communist violence, or to seeing their old fathers bashed on the head by roughs, or returned troops spat on (yes, physical sputum) by idem.

In working with the Pound archive, I have yet to come across any real critique of fascism by Pound during his years of institutionalisation. And that is "fascist" with a "Small F," of course—referring to the generic ideology—not just Mussolini's PNF, as one of his earliest letters to Dudek, probably from early 1950, makes plain regarding Hitler's 1925 autobiography:

> HAS DUDEK
> ever read Mein Kampf? preferably in the original, or passably in Italian. (no knowledge of what it may hv/ been distorted to in frog or eng.) [....I] left it unread for years. slop journalism and the kind of smear that the british and murkn press can spread//[14]

Parenthetically, Pound's encounter with *Mein Kampf* came in April 1942 through an Italian translation—titled *La mia battaglia*, issued by the Milanese publisher Valentino Bompiani, which ran to fully 20 editions from 1934 to 1943—and wrought important changes to his wartime propaganda strategies thereafter. The years, moreover, saw Pound write and broadcast literally thousands of wartime radio items—a long neglected issue on which the enormous dimensions are only now becoming known (for instance, he composed radio typescripts under more than 10 different factiously-created names).[15] Considering the level of venom he directed at the Allies over the microphone, it should be obvious that these phrases do not make for comfortable post-war bedfellows—particularly amongst ultra-nationalists. Two examples amongst scores more presented in Leonard Doob's edited collection, *"Ezra Pound Speaking,"* unmistakably mark out Pound's views on Britain:

> **"England," Broadcast 15th of March 1942**
> You let in the Jew and the Jew rotted your empire, and you yourselves out-Jewed the Jew. [...] YOU HAVE NO RACE left in your government. God knows if it can be found still scattered in England. It must be found scattered in England. The white remnants of England, the white remnant of the races of England must be FOUND and find means to cohere; otherwise, you might as well lie down in your grave yards. Is there a RACE left in England? Has it ANY will left to survive? You can carry slaughter to Ireland. Will that save you? I doubt it. Nothing can save you, save a purge.
>
> **"Soberly," Broadcast 23rd of May 1943:**
> Usury has gnawed into England since the days of Elizabeth. First it was mortgages, mortgages on Earl's estates; usury against the feudal nobility. Then there were attacks on the common land, filchings of village common pasture. Then there developed a usury system, an international usury system, from Cromwell's time, ever increasing. That system gave you your slums. It brought in that civic leprosy that has made England a byeword. It has taken the shock of this war, three years of war to jog your memory, to bring your slums up again into headlines. EVERY social reform that has gone into effect in Germany and Italy should be defended. And the best men in England know that as well as I do.[16]

Notwithstanding his exoriation of virtually everything British before 1945, Pound was one of the very few, as the remainder of this chapter will show, to advance both "first wave" fascism for Mosley's BUF during the "fascist epoch" in 1930's and 1940's; *as well as* a post-war, "second wave" fascism via publicism for Mosley's re-launched Union Movement in the 1950's, most notably via its aforementioned "intellectual" house journal, *The European*. According to one of Mosley's recent critics, this journal, edited by Oswald's wife Diana, was a key vehicle for the advocacy of a Europe ruled by neo-fascist, 'third way' corporatist principles. This was undertaken via Mosley's reheated attempt to place fascist thought on "a[n] intellectual plane," thus revealing his persisting "attempts at a more cerebral brand of fascism":

Whilst *The European* served as a crucible for a number of young fascist ideologues, like Desmond Stewart and Alan Neame who had become sympathisers... it also attracted a group of writers fixated with the poetry of Ezra Pound, not to mention soliciting the occasional article from Pound himself; who recently been released from a mental hospital in America, where had been incarcerated following his arrest in 1945 for broadcasting for Mussolini. *The European* also served as a forum through which Continental fascists could appraise Mosley's concept of "European Socialism," which he wished to be accepted as a common programme for all European fascist movements, a drive that culminated in his participation in the Conference of Venice in 1962, and the foundation of the National Party of Europe (NPE), a grandiose pan-European edifice "for which I have striven during the past fifteen years," but which began to crumble almost immediately afterwards.[17]

Interestingly, this overview echoes Pound's call for a "United States of Europe" fully a generation earlier in Mosley's propaganda mouthpiece, *Action*. In an Orwellian inversion, as suggested above, fascist ultra-nationalism was now to become "European socialism"—as Oswald Mosley was fond of declaring at time. One readily available example derives from a May 1956 article of that name, published in both the neo-fascist *Nation Europa* and reprinted in his movement's journal, *The European*:

> the development by a fully united Europe of all the resources in our continent for the benefit of all the peoples of Europe, with every energy and incentive that the active leadership of European government can give to private enterprise, workers' ownership or any other method of progress which science and a dynamic system of government find most effective for the enrichment of all our people and the lifting of European civilization to ever higher forms of life.[18]

Not least given his putative "insanity" at the time, Pound's visibility in *The European* was remarkable—all the more so, indeed, as this relationship has been virtually ignored by scholars of either fascism or modernism. For the journal's very first issue, Pound contributed a note entitled "Sovereignty"—for which, read anti-Semitic railing against perceived "usury" by liberal democrats. At the same time, behind the scenes, Pound was trying to help as best he could from his position of confinement; for instance, in a letter written on 26th of June 1953, Pound asked Dudek for $50 to help reach the estimated $300 needed to continue publishing *The European*, a journal, as he put it, "standing for maximum awareness."[19] This admiration was mutual, of course, especially by some of the younger fascists braying within *The European*'s stable. One of these, Harvey Black, a member of the UK's committee advocating Pound's release, penned "The Story of Ezra Pound" for the November 1956 issue. This text offered a useful barometer of the way in which fascists viewed his quite unique legal position, since Pound's only so-called "crime" was the expression of his personal opinions on the Italian Radio during the years when American was at war with Italy... a cursory glance at them brings home the absurdity of treating such material as "treason," or even as propaganda. The ill-treatment meted out to him by the Americans in 1945 still reads as one of the more notorious scandals of recent history.[20]

Similarly, over the six years of *The European*'s short lifespan, there were no fewer than 7 essays by Alan Neame on Pound's *Pisan Cantos* sequence. Neame, another neo-fascist disciple of Pound's based in Britain, had come to Pound's attention in 1947 as a potential translator of Jean Cocteau's 1945 *Léone*; their relations first came to view in a May 1951 text for the Oxford-based Catholic journal, *New Blackfriars* (volume 32, number 374) entitled "Ezra Pound Reconsidered."[21] Following this neutral overview, Neame washed up in the fourth issue of *The European* two years later, offering an annotated reading of Pound's poetry in June 1953; in this case, of Canto 74, the first in *The Pisan Cantos* sequence. From a decidedly non-fascist viewpoint, Pound scholars like Ron Bush have long noted that *The Pisan Cantos* represent not so much a rejection of Pound's fascist activism as a lament that his political faith had been strung up with Mussolini; a laughing stock and warning to others. As John Whittier-Ferguson notes of Canto 74, that with "the death of Il Duce, or 'The Boss', as Pound often called him, this epic-in-progress lost its heart," for the "vital centre of Pound's poem, its chief 'artifex' who had literally been founding a new nation—who had, in other words, been planning and building in the present moment the 'patterned streets' Pound had been called for in poetry and prose at least since Canto V"[22]—was unceremoniously strung up with his mistress, Clara Petacci, and a handful of regime sycophants (like the notorious Fascist anti-Semite, Roberto Farinacci) trying to flee the dying days of war in Italy:

> The enormous tragedy of the dream in the peasant's bent shoulders
> Manes! Manes was tanned and stuffed,
> Thus Ben and la Clara *a Milano*
> by the heels at Milano
> That maggots shd/ eat the dead bullock
> DIGONOS [twice-born; also written in Greek], but the twice crucified

The poem's reference to the heretical founder of Manichaeism, allusions to the Dionysian, Christ-like "twice crucified"—Mussolini was first deposed from power on 25 July 1943 and, after a stint as head of the Salò Republic, executed on 28 April 1945—and the "twice born," or *Digenes* (for Neame, "a term common to mystery religions, denoting the initiate as against the uninitiated") all point to the perseverance of Pound's political faith after WWII. Indeed, the very first line, that tragic outcome of the fascist "dream" was one of *The Pisan Cantos*' three major themes, as Neame rightly intuited: "the loss of a familiar world; the frustration of an ideal world; and the imperishability of once-apprehended beauty."[23]

Neame was only getting started. His subsequent article on Pound, from the final issue of *The European* in 1953, annotated a further ten lines from Canto 75 before returning to the pivotal Canto 74 in Sept. 1954 via a classic trope of WWII revisionism: the Allies were the war's actual villains, not the Axis:

> Hence, in Europe, we subject ourselves with beastly periodicity to the horrors of fraternal warfare, warfare in which some nameless agency decrees that in the same city of Frankfurt-am-Main the Goethehaus shall be razed but the Farbenfabrik shall be spared; that Monte Cassino and Dresden shall as non-military objectives be reduced to rubble; that three hundred years of cultural endeavour shall lie under permanent threat
> "at the mercy of a tack hammer
> thrown through the roof"

Writing precisely on these last two lines in his 1995 study of *The Pisan Cantos*, Ron Bush rightly asserts that the "Fascist orientation of this desire continues to pervade *The Pisan Cantos* and remains firmly rooted in the ideological passions of the last year of the Second World War."[24]

Thereafter, bookending the dozen monthly issues of *The European* in 1955, Neame provided two additional articles on Pound's Pisans. These annotated another 20 lines from Cantos 74 and 75 prior to ideologically "coming clean" in his sixth, penultimate essay of August 1956, "A Musical Interlude": "these poems are more than a record of the suffering of one man crushed by the political machine. They record also something more catastrophic, the shattered life of a continent, of *a culture and a myth* that for many people came to a fiery end on May 1 [8th—sic], 1945."[25] The next year saw Neame publish his translation of Cocteau's *Léone* with the Australian journal *The Edge*; interestingly, in the previous issue of that journal Pound published an anonymous translation of his own Mussolini's "Notes in Captivity," composed in the weeks after being deposed in July 1943.[26] The former, Neame's translation, was dedicated to Camille Chamoun, then-President of Lebanon, in the hopes he would assist in seeking Pound's release from St Elizabeths sanatorium, as evinced by this striking letter that Neame addressed to Chamoun on 21 May, 1957:

> Those held responsible for the war of 1939-1945, even those whose hands had shed most blood, are for the most part either dead or pardoned [....] my master, who was neither a murderer nor was ever formally condemned, has not yet been set free, although now over seventy... I make bold to beg you, as you condescend to accept this poetic tribute, to pity the wretched lot of Ezra Pound and to ask at the hands of the President of the United States the release of the release of a poet whose greatness has only increased with his misfortunes...[27]

In his final missive from February 1958—only a year before the closure of *The European*—Neame demonstrated his own commitment to the continuing "political religion" of fascist ideology via *The Pisan Cantos* of "his master." Returning to the hanging of war criminals at Nuremberg on 16 October 1946, when the "folk-mind was restocked with martyrs," Neame avers: "By a curious coincidence the Nuremberg executions took place on the sixth day of the Feast of Tabernacles, when Jews celebrate the mystical victory of Messiah over Leviathan." The tone of Neame's article, like that in the many anti-Semitic passages in Pound's post-1933 poetry, suggests that "coincidence" was the furthest thing from his mind:

> Saints, martyrs and divine kings are not the only people to rule from the tomb; and poets sometimes rule from the prison house… if we live in the Era of the Asylum, it is only so because it is at the same time the Era of the International Loan with Strings Attached.[28]

Beyond Neame's hero-worship across its pages, *The European* was itself Poundian in virtually every manner conceivable. Reviews of Pound's favourite authors stuffed its pages—such as otherwise obscure economic conspiracists like the Americans Alexander del Mar and Brooks Adams—in addition to frequent reviews of his 1950's publications of poetry and translations, including: *The Classic Anthology defined by Confucius* (June 1955); *Section: Rock-Drill, 85-95 de los Cantares* (April 1956); alongside a review article by Denis Goacher entitled "The Critics and the Master," reviewing *The Translations of Ezra Pound; Literary Essays of Ezra Pound; and Sophokles Women of Trachis: A version by Ezra Pound* in May 1954. Still other essays, like Denis Goacher's "Dr. Leavis or Mr Pound?"—which argued that "Mr. Pound is so far from being 'purely literary in interests' that it would take some pages to tabulate his activities"—including, putting it mildly, becoming "embroiled in world politics"—witnessed a lively correspondence over a number of ensuing issues.[29] It is no overstatement to say that Pound's literature and politics were an indispensable touchstone for this neo-fascist journal.

Tellingly, two texts were contributed to *The European*'s final issue in 1959 by Pound's authorised biographer, Noel Stock. While the latter's 1970 *The Life of Ezra Pound* remains the gold standard of Pound biographies, there can be little doubt Stock had been drinking deeply from the radical right Kool-Aid but a decade earlier. As one of the disciples helping to disseminate Pound's postwar "political religion" during the later 1950's—including his editorship of the aforementioned Melbourne journal, *The Edge*, during 1956 and 1957—Stock was clearly taken with the phrase "blackout on history." In actual fact, this was the title of his first of two articles for *The European*. For his part, Pound had been using the phrase in his correspondence several years earlier, as with the neo-fascist Olivia Rossetti Agresti. The phrase, in turn, is almost certainly a reference to Harry Elmer Barnes's introductory chapter, "Revisionism and the Historical Blackout," from his 1953 book, *Perpetual War for Perpetual Peace*. For his part, Barnes is notorious as a pioneer of Holocaust Denial writings—or what he dubbed "WWII revisionism." That this was simply an ideological repackaging of fascist anti-Semitism is made clear by the likely source for the title of Barnes's 1953 chapter; namely, *The Protocols of the Learned Elders of Zion* (which Pound had already read in April 1940). This infamous Tsarist forgery has been traced by Archie Henderson as Pound's inspiration for his, and subsequently, Stock's use of the phrase "blackout on history:"

> On the historical blackout, see Protocol 16.4: "Classicism as also any form of study of ancient history, in which there are more bad than good examples, we shall replace with the study of the program of the future. We shall erase from the memory of men all facts of previous centuries which are undesirable to us, and leave only those which depict all the errors of the government of the GOYIM."[30]

In his 1959 article by that name, Stock went so far as to praise Barnes as the "one professor who has made a fight for some sort of decency inside the historical profession." Stock concludes, through a veiled anti-Semitic reference preferred in *The European* to open Judeophobic references: "My purpose here has been to indicate that history is largely in the hands of men who in many cases seem to be hamstrung by attachment to 'vested interests.'"[31]

That same year also witnessed Pound contributing a further three items to the final two issues of *The European* in 1959—with the journal in danger of collapse and Pound now out of the asylum—one short prose text; three doggerel poems; and most importantly, Canto 101, taken from the sequence *Thrones de los Cantares* (Cantos 96-101; reviewed in the May 1960 issue of *Action*) which, Pound explained, referred to the "thrones in Dante's *Paradiso* [which] are for the spirits of the people who have been responsible for good government… and to establish some definition of an order possible or at any rate conceivable on earth."[32] Given this explanation, it is perhaps easier to understand Pound's inclusion of two well-known Fascist apparatchiks, Edmondo Rossoni and Carlo Delcroix, in the canto, which appeared on the final page *of The European*'s February 1959 issue:

> Rossoni "così lo stato …" etcetc [thus the state…]
> Delcroix: "che magnifica!" [how magnificent!][33]

In a way, the explicit appearance of this Canto in a fascist publication in 1959 is unsurprising. Pound felt censored in St Elizabeths, and usually sent out items for publication anonymously or pseudonymously—albeit for much different reasons than during the war—for doing otherwise might jeopardise his insanity claim. Likewise, a second, perhaps tactical, consequence follows from this: Pound was becoming more extreme and unguarded in his endorsement of "first wave" biological racism precisely at the same time Mosley was repudiating many of his earlier views in favour of a "second wave" fascism—one stressing a less seemingly dictatorial "Europe of nations" alternative. Mosley's attempted "reframing" of some of the key points of fascist ideology in light of wartime experiences stood in stark contrast to Pound's anti-black racism and especially anti-Semitism; for example, his award-winning *Pisan Cantos* lifts phrases directly from the aforementioned forgery *The Protocols of the Learned Elders of Zion*: "goyim are cattle" and "blackout on history."[34] Indeed, at the same time as Pound was contributing to *The European*, he lavished praise on *Hitler's Table Talk* in his correspondence, or loaned out Mussolini's 1943 diaries in captivity to his disciples. For Mosley's part, in light of the Holocaust—for the radical right knows actual history as well as anyone—any recourse to anti-Semitism was likely to be wrapped in the dog-whistle phrase "international financiers" (much like "cultural Marxism" today).

Yet by this time, what must be frankly called Pound's white supremacist variant of fascism was rather more unreconstructed than that of Mosley's more sophisticated approach to the failings of the fascist past. Nonetheless, Archie Henderson further reports, this unlikely duo appeared together on the 20th of March 1961, when "Mosley held a press conference in Rome and Pound was among those in attendance. Afterwards, he said that he believed that the day would come for European unity, a concept wholly endorsed by Mosley."[35] Yet intellectually at least, all was not as it seems.

To spell out this post-war divergence between "first wave" and "second wave" fascism, a brief look of two radical right ideologues directly inspired by Ezra Pound—John Kasper and Eustace Mullins—points in an entirely different direction from that of Mosley's preferred, watered-down neo-fascism: essentially "doubling down" on interwar fascism and biological racism. Eustace Mullins, who died in 2010, was to become one of the leading ideologues of the American radical right, with pamphlet titles such as *The War on Christianity; Jewish TV: Sick, Sick Sick;* and *Jewish War against the Western World*.[36] Still another revealing text was written just before Mullins wrote the earliest biography of Pound in 1961. This was "Hitler: An Appreciation," flagged by the House on Un-American Activities Committee "Preliminary Report on Neo-Fascist and Hate Groups" (ironically, he had worked as a congressional researcher until being dismissed in 1952).[37] Mullins's later writings were still more extreme, and extended to enthusiastic Holocaust Denial, neo-Nazism and uncompromising racism—as indicated by his 1985 book, published by none other than the far-right Ezra Pound Institute, *The World Order: A Study in the Hegemony of Parasitism*. In addition to his unabashed neo-Nazism, Mullins was a roommate and close friend of Matt Koehl, soon to lead the American

Nazi Party following the murder of George Lincoln Rockwell in 1967. Indeed, at the time when Koehl and Mullins were closest, in the mid-1950's, Mullins also headed the Aryan League of America. Under its letterhead he corresponded frequently with Pound during his internment, this 1956 letter being one example:

> I have the hard core of a group of determined fanatics who are willing to [go—sic] to the limit with me. I have done my country a great service by acting as a restraining influence and preventing them from assassinating some of our great public-spirited leaders, but perhaps I will not be able to hold them in check much longer. Quien sabe?[38]

Yet the more dangerous of Pound's two protégés—who truly purred at his feet at St Elizabeths Hospital—was the head of the Seaboard White Citizens' Council in the 1950's, essentially the non-hooded face of the campaign against desegregating schools in the American South. He called Pound "Grandpa" and hung on his every word, even mimicking Pound's style and ideas—right down to that of framing the issue of American "civil rights" as a states rights issue; in fact, he needed only ten days in Clinton, Tennessee, to initiate race riots so severe that the National Guard was called in and thereafter assumed law and order in the town.[39] Kasper's justification for doing so was made plain in a letter to Pound of 30 June 1956:

> It is 1956 Fascism. It is Jeff/ and Jacksonian and J. Adams.
>   LONG LIVE THE ANGLO SAXON   DEATH to his ENEMIES.

Two final letters further underscore this point: two months earlier, Kasper wrote to Pound, explicitly asking him to draft pro-segregation speeches:

> Dear Gramp:
> COPY COPY. Can you write some short quotable slogans. Nothing highbrow. Stuff to stick in mass-mind. Repeated over and over so they don't forget.
>   And 5 minute speeches and 15 minute speeches.
>   on Segregation/ States Rights
>   Mongrelization/ Separation of Races.
>   NIGGERS
>   And JEWS: the Admiral [Crommelin] has taken up THE Question openly and it hasn't hurt him. The kike behind the nigger.
>   No war to save Israel.
>   Awful busy here.

Alec Marsh has rightly suggested that Pound continued assisting in the construction of these violently racist slogans and speeches.[40] Only a month later, furthermore, responding to a program called "Virginians on Guard" written by Kasper—which his mentor clearly had a hand in editing (see image 2[41])—Pound replied on 17 May 1956:

> You can NOT say: Nationalist
> You can not put segregation as BASIC.
> You cannot say, Douglas (C.H.) or Social Credit or Gesell.
> You must use a formula which allows you to plug for what is correct in all three.
>
> You can say local control of local affairs.
> You can not SAY local control of local pur/pow which is the only way to GET loc. cont. loc. af. … Get the ku kluxers to keep their eye on main issue, not the immediate irritant…

The historian Benjamin Muse remarks that Kasper "had a large hand in the violence" surrounding desegregation—for instance, the aforementioned "ku kluxers," or KKK, were responsible for no fewer than 118 bombings between 1956 and 1963 in the American South—and was sentenced to federal prison in May 1958. Kasper apparently entered the penitentiary with Hitler's *Mein Kampf* under his arm.[42] His aims and targets were crystal clear by this time, as his contemporaneous pamphlet entitled "Segregation or Death" reveals, arguing that Jews were engaged "in a fanatical effort to subvert existing Gentile order everywhere." The cartoon on page 4 depicts a snake with a stereotypically Jewish head, winding around the White House, U.S. Capitol building, Supreme Court and, of course, the United Nations.[43] Not to be outdone by Kasper, two months later Pound, following his release from St Elizabeths and return to Italy in July 1958—which was to be his home for the final 14 years of his life—greeted the waiting photographers not with a wave, but with a "first wave" fascist salute (see image 3).

Image 1: Mussolini's "Believe, Obey, Fight"

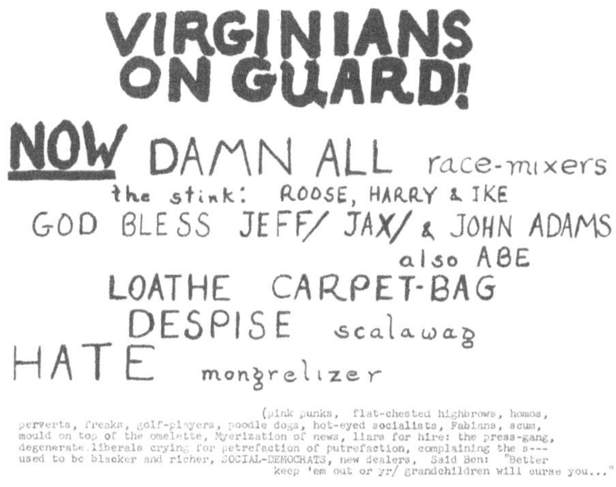

VIRGINIANS ON GUARD!

<u>NOW</u> DAMN ALL race-mixers
the stink: ROOSE, HARRY & IKE
GOD BLESS JEFF/ JAX/ & JOHN ADAMS
also ABE
LOATHE CARPET-BAG
DESPISE scalawag
HATE mongrelizer

(pink punks, flat-chested highbrows, homos, perverts, freaks, golf-players, poodle dogs, hot-eyed socialists, Fabians, scum, mould on top of the omelette, Myerization of news, liars for hire: the press-gang, degenerate liberals crying for petrefaction of putrefaction, complaining the a--- used to be blacker and richer, SOCIAL-DEMOCRATS, new dealers. Said Ben: "Better keep 'em out or yr/ grandchildren will curse you..."

Image 2: "Ezra Pound returned to Italy today and hailed his adopted nation with a Fascist salute," *The New York Times*, 9 July 1958

Image 3: First page of *Virginians on Guard* (Seaboard White Citizens' Council, 1956)

Endnotes

[1] Pound's MI-5 files are catalogued as follows: Ezra Pound TNA KV2 series, KV/875 and KV/876; cited KV/875, 31a and 2a. For discussion of these materials see Ira Nadel, "Ezra Pound and MI-5", *Paideuma: Modern and Contemporary Poetry and Poetics* 40 (2013), pp. 327-347.

[2] Ezra Pound, Statement to FBI, War Office File 204/12602, 8 May 1945, 13a and 13b. Pound's statement is very similar to a remarkable interview he made earlier that day; partially reprinted in Noel Stock, *The Life of Ezra Pound* (London: Routledge and Kegan Paul, 1970), p. 407. These statements are substantially different in tone and content from a longer, more formal statement, also contained in WO/204 (13c-13h), versions of which are reproduced in: Noel Stock, "Ezra Pound in Melbourne," *Helix* 13-14 (1983), pp. 129-32; Richard Sieburth, "Ezra Pound: Confession," *The Paris Review* 128 (1993), pp. 194-206; and most recently, in Omar S. Pound; Robert E. Spoo and Dorothy Pound, eds., *Ezra and Dorothy Pound: Letters in Captivity, 1945-1946* (Oxford: Oxford University Press, 1999), pp. 59-68.

[3] For key works on Pound and fascism, see: Tim Redman, *Ezra Pound and Italian Fascism* (Cambridge: Cambridge University Press, 1991); Leon Surette, *Pound in Purgatory: From Economic Radicalism to Anti-Semitism* (Chicago: University of Illinois Press, 1999); "Pound and Fascism," in Miranda Hickman, ed., *One Must not Go Altogether with the Tide: The Letters of Ezra Pound and Stanley Nott* (London: McGill-Queen's University Press, 2011), pp. 278-299; and on the post-1945 period see, for example, "Ezra Pound: Anti-Semitism, Segregationism and the 'Arsenal of Live Thought'", in Alex Houen, *Terrorism and Modern Literature* (Oxford: Oxford University Press, 2002), pp. 143-91. On Mussolini's well-known slogan, see Tracy H. Koon, *Believe, Obey, Fight: Political Socialization of Youth in Fascist Italy, 1922-1945* (London: University of North Carolina Press, 1985); see also Image 1, c. 1940, TNA INF 2/1, Part 3, available online at: www.nationalarchives.gov.uk/education/heroesvillains/g3/cs1/g3cs1s2.htm (all websites last accessed 23 February 2020).

[4] Emilio Gentile, "The Sacralisation of Politics: Definitions, Interpretations and Reflections on the Question of Secular Religion and Totalitarianism," in *Totalitarian Movements and Political Religions* 1.1 (2000), pp. 18-19. See also Gentile, "Political Religion: A Concept and Its Critics—A Critical Survey," in *Totalitarian Movements and Political Religions*, 6/1 (2005), pp. 19-32; and more expansively, Gentile, *Politics as Religion*, trans. George Staunton (Princeton: Princeton University Press, 2006). For the most definitive Anglophone works on political religion, see Hans Maier, ed., *Totalitarianism and Political Religions: Concepts for the Comparison of Dictatorships*, 3 vols. trans. Jodi Bruhn (London: Routledge, 2004-2007).

[5] Ezra Pound, "The Exile III," in *Exile* 3 (1928), reprinted in Ezra Pound, *Impact: Essays on Ignorance and the Decline of American Civilisation*, ed. Noel Stock (Chicago: H. Regnery, 1960), p. 222.

[6] Herbert Schneider, *Making the Fascist State* (Oxford: Oxford University Press, 1928), pp. 228-29, 241.

[7] Benito Mussolini, *My Autobiography*, with a foreword by Richard Washburn Child (New York: Charles Scribner's Sons, 1928), p. 69, cited in Roger Griffin, *Modernism and Fascism* (Basingstoke: Palgrave, 2007), p. 220.

[8] Alec Marsh, *Ezra Pound: Critical Lives* (London: Reaktion Books, 2011), pp. 105-106.

[9] Eric Bulson, "Journalism," *Ezra Pound in Context* (Cambridge: Cambridge University Press, 2011), p. 94.

[10] Pound, "The Criterion Passes," *British Union Quarterly* 3/2 (1939), 67; and Pound, "Britain, who are your Allies?" *Action*, 9 April 1938.
[11] Pound to Alexander Raven Thomson, intercepted letter of 5 July 1939, KV/876 20a; cited in my *Ezra Pound's Fascist Propaganda, 1935-45* (Basingstoke: Palgrave, 2013).
[12] G.C. Webber, "Patterns of Membership and Support for the British Union of Fascists," *Journal of Contemporary History* 19/4 (1984), p. 580.
[13] This document is reproduced in my "The 'Pound Case' in Historical Perspective," in *Journal of Modern Literature* 35.2 (2012), p. 90.
[14] Pound, cited in Louis Dudek, ed., *DK: Some Letters of Ezra Pound* (Montreal: DC Books, 1974), pp. 17, 56; all "Poundian" capitalization and grammar in original.
[15] *Ezra Pound's Fascist Propaganda, 1935-45*, Sections 5 and 6.
[16] Pound, "England" and "Soberly," reprinted in Leonard Doob ed., *"Ezra Pound Speaking": Radio Speeches of World War II* (Westport, CT: Greenwood Press, 1978), speech numbers 16 and 90, respectively.
[17] Graham Macklin, *Very Deeply Dyed in Black: Sir Oswald Mosley and the Resurrection of Fascism after 1945* (London: I.B. Tauris, 2007), pp. 135-36.
[18] Mosley, "European Socialism," reprinted in *The European*, 6/39 (1956), 13-29, available online at www.feastofhateandfear.com/archives/oswald.html.
[19] Pound, "Sovereignty," *The European* 1.1 (Mar. 1953), p. 51; and Pound, cited in *DK: Some Letters of Ezra Pound*, p. 102.
[20] Harvey Black, "The Story of Ezra Pound," *The European*, 4/45 (Nov. 1956), pp. 163-164.
[21] The first page of Neame's essay is available online at https://onlinelibrary.wiley.com/doi/10.1111/j.1741-2005.1951.tb06650.x.
[22] John Whittier-Ferguson, "Ezra Pound, T.S. Eliot, and the Modern Epic," in Catherine Bates, ed., *The Cambridge Companion to the Epic* (Cambridge: Cambridge University Press, 2010), pp. 226-27.
[23] Alan Neame, "Canto LXXIV", in "The Pisan Cantos: An Approach," *The European*, 1/4 (Jun. 1953), pp. 42, 38.
[24] Neame, "Canto LXXIV," in "The Pisan Cantos III: Oxford Episode," *The European* 2/19 (Sept. 1954), p. 25; and Ron Bush, "Art versus the Descent of the Iconoclasts: Cultural Memory in Ezra Pound's *Pisan Cantos*," *Modernism/modernity* 1.1 (1995), pp. 71-95, at 92.
[25] Neame, "The Pisan Cantos, Canto LXXV: A Musical Interlude," *The European* 11/66 (Aug. 1956), p. 371; italics added.
[26] See Neame and Pound, in *The Edge*, Feb. and Mar. 1957, respectively. I am grateful for Archie Henderson's assistance with this journal; for further details, see his *"I Cease Not to Yowl" Reannotated: New Notes on the Pound/Agresti Correspondence* (Houston, TX: Private publication, 2012), p. 920.
[27] Neame, cited in Desmond Stewart, "Men and Books VI: Cocteau: The Last Imagist Poet," *The European* 5.55 (Sept. 1957), pp. 38-39.
[28] Neame, "The Pisan Cantos VI [sic; should read VII]: Speech and Penalty," in *The European* 6.60 (Feb. 1958), pp. 357, 360.
[29] Denis Goacher, "Dr. Leavis or Mr Pound?" *The European* 1/1 (Mar. 1953), p. 46.
[30] Henderson, *"I Cease Not to Yowl" Reannotated*, pp. 509-10. For Pound's reading of the *Protocols of the Elders of Zion* in April 1940, see Tim Redman, *Ezra Pound and Italian Fascism* (Cambridge: Cambridge University Press, 1991), p. 202.
[31] Noel Stock, "Blackout on History," *The European*, 7/72 (Feb. 1959), pp. 337, 343.
[32] Pound, cited in Humphrey Carpenter, *A Serious Character: The Life of Ezra Pound*, p. 854.

[33] Ezra Pound, "CI de los Cantares," *The European*, Feb. 1959, p. 384. Translations are suggested by Carroll F. Terrell's *A Companion to the Cantos of Ezra Pound: vol. 2, Cantos 74-117* (Berkeley, CA: University of California Press, 1984), p. 658.

[34] Pound, "Canto 74" in *The Cantos* (London: Faber and Faber, 1986), p. 459. I am grateful to Archie Henderson for his insights into *The Pisan Cantos*.

[35] Cited in Archie Henderson, "Pound, Sweden, and the Nobel Prize: An Introduction," in Richard Taylor, and Claus Melchior, eds., *Ezra Pound and Europe* (Atlanta: Rodopi, 1993), p. 164.

[36] These and other conspiratorial texts are available on Mullins' website, maintained by a protégé and headed by four images at the top of the main site: two pictures of Mullins late in life, alongside two pictures of his mentor, Ezra Pound; available online at http://www.eustacemullins.us/.

[37] See the House of Representatives' Committee on Un-American Activities report on "Neo-Fascist and Hate Groups", 17 April 1954, online at: http://debs.indstate.edu/u588n4_1954.pdf.

[38] Eustace Mullins to Pound, undated letter from 1956, Yale University's Beinecke Library Pound Collection, YCAL MSS Box 43, Folder 1500.

[39] An excellent account of John Kasper's actions in Clinton, TN is provided by Clive Webb's *Rabble Rousers: The American Far Right in the Civil Rights Era* (Athens, GA: University of Georgia Press, 2010), ch. 2.

[40] John Kasper to Pound, letter of 10 April 1956, Yale University's Beinecke Library Pound Collection, YCAL MSS Box 26, Folder 1127; and Alec Marsh, "Politics" in Ira B. Nadel, ed., *Ezra Pound in Context* (Cambridge: Cambridge University Press, 2011), pp. 101-104.

[41] I am especially grateful for Alec Marsh's assistance with this 36-page document, the first page of which is reproduced here.

[42] William Randel, *The Ku Klux Klan: A Century of Infamy* (Philadelphia: Chilton Books, 1965), p. 36.

[43] A major exception to the silence on these issues by Pound scholars is the writings of psychiatrist E. Fuller Torrey, who details some of the views of Mullins and Kasper; see *The Roots of Treason* (London: Sidgwick & Jackson, 1984), p. 230; see also John Kasper, "Segregation or Death," *The Virginia Spectator* 118.8 (May 1957), pp. 21, 34-37, available online at https://faulkner.lib.virginia.edu/media%3Fid=spectator12.html. Roughly a year later, by which time Kasper was in prison, the Seaboard White Citizens' Councils reprinted his article as a pamphlet with illustrations. I am grateful to Archie Henderson and Alec Marsh for their assistance with these texts.

7. 'Penny-wise...':
Ezra Pound's Posthumous Legacy to Fascism

Andrea Rinaldi and Matthew Feldman

Certainly a leading American modernist at his death in 1972, aged 87, Ezra Pound's influence continues to extend far beyond poetry. Although almost entirely neglected by Pound Studies, another, darker side of Pound's legacy is charted here.[1] As this unlikely case study demonstrates, Pound has inspired ideologues of post-war, or 'neo' fascism (often taxonomically understood as the 'extreme right', which will be used here as an umbrella term)—on both sides of the Atlantic, both during his lifetime and since. This article argues that Pound remains an important touchstone for different shades of extreme right thought—most notably in the US, Britain and Italy, places in each of which he spent more than a decade of his long life. Whether in British, Italian or American contexts, Pound's political views have an unexpected relevance to the international networks and converging ideas that recent scholarship has helpfully understood in terms of 'transnational fascism'.[2]

It is widely agreed that disgust at the economic meltdown of the 1929 'Great Depression', by no means an exclusively fascist attitude, brought Pound's economic ideas to a boil in the 1930s, intensifying his pre-existing vitriol against bankers, financiers and (increasingly Jewish) usurers between the wars. In fact, during World War I Pound lost two of his best friends, including the leading intellectual of *The New Age*, T.E. Hulme, and especially the sculptor Henri Gaudier-Brzeska. This, combined with the huge and terrifying death toll in the war itself, had a strong effect on Pound's sensitivity and, eventually, upon his political convictions. The idea that the Great War revealed a "botched civilization", an "old bitch gone in the teeth," as Pound wrote in his 1920 sequence, *Hugh Selwyn Mauberley*, would drive him toward the putatively social, political, and above all, economic causes of the conflict.

Within a year of the war's conclusion, Pound met Clifford Hugh Douglas, a retired Scottish engineer who had devoted himself to the construction of the project of social and economic reform known as "Social Credit". The meeting took place at the editorial offices of *The New Age* magazine, where Pound was the only regular salaried employee. A. R. Orage, *The New Age*'s editor, was the first to try to popularise Douglas' ideas through the magazine, whose Guild Socialist background was to become the principal means of diffusion for Social Credit theory in the 1920s (Marsh 80-110). In Pound's mind, Douglas' project gained a much wider significance, and became part of a larger program for a new cultural and social renaissance that was to be ultimately inextricable from fascism in Britain, the US, Italy and even Nazi Germany. Increasingly, for Pound, fascist Italy came to represent a key example of his economic ideas being put into practice and, consequently, the best prospect for a spiritual renaissance of Western civilisation. From Pound's point of view, Italian Fascism was capable of instigating the new, occidental renaissance because of its alleged superiority over both democracy and communism. As maintained long ago by Niccolò Zapponi:

> In the political events surrounding Ezra Pound we can perhaps identify the unique case of a man of letters who came to sympathise with fascism via the economy: for nearly twenty years, the American poet advocated the absolute need for monetary and taxation reforms, and believed that Italian Fascism was oriented towards their gradual implementation. In practice, this was not true in any way, but the actual reality of the policy never affected Pound's conviction that Mussolini was an economist of genius (Zapponi 11).[3]

Thus, argues Zapponi, Pound became a sort of "Buddhist monk of republican fascism" who, despite his extraordinary "acts of faith" in fascism, could not recognise that, under Mussolini, the Italian political economy scarcely took the direction advocated by Douglas. Accordingly, the large number of publications Pound dedicated to Italian economics—even during the notorious months of the Salò Republic—show him praising Fascism's adoption of Douglas' theories (Zapponi 32-47).

Furthermore, recent scholarship has argued that, for much of his life, Pound was a committed fascist ideologue and anti-Semite—at his peak, acting as a key propagandist for what he termed, in one talk, "The United States of Europe"— delivering perhaps as many as two thousand radio items for the wartime Axis.[4] One revealing and representative example must suffice at the outset here, taken from Pound's widely available transcripts reproduced in Leonard Doob's 1978 collection of 120 radio broadcasts, *Ezra Pound Speaking*:

> You with your cheatings and with your Geneva and sanctions, set out to crush it, in the SERVICE of Jewry, though you do not even yet KNOW this. And you have not digested the proposals or instructions of Jewry. And you have NOT understood fascism, or nazism for that matter. Very few of you have read the writings of either leader. It is and has been for 20 or more years, God knows, nearly impossible to print news from or to Italy or translations from Italy in your country. You have NOT read Mussolini, and I don't suppose you could now get hold of his speeches in coherent order: not many of you; or understand the points and situations that they apply or applied to.[5]

This excerpt exemplifies Pound's wartime vitriol on behalf of the Italian Fascist regime. There are many similar passages in Doob's collection, which itself only scratches the surface of his activism for the Axis. As a result of these activities, Pound was ultimately imprisoned for twelve and a half years in St Elizabeths asylum after the Second World War.[6]

Emblematic of his continued support for fascism, upon his release and return to Italy in late June 1958, Pound made the fascist salute to waiting reporters. Nowadays, the famous shot is proudly exhibited on the web page of the group of artists who gather around CasaPound Italia, the neo-fascist group described below (see image).[7]

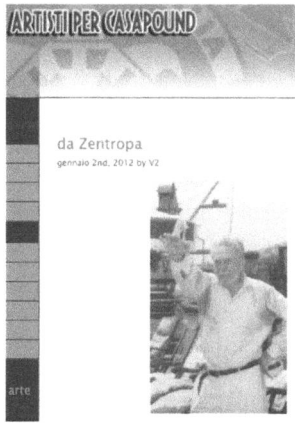

Celebrating his Italian arrival were a group of neo-fascist activists for the *Movimento Sociale Italiano* and "over-enthusiastic nostalgics for the old regime who", in the words of his long-time friend and protégé John Drummond, "would like to transform your arrival into a political triumph". In his letter of 5 June 1958, Drummond continued: "There was even a scheme to have you taken off the ship at Naples and borne north in triumph in a fleet of escorted cars, banners and gagliardetti flying, etc."; moreover, in Italy, the

> present neofascist parties may or may not have something to be said for them, though my own opinion is that they are quite unworthy to represent any of the things that were good in Fascism, and might still have validity today. But the point is that their motives for wanting to make a political celebration of your return are wholly self-interested, and for this reason alone they should not be given the chance.[8]

Back in Italy, Pound resumed contact with a number of far-right ideologues including Valerio Borghese, Vanni Teodorani and Ugo Dadone. On the latter, one of Pound's biographers, Humphrey Carpenter, has noted that, in Spring 1961, Pound stayed with Dadone, who was involved with the neo-Fascist *Movimento Sociale Italiano* and regularly wrote articles about them in right-wing journals. They held a May Day parade, wearing jackboots and black armbands, displaying the swastika, shouting ant-Semitic slogans, and goose-stepping. Among those photographed at the head of the parade was Ezra.[9]

Also in 1961, on 20 March Pound attended a press conference in Rome held by Sir Oswald Mosley.[10] Since founding the Union Movement several years after his release from wartime internment (as the leader of the British Union of Fascists and National Socialists, or BUF), the latter advocated a decidedly "transnational fascist" concept of "Europe a Nation" in his post-war journal, *The European*.[11] Pound's activities in 1961 alone suggest that this was scarcely the last time that his political activism would be instrumentalised by extreme right ideologues with pretentions of international influence.

More specifically, this article considers three distinct strands of the post-war extreme right since the Axis dénouement of 1945 that have explicitly, and repeatedly, emphasised their Poundian influence. In doing so, this contribution can only scratch the surface of what is an unusually diverse legacy amongst the post-war extreme right. The first of these strands, white nationalism and biological anti-Semitism, is most often associated with neo-Nazism; namely, the attempted ideological preservation of values and traditions from the Third Reich, above all its symbols and belief in a Jewish conspiracy. A second strand, conscious of the stigma of the Axis war and Holocaust, has long flourished in post-war Europe. It typically traces its legacy to non-Nazi forms of fascism; most notably those associated with Mussolini's Italian Fascism, and represents deliberate attempts to update fascist ideology through studious revision, even selective rejection, of past fascist policies. This is sometimes referred to as "Fascism of the Third Millennium", which may be best observed in the case of the explicitly fascist movement CasaPound Italia—a movement so indebted to Pound's legacy that his daughter, Mary de Rachewiltz, has threatened litigation for using the poet's name for unabashedly fascist purposes.[12] Finally, a third strand touched upon here, represented by Britain's New Right, emphasises European 'Tradition' and a metapolitical, ideas-driven ideology that has similarly championed Pound as a kind of cultural martyr for fascist ideas during and after WWII. Albeit briefly given the constraints of space and scope, each of these three 'faces' of post-war fascism will be considered through the surprisingly significant legacy of a leading modernist poet turned extreme right ideologue.

Naturally, Pound's legacy is not of the same influence or character as the key fascist pantheon of post-war ideologues of Julius Evola and Léon Degrelle, or even lesser-known figures like Oswald Mosley or Colin Jordan. This is largely due to the fact that academics debating Pound's influence upon right-wing extremists have confined themselves to the effective diffusion—or otherwise—of Pound's poetry and prose within extreme right circles. Academics believed, rightly, that most of these extreme right activists and sympathizers would neither understand nor really appreciate texts like *Guide to Kulchur* or *The Cantos* which, on the whole, seems to have led to an underestimation of neo-fascist appropriation of Pound. The question they ask is—to employ John Lauber's characterisation—did Pound's work from the mid-1930s constitute a kind of "fascist epic"?[13] The subject is largely taboo in Pound Studies, and those even raising the issue frequently receive undue opprobrium. But Pound's legacy is of another order altogether. Indeed, Pound's infamous case remains relevant to the extreme right beyond his literary production and his radio-propaganda. It is, rather, his life as a fascist 'martyr' that has really impressed the audience of the contemporary extreme right. Pound's 13-year punishment for the fascist cause is a significant legacy in its own right.[14] The alleged hypocrisies of incarcerating (mostly in a sanatorium) a non-convicted man, in fact, became an iconic example for right-wing extremists, one far more significant than the esotericism of *The Cantos*.[15]

Pound and the Anglo-American Extreme Right since 1945

In the wake of his arrest on treason charges in 1945, Pound was declared insane and institutionalised until 1958. Drawing upon his earlier interwar relationship with the BUF, from his residence at St Elizabeths asylum near Washington, D.C., Pound both raised money and smuggled out texts for Oswald Mosley's neo-fascist Union Movement.[16] This extended to publishing several texts in the organisation's short-lived house journal, *The European*—including the first publication of *Canto CI* and several shorter texts. This short-lived publication (1953-1959) touted "Mosley's concept of 'European Socialism', which he wished to be accepted as a common programme for all European fascist movements".[17] Amongst the younger fascists in Mosley's stable responding to Pound's work were Denis Goacher, Harvey Black, Desmond Stewart and, most fervently, Alan Neame.

Interestingly, Pound's British influence extended beyond the United Kingdom to the post-war Commonwealth as well. This is especially the case with the Australian writer, Noel Stock, a one-time devotee who was tirelessly seeking to establish Pound's place in modern English verse—and extreme right politics. In 1953, Stock wrote to the leading modernist critic, Hugh Kenner, who advised him to get in contact directly with Pound. Even if the two only met personally in 1958 in Brunnenburg Castle—Mary (Pound's daughter) and Boris de Rachewiltz's residence in the Italian Tyrol—Stock and Pound had an extended correspondence of "more than a hundred letters (between forty-five and fifty thousands words)" during the previous five years. Published in 1970, Stock's *The Life of Ezra Pound* revealingly states:

> I well remembered Kenner's warning in 1954 to be careful of Pound's politics; I paid little heed and was soon involved in Social Credit and similar activities. I joined a Social Credit newspaper, *The New Times*, and to Pound's great satisfaction began to publish unsigned or pseudonymous items which he sent from Washington (Stock xiii).

Doubtless encouraged by Pound, Stock contributed two texts to *The European's* final issue in 1959, one of which was entitled the 'Historical Blackout'. Linking these more opaque phrases to explicitly fascist writings, moreover, only two years earlier, Stock had also published Pound's translation of Benito Mussolini's summer 1943 diary composed while under house arrest, "In Captivity: Notebook of Thoughts in Ponza and La Maddelena". This anonymised text appeared in Stock's Australian journal, *Edge* (appearing in 1957-1958); that is, at a time when Stock was clearly receptive to the neo-fascist ideas circulating amongst the Poundian acolytes at St Elizabeths.[18] Likewise revealing Pound's transnational relevance to neo-fascism today, another Antipodean extreme right ideologue, the New Zealander Kerry Bolton, has published a short biography of Pound at Oswald Mosley's homage website—still hosted by the far-right 'Friends of Oswald Mosley' group—affirming in the final paragraph: "On 30 June 1958, Pound set sail for Italy. When he reached Naples, he gave the fascist salute to journalists and declared 'all America is an asylum.' He continued with *The Cantos*, and stayed in contact with political personalities such as Kasper and Oswald Mosley."[19]

Yet Stock was not the first biographer to sit at the feet of the modernist patriarch; rather, it was the American conspiracy theorist Eustace Mullins—another pivotal transnational figure on the post-war extreme right. Since Mullins's death in 2010, a devotional website has been launched, republishing many works following his 1961 biography *This Difficult Individual, Ezra Pound*. Perhaps unsurprisingly, one text not included on this site was published only a year before Mullins's whitewashing biography, entitled "Adolf Hitler: An Appreciation". Rather than explicit neo-Nazism—which Mullins never recanted, in fact—pictures of Pound festoon the homepage at www.eustacemullins.us, including the latter's infamous mugshot—taken in captivity on 26 May 1945 (see image[20]).

Further underscoring this connection with the poet is Mullins's biography, found on the homepage:

> Eustace Mullins (born 1923) is an American political writer, author, biographer, and the last surviving protege of the 20th century intellectual and writer, Ezra Pound [....] Mullins was a student of the poet and political activist Ezra Pound. He states that he frequently visited Pound during his period of incarceration in St. Elizabeth's [sic] Hospital for the Mentally Ill in Washington, D.C., between 1946 and 1959 [sic—Pound was released in May 1958]. Mullins claimed that Pound was, in fact, being held as a political prisoner on the behest of President Franklin D. Roosevelt. Mullins' most notable work, *The Secrets of the Federal Reserve*, was commissioned by Pound during this period.[21]

Tellingly, at the time of writing Pound's biography Mullins headed the Aryan League of America—upon whose headed stationery Mullins corresponded with Pound at St Elizabeths during the 1950s. According to the neo-Nazi right activist, Pound expressly started him on the first of his conspiratorial writings, *The Secrets of the Federal Reserve*, paying him "ten dollars a week" and hosting him at St Elizabeths Hospital during the book's research in the nearby Library of Congress. This is highlighted by the following Preface, added to the book in 1983:

> Here are the simple facts of the great betrayal. Wilson and House knew that they were doing something momentous. One cannot fathom men's motives and this pair probably believed in what they were up to. What they did not believe in was representative government. They believed in government by an uncontrolled oligarchy whose acts would only become apparent after an interval so long that the electorate would be forever incapable of doing anything efficient to remedy depredations.

(AUTHOR'S NOTE: Dr. Pound wrote this introduction for the earliest version of this book, published by Kasper and Horton, New York, 1952. Because he was being held as a political prisoner without trial by the Federal Government, he could not afford to allow his name to appear on the book because of additional reprisals against him. Neither could he allow the book to be dedicated to him, although he had commissioned its writing. The author is gratified to be able to remedy these necessary omissions, thirty-three years after the events.)[22]

Whether or not Pound explicitly considered him as his protégé, it is clear that their relationship was both close—especially in the 1950s—and of primary importance for Mullins over the ensuing decades of extreme right activism.

One influence upon Mullins during Pound's incarceration, surely, was the encoding of anti-Semitic conspiracy theories. Accordingly, the word 'Jew' does not appear in *The Secrets of the Federal Reserve*—favouring the dog-whistle term 'international financiers' instead—although Mullins was to become much more explicit in his prejudices after Pound's death. In fact, Mullins's publications became increasingly anti-Semitic as his star began to rise in the US neo-fascist firmament. Thus, works over the ensuing decades included *Jewish TV: Sick Sick Sick* and *Mullins' New History of the Jews*, which opens: "Throughout the history of civilization, one particular problem of mankind has remained constant. In all of the vast records of peace and wars and rumors of wars, one great empire after another has had to come to grips with the same dilemma... the Jews." Later, contributing to perhaps the most enduring anti-Semitic conspiracy of the twentieth century, Mullins's chapter "Jews and Communism" then avers:

> The poet Ezra Pound, who criticized the Jews for plunging the world into the horrors of the second world war, spent thirteen years in the Hellhole of St. Elizabeths, a Federal mental institution in Washington, D.C. for political prisoners. Pound won a number of prizes for his writings while the Jews had him locked up as a madman. Many visitors to the ward, including this writer, commented that the stench of the place was exactly like that of the cities in Europe which had fallen to the Jewish Communists.[23]

This was not the only conspiracy theory Mullins was spinning as a leading ideologue of the extreme right, both in the US and internationally. Only a year earlier, Mullins argued in *The Secret Holocaust* that Jews had been engaged in genocidal activity toward gentiles long before the Second World War. But that was not to say the Nazis' attempted Judeocide was justified; instead, Europe's Jews had conspired to construct the Holocaust to elicit sympathy and financial reparations after 1945. As one of the earliest Holocaust deniers in the US—alongside Harry Elmer Barnes, to be sure—for Mullins, this ruse "might have more validity had it not been for one unfortunate oversight by the Jews—they did not build the gas chambers at Auschwitz until after World War II had ended" (*Secret Holocaust*). In keeping with Pound's turn toward the US movement of white supremacism—to the extent of assisting the Ku Klux Klan in the mid-1950s in attempting to retain the segregation of American schools following the Supreme Court's 1954 *Brown v. Board of Education* ruling—Mullins similarly linked US racial desegregation to alleged Jewish control and rejection of 'Aryan' values.

Given Mullins's decades-long trafficking in Holocaust denial, it should come as no surprise that, as his hagiographic website avers, he was on the "editorial staff of far-right Willis Carto's American Free Press. He is also a contributing editor to the Barnes Review"—the latter, of course, named after the aforementioned Harry Elmer Barnes.[24] As the publisher of the American Free Press and *The Barnes Review*, Willis Carto's Liberty Lobby has long acted as the main disseminator of Holocaust 'revisionism'—both in book and serialised form. Which is to say, of course, that Carto's veneration for Pound is likely less for his poetic achievements than for his extreme right politics, as the following vignette from the late Christopher Hitchens underscores:

> I was once introduced, in the Cosmos Club in Washington, to Willis Carto of the Liberty Lobby, a group frequently accused of being insufficiently philo-Semitic. Mr Carto unburdened himself of quite a long burst about the power of finance capital, whereupon our host, to lighten the atmosphere, said, 'Come on Willis, you're sounding like Ezra Pound'. 'Ezra Pound!' exclaimed Mr Carto. 'Why, I love that man's work. Except for all that goddam poetry!' I thought then that if one ever needed a working definition of an anti-Semite, it might perhaps be an individual who esteemed everything about Ezra Pound except his Cantos.[25]

It bears noting that *The Barnes Review*, and especially its parent organisation, The Institute for Historical Review (IHR), has remained the most influential publishing outlet for the transnational extreme right for decades. In this light, Carto's otherwise curious interest in a modernist poet (if not modernist poetry) becomes explicable, as George Michael's recent study maintains:

> In the realm of literature, Carto exalts Ezra Pound as one of America's greatest poets, and for heroically opposing FDR's pubs for war in Europe. Pound's service as a radio propagandist in Fascist Italy is characterised as an admirable effort to inform Americans that their system of government and society had been taken over by 'alien forces dedicated to achieving their own goals, trampling over American interest in the process.[26]

Despite the linguistic encoding so readily deciphered by Hitchens and others, the identity of these conspiring "alien forces" is undoubted and in keeping with the views of an overwhelming majority of Holocaust 'revisionists': Jews. Moreover, given the confluence of Holocaust denial and devotion to Ezra Pound, it is only to be expected that Liberty Lobby publications would feature texts on the canonical modernist as a free-speech 'martyr' and purveyor of unpalatable 'truths' about putative Jewish control. In fact, *The Barnes Review* dedicated a special issue to Pound in July 1995. Following that issue three years later was an overview in the same journal by Michael Collins Piper, entitled "What Did Ezra Pound Really Say?"—representing little more than a defence of Pound's conspiracy theories, fascism and vituperative anti-Semitism. Piper's essay was widely re-published—including from Carto's Historical Review Press, an arm of The Institute for Historical Review—while the themes remained central to Piper's anti-Semitic oeuvre. His 2009 study, *The New Babylon, Those Who Reign Supreme,* was naturally published via Willis Carto, with whom he has "worked closely with" for "over 25 years" as "the public face of Liberty Lobby".[27] Other tellingly titled texts include *The Rothschild Empire: The Modern-Day Pharisees, and the Historical, Religious, and Economic Origins of the New World Order*. In particular, the latter potboiler basks in Poundian anti-Semitic conspiracies, as made clear by the book's inside cover:

> Examining the New World Order's religious and philosophical roots in the Jewish book of laws known as the Talmud, a product of ancient Babylon, Piper explores the manner in which followers of the Talmud rose to titanic heights in the arena of finance, culminating in the establishment of the Rothschild Empire as the premiere force in the affairs of our planet. Today, with the Rothschild power network firmly entrenched in American soil, the United States today has emerged as "The New Babylon" from which these modern-day Pharisees are working to set in place a global hegemon: The New World Order.[28]

In addition to Jewish control of world financial markets, other writings by Collins Piper allege that Israel was behind the assassination of John F. Kennedy and Martin Luther King, Jr., as well as having foreknowledge of the terrorist attacks on September 11, 2001. Indeed, such is his antipathy to Jews that Collins Piper has attempted to forge an alliance with Middle Eastern anti-Semites. Further highlighting the way in which anti-Semitic conspiracy theories increasingly transcend borders, and even cultures—often in an updated and repackaged form—Collins Piper spoke at a notorious Holocaust 'revisionist' conference hosted by Iranian President Mahmoud Ahmadinejad in December 2006. That same year, ironically enough, Collins Piper launched a radio talk show entitled "The Piper Report". One of his first guests, naturally enough, was "his friend of some 25 years, Eustace Mullins". On that programme, in turn, Mullins reflected on his

> long-time friendship with famed poet Ezra Pound who was illegally detained in a mental institution in Washington, DC for many years on trumped-up suspicion of "treason" for having dared to criticize the war policies of Franklin Delano Roosevelt. It was Pound who first directed Mullins into research into the Federal Reserve racket and things have never been the same since. There is hardly anything of serious consequence written on the subject of the Federal Reserve today that does not owe its debt to the original research by Mullins, acting under the advice and direction of his friend Pound.[29]

By the early 2000s, another friend of Mullins, his one-time roommate from the 1950s, Matthias Koehl, had gone further than any of the above with respect to white supremacism. Under the tagline "BUILDING A BETTER WORLD FOR FUTURE ARYAN GENERATIONS", Koehl had literally turned National Socialism into a fully-fledged religion. In doing so, Koehl placed a quote from the extreme right occultist Savitri Devi on the homepage of his website, *New Order* (with the 'O' in Order tellingly encircling a swastika):

> National Socialism is infinitely more than a mere political creed; the fact is that it is a way of life, a faith in the fullest sense of the word—one could say a religion, however different it may at first appear, from every existing system thus labelled in current speech. Religions are not as easy to uproot as mere political creeds.[30]

The movement's neo-Nazi aims are set out opposite Devi's quotation, under a paragraph entitled 'The Alternative'—representing an exemplary expression of fascist ideology, as understood by contemporary scholars on the subject.[31]

> Today we live under an Old Order. It is a sick, degenerate system of rat-race materialism, self-fixation, drugs, pollution, miscegenation, filth, chaos, corruption and insanity. It is a way of alienation—and Death. But there is a better way, a way of Life. That way calls for a rebirth of racial idealism and reverence for the eternal laws of Nature. It involves a new awareness, a new faith, a new way of life—a New Order. If you would like to find out more about a great historic movement of white men and women working to build a better future, contact us today.[32]

Koehl's support for National Socialist ideas—to the point of venerating them as a religious faith—had developed over more than half a century. In fact, it seems that his overt embrace of neo-Nazism began to develop in the 1950s, when he was the roommate of none other than Eustace Mullins. As might be expected, Koehl was brought by Mullins to St Elizabeths in order to meet his mentor, Ezra Pound. At the very least, this surely did not hinder Koehl's subsequent advocacy for his longed for "Fourth Reich". By the 1960s he had gravitated toward the US branch of the World Union of National Socialists (WUNS), the American Nazi Party, rising to the rank of second-in-command under infamous neo-Nazi George Lincoln Rockwell. Following the latter's murder in 1967 at the hands of a disaffected follower, Koehl became the movement's commander and editor of the movement's journal, *National Socialist World*.

From there, Koehl attempted to add intellectual discourse to the movement in the 1970s, implied through changing the organisation's name to the National Socialist White People's Party. Such were Koehl's attempts to raise the level of discourse amongst the US neo-Nazis that, by summer 1980, he had re-launched the movement's neo-Nazi publication. Amongst the articles in the journal's second iteration, *The National Socialist*, was an article by Koehl entitled "The Revolutionary Nature of National Socialism", and another anonymous text, "Program of the National Socialist White People's Party". Most strikingly, the preceding text was titled "Artemis' Compleynt"– a republication of the first quarter of *Canto XXX* by Ezra Pound. It remains an astonishing admission of Pound's influence upon American neo-Nazi discourse (see image[33]).

Indeed, as exemplified both by the journal's unabashedly neo-Nazi title—no less than by the movement's second in command, the British neo-Nazi Colin Jordan—to this day WUNS continues to tout an international extreme right activism based, above all, upon the mythic 'Aryan' race. An individual or small group need only therefore self-identify as a 'White-Aryan' dedicated to the cause of a revolutionary rebirth in order to join WUNS: no membership cards, political meetings or codes of conduct are needed. As borne out by the 'Participating Members' webpage of the recently-reformed National Social Movement—naturally headquartered in the United States since its September 2006 re-launch—affiliated countries range from Spain to Serbia in Europe to Mexico, Costa Rica and beyond; there is even, apparently, an affiliated group called the Naska Party in Iran.[34]

Albeit far less overt, another insightful snapshot of Pound transnational influence upon today's extreme right can be seen in the burgeoning New Right in Britain, the US and elsewhere. Deriving from the French-led *Nouvelle Droite* launched by Alain de Benoist in the late 1960s, in Roger Griffin's summation, these avowedly metapolitical advocates of an 'Indo-Europeanism' have been a major factor in the overhaul of intellectual fascism since the 1970s. By concentrating on the primacy of 'cultural' over 'political hegemony' (perversely enough, the New Right draws upon the theories of the Italian Marxist Antonio Gramsci), and by stressing a pan-European philosophy of contemporary history, this current of palingenetic ultra-nationalism enables modern fascists to dissociate themselves from the narrower nationalisms of the interwar movements. Their common denominator is that they are all in one way or another linked to anti-reductionism, anti-materialism, and anti-egalitarianism, but free of links with Fascism or Nazism in the public mind.[35]

Yet explicitly culturalist attempts to distance the New Right from the unreconstructed, overtly fascist Old Right have been rumbled by the work of Griffin, and even more so, the brilliant historical research of Pierre-André Taguieff, who reminds readers of the Nouvelle Droite's repackaged prejudice—now going by the fancy-sounding term 'ethno-differentialism'—

> Neither "fascism" nor "racism" will do us the favor of returning in such a way that we can recognize them easily. If vigilance was only a game of recognizing something already well-known, then it would only be a question of remembering. Vigilance would be reduced to a social game using reminiscence and identification by recognition, a consoling illusion of an immobile history peopled with events which accord with our expectations or our fears. Magical vigilance: one declares oneself "vigilant" to prevent the return of the "old devils." If vigilance was only a game of recognising something already well-known, then it would only be a question of remembering.[36]

This injunction certainly applies to New Right iterations in the US and Britain, both drawing heavily upon Ezra Pound's post-war legacy. In the US, Greg Johnson's online outlet for the North American New Right, *Counter-Currents Publishing,* has made heavy use of Pound's writings over the last few years, including the 1939 standalone BUF pamphlet on 28 October 2011, *What is Money For?*; the 1935 *Social Credit: An Impact* on 30 October 2012; and, in five parts, the 1933 *ABC of Economics* in December 2012. More recently, Johnson has continued lauding Pound's writing, posting some of his early poetry on January 27 and October 30, 2013; a video containing Pound's reading of *Canto I* on February 28, 2013; and then, in five parts, reposting the entirety of Pound's 1933 screed, *Jefferson and/or Mussolini*—which commenced Pound's interwar activism for fascism in Italy and Britain[37]—between 28 October and 1 November. It seems these autumn dates were specifically chosen, as Johnson maintains, to coincide with Pound's birth- and death-days:

> The end of October is one of my favorite times of the year, and not just because Halloween falls on the 31st. On the 30th, we celebrate the birthday of Ezra Pound, poet and prophet of a just social and economic system, and on November 1st, we commemorate his death.[38]

John Drummond's translation of Pound's 1944 text, *Oro e Lavoro*, explicitly written for the Nazi-occupied Salò Republic, is the most recent of Pound's writings to be uploaded on Johnson's *Counter Currents* site—with thanks to "Kerry Bolton for making a copy available for scanning."[39] Even in the transnational arena of metapolitical activism, it seems—especially with the rise of online connectivity in the last generation—the world remains a very small place for extreme right ideologues. To be sure, this internationalisation of New Right celebration of Pound's poetic and political writings bears out Federico Finchelstein's recent claim that, "[i]n order to grasp the global and transnational dimensions of fascism it is, however, necessary to understand its history, first in its national articulation and second to relate this manifestation of fascism to intellectual exchanges across the Atlantic Ocean and beyond."[40]

This "beyond" doubtless embraces Britain's New Right as well, launched through the aegis of long-time extreme right activist Troy Southgate—once of Britain's avowedly neo-Nazi National Front in the 1970s; the International Third Position in the late 1980s (in collaboration with Nick Griffin, current leader of the neo-fascist British National Party; BNP), and a pioneer of 'metapolitical fascist', or *apoliteic*, music.[41] Southgate launched Britain's New Right in January 2005, with Jonathan Bowden as the guest speaker at the launch event. Testifying to the intimate connections between the 'metapolitical' New Right and the revolutionary Old Right, Bowden was intimately connected to Griffin's BNP at the time, rising to the role of Cultural Officer and Advisory Council Member in 2007. In an interview with Southgate in 2010, published under the revealing title "Revolutionary Conservative", Bowden advocates "the mixing together of ultra-conservative and neo-fascist ideas; second, a belief in the importance of meta-politics or cultural struggle." It is this "creative vortex" that Bowden understands as the extreme right attempt "to back past verities in new guises"; moreover, "the New Right recognises that fascism and national socialism were populist or mass expressions of revolutionary conservative doctrines."[42]

For Bowden's part, this more culturally inflected extreme right activist had long counted Pound as one of his political idols; for example, he is cited twice in the aforementioned 2010 interview with Southgate. Bowden is yet more explicit about the role of Pound in British New Right thinking in another interview with a 'metapolitical' activist, the Croatian ideologue Tomislav Sunić:

> I agree with Ezra Pound that the artistic community is like the antennae of the civilization that they're a part of and that they feel the tremors in the web or in the ether before anyone else [....] It's interesting to note, in relation to modernism for example, many of the early modernists—Eliot, Wyndham Lewis, Marinetti, Céline, Ezra Pound, and so on—were deeply attracted to the extreme Right. They were attracted because they saw in it fundamentalist cultural energies.[43]

Given the international linkages amongst the contemporary extreme right—above all, exemplified by the Euro-American New Right—it should come as no surprise that Sunić's interview with Bowden is available on Greg Johnson's North American New Right website, Counter-Currents Publishing (where, alongside Kerry Bolton, Bowden is listed as one of "Our Authors"). So too is the *pièce de résistance* of Bowden's Poundian interest: an hour-long hagiography on the American modernist at the 33rd meeting of Troy Southgate's London New Right on 11 June 2011—some nine months before the latter's death. In fact, the entire text is available to audit on *Counter-Currents Radio*.[44] Perhaps by way of tribute, Southgate's publishing outlet, Black Front Press, published an edited collection on Pound in 2012 entitled *Ezra Pound: Thoughts and Perspectives, Volume Six*. Again highlighting the transnational nature of Pound's influence, contributors included Southgate and Mariella Shearer from the UK and Dimitris Michalopoulos from Greece, alongside republished articles from the New Zealander Kerry Bolton and the American Michael Collins Piper.[45] Were there any question about the international and ideological *bona fides* of this volume and its parent series, other volumes in Southgate's Thoughts and Perspectives collection include books devoted to Jonathan Bowden (Volume 9)[46]; the Italian Fascist and key post-war extreme right ideologue Julius Evola (Volume 1)[47]; Corneliu Codreanu, leader of the interwar Romanian Iron Guard (Volume 5)[48]; the German 'Conservative Revolutionary' Ernst Jünger (Volume 11)[49]; and, with a Poundian ring, even the extreme right author from Japan, Yukio Mishima (Volume 8).[50] Likewise the National-anarchists, headed by Southgate since the 1990's, claim an influence from Pound—emphasised in the website's Italian version—in a page dedicated to economics, where the group closely mirror's Pound's programme.[51]

Pound and Post-war Italy: 'Fascists of the Third Millennium'

Considering the importance of Pound's case to white nationalism in the US, it should come as no surprise that his influence was also felt by the far-right across the Atlantic. As noted above, this has been the case, above all, with CasaPound in contemporary Italy. CasaPound Italia (often abbreviated as CPI) has its roots in the hard rock band Zetazeroalfa, born in 1997 and headed by Gianluca Iannone. CPI's activists, sometimes referred to as a *santa teppa* [holy mob]—reflected in the text of a Zetazeroalfa's song—unabashedly declare themselves to be fascists, despite the fact that longstanding Italian laws prohibit the formation of explicitly Italian Fascist parties. Similarly, the band '270bis', provocatively named after the article of the Italian penal code that punishes management of or membership in terrorist or subversive associations[52], often airs on Radio Bandiera Nera [Black Flag Radio] CPI's online broadcasting arm; their song *Bomber nero* [black bomber jacket], claims they are youths who "love Hitler and Mussolini'" and yell "*Sieg Heil*" outstretching their arms."[53] Over the last decade, CPI has been a growing force in both Italian, and especially in Roman, politics.[54]

> The introduction of CPI's political programme declares:
>
> The Italian nation must again become a living organism with tasks, life and means superior, for strength and power, to that of individuals [...] it must be a moral, political and economic unity that is integrally realised within the State. The State we want is an ethical, organic, inclusive [...] state. [...] A social and national Italy, according to the vision of the Risorgimento, of Mazzini, Corridoni, Futurism, D'Annunzio, Gentile, Pavolini and Mussolini.[55]

Given his overt valorisation of Mussolini, Iannone is among those to have recently created an honour guard standing continuously outside Mussolini's tomb in his birthplace, the small town of Predappio. CPI's socio-political project explicitly refers to key tenets of fascist ideology.

Equally, in their online "Ideodromo"—described by Iannone as "the place where our ideas take form"—CasaPound's spokesperson, Adriano Scianca, claims that the main reason for CPI taking the North American poet as their main example is "because Pound was fascist". In facts, these self-proclaimed "fascists of the third millennium" look to Pound as a model for contemporary applications of fascist ideology. This owes much, in turn, to Pound's conception of fascism as a "third way" to both liberal democracy and socialism. Correspondingly, Scianca is surely right in saying that Pound's writings on radical economics appear prophetic for many contemporary readers on the far-right. A fitting example can be found in what Pound wrote in his 1944 Italian essay *Lavoro e Usura* [Work and Usury]:

> The insidiousness of banking has always followed the same road--abundance–any kind of abundance tends to create optimism. This optimism is exaggerated, usually with the help of propaganda. Sales increase; prices of land, or of shares, rise beyond the possibility of material revenue. The banks that favour exaggerated loans, in order to manoeuver the increase, restrict, recall their loans, and presently panic overtakes the people.[56]

While the above characterisations of Pound's political propaganda are still contentious—albeit uncontested by CPI itself—a consistent attempt has been made to play down Ezra Pound's own racism and, especially, his virulent anti-Semitism.

In the words of Scianca: "It's important to remember that he renounced anti-Semitism, but never fascism".[57] In turn, this disavowal of anti-Semitism is in keeping with a longstanding attempt by extreme right protégés of Pound to distance their mentor from his visceral radio attacks on Jews during WWII. Thus, in an interview with Alexander Baron from 1993, Eustace Mullins asserted "he [Pound] wasn't an anti-Semite, and neither am I myself!"[58]

Finally, the most recent book-length account from CasaPound, *Ezra fa surf: Come e perché il pensiero di Pound salverà il mondo* [*Ezra surfs: How and why Pound's thought will save the world*] was written by the aforementioned Adriano Scianca, who has been responsible for the cultural section of CasaPound since 2008. The short outline of the book, on the publisher's website, proclaims:

> A rocker Ezra Pound who will save the world? His thought, even if it belongs to the past century, appears as extremely timely [....] A Pound who is philosopher and economist that can be considered a master of ethical anti-conformism for such personalities as Bukowski, Allen Ginsberg and Pasolini, [...] Patti Smith and the Velvet Underground [...] carrier of a message of dialogue which is typically Mediterranean, anti-chauvinist, and against any xenophobia and prejudice.[59]

Ezra surfs was released on 19 September 2013, and in an interview the author declared that the title refers to William Kilgore's phrase from *Apocalypse Now*, "Charlie don't surf!" ('Charlie' was the derogatory term for the Vietcong used by American forces in South Vietnam.) For Kilgore, 'Charlie' is not cool because he doesn't surf. In the film, Kilgore is the "classic obtuse Yankee", convinced that US forces would win the war in Vietnam because Charlie is a "loser". In turn, Scianca views him as a kind of anti-Pound, as the lieutenant colonel is a close-minded militarist—whereas the poet criticises the usurious "war system". For Scianca, "Pound surfs because he is more fresh, free, original, revolutionary of all today's fashionable scribblers".[60] The idea of Pound surfing, like the reference to Bradbury's Casa Montag, further underscores with willingness of CasaPound to borrow cultural references from across the Atlantic. Here, too, a strictly national understanding of these self-proclaimed "fascists of the third millennium" can miss the transnational wood for the more parochial trees.

Furthermore, Scianca argues that the contemporary world expresses itself through recourse to slang references to the sea, such as the "navigation" on the internet; thus "to surf on the present condition has somehow the same sense of Julius Evola's *Riding the Tiger*, which means being within modernity, but fighting for a different modernity." This "surfer" Pound is also the inspiration for CPI's approach to the issue of immigration. Contained in the "Ideodromo" is a section titled *Perché ci piace Ezra Pound* [Why we like Ezra Pound], where Scianca states that:

> In a world that piles up disorderly languages and cultures, devouring human flesh and covering up this genocide behind facades of nice and colourful babble, Pound has shown the way for a sane cosmopolitanism, one that pays attention to differences but without forgetting one's roots.[61]

Yet Pound's anti-Semitism was long based on the supposed character of Jews themselves as exclusive, exclusionary and rejecting of cultural diversity. As Pound said in his 1935 article "Germany Now" in *The New English Weekly*, "the idea of a chosen race is thoroughly semitic".[62] This gave the right to Pound, and today to the CPI's activists, to defend "Roman sanity" from alien influences, "for developing the real differences, beyond the multi-racist society", as expressed in CPI's political programme remarkably called *Una Nazione* [One Nation]. This programme (cf. point 3) evokes various far right measures for the control of immigration, and for defending Italian society from supposedly intolerant cultures, extending to the suspension of the Schengen Treaty (allowing free movement of citizens within Europe) and the repatriation of illegal immigrants (3-4). As examined by Pierre-André Taguieff and other scholars working on the contemporary extreme right, this discourse may be seen as a kind of upside down racism, and is most prominently associated with the *Nouvelle Droite*'s chief 'metapolitical' ideologue, Alain de Benoist.[63] Thus, the assumed racism of multicultural "race-mixing" justifies policies familiar from last century: segregation of different ethnic groups, and repatriation where possible.[64]

Pietrangelo Buttafuoco, a notable journalist and writer who worked for a number of different Italian newspapers (*La Repubblica*, *Il Giornale*, *Il Foglio Quotidiano*), magazines (*Panorama*) and television stations (LA7 and Berlusconi's Canale 5), wrote the preface to Scianca's *Ezra fa surf*. Pietrangelo is the son of Antonio Buttafuoco, a former deputy in the 'post-fascist' Movimento Sociale Italiano (MSI, or Italian Social Movement), and a member of the central committee of the party.[65] As emphasised in Buttafuoco's preface, the book recounts aspects of Pound's economic and social vision, since he demonstrated that the only alternative to the uncontrolled dominance of the "market" is not "democracy" but the "temple":

> The biggest insult that democracy has committed against Ezra Pound is not having locked him in "the gorilla cage". Nor, by itself, the fact of having thrown him in the 'hell hole' of St. Elizabeths for thirteen years. The real bleeding shame of Pound's case, instead, is the power of violence by the enemy of beauty and goodness.[66]

Pietrangelo Buttafuoco thus writes on behalf of a very different 'face' of the post-war far-right from that of Eustace Mullins, Willis Carto or even his father, yet he likewise finds in Ezra Pound's outlook direct inspiration, even a future direction. In underscoring this point in his revealing preface, Buttafuoco then cites a verse of *Canto XCVII*, from the sequence *Thrones de los Cantares* where Pound reaffirms his beliefs in the continued religiosity of the west no less than those on usury: "the temple is holy because it is not for sale".[67] This is in order to assert, characteristically—if rather more opaquely than in the past—that the "perfect revolution is the one that doesn't chatter about rights, but evokes gods":

> There is no solution outside the temple. Because religion is man's basic instinct of survival. Religiosity is the key. And, likewise, there is no revolution without Pound. [...] against the queen of mystifications, that macabre dance of the fight between civilisations, consciously organized by those with an interest in perpetuating wars. That is a system that creates wars serially, as the poet shouted, without being heard, from the microphones of Radio Roma.[68]

While but scratching the surface, this article has shown that Pound's influence amongst extreme right ideologues is equally transnational and persevering. Of the former, activists from New Zealand to Italy, and Britain to the United States, testify to his continuing relevance in—at least—three 'faces' of the contemporary extreme right: white supremacism, neo-fascism, and New Right 'metapolitics'. In each, he is lauded as a political martyr and cultural icon. Of the latter, the continued relevance of Pound's fascist legacy is such that, from the present perspective, it is unlikely to be circumvented anytime soon. Despite what his many poetic admirers and academic analysts may wish to be the case, it is clear that Pound's memory is alive and kicking on the extreme right. This may be so much the case that what his fellow Anglophone poet, Basil Bunting, had to say of his modernist writing may also be true of his revolutionary right-wing politics:

> There are the Alps. What is there to say about them?
> They don't make sense [....]
> There they are, you will have to go a long way round
> if you want to avoid them.
> It takes some getting used to. There are the Alps,
> fools! Sit down and wait for them to crumble![69]

Endnotes

[1] For more on Pound and fascism see, for example, Niccolò Zapponi, *L'Italia di Ezra Pound* (Roma: Bulzoni, 1976); Tim Redman, *Ezra Pound and Italian Fascism* (Cambridge: Cambridge UP, 1991); Alex Houen, "Ezra Pound: Anti-Semitism, Segregationism," *Terrorism and Modern Literature: From Joseph Conrad to Ciaran Carson* (Oxford: Oxford UP, 2002), Ch. 3.

[2] For recent studies of 'transnational fascism', see for example, Arnd Bauerkämper, "Transnational Fascism: Cross-Border Relations between Regimes and Movements in Europe, 1922-1939," *East Central Europe* 37.2-3 (2010): 214-46; Michael Whine, "Trans-European trends in right-wing extremism", Andrea Mammone, Emmanuel Godin, and Brian Jenkins (eds.), *Mapping the Extreme Right in Contemporary Europe: From Local to Transnational* (London: Routledge, 2012); and Jim Wolfreys, "The European extreme right in comparative perspective", Andrea Mammone, Emmanuel Godin, and Brian Jenkins (eds.), *Varieties of Right-wing Extremism in Europe* (London: Routledge, 2013), Ch. 1.

[3] "Nelle vicende politiche di Ezra Pound si può forse individuare l'unico caso di un uomo di lettere giunto a simpatizzare per il fascismo attraverso l'economia: per circa vent'anni, il poeta americano sostenne infatti l'assoluta necessità di alcune particolari riforme monetarie e fiscali, e credette che il fascismo italiano fosse orientato verso la loro progressiva attuazione. All'atto pratico, ciò non era vero in alcun modo, ma la realtà effettiva della politica non intaccò mai la convinzione poundiana, che Mussolini fosse un economista di genio". See Zapponi, p. 11; translated by the authors.

[4] It is difficult to precisely establish exactly the number of Pound's broadcasts—some are longer radio speeches, others merely slogans that may, or may not, have ultimately been broadcast—although the Pound archive at Yale's Beinecke Library contains more than 8 boxes of radio material. For further discussion on this issue, see Matthew Feldman, *Ezra Pound's Fascist Propaganda, 1935-45* (Basingstoke: Palgrave, 2013), pp. 65-79.

[5] Ezra Pound, "Brain Trust: Second Spasm" (31 May 1942) in Ezra Pound, *"Ezra Pound Speaking": Radio Speeches of World War II*, edited by Leonard W. Doob (Westport, CT: Greenwood, 1978), #43.

[6] Ezra Pound was interned in St. Elizabeths psychiatric hospital 'a few days before Christmas of 1945', his charge was dismissed on 18 April 1958, and he was formally officially released on 7 May of that year. For further details, see John Tytell, *Ezra Pound: The Solitary Volcano* (New York: Anchor, 1987), 289, 326.

[7] "Pound, In Italy, Gives Fascist Salute; Calls United States an 'Insane Asylum'." *The New York Times* 10 July 1958. The image is a screenshot taken by the authors from http://www.artistipercasapound.org. Artisti per CasaPound, 2 Jan. 2012. Web. 18 Nov. 2014. http://www.artistipercasapound.org/index.php?s=zentropa.

[8] John Drummond to Ezra Pound, 5 June 1958, in "Ezra Pound Papers", Beinecke Rare Book and Manuscript Library, Library, Yale University, YCAL MSS 43 Box 13, folder 615.

[9] Humphrey Carpenter, *Ezra Pound: A Serious Character* (London: Faber and Faber, 1988), pp. 873–4.

[10] Pound had been in contact with the British Union of Fascists from 1934, as shown in his correspondence with, amongst others, the chief propagandist for the BUF, Alexander Raven Thomson. Box 52, folders 2338-2353. YCAL MSS 43 Ezra Pound Papers. Beinecke Rare Book and Manuscript Library, Library, Yale University. For an overview of this correspondence: Andrea Rinaldi, "Tracking Fascism Across Boundaries: The Ezra Pound/Alexander

Raven Thomson Correspondence 1934-1940." http://backdoorbroadcasting.net. Proc. of British Fascism, Anti-Fascism and Jewish Defence, The Wiener Library, London. Academic Podcasts, 10 Mar. 2013. Web. 15 Nov. 2014. http://backdoorbroadcasting.net/2013/03/andrea-rinaldi-tracking-fascism-across-boundaries-the-ezra-poundalexander-raven-thomson-correspondence-1934-1940/.

[11] For more on the extreme right in Europe during this period, see Stephen Dorril, "The Neo-Fascist Internationals," *Blackshirt: Sir Oswald Mosley and British Fascism* (London: Penguin, 2007), 594-612.

[12] See: Tom Kington, "Ezra Pound's Daughter Fights to Wrest the Renegade Poet's Legacy from Fascists," *The Guardian*, 14 Jan. 2012. Web. 15 Nov. 2014. http://www.theguardian.com/world/2012/jan/14/ezra-pound-daughter-fascism; Mary de Rachewiltz, "Giù le mani da mio padre Ezra Pound." Interview by Breda Marzio, *Il Corriere della sera* [Milan] 1 Apr. 2010: 44-45. *Archiviostorico IlCorriere.it*. Web. 15 Nov. 2014. http://archiviostorico.corriere.it/2010/aprile/01/Giu_mani_mio_padre_Ezra_co_9_100401073.shtml.

[13] See John Lauber, "Pound's 'Cantos': A Fascist Epic," *Journal of American Studies* 12.1 (1978): 3-21. *JSTOR*. Web. 16 Nov. 2014. http://www.jstor.org/stable/10.2307/27553361?ref=no-x-route:e81bbd5e02a4b78976c21d2d20334d2f.

[14] In Pound's words: "If a man isn't willing to take some risk for his opinions, either his opinions are no good or he's no good." Cited in Charles Norman, "The Case for and Against Ezra Pound," *PM* (25 Nov. 1945), online at: www.fultonhistory.com/Newspaper%2018/New%20York%20NY%20PM%20%20Daily/New%20York%20NY%20PM%20Daily%201945/New%20York%20NY%20PM%20Daily%201945%20-%203996.pdf. I am grateful to Archie Henderson for his assistance with this reference.

[15] There are many online examples of extreme right-wing websites exalting Pound's life. A leading example is the homepage of CasaPound Italia, the neo-fascist movement discussed below, which is dedicated to Pound, and where the *Cantos* are not even mentioned, see for example: CasaPound Italia. Web. 17 Nov. 2014. http://www.casapounditalia.org/p/ezra-pound.html. On the relevance of Pound's life on post-war fascists in the US, especially neo-Nazism, see: Carlo Pacelli, "Ezra Skinhead: The Cantos as 'The Anthem of Fascism'", *Flashpoint*. Web. 17 Nov. 2014. http://www.flashpointmag.com/skin.htm.

[16] For further discussion of these texts—including the publication of "Canto CI" in *The European*, see Matthew Feldman, "Ezra Pound's Political Faith from First to Second Generation; Or, 'It Is 1956 Fascism'", Erik Tonning, Matthew Feldman, and David Addyman (eds.), *Modernism, Christianity and Apocalypse* (Leiden: Brill, 2014), Ch. 15.

[17] Graham Macklin, *Very Deeply Dyed in Black: Sir Oswald Mosley and the Resurrection of Fascism after 1945* (London: I.B. Tauris, 2007), pp. 135-136.

[18] Pound, Ezra, trans. "In Captivity: Notebook of Thoughts in Ponza and La Maddelena." *Edge* 4 (1957): 10-26. Noel Stock, *The Life of Ezra Pound* (London: Routledge and K. Paul, 1970), 444. Ezra Pound, *"I Cease Not to Yowl": Ezra Pound's Letters to Olivia Rossetti Agresti*, ed. Demetres P. Tryphonopoulos and Leon Surette (Urbana: U of Illinois, 1998), 251-253.

[19] Tytell asserts the "couple" of *The Cantos* Pound included in the second volume he wrote while he was hold captive in St. Elizabeths Hospital (the volume known as *Thrones*), were first published by *The European*; see Tytell, *Ezra Pound: The Solitary Volcano*, 329. Kerry Bolton, "Ezra Pound." *Oswald Mosley RSS*. N.p., n.d. Web. 16 Nov. 2014. http://www.oswaldmosley.com/ezra-pound. For more on Bolton's extreme right past—including stints with the New Zealand National Front and the short-lived New Zealand Fascist Union—see Paul Spoonley, *The Politics of Nostalgia: Racism and the Extreme Right in New Zealand* (Palmerston North, N.Z.: Dunmore, 1987), 167-171. For greater detail on Bolton's activities in

New Zealand, see the contentious University of Waikato Master's thesis from 2008 by W.R. van Leeuwen, "Dreamers of the Dark: Kerry Bolton and the Order of the Left Hand Path, a Case-study of a Satanic Neo-Nazi Society", listing fully 9 publications by Pound for sale by Bolton's Renaissance Press. See also: K. R. Bolton, *Thinkers of the Right: Challenging Materialism* (Luton: Luton Publications, 2002), containing chapters on, amongst others, Ezra Pound, Marinetti, D'Annunzio, Knut Hamsun, Oswald Spengler and Julius Evola.

[20] US Armed Force. *Ezra Pound 1945 May 26*. Digital image. Web. 18 Nov. 2014. http://it.wikipedia.org/wiki/Ezra_Pound#mediaviewer/File:Ezra_Pound_1945_May_26_mug_shot.jpg.

[21] See www.eustacemullins.us; for further online claims regarding the connections between Pound and Mullins, see the far-right publication *The Occidental Quarterly*; homage to the latter in the wake of his 2010 death: Beatrice Mott, "This Difficult Individual Eustace Mullins—and the Remarkable Ezra Pound," now in *Occidental Observer*. 20 Mar. 2010. Web. 18 Nov. 2014. http://www.theoccidentalobserver.net/authors/Mott-Mullins.html.

[22] Eustace Mullins, *The Secrets of the Federal Reserve*, online at: www.arcticbeacon.com/books/Eustace_Mullins-SECRETS_of_the_Federal_Reserve_Bank.pdf (last accessed 24 April 2014), 85.

[23] Eustace Mullins, *Mullins' New History of the Jews* (Staunton, The International Institute of Jewish Studies, 2007), 101.

[24] For further details see, amongst other readily available sources, "Barnes Review," *http://www.splcenter.org*. The Southern Poverty Law Center, n.d. Web. 17 Nov. 2014. http://www.splcenter.org/get-informed/intelligence-files/groups/barnes-review; "one of the most virulently anti-Semitic organisations around […embracing] antigovernment extremists, anti-Semites, white supremacists, and racist conspiracy theorists'".

[25] Christopher Hitchens, "The New Anti-Semitism? How Ancient Prejudice and Outright Hostility Have Re-Emerged Since the Nuremberg Trials", *The Times Literary Supplement*, 19 November 2008: www.the-tls.co.uk/tls/public/article758321.ece (last accessed 24 April 2014).

[26] George Michael, *Willis Carto and the American Far Right* (Gainesville, FL: University of Florida Press, 2008), 154. Further highlighting Carto's interest in a text from 1996, containing a reference to Pound—sandwiched between the names of Father Charles Coughlin and Eustace Mullins—amongst the 'Great Americans Who Understood Money': A Special Report On The Bogus Budget From. "8 Reasons Why the Budget Is a Fraud." *American Free Press Newspaper* (n.d.): *http://americanfreepress.net*. Web. 17 Nov. 2014. http://www.americanfreepress.net/Eight_Reasons_Supplement_2.pdf. The authors are grateful to Archie Henderson for his assistance with both this and the in text reference.

[27] George Michael, "Michael Collins Piper: An American Far Right Emissary to the—Islamic World", *Totalitarian Movements and Political Religions*, 9/1 (2008), 61-78 (at 61, 62), online at https://www.researchgate.net/publication/233199329_Michael_Collins_Piper_An_American_Far_Right_Emissary_to_the_Islamic_World.

[28] Michael Collins Piper, summary of *The New Babylon. Those Who Reign Supreme*, online at: www.amfirstbooks.com/catalog/product_info.php?products_id=54 (last accessed 24 April 2014).

[29] Collins and Mullins, *The Talk Show*. See www.mikepiperreport.com/Talk_Show_Archive/TalkShowIndex.htm (last accessed 24 April 2014).

[30] See www.theneworder.org (last accessed 24 April 2014).

[31] Roger Griffin and Matthew Feldman, *Fascism: Critical Concepts in Political Science*. Vol. I (London: Routledge, 2004); see also: Aristotle A. Kallis, Introduction. *The Fascism Reader* (London: Routledge, 2003), 1-42.

[32] For further details see: "New Order". *The New Order*. Matthias Koehl, n.d. Web. 17 Nov. 2014. http://www.theneworder.org/.
[33] Image scanned by the authors from a private copy.
[34] See 'National-Socialist Unity'. *World Union of National Socialists Membership Directory: W.U.N.S.* N.p., n.d. Web. 17 Nov. 2014. http://nationalsocialist.net/members.htm; "NASKA PARTY." *NASKA PARTY*. N.p., 20 Apr. 2006. Web. 17 Nov. 2014. http://www.naskaparty88.blogspot.no/.
[35] Roger Griffin, "Europe for the Europeans: Fascist Myths of the European New Order 1922–1992", in Matthew Feldman (ed.), *A Fascist Century: Essays by Roger Griffin* (Basingstoke: Palgrave, 2008), 166.
[36] Pierre-André Taguieff, "Discussion or Inquisition: The Case of Alain de Benoist", *Telos*, 98–9 (1993/1994), 54; see also: Tamir Bar-On, *Where Have All the Fascists Gone?* (Aldershot, England: Ashgate, 2007); and Tamir Bar-On, *Rethinking the French New Right: Alternatives to Modernity* (London: Routledge, 2013).
[37] See Matthew Feldman, "The 'Pound Case' in Historical Perspective: An Archival Overview", *Journal of Modern Literature* 35.2 (2012): 83-97.
[38] Ezra Pound, "Author Archives: Ezra Pound", *CounterCurrents Publishing Posts by Ezra Pound*. Ed. Greg Johnson. Counter-Currents Publishing, n.d. Web. 17 Nov. 2014. http://www.counter-currents.com/author/epound/.
[39] Ezra Pound, "Gold and Work," *CounterCurrents Publishing*. Ed. Greg Johnson. N.p., 4 Nov. 2013. Web. 17 Nov. 2014. http://www.counter-currents.com/2013/11/gold-and-work/#more-43280 with editor's notes. For details of the British and Italian fascist context of Pound's 1930s publications, see Feldman, *Ezra Pound's Fascist Propaganda, 1935-45*, chs. 3 and 7.
[40] Federico Finchelstein, "On Fascist Ideology", *Constellations* 15/3 (2008), 321.
[41] Anton Shekhovtsov, "European Far-Right Music and its Enemies", in Ruth Wodak and John E. Richardson (eds.), *Analysing Fascist Discourse: European Fascism in Talk and Text* (London: Routledge, 2013), 279; for further details on Southgate's 'metapolitical' music, see: Anton Shekhovtsov, "Apoliteic Music: Neo-Folk, Martial Industrial and 'metapolitical fascism'", *Patterns of Prejudice* 43.5 (Dec. 2009): 431-57. For a very good introduction to Southgate's far-right politics see: Strelnikov, "Troy Southgate, the New Right and Old Nazis", *Who Makes the Nazis?* N.p., 26 Nov. 2010. Web. 17 Nov. 2014. http://www.whomakesthenazis.com/2010/11/troy-southgate-new-right-and-old-nazis.html.
[42] Jonathan Bowden, "Revolutionary Conservative". Interview by Troy Southgate. *http://www.wermodandwermod.com*. Wermod and Wermod Publishing Group, 27 Oct. 2010. Web. 17 Nov. 2014. http://www.wermodandwermod.com/newsitems/news271020101553.html.
[43] Jonathan Bowden, "Tom Sunić Interviews Jonathan Bowden (Transcript)". Interview by Tom Sunić. *http://www.counter-currents.com*. CounterCurrents Publishing, n.d. Web. 17 Nov. 2014. http://www.counter-currents.com/2013/12/tom-sunic-interviews-jonathan-bowden-transcript.
[44] Jonathan Bowden, "Ezra Pound". *http://www.counter-currents.com*. CounterCurrents Publishing, 24 Jan. 2014. Web. 17 Nov. 2014. http://www.counter-currents.com/2014/01/jonathan-bowden-on-ezra-pound.
[45] https://web.archive.org/web/20120118183208/http://www.arktos.com/thoughts-and-perspectives-pound.html. Web. 22 Feb. 2020.
[46] https://web.archive.org/web/20150307055213/http://www.arktos.com/thoughts-and-perspectives-bowden.html. Web. 22 Feb. 2020.
[47] https://web.archive.org/web/20120126204345/http://www.arktos.com/evola-thoughts-perspectives.html. Web. 22 Feb. 2020.

[48] https://web.archive.org/web/20120126215345/http://www.arktos.com/thoughts-and-perspectives-codreanu.html. Web. 22 Feb. 2020.
[49] https://web.archive.org/web/20150308092407/http://www.arktos.com/thoughts-and-perspectives-junger.html. Web. 22 Feb. 2020.
[50] https://web.archive.org/web/20150308094806/http://www.arktos.com/thoughts-and-perspectives-mishima.html. Web. 22 Feb. 2020.
[51] For further details: "L'economia Secondo Ezra Pound." *http://nazionalanarchismo.jimdo.com*. Nazional-Anarchismo, n.d. Web. 17 Nov. 2014. http://nazionalanarchismo.jimdo.com/economia/.
[52] "Art. 270-bis (Associazioni con finalità di terrorismo anche internazionale o di eversione dell'ordine democratico).—Chiunque promuove, costituisce, organizza, dirige o finanzia associazioni che si propongono il compimento di atti di violenza con finalità di terrorismo o di eversione dell'ordine democratico è punito con la reclusione da sette a quindici anni. Chiunque partecipa a tali associazioni è punito con la reclusione da cinque a dieci anni." ["Article 270-bis (Associations for purposes of terrorism including international or for subversion of the democratic order).—Whoever promotes, sets up, organizes, manages or finances associations whose purpose is the committing of acts of violence for terrorist ends or for subversion of the democratic order is punishable by imprisonment from seven to fifteen years. Whoever takes part in such associations is punishable by imprisonment from five to ten years."] See https://www.gazzettaufficiale.it/atto/serie_generale/caricaArticoloDefault/originario?atto.dataPubblicazioneGazzetta=2001-12-18&atto.codiceRedazionale=01A13875&atto.tipoProvvedimento=TESTO%20COORDINATO%20DEL%20DECRETO-LEGGE and https://www.imolin.org/doc/amlid/Italy/Italy_Law_438_of_2001.pdf. Web. 22 Feb. 2020.
[53] Zetazeroalfa. *Santa Teppa*. Rupe Tarpea, n.d. *http://archiviononconforme.blogspot.no*. Web. 17 Nov. 2014. http://archiviononconforme.blogspot.no/2008/03/zetazeroalfa-santa-teppa.html; Zetazeroalfa. *Bomber Nero*. Rupe Tarpea, n.d. *http://archiviononconforme.blogspot.no*. Web. 17 Nov. 2014. http://archiviononconforme.blogspot.no/2008/04/270-bis-bomber-nero.html.
[54] For further details on CPI's far-right activities see, for instance, the biography of the movement written by one of its activists: Domenico Di Tullio, *Nessun dolore* (Milano: Rizzoli, 2010). According to the newspaper *Il Fatto Quotidiano*, CPI has more than 4,000 activists and 40 regional parliamentary: "CasaPound, Il Reportage Su Le Monde—Il Fatto Quotidiano." *http://www.ilfattoquotidiano.it*. *Il Fatto Quotidiano*, 19 May 2014. Web. 17 Nov. 2014. http://www.ilfattoquotidiano.it/2014/05/19/casapound-il-reportage-su-le-monde/990388/. The movement caught the attention of the international press too, with the French newspaper *Le Monde* recently filing a large report: "CasaPound, Sous la carapace du nouveau fascisme italien," *Le Monde.fr*. *Le Monde*, 4 Apr. 2014. Web. 17 Nov. 2014. http://www.lemonde.fr/monde-academie/visuel/2014/04/04/casapound-sous-la-carapace-du-nouveau-fascisme-italien_4395746_1752655.html. For a more detailed sociological study on CPI, see: Daniele Di Nunzio and Emanuele Toscano, *Dentro e fuori CasaPound: Capire il fascismo del Terzo Millennio* (Roma: Armando, 2011); the authors also created a blog: Daniele Di Nunzio and Emanuele Toscano. Web log post. *Dentro e fuori CasaPound*. Wordpress, 28 Nov. 2011. Web. 17 Nov. 2014. http://dentroefuoricasapound.wordpress.com/. For CPI's political programme see: Italy. Ministry of Interior. *Programma Politico CasaPound Italia*. By CasaPound Italia. N.p.: n.p., n.d. *http://www.interno.gov.it/mininterno/export/sites/default/it/*. Web. 17 Nov. 2014. http://www.interno.gov.it/mininterno/export/sites/default/it/assets/files/25_elezioni/17_CASAPOUND_ITALIA.PDF/mininterno/export/sites/default/it/assets/files/25_elezioni/17_CASAPOUND_ITALIA.PDF. For an Anglophone analysis of CasaPound

Italia, see: Anna Castriota and Matthew Feldman, "Fascism for the Third Millennium": An Overview of Language and Ideology in Italy's CasaPound Movement," *Doublespeak: The Rhetoric of the Far Right since 1945*, ed. Matthew Feldman and Paul Jackson (Stuttgart: ibidem, 2014), Ch. 11; Pietro Castelli Gattinara, Caterina Froio, and Matteo Albanese, "The Appeal of Neo-fascism in times of Crisis. The Experience of CasaPound Italia," *Journal of Comparative Fascist Studies* 2 (2013): 234-58; Pietro Castelli Gattinara and Caterina Froio, "Discourse and Practice of Violence in the Italian Extreme Right: Frames, Symbols, and Identity-Building in CasaPound Italia," *International Journal of Conflict and Violence* 8.1 (2014): 154-170, online at https://spire.sciencespo.fr/hdl:/2441/6aj2qf82mq9q191mahpr2fft 06/resources/2014-discourse-and-practice-of-violence-in-the-italian-extreme-right.pdf; Jamie Bartlett, Jonathan Birdwell, and Mark Littler, "The Rise of Populism in Europe Can Be Traced through Online Behaviour...". *http://www.demos.co.uk*. DEMOS, n.d. Web. 17 Nov. 2014. http%3A%2F%2Fwww.demos.co.uk%2Ffiles%2FDemos_OSIPOP_Book-web_03.pdf %3F1320601634.

[55] Downloaded from http://204.45.55.21/~casapoun/images/unanazione.pdf (last accessed 24 April 2014).

[56] Ezra Pound, *Lavoro ed usura: tre saggi* (Milan: All'insegna del pesce d'oro, 1954), 106–7.

[57] Stephan Faris, "A Poet's Legacy: As Neo-Fascists Claim Ezra Pound, His Family Says, 'Hands Off'", *Time*. Time Inc., 31 Jan. 2012. Web. 17 Nov. 2014. http://content.time.com/time/world/article/0,8599,2105702,00.html.

[58] Alexander Baron, *Eustace Clarence Mullins: Anti-Semitic Propagandist or Iconoclast?: The World's Premier Conspiracy Historian on the Jews, the Fed and the "New World Order": Including Notes on "Global Deception"*, January 1993 (London: InfoText Manuscripts, 1995), Ch .17 and 20.

[59] Adriano Scianca, *Ezra Fa Surf. Come e perché il pensiero di Pound salverà il mondo* (Milan: ZERO91, 2013). For the quote see: Introduction. *http://www.zero91.com*. ZERO91. Web. 17 Nov. 2014. http://www.zero91.com/prossime-uscite/13-libri/254-ezra-fa-surf-adriano-scianca.html.

[60] Adriano Scianca, "Ezra fa surf, il nuovo libro di Adriano Scianca." Interview. *Affaritaliani.it*. N.p., 4 Dec. 2013. Web. 17 Nov. 2014. http://www.affaritaliani.it/culturaspettacoli/ezra-fa-surf-il-nuovo-libro-di-adriano-scianca.html.

[61] See *www.ideodromocasapound.org*. CasaPound Italia, n.d. Web. 14 Apr. 2014. www.ideodromocasapound.org%2F%3Fp%3D1031. (This site belongs now to another company, the 'Ideodromo' now exists only as a page on Facebook).

[62] Today in: Ezra Pound, *Ezra Pound's Poetry and Prose: Contributions to Periodicals*, ed. Lea Baechler, A. Walton Litz, and James Longenbach (New York: Garland, 1991), Vol VI, 316. In December 1941, the Grand Mufti of Jerusalem told Hitler, to the latter's astonishment, "The chosen people of God are not the chosen people, but the chosen race and that blood carries the soul. And this chosen race must keep its blood pure. It must not mix its blood with non-Jews, the foreigners, the subhuman beasts called the goyim, are inferior to the Jewish master race. The genocide order of God in the fifth book of Moses and in the book of Joshua. The race laws of Ezra and Ishmael. All of these things are in the Old Testament." Cited in George Michael, *The Enemy of My Enemy: The Alarming Convergence of Militant Islam and the Extreme Right* (Lawrence, Kan.: University Press of Kansas, 2006), pp. 115-16.

[63] Tamir Bar-On, *Rethinking the French New Right: Alternatives to Modernity* (London: Routledge, 2013).

[64] Pierre-André Taguieff, *The Force of Prejudice: On Racism and Its Doubles* (Minneapolis, MN: U of Minnesota Press, 2001)

65 Pietrangelo Buttafuoco, "Dieci domande a Pietrangelo Buttafuoco." Interview by Filippo Giunta. *Siciliaevents.it.* Web. 14 Apr. 2014, online at: https://web.archive.org/web/200 30504041900/http://www.siciliaevents.it/SEvents/number/00/n1/Dieci%20domande%20a%20Pietrangelo%20Buttafuoco.htm.
66 Pietrangelo Buttafuoco, "Serve il coraggio di Pound per salvare tutto il mondo." *http://www.ilgiornale.it. Il Giornale*, 18 Sept. 2013. Web. 17 Nov. 2014. http://www.ilgiornale.it/news/cultura/serve-coraggio-pound-salvare-tutto-mondo-sei-stagioni-951110.html.
67 For the entire *Canto XCVII* see: Ezra Pound, *The Cantos of Ezra Pound* (New York: New Directions, 1970), 688-703.
68 Buttafuoco, op. cit.
69 For an excerpt from Basil Bunting see: Basil Bunting, "On the Flyleaf of Pound's Cantos." *Poetryarchive.org.* The Poetry Archive, n.d. Web. 17 Nov. 2014. http://www.poetryarchive.org/poem/flyleaf-pounds-cantos.

8. "Fascism for the Third Millennium": An Overview of Language and Ideology in Italy's CasaPound Movement

Anna Castriota and Matthew Feldman[1]

> We want to become protagonists of our times and not just some extras in a show whose script has already been written, giving us the part of being evil, subversives, fanatical. We will please our enemies if we would behave like this. We are not going to hide in the basements to conspire in the shadow. Commander D'Annunzio, accused of a plot against the regime, of which he was a fierce adversary, answered: "I dare, not conspire." This is also our motto.

Introduction: 'Set keel to breakers, forth on the godly sea'[2]

At first sight, CasaPound seems a raft of contradictions. On one hand, this is an Italian far-right movement whose loosely affiliated supporters, according to the first Anglophone report on their online profile, are more likely to advocate violence than any other 'populist group' in contemporary Europe.[3] On the other hand, this still-predominately social movement blossomed via traditionally left-wing housing occupations; and moreover, owes its name to the (in)famous American poet, Ezra Pound: hardly traditional fare for the notoriously influential far-right in postwar Italy. Furthermore, CasaPound openly praises Mussolini and advocates a return to Italian Fascism, yet at the same time disseminates its message and organises its activities chiefly through new media technologies. So just what gives with CasaPound?

This lack of clarity extends to the few commentators who have thus far tried to explain CasaPound. According to the Swiss historian Aram Mattioli, for instance, CasaPound should be considered within the context of flourishing radical right groups in Italy following the collapse of the Soviet Union and the close of Italian First Republic in the first half of the 1990s.[4] To be sure, the demise of communism and the Italian political scandal dubbed 'Mani Pulite [Clean Hands]' created a completely new scenario in the country, doubtless contributing to the rise of a populist far-right in Italy over the last generation.[5] In stark contrast, sociologists Daniele di Nunzio and Emilio Toscano note the originality of CasaPound with respect to Italian far-right groups this century: 'From the sociological analysis here, the distance of CasaPound from the cultural references, political and social composition of the Italian radical right emerges clearly, by their proposing a new interpretation of fascism aimed to overcome the dichotomy right-left'.[6] So which is it? Or can it be both: that CasaPound is part and parcel of Italy's well-entrenched far-right; *and* that the movement's 'originality' marks it out as something different from Italian far-right movements like the Northern League [Lega Nord; LN]; the National Alliance [Alleanza Nazionale; AN, before 1995 the influential MSI, or Movimento Sociale Italiano]; and most recently, the Tricolored Flame [Movimento Sociale-Fiamma Tricolore; MS-FT]?[7]

As perhaps Italy's most recent and novel in a rash of post-, neo- and unashamedly fascist movements since 1945—the year that itself concluded nearly 23 years of political domination by Benito Mussolini's Italian Fascists [Partito Nazionale Fascista, or PNF]—CasaPound first 'officially' appeared in 2003 under the leadership of the long-time far-right activist and musician, Gianluca Iannone, a self-defined 'fascist of the third millennium'. For all the movement's socio-political attempts to 'Make it New', to use Ezra Pound's celebrated advice for modernist cultural production, twentieth century precursors and influences are clearly apparent over the first decade of CasaPound's development. In this respect, it bears noting that Ezra Pound's catchphrase was itself adapted from a washbasin inscription by Chinese emperor Tching Tang of the Shang dynasty (1766–1753 BC): 'Make it new day by day make it new'.[8] So, too, with CasaPound's relationship with fascism in Italy, both before and after the watershed year of 1945: there is little of substance that is new here under the Italian sun.

As suggested by the above, this chapter provides a thematic overview of the CasaPound movement, paying especial attention to its use of language along the way—particularly that of Iannone, unmistakably the movement's 'charismatic personality'. That a canonical poet-turned-fascist is 'name-checked' in the movement's very title, moreover, suggests the utility of this discursive approach.[9] That the role of language, since time immemorial a reservoir for poets and writers, was key to Pound himself is announced, for instance, in his 'Addendum for C' notes toward his self-defined 'epic poem including history', *The Cantos*:

> "A pity that poets have used symbol and metaphor
> and no man learned anything from them
> for their speaking in figures."[10]

Pound composed these lines during WWII, when his support of Fascism facilitated many hundreds of pro-Axis radio scripts; in turn leading to his indictment for treason by the US government. This was not, of course, lost on CasaPound's founder; for instance, in an interview from 2012:

> Ezra Pound was a poet, an economist and an artist. Ezra Pound was a revolutionary and a fascist. Ezra Pound had to suffer for his ideas, he was sent to jail for ten years to make him stop speaking. We see in Ezra Pound a free man who paid for his ideas; he is a symbol of the "democratic views" of the winners.[11]

These 'ideas' included advocating a spiritual and economic vision of fascist ideology and, without doubt, in keeping with Axis wartime propaganda, anti-Semitism was a major part of Pound's rhetoric at this time. Revealingly, the symbol referred to in the 1941 fragment cited above was *'neschek'*—'the crawling evil / slime, the corrupter of all things'—an ancient Jewish word for usury; by that time closely connected in both Pound's poetry and wartime broadcasts, with the latter bringing about treason charges in July 1943. Considering the prominence of the 'Pound Case' during these years and, indeed, since, scholars have exhaustively analyzed the depths and drivers of Pound's often-scurrilous anti-Semitism.[12] To cite but three excerpts published as long ago as 1976—taken from literally scores contained in Pound's 1,516 page FBI file—in his shortwave broadcasts from Radio Rome to the US and UK, Pound announced:

> Nothing can save you, save a purge. Nothing can save you, save an affirmation that you are English. Hore-Belisha is not. Isaacs is not. No Sassoon is an Englishman racially. No Rothschild is English, no Streiker is English, no Roosevelt is English, no Baruch, Morgenthau, Cohen, Lehman, Warburg, Kuhn, Kahn, Schiff, Sieff or Solomon was ever yet born Anglo-Saxon. And it is for this filth that you fight. (15 March 1942)

> Don't start a pogrom. That is, not an old style killing of small Jews. That system is no good, whatever. Of course, if some man had a stroke of genius, and could start a pogrom at the top. (30 April 1942)

> Just which of you are free from Jewish influence? Just which political and business groups are free from Jew influence, from Jew control? Who holds the mortgage, who is the dominating director? (19 March 1943)[13]

Obviously, Pound's anti-Semitism was neither a debatable case like, say, T.S. Eliot's; nor a purely literary one, as with J.F. Céline. Instead, this was Nazi-style anti-Semitism, enthusiastically undertaken for Fascism throughout the Holocaust. Nonetheless, in the aforementioned interview with the founder of CasaPound, Iannone made this remarkable claim about Pound's anti-Semitism:

> To associate Ezra Pound and anti-Semitism is an absolute twist. It is the same for CasaPound, it makes no sense. It is true that we are against Israel['s] politics towards Palestinians, against the bombing of civilians, and the embargo on international aid. To say so does not mean to be anti-Semitic, it means analyzing facts.[14]

As this single example highlights, then, language can be used as much to conceal as clarify. In keeping with many Italian far-right movements since the watershed of 1945, moreover, this is of particular relevance to CasaPound—even if its online presence and the social movement aspects of its organization clearly mark it out as a manifestation of the European 'new far right'[15]—indeed, more specifically as a kind of 'Fascism for the third millennium'. Before moving on to a closer examination of CasaPound, however, a brief consideration of this term is in order.

In twenty-first century Italy there remain several 'fascist', 'neo-fascist' and even 'post-fascist' political movements. This spectrum is broad enough to range from legitimate *democratic* political parties sitting in Parliament to far more *revolutionary* expressions of fascist ideology. This may seem to the observer a kind of *contradictio in terminis*, or may at least signify a failure in the process of de-fascistization that the country went through after WWII.[16] This is borne out by an interview with the far-right journalist, Marcello Veneziani, in response to one of the authors' questions about how it was possible to have an openly xenophobic party like Lega Nord sitting in the Italian parliament. Veneziani replied that they were 'post-fascists' or 'fascists of the third millennium', who believed in an exclusive form of democracy rather than an inclusive one.[17] Lega Nord is not alone in this approach; there are other 'post-fascist' movements in Italy which similarly propose a new version of Fascist ideas in an attempt not simply to re-affirm their shared ideology but, rather, to revitalize—in a different format and context—the same ideological core; sometimes expressed as a 'return to the future'.[18]

In much the same way, CasaPound reveals key elements of continuity with the past *as well as* updating core fascist concepts and forms of self-representation. Especially relevant in terms of the latter is the prominent use of the new media (notably the internet) not only for organisational messages and discussion but also for the cultural dissemination of the arts, music, and so on. Yet whatever its audiovisual effectiveness, even a cursory analysis of the movement reveals a strong impulse to openly declare their radical ideological and political inclinations. This, too, is correspondingly borne out in another interview with Iannone from late 2011.

> CasaPound is based around four principles: culture, solidarity, sport and (obviously) politics. These four domains can be seen as social actions in one way or another. CPI organize book presentations, plays, concerts, debates about movies and has a monthly publication (Occidentale) [....] We try to communicate in a radical mode and renew our dream. We want to launch it and give it a new spin. It could be through music or art.[19]

CasaPound Italia: '"Noi ci facciam scannar per Mussolini"'

'CasaPound Italia', to give the movement its full name (often abbreviated as CPI, as above), is an association or movement of recent formation. In fact, the movement's 'unofficial' birth occurred on 12 July 2002, when a group of well-known far-right activists occupied a long-empty public building in order to house some of those unable to rent or own. As is usually reported in media accounts of Casa-Pound, this type of squatting is generally regarded as 'socialist', and has long been the preserve of radical left wing groups.[20] The occupied building in Rome was renamed 'CasaMontag'—after Guy Montag, protagonist of Ray Bradbury's science fiction novel *Fahrenheit 451*—first giving rise to what were called ONCs [Occupazioni Non Conformi, or Non-conformist occupations]. On 26 December 2003, the same group then occupied a building on Via Napoleone in Rome and renamed it 'CasaPound Italia'. Interestingly, in the movement's own account of its origins on its website, the illegal occupation of derelict buildings is referred to as 'mine vaganti [loose cannon]' operations. Here too, stress is placed upon the voluntarism of the movement and its 'non-conformist' stance. In this sense, CasaPound is clearly different from more party-political tendencies within the Italian far-right. In fact, Iannone and the movement largely reject any association with established far-right groups, claiming to operate on a different level:

> Q: What kind of relationship does CasaPound have with the other parties of the so-called 'Radical Right'?
> A: CPI is external to and independent of any party. Being independent means that we can dialogue and cooperate with any party which is willing to have an honest debate, whether this party would be internal or external to the 'Radical Right'.[21]

Here again, language plays its part in casting the movement as 'independent'. In reinforcing this sense of a seemingly amorphous political grouping, another interview by Iannone responds directly to the charge that CasaPound is a far-right organization:

> First of all, linking CP to the right wing is a bit restrictive. CasaPound Italia is a political movement organised as an association for social promotion. It starts from the right and goes through the entire political panorama. Right or Left are two old visions of politics; we need to give birth to a new synthesis.[22]

In making such declarations of political and ideological neutrality, the group's 'frontstage' rhetoric aims to portray an openness toward those with different ideas and perspectives. Yet in also signalling to a more hardcore 'backstage', the attentive reader can detect in Iannone's characterization of CasaPound as transcending the right and left a hallmark of fascism's self-representation. Fascism was identified by the late, brilliant George Mosse, as 'a revolution attempting to find a 'Third Way' between Marxism and capitalism'.[23] These ideas were clearly delineated as long ago as Benito Mussolini and Giovanni Gentile's widely-circulated, 1932 *Enciclopedia Italiana* entry for 'The Doctrine of Fascism':

> Fascism is totalitarian, and the Fascist State, the synthesis and unity of all values, interprets, develops, and gives strength to the whole life of the people... Therefore Fascism is opposed to Socialism, which confines the movement of history within the class struggle [....] Fascism is opposed to Democracy, which equates the nation to the majority, allowing it to the level of that majority.[24]

Correspondingly, and as proclaimed by CasaPound's official website, the idea of a movement approaching political action like the postwar Italian left was initially conceived in 1997, when a group of far-right activists frequenting the neo-fascist pub 'The Cutty Sark' in Rome decided to create a more structured political identity for their meetings. The hagiographical account on CasaPound's website further announces that, far from being a ragtag collection of neo-Nazis or skinheads, these activists were instead a 'group of rebel souls'.[25] CasaPound's opaque use of the expression 'rebel souls' discursively appears non-political—simply referring to those rejecting the suggested socio-political conformity of contemporary Italy. However, from their own, sanitized history of the movement, it seems that the expression 'rebels' is an overture toward a broader section of 'non-conformist' society than that consisting simply of those defining themselves as 'fascists' or far-right supporters. The expression 'rebel souls' additionally recalls the enthusiasm and energy surrounding the avant-gardist movement in the years leading up to the Great War. Here too, another not-so-concealed fascist element may be identified. Published in 1909 by Filippo T. Marinetti, the first *Futurist Manifesto* advances strikingly similar views of 'freedom' and 'rebellion' to those found in CasaPound's official declarations.

Indeed, two groups stemming from the main movement of CasaPound bear close resemblance to Italian Futurism, an avant-garde movement that was, in many respects, the midwife of Mussolini's subsequent *Fascismo*. The first is called 'Turbodinamismo' [Turbodynamism], a group whose link appears on CasaPound's official webpage. Without mincing words, the Manifesto del Turbodinamismo proclaims that 'Turbodynamism is the glorification of the gratuitous, violent and inconsiderate gesture.'[26] In fact, the group's very name recalls central elements of the Futurist message: 'Except in struggle, there is no more beauty. No work without an aggressive character can be a masterpiece. Poetry must be conceived as a violent attack on unknown forces, to reduce and prostrate them before man.'[27] Both Italian manifestos, moreover, emphatically praise recourse to violent action as the privileged means of self-affirmation.

A second artistic sub-group deriving from CasaPound is named 'Artisti per CasaPound [Artists for CasaPound]'. Once more, there is a thread connecting Italian Fascism and Futurism: 'This group is a group of artists who express themselves in the arts projects devoted to the idea of beauty and freedom; they can only find such freedom of expression in the non-conformist culture always promoted by CP.'[28] A similar aim of creating a 'new man' able to rise above the constrictions of middle-class mediocrity is another commonplace in Fascism ideology; long ago articulated as the *homo fascistus* so dear to Mussolini. Fascist Party Secretary Achille Starace—who declared in November 1933 that 'Duce' could only be spelled in all capitals—phrased this myth of the *uomo nuovo* succinctly in a laudatory speech just before the outbreak of World War Two: "The creation of the man, of Mussolini's new Italian, capable of believing, of obeying, of fighting, has been our constant objective, towards which the Party has channeled all its forces."[29]

Yet another key continuity with Mussolini's Italy as updated by CasaPound is the importance of youth—the very name of Mussolini's Fascist Anthem ('*Giovinezza*'). Writing as Party Secretary for Mussolini's PNF in 1931, Giovanni Giuriati stressed: 'It is among the young that all the great movements in history have found their prophets, their soldiers, their martyrs. It is well known that the more life is held in contempt, the more value it acquires, and the young, since they are more prepared to embrace a faith are precisely for this reason more prepared to pay the final sacrifice for it.'[30] In turn, it is important to notice that the average age of a CasaPound member is between 18 and 30. This owes much to the movement's active promotion of social and cultural events, especially sport:

> CPI works on everything that concerns the life of our nation: from sport to solidarity, culture and of course politics. For sports, we have a soccer team and academy, we do hockey, rugby, skydiving, boxing, Brazilian jiu-jitsu, scuba diving, hiking groups, caving, climbing. For solidarity, we have first aid teams, we do fundraising activities for the Karen people, and we provide help to orphans and single-mums. A phone line called "Dillo to CasaPound" (tell it to CasaPound) is active 24/7 to give free advice on legal and tax issues. On the cultural front, we host authors and organize book presentations; we have an artist club, a theater school, free guitar, bass guitar and drum lessons, we created an artistic trend called Turbodinamismo, we have a publishing company, dozens of bookshops and websites. Politically we propose various laws like the Mutuo sociale (social mortgage), Tempo di essere Madri (Time to be a mother) or against water privatization and so many more. Speaking about CPI is never easy because all these things are CASAPOUND. All of these represent our challenges and projects for now and the millennium.[31]

Furthermore, Iannone is only in his mid-forties, and cultivates the image of youth as the lead singer in the movement's 'house band'. Indeed, one of the first acts in the movement's 'pre-history' was the 1997 formation of the punk band Zetazeroalfa. Given that, like sport, music typically regarded as a privileged tool of communication with young people, the presence of a populist rock band has undoubtedly contributed to the resonance of CasaPound's political message.

This valorisation of youth, moreover, is a constant trait. One of CasaPound's favored slogans is 'ho 17 anni per sempre [I am seventeen forever]', underscoring the ideological role of youth for the movement. Violently bearing this out is another practice as revealing as it is notorious: '*Cinghiamattanza*' (literally, belt-fighting). Iannone's band, Zetazeroalfa, plays a song aimed at whipping up frenetic energy in 'mosh pits' with the following lyrics:

> One, I take off the belt, Two, the dance will start, Three, I will get to choose my target, Four, Cinghiamattanza!... Here there is the whip, the room is on fire, the life of the Ardito is burning, you will yell Cinghiamattanza![32]

This practice has become a trademark for CasaPound's image, and even has an associated blogspot, declaring that 'Cinghiamattanza is a macabre dance that we have among camerati [*sic*], a physical expression of style and force. Cinghiamattanza is honour, is street fighting but with an ethics of its own; constructive confusion, sweat and will. Ultimately, Cinghiamattanza is an act of love.' After music performances or even belt-fighting tournaments, the injuries thus obtained are often exhibited online as quasi-'war' wounds (particularly evident through social networking sites, as well as www.youtube.com and a range of dedicated webpages).[33] On occasion, CasaPound's leadership tries to play down the culture of Cinghiamattanza, claiming it is merely a way for youths to channel their natural force and vitality. Yet whatever the frontstage presentation, in practice, Cinghiamattanza is also employed when members of CasaPound are involved in clashes with political opponents. Cinghiamattanza may thus be considered a twenty-first century version of castor oil.

Another characteristic revealing 'updated continuities' with the historical experience of Fascism in Italy is that of voluntarism and the cult of action. A similar impulse to radically effect change leads CasaPound's website to proclaim: 'To us politics is action, direct and popular participation is the most simple way to solve conflicts and social injustices.'[34] This stress upon politics as action recalls another core principle of Italian Fascism. This, too, can be traced to Iannone's band Zetazeroalfa; for instance, in the lyrics of the '*Nel Dubbio, Mena*' [When in doubt, just fight]:

> When in doubt, fight! I miss the synopsis, I miss the photocopy, I miss the pain of living, I miss the sunshine of the future, I miss what is right, I miss our world, I miss a new fridge and everything else, I miss also the hairdryer with whom I don't do a fuck, I please myself and then I am not longer embarrassed. No, don't be worried! In doubt, fight and you will see that you will live longer! No, don't be worried! In doubt fight and you will see that you will live longer, longer, longer!!!![35]

The lyrics express a *malaise de vivre* of youth and the failure of socialism (referred to as the 'sunshine of the future') and the bourgeois assumptions of capitalism (the fridge and the hairdryer). This homage to youth—to whom the song is clearly addressed—is not one of despair but instead an encouragement to activism. Correspondingly, the concluding verses of the song quite simply glorify violence; fighting is valorized in order to feel more alive, to live longer. In other words, the song is a hymn to the use of violence as an expression of vitalistic, youthful force, one that is considered a positive response to socio-political elements of the day. It is not quite Mussolini's favoured slogan '*Libro e moschetto—fascista perfetto*' [Book and rifle—perfect fascist], but the similarities are palpable.

More generally, CasaPound refers to Zetazeroalfa as a 'challenge to the world of the equals', that cornerstone of liberal democracy.[36] This objection is no mere anachronism of the movement, but is better understood in light of Mussolini's well-known criticism of democracy—advanced in the 1932 'Doctrine of Fascism', notes John Pollard, 'in the clearest terms, a rejection of the liberal-democratic doctrine of individual, imprescriptible human rights: 'The principle that society exists solely for the well-being and liberty of the individuals who compose it does not seem to fit with the laws of nature, laws which only take the species into consideration and sacrifice the individual.'[37] Understood in this sense, equality becomes little more than a 'false impression' provided by liberalism. Nor is the connection fanciful: Gianluca Iannone is among those creating an honour squad standing continuously outside Mussolini's tomb in his birthplace, the small town of Predappio.

In explicitly defining themselves as 'fascists', moreover, the documents from the Fascist era most frequently invoked by CasaPound are the *Carta del Lavoro* (*Labour Charter*, 1927) and the *Discorso di Verona* (*Verona Manifesto* for the Salò Republic, 1943). These two texts exemplify the Fascist 'third way' attempts at socialism for the nation and, despite being written sixteen years apart and in quite different historical circumstances, were nevertheless attempts to balance the social injustices in the Italian system. The 1927 *Carta*, for instance, represents an answer to the socialist and communist trade unions that had just been banned. The *Carta* thus superseded all prior laws used to regulate labour questions in Italy. The document is simple, containing an introduction and 18 points detailing the economic matters to be regulated. The *Verona Manifesto*, for its part, was proclaimed under Nazi occupation in Autumn 1943; it is in this respect less 'third way' than 'radical right'. More generally, in comparing the *Carta* and Mussolini's 1943 *Verona Manifesto* with the CasaPound political program, a number of interesting parallels arise. The latter declares: 'Because of its history and its destiny, Italy has to be again a forerunner within a Europe that has to be united, independent, sovereign, at peace and peaceful'.[38] Interestingly enough, this is directly evocative of the *Verona Manifesto*'s endorsement of 'the creation of a "European community" through the federation of all nations'.[39] Fascism's advocacy of a pan-European federation is an important aspect of CasaPound's vision—and a decidedly anti-EU one. In this connection, the movement's official website offers the following explanation for the name of CasaPound's monthly magazine, *L'Occidentale:* 'The West (Occidente), etymologically, means *sol occidens*, the setting sun. It is, historically and geopolitically, that strip of land born as a result of hate for Europe and which then reabsorbed the old continent with the sound of phosphorus bombs, imposing upon the world a regime made of arrogance, robbery and approval'.[40] Revealingly, *L'Occidentale*, a "magazine that has existed for 40 years"[41] with a long history of strong ties to Italian neo-fascism, lapsed before resuming publication under CasaPound.[42]

Yet in contrast, more difficult to pinpoint is the degree of xenophobia and racism—that hallmark of far-right movements in Europe for literally decades—advocated by CasaPound. The movement seeks to actively advance the notion that they are not racists at all. A good example highlighted on the movement's website is a 'mission' undertaken by CasaPound members to bring food, medicines and general relief to the Serbian enclaves in Kosovo. Importantly, the aid was addressed to the Christian Serbs and not, for instance, to Muslim Albanians in Kosovo. This is needed, CasaPound declares, because '[Serbian] villages, homes, schools, hospitals are 'hostages' of an Albanian electricity company which manages the distribution of electricity in the area.'[43] CasaPound's relief mission may thus be interpreted as an attempted defence of a white, Christian minority within an area of Muslim majority—a trend strikingly in keeping with the contemporary far-right across Europe. When challenged on controversial topics like religious tolerance or xenophobia, CasaPound's 'frontstage' answer seems one of openness to 'diversity'. Yet here too, careful reading suggests a language used to signal key 'backstage' fascist traits:

> Q: Is CasaPound a xenophobic movement? A: Absolutely not. Phobias are by their own definitions for all those weak intellects and fearful hearts. CPI wants to do an analysis [of the problem of immigration] and provide solutions, not feed obsessions. We want radical analysis and non-conformist solutions without looking for the simplest solution, or looking for scapegoats. We are not interested in a war between paupers, and the fears of the bourgeoisie. That said, this does not mean that our condemnation of mass migration, of the multi-racist society is any less strong.[44]

What is interesting to notice in the above passage is a conciliatory tone at the start, quickly followed by an affirmation of xenophobia. Use of the term 'multi-racist' rather than 'multi-racial' is not accidental, for 'multi-racist' underlines the notion that human groups can be neatly divided into 'races', which are ultimately better off remaining 'pure' rather than 'mixed'. This interpretation is supported by CasaPound's position on immigration, as set out in their political program:

> The infernal migratory mechanism is one of the main elements of loss of identity and social, cultural and existentialist impoverishment of all the populations involved in it, whether hosts or guests. In this system designed to kill peoples, there do not exist winners but only an elite of few private groups with their own ideological prejudices and an anti-national group with its own economic interests.[45]

Thus, the anti-immigration element is concealed by apparent compassion toward those migrating. Migration is therefore perceived as an impoverishment for different ethnic groups coming together. The associations or groups that tend to protect or insert the immigrants into the local culture are simply labelled as 'anti-national' (itself, arguably, another coded anti-Semitic reference). CasaPound's diagnosis of the problem of migration, no less than its solution, is simple:

> Against the infernal machine of the multi-racist society we propose the removal of the problems created by migration by means of: total blockade of the waves of immigrants; [...] cooperation with the economic areas outside Europe with a view to their development and liberation from the yoke of the multi-nationals; [...] support to all those extra-European identitarian movements that favour the resettlement of indigenous populations.[46]

The movement's program continues in much the same vein in recommending suspension of the Schengen agreement (allowing for the free circulation of European citizens). In reference to the recent immigration wave from Western Europe by recent EU accession states from Central and Eastern Europe, the program declares: 'An "internal Third World" cannot exist in Europe, which would export slaves and delinquents towards the most economically advanced areas of the continent.'[47] Once again, here the message appears encoded for, on a superficial reading, it looks like CasaPound takes a largely supportive attitude towards immigrants. Yet whatever the linguistic obfuscation, the 'help' on offer is toward repatriation of migrants to their native countries of origin, further underscoring CasaPound's views regarding the separation of peoples. It is not for nothing that the movement's symbol is a turtle: a creature always bringing along its own home.

In this respect, CasaPound's endorsement of so-called 'ethno-differentialism' is right out of the 'new far-right's' playbook. Summarizing this recent development in far-right propaganda, Steve Bastow notes that this view is 'presented as an anti-racist recognition of cultural difference. True racism, as the ND [Nouvelle Droite in France] also argues, is the attempt to integrate immigrants, undermining both cultures; that of host and of immigrant.[48] In this sense, as Pierre-André Taguieff has impressively shown, racism is thus turned on its head, with those advocating multiculturalism branded racists for diluting the cultural—not racial—homogeneity of otherwise 'pure' ethnic blocs (e.g. Europe, Africa).[49] While the same ends of racial separation are served as more 'unreconstructed' forms of ethnic prejudice and the recommendations are notorious far right fare—repatriation, closing borders, banning 'foreign' religious symbols, and so on—the discourse is starkly different. This form of 'right-wing Gramscism', Roger Griffin argues, seeks

> to undermine the intellectual legitimacy of liberalism by attacking aspects of actual existing liberal democracy: materialism, individualism, the universality of human rights, egalitarianism, multi-culturalism, and so on. "Metapolitical fascism" did so not on the basis of an aggressive ultra-nationalism and axiomatic racial superiority, but in the name of a Europe restored to the (essentially mythic) homogeneity of its component primordial cultures, and by the application of a "differentialist" ideal which seeks to put an end to rampant "vulgarisation" and ethnic miscegenation that they see endemic to modern societies.

In what sounds like a template for CasaPound's hybrid form of fascism, Griffin continues:

> Later versions of the extraordinarily prolific, logorrheic New Right have placed increasing stress on the need to transcend the division between Left and Right in a broad anti-global front. In short, the metapolitical perpetuation of inter-war fascism's crusade against liberal decadence advocates in its varied factions the inauguration of a new global order which would preserve or restore (through policies and measures never specified) unique ethnic and cultural identities (first and foremost European/Indo-European ones) allegedly threatened by globalization.[50]

If, by 'metapolitical', Griffin understands a *tout court* rejection of democratic elections, then this, too, only partly characterises CasaPound. For instance, some members of the group have participated in the Rome local elections within the rank and file of La Destra, a populist right party founded by one time neo-Fascist, Francesco Storace; the openly radical right party Tricolored Flame, created by the well-known neo-fascist activist and politician, Pino Rauti; and even a handful standing under Berlusconi's PDL (Partito delle Libertà; the Party of Liberty).[51] Even in terms of more indirect political engagement, CasaPound's connection is unusual, if nevertheless perceptible. Thus, Pino Rauti's son-in-law, Gianni Alemanno, at the time of writing Mayor of Rome, attempted to 'donate' CasaPound's squatted headquarters via an €11.5 million purchase from Rome's municipal treasury.[52] But this must be counted against far more visible, unconventional CasaPound centres now dotted across Italy, reputedly housing 5,000 members; an active student group called 'Blocco Studentesco' [Student's Bloc]' which, tellingly, employs the BUF's encircled lightning flash as their logo; the aforementioned cultural groups (Artisti per CasaPound and Turbodinamismo), in addition to 15 bookshops, 20 pubs, 8 sport associations, and a web radio station; the (in)famous *Radio Bandiera Nera* [*Black Banner Radio*]—where the use of the colour 'black' is a clear reference to Italian Fascism (in particular, the reference here is to the 'Black Shirts'). Similar to the undertakings of Alain de Benoist's GRECE—creator of this 'metapolitical' approach[53]—CasaPound has held more than 150 conferences around Italy and, as noted above, continues monthly publication of *L'Occidentale* and remains involved in *Solidarité-Identités*, a non-profit organization which promotes aid to developing countries like Kosovo.

As noted at the outset, perhaps CasaPound's hybridization of 'neo-fascism and the third way'[54] tradition of Italian Fascism is most conspicuously and idiosyncratically evident in CasaPound's approach to social housing and poverty relief—hardly the stuff of European far-right stereotypes since 1945. In fact, CasaPound's occupation of unused buildings to provide shelter for those otherwise unable to afford it doubtless carries sharp overtones of social justice. This initiative is part of their program of 'social mortgage' [mutuo sociale], in which they propose that the family occupying a given building can acquire a flat, paying only the costs of construction.[55] Although traditionally associated with left wing groups, these occupations are nevertheless closely related to their core ideology. For example, there are certain rules to respect to be accepted to live in one of the CasaPound buildings: no drugs, guns or prostitution; and in striking contrast to these behavioural codes, having Italian citizenship. Furthermore, the association is committed to volunteer work. CasaPound has also organized squads to help the recent victims of floods striking northern Italy in April 2009; these same volunteer squads later assisted in relieving the Abruzzi region after a major earthquake.

Once more, seeming contradictions arise. How are images of volunteers in natural catastrophes reconciled with activists loyal to Fascist ideology? Quite easily, actually, in light of the 'new consensus' on fascism. Attempts to regenerate the 'national community' through voluntaristic social initiatives—in this case, housing the homeless, or organizing volunteer squads for natural disasters—in no way precludes radical right ideology. To this end, consider Roger Griffin's definition of the 'broadly congruent' understanding of fascist ideology over the last generation: '*fascism is a genus of modern, revolutionary, "mass" politics which, while extremely heterogeneous in its social support and in the specific ideology promoted by its many permutations, draws its internal cohesion and driving force from a core myth that a period of perceived national decline and decadence is giving way to one of rebirth and renewal in a post-liberal new order*'.[56] That CasaPound activists would recognize such a harmony between social welfare and fascist praxis, and indeed even endorse a perspective like Griffin's, is borne out by numerous interviews with leading figures in the movement. In the words of the online broadcaster for CasaPound's *Black Banner Radio*:

> 'We are an organisation of social advancement that aims to use the power of volunteering to defend its social visions' [....] 'What we love of fascism is the attention to justice, the great social and administrative achievements in the interest of the entire national community,' Cristiano Coccanari declares, 'and the work done to render Italy a destined community from the Alps to Sicily, and not a mere geographic expression.'[57]

More recently, and in similar vein, an interview with CasaPound's official spokesperson maintains: "Q: What is the main concern of CasaPound? A: Politics. Namely, we are concerned of the good of the polis. In other words, to give hope, dignity, strength, will to a population that has been exhausted and tired'.[58] This willingness to help the polis thorough volunteer organizations finds its roots in any number of Fascist declarations; perhaps most prominently, from the final clause in the aforementioned *Verona Manifesto* from 1943, often cited by CasaPound activists:

> With this preamble to the Constituent Assembly, the Party shows not only that it is going to the people, but that it stands by the people. For its part, the Italian people must realize that there is only one way for it to defend its conquests of yesterday, today, tomorrow, namely to repel the enslaving invasion of Anglo-American plutocracies, which have given a thousand signs of their desire to increase the distress and misery of Italian life. There is only one way to achieve all its social goals: fight, work, win.[59]

In this way, the putatively 'leftist' actions and fascist ideology of CasaPound not only are compatible, but they are also inextricable.

Conclusion: 'I tried to make a paradiso terrestre'

Perhaps on account of its recent vintage, it has been journalism rather than academic scholarship with has, to date, best squared the perceived circle presented by CasaPound's iconoclastic ideology. In charting CasaPound's development for the UK-based *Guardian* in 2011, Tom Kington's analysis seamlessly merged the historic ('Mussolini') and the contemporary ([new] 'far-right'):

> CasaPound's approach to economics is pure Mussolini[.] "We would like to see communications, transport, energy and health renationalised and the state constructing houses which it then sells at cost to families," said Di Stefano. On immigration, the stance is typical of the far right. "We want to stop it," says Di Stefano. "Low-cost immigrant workers mean Italians are unable to negotiate wages, while the immigrants are exploited."[60]

So too with CasaPound's discourse and ideology generally: this is—quite self-consciously— 'fascism of the third millennium'. As shown above, this example of a twenty-first century European far-right movement advocates a revolutionary, socialist and 'ethno-differentialist' form of fascism. Examination of CasaPound's politics thus reveals an engagement with an Italian [postwar] Fascism of the origins, of the *fasci di combattimento* and even the Salò Republic. Yet as underscored by a global, multilingual blog, 'metapolitical' website and online merchandizing, CasaPound is not merely nostalgic.[61] This is not simply a re-run of the (ignominious) past, but is instead a 'return to the future'; a contemporary version of fascist ideology.

Correspondingly, CasaPound cannot be easily explained as just another 'neofascist' group *sic et simpliciter*. In researching this chapter, for instance, the authors contacted a CasaPound member for a background interview, who rejected the label 'neo-fascist'. 'I am a fascist', he said. There was no need to add anything else. In much the same way, CasaPound's adoption of political tactics typical of the postwar left—such as disaster relief or creating 'centri sociali' [community centres]—is no paradox; instead, this is an attempted application of Fascism's 'third way' to contemporary Italian realities. As CasaPound activists know only too well, it was the original 'daring ones', the Arditi under D'Annunzio, who occupied Fiume after World War One; while at Milan in 1919, their principal inspiration, Mussolini, launched his first Fascist manifesto from an occupied building in the Piazza San Sepolcro.

Finally, that words have consequences was tragically witnessed by Mussolini's dictatorial drive to 'regenerate' Italy, it should be recalled, when 'the Fascist regime's seizure of power, repression and wars left a "body count" of an estimated one million dead.'[62] Yet one need only look to fascism's more recent history in Italy to draw a similar conclusion. And here, too, CasaPound Italia is at the forefront of developments. That language matters was not lost on Italy's Foreign Ministry, for instance, upon finding that its Consul-General in Japan, Mario Vattani, was filmed giving a Fascist salute and praising the Salò Republic while performing at a CasaPound event with his band '*Sotto Fascia Semplice*' [*Under a Simple Fascist Banner*].[63] Nor was this lesson lost upon Ezra Pound's daughter, Mary de Rachewiltz, who recently undertook legal action in Italy to force the movement to change its name. Her efforts were redoubled, she declared, upon learning of the shooting rampage by a CasaPound member in December 2011.[64] Before killing himself, the author and accountant Gianluca Casseri murdered two street vendors in Florence and paralyzed a third.[65] For all CasaPound's doublespeak about non-racist 'ethno-differentialism' and for all its attempts to portray a 'friendly fascism' through welfare voluntarism, Casseri targeted only black African migrants. That he had been, at least to some degree, radicalized by CasaPound's tireless injunctions to action and violence is but a further reminder that language—in particular, far-right language, however sanitized and 'reconstructed'—is all too often a spur to action. Cutting through CasaPound's ideological sophistry and pointing this out fell to one of the Senegalese street traders being victimized, and potentially made into victims, by this all-too-familiar 'fascism of the third millennium':

> "Don't tell us he was a madman," said one, "because if he was he would have killed whites as well as blacks".[66]

Endnotes

[1] Matthew Feldman would like to thank the Berendel Foundation, London, for a Senior Research Fellowship facilitating the completion of this text.

[2] This chapter's epigraph is taken from an interview on CasaPound's official website, available online at: http://www.casapounditalia.org/ (all websites last accessed 19 February 2020). All translations from the Italian are by Anna Castriota. All websites last accessed 28 May 2012 (unless otherwise noted). Finally, each of three section titles are taken from Ezra Pound, *The Cantos* (London: Faber and Faber, 1998) pp. 3 (Canto I); 202 (Canto XLI), and 816 [Notes for CXVII et seq], respectively.

[3] Jamie Bartlett, Jonathan Birdwell and Mark Littler, *"The rise of populism in Europe can be traced through online behavior...": The new face of digital populism* (London: Demos, 2011), pp. 96-98. Alongside this report, a bespoke study of CasaPound's online profile is also available online at http://www.demos.co.uk/projects/populismineurope.

[4] See Aram Mattioli, *"Viva Mussolini": Die Aufwertung des Faschismus im Italien Berlusconis* (Paderborn: Ferdinand Schöningh Verlag, 2010).

[5] Following the 'Mani Pulite' scandal in 1994, fully 77.6% of the Italian electorate supported 'Anti-political Establishment Parties' according to Amir Abedi, *Anti-Political Establishment Parties: A Comparative Analysis* (London: Routledge, 2004), pp. 52-55, cited p. 53.

[6] D. Di Nunzio and E. Toscano, 'Can We Still Speak about Extreme Right Movements? CasaPound in Italy between Community and Subjectivation Drives'; presented at the XVII Congress of the International Sociological Association, Gothenburg, Sweden, 11-17 July 2010.

[7] For effective Anglophone studies of each of these movements, see Anna Cento Bull and Mark Gilbert, *The Lega Nord and the Northern Question in Italian Politics* (Basingstoke: Palgrave, 2001); and Antonio Carioti. 'From the Ghetto to Palazzo Chigi: The Ascent of the National Alliance', in Roger Griffin with Matthew Feldman, eds., *Fascism: Critical Concepts*, Vol. V (London: Routledge, 2004), pp. 57–78. On the MSI, see Piero Ignazi, *Extreme Right Parties in Western Europe* (Oxford: Oxford University Press, 2003), pp. 35-44. More recent comparative studies include Jonathan Hopkin and Piero Ignazi,'Newly governing parties in Italy: comparing the PDSI/DS, Lega Nord and Forza Italia', in *New Parties in Government*, Kris Deschouwer, ed. (Abingdon: Routledge, 2008), pp. 45-64; Marco Tarchi, 'Recalcitrant Allies: The Conflicting Foreign Policy Agenda of the *Alleanza Nazionale* and the *Lega Nord*', in *Europe for the Europeans: The Foreign and Security Policy of the Populist Radical Right*, ed. Christina Schori Liang (Aldershot: Ashgate, 2007), pp. 187-207. On the Tricolored Flame, see Anna Cento Bull, 'Casting a long shadow: The legacy of *stragismo* for the Italian extreme right', in *The Italianist* 25 (2005), pp. 260-279, esp. pp. 272-274.

[8] Cited in the most recent biography by Alec Marsh, *Ezra Pound: Critical Lives* (London: Reaktion Books, 2011), p. 47, which continues: 'In this sense modernism is really about *re*newal; its innovation are meant to *re*novate the world. Modernism is about beginning gain. From the beginning, Pound always looked to reprise the Renaissance.'

[9] For three recent discussions of Pound and fascism, see Serenella Zanotti, 'Fascism', in *Ezra Pound in Context*, ed. Ira B. Nadel (Cambridge: Cambridge University Press, 2011), pp. 376-390; Matthew Feldman, "The 'Pound Case' in Historical Perspective: An Archival Overview", in the *Journal of Modern Literature* 35/2 (2012), pp. 83-97, online at https://www.academia.edu/14687555/Proofs_for_The_Pound_Case_in_Historical_Perspective_An_Archival_Overview; and Leon Surette's *Dreams of a Totalitarian Utopia: Literary Modernism and Politics* (Montreal: McGill-Queen's University Press, 2011), pp. 220-250.

10. Ezra Pound, 'Addendum for C', in *The Cantos*, p. 813. For a discussion of this 'epic' poem see, for example, Lawrence Rainey, ed., *A Poem Containing History: Textual Studies in* The Cantos (Ann Arbor, MI: University of Michigan Press, 1997).
11. See "An Interview with Gianluca Iannone", posted at *Folkadvance* on 6 Feb. 2012; available online at: http://folkadvance.org/italy/gianluca-iannone-interview.
12. Pound, 'Addendum for C', 812-813. For academic accounts of Pound's anti-Semitism, see Flory's uncompromising view that Pound's anti-Semitism was born of a mental breakdown around 1935 in her "Pound and antisemitism", in the *Cambridge Companion to Ezra Pound*, ed. Ira B. Nadel (Cambridge: Cambridge University Press, 1999), pp. 284-300. For more general, empirically substantiated accounts of Pound's unmistakeable anti-Jewish vitriol, see the general accounts by Robert Casillo, *The Genealogy of Demons: Anti-Semitism, fascism and the myths of Ezra Pound* (Evanston, IL: Northwestern University Press, 1988); and rather more charitably, Leon Surette, *Pound in Purgatory: From Economic Radicalism to Anti-Semitism* (Urbana, IL: University of Illinois Press, 1999). Finally, Ezra Pound's radio broadcasts for Fascist Italy have been widely circulated and, more than four decades ago, culminated in the publication of fully 120 radio broadcast scripts under the title '*Ezra Pound Speaking': Radio Speeches of WWII*, ed. Leonard Doob (Westport, CT: Greenwood Press, 1978).
13. These excerpts, and many others, were long ago reproduced in C. David Heymann's unflinching account of Pound's politics, *Ezra Pound: The Last Rower* (New York: Viking Press, 1976), pp. 116-122. Following his release from St Elizabeths sanatorium in 1958 Pound returned to Italy, where he resumed contact with a number of far-right ideologues, including Valerio Borghese, Vanni Teodorani and Ugo Dadone. Of the latter, revealingly, one of Pound's biographers has noted that, in Spring 1961, Pound stayed with Dadone, who 'was involved with the neo-Fascist Movimento Sociale Italiano and regularly wrote articles about them in right-wing journals. They held a May Day parade, wearing jack-boots and black armbands, displaying the swastika, shouting ant-Semitic slogans, and goose-stepping. Among those photographed at the head of the parade was Ezra.' See Humphrey Carpenter, *Ezra Pound: A Serious Character* (London: Faber and Faber, 1988), pp. 873-874.
14. See http://folkadvance.org/category/casapound.
15. For a brief overview of the term "new far right", see Paul Jackson et. al., *The EDL: Britain's 'New Far Right Social Movement'* (Northampton: RNM Publications, 2011); available online at https://web.archive.org/web/20120121031539/http://www.radicalism-new-media.org/wp-content/uploads/2011/09/The_EDL_Britains_New_Far_Right_Social_Movement.pdf, pp. 7-11.
16. Although now slightly dated, the best Anglophone account of the development of the Italian far-right since 1945 remains Franco Ferraresi's excellent *Threats to Democracy* (Princeton: Princeton University Press, 1996), esp. chapters 1, 4, 6 and 7.
17. Marcello Veneziani, unpublished interview with Anna Castriota, August 2007.
18. See, for example, Marco Tarchi, "Italy: A Country of Many Populisms", in *Twenty First Century Populism*, eds. Daniele Albertazzi and Duncan McDonnell (Basingstoke: Palgrave, 2008), pp. 84-99; and for a more focused view of revolutionary youth activism, see Stéphanie Dechezelles, "The Cultural Basis of Youth Involvement in Italian Extreme Right-Wing Organisations", in the *Journal of Contemporary European Studies* 16/3 (2008), pp. 363-375.
19. "Retake Everything!", interview with Gianluca Iannone posted at *Open Revolt!* on 15 Dec. 2011; available online at: https://web.archive.org/web/20200217053157/https://openrevolt.info/2011/12/15/casa-pound/.
20. See, for example, 'CasaPound and the new radical right in Italy', posted at *libcom.org* on 28 June 2011; available online at: http://libcom.org/library/casa-pound-new-radical-right-italy#footnote2_2kk6qu4.

[21] See 'Le FAQ di CPI' [Frequently Asked Questions] on CasaPound's official website; available online at: https://web.archive.org/web/20091101042525/http://www.casapounditalia.org/index.php?option=com_content&view=category&id=40&Itemid=66. For a similar interview with CPI's founder Gianluca Iannone on the subject of Italian fascism, see Alessandro di Capriccioli, 'Roma, CasaPound spiazza tutti", *l'Espresso*, 8 February 2012; available online at: http://espresso.repubblica.it/dettaglio/roma-casapound-spiazza-tutti/2173562. Tellingly, this interview was translated and cross-posted on the leading "White Pride World Wide" website, *Stormfront* (available online at: www.stormfront.org/forum/t866233/):

> ...at that time [under Mussolini] there was more freedom of expression than it is now. Anyway, we claim the freedom to say that fascism did many good things, and we want to speak about those things. We live in a country which fascism lasted twenty years and anti-Fascism lasted sixty-six. There is the consolidation of power positions behind the word "anti-fascism." They muted you, your demonstrations and activities are prohibited, even when there is a flood in Genova and your militants go to help out, even when you spend your forces on volunteering.

[22] Interview with Gianluca Iannone, posted on *Tumblr*; available online at: www.tumblr.com/tagged/iannone.

[23] For an overview of frontstage/backstage discourse, see Cas Mudde, *The Ideology of the Extreme Right* (Manchester: Manchester University Press, 2000), pp. 20ff.; and for a brief characterisation of fascism as a 'Third Way', see George Mosse, cited in Roger Griffin, ed., *Fascism* (Oxford: Oxford University Press, 1995), pp. 303-304.

[24] Benito Mussolini and Giovanni Gentile, 'The Doctrine of Fascism', partially reprinted in John Whittam, *Fascist Italy* (Manchester: Manchester University Press, 1995), cited p. 156.

[25] See *CasaPound*, 'La Storia', available online at: https://web.archive.org/web/20091102075354/http://www.casapounditalia.org/index.php?option=com_content&view=category&id=36&Itemid=61.

[26] 'The Manifesto of Turbodynamism', available online at https://web.archive.org/web/20140801114732/http://zentropaville.tumblr.com/post/26969144436/amour-absinthe-revolution-the-manifesto-of.

[27] Filippo Tommaso Marinetti, "The Founding and Manifesto of Futurism', in Umbro Apollonio, ed., *Futurist Manifestos* (New York: Viking Press, 1973), pp. 19-24, cited p. 21.

[28] See "Artisti per CasaPound", available online at: http://www.artistipercasapound.org/.

[29] Cited in Emilio Gentile, *The Struggle for Modernity: Nationalism, Futurism and Fascism* (Westport, CT: Praeger, 2003). Also cited in *ibid*. (p. 84), for instance, Mussolini claimed: 'We must scrape and pulverize, in the character and mentality of the Italians [....] It is an immense labor. The Risorgimento was but the beginning, because it was the work of tiny minorities; the world war, instead, was profoundly educational. Now it is a matter of continuing, day by day, this remaking of the national character of the Italians.'

[30] Giovanni Giuriati, 'The Young and the Party', translated and reprinted in Roger Griffin, ed., *Fascism*, cited p. 68.

[31] See Colin Liddell, "In the House of Pound: An Interview with Gianluca Iannone," Alternative Right—An Online Magazine of Radical Traditionalism, 5 February 2012, https://web.archive.org/web/20120511085054/http://www.alternativeright.com/main/the-magazine/in-the-house-of-pound/, reprinted in Folk Advance, February 6, 2012, https://web.archive.org/web/20120603203655/http://folkadvance.org/italy/gianluca-iannone-interview.

[32] Lyrics from the song "Cinghiamattanza", taken from CasaPound's official website.

[33] See, for example, www.cinghiamattanza.blogspot.com.

[34] Communication on CasaPound's official website, 18 October 2009; available online at: www.casapounditalia.org.
[35] Lyrics from the song "Nel Dubbio Mena" taken from CasaPound's official website.
[36] See 'Le FAQ di CPI', www.casapounditalia.org/index.php?option=com_content&view=category&id=36&Itemid=61.
[37] See John Pollard, *The Fascist Experience in Italy* (London: Routledge, 1998), cited p. 126.
[38] See 'Il Programma' on CasaPound's official website, titled 'Una Nazione [A Nation]', cited pp. 1-2; available online at: https://web.archive.org/web/20150317223503/http://issuu.com:80/di_stefano/docs/unanazione.
[39] 'The Verona Manifesto of the Republican Fascist Party', partially translated and reprinted in Griffin, *Fascism*, ed., p. 87.
[40] See 'Occidentale' on CasaPound's official website, available online at: https://web.archive.org/web/20110704053828/http://www.casapounditalia.org/index.php?option=com_content&view=article&id=70&Itemid=95: "'Occidente' è, etimologicamente, sol occidens, sole che declina. È, storicamente e geopoliticamente, quel lembo di terra nato per odio dell'Europa e che poi ha riassorbito il vecchio continente a suon di bombe al fosforo, imponendo al mondo intero un regime di arroganza, rapina e omologazione. È occidentale per rivendicare questo Occidente, il nostro Occidentale? Certo che no, e su questo non sussistono ambiguità di sorta."
[41] *Ibid.*
[42] On the origins of the periodical *Occidentale* see Enrico Sermonti, "Le battaglie di OCCIDENTALE e il motivo del suo nome," *Occidentale: Rivista di critica radicale*, anno XXXVI (2005), https://web.archive.org/web/20050407170846/http://www.occidentale.org/sermonti.html and https://forum.termometropolitico.it/362001-occidentale-rivista-di-critica-radicale.html.
[43] https://lucanianonconforme.wordpress.com/2011/01/03/396/. On the "Attività" tab of CasaPound Italia's home page (https://web.archive.org/web/20110907200657/http://www.casapounditalia.org/index.php?option=com_content&view=section&id=8&Itemid=69), there is a link to https://web.archive.org/web/20110830223011/http://www.solidarite-identites.org/.
[44] See www.casapounditalia.org/index.php?option=com_content&view=category&id=40&Itemid=66
[45] 'Il Programma', p. 4, available online at: https://web.archive.org/web/20150317223503/http://issuu.com:80/di_stefano/docs/unanazione.
[46] *Ibid.*, p. 4.
[47] *Ibid.*, p. 4.
[48] Steve Bastow, 'A neo-fascist third way: the discourse of ethno-differentialist revolutionary nationalism', reprinted in Griffin with Feldman, eds., *Fascism*, Vol. V, cited p. 77.
[49] In Christopher Flood's impressive summary, '[h]aving tracked de Benoist's theoretical trajectory from white-supremacist biological racism to ethno-differentialism, Taguieff came to the view that de Benoist's positions in this and other areas had evolved to such a degree that he could no longer be classed straightforwardly as a thinker of the extreme right or even be conveniently pigeonholed in conventional left-right terms at all. 'Pierre-André Taguieff and the dilemmas of antiracism', in *l'esprit créateur* 37/2 (1997), pp. 68-78, cited p. 69.
[50] Roger Griffin, 'Fascism's New Faces (and New Facelessness) in the "post-fascist" Epoch', reprinted in Matthew Feldman, ed., *A Fascist Century* (Basingstoke: Palgrave, 2008), cited pp. 195-196.
[51] Some CasaPound activists participated as candidates in the local elections held in 2008; for a general overview, see www.casapounditalia.org/politica.

[52] 'Il Campidoglio acquista sede Casapound Il Pd insorge: è una vergogna', as reported in *Il Messaggero Roma* on 25 April 2012; available online at: http://www.ilmessaggero.it/articolo.php?id=192603&sez=HOME_ROMA (currently online at https://controinformazion.wordpress.com/2012/04/25/la-storiella-dei-topi-non-conformi/). The authors are grateful to Andrea Rinaldi for drawing this development to their attention. Gianni Alemanno's apparent attempt to purchase the building for CasaPound activists was recently struck down by the Italian Audit Court; see Lorenzo D'Albergo, 'La Corte dei conti boccia i bilanci del Comune' in *La Repubblica Roma*, 25 Maggio 2012; available online at: http://roma.repubblica.it/cronaca/2012/05/25/news/la_corte_dei_conti_boccia_i_bilanci_del_comune-35865319/.

[53] For detailed analysis of De Benoist's pedigree and intellectual trajectory, see Pierre-André Taguieff, 'The New Cultural Racism in France', in *Telos* 83 (1990), pp. 109-122; and Pierre-André Taguieff, 'From Race to Culture: The New Right's View of European Identity', in *Telos* 98/99 (1993), pp. 99-125.

[54] For an excellent overview, see the chapter by this name in Steve Bastow and James Martin, *Third Way Discourse: European Ideology in the Twentieth Century* (Edinburgh: Edinburgh University Press, 2003), ch. 4.

[55] See 'Il Programma', p. 10, available online at: https://web.archive.org/web/20150317223503/http://issuu.com:80/di_stefano/docs/unanazione.

[56] Roger Griffin ed., *International Fascism: Theories, Causes and the New Consensus* (London: Arnold, 1998), cited p. 14; italics in original.

[57] Cristiano Coccanari, cited in 'Casa Pound Italia: Neo-fascism on the rise', posted at *cafebabel.com* on 23 March 2010; available online at: http://www.cafebabel.co.uk/article/33321/casa-pound-italia-fascism-neo-fascism-duce.html.

[58] See 'Le FAQ di CPI', www.casapounditalia.org/index.php?option=com_content&view=category &id=40&Itemid=66

[59] Griffin, ed., *Fascism*, p. 87.

[60] Tom Kington, "Italy's Fascists Stay True to Mussolini's Legacy", *The Guardian*, 6 November 2011, available online at: http://www.guardian.co.uk/world/2011/nov/06/italy-fascists-true-mussolini-ideology?INTCMP=SRCH.

[61] See, respectively, http://zentropa.info/; http://www.ideodromocasapound.org/; and www.zazzle.co.uk/casapound+gifts.

[62] Michael R. Ebner, *Ordinary Violence in Mussolini's Italy* (Cambridge: Cambridge University Press, 2010), cited p. 11.

[63] 'Italy's Osaka consul recalled over fascist rock band links', *The Telegraph*, 24 January 2012; available online at: www.telegraph.co.uk/news/worldnews/europe/italy/9034972/Italys-Osaka-consul-recalled-over-fascist-rock-band-links.html.

[64] Tom Kington, 'Ezra Pound's daughter aims to stop Italian fascist group using father's name', *The Guardian*, 23 December 2011; available online at: http://www.guardian.co.uk/world/2011/dec/23/ezra-pound-daughter-italian-fascist.

[65] See, for example, 'CasaPound runs riot in foreign market', *SchNEWS*, 16 December 2011; available online at: http://www.schnews.org.uk/stories/CASAPOUND-RUNS-RIOT-IN-FOREIGN-MARKET/.

[66] Tom Kington, 'Florence gunman shoots Senegalese street vendors dead', *The Guardian*, 13 December 2011; available online at: http://www.guardian.co.uk/world/2011/dec/13/Florence-gunman-shoots-street-vendors.

Part 2
War and Empire:
The Fascist Way and the Liberal Way

9. The Holocaust in the NDH: Genocide between Political Religion and Religious Politics

Catholic Nuns march in step with Ustaša troops

Duro Schwartz survived what he called the 'inferno' of Jasenovac—the only non-Nazi extermination centre active during the Holocaust—and in 1945 composed a detailed memoir about his travails in the Ustaša-run camp. After witnessing a catalogue of scarcely believable actions savagely and ritually carried out over his eight months of imprisonment between Autumn 1941 and Spring 1942, Schwartz concluded: "If all those who had gone through the camp could join their voices and the despair in their hearts into one voice and one despair, the thunder and horror of the day of judgment would make itself heard."[1] This chilling account, which could only be written due to Schwartz's release on account of his marriage to a non-Jewish woman, was still bound to fall short in the eyes of the author, for "human language is not powerful enough to even approximate the reality of existence there."[2]

Despite noting the necessity of trying to speak about an ultimately inexplicable horror—a paradox noted in the accounts of many Holocaust survivors—this did not stop Schwartz from recording, hiding, and later writing up his notes on everyday life at Jasenovac. Another excerpt from his testimonial serves to evoke the brutality of Ustaša guards toward, especially, Jews, Serbs, and Roma and Sinti travelers:

> To break the monotony an Ustaša walks up to us now and then and hits us with the butt of his rifle .... Some more naïve prisoners tried to appease the Ustaša "psychologically," or, as they put it, "in a nice fashion." Dr. Vlatko Donner, for example, said, "They are human beings, after all! One should always be polite to human beings. Wait and see that he will be polite toward me." Lo and behold, when an Ustaša came to him and hit him with the butt of his rifle, Donner reproached him with a plaintive voice: "Brother, don't hit me, can't you see I am weak and ill?" But the reaction was the opposite of what he expected, as the "brother" landed a blow on his head that stunned and knocked him down. Then the "brother" gave him a few kicks for good measure. This was the harvest of psychology and pedagogy.[3]

By appearing silent and invisible, yet at the same time as a skilled builder and team leader, Schwartz survived the arduous winter of 1941/2. During this time, he was put to work expanding the camp infrastructure by building two of the five camp sites ultimately comprising Jasenovac—not for nothing was this place of death termed the 'Yugoslav Auschwitz'.[4] His writing gives us insight into how the camp operated, and what it took for someone to stay alive with leaders who took a sadistic interpretation of their directives. Despite actions in the short-lived Independent State of Croatia (*Nezavisna Država Hrvatska*; hereafter NDH)—leading even the Third Reich's envoy to describe the Ustasha regime as 'raging mad'—most accounts of the Holocaust simply exclude wartime Croatia, or treat it summarily as part of the wider Nazi 'Final Solution to the Jewish Question'.[5] Yet this was autonomous genocide in the Balkans, with some of the highest percentages of violent deaths anywhere in Axis Europe.[6]

As this suggests, seventy-five years on, historians have only scratched the surface of the psychology shaping actions by the Ustaša. Sexual piety, Catholic asceticism, and even a movement against swearing were coupled with truly savage killings of Serbs, Jews, Roma and Sinti in a 'revolution of blood' sparked by the Third Reich's invasion of Yugoslavia in April 1941. As recent Anglophone work has shown, the Ustasha has been cast as a racial state similar to Nazi Germany; a death cult of fanatical anti-Serb (as well as anti-Jewish and anti-Roma) genocidaires, and a fascist movement very much in the interwar European cast.[7] All this is true, and more. Yet too little has been said about the religious dimension of this genocidal hybrid between crucifix and dagger. For the Catholic Church in Croatia, the temptation of irredentist nationalism was considerable: more than 200 priests joined the Ustaše ranks, blessing flags and battle units, taking part in Ustaša funerals and holding ritual masses; of these, more than half were decorated with Ustaša medals for their service to the NDH.[8]

From its 1929 founding the Ustaša movement, under its 'chieftain', Ante Pavelić, looked as much as a medieval Crusading order as European fascist movement. Most of the Ustaša abroad were supported by Fascist Italy and then Nazi

Germany in the 1930s, biding their time for the destruction of the multiethnic Yugoslav state that had always been predicted. After the defeat and occupation of Yugoslavia in April 1941, the NDH were given comparative autonomy on a large strip of Dalmatia under control of Fascist Italy and Nazi Germany. With a free hand against alleged racial and ideological enemies, the Ustaše was free to implement its notorious policy of 'thirds': kill one third, deport one third, or forcibly convert one third of Jews, Serbs and Travelers in the Independent State of Croatia. So brutal was its rule that civil war had already broken out in Croat territory by the end of 1941, with the NDH regime staggering on through terror until the end of the war. Perhaps most offensively, Pavelić—a man known to keep the eyeballs of victims beside his desk—availed himself of the so-called 'ratline' that spirited him out of wartime Croatia, allowing him to die peacefully in 1957 atop an Argentine bed.[9]

What, then, can one say about the role of religion in the Independent State of Croatia, and its influence in genocide? Wading through oftentimes politically-charged scholarship—which, reflecting Yugoslavia's tumultuous history, may be anti-clerical, nationalist, Marxist or liberal humanist (let alone their opposites)—underlines the difficulty of comprehensive responses to such a question. In the limited number of Anglophone texts on the NDH to date, one thread of particularly hostile interpretation has been the persistent assertions that the Catholic Church was not only complicit in, but even acted as the principal vehicle for, "the development of the Croatian Catholic movement into terroristic clero-fascism." In this view, Catholicism as a whole bears chief responsibility for "the leading role in the ideological preparation and justification for these mass crimes."[10] Such angry criticisms have recently been laid at the foot of the Vatican, and in particular Pope Pius XII, who headed the Catholic Church from 1939 until his death in 1958, for culpability in the genocide against European Jewry of a variously moral, indirect, and even collaborative nature. In more balanced renderings, Catholic clerics were found not to be mavericks like the short-lived commandant of Jasenovac, Miroslav Filipović-Majstorović (who was ultimately defrocked), but were instead representative of long-held anti-Semitism and radically reactionary politics held to be historically intrinsic within the Catholic Church. To be sure, these are serious charges. And even if most commentators fall short of accusing Pius of being 'Hitler's Pope', the claim that the Church was fundamentally compromised by decisions at the top and actions at the bottom remains a persistent accusation.[11]

Yet a closer look suggests that much of this debate is misdirected. In David Dalin's insightful narrative, this has little to do with World War Two and the Holocaust, and rather more to do with ulterior political agendas, from the earlier "standard Communist agitprop" holding that Pope Pius XII harbored Nazi sympathies. This argument extends to more recent and surprising calumnies by liberal ex-seminarians and Catholic priests similar to John Cornwell, such as James Carroll and Garry Wills, who are "using the sufferings of Jews fifty years ago to force changes upon the Catholic Church today." "The technique for recent attacks on Pius XII," Dalin continues, "is simple. It requires only that favorable evidence be read in the worst light and treated to the strictest test, while unfavorable evidence is read in the best light and treated to no test."[12] Another historiographical survey finds the same methodological partiality:

> Most of the Pope's critics tend to extremism, while defenders tend toward moderation. This is because the critics have taken the position that the Holocaust would have been much diminished, or even averted, by strong papal action, while defenders of the Pope argue more convincingly that a strong papal protest would have had little effect upon the Nazi machine of destruction.[13]

Interesting circumstantial evidence may be found in Bottum and Dalin's recent book, *The Pius War: Responses to the Critics of Pius XII*. In an extensive catalogue of works on the debate over Pius XII, included in the book, William Doino Jr. provides hundreds of titles under the twin headings "Major Attackers" and "Major Defenders." The distinction between extremism and moderation in the titles alone is instructive.[14] Such revisionist attacks on wartime Catholicism, however, as Thomas Woods points out, have to contend with (or, indeed, ignore) the fact that "Pope Pius XII was deeply admired in his day and in the years following his pontificate" by Holocaust survivors and scholars alike.[15] To Holocaust survivors, members of Pius XII's inner circle, Jewish leaders, and diplomats on the spot, the Vatican's interventions on behalf of Jews during World War Two were frequent, dangerous, and heroic. Here, two points are worth mentioning which seem, to me least, decisive.

The first is the catalogue of actions and material aid directed to those in need, including, for example, arranging transit visas and facilitating emigration outside Europe until 1943, opposing deportations, and hiding persecuted Jews after major deportations had been carried out. More than 3,000 Jews hid in the Pope's summer residence at Castle Gandolfo, showing the Pope's personal commitment and exposure. Eighty percent of Italian Jews survived the Holocaust, compared to the sobering figure of 80 percent of European Jews who did not; this speaks volumes for Pope Pius XII's impact within his circle of influence. Doubtless, specific mistakes were made, or opportunities to save lives shamefully squandered. But the thrust of Vatican policy was just and humane, as was widely recognised at the time. This is because, far from being a Nazi sympathizer, Pius XII, according to Pierre Blet's judicious study, "employed all the means at his disposal to save [Jews]. As much as possible he took care to limit what he said in public, expecting nothing worthwhile to come of this. He did not speak, but he took action."[16]

A second point seems equally decisive, one also obscured in recent revisionist accounts: the Nazis regarded Pius XII as a "Jew-loving" Pope and an implacable enemy of the Third Reich. The Pope knew he had no favour with Hitler and the regime; indeed, even listening to the Vatican Radio (set up by Eugenio Pacelli in 1930) was punishable by death in wartime Germany and Poland. The Vatican's own views were clear to leading Nazis following the publication of the 1937 encyclical *Mit brennender Sorge* [*With Burning Concern*]—one of a number of attacks on racial doctrine penned by then-Vatican Secretary of State Eugenio Maria Giuseppe Giovanni Pacelli—which goes a long way to explaining why the Nazis opposed, rather than celebrated, Pacelli's ascendance to the papacy in 1939. Thereafter, abortive attempts by the Nazis up to 1944 to kidnap or even kill the Pope for obstructing the Final Solution suggest that Pius XII was no friend to the Nazis; quite the opposite.

No matter what some commentators may argue today—through sometimes injudicious interpretation—no one misunderstood at the time of its delivery the Pope's Christmas message of December 1942: "humanity owes to the hundreds of thousands of people, who, without any fault of their own and sometimes because of their nationality or race alone, have been doomed to death or to progressive extermination."[17] Nazi agents certainly grasped the point of this address, far better than many later interpreters: "He virtually accuses the German people of injustice toward the Jews, and he makes himself the spokesman of the Jews, who are war criminals."[18]

Yet even before Rolf Hochhuth's notorious hand grenade, the 1963 play *Der Stellvertreter: Ein christliches Trauerspiel* [*The Deputy: A Christian Tragedy*], savaged Pope Pius XII—and by extension, wartime Catholicism as a whole—for "silence" in the face of the Nazis' Final Solution, such hyperbolic charges had been familiar enough. To varying degrees, scholars have largely held the Catholic hierarchy, both in the Vatican and in the Croatian Archbishopric under Alojzije Stepinac, somehow complicit in the Holocaust. Edmond Paris' account of the influence genocidal policies in Croatia 1941-1945 interprets the NDH as a kind of chameleon colored by imported Nazism and Rome-led clericalism. He describes collusion between the NDH and the Croatian Catholic clergy—especially Archbishop Stepinac—in forced conversions, torture and mass murder. This led understandably, if wrongly, to maximalist evaluations of Catholic complicity in NDH's genocidal campaign. That said, those pivotal themes already identified by Paris and others in the 1960s and 1970s—ideology, religion and genocide—have remained central to scholarship on the Ustaša since that time.[19] Needless to say, the examination of application of such massive and contentious themes and how the Ustaša state operated is challenging, and this exploration will only attempt to sketch these by way of drawing heavily upon recent Anglophone scholarship.

Perhaps what Duro Schwartz called the Independent State of Croatia's "harvest of psychology and pedagogy" cannot, and moreover perhaps should not, simply give way to detached comparative summary or biased politicized explanation. In short, one may be able to tally up the figures and cite the reasons, but the crimes committed in wartime Croatia must, surely, baffle attempts at humanistic understanding. There was a murderous interplay of religion and politics in the NDH; one must concede that the Ustaša's "psychology and pedagogy" may not allow for a straightforward accounting for it—let alone any inflexible or essentialist one.

With this in mind, it may be useful to revisit three pivotal themes: ideology, religion and genocide. Upon close examination, we can find statements linking these three themes starkly, like the following, made by a priest and cabinet minister, Dionizije Juričev, in his role as Head of State Direction for Renewal on 22 October 1941:

> In this country only Croats may live from now on, because it is a Croatian country. We know precisely what we will do with the people who do not convert. I have purged the whole surrounding area, from babies to seniors. If it is necessary, I will do that here, too, because today it is not a sin to kill even a seven-year-old child, if it is standing in the way of our Ustaša movement ... Do not believe that I could not take a machine gun in hand just because I wear priests vestments. If it is necessary, I will eradicate everyone who is against the Ustaša state and its rule—right down to babies![20]

Ideology

"'Ustašism: 'the catastrophe of our Independent State of Croatia had a moral cause.'" This quote, from a postwar article by the regicidal Ustaša functionary Eugen Dido Kvaternik, provides a starting point for discussion of Ustaša ideology; even more so when placed next to Juričev's Direction for Renewal quoted above.[21] For Kvaternik was the "planner and organizer of genocide" and was regarded at the time as the "symbol of Ustaše terror in the NDH" in Ivo Goldstein's assessment. Supporting this view is a quotation from German Plenipotentiary Edmund Glaise von Horstenau, who viewed Kvaternik as a destabilizing threat, and described him as "the most hated man in the land."[22]

Indeed, Kvaternik hangs like a vulture over Juričev's decree. Yet if the former's "moral cause" could hypothetically be maintained in the face of a declared willingness to execute children, "morality" must be understood—not in Kvaternik's attempted exculpation in terms of "goodness" or any other sort of backdoor justification—but in the definitional sense of the word as "a system of values and moral principles" whereby the latter concern "the distinction between right and wrong and good or bad behavior".

If one is willing to grant fascist ideology the possibility of morality, that is, if fascist movements can be understood in their own terms containing a system of values helping to shape behavior, then one may technically accept the accuracy of Kvaternik's comment while emphatically rejecting the mindset guiding it, either before or after 1945. This, in turn, begs the question of what values a fascist like Dido Kvaternik might hold.

By way of response, it is worth cautioning that Fascist Studies is a contentious area, even if Roger Griffin perceived a new consensus emerging in the field toward the end of the 1990s. While this is not the place to repeat this important debate about the generic nature of fascist ideology, it suffices to say that many more researchers are now willing to grant fascism status as a political ideology of hypernationalistic inclination. That is, fascism can be seen to hold both "positive" values (e.g. being "for" something; as with Griffin's use of the term palingenesis) and "negative" values (being "against" something; such as anti-Semitic scapegoating and demonisation). This can be seen in movements across interwar Europe—and likely beyond, both in terms of geography and period.[23]

In what follows, fascism is understood as a specifically modern form of secular "millenarianism" constructed culturally and politically, not religiously, as a revolutionary movement centring upon the "renaissance" of a given people (whether perceived nationally, ethnically, culturally, or religiously) through the total reordering of all collective energies towards a utopia; fascism as an ideology is implacably hostile to democratic representation and socialist materialism, equality and individualism, in addition to any specific enemies perceived as alien or oppositional to their secular myths.

In practice, however, many scholars have long omitted the Croatian Ustaša as well as the NDH regime from comparative discussions of fascism, seeing them as alternatively "semi-fascist" (Hory and Broszat)[24], "proto-fascist" (Griffin)[25], or, more typically than these two examples, simply omitting the movement from taxonomic considerations altogether. Those confronting the problem have often perceived too much emphasis on Catholicism within Ustašism for it to be seen as a genuinely secular political ideology; instead, they describe it as a form of "clerical fascism" (of which more presently). Other views declare that the lack of any Croatian "nation" as such (unlike Western and Central European states)—in terms of complete political sovereignty over Croatian territory—*ipso facto* denies the Ustaša status as a nationalistic movement, and hence containing just an idiosyncratic, localized political credo. It is precisely this milieu—the interplay of religion and nationalism in interwar Croatia—that has offered a consistent challenge to interpretations of comparative fascism in respect of both the Ustaša movement and NDH regime. Before considering the Ustaša movement in terms of a fascist movement—and consequently, a political religion—along the interpretative lines indicated above, a few contentious points ought to be highlighted. First of all, "nationalism" is a notoriously tricky topic, possibly even more difficult to characterize than "religion".

Nonetheless, one can advance some assertions regarding the Croatian case. Most importantly, the fact that there had been no sovereign Croat state since 1102 in no way precludes Croatian nationalism. In fact, the classical liberal ideal espoused by Starčević in the 19th century was not far different from that of contemporaneous European nationalists like Garibaldi. That the latter succeeded in creating a territorially-defined state from a national ideal while his Croatian counterpart did not, moreover, may have actually served to augment Croatian nationalism throughout the succession of crises and conflicts plaguing interwar Yugoslavia. This reading of nationalism is certainly in keeping with major theories on this particular badge of identity as a distinct, modern (initially European) phenomenon that Elie Kedourie describes as "a comprehensive doctrine which leads to a distinctive style of politics." Amongst other points of direct relevance to Ustaša nationalism, "Nationalists make use of the past in order to subvert the present." Finally, in this nationalist doctrine, language, race, culture, and sometimes even religion, constitute different aspects of the same primordial entity, the nation. Kedourie continues:

> What is beyond doubt is that the doctrine divides humanity into separate and distinct nations, claims that such nations must constitute sovereign states, and asserts that the members of a nation reach freedom and fulfilment by cultivating the peculiar identity of their own nation and by sinking their own persons in the greater whole of the nation.[26]

As such, the Croatian people's own historical narratives, linguistic and ethnic ties, and—most importantly—perceived sense of its own collective community and distinctive, providential history, locates a majority of Croats as nationalistic within Yugoslavia on the eve of World War Two. And while the distinction between generic nationalism and fascism's hyper-nationalism (or ultra-nationalism) is similarly challenging, the difference in rhetoric separating the Croat Party of Right/Ustaša from the Croat Peasant Party [HSS] and Populists [HPS] is not.

The chasm is unmistakable: the former is unabashedly revolutionary, whilst the latter two are essentially conservative. For there remained a clear division between Croatian rejectionists and reformists, that is, between those willing to work within the federal structure of Yugoslavia established in 1918, and those who, like the Ustaša, were bent upon its destruction—a distinction placed in sharp relief by the autonomy brought about by the August 1939 *Sporazum,* or federal agreement on devolution. In the context of fractious Croatian and Yugoslav politics up to 1941, then, it seems safe to equate what Biondich calls the sizeable "hard opposition" of Croatian nationalists with an ultra-nationalism indispensable to interwar fascist ideology. At the same time, however, this is not to say that all Croatian ultra-nationalists necessarily became supporters of the NDH. Moreover, the invocation of state religion is characteristic of all nationalist movements. That the Ustaša drew heavily upon Catholicism as a form of community identity in no way compromises its fascist bona fides (as a glance at the appropriation of Christianity by the Romanian Iron Guard, the Spanish Falange, or the Afrikaner Ossewabrandwag demonstrates).

Here, it is a question of first principles. If interwar fascist ideology was focused upon the mythic "nation", its self-selective criteria for community inclusion—both racial and religious under the later NDH regime—must always vary from location to location. Just as German culture emphasized a technocratic scientism of race as the defining feature of its (religiously divided) "Aryan" *Volksgemeinschaft [Racial Community]*, so the Ustaša emphasized centuries as a Catholic "bulwark" in the east as an identifying characteristic of the Croats' own championed *Volksgemeinschaft*. (Of course, this does not mean that eugenic thinking and the like was absent from either Croatian intellectuals or Ustašism.[27]) Like all fascist movements enjoying power, the NDH "tried to portray itself as an organic part of Croatian culture and history", amongst which, Ramet argues in *The Three Yugoslavias,* meant appropriating existing Croatian Catholicism toward secular political ends. By placing Catholicism within the cosmology of the (ultimately abortive) totalitarian state, the NDH doubtless wanted people to worship in a Ustaša style. The party program of June 1941 asserted that in "the Ustaša state, created by the *poglavnik* [leader] and his Ustaše, people must think like Ustaše, speak like Ustaše and—most important of all—act like Ustaše. In a word, the entire life in the NDH must be Ustaša-based".[28]

Yet this was a secular, not a religious, regime, one that appealed to (and ultimately perverted) centuries-long Croatian traditions of Roman Catholicism to initially legitimate its rule. How else can one interpret propaganda spouted by daily newspapers like *Hrvatski Narod [The Croatian People]* that seamlessly equated Catholicism, "Croatianness" and the Ustaša? Thus in terms of causality, for those Croatian fascists who placed the state before God—such as the 300 or more Ustaša ultra-nationalists exiled with Ante Pavelić in Italy, later to become the central apparatchiks of the regime between 1941 and 1945[29]—religion was but a constituent part of a Greater Croatian "nation" always intended to be (re-)created and "purified" through widespread violence. Now, a host of other features also show that Ustašism contained problematic characteristics when compared to rival fascist movements in practice. Foremost here, Pavelić did not fit the classic fascist mold as a charismatic leader, despite his 1933 adoption of the title *Poglavnik* and his penning the movement's ideological tract, *Principles of the Ustaša Movement*.[30] Whatever else he was, Pavelić was not an accomplished demagogue like Hitler or Mussolini.

Yet if the NDH was indeed a fascist state, and a defining feature of fascist states is expansionistic power politics as the outward expression of national rebirth, it is salutary to note that this does not extend to a total unwillingness to compromise. Both the Nazis and Fascists fully realized this factor when accommodating other elite (largely conservative) groups once in power. For its part, the Independent State of Croatia was simultaneously willing to negotiate out of political necessity (one may even include the 1942 enforced creation of the Serbian Orthodox Church as an example here), while showing no mercy to those ideological outcasts within its grip. The point is, conflating the practical policies of a fascist state with its idealized worldview risks mistaking an ideological core with its specific political manifestations, or in Michael Freeden's terminology, "adjacencies."[31] Keeping the two separate becomes all the more important in the case of the NDH, not least because of the speed in which political events initially transpired in the revolutionary days of spring 1941.

Political Religion

The theory of political religion may facilitate a closer understanding of the NDH. This approach, in brief, holds that the human sense of the sacred is often temporally manifested through phenomenological behavior that need not be directed toward the supernatural, or the divine.[32] Marxist-Leninism, of course, directs faith-based actions at the proletariat, while it was with the nation or race that fascist ideology insisted on investing with a sense of the numinous or divine; yet both ideological systems and their attendant political permutations in the 20th century are, in this reading, ultimately intelligible as secular forms of devotion. Thus, the "*tremendum et fascinosum*" of religious experience dissipates in the face of modernizing Europe's charging horsemen of the apocalypse—anomie, secularisation, consumerism and sweeping technological change, to name but four. At the same time the ideology of the state or *Volk* becomes the new hymn-sheet for the re-christened masses under fascist regimes. The nation therefore becomes both the main icon and cathedral for collective worship.

So long as one can separate the "'technical' aspects of the bid for and assertion of power" (such as political compromise or organisational structure) from their ideological underpinnings, Hans Maier emphatically argues that the concept of political religions helps to explore the latter, for this theory "directly addresses the logic justifying modern despotisms and, with the help of categories from sociology and the psychology of religion, can help us understand it better." [33]

While the features of political religion are more evident in relation to (even dysfunctional) totalitarian states with a period of peacetime consolidation like Nazi Germany and Fascist Italy, the NDH had neither the time nor organisational strength to "convert" a citizenry quickly sliding into civil war against Serbian Chetniks and (mostly communist) partisans; in the summer of 1941, the population was more concerned with daily bread than being a deified nation. Yet the Ustaša never even tried to instill a functional political religion into the Independent State of Croatia. By way of brief example, the object of worship in Slavko Kvaternik's infamous proclamation of independence on 10 April 1941, despite its first word, is not God, but the sacralized nation:

> God's providence and the will of our ally, as well as the hard centuries-long struggle of the Croatian people and the great efforts of our Poglavnik Dr Ante Pavelić and the Ustasha movement both at home and abroad, have determined that today, the day before Easter, our independent Croatian state arise.[34]

Christ's celebrated resurrection during Easter was but the occasion for an even holier, more inspiring resurrection: that of the Croatian nation. The difference is fundamental.

The NDH, not the Catholic orders, oversaw forced conversions; it was Ustaša ideology behind the influx of racial—not religious—anti-Semitism in 1941; and it was the latter's secular ideology that was the driving impetus in the NDH's sanguinary pogroms. By way of example, an avalanche of laws ensuring the "purity" of Croatia from April 1941 (language, culture, race, morality and so on) was largely undertaken against Catholic dogma. This points to Ustašism as not a politicized religion, but a political religion—a sacralized form of secular politics, and hence a travestied form of Christianity (albeit one aided and abetted by a genuine faction of "clerical fascists", which we shall consider presently). Both the fascist ideology long held by Pavelić and his ideologues, as well as their practical decision-making that knowingly increased the Church's marginalization between 1941 and 1945, should not leave in doubt the ultimately secular character of the regime—one brandishing Catholicism like a murderer wields a loaded gun.

Genocide: Murder Weapons in the Hand of the Religious

Shockingly, a Bishop's letter from 1941 lauded "priests in whose hands revolvers might better be placed than a crucifix."[35] This is not unique to Christianity, of course, insofar as religious orders and rituals can get hijacked for a revolutionary cause. Much has been written of late about Islamic fundamentalism as a radical variant, perhaps bastardization, of the Muslim faith, especially since the horrific terrorist bombings of 11 September 2001. Scholars working in this area of political science—calling themselves "Islamicists"—have settled on "Islamism" (rather than "Islamo-fascism", Islamic fundamentalism, or "jihadism") as the preferred term to describe these extremist, frequently violent movements—groups usually traced back, both ideologically and organizationally, to Islamic ideologues like Sayyid Qutb and Hassan al-Banna.[36]

It seems clear that such groups may be profitably categorized within the genre of religious politics rather than political religion. Religious politics, in diametrical contrast to political religions, politicizes an existing faith, meaning that their raison d'être, the core of this worldview, is an earthly-manifested belief in a sacred (supernatural) rather than secular (ideological) cause. But one may ask whether the capacity for organized religion's radical politicization is limited to the Muslim faith, to the postwar world, let alone simply to "terrorists." Those in glass houses ought to be more wary of casting stones: if Islamism may be dispassionately and objectively explored as a radical form of religious politics, might not the same be said about an historic and/or existing "Christianity"?

Compelling evidence has long suggested that Christianity is no more inured to extremist applications of the faith than Islam, with groups no less revolutionary continuing to crusade under a Christian banner in places like the United States, to cite a recent example. And, parallel to the creation of Islamism by the Muslim Brotherhood in 1928, a radical form of Christian religious politics arose in the interwar period. Across Europe in the 1920s and 1930s, a cross-section of Orthodox, Protestant and Catholic clerics—and occasionally their religious organizations—gave material support to radical right and fascist movements. While comparative research on this phenomenon is in its infancy, a few claims can be made that, however tenuously, bear directly upon the case of the NDH.

Like elsewhere in Europe, in the new Yugoslav kingdom political Catholicism and its lay institutions (most notably Catholic Action) were of recent vintage. These movements came to prominence, in no small measure, as a proactive response to many of the same perceived decadences of modern life that fascism likewise arose to combat in the wake of World War One: Marxism and materialism, liberalism and individualism, capitalism and cosmopolitanism. This amorphous movement may be regarded as a fellow-traveler of fascism, with an important article of faith separating their paths: the Christian God (in an extensively elaborated and "revised" version) came first for clerics intervening in politics where, for fascists, the nation became revered, ersatz god. No hard and fast distinction as yet exists in the realms of experimental psychology to show how one "chooses" a particular worldview as a formative organizing principle, but this is arguably the key distinction between political religions—frequently keen to appropriate a particular community's religious tradition as an indicator of its unique cultural identity and nationhood—and religious politics.

The former translate into pseudo-religious categories a secular entity (class, race, nation, and so on). The latter are fundamentally religious interventions into politics. Notwithstanding the terms' semantic similarities, the ideological difference remains immense in works devoted to the study of political religions (e.g. Maoism, Stalinism, Fascism and Nazism). For distinct (indeed, incommensurate) basic mindsets are at work; even if members and their "Christianist" allies in Croatia butchered Serbs side by side, the latter did this out of a wholly misguided application of Catholicism to the moral justification of racial hatred, while for the former, Catholic morality in toto was only useful insofar as it helped realize the utopian state sacralized and deified by an ultimately secular Ustašism. This summary, perhaps, offers an interpretive brush with which to paint Catholic actions during World War Two, capable of distinguishing between secular and religious extremism rather than simply conflating the two. Yet it does not simply exonerate the Catholic Church from all actions taken by men of the cloth within the NDH.

Still, holding individual members of the Catholic clergy accountable for decisions taken in wartime Croatia (or failures to take opposing steps) is an altogether different proposition from holding Catholicism itself accountable for crimes in the NDH that it did not foresee or prevent (although, given the Ustaša's pre-existing credentials for murder, perhaps it should have). Clearly scores of Catholics, within and outside the Church alike, behaved devilishly. But there were also scores of Catholic priests and even more lay Catholics who joined the Partisans in order to fight fascism. That the hierarchy of the Catholic Church in Croatia made a Faustian bargain for long-awaited political sovereignty in 1941 does not itself make its priests, laity or institutions, of necessity, evil. It does, however, raise a final question: What actual proportion of this Catholic congregation may be considered "clerical fascist", or more confessionally specific, "Christianist"?

In the first place, "clerical fascism" may well be an oxymoron when applied beyond clerics, theologians or lay organizations (none of which was enthusiastically embraced by the various fascist movements during the interwar period). In 2008, along with my colleagues Marius Turda and Tudor Georgescu, I edited the first comprehensive academic investigation of the collusion between fascist politics and radicalized Christianity in interwar Europe to date, *Clerical Fascism in Interwar Europe*. Looking at the many examples of clerical fascism together, Croatia's swirling currents of religious politics and political religion are revealed as far from unique. The precise relationship between the two becomes more comprehensible when placed in its international context, and when it is explored heuristically within the context of Griffin's definition of "clerical fascism":

> The ideology and political praxis of clerics and theologians who either tactically support fascism as a movement or regime while maintaining a critical distance from its totalising, revolutionary, and basically secular objectives, or integrate elements of fascist values and policies into the way they conceptualise their mission on earth as devout believers in a divinely ordained world. As such, clerical fascism can never be a movement in its own right with a clerical leadership, independent ideology, and autonomous organisational structure, though it may operate as a discrete faction or constituency within a fascism regime with which it enters a symbiotic relationship.[37]

Wartime Croatia abounded with examples of both tactical support and symbiosis.

A deeper examination of these movements that emerged when editing *Clerical Fascism in Interwar Europe* showed that a certain demographic pattern may also be discernible in terms of clerical adherents to national fascist movements. Mark Biondich's contribution on the Croat clergy notes that "[t]he younger generation of radical Catholics, particularly those reared in the crusader organisation, supported the Ustaša regime with considerable enthusiasm, while the older generation of Croat Populists [HSS] was more reserved and in some cases overtly hostile"[38]; Biondich cites Augustin Juretić's report on the Zagreb Archbishopric of June 1942 which found that "the younger clergy raised in the so-called Crusader organisations is, with few exceptions, completely Ustaša. The majority does not condone the killings—one small part has in general lost all *sensum moralem*."[39]

To be sure, this demography saw radical, especially younger, clerics of all major Christian confessions swept into the ambit of individual fascist movements throughout Europe. In Croatia, the generational gap between conservative and radical Catholic priests in the nearly thousand-strong Zagreb Archdiocese was also divided by: region (and particularly urban centers); order (e.g., Franciscans were more prominently associated with the Ustaša than were, say, the Salesians); geographical location of churches and bishoprics; a given priest's place within the Church hierarchy (with more senior clerics generally disassociating themselves from the NDH); and of course, a wide range of personal experiences and values. Despite the fact that Croatian Catholicism "was a heterogeneous and politically divided movement", the drift of Yugoslav politics increasingly led Catholics in Croatia—lay and clergy alike—toward a wholesale rejection of their fractious interwar state; in practice, Biondich finds, this means "the Catholic movement largely committed itself to Croatian statehood"—a movement itself strongly conditioned by conditions in interwar Yugoslavia—and "the interwar nationalism and growing radicalism of the Catholic movement in Croatia."[40] Patient reform of Yugoslav federal structures therefore gave way to the siren-call of some form of politico-spiritual revolution amongst the Croatian clergy—ends, if not means to those ends, shared by the outlawed Ustaša movement.

As the 1930s Royal Dictatorship wore on, the politicization of Catholicism in Croatia was, without doubt, increasingly tied to Croatian state sovereignty. Faced with the choice between supporting a paralyzed Yugoslav federation and an idealized Independent State of Croatia, the clergy, from Stepinac on down, placed themselves on the side of Croatian sovereignty—and thereby Ustaša rule—in April 1941. It appears to have been an informal, collective decision made at a critical period, one that found the Catholic movement's religious politics seemingly overlapping in a favorable way with Ustašism. That the slaughter unleashed by the NDH caused most of these clerics to rethink this support as early as the summer of 1941 is a vital point to remember before one judges their naïve expectations of Croatian statehood.

But the early endorsement of the Independent State of Croatia—in the interests of crowning the new state at a time when the Croatian clergy, let alone their flock, were caught between rival factions—was a decision held against Catholicism ever since 1941. Indeed, this was a persistent problem throughout the war, as Marcus Tanner's study of Croatia maintains: "The [Catholic] right wing and the clericals were held back from opposing the NDH by their conviction that Croatian independence was a good thing, even if the form that it took under Pavelić was not." [41] This view stands in stark contrast to the unworkably neat division between religion and nation offered by Jelinek: "One may go as far as to say that certain Croat priests became 'schizophrenic' when national and religious demands called for split loyalties; and in nationalistic zeal often breached the Ten Commandments."[42] Whereas religious politics, in a banal sense at least, may be observed wherever clerics become directly involved in politics, the term "Christianism" is intended to denote a more radical, revolutionary approach to secular politics nonetheless also arising from the Judeo-Christian tradition.

The connecting thread is, without doubt, a long one. At one end of the spectrum are the familiar expressions of religious politics, such as a clerical blessing at a political ceremony or event. At the other end are extremist manifestations, such as the German Christians [*Deutsch Christen*] of the 1930s, or The World Church of the Creator today—versions of Christianity predicated on antisemitism and white supremacy—both prime examples of radical right "clerical fascism." And along the axis of religious politics there are many stopping-off points, with Stepinac and most within the Catholic hierarchy in Croatia taking a politically reformist stance to the NDH; certainly not a "Christianist" one. But this does not mean that wartime Croatia was without its share of "Christianists", and more specifically, "clerical fascists." This designation demarcates not only those who personally committed violent acts against the innocent, but also those who knowingly put their religious faith at the disposal of a genocidal state whose aims were clear within several months of taking power. Critically, this view is based on the political fusion, or hybridization (not simply intellectual schizophrenia, or religious "bad faith"), of Catholicism and "Croatianness" by clerics like Archbishop Ivan Šarić of Vrhbosna. And if for these "Christianists", as opposed to secular-minded fascists worshipping the Croatian state via Ustašism, Catholicism's God remained the source of their own first principles, these were truly savaged and perverted.

For the right-wing "Christianists" serving the Independent State of Croatia took Catholicism and transmuted it into a chauvinist, racist, and murderous doctrine, one antithetical to the Jewish Ten Commandments and Christian Beatitudes alike. By way of illustrating the religious zeal within which such "clerical fascists" swaddled their infant state, consider the song for Christmas 1941 by a leading "clerical fascist" and devotee of the NDH, Šarić, entitled "Dedicated to the Poglavnik":

> The poet saw you in the holy city
> in Saint Peter's basilica.
> His presence was as dear to him
> as is our homeland ...
>
> You are both idol of the Croatians,
> you defend the ancient sacred rights.
> The sun beams with you, our noble ones.
> Eternal fame to you!
>
> You are totally dedicated to the homeland,
> you live from the faith, you hero, bold warrior.
> You stand up for freedom of the homeland,
> divine Ustaša ...
>
> Against the greedy Jews with all their money,
> Who wanted to sell our souls,
> betray our names,
> those miserable ones.
>
> You are the rock on which rests
> homeland and freedom in one.
> Protect our lives from hell,

From Marxism and Bolshevism ...[43]

Conclusion

Of all the circumstances plaguing interwar Yugoslavia and wartime Croatia, the interplay of Ustaša political religion and "Christianist" religious politics may be the most noxious and elusive, not to mention destructive. Although this was a marriage of convenience, sharing many common enemies and, above all, an overarching desire for political sovereignty, religion and nation were not the inseparable couple in Croatia that they have sometimes been made out to be.

The interplay was more complex, and less susceptible to neat historiographical analysis. For both radical Catholicism and Ustašism had their own, only partially intertwined, histories. Once pulled apart, these histories are subsumed within comparative studies of fascist political religion and of "clerical fascist" religious politics, respectively. In turn, both belong to the integrated history of modern Europe, not just the abortive and disastrous Independent State of Croatia. In a recent work on the latter subject Jozo Tomasevich concluded, the "Ustaše and their Clericalist allies who constantly stressed that Croatia belongs to the Western world because of its religion, culture, and tradition practiced a politics and ideology that were the antithesis of Western ideals."[44]

These final words offer a comforting thought, but it should not be forgotten that rationally-constructed extermination camps, eugenic racism, as well as secular and divine millenarianism are also, and have long been, integral components of Western modernity, no matter how reluctant historians who uphold the ideals of Enlightenment or Christian humanism are to acknowledge it. That the Ustaša movement turned its back on Christian ideals and resolutely pursued its own bloody path to an alternative modernity through the former set of "values" remains a distasteful subject to consider, but one that must be faced by historians without resorting to crude stereotypes, generalizations, or assumptions about a Croatian Sonderweg. The resulting scholarship may yield further insights not only into the nature of the NDH, but also into the capacity for genocidal excess by "faith-based" protagonists of a new order that would resolve the chaos of early 20th-century history. Certainly, the dehumanizing trajectory of Ustaša barbarism needs to be examined in its own right, through important archival studies like those presented here—employing, where appropriate, heuristic tools like political religion and fascist ideology from a secular perspective, and "Christianism" and "clerical fascism" from a religious one.

In tandem with this, the NDH's place within a broader European "politics and ideology" needs to be explored more thoroughly, in order to illuminate both the specific case of the NDH, as well as the panoramic vistas afforded by the comparative study of religion, ideology and genocide in wartime Croatia. Yet, in doing so the importance of empirical reconstruction and theoretical explanation ought never obscure the fate of millions of innocent civilians, like Duro Schwartz, condemned to experience this manmade apocalypse "on the skin":

Just as in our existence as slave prisoners in this inferno the camp was a world diametrically opposite to the rest of the world, so the people, former prisoners, who had experienced in the depths of their being and on their flesh the satanic side of man and the injustice reigning in all of nature, forever ceased to resemble human beings, equal to the rest of humanity.[45]

Endnotes:

1. Duro Schwartz, "The Jasenovac Death Camps", in Aharon Weiss (ed.), *Yad Vashem Studies*, XXV (Jerusalem: Daf Noy Press, 1996), p. 430. Another harrowing account is provided in Egon Berger, *44 Months in Jasenovac* (Austin: Sentia Publishing, 2017).
2. Schwartz, "The Jasenovac Death Camps", p. 384. Discussion of the difficulty of representing the Holocaust is brilliantly provided in Saul Friedländer (ed.), *Probing the Limits of Representation: Nazism and the Final Solution* (Cambridge, MA: Harvard University Press, 1992).
3. Schwartz, "The Jasenovac Death Camps", p. 386. For general background on NDH genocide, see Ivo and Slavko Goldstein, *The Holocaust in Croatia* (Pittsburgh: University of Pittsburgh Press, 2016).
4. Vladimir Dedijer, *The Yugoslav Auschwitz and the Vatican* (Buffalo: Prometheus Books, 1992).
5. Edmund Glaise von Horstenau, cited in Dan Stone, *Histories of the Holocaust* (Oxford: Oxford University Press, 2010). This otherwise superb account of themes and debates in Holocaust Studies does not view the NDH as an example of an 'independently executed' genocide during World War Two, p. 37.
6. Tomislav Dulić, "Mass killing in the Independent State of Croatia, 1941–1945: a case for comparative research", *Journal of Genocide Research* 8/3 (2006), pp. 255-281.
7. For recent scholarship, see, respectively, Nevenko Bartulin, *The Racial Idea in the Independent State of Croatia: Origins and Theory* (Leiden and Boston: Brill, 2014); Rory Yeomans, *Visions of Annihilation: The Ustaša Regime and the Cultural Politics of Fascism, 1941-1945* (Pittsburgh, University of Pittsburgh Press, 2015); and Aristotle Kallis, "Recontextualizing the Fascist Precedent: The Ustasha Movement and the Transnational Dynamics of Interwar Fascism" in Rory Yeomans, *Life and Death in Wartime Croatia* (Rochester, NY: University of Rochester Press, 2015), pp. 260-283.
8. See "Decorations for Roman Catholic Priests for meritorious Service to the Ustasha State", in Dedijer, *The Yugoslav Auschwitz*, pp. 103-11.
9. For an overview of Croatian nationalism and the revolutionary ideology of the Ustaša, see Goran Miljan, "From Obscure Beginnings to State 'Resurrection': Ideas and Practices of the Ustaša Organization", *Fascism*, 5/1 (2016), pp. 3-25; and for more on the NDH regime, see Jonathan Steinberg, *All or Nothing: The Axis and the Holocaust* (London: Routledge, 2002), pp. 27ff.
10. The preceding two quotations are taken from Dedijer, *The Yugoslav Auschwitz and the Vatican*, pp. 41, 73.
11. John Cornwell, *Hitler's Pope: The Secret History of Pius XII* (London: Penguin, 2000). See also Daniel Jonah Goldhagen, *A Moral Reckoning: The Role of the Catholic Church in the Holocaust and its Unfulfilled Duty of Repair* (Boston: Little, Brown, 2002), for another highly problematic book that takes much the perspective. For a devastating critique of Cornwell's thesis and methodology, see Ronald Rychlak, *Hitler, The War, and The Pope* (Huntington: Our Sunday Visitor, 2000), especially the Epilogue.
12. See David Dalin, "Pius XII and the Jews", *The Weekly Standard* 6/23, 26 February 2001, reprinted online at: www.washingtonexaminer.com/weekly-standard/pius-xii-and-the-jews-1806 (all websites last accessed 17 February 2020).
13. José Mariano Sánchez, *Pius XII and the Holocaust: Understanding the Controversy* (Washington, DC: Catholic University of America Press, 2002), p. 177.

14. William Doino Jr., "An Annotated Bibliography of Works on Pius XII, the Second World War, and the Holocaust", in Joseph Bottum and David G. Dalin (eds.), *The Pius War: Responses to Critics of Pius XII* (Lanham: Lexington Books, 2004); see especially Parts Four and Five, pp. 158-211.
15. See Thomas Woods, review of David Dalin's *The Myth of Hitler's Pope*: "How Pope Pius XII Rescued Jews from the Nazis", online at: www.lewrockwell.com/woods/woods48.html.
16. See Pierre Blet, *Pius XII and the Second World War: According to the Archives of the Vatican*, trans. Lawrence J. Johnson (Hereford: Gracewing, 1999), pp. 139-81; quoted p. 167.
17. *Ibid.*, p. 161.
18. *Ibid.*
19. Edmond Paris, *Genocide in Satellite Croatia, 1941-1945* (Chicago: Institute for Balkan Affairs, 1962). The anonymously edited *The Third Reich and Yugoslavia* (Belgrade: Institute for Contemporary History, 1977) contains essays in several different languages. By contrast, Sabrina Ramet's special issue of *Totalitarian Movements and Political Religions*, "The Independent State of Croatia, 1941-45", 7/4 (2006), was composed solely of English-language articles (articles published in *TMPR* were by Sabrina Ramet, Stanley Payne, Ivo Goldstein, Mark Biondich, Mario Jareb and Nada Kisić Kolanović).
20. Quoted in Dedijer, *The Yugoslav Auschwitz*, p. 317.
21. See Jozo Tomasevich, *War and Revolution in Yugoslavia 1941-1945: Occupation and Collaboration* (Stanford, CA: Stanford University Press, 2001), 781. Relevant, too, is an earlier volume by the same author, dealing almost exclusively with the Greater Serbian movement of Chetniks: *War and Revolution in Yugoslavia 1941-1945: The Chetniks* (Stanford, CA: Stanford University Press, 1975).
22. Ivo Goldstein, "The Independent State of Croatia in 1941: On the road to Catastrophe", *Totalitarian Movements and Political Religions*, 7/4 (2006) p. 422.
23. Roger Griffin (ed.), *International Fascism: Theories, Causes and the New Consensus* (London: Arnold, 1998). For shorter, pivotal extracts of scholarly interpretations of fascism, also see Aristotle Kallis' edited *The Fascist Reader* (London: Routledge, 2003); for longer analyses of fascism, consult Roger Griffin with Matthew Feldman (eds.), *Fascism: Critical Concepts*, 5 vols. (London: Routledge, 2004).
24. Cf. Bela Vargo, writing in 1976: "The authors of a detailed scholarly work about the Croatian State—Andreas Hory and Martin Broszat—suggest the term *pre-fascist* or *semi-fascist* for the movement. And in [Ernst] Nolte's view there is no certainty whatsoever that the Ustasha movement actually qualifies as fascist at all." From "Fascism in Eastern Europe," cited in Walter Laqueur (ed.), *Fascism: A Reader's Guide* (Berkeley & Los Angeles, CA: University of California Press, 1976), p. 248.
25. See Roger Griffin, *The Nature of Fascism* (London: Routledge, 1993), p. 120.
26. Elie Kedourie, "Nationalism and Self-Determination", cited in Anthony Smith (ed.), *Nationalism* (Oxford: Oxford University Press, 1994), quoted pp. 49-51.
27. Currents of eugenics and racial anthropology in Croatia also no doubt contributed to the construction of the "new Croatian man", which Rory Yeomans effectively documents in "Of 'Yugoslav Barbarians' and Croatian Gentlemen Scholars: Nationalist Ideology and Racial Anthropology in Interwar Yugoslavia", in Marius Turda and Paul Weindling (eds.), *Blood and Homeland: Eugenics and Racial Nationalism in Central and Southeastern Europe, 1900-1940* (Budapest: Central European Press, 2006), pp. 83-122, especially pp. 102-16.
28. Cited in Ivo Goldstein, *Croatia: A History* (London: Hurst and Company, 1999), p. 135.

[29] See *ibid.*, which further notes that "Pavelić was welcomed by about 2,000 'sworn' Ustaše who had been working underground in the country", followed by some "100,000 members who had sworn the Ustasha oath" by May 1941, pp. 133-4.

[30] See Ivo Goldstein, "Ante Pavelić, Charisma and National Mission in Wartime Croatia", in António Costa Pinto, Roger Eatwell, and Stein Ugelvik Larsen (eds.), "Charisma and Fascism in Interwar Europe", *Totalitarian Movements and Political Religions* 7.2 (2006), pp. 225-34.

[31] For the distinction between "core" and "adjacent" ideological manifestations, see Michael Freeden, "Political Concepts and Ideological Morphology", *Journal of Political Philosophy* 2.2 (1994), pp. 140–64.

[32] The theory is given currency within political science by Eric Voegelin (and, to a lesser extent, Raymond Aron, building upon Weber, Durkheim, Eliade and others), but is now associated especially with Emilio Gentile and Hans Maier.

[33] Hans Maier "Concepts for the comparison of dictatorships", in Hans Maier (ed.), *Totalitarianism and Political Religions*, vol. 1 (Abingdon: Routledge, 2004), quoted pp. 205, 209 (my emphasis). For further discussion of political religion theory in relation to fascist ideology, see Maier's three volumes of *Totalitarianism and Political Religions* (Abingdon: Routledge, 2005/8) and Emilio Gentile's *Politics as Religion*, trans. George Staunton (Princeton, N.J. & Oxford: Princeton University Press, 2006).

[34] See Tomasevich, *Revolution and Occupation*, p. 53. The similar message, but with an explicitly different object of veneration, is striking in comparison with the opening of Stepinac's pastoral letter from 28 April 1941: "There is no one among you who in recent times has not been witness to the important events in the life of the Croatian people, in which we as messengers of Christ's gospel have been active ... And who can chastise us when we as spiritual leaders contribute our part to the joy and the enthusiasm of the people, when we full of deep emotion and warm gratitude turn to the divine majesty", cited in Dedijer, *The Yugoslav Auschwitz*, p. 95.

[35] Dr Franjo Butorac, Bishop of Koto, letter to Stepinac of 4 Nov. 1941, cited in Herbert Butler, "The Artukovitch File", in R. F. Foster (ed.), *The sub-prefect should have held his tongue, and other essays* (London: Allen Lane, 1990), p. 289.

[36] For a valuable summary of the development of Islamism, as well as details about Sayyid Qutb, Hassan al-Banna, and the founding of the Muslim Brotherhood, see Sayed Khatab, *The Power of Sovereignty: The Political and Ideological Philosophy of Sayyid Qutb* (London: Routledge, 2006); and Richard Paul Mitchell, *The Society of the Muslim Brothers* (Oxford: Oxford University Press, 1993). For a general and more recent analysis, see Malise Ruthven, "Can Islam be criticized?", *New York Review of Books Daily*, 11 October 2012, online at: www.nybooks.com/daily/2012/10/11/can-islam-be-criticized/.

[37] Roger Griffin, "'The 'Holy Storm': 'Clerical Fascism' through the Lens of Modernism", in Matthew Feldman and Marius Turda with Tudor Georgescu (eds.), *Clerical Fascism in Interwar Europe* (Abingdon: Routledge, 2008), p. 5.

[38] Mark Biondich, "Radical Catholicism and Fascism in Croatia, 1918-1945", in Matthew Feldman and Marius Turda (eds.), "'Clerical' Fascism in Interwar Europe", *Totalitarian Movements and Political Religions*, 8.2 (June 2007), p. 393, reprinted in Feldman and Turda with Georgescu (eds.), *Clerical Fascism in Interwar Europe*, p. 181.

[39] Mark Biondich, "Controversies Surrounding the Catholic Church in Wartime Croatia, 1941-45," in Sabrina P. Ramet (ed.), "The Independent State of Croatia (NDH), 1941-45", *Totalitarian Movements and Political Religions* 7.4 (Dec. 2006), p. 445. Biondich also notes: "As Aleksa Djilas has quite correctly pointed out, Catholicism for the Ustaše 'was primarily an

instrument for strengthening the state rather than a goal in itself', which distinguished the Ustaše markedly from the Hlinka movement in Slovakia, which was genuinely Catholic and led by priests". *Ibid.*

[40] Biondich (2007), pp. 387, 393, reprinted in Feldman and Turda with Georgescu (eds.), *Clerical Fascism in Interwar Europe*, pp. 175, 181.

[41] Marcus Tanner, *Croatia: A Nation Forged in* War (New Haven, Conn., and London: Yale University Press, 2001), p. 156.

[42] See Yeshayahu Jelinek, "Clergy and Fascism: The Hlinka Party in Slovakia and the Croatian Ustasha Movement", in Stein Ugelvik Larsen, Bernt Hagtvet and Jan Petter Myklebust (eds.), *Who Were the Fascists?* (Bergen: Universitetsforlaget, 1980), pp. 367-78, quoted p. 371.

[43] Ivan Šaric, "Thoughts at Christmas Time", reproduced in Dedijer, *The Yugoslav Auschwitz*, pp. 97-98.

[44] Cited in Tomasevich, *Revolution and Occupation*, p. 783.

[45] Schwartz, "The Jasenovac Death Camps", p. 430.

10. Showing the 'Unshowable'?: A Generation of "Mainstream" Films on the Shoah

In mid-August 2008, it emerged that Quentin Tarantino, director of popular Hollywood films including *Pulp Fiction, Death Proof*, and *From Dusk Till Dawn* "and master of bloodbath cinema", had his 165-page film-script for *Inglourious Basterds* [sic] leaked online.[1] Given that this remake of Enzo G. Castellari's 1978 *Quel Maladetto Treno Blindato* centres upon 8 Jewish-American soldiers sent to take Nazi scalps behind enemy lines against the backdrop of the Holocaust in wartime Europe, objections have already been raised on grounds of propriety, historical appropriateness and, quite simply, taste.[2] Put another way, in the generation since the landmark *Schindler's List* from 1993, has the Holocaust become yet one more kitsch setting for mainstream films? Consider the following dialogue from the script, ultimately given to Brad Pitt's lead character, Lt. Aldo Raine in the 2009 film, *Inglourious Basterds*:

> We're gonna be dropped into France, dressed as civilians. And once we're in enemy territory, as a bushwackin' guerilla army, we're gonna be doin one thing, and thing only, Killin Nazi's. The members of the Nationalist Socialist Party, have conquered Europe through murder, torture, intimidation, and terror. And that's exactly what we're gonna do to them. ... But I got a word of warning to all would be warriors. When you join my command, you take on debit. A debit you owe me, personally. Every man under my command, owes me, one hundred Nazi scalps. And I want my scalps. And all y'all will git me, one hundred Nazi scalps, taken from the heads of one hundred Nazi's or you will die trying.[3]

On account of the tremendous shadow cast by the Shoah, debates are likely to persist over how mainstream cinema represents, and ought to represent (or indeed, not represent), the Nazis' murder of 6 million innocent European Jews. Amidst the furore caused by Tarantino's staging of action-adventure film, it seems rather more general principles over Holocaust films merit reflection and contextualisation. In doing so, this chapter will focus upon in the general way in which the Final Solution has been presented—*pace* Theodor Adorno's well-known view—in the light of an *ineffability*, an unrepresentability or 'unshowability', posed "after Auschwitz". Adorno's famous objection suggests that representing this most perfected of inhumane genocides is perhaps not within the traditional capacity of a European art, which is conceived as humane, mimetic, and representational. Indeed, it is telling that Adorno's two exceptions to his (later partially-retracted) dictum that "poetry after Auschwitz is barbaric", Samuel Beckett and Paul Celan, are philosopher-poets who, though in many ways dissimilar, both pushed against the boundaries of representation, of speech and silence, of the very nature of narration itself—as suggested even by titles such as Beckett's *Worstward Ho* or Celan's "textvoid".[4] Yet if art of a striking variety (and quality) continues to be produced 'after Auschwitz', a narrower question in this paradoxical spirit may be posed: are films made *about* Auschwitz (and more generally, the Shoah)—especially faced by this problem of the ineffable, given the subject matter's scope and brutality—capable of adequately depicting their subject? And in mainstream films necessarily oriented toward profit, no less?

It is first worth recalling that these were certainly *not* questions that greeted Allied liberators of Nazi camps in 1945, nor were they generally posed in the immediate aftermath of the Second World War. Importantly, it was really only in the last forty-five years or so that the Shoah became recognisable as a separate, or at least distinct, aspect of the Third Reich—usually understood as taking place between the onset of war with Poland on 1 Sept. 1939 and the surrender of Germany on 8 May 1945 (although sometimes the Final Solution is understood to have lasted nearly double this time, from Hitler's assumption of power on 30 January 1933).[5] To be sure, one reason for a shift in examining the Shoah in its own right was the 1961 Israeli trial of Adolf Eichmann, so capturing the world's attention. It also located the Shoah as a central plank of Nazi wartime planning and policy, in addition to making available many thousands of documents for scholarly study. That same year, Raul Hilberg's groundbreaking study was first published, *The Destruction of the European Jews*. In part, thanks to his and other contributions—from the 1960s onwards, in particular (with no slight to Gerald Reitlinger's 1953 *The Final Solution* intended)—historians' impressive labours on the Shoah have resulted in an unusual distinction: the Final Solution is the best-documented genocide in human history. To necessarily summarise a rich and nuanced historiography, it might be fair to say that historians now broadly conceive of the Third Reich as fighting two, sometimes overlapping, wars from September 1939, and certainly from June 1941: one against soldiers and other combatants, including partisans; the other against civilians deemed ideological enemies—the disabled, Roma and Sinti travellers, or Gypsies; and above all, European Jewry *in toto*.

And what about the general public in the initial decades after 1945? Many would have read the Eichmann Trial reportage between April and August 1961 by Hannah Arendt in the *New Yorker* (published in book form in 1963 as *Eichmann in Jerusalem: A Report on the Banality of Evil*), while some also bought Hilberg's book released in the year of the trial. Yet surely most—then as now—had their understanding of the Shoah largely mediated by film and, to a lesser extent, radio. The vast majority of early films on the Holocaust were documentaries, news reports or memoirs of one type or another, ranging in style from BBC documentaries on the liberation of Bergen-Belsen in Spring 1945 and Alain Resnais' influential *Night and Fog* [*Nuit et Brouillard*] a decade later, to George Stevens's *The Diary of Anne Frank* in 1959, which won three Oscars. Yet surely, such films cannot be called 'fiction' in the same way that, say, Elem Klimov's Hungarian film from 1985, *Come and See*, or Alan Pakula's 1982 *Sophie's Choice* (based on William Styron's 1979 novel of the same name) are understood as fictional—neither of the latter films are 'Based upon a True Story', although both deploy a largely historically accurate backdrop of Nazi occupation in wartime Europe in their representations.

Moreover, it may be that the revelations of the former facilitated the creativity of the latter; that is to say, the rich but infrequent stream of informative documentaries on the Final Solution may have created the public space whereby fictional accounts could be subsequently contemplated as marketable films. As 'mainstream', internationally-released and widely-screened films are the thrust of this contribution—for example, Roberto Benigni's *Life is Beautiful* was released over Christmastime 1997, the traditional period for Italian domestic competition with imported films, usually from Hollywood—it merits pausing over two preceding Holocaust films that can justly claim to have brought the Final Solution to widespread public attention, even perhaps helping to usher in subsequent films taking greater 'creative license' with the Shoah. Perched atop the pinnacle of this simultaneously informative and memorialising filmmaking endeavour is certainly Claude Lanzmann's 1985 *Shoah*, a nearly 10-hour series of interviews with victims and perpetrators of the Final Solution (followed by the publication of the film's transcript in 1986). Yet even this cinematic triumph had built upon the 'small screen' some dozen years earlier, in the form of ITV's 26-part mini-series shown weekly in the UK for six months over 1973-74, *The World at War*. In the Anglophone media at least, the latter continues to be hailed as the best documentary of World War Two ever produced, and fully three of the 26 fifty-minute episodes are devoted to Nazi genocide and the Final Solution. With Lanzmann's *Shoah*, it is also considered the best of the genre dominating early filmic representations of the Shoah: documentaries probing the enormity of Nazi genocide against European Jewry. In one excerpt from the 27 March 1974 *World at War* episode "Genocide: 1941-1945", for example, footage of the liberation of Majdenek is followed by an interview with a Hungarian *Sonderkommando* named Dov Paisikovic:

> I was present when the Gypsies were brought for burning, for gassing. A terrible sight. There were cries to the sky. Cries in the bunker and the crematoria and the gas chamber were horrible. I still wonder today how God didn't hear these cries. It's a wonder to me today that He didn't hear such a thing. They were horrible, the cries to the sky.

Perhaps it is just distance, the passage of time, which dictated that earlier films on the Shoah were austere and documentary, but which allowed later directors, producers and screenwriters a degree of representational freedom that was unthinkable in the 1950s, 1960s and 1970s—the decades closest to the events depicted. But it seems that there is another impulse at work in subsequent feature films placed on general release: a ubiquitous need to 'tell a story'—specifically, one showing that things are bad, but that the real horror is taking place outside the world portrayed onscreen; one only alluded to, gestured at. One might here refer to Beckett's elliptical use of Shakespeare's King Lear soliloquy in his 1983 *Worstward Ho*: "The worst is not, so long as we can say, this is the worst". With this seemingly opaque analogy in mind, this chapter will now broach several cases of filmic representations of the Shoah since 1993.

In *The Guardian*'s October 2007 review, "The Bitterest Pill", Jonathan Freedland detects "a subtle form of evasion" in Stefan Ruzowitzky's *The Counterfeiters* [*Die Fälscher*] from the same year. Freedland finds the trope to be "the perennial obstacle confronting all films about the Holocaust, namely how to portray the unportrayable (clearly no actors can ever be as bone-thin, as starved, as the camps' real victims)".[6] To make this point, however, one might have instead turned to the words of an academic rather than a journalist. For example, writing in an important 2005 edited collection, *Holocaust and the Moving Image*, Trudy Gold begins her survey of mainstream American films on the Final Solution by declaring: "The story of the Holocaust can never really be realistically told. Six million [Jewish—sic] men, women and children were murdered, six million untold stories. Consequently all the feature filmmaker can ever do is to recreate a small part of the tragedy".[7] And this essential interpretative thread linking so many films dealing with the Shoah was already captured by the title of Annette Insdorf's groundbreaking work fully a generation earlier, *Indelible Shadows: Film and the Holocaust*. In praise of Insdorf, "the best critic in America on Holocaust films", Elie Wiesel returned to the dilemma of representation in his 1989 "Foreword" to Insdorf's second edition (now revised and in third edition as of 2003): "An ontological phenomenon, "The Final Solution" is located beyond understanding [….] One does not imagine the unimaginable. And in particular, one does not show it on screen". This leads Wiesel to ask, "if we allow total freedom to the mass media, don't we risk seeing them profane and trivialize a sacred subject?"[8]

Here is the dilemma starkly facing films of the Holocaust over, at the very least, the last generation. Various demands pull upon each other: film companies' drive for profit; the canonical audience reassurance of a 'happy ending'; both ranged against the horror of actual events, and the ethics demanded of contemporary cinema in depicting these. And underlying all of these is still another challenge. As forcefully expressed by Saul Friedländer's pivotal "Introduction" in his edited *Probing the Limits of Representation*, "we are dealing with an event which tests our traditional conceptual and representational categories, an 'event at the limits' [....] there are limits to representation *which should not be but can easily be transgressed*".[9] Intriguingly, Friedländer cites Paul Celan's poetry and Lanzmann's *Shoah* as instances where "the unsayable is almost directly presented", in a form of *"allusive or distanced realism"*, clearly his preference for artistically presenting the Final Solution: "Reality is there in its starkness, but perceived through a filter: that of memory (distance in time), that of spatial displacement, that of some sort of narrative margin which leaves the unsayable unsaid."[10] Before returning to the 'big picture' offered here on mainstream films dealing with the Shoah—or rather, many of these films' tendency to circumvent, avoid and perhaps minimise those un-representable realities comprising the Final Solution—there are (at least) two very different objections to analysing how this "unsayable" has been expressed, or rather more narrowly, how the 'unshowable' has been screened. One of these concerns the aesthetics of the medium of film generally, while the other is more specifically concerned with the politics of filmic representation. Both of these should be acknowledged, if ultimately side-stepped for reasons peripheral on brevity and relevance to the subject at hand.

The first problem is how to realistically represent *anything* through the medium of film. Techniques such as editing and cutting, music, sound effects and "the simultaneous use of several systems of expression";[11] questions of narrative and selection (meaning what is shown by the camera as opposed to what is not); and of course the perceptual distortions intrinsic to film—all of these are long-running objections to filmic mimesis that cannot be given space here.[12] Suffice it to say, a film is not the same as real life. Yet at the same time, film remains valid as 'evidence' of all kinds, from CCTV and courtroom prosecutions to archival footage of the 27 January 1945 liberation of Auschwitz-Birkenau (which has since become the annual commemorative date for Holocaust Memorial Day). Indeed, despite its constraints, filmic representations of the past may be seen as new ways of 'doing history', as witnessed in Robert Rosenstone's plea for historians to investigate film's "rules of engagement with the traces of the past, and investigating the codes, conventions, and practices by which they bring history to the screen".[13] The contention underlying Rosenstone's three categories of historical film—"the dramatic feature film", "the documentary film", and "the baggy category" that constitutes "opposition or innovative film"—is that cinematic representation of the past faces a fundamentally different challenge from that of doing traditional history 'on the page': comparing the two is like comparing fish and fowl.[14]

A second, distinct objection follows from what Norman Finkelstein has mischievously termed "The Holocaust Industry"; that is, an "ideological representation" of the actual events surrounding the Nazis' genocide against European Jewry. Financial considerations, "vulgarization" and trivialisation of complex historical events, and the putative advancement of a pro-Zionist agenda all feature in Finkelstein's outspoken critique: "Too many public and private resources have been invested in memorializing the Nazi genocide. Most of the output is worthless, a tribute not to Jewish suffering put to Jewish aggrandizement."[15] Even if Finkelstein goes overboard, the implication for feature films on the Shoah is clear: the historical "modes of emplotment"—here I refer to Hayden White's similar view of how the past is made a narrative, with varying constraints, by largely "modernist" modes of representing the past[16]—are bounded by certain values and agendas; in the case of film, institutional constraints producing a subtly ideological and entertaining, rather than an informative or didactic, portrait of the Final Solution. Granted that they do so to a far less polemical degree, similar works like Peter Novick's *The Holocaust in American Life* have also raised important questions about the 'ownership' of memory and representation, with especial emphasis upon a perceived "Americanization" of the Shoah.[17]

These are substantial points worth exploring further, doubtless impacting upon the cultural influence of Hollywood's global reach; and consequently, upon representations of the Final Solution through cultural mores derived from the United States' film industry—not an entirely comforting thought, contra Rosenstone's view. To circumvent some of these objections—in a volume focussing upon Britain and the Holocaust, no less—consideration will be squarely placed upon five 'mainstream' Holocaust films with very different profiles: *Schindler's List* (1993), *Life is Beautiful* [*La Vita è bella*] (1999), *Jakob the Liar* (1999), *The Pianist* (2003), and briefly in conclusion, *Black Book* [*Zwartboek*] (2006). In addition to broaching how such a diverse range of international films have navigated this 'showing the unshowable' of the Shoah, some attention will be given to each of these films' reception by British theatres and audiences. With respect to the films cited here, the following table provides some details for British releases:

TABLE 1

Film Title	UK Release Date	UK Box Office Total Gross	Opening Weekend	Highest # of Screens
Schindler's List	18/2/1994	£13,828,187	£229,855	225
Life is Beautiful	14/2/1999	£1,981,831	£87,818	76
The Pianist	24/1/2003	£2,564,468*	£204,501*	93
Black Book	19/1/2007	£210,527*	£791,569*	85
The Counterfeiters	12/10/1997	£152,858*	£844,818*	68
The Boy in the Striped Pyjamas	12/9/2008	£4,768,092	£513,653	201
The Reader	4/1/2009	£5,371,138	£671,064	226
Defiance	8/1/2009	£3,309,017	£1,198,425	328

Compiled via official details provided by *The Independent Movie Database* (imdb), available online at www.imdb.com; and *Box Office Mojo*, available online at www.boxofficemojo.com/movies. Figures not adjusted for inflation.
* Figures converted from US dollars and rounded to the nearest GB pound, based upon currency rates as of 11/10/11.

Although two miniseries originally aired in the United States had previously been screened to great notoriety—*Holocaust* (1979) and *War and Remembrance* (1988)—Steven Spielberg's *Schindler's List* is justly credited with being the first big-budget Hollywood treatment of the Shoah as subject (unlike, say, Stanley Kramer's 1961 *Judgment at Nuremberg*), garnering 7 Oscars and literally tens of millions of viewers. In Britain, interestingly, viewers flocked to see the film: screenings of *Schindler's List* took nearly 10% of the total foreign income for the film ($225,240,537), making it the fourth highest grossing country (at $21,170,107), behind only Germany ($38,500,174), Japan ($32,785,635) and of course the United States ($96,065,768).[18] Shot in black and white—excepting a little girl in a red dress and a closing scene featuring a tribute at Schindler's gravesite—the film centres around Liam Neeson's protagonist, Oskar Schindler, whose character progressively shifts from that of a venal businessman and war profiteer, willing, earlier in the film, to both exploit suffering Jews from the Krakow Ghetto and sell his wares to Nazi officials (most prominently represented by Amon Goeth, played by Ralph Fiennes). This creates an initially fractious relationship with Itzak Stern (Ben Kingsley), which changes after Schindler encounters the now-dead girl in a red dress at a horrific cremation site.

Here, perhaps, viewers see more than just a "corner of the calamity": sadistic guards enjoying their 'work'; bodies dumped onto makeshift crematoria to dispose of evidence; the labours of the *Sonderkommandos* very similar to those recounted in *The World at War*. Immediately following this pivotal scene, in which Schindler sees the dead body of the little girl in the red dress being carried on a cart toward the makeshift crematoria, he makes a list in order to save 1,100 Jews from deportation to Auschwitz, and is memorably told by Stern: "The list is an absolute good.

The list is life. All around its margins lies the gulf". Yet saving Jews in Czechoslovakia bankrupts Schindler, who is later told the news by Stern; another quick cut to the next scene then presents Churchill's announcement of Nazi Germany's surrender over the radio. The film ends with "Schindler's Jews" marching forward collectively, transposed into colour images for the final shot; namely, a sequence of rescued Jews and their descendants named in the film, each setting memorial stones at Oskar Schindler's historical grave. In this way, despite the unprecedentedly negative subject matter, *Schindler's List* provides viewers with a (relatively) 'happy ending', one that concludes by merging the artistic rendering of history into the commemorative act made by actual survivors and their families.

Like *Schindler's List*, Roman Polanski's *The Pianist*, winner a decade later of the *Palme d'Or* at the Cannes Film Festival, was inspired by published events. Unlike Thomas Keneally's *Schindler's Ark*, however, *The Pianist's* real-life protagonist, Władysław Szpilman, had written an autobiographical work, posthumously published in 1999 as *Das wunderbare Überleben* [*The Miraculous Survival*]. Polanski, a Polish director and survivor of the Krakow Ghetto whose mother and sister died in the Nazis' Final Solution, had earlier turned down the opportunity to direct *Schindler's List* as it "seemed too close to his own experience".[19] Yet for its part, *The Pianist* centres on a Jewish pianist in occupied Poland, played by the American actor, Adrien Brody, who survives the inferno of several ghettos and camps despite the murder of his family at the hands of the Nazis.

And in *The Pianist* there are further, relevant parallels with *Schindler's List*. One cluster of similarities is cinematic: German is not rendered into English via subtitles, for example, conveying a sense of distance from the perpetrators in both films (considering that both were initially Anglophone releases initially). Another parallel is the way in which, after his miraculous survival in increasingly horrific conditions, Brody's rendering of Szpilman concludes with a scene of his playing the piano in wartime Warsaw—albeit not the same Bach English Suite used in the Krakow Ghetto clearance scene of *Schindler's List*—as the film then cuts to a reinvigorated Szpilman, continuing to play, but now in a packed auditorium in postwar Poland. This raises a second set of parallels with *Schindler's List*, and indeed, with Freedland's comments about *The Counterfeiters*. Once again viewers are presented with a comparatively positive conclusion to the film, brought about by Szpilman—and as a result, the camera—remaining outside 'the worst' of the violence. Giving voice to a number of these events depicted in *The Pianist*, Szpilman watches the Warsaw Ghetto uprising brutally suppressed by Jürgen Stroop through a secluded window, lamenting, "I should have stayed". While the fragility of life in wartime Poland is powerfully conveyed in both films, a sense of distance and comparative 'luck' nevertheless remains, of better material circumstances shared by both 'Schindler's Jews' and Salomon Sorowitsch's counterfeiters (the latter also based on a memoir; in this case Adolf Burger's 2007 *The Devil's Workshop* [*Die Fälscher*]; the character played by August Diehl in *The Counterfeiters*).

With these "dramatic feature films" a number of overlapping features emerge. First, there is a trope of Hollywood-style positive endings at historical variance with the Shoah: some 80% of Europe's Jews perished in the Holocaust, whereas most Jews in films representing the Final Solution survive. The vast majority of victims and their families were brutally murdered *without* privileged conditions; *without* the comparative safety of Szpilman's (or Anne Frank's) attic or Schindler's and Sorowitsch's workshops; and of course, *with* all those terrifying things that naturally cannot be rendered onscreen: the smell, the fear, the hunger, the omnipresence of murder. This distancing from events may be necessary for dramatic representation of the Final Solution; it may even be a technique expected by critics tuned into the 'unrepresentability' of either film generally or Shoah films specifically. But this is a presentation of history fundamentally different from that of the printed page and the archive, and necessarily so. Nor, surely, would it do to simply dispense with the latter. For example, it is easy to leave a viewing of the 2008 *Valkyrie*, Bryan Singer's reconstruction of the July 1944 assassination attempt against Hitler, with the impression that the Wehrmacht were a pretty democratic, peace-loving lot. Broadly speaking, the problems of historical faithfulness would not have such immediacy if the same number of viewers had read, say, the work of Omer Bartov or attended the Hamburg Institute's "Crimes of the Wehrmacht 1941-1944" exhibition.[20]

And yet, for all of its seeming faults of sentimentality and representational evasion, this genre of Shoah film has been remarkably successful. Here, the gold standard remains *Schindler's List*, whose success can be measured on three fronts: it has been seen by a quarter of the United States population and tens of millions beyond; hailed by a majority of critics and numerous awarding bodies; and thirdly, significantly, also credited by survivors and educators with piquing much greater public interest in the Shoah. In the words of one Holocaust survivor: "that lousy film of *Schindler's List* is a tremendous help. I lecture in schools all the time, and wherever *Schindler's List* has been shown in advance there is the most incredible attendance." Indeed, added another survivor at this round-table event, it "opened the doors for us into schools, into universities […] I think it was a very valuable film, even though it has got its weaknesses". In fact, a number of other survivors also specifically cite this film as a turning point in public understandings of the Final Solution, at least in the case of the US: "before it there was very little talk about the Holocaust. It was suppressed. In my case, for fifty years I didn't touch it, because I didn't think people would believe me. So it was the Schindler film that broke the silence." Thus in terms of engendering a public response, and pointing to the reality of the Nazi concentration and death camps—however sanitised—Holocaust films have also been lauded for raising consciousness and debate:

> We've been speaking to schools for a number of years, long before *Schindler's List*. But no matter how much hard work we did, it didn't mean very much. *Schindler's List* put us on the map. Whether we like the film or we don't like it is not important at all, that fact is that it depicts what happened. Whether there is some fellow who is a Nazi, whatever Schindler was, it's unimportant—it shows the camps. I know some of these camps, and it gets absolutely right what happened there. Therefore when we go into schools now there is more credence to our memories.[21]

From a didactic and educational perspective, still more problematic are 'fables' of the Final Solution, which demonstrate less fidelity to events; even to the point of backgrounding them, as Giacomo Lichtner has effectively concluded in his analysis of Roberto Benigni's 1997 *La vita è bella* [*Life is Beautiful*]:

> this film is not really about the Holocaust as much as it is about a father-child relationship and the faith in innocence as a shield against life's 'ugliness'. Because in spite of its title and its artificial ending, in spite of its own simplistic message, what one can discern in Benigni's film is in fact that life is not always beautiful. Indeed, immediately after the characters' arrival in the concentration camp, Benigni seems to begin to deconstruct his films own fairytale structure and reject its axiom. The climax of this rejection is reached with the father's (Guido's) death, but suddenly denied by the child's (Giosuè's) triumphant exit aboard a US tank, to re-establish the dominant ethics of the film.'[22]

Prior to the climactic scene featuring his (yet again) off-camera execution, Guido cross-dresses to gain entry into the women's section of this unnamed camp in order to see his wife—the basis of the first half of the film, a love story. In keeping with the narrative of the second half of the film, Guido instructs his son Giosuè to hide in a metal box in order to win the game they are playing: this is to shield him (and indeed the audience as well) from the brutality against, and expected extermination of, inmates in the camp. While the Nazis are razing the buildings, Guido is caught trying to enter the women's camp and marched past his son to his death, where events are once again viewed through a visual 'screen'. While also internationally acclaimed (and sometimes recognised as raising public consciousness through debate in a manner similar to *Schindler's List*), many more critics found the tone in *Life is Beautiful* to be overly sentimental and light-hearted. For this new genre of non-"dramatic feature films" on the Holocaust begs Saul Friedländer's question once more: *How much* license should screenwriters, directors and producers have with this subject-matter? To put this another way: is the tragic and/or dramatic the only appropriate perspective for filmic representations of the Final Solution?

Above all, just such questions were piqued by films like Benigni's *Life is Beautiful* and *Jakob the Liar* (directed by Peter Kassovitz and released in 1999). Both employ humour structurally—sometimes slapstick in the tradition of Chaplin's *The Great Dictator* (1940), and more frequently black humour (recalling the montage scene of Hitler and Stalin dancing in Agnieska Holland's 1990 *Europa Europa*) — in order to circumvent the most brutal aspects of the Shoah. In response, a number of trenchant critiques, for instance, found Benigni's *Life is Beautiful* by turns implausible, inappropriate, and unduly "reassuring like *Schindler's List*". Even more damningly, wrote Thane Rosenbaum:

> *Life is Beautiful* may be yet another example of society's obsession with exploiting the images and symbols of the Holocaust, in order to satisfy a popular culture that depends on atrocity for entertainment [....] The camps were foremost about death, and, in their aftermath, memory, but on no occasion should they be used as a soundstage for slapstick.[23]

If difficult, a historical riposte might nonetheless be advanced: did ghettoised Jews use humour itself as a defence or protective mechanism? This contentious view is explicitly engaged in the "Extra Features" section of the DVD release for *Jakob the Liar*. Interspersed with light-hearted moments form the film, Robin Williams, who plays the eponymous hero, states in an interview:

> It's weird because people who, survivors who've read the script said please don't be afraid of the humour. They knew it happened. It's the little things—especially in the ghetto and especially in that time—little moments of human kindness. This goes back and forth between being very funny and very tragic within moments. Shards of the tiniest thing meant the world.

Based like *The Pianist* on a memoir—Jurek Becker's acclaimed 1969 *Jakob der Lügner*, first made into a 1974 East German film directed by Frank Beyer—Kossovitz's 1999 reworking is set "somewhere in Poland" in "Winter 1944", and features the American comedian Robin Williams as Jakob Heym. Throughout, humour is used as a defence against Nazi occupation, right from the opening joke about Hitler's death being a cause for a Jewish holiday, followed by the critical voice-over offered by the protagonist:

> So you ask me as a Jew, 'How can you tell a joke like that a time like that?' That's how we survived, and those are some of the things that kept us going. Everything else the Germans had taken. They built high walls covered in barbed wire to shove us in the ghetto. We were isolated from the rest of the world for years without any news. So we relied on the little things, a dark joke, a sunny day, a hopeful rumour..."

With this *apologia*, the premise of the film unfolds: Jakob invents positive radio broadcasts to inspire hope and resistance in an unnamed Jewish ghetto, subsequently risking his own life to protect a young girl and counter the apparent hopelessness of their enslavement. In doing so, he ultimately dies after courageously standing up to a Nazi 'waterboarding' and enforced public confession, which he defiantly refuses to proffer.

While space does not permit a thoroughgoing comparative analysis, it is worth noting a final similarity linking these Shoah 'fables' set in Nazi camps. As with Benigni's film, the generalised setting and comic approach in Kossovitz's *Jakob the Liar* have the effect of distancing audiences from specific details surrounding the Nazis' brutality. The characters generally appear relatively healthy, and crucially, survive—with the exception of the two respective protagonists. Both films conclude with the 'suspension of disbelief', yet in a manner far different from that of the transposed final scenes of *The Pianist* or S*chindler's List*. Following the triumphant liberation of the camp by American forces (!), an adult Giosuè, having found his mother in a long column of rescued camp survivors, offers a triumphant voice-over to *Life is Beautiful*, not in the spirit of a 'fairy tale', but that of a 'survivor's tale': "This is my story, this is the sacrifice my father made for me."

A similar manoeuvre is used to conclude *Jakob the Liar*. Having opened with the value of "a dark joke" in the ghettos, Jakob Heym is ultimately depicted shot and dying at the gallows for having mocked his executioner, not wholly unlike Guido's 'tragicomic' last moments, light-heartedly marching in front of his hidden son. An omniscient narrator book-ends both films, in the former case by explicitly returning to the 'fable' motif. As the camera shows a dying Jakob Heym, and the ghetto residents are herded onto trains toward ostensible annihilation, Robin Williams' voice-over inverts the expected reality—even the film's own 'reality'—by interrupting the final sequence with this declaration:

> Yes that's how it ended.
> And they all went off to the camps, and were never seen again.
> But maybe, it wasn't like that at all. Because you know, as Frankfurter says, "Until the last line has been spoken the curtain cannot come down".
> About 50 miles out of town the train was stopped by Russian troops…

Here too tragedy—yet again, only a personal tragedy partially rendered on-screen, as symbolised by the protagonist's death—is replaced by triumph as the Soviet liberators stop the train, and Jakob is seen a final time, through a wire-mesh train window, by the young girl he had earlier saved from the Nazis' process of selection.

As should be clear, neither *Jakob the Liar* nor *Life is Beautiful* are educational films; they do not set out to be. But can they be legitimately said to be another way of "doing history", of faithfully engaging with the past in a thought-provoking and entertaining way? It is perhaps Shoah 'fables' that raise these questions most starkly. In conclusion, however, a distinction should not be drawn too greatly between the former two films, or Mark Herman's 2008 adaptation *The Boy in the Striped Pyjamas*, on the one hand; and, on the other, two further 2008 releases *The Reader*, starring Kate Winslet, and *Defiance*, starring Daniel Craig (directed by Edward Zwick and Steven Daldry, respectively). For the visual screen acting as a metaphor for cinematic distance, the central role afforded innocence by the protected child, but most of all, the very act of survival—especially as enforced by narrative fiat through recourse to the 'fairytale' genre—all bring these seemingly different, humorous films into line with other filmic representations of the Final Solution.

It merits closing with a final glance at another recent film, Paul Verhoeven's 2006 *Zwartboek* [*Black Book*], which draws together some of these disparate strands. More loosely 'Based on a True Story' similar to Claude Berri's 1997 *Lucie Aubrac*, the backdrop is provided by resistance to (and collaboration with) Nazi occupation, in this case via the "Den Haag" organisation in Holland from September 1944. Revealingly, the protagonist, Rachel Stein (played by Carice van Houton), an assimilated Dutch Jew, frames *Black Book* through her newfound life on a Kibbutz in Israel more than a decade later. In contrast to the previous films surveyed, the entire film is constructed as a mystery, whereby Stein assumes the guise of Ellis de Vries to gather information for the Dutch resistance from the local SD chief, Ludwig Müntze (played by Sebastian Koch). Not the least of the ways that the Shoah looms as an ultimately unexpressed threat is the film's distance from the scene of the action: it is set in Western Europe. Most characters are ambivalently drawn; the real villain appears only as reluctant hero until the film's climax, and *vice versa* with both Müntze and Stein—one of several 'false' 'happy endings' toward the end of *Black Book*. Yet most intriguingly, the film ends on a note of apparent reprisal rather than triumph, and with unmistakable ambiguity rather than cautious optimism. Does the final scene raise the ominous spectre of continued Jewish persecution, or alternatively, is this a portrayal of collective Jewish defence represented by the state of Israel? Given the subject matter at hand, this seems an appropriate way in which to finish this contribution; that is, without drawing explicitly drawing conclusions or value judgments. For when it comes to art, if the best poets and filmmakers can—with their best, most humane and sensitive efforts, no less—only show a "corner of the calamity", surely a historian can, and possibly even should, assert even less.

Selected Films on the Shoah since 1993:

Band of Brothers, "Why we Fight" (Episode 9), David Frankel: USA, 2001

Black Book [*Zwartboek*], Paul Verhoeven: Holland/Germany/Belgium, 2006

The Boy in the Striped Pyjamas, Mark Herman: USA/UK, 2008

The Grey Zone, Tim Blake Nelson: USA, 2001

The Counterfeiters [*Die Fälscher*], Stefan Ruzowitzky: Germany/Austria, 2007

Defiance, Edward Zwick: USA, 2008

Inglourious Basterds, Quentin Tarantino, USA, 2009

Jakob the Liar, Peter Kassovitz: UK, 1999

Life is Beautiful [*La Vita è bella*] Roberto Benigni: Italy, 1999

Lucie Aubrac, Claude Berri: France, 1997

The Pianist, Roman Polanski: France/Germany/UK, 2002

The Reader, Stephen Daldry: UK/Germany, 2008

Schindler's List, Steven Spielberg: USA, 1993

Endnotes

[1] For details of this story, see https://time.com/1903/quentin-tarantino-is-suing-gawker-after-script-leak/ (all websites last accessed 1 March 2020).

[2] Kate Connelly provided an insightful review in *The Guardian* on 15 Aug. 2008, available online at: www.guardian.co.uk/film/2008/aug/15/quentintarantino.secondworldwar.

[3] Mistakes in original; online at: www.imsdb.com/scripts/Inglourious-Basterds.html.

[4] See, for example, Matthew Feldman and Mark Nixon, eds., *Beckett's Literary Legacies* (Cambridge: Cambridge Scholars Publishing, 2007), especially chs. 1 and 9.

[5] For an overview of recent historiographical and interpretative readings of the Holocaust, see my review article "Debating Debates in Holocaust Studies", in *Holocaust Studies* 16/3 (Dec. 2010), pp. 156-174, available online at: https://www.academia.edu/14688322/Debating_Debates_in_Holocaust_Studies.

[6] See Jonathan Freedland, "The Bitterest Pill", *The Guardian*, 12 Oct. 2007, available online at: http://film.guardian.co.uk/features/featurepages/0,,2188718,00.html. The passage in question regarding *The Counterfeiters* continues: "The captives are well-fed, sleeping on beds with real sheets and blankets—conditions utterly unlike those elsewhere in Sachsenhausen or in any other concentration camp. More importantly, they are ruled over by an SS officer who is venal, but not murderous. Now, this exceptional situation at least provides The Counterfeiters with a way around the perennial obstacle confronting all films about the Holocaust, namely how to portray the unportrayable (clearly no actors can ever be as bone-thin, as starved, as the camps' real victims). And, to its credit, it repeatedly reminds the audience that what it is witnessing is atypically moderate by Nazi standards. Characters say as much explicitly—'We have it so good in here, while out there ...'—and occasionally reality intrudes. At one point a bullet, fired in an execution in Sachsenhausen proper, pierces the wall of the forgers' enclave."

[7] Trudy Gold, "An Overview of Hollywood Cinema's Treatment of the Holocaust", in Toby Haggith and Joanna Newman, eds., *Holocaust and the Moving Image* (London: Wallflower Press, 2005), p. 193.

[8] Elie Wiesel, "Foreword" to Annette Insdorf, *Indelible Shadows: Film and the Holocaust*, Third Edition (Cambridge: Cambridge University Press, 2003 [1983, 1989]), pp. xi-xii.

[9] Saul Friedländer continues, quoting Habermas' well-known position that "Auschwitz has changed the basis for continuity of the conditions of life within human history", and asserts: "What turns the 'Final Solution' into an event at the limits is the very fact that it is the most radical form of genocide encountered in history: the wilful, systematic, industrially organized, largely successful attempt totally to exterminate an entire human group within twentieth-century Western society", *Probing the Limits of Representation: Nazism and the "Final Solution"* (London: Harvard University Press, 1992), cited p. 3; italics in original.

[10] *Ibid.*, p. 17.

[11] Pierre Sorlin, *The Film in History: Restaging the Past* (Oxford: Basil Blackwell, 1980), p. 211.

[12] For an introduction to the debates around Film Theory, see Leo Braudy and Marshall Cohen, eds., *Film Theory and Criticism* (Oxford: Oxford University Press, 1999).

[13] Robert A. Rosenstone, *History on Film / Film on History* (Harlow: Pearson, 2006), pp. 13ff.

[14] *Ibid.*, p. 159; where Rosenstone adds: "To accept film makers as historians, as I have been proposing throughout this book, is to accept a new sort of history. The medium and its practices for constructing a past—all ensure that the historical world on film will be different

from that on the page. In terms of informational content, intellectual density, or theoretical insight, film will always be less complex than written history. Yet its moving images and sound scapes will create experiential and emotional complexities of a sort unknown upon the printed page. Like the Buddhist paintings, the historical film can convey much about the past to us and thereby provide some sort of knowledge and understanding—even if we cannot specify exactly what the contours of such understanding are."

[15] Norman G. Finkelstein, *The Holocaust Industry: Reflections on the Exploitation of Jewish Suffering* (London: Verso, 2000), cited pp. 3, 144, 150.

[16] Hayden White, "Historical Emplotment and the Problem of Truth", in *Probing the Limits of Representation*, pp. 37-53.

[17] Peter Novick, *The Holocaust in American Life* (London: Bloomsbury, 2000).

[18] As with the figures in GBP given from the table, these amounts in USD are not adjusted for inflation; available online at: www.boxofficemojo.com.

[19] Terrence Rafferty, "Polanski and the Landscape of Aloneness", *The New York Times*, 26 Jun. 2003, online at: www.nytimes.com/2003/01/26/movies/film-polanski-and-the-landscape-of-aloneness.html.

[20] Following its release in December 2008 (US) and Jan. 2009 (in the UK), *Valkyrie* grossed more than $200m worldwide; details online at https://www.boxofficemojo.com/title/tt0985699/?ref_=bo_se_r_1. See also Omer Bartov, *The Eastern Front, 1941-1945: German Troops and the Barbarisation of Warfare* (Basingstoke: Palgrave, 2001); and on the public debate over the 1995 "The Crimes of the Wehrmacht Exhibition", for example, see Bartov, "German Soldiers and the Holocaust: Historiography, Research and Implications", *History and Memory* 9/1-2 (1997), pp. 162-188; and "Reaction to the Wehrmacht Exhibitions", forming Part 3 of Hannes Heer, Walter Manoschek, Alexander Pollak and Ruth Wodak, eds., *The Discursive Construction of History* (Basingstoke: Palgrave, 2008).

[21] Frank Reis, Joan Salter, Fred Knoller, and Harry Fox, quoted in "The survivors' right to reply', in *Holocaust and the Moving Image*, pp. 244ff.

[22] Giacomo Lichtner, "For the few, not the many: delusion and denial in Italian Holocaust Films", in *ibid.*, p. 337.

[23] *Indelible Shadows*, p. 289.

11. "Intellectual" Discourses on the Radical Right: From Double-Speak to Holocaust Denial

Being "on message" is no less vital for mainstream politicians in Europe and the US today than it has been for members of the radical right, even if this is manifested in a much different way. For the latter network of groups—typically characterized by ethno-nationalism, prejudice against scapegoated minorities and aggressive populism[1]—the issue is ultimately simpler: veil your true colors. Radical right activists have long tended toward racism or xenophobia and, since 1945, are frequently sympathetic to fascism and to anti-Semitic ploys like Holocaust denial (or its cousin, Holocaust "revisionism").[2] In postwar Europe and the US, these views—at least when put baldly—are not vote-winners. As a consequence, the radical right in both countries has had to go much further in "shaping the message" than mere political triangulation—something perhaps better described as "fifth column discourse": a radical right rhetoric and organizational self-censorship by an extremist party that is sanitized in order to challenge liberal democracy from within. By no means limited to a single movement or ideology, it is nevertheless the case that a "mainstreaming" of previously "taboo" racial and religious prejudices has been a sustained and significant project for contemporary radical right discourse.[3]

The term "fifth column" was first attributed to a Nationalist general during the opening months of the Spanish Civil War. As his army converged on Madrid in October 1936, Emilio Mola Vidal claimed to have four columns of troops surrounding the city, with a fifth column inside the city itself, in order to attack it from within. Extending this term, "fifth column discourse" is thus a rhetorical form intended to bring an enemy down from within; in this case, by mimicking the language of liberal democracy. Exemplifying this longstanding phenomenon is the one-time openly neo-Nazi, Nick Griffin, "modernizing" leader of the British National Party between 1999 and 2014—a period in which the party won scores of local government seats, and even secured two MEP in the north of England in May 2009—to date the UK's most successful radical right party. He called this embrace of euphemistic language "verbal judo" shortly after taking over leadership of the BNP in 1999:

> Of course, we must teach the truth to the hardcore [... but] when it comes to influencing the public, forget about racial differences, genetics, Zionism, historical revisionism and so on [...] It's time to use the weight of democracy's own myths and expectations against it by side-stepping and using verbal judo techniques.[4]

This separation between "hardcore" revolutionary rightists and "the public" was clearly identified in Cas Mudde's landmark study from 2000, *The Ideology of the Extreme Right*, which noted that such groups typically have a more "moderate 'front-stage'" intended for public consumption and "a radical 'back-stage'"[5] targeted at neo-fascist activists. Even earlier, another scholar on radical right ideology, Roger Eatwell, noted an "exoteric" and "esoteric" division in the 1980s National Front,[6] one that doubtless also extended to the BNP in the early 1990s, when it won its first council seat under the 1990s "rights for whites" banner in London's Tower Hamlets. Applying this formula to the party as a whole under his modernizing leadership, Nick Griffin's understanding of "verbal judo" was made abundantly clear exactly a decade later. In April 2009, a leaked internal document in the lead-up to the European elections that May was circulated, under the revealing title "BNP Language and Concepts Discipline Manual."[7]

As this document makes plain, when the first of the 13 internal rules is "We are not a 'racist' or 'racial' party" (just "ethno-nationalist"), it likely means they have something to hide. Some of the BNP's other "rules" are equally telling in terms of "verbal judo", exoteric/esoteric, front-stage/backstage—or however one wishes to call this turn toward euphemism. It is effective because it deploys the language of inclusion and democracy for xenophobic and illiberal ends. It seduces under a populist banner by appealing to "the masses", but it is ultimately deceptive of its ulterior aims. For these radical right ideologues and movements, in short, leopards have not changed their spots so much as found better camouflage. In looking into the varying shades of deception, this chapter will examine some of the principal developments in this fifth column discourse as it relates to the post-war radical right. Of course, there are a number of other ideologies, events and contexts that could be cited here—in particular, the recent rise of anti-Muslim hatred[8]— even if the aim of this short text is to identify some of the more salient euphemistic patterns in radical right rhetoric since 1945.

First of all: why 1945? To start off with, the scale of defeat of the Axis powers—and with it any support for extreme right, neo-fascism in Europe and the US—made that ideology wholly toxic. While long associated with violence and militarism, fascist praxis swiftly became synonymous with brutality and extermination in the European and American mind. And for good reason: 50 million dead in Europe, six million of them Jews, systematically murdered in specially-constructed death chambers in the so-called "Final Solution to the Jewish Question." Put simply, "classic" fascism of Nazism's and Fascism's stripe was so wholly discredited—and in many parts of Europe, made illegal—after 1945, that politically drawing upon its legacy was simply impossible. To this day, the image of Hitler is often synonymous with "evil" in the public mind in most Western countries.

Some of the more sophisticated members of the "old guard," like Oswald Mosley in Britain or Maurice Bardèche in France, realized that, at the very least, the outward trappings of fascism—the shirts and rallies, the overt anti-Semitism and revolutionary politics—needed to be consigned to socio-political history. Bardèche, for one, maintained in his 1962 text *What is Fascism?* [*Qu'est-ce que le fascisme?*]:

> The single party, the secret police, the public displays of Caesarism, even the presence of a Führer are not necessarily attributes of fascism, let alone the reactionary thrust of political alliances...The famous fascist methods are constantly revised and will continue to be revised. More important than the mechanism is the idea which fascism has created for itself of man and freedom... With another name, another face, and with nothing which betrays the projection from the past, with the form of a child we do not recognize and the head of a young Medusa, the Order of Sparta will be reborn.[9]

To remain with France for a moment; here, a fascist ideology emerged after the slaughter of the Great War, incubated by the likes of Georges Sorel or Charles Maurras's *Action Française*. A new type of radical right politics gradually matured, taking Bardèche's warnings to heart. In the words of a leading scholar of the French radical right, Jens Rydgren, writing in 2005:

> an innovative master frame was constructed in France during the late 1970's and early 1980's, and was made known as a successful frame in connection with the electoral breakthrough of the Front National in 1984. As the old master frame of the extreme right ... was rendered impotent by the outcome of the Second World War, it took the extreme right a long time to establish a new, potent master frame that simultaneously met the conditions of: being flexible enough to fit (in modified form) different political and cultural contexts; sufficiently resonated with the lived experiences, attitudes and preconceptions of many people ... and was sufficiently free from stigma. The master frame combining ethnonationalist, cultural racism and anti-political establishment populism met these requirements.[10]

This euphemistic "master frame" met with surprising success in 1984, when a suited Jean-Marie Le Pen appeared on French television to discuss his party, the *Front National* (FN). Crucially, he came across as reasonably moderate while advancing prejudicial ideas. In keeping with this new shift of emphasis in mainstream discourse, rather than engaging in anti-Semitic conspiracism, in 1987 Le Pen notoriously declared: "I'm not saying the gas chambers didn't exist. I haven't seen them myself. I haven't particularly studied the question. But I believe it's just a detail in the history of World War II."[11] He was convicted in France and, later, in Germany, for these and similar remarks, which he reiterated in 2015.[12] This was classic dog-whistle politics for the hardcore supporters, while at the same time not attempting to deny, just "revise", public understandings of the Holocaust. One explanation for Jean-Marie's recent reiteration of Holocaust revisionism is that his daughter, Marine—who now leads the party he founded in 1972—has moved in a still more publicly moderate direction, shifting her focus (as has been common amongst what is sometimes called the "new far right" over the last generation) away from anti-Semitism and toward anti-Muslim prejudice, immigration and hostility to the EU.[13] This change in focus led to Jean-Marie Le Pen's expulsion from the FN by his daughter, whom he in turn disowned; meanwhile, she has taken his party forward and now, as National Rally, leads one of the largest political parties in France.

From this new "master frame" also emerged the public stirrings of Holocaust denial in the late 1960s and early 1970s, which tried to sanitize fascism and especially Nazism by claiming to "debunk" the Holocaust narrative. At first, writes Sir Richard Evans, this type of writing was instead "mostly distributed by mail order," and of a caliber that "seemed to belong in the world of sensational newspapers such as you could buy in American supermarkets, recounting the experiences of people who had been abducted by little green aliens or who had seen Elvis Presley still alive."[14] Motivations for Holocaust denial, to this day, are overwhelmingly advanced for racist and ideological reasons, especially anti-Semitism and fascism. It is understandable, therefore, that many people feel passionately that there is no debate to have with deniers. The Holocaust took place, and spending even a second on the subject of Holocaust denial is simply a waste of time. True, there is indeed no benefit in debating whether the Holocaust "happened" with those who think, against the mountains of evidence, that it did not. Yet it does not follow that simply ignoring this phenomenon altogether is the best way forward. James Najarian, a wise interpreter of the various methods involved in denying the Holocaust, has employed this analogy: "Flat-earthers believe that the earth is flat and the United States space program is a hoax. This does not make the rest of us round-earthers; we don't need a name for ourselves."[15]

As described above, the perpetrators of the Holocaust were the first to try to hide, cover up, and obscure the facts of the Holocaust. But they are not the only ones. Most Holocaust deniers today accept that the world is round, and try to find ways of occluding the accepted view of history. Some of the more dangerous forms of Holocaust denial, in fact, go by the tag "Holocaust revisionism", so as to appear moderate and convincing—as simply another "point of view" that everyone's entitled to. A correspondingly slick surface can be seen on professional websites and many books aiming for the look, scholarly apparatus and jargon of academic respectability. It is this more "intellectual" form of Holocaust denial—such as Jean-Marie Le Pen's claims examined above—that is illegal in most of the European Union today (including France, Germany and Austria, but not Britain).

To throw this point into some relief, we have but a handful of authentic sources about the Spanish Armada, or the Great Fire of London in 1666—the latter, for example, recounted in less than a dozen accounts surviving from that year, of which the diary by the parliamentarian Samuel Pepys is certainly the best known. Yet to my knowledge, no one has carbon-dated Samuel Pepys's diaries for authenticity, forensically analyzed his handwriting for veracity, or produced a 250-page report on the diary's legitimacy—as the Netherlands State Institute for War Documentation felt compelled to do with Anne Frank's diary in the 1980s. This was largely a result of systematic forgery claims by well-known deniers such as Richard Harwood (aka Richard Verrall of Britain's National Front, who wrote *Did Six Million Really Die?* in 1974), Ernst Zündel and of course, the gold standard of these historical deceivers, David Irving, whose trial is discussed below.

We could just dismiss the conspiracy theories, denying them our attention. On the other hand, perhaps by familiarizing ourselves with the central arguments and post-war history of Holocaust denial, however nauseating and noxious they may be, we may find it possible to discern the attempts by extremists to hide behind scholarly facades and seemingly informed arguments. Particularly with the possibilities for communication offered by the internet and social media, recognizing these weavers of deception for what they are—and indeed always have been—has never been so important as it is today. One reason is obvious: on some search engines, typing in "Holocaust" as a keyword will bring up a denial site amongst the first pages of hits. This century, there is no doubt that we have entered Holocaust denial 2.0. Simple Holocaust denial slogans are used on Facebook and social media every day. Anyone can favorite or share a tweet that simply says #Holohoax. While this does not *necessarily* make that person a Holocaust denier, it is nonetheless hateful, and it is offensive. Online, comments denying the Holocaust are often simply substitutes for hatred of Jews.

There is, for instance, the highly visible website Codoh—"Committee for Open Debate on the Holocaust"—which hides behind the "intellectual freedom" that it claims to advance "with regard to this one historical event called 'Holocaust,' which in turn will help advance the concept of intellectual freedom with regard to all historical events."[16] Another example can be seen in the conspiracy website Solar General, touting itself as "The Most Controversial, Censored and Forbidden Web Site in the World." It boasts a professional layout, highlighting the first three topics: "105 Questions on the Holocaust"; "Adolf Hitler: Life of a Leader"; and "Anne Frank Fraud"—which should tell you all you need to know about this hate-inspiring "Holocaust revisionist" website.

While ignoring Holocaust denial is certainly preferable, the ubiquity of the Internet and social media makes that nearly impossible today. So, we must call out and contest their vitriol, knowing that Holocaust denial is a ruse for an assault on the past to advance racism and radical right values. In Britain, a classic example is the previously-mentioned 1974 pamphlet called *Did Six Million Really Die?*, written by a "Richard Harwood"—the pseudonym for the neo-Nazi National Front deputy chairman Richard Verrall. Britain's NF was thoroughly anti-Semitic. Such anti-Jewish hatred, in fact, returns us to the wartime Holocaust: the most totalizing expression of anti-Semitic hatred, and of genocide, in history. For, vitally, it bears remembering that the first people to systematically deny extermination of Europe's Jews were the Nazis themselves and their wartime collaborators. It was elites in the Third Reich who destroyed evidence, ranging from documents to crematoria; who exhumed and burned already-desecrated corpses[17]; and who kept the existence of their so-called "Final Solution to the Jewish Question" as great a secret as possible during the Second World War.

An architect by trade, the 46-year-old Paul Blobel commanded the infamous *Einsatzgruppe* 4a in Ukraine that followed the Wehrmacht into the Soviet Union on June 22, 1941. Although Jews had been persecuted for the preceding eight years under the Third Reich, and thousands of Polish Jews had already been killed since the onset of the Nazi occupation there from September 1939, the invasion of the USSR, codenamed Operation Barbarossa, immediately marked a step-change in the targeting and mass murder of Jews. At first shooting thousands of Jewish men as partisans, soon the *Einsatzgruppen* roving units began murdering tens of thousands of the elderly, women, and children a month. In September 1941, Blobel organized the largest recorded murder in history to that date: the shooting of 33,771 Jews at the Babi Yar ravine just outside of Kiev, as meticulously documented in the *Einsatzgruppen* situation reports.

In order to conceal the growing scope of these activities in the East, the Nazi leadership looked for alternatives for mass shooting that would provide greater secrecy. In the closing months of 1941, new decisions were taken on what had moved from mass murder to systematically-planned genocide. On September 3, gassing with Zyklon-B was tested at Auschwitz-Birkenau; from November 1, 1941, construction began on new extermination camps at Bełżec and Chełmno, with the latter starting to murder Jews by carbon monoxide on December 7, 1941, in occupied Poland.

These methods were derived from earlier programs to murder disabled people using reinforced gas vans; when the so-called "euthanasia program" was concluded in August 1941—revealingly, due to a public outcry raised by Bishop von Galen—these secretive vans were sent to the *Einsatzgruppe* still operating behind the front lines. Paul Blobel's *Einsatzgruppen C Kommando* received two of these gas vans in November 1941, and were the first to use them in the occupied East. By the time of the infamous Wannsee Conference on January 20, 1942, that informed, coordinated and set to work the Third Reich's different agencies of state in carrying out the genocide of all of Europe's Jews under Nazi control, another so-called "problem" needed a "solution": tens of thousands of bodies buried in shallow graves were impossible to conceal; they also took to poisoning water tables from the Baltic in the north to the Balkans in the south. In mid-1942, Blobel was put in charge of the exhumation and cremation of these bodies, under the code-name *Sonderkommando 1005*. Its job was to erase as much of the evidence of Nazi crimes as possible, extending to exhuming and burning bodies in open air pits. This evolved grisly techniques to efficiently cover up many Holocaust sites in central–Eastern Europe; for example, Chełmno was partially demolished, and Bełżec was completely destroyed, with a Ukrainian farming family placed on top to hide the minimum of 434,508 Jews murdered there in nine months.

The role played by Blobel, who was hanged in Germany in 1951 for his crimes, is horrifyingly instructive. He helped organize the mass shootings of Jews in the second half of 1941. In 1942, when more secretive extermination camps began operating, Blobel organized the removal of evidence of Nazi genocide, and testified about his activities in the 1948 *Einsatzgruppen* trial. But above all, the case of Paul Blobel provides clear evidence that Holocaust denial was undertaken by the very murderers themselves, in order to eliminate all traces of their unprecedented crimes. Holocaust denial, then, was originally deployed during World War II itself by the Nazis for self-serving, sanitizing and, above all, anti-Semitic reasons. The Third Reich's attempt to murder every European Jew under their control and, more relevantly, their systematic attempt to conceal this unparalleled crime, were both unsuccessful: millions of Jews survived the occupation of the Third Reich, and Holocaust deniers must contend with literally thousands of corresponding testimonies by perpetrators and victims alike; they must ignore tens of millions of pages of contemporaneous documents; and they must argue in the face of such evidence that both general understandings of history and generations of academic historians are deluded, deceitful or conspiratorial in their scholarship on the Holocaust.

These early Holocaust deniers were clearly writing from within an anti-Semitic framework, typically alleging Jewish conspiracies to invent, inflate or exploit the *Shoah*—an ancient Hebrew word meaning utter destruction, used by Jews when talking about the Holocaust. Yet in the US, too, fifth column discourse was able to wrap the message in superficially innocuous language. Think of the Institute for Historical Review, a clearing-house of nearly four decades for well-circulated, now online, Holocaust "revisionism." Scarcely by coincidence, the organization's longstanding acronym has been IHR: all too easily confused with London's renowned Institute for Historical Research—and deliberately so (the web address of the former is www.ihr.org, while that for the latter is www.ihr.ac.uk). At the time of writing, The Institute for Historical Review is directed by Mark Weber, earlier of the white supremacist, anti-Semitic National Alliance; moreover, from 1978 he helped edit the movement's openly fascistic journal, *National Vanguard*. Styling himself as a disinterested "historian", in 2012 Weber described Holocaust memorialization in the following terms:

> Lurid falsehood and outright lies are routinely promoted, even by supposedly reputable media, as part of the seemingly endless campaign of 'Holocaust Remembrance' ... Such historical deceit is a routine part of the relentless 'Holocaust' campaign, which plays such an important role in our society because it's an expression of Jewish-Zionist power, and is meant to further Jewish-Zionist interests.[18]

More recently, Weber appeared in London at an April 2015 meeting of more than 100 fellow "Nazi sympathisers, Holocaust deniers and their supporters from across the world", where he gave a speech entitled "The Challenge of Jewish-Zionist Power."[19]

Without doubt the gold standard of historical deceivers, David Irving, had long been a denier of the Holocaust—calling it an Allied "propaganda exercise"; crucially, however, he posed as a reasonable, "revisionist" historian while doing so (his books are heavily laden with footnotes, academic jargon and other forms of intellectual camouflage). Irving had an important fringe following in the 1980s and 1990s, especially among the radical right, when he sued Penguin Books and Deborah Lipstadt for libel after she claimed, in her 1993 *Denying the Holocaust: The Growing Assault on Truth and Memory*, that Irving was an influential mouthpiece for Holocaust denial. A famous case in 1996 then saw several historians of Nazism and the Holocaust testify for the defense, including the aforementioned Richard Evans, who concluded:

> The supposed evidence for the Nazis' wartime mass murder of millions of Jews by gassing and other means, he [Irving] claims, was fabricated after the war. He has referred repeatedly to the 'Holocaust myth' and the 'Holocaust legend' and has described himself as engaged in a 'refutation of the Holocaust story.'[20]

After a four-month trial, it was found that "Irving had 'significantly' misrepresented, misconstrued, omitted, mistranslated, misread and applied double standards to the historical evidence in order to achieve his ideological presentation of history". Judge Gray's ruling also found that Irving was an "active Holocaust denier; that he is anti-Semitic and racist, and that he associates with right-wing extremists who promote neo-Nazism."[21] In attempting to invert the role of Nazis and Jews, then, this most sophisticated of Holocaust "revisionists" was shown to be a fraud shaping historical evidence for ideological ends.

As this suggests, anti-Semitic conspiracy theories have remained an essential recourse for radical right movements in this century. For instance, commenting upon the German radical right scene in 2002, a report by the Office for the Protection of the Constitution maintained that hatred of Jews remained an "essential ideological ingredient of the radical right" in Germany—but with this caveat:

> Although all relevant extreme right parties and factions work with anti-Semitic stereotypes, and anti-Jewish feeling is always present, no organization has hitherto placed the central focus of their propaganda on anti-Semitism. Recently, however, the use of anti-Semitic stereotypes has increased. Putative taboo-breakers could (unintentionally) break the 'communication latency' down.[22]

Bearing in mind this persistence of anti-Jewish stereotypes, it is useful to move across the Atlantic in order to consider an exemplary case study in this "communication latency." Indeed, exemplary of this wolf in sheep's clothing is a political activist who notoriously declared in the late 1970s:

> It is not necessary to wear brown shirts to be a fascist ... it is not necessary to wear a swastika to be a fascist ... It is not necessary to call oneself a fascist to be a fascist. It is simply necessary to be one![23]

This quotation forms the frontispiece to Dennis King's 1989 exposé of Lyndon Hermyle LaRouche, Jr., a cultish radical right ideologue who died in 2019, aged 96. Charting the development of LaRouche's charismatic domination over his veritable political cult, from its left-wing origins to an embrace of radical right milieu in the 1970s, King's "Afterword" concludes: "As early as 1976-77, recognition that LaRouche had gone fascist could be found in places as diverse as the newsletter of the *Christian Anti-Communist Crusade* and the Op-Ed page of *The Washington Post*."[24] Likewise, in 2003, Helen Gilbert described LaRouche in the following terms:

> There's something strange and cultish about LaRouche—but it's hard to figure out exactly what he's up to. Much of his message appears to be innocuous, kooky, contradictory, esoteric or shamelessly inflammatory. But underneath the weirdness lies a radical right worldview ... LaRouche's brand of politics both employs standard elements of fascism and revisions that may initially throw some people off track.[25]

Similar views by experts abound on the convicted fraudster and eight-time Presidential hopeful—running seven of those times on the Democratic ticket; experts tend to emphasize his coded anti-Semitism and oftentimes-bizarre talking-points (such as the Queen of England allegedly running the global drugs trade).

In the main, LaRouche's idiosyncrasies have usually seen him dismissed as a fringe figure, allowing him to build a substantial intelligence-gathering organization; an international network of affiliated groups with hundreds—at times perhaps thousands—of dedicated, cult-like followers; and an outsized propaganda arm. To be sure, when it comes to the LaRouche group, there is no shortage of material: publishing is one thing this movement does exceedingly well. For example, the following are a few recent or ongoing publications owing fealty to the convicted fraudster: the *New Federalist* newspaper (defunct as of spring 2006) and its predecessor, *New Solidarity*; *Nouvelle Solidarité*; *Neue Solidarität*; *Executive Alert Service*; *Executive Intelligence Review*; *21st Century Science & Technology* and its predecessor, *Fusion*; *The Campaigner* (now defunct) and its successor, *Fidelio* (also defunct); *Ibykus*; and *The New Citizen* (Australia).

Over the years, these publications have evolved a sophisticated method of encoding their anti-Semitism and radical right politics. As with the radical right more broadly, this rhetorical throwing "some people off track" best comes into focus by taking the long view. In this vein, two methods applied by the LaRouche movement will be examined in the remainder of this chapter as exemplars of this radical right manipulation of language, especially as it relates to anti-Semitism and "Holocaust revisionism." The first, an innovative method by LaRouche, might be dubbed *metonymy*; that is, using individual Jews as shorthand for the entire group. Joseph Goebbels was particularly skilled at this technique, selecting for representative condemnation the Jewish deputy police chief in Weimar Berlin, Bernhard Weiss, calling him "Isidor" in the Nazi paper *Der Angriff* [The Attack]. According to Peter Longerich's recent study of Goebbels,

> this distorted image of 'Isidor Weiss' was to pillory the alleged dominance of "the Jews" in the Weimar "system". Under the steady barrage of this smear campaign, the person of *Weiss became a type and the name 'Isidor Weiss' a byword*. This confirmed the motto with which Goebbels prefaced [one of his] Isidor book[s]: 'Isidor: not a person or an individual in the legal sense. Isidor is a *type, a mentality, a face*.[26]

For just these reasons, over the years a diverse group of organisations have adjudged the LaRouche movement to be akin to a radical right political cult that is, at core, anti-Semitic. For the US-based Anti-Defamation League, LaRouche is a "longtime anti-Semitic conspiracy theorist" and, in the words of ADL President Abe Foxman, is "a man who has a long track record of anti-Semitic fear mongering". The *Encyclopedia Judaica* defines LaRouche as a "notorious anti-Semite" whose "international organization" is today a "major source of ... masked antisemitic theories globally". Also in the US, Chip Berlet, a long-standing LaRouche watcher, likewise asserts: "The LaRouche organization is currently the world's largest distributor of literature based on 'coded anti-Semitism', rooted in the false allegation of the Protocols of the Elders of Zion."

In Germany, as early as 1994 the Bundestag described LaRouche's political arm based in Wiesbaden, Civil Rights Solidarity Movement (Bürgerrechtsbewegung Solidarität, or BüSo), as a "political sect". German Green MP Hans-Christian Ströbele later characterised the German organisation as "anti-Semitic and extremely right-wing". In similar vein, Germany's *Aktion für Geistige und Psychische Freiheit Bundesverband Sekten- und Psychomarktberatung e.V.* considers the LaRouche movement in Germany to be "part of a political sect which aims at completely capturing its members through conspiracy theories and anti-Semitic content." With respect to the LaRouche movement's activities in Australia, operating as the Citizens Electoral Council, Dr Paul Gardner, Chairman of the B'nai B'rith Anti-Defamation Commission in Australia, maintains that the "LaRouche organisation spreads anti-Semitic propaganda throughout the world and in many place acts like a cult group which attempts to indoctrinate young people with its ideology. They are accused of propagating incitement to hatred towards the Jews, the British and the Anti-Defamation League. Coupled with this they stand accused of using sinister secretive methods of recruitment."

In post-war America, more specifically, some of LaRouche's preferred *bêtes noires* have long included Henry Kissinger, Leo Strauss, the Rothschilds and other prominent Jews. When paired next to more familiar forms of encoded language, such as reference to "special interests" or "international financiers", these anti-Semitic tropes can be bewildering, and difficult to detect for a "front-stage" (mainstream) audience; yet at the same time, the words appeal to more informed activists "back-stage." To return to the words of LaRouche's biographer in 2009, Dennis King, 20 years after the publication of his exposé:

> *Anti-Semitism lies at the core of LaRouche's beliefs.* He uses a mixture of hate and scorn; thinly-veiled euphemisms and conspiracy theories involving Jewish banking families. His methods are to build up *prominent Jews as symbolic hate figures,* developing new forms of 'blood libel', and the concoction of the myth of an evil 'oligarchy'—also known as the 'Zionist-British organism', the 'Venetian party' or simply 'the British'. This 'oligarchy' is the target of the LaRouche organization's most violent abuse; naming them as utterly evil and parasitical.[27]

A second effective linguistic techniques can be called *inversion*; that is, calling others fascists and Nazis. This has the effect of discrediting opponents, while distancing one's own position from the radical right. Amongst the finest examples of this tactic was one furnished by the aforementioned Nick Griffin in 2007, then head of the BNP. Having been invited to debate alongside the notorious Holocaust denier David Irving at the Oxford Union Society, he found the event disrupted by protesters whom he described as "a mob which would kill." Griffin went on to add: "Had they grown up in Nazi Germany they would have been splendid Nazis."[28] While this may have been an opportunistic comment at the time, this paradigm is a recurrent one amongst radical right ideologues.

It is useful to examine together these two general techniques in the radical right's 'fifth column discourse', namely *metonymy* and *inversion*. The LaRouche movement utilized progressive encoding of demonizing language, from the 1970s to the 2010s. Amongst the scores of articles and editorials assembled by the anti-LaRouche website, LaRouche Planet,[29] LaRouche's main publishing arm, *New Solidarity*, offers an array of revealing statements. Consider the following, pretty unreconstructed radical right language in 1978:

> America must be cleansed for its righteous war by the immediate elimination of the Nazi Jewish Lobby and other British agents from the councils of government, industry, and labor.[30]

That same year, one of increased contact with Willis Carto, the notorious anti-Semite and founder of the aforementioned Institute for Historical Review, LaRouche's language started to become progressively more veiled in terms of anti-Semitism:

> Even on a relative scale, what the Nazis did to Jewish victims was mild compared with the virtual extermination of gypsies and the butchery of Communists. The point is that Adolf Hitler was put into power largely on the initiative of the Rothschilds, Warburgs and Oppenheimers, among other Jewish and non-Jewish financial interests centered in the City of London [...] The Jews who did die at the hands of Nazism were the victims of fascism, the victims of the Schactian form of "fiscal austerity." The "Holocaust" simply proves that the failure of the Nuremberg tribunal to hang Hjalmar Schacht made the whole proceeding a travesty of justice. The murderers of the million and a half or more Jews who died in the "holocaust" are any group, Jewish or non-Jewish, which supported then or now the policies advocated by Felix Rohatyn or Milton Friedman. Either you, as a Jew, join with the U.S. Labor Party to stop Rohatyn, Friedman the Mont Pelerin Society now, or you are implicitly just as guilty of the death of millions of Jews as Adolf Hitler.[31]

As noted above, these views unmistakably attempt to deny central aspects of the Holocaust: to marginalize suffering, relativize guilt, question facts, and shift blame away from the perpetrators of the Holocaust. Secondly, they try to sanitize fascist practice by referring to one's enemies as Nazis, fascists, and so on. Through this technique of inversion, fascism's crimes are both normalized and applied to perceived enemies.

Finally, LaRouche's rhetoric makes use of individual Jews as anti-Semitic code: reference to Rohatyn and Friedman above, therefore, can be usefully understood as a symbolic metonymy for Jews generally. In this way, anti-Semites deliberately disguise their attacks on Judaism by singling out "bad" Jews—wealthy or powerful individuals, political supporters of Zionism and, of course, anything relating to Israel (which is consistently portrayed in LaRouche propaganda as a Nazi-like regime). As a result, actual fascist and Nazi actions—especially the Final Solution—are systematically trivialized; they return within the boundaries of normal human activity. Likewise, enemies are vilified and demonized: they are the ones considered to be conspirators and genocidaires; the very embodiment of evil. These individuals are typically Jews prominent in public life. To again cite LaRouche's "New Pamphlet to Document Cult Origins of Zionism" from 1978:

> The impassioned sophistry which the Zionist demagogue offers to all foolish enough to be impressed with such hoaxes as the "holocaust" thesis: that the culmination of the persecution of the Jews in the Nazi [H]olocaust proves that Zionism is so essential to 'Jewish survival' that any sort of criminal activity is justified against anti-Zionists in memory of the 'six million.' This is worse than sophistry. It is a lie. True, about a million and a half Jews did die as a result of the Nazi policy of labor-intensive "appropriate technology" for the employment of "inferior races", a small fraction of the tens of millions of others, especially Slavs, who were murdered in the same way that Jewish refugee Felix Rohatyn and others of his ilk propose to revive today.[32]

In this reading, "Zionists" act as the *real* Nazis, and combatting them was the task for "humanism." LaRouche argues that there is a nefarious oligarchy, identified as a Jewish-British conspiracy (earlier put forward by a number of early and mid-20th century American racists).

The message was received clearly by racists, and was repeated for years by LaRouche with growing sophistication. A few decades later, LaRouche was still at it—the same radical right ideology, albeit with more encoded language. Thus, in 2003, LaRouche's "Physical Geometry as Strategy" declared:

> Who's behind it? The people I referred to, in January 2001: the independent central-banking-system crowd, the slime-mold. The financier interests. The same type of financier interests: descendants of the same interests that were behind the Hitler project, when the head of the Bank of England, backed by Harriman money, and by the grandfather of the present President of the United States, moved the money to refinance the Nazi Party, and the pressure to bring Hitler to power, on Jan. 30, 1933: This is what is happening now.[33]

The world is thus divided into two—the enemy, characterized as implacably evil (the British monarchy and their Jewish agents)—versus the putative saviors of humanity; namely, LaRouche and his fanatical followers. Major world events, like September 11th, 2001, are consequently viewed through the prism of a global conspiracy, of which only LaRouche is fully cognizant. From the same year, consider his words in "War, Hitler and Cheney":

> The Nazi-like doctrine adopted by the Bush administration—merely the lackeys of the circles of influence emanating from Leo Strauss are hell bent on war and destruction along Nazi lines and what faces the world is "virtually endless world war" unless stopped.[34]

That same year, moreover, exactly 70 years after Goebbels organized the burning of Jewish and other "decadent" books in 1933, the LaRouche Youth Movement published a text called "Burn the Textbooks" shortly after a youth training and "pedagogical" weekend in Germany at the end of May 2003.[35] It is difficult to view this move as pure coincidence, or to mistake the echo of fascism.

For LaRouche it is the British, Jews and their supporters who stand accused of being fascists and Nazis; and of course, following that well-worn conspiracy theory, of being monopolistic controllers of the budgets, the politics, and the wars. It is not merely that LaRouche uses esoteric language and seemingly eccentric redefinitions to hide references to the Jews; he deploys Jewish "sounding" names or stereotypical Jewish references to convey his underlying message. Connected to this, there is also a proliferation of obvious epithets and codes such as "usurer", "cabalist", "Venetian", "locust" or "Babylonian". This may puzzle the uninitiated, but strikes an unmistakable chord with contemporary right-wing extremists.

Through these techniques of inversion and metonymy, LaRouche's propaganda outlets return to blaming Jews for the problems facing the world. Yet when it comes to the 93-year-old (as of 2015) activist, a familiar response is that he is so eccentric as to be dismissed. That may be true for the uninitiated, but as with the wider radical right's "fifth column discourse" more broadly, such a view misses the point. His eccentricity is a veneer, and writing it off as one man's loony leanings fails to see the power he exercises, consistently, over decades. The radical right will not simply show the same face, with the same jackboots, salutes and manifestos of old; for they, too, know their (toxic) history. For the radical right, versatile language is an indispensable key in unlocking populist respectability. Tracing this genealogy over the post-war decades remains a daunting task, even if some of the patterns are discernible across seemingly disparate radical right movements in Europe and the US.

This conclusion is similar to that reached by Deborah Lipstadt 20 years ago, in her watershed book of the same time, *Denying the Holocaust*. Given her refusal to be cowed by Holocaust deniers like David Irving, no less than her principled refusal to engage with their pseudo-intellectual shenanigans long before the problem of Holocaust denial manifested itself online, her closing words remain true:

> We must vigilantly stand watch against an increasingly nimble enemy ... When we witness assaults on truth, our response must be strong, though neither polemical nor emotional. We must educate the broader public and academe about this threat and its historical and ideological roots. We must expose these people for what they are. The effort will not be pleasant .... We will remain ever vigilant so that the most precious tools of our and our society—truth and reason—can prevail. The still, small voices of millions cry out to us from the ground demanding that we do no less.[36]

Endnotes

[1] Ruth Wodak, *The Politics of Fear: What Right Wing Populist Discourses Mean* (London: Sage, 2015).

[2] For further analysis of this neglected issue, see the following recent studies: Andrea Mammone, "*The Eternal Return?* Faux Populism and Contemporarization of Neo-Fascism across Britain, France and Italy", *Journal of Contemporary European Studies* 17, no. 2 (Aug. 2009): 171-192; C. Wood and W. M. L. Finlay, "British National Party representations of Muslims in the month after the London bombings: homogeneity, threat, and the conspiracy tradition", *The British Journal of Social Psychology* 47, no. 4 (Dec. 2008): 707-726; and Pedro Zúquete, "The European extreme-right and Islam: New directions?" *Journal of Political Ideologies* 13, no. 3 (Oct. 2008): 321-344, available online at https://www.research gate.net/publication/240524859_The_European_extreme-right_and_Islam_New_directions.

[3] Aristotle Kallis, "When Fascism Became Mainstream: The Challenge Of Extremism in Times of Crisis", *Fascism: Journal of Comparative Fascist Studies* 4, no. 1 (Apr. 2015): 1-24 (at 21), available online at https://www.researchgate.net/publication/275247298_When_ Fascism_Became_Mainstream_The_Challenge_of_Extremism_in_Times_of_Crisis_Secon d_Lecture_on_Fascism_-_Amsterdam_-_April_9_2015.

[4] Nick Griffin, cited in Matthew Feldman and Paul Jackson, eds., *Doublespeak: The Rhetoric and Framing of the Far Right since 1945* (Düsseldorf: Ibidem, 2014), p. 11.

[5] Cas Mudde, *The Ideology of the Extreme Right* (Manchester and New York: Manchester University Press, 2000), p. 20.

[6] Roger Eatwell, "The Esoteric Ideology of the National Front in the 1980s", in Mike Cronin, ed., *The Failure of British Fascism* (Basingstoke: Palgrave, 1996), p. 100.

[7] http://www.reportingthebnp.org/wp-content/uploads/language_discipline.pdf updated April 2009.

[8] For academic views on anti-Muslim rhetoric and hate crimes against Muslim, see my co-authored reports with Mark Littler on reporting of anti-Muslim hatred in Britain by the leading third sector organisation Tell MAMA, for the years 2014 (www.tellmamauk.org/wp-con tent/uploads/pdf/Tell%20MAMA%20Reporting%202014-2015.pdf) and 2015 (https://re search.tees.ac.uk/ws/portalfiles/portal/4250550/Tell_Mama3.pdf). See also the 2019 report, co-authored with William Allchorn, relating to a working definition of anti-Muslim hatred, published by openDemocracy: https://cdn-prod.opendemocracy.net/media/documents/Wor king_definition_Islamophobia.pdf.

[9] Maurice Bardèche, cited in Roger Griffin, ed., *Fascism* (Oxford: Oxford University Press, 1995), pp. 318ff.

[10] Jens Rydgren, "Is extreme right-wing populism contagious? Explaining the Emergence of a New Party Family", *European Journal of Political Research* 44, no. 3 (2005): 413-37, available online at http://www.jensrydgren.com/Is%20extreme%20right-wing%20populism. pdf.

[11] Hate Speech International, 20 December 2013, online at: www.hate-speech.org/le-pen-fined-for-roma-remark/.

[12] Lewis Smith, "Jean-Marie Le Pen to be prosecuted for comments on Nazi gas chambers", *The Independent*, 24 February 2015, online at: www.independent.co.uk/news/world/Europe /jean-marie-le-pen-to-be-prosecuted-for-comments-on-nazi-gas-chambers-10415223.html.

[13] See Paul Jackson and Matthew Feldman, eds., *The EDL: Britain's 'New Far Right' social movement* (2011), online at: http://nectar.northampton.ac.uk/6015/7/Jackson20116015.pdf.

14 Richard Evans, *Lying about Hitler* (New York: Basic Books, 2001), pp. 107-108.
15 James Najarian, "Gnawing at history: the rhetoric of Holocaust Denial", *The Midwest Quarterly* 39, no. 1 (1997), p. 84, available online at https://codoh.com/library/document/523/?lang=en.
16 https://codoh.com/about/.
17 For further examples see, for example, Holocaust Research Project entries on the Einsatzgruppen leadership, including Paul Blobel: www.holocaustresearchproject.org/einsatz/blobel.html.
18 http://www.ihr.org/mwreport/2012-04-25.
19 Nick Craven, Paul Cahalan And Simon Murphy, "Nazi invasion of London Exposed: World's top Holocaust deniers... filmed at secret race hate rally where Jews are referred to as the 'enemy'", *The Daily Mail*, 26 May 2015, online at: www.dailymail.co.uk/news/article-3045115/Nazi-invasion-London-EXPOSED-World-s-Holocaust-deniers-filmed-secret-race-hate-Jews-referred-enemy.html.
20 Richard Evans, cited in "David Irving, Hitler and Holocaust Denial: Electronic Edition", *Holocaust Denial on Trial*, online at: www.hdot.org/en/trial/defense/evans/360.html.
21 Justice Gray, cited in "Trial Materials", *Holocaust Denial on Trial* (2018), online at: www.hdot.org/en/trial/.
22 Cited in Gideon Botsch and Christoph Kopke, "A case study of anti-Semitism in the language and politics of the contemporary far right in Germany", in Feldman and Jackson, eds., *Doublespeak*, p. 209.
23 Lyndon LaRouche, as cited in Dennis King, *Lyndon LaRouche and the New American Fascism* (New York: Doubleday, 1989), available online at https://web.archive.org/web/20071015143131/http://www.lyndonlarouche.org/newamericanfascism.htm.
24 *Ibid.*, p. 372, available online at https://web.archive.org/web/20080512202412/http://lyndonlarouche.org/fascismafterword.htm.
25 Helen Gilbert, *Lyndon LaRouche: Fascism Restyled for the New Millennium* (Seattle, WA: Red Letter Press, 2003), available online at: https://www.redletterpress.org/LaRouche_Fascism%20Restyled.pdf, cited pp. 5-6.
26 Peter Longerich, *Goebbels: A Biography*, trans. Alan Bance, Jeremy Noakes and Lesley Sharpe (London: The Bodley Head, 2015), p. 94, emphasis added.
27 Dennis King, *Lyndon Larouche and the New American Fascism*, p. 284.
28 Matthew Taylor, "Irving and Griffin spark fury at Oxford Union debate", *The Guardian*, 27 November 2007, online at: www.theguardian.com/uk/2007/nov/27/highereducation.studentpoliticseducation.
29 LaRouche Planet, online at: http://laroucheplanet.info/pmwiki/database/archives_larouche.htm.
30 http://laroucheplanet.info/pmwiki/pmwiki.php?n=Library.Awarwinningstrategy.
31 http://laroucheplanet.info/pmwiki/pmwiki.php?n=Library.CultOriginsofZionism3.
32 *Ibid.*
33 https://larouchepub.com/lar/2003/3013badschwal_kynt.html0.
34 https://larouchepub.com/eiw/public/2003/eirv30n13-20030404/eirv30n13-20030404_050-war_hitler_and_cheney-lar.pdf.
35 http://laroucheplanet.info/pmwiki/pmwiki.php?n=Cult.BurnBooks.
36 Deborah Lipstadt, *Denying the Holocaust: The Growing Assault on Truth and Memory* (London: Penguin, 1994), p. 222.

12. On Radical Right Mainstreaming in Europe and the US

The Far Right's Challenge to Liberal Democracy

Liberal democracies are facing an increasingly clear challenge today: the development and effects of a congealing 'far right' in Europe. At the time of writing, what have been called 'post-fascist' parties have entered coalition government in Austria (the Austrian Freedom Party) and Italy (La Lega Nord, now shorthanded as 'Lega'), on the one hand; while on the other, once centre-right and now increasingly 'illiberal democracies' in Poland, Hungary and the US erode fundamental democratic norms by embracing far-right positions on nativism and authoritarianism. This pincer movement towards what can be called a near-right politics is, in turn, the long-term result of the mainstreaming of previously radical right policies—above all 'Fortress Europe' and 'Fortress US' for non-white migration—which are posing acute challenges to the post-war Euro-American settlement. In taking the long view of some of these converging developments, this chapter returns to a pressing interwar question, so long dormant, that is emerging once again: 'Could it happen here?'

Recognizing and then defining the 'it' of far-right politics, and its connection to historical fascism, remains a vexatious issue (for example, Camus & Lebourg 2017: 53ff.). Protestors and left-wing activists see fascism in the politics of Trump, Orbán, and Salvini, to name but three political elites. Conservatives tend to be less sure, even if they see a clear divide between themselves and nativist, often explicitly racist, campaigns by insurgent parties such as Alternative for Germany (Alternative für Deutschland, AfD) or the Sweden Democrats (Sverigedemokraterna, SD)—parties that entered national parliaments in 2017 with 13 per cent and 17 per cent of the vote in 2018, respectively. To this challenge, historians and political scientists bring forth small libraries of commentary and analysis, with often sharp disagreement over terminology (on the debate over the definition of the radical right, see, for example, Eatwell 2000; and Mudde 1996, 2017). Without getting too bogged down in an article concerned with different issues, it nevertheless remains the case that what is variously called the (neo-)fascist, radical right, far right, or, most opaquely, national populist usually boils down to a handful of commonly identified features. These Wittgensteinian family resemblances, or 'faces' of the far right, have been usefully summarized in a book whose title identifies one of the principal challenges to liberal democracies at present, *Trouble on the Far Right*:

far-right activism should be understood as tactically oriented in the short run; at the same time, it may also target gradual changes in mindset, discourse, values, loyalties and legitimacy in the long run. One aspect of the long-term strategy is the professionalised political appearance of many right-wing organizations, which has contributed to the gradual disappearance of a cordon sanitaire: a figurative firewall that the political mainstream would previously use to block far-right influences. (Actors base their ideology and action on the notion of inequality among human beings, combining the supremacy of a particular nation, 'race' or 'civilization' with ambitions for an authoritarian transformation of values and styles of government.) (Fielitz & Laloire 2016: 16)

Rather than perpetuating 'the academic "war of words" on far-right definitions' or 'simplistic schemes of plug and play designs' (Fielitz & Laloire 2016: 18), the editors helpfully

use far right as an umbrella term to subsume actors, attitudes and behaviours, spanning from those which articulate dissent within the framework of representative democracy but are not geared toward the entire system (radical right) to those which deny the values, rules and arenas of democracy, impelling a revolutionary overthrow ('extremist right'). [As a distinct ideological world view] actors base their ideology and action on the notion of inequality among human beings, combining the supremacy of a particular nation, 'race' or 'civilization' with ambitions for an authoritarian transformation of values and styles of government. (Fielitz & Laloire 2016: 17–18)

Seen in this way, the far right is a praxis of revanchist ethnonationalism, hostile to many of the fundamental principles of liberal democracy.

Fully twenty-five years ago, a pioneer in this area of study, Hans-Georg Betz (1993: 413), defined 'radical, right-wing populist parties' in definitive terms, setting out their key platforms and ideas:

Radical right-wing populist parties are radical in their rejection of the established sociocultural and sociopolitical system and their advocacy of individual achievement, a free marketplace, and a drastic reduction of the role of the state. They are right-wing in their rejection of individual and social equality, in their opposition to the social integration of marginalized groups, and in their appeal to xenophobia, if not overt racism. They are populist in their instrumentalization of sentiments of anxiety and disenchantment and their appeal to the common man and his allegedly superior common sense.

A generation on, it is remarkable how far this scholarly convergence on the ideological tenets of populist radical right parties has advanced. To take just two recent examples, Elise Saint-Martin (2013: 4) offered a sophisticated template for European radical right parties in the twenty-first century:

radical right parties rely on appeals to national sentiments defined in ethnic terms; reject cosmopolitan conceptions of society; react to rising non-European immigration; oppose globalization and reject European integration which they see as undermining national sovereignty and identity; and brand themselves as anti-parties, criticizing domestic political elites as corrupt and removed from the 'common people' ... I have chosen to categorize the radical right according to three (3) defining features: nativism, socio-authoritarianism, and populism.

And as Ov Cristian Norocel rightly argued in a recent doctoral thesis, these and similar features (most recently, antisemitism and anti-Muslim prejudice) form the core of radical right ideology, which extends from parties to less formal movements and groups:

The ineliminable components of radical right populist ideology are the identification of a Manichean opposition between a 'corrupt elite' and a 'pure *people*'. The said *people* of radical right populist ideology is not only pure, but also constitutes an indivisible whole, whose sovereign will finds its most appropriate manifestation in the figure of a respected leader. What is worth underlining here is that the aforementioned purity of *people*, and the intrinsically interrelated fear of pollution, rests on exclusivist definitions of the 'rightful' inhabitants of a certain nation–state, in a decidedly nativist nationalist manner. [. . .] This has a key economic aspect—namely, welfare chauvinism—which delineates the 'pure' *people* and their birthright to the nation–state's welfare infrastructure from those underserving Others: a dynamic category that may include allegedly parasitical social groups, resented ethnic/'racial', religious, and/or sexual minorities, along a logic of nationalist solidarity. (Norocel 2013: 18)

From Betz and Mudde to early career researchers today, the radical right has become a well-understood phenomenon amongst scholars of political science, history, sociology, gender studies, and psephology. As this suggests, the varying organizational faces of the far right—street marches, populist politicians, even political violence and terrorism—have been the subject of commentary that dwarfs the coverage of other ideological groupings.

Put another way, everyone seems to be talking about the far right. So what is all the buzz about? Is the far right 'back', and if so, how can liberal democracy best respond?

Historical Parallels as a Double-Edged Sword

While historical parallels have their place, the far right today poses challenges that differ from those of the interwar fascism that preceded it. Indeed, perspectives from the interwar history of fascism can cloud as much as illuminate views of the far right today. History does not repeat itself—can never simply replicate itself—but it does sometimes echo, point, or even nudge. For the far right, the historical experience of transnational fascism (Bauerkämper 2010) after the Great War often boils down to the wartime Axis, the lasting stigma of which the far right, in its various guises since 1945, has consistently tried to negate, excuse, or otherwise overcome (Feldman 2015: 9). For several decades after the Second World War, the results of what should be properly called neo-fascist distancing tactics were mixed at best (Bastow 2002). Indeed, the early twenty-first-century context is so different from that of 1930s Europe that political, mobilizational, and even intellectual responses are just as likely to provide counterproductive historical examples for our current milieu. It bears repeating that historical analogies are a double-edged sword, which, at least when it comes to the far right today, can be used as much for defence—such as drawing lessons from the interwar rise and consolidation of fascism in Europe—as for attack, whether in terms of Antifa street confrontations, or in rhetorically tarring far-right groups as Nazis and fascists (as can be seen in countless placards at any counterdemonstration against the far right today) (see Wodak & Forchtner 2014, which includes an example from Vienna). Equally, history provides more nuanced explanations than slogans such as '¡No pasarán!' allow (from the Spanish Civil War)—a blunderbuss that risks making the issue of far-right legitimization worse rather than better. Care should be taken in drawing the historical parallels between fascism and the contemporary far right.

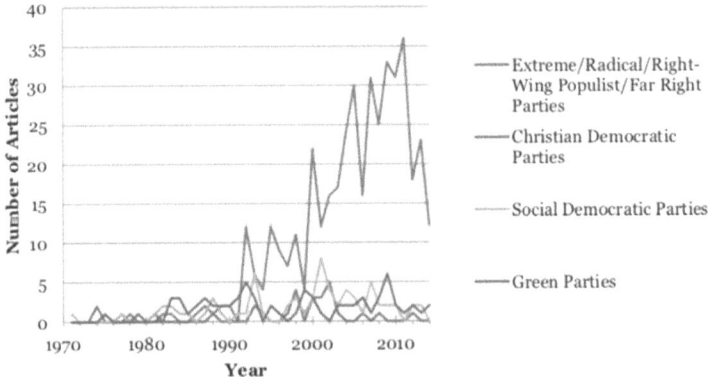

Figure 1.1. Scholarly articles about the far right (adapted from Mudde 2017: 2).

It scarcely needs be said, however, that most journalism and non-specialist literature compound these problems. In terms of historical fiction, for example, consider the October 1935 publication of *It Can't Happen Here*, Sinclair Lewis's novel republished in 2017—which sold like hot cakes following Donald Trump's inauguration in January of that year. Offering a standard Marxist view of fascism long ago discarded by most scholars (Griffin 2008), Lewis imagines big business as the reactionary hand behind a semi-legal dictatorial regime—a mix of Nazi racism and Fascist economic corporatism, sprinkled with heavy doses of paramilitary violence:

> Pushing in among this mob of camp followers who identified political virtue with money for their rent came a flying squad who suffered not from hunger but from congested idealism: Intellectuals and Reformers and even Rugged Individualists, who saw in Windrip, for his clownish swindlerism, a free vigor which promised a rejuvenation of the crippled and senile capitalistic system. (Lewis 2017: 79)

By this account, American liberalism had become 'cramped by a certain respect for facts which never enfeebled the press-agents for Corporism' (Lewis 2017: 283) which oversees concentration camps and summary executions, arrests much of Congress and later invades Mexico 'as a protection against the notorious treachery of Mexico and the Jewish plots there hatched'. The regime ultimately brings about another American civil war. Opposing the aggressive tyrants, Buzz Windrip and his henchmen, who whip up extremes of nationalist hysteria, is the journalist-cum-protagonist, Doremus Jessup, a sort of prototype 'Liberal American Humanitarian' (58). Revealingly, he is hampered by 'a certain respect for facts' (283); troubled by bad educational standards, he is only too aware that all utopias 'end in scandal, feuds, poverty, griminess, disillusion' (114). Watching with horror as a 'program for revitalizing the national American pride' turns swiftly into a bloody dictatorship, Jessup concludes, 'It can happen here' (243).

At the point in which Lewis's warning was written, of course, fascist movements were very much on the march in Depression-era Europe. It was concern at the rise of fascism in Europe that led Lewis to write the novel in the summer of 1935—even though events were to swiftly overtake his fiction. Ahead of a 1-million-strong rally in September 1935, the Third Reich hurried to introduce the so-called Nuremberg Laws, that quintessence of administrative inequality, making Jews legal aliens in Germany (Knox 2000: 145). Less than three weeks later, Fascist Italy invaded Abyssinia, with a trail of chemical weapons in their expansionist wake. These events markedly changed the picture of interwar Europe, generating the classic, indeed rightly indelible, picture of fascist aggression and legalized persecution. *It Can't Happen Here*'s seductive warning of imminent fascist dictatorship fit the roiling times of crumpling democracies and militaristic nationalism in Europe, but less so the US in the 1930s, with its puny Silver Shirt movement (Steigmann-Gall 2017: 108), and far less so in our day—save for those crying wolf by denouncing Trump as some kind of fascist dictator.

'If Trump as fascist dictator' does not warrant analytical scrutiny in terms of historical parallels (Matthews 2016), surely more helpful is the view that many fascist tropes were dangerously mainstreamed in interwar Europe. Extreme ideas, as the historian Aristotle Kallis (2013: 55–6) rightly reminds us, 'begin their life cycle as politically and socially marginal and radical counterpropositions to established "mainstream" cognition. By transgressing the widely accepted boundaries between "acceptable" and "unacceptable" premises or prescriptions, they are essentially attempting to remap these established cognitions and subvert the mainstream "frames" that support them.' In the context of the 1930s, what Kallis elsewhere calls the 'fascist effect' became a kind of 'brand' that even non-fascists wished to emulate. To take just one historical instance, consider the impact of the Nazi race laws:

> When one looks at the diffusion of the 'racial' anti-Jewish paradigm in 1930s Europe, it becomes obvious that the model pioneered by the Nazi regime with the 1935 'Nuremberg Laws' broke taboos and, in so doing, activated and/or empowered pre-existing, yet latent or partly suppressed, anti-Jewish demand in other countries. This contributed critically to its reproduction—in a 'domino effect' style—across other European countries between 1936–9. It also served as both a legitimizing (viewed as 'successful') precedent *and* a 'successful', bold model for shaping similar 'solutions' to the so-called Jewish problem outside Nazi Germany. (Kallis 2013: 56)

From this perspective, in several European states between the wars, the danger was in fascism's becoming normalized or domesticated, or rather in the mainstream's becoming fascistized. A paradigmatic instance was the conservative elite, like the Junkers and civil servants in early 1930s Germany who were disdainful of democracy and willing to co-opt Nazism as a bulwark to smash what they broadly understood to be 'the left'—or so they thought. As it turned out, fascism's political opportunism and mobilizational appeal, first in Italy and then in Germany, soon overwhelmed the reactionary elites once it had its hands on the machinery of state power (Knox 2000). It should be remembered that Nazism rested on widespread popular appeal—including 40 per cent of the working-class vote—and most of the Gestapo's later arrests came from denunciations made by ordinary informants (Gellately 2001: 136ff.). These were as much 'consensus dictatorships' as autocratic tyrannies. Across Europe, new democracies established after the Great War fell one after another to right-wing authoritarianism, like shakily placed dominoes, until fewer than a dozen democracies remained in the west and north on the eve of the Second World War. In much of the former Russian, German, and Austro-Hungarian empires, democracy failed to put down solid roots or galvanize widespread popular support, such that the UK, France, Switzerland, Belgium, the Netherlands, Ireland, Denmark, Sweden, Norway, and Finland were the only remaining democracies in Europe by the outbreak of the Second World War (Linz 2003: 226).

From the Margins to the Mainstream Revisited

Perhaps the last time the mainstream felt such a sense of acute alarm was in the years following the fall of the Berlin Wall. Speaking for many, exactly sixty years after Sinclair Lewis's warning, the celebrated novelist and intellectual Umberto Eco penned 'Ur-Fascism' (1995) for the *New York Review of Books*, widely disseminated then, and since taken as a popular guide for gauging whether a particular country is 'going fascist'. His concern had been triggered by what Martin Lee and others have called an 'ideological facelift' by the far right (2000: 388)—one starting to pay dividends following the demise of the once great enemy, the Soviet Union.

Perhaps the best example came from Eco's native Italy, where, in 1994, a relaunched, explicitly 'post-fascist' Alleanza Nazionale (AN), tracing its now-rejected heritage to ex-Fascist militants who established the Movimento Sociale Italiano in 1946, joined the first Silvio Berlusconi government alongside the more extreme La Lega Nord, together comprising 33 of 64 members of the government (ironically enough, a rebranded La Lega joined a right-wing coalition Italian government in early 2018). In January 1995, the AN restyled itself as a mainstream party at the pivotal Fiuggi Conference (Carioti 1996), which positioned the movement alongside the Belgian Vlaams Blok (VB), the French Front National, and the Austrian Freedom Party as allegedly mere populists vying for national office. Even though the *New York Times* reported on 31 March 1994 that 'several hundred young skinheads gave straight-arm neo-Fascist salutes while mingling with a crowd of National Alliance supporters at a victory rally' (Cowell 1994), this did not stop polls from finding AN leader Gianfranco Fini to be the most popular politician in Italy by early 1995. That same year, in 'Ur-Fascism', Eco grudgingly admitted, 'I have no difficulty in acknowledging that today the Italian Alleanza Nazionale ... has by now very little to do with the old fascism' (Eco 1995: 407).

Next door in Austria, more troublingly, the FPÖ, a party founded by ex-Nazi activists in 1955, had sufficiently distanced itself from its past, under the charismatic Jörg Haider's march to the mainstream, that it received more than 1 million votes—22.5 per cent of the national vote and 43 seats in 1994 (Fallend 2004). In part, it was these kinds of electoral breakthroughs that moved Eco to declare:

> Ur-Fascism is still around us, sometimes in plainclothes. It would be so much easier for us if there appeared on the world scene somebody saying, 'I want to reopen Auschwitz, I want the Blackshirts to parade again in the Italian squares.' Life is not that simple. Ur-Fascism can come back under the most innocent of disguises. (Eco 1995: 415)

Eco's sentiments are still apposite today. Yet just as importantly—although it is a more neglected point—there is a key difference between fascism and the far right implied by Ur-Fascism: that the latter is more than just a disguise for the former.

Specialists—let alone those unfamiliar with the extensive literature—are likely then to misdiagnose the dangers to liberal democracy by approaching the far right today principally through the lens of historical fascism. If we are going to historicize, we may do it better by taking as our starting point the sociologist Juan Linz's contention (as summarized by Kallis 2015: 9) that interwar fascism's ascendency was due mostly to 'a profound institutional crisis that deprived the liberal-democratic systems of their much-needed legitimacy in the eyes of elites and public opinion alike'. Linz has rightly been lauded for showing the way in which Axis regimes influenced other authoritarian practices in interwar Europe. Yet perhaps more timely is his identification of unsuccessful liberal hegemony across continental Europe in the years following the Great War—so starkly at variance with its history after 1945. For Linz, the 'crisis and breakdown of democracy' between the wars was as much a product of liberal-democratic failure as radical right success:

> Failure of the liberal-democratic political class and governmental instability or inefficacy were even more important; these allowed small groups of conspirators to end democracy or democratization with the passive acquiescence of kings, non-conspiratorial militaries and populations that were unwilling to support the regime and even welcomed the dictatorships with a sense of relief and even hope. (Linz 2003: 248)

The parallels between historical fascism and the far right can distract as much as instruct, for at least two reasons. On this point, Pierre-André Taguieff has argued that

> Neither 'fascism' or 'racism' will do us the favour of returning in such a way that we can recognise them easily. If vigilance was only a game of recognizing something already well known [sic], then it would only be a question of remembering. Vigilance would be reduced to a social game using reminiscence and identification by recognition, a consoling illusion of an immobile history peopled with events which accord to our expectations or our fears. (Taguieff 1993: 54)

This assessment was made in reference to the Nouvelle Droite (ND), and it introduces, if indirectly, one of two essential changes that took place among neo-fascists in the Cold War era. The first of these is ethno-pluralism, which Taguieff denounces as 'differentialist racism': 'the tactical dressing of inegalitarian racism, as an *acceptable reformulation* making an appeal to an ideological keyword (*difference*)' (2001: 212, original emphasis).

After May 1968, faced with the despised 'cultural hegemony' of a liberal-left France, the ND brought together neo-fascist activists for pivotal ideological revisions. The movement and its many publications were avowedly 'metapolitical', since the ND claimed not to seek political influence, setting as its task ahead a

'Gramscism of the right': an assault an assault on the so-called 'laboratories of thinking' in the media, universities, and government. According to the group's main interpreter today, Tamir Bar-On, 'De Benoist's logic was that if he explicitly recognized other cultures according to cultural elements rather than biological ones and rejected the notion of cultural superiority, then how could he be labelled a "racist"?' (2013: 14). This differentialism undertook a long march, over decades, in rejecting a key tenet of historic fascism: white—or national—supremacy. In its place was the 'right to difference' and the countercharge that it was the multicultural 'race-mixers' who were the real racists. Instead, the ND alleged it valued all cultures equally—but it was the integrity of the ethnos that mattered above all.

Given the well-established radical-right pedigree of its chief ideologues across Europe (Aleksandr Dugin, Guillaume Faye, Dominique Venner, Pierre Krebs, and Michael Walker), it appears this was simply white separatism through the back door: fascist 'blood and soil' in politically correct language.[1] Yet its cumulative effect over more than two generations has been staggering—and perhaps successful in its aims. Indeed, according to Camus and Lebourg, the ND has 'taken root in a lasting matter as an intellectual project' (2017: 151). Crucially, it has provided intellectual cover for far-right groups to publicly move away from claims of racial superiority in favour of protecting national–cultural identities. In this view, all ethnies are purportedly equal so long as they are not weakened by immigration, multiculturalism, or intermixing.

By replacing race with identity, a populist doorway could be opened by once-toxic movements and political parties, with a new message aimed at mainstream audiences. Differentialism has been adopted lock, stock, and barrel by far-right groups aiming for mainstream, populist appeal—presenting anti-immigration, anti-multiculturalism and racial nationalism as merely the defence of indigenous cultures globally and no more than a 'first amongst equals' preference. Shorn of its neo-fascist trappings, 'the foreign' can once more be directly and allegedly 'unprejudicially' against 'the native'—an attempted end-run around conventions against inciting prejudice and discrimination. The baleful achievements of this idea can be seen insomuch as the recent refugee crisis seems to have led to a greater mobilization in far-right support than the earlier financial crisis (with the exception of Golden Dawn in the special case of post-bailout Greece, see Pirro & van Kessel 2017).

Alongside this slow change was the second, more practical calculation noted above: far-right parties, in attempting to influence public policy in Europe, jettisoned the revolutionary and totalitarian dynamics of interwar fascism. This, incidentally, is also what separates them from more minor, extreme-right groups of neo-fascists and neo-Nazis. The calculus was a straightforward one: anti-establishment populism within an entrenched liberal framework. Parenthetically, populism is not a core feature of either fascism or the far right, it is a mobilizational and communications strategy used by right and left alike (think of Podemos in Spain or Syriza in Greece, for example—usually distinguished between populist radical right and populist radical left, as in Rooduijn et al. 2017), and it is absent in many smaller, elitist fascist and far-right movements—not least the Nouvelle Droite. In order for far-right parties to be 'de-demonized', in the words of Marine Le Pen (Lichfield 2015), there could be no reminder of the infamous fascist style: no paramilitarism, no semi-divine leader, no fascist chants or salutes, and certainly no parading blackshirts.

Accordingly, the revolutionary-right challenge of yesteryear is not that faced today. There will be no replay of coloured shirts from the past, nor the totalitarian dynamic of historical fascism before 1945. Today, the descendants of this ideology wear suits, are often hostile to their parentage, and, above all, have accepted, at least for now, the hegemony of liberal democracy in Europe. To date, no country that became a liberal democracy in post-war Europe has succumbed to dictatorship, even if some, like Hungary, Poland, and perhaps the US, have become 'illiberal democracies'—that is, retaining the majoritarian trappings of democracy, while curtailing civil and political rights for opponents and minorities. In this way, the spectre of fascist war and racial tyranny may not be a useful historical lesson for the present; by contrast, populist appeal and a crisis of legitimacy in the mainstream raise awkward questions.

Do Leopards Change their Spots?

True, many of the recognisable far-right characteristics Eco so perceptively noted are still discernible, such as conspiracy theorizing, authoritarian governance and anti-liberalism/socialism. Yet broadly speaking, these movements have truly learnt to speak the language of reform rather than revolution. In Gianfranco Fini's populist transition of the Alleanza Nazionale from neo-fascism to post-fascism, for instance, the previous leader, Pino Rauti, maintained a hardline stance that brought about a party split and the formation of the neo-fascist (and unashamedly pro-Republic of Salò) Movement Tricolour Flame. Variations on this discordant Italian theme were repeated by France's Front National in the west, by the Sweden Democrats in the north and the Slovak National Party in the east (which took 8.6 per cent of the 2016 national vote and 15 parliamentary seats). All of these parties purged their more extreme activists in a bid for greater legitimacy. Even Marine

Le Pen's father, Jean-Marie, was dismissed from the Front National for his antisemitism—a new taboo for far-right parties so keen to swap historical Judeo-prejudice for Islamo-prejudice today (see, for example, Camus & Lebourg 2017; Richardson 2018).

Alongside shedding the most militant, unbending, or outspoken neo-fascists, a second path to legitimacy while keeping committed activists aboard is to develop a kind of coded language that can be termed doublespeak (Feldman & Jackson 2014; Richardson 2018). Of course, all political parties triangulate in order to 'manage their message', but this is far closer to deception for far-right parties. Scholars talk about a 'front-stage' of moderation and reform presented to the outside world against a persisting 'backstage' of committed extreme-right activists largely kept out of public sight (Feldman & Jackson 2014: 10). Bridging the two are dog-whistle terms (such as 'international financiers' to mean Jews) and populist themes such as immigration or law and order.

A perfect example of this front-stage–backstage dynamic could be seen in the now nearly defunct British National Party (BNP), which in its heyday had scores of local and parish councilors in Britain, and, from May 2009, two MEPs. Only a decade earlier, photographs had showed then-leader John Tyndall dressed in Nazi regalia and depicted him with David Copeland, who killed several and maimed dozens more in an April 1999 attack on gay and ethnic minority areas in London. With 'modernization' pledges patterned on the examples of the far right in France, Austria and Italy, Nick Griffin took over later that year, attempting to balance a front-stage stress on identity and monoculturalism with backstage activism by neo-fascist militants. Again and again, Griffin insisted that a desire to 'teach the truth to the hardcore' needed to be subordinated to the populist moderation that he believed would spell electoral breakthrough (cited in Feldman & Jackson 2014: 7). In fact, only a month before the European elections in 2009, which took Griffin and Andrew Brons into the European Parliament with nearly one million votes (6.3 per cent), the BNP released an astonishing 'Language and Concepts Discipline Manual' for use by 'backstage' activists (for instance, Rule 1 fancifully states: 'We are not a "racist" or "racial" party'; cited in Feldman 2015: 8). If to a less stark degree, this front-stage–backstage dynamic was replayed all over Europe as part of the legitimizing march by far-right parties. It also should be remembered, moreover, that neo-fascists and the far right know their history as well as anyone (for an excellent analysis of radical right doublespeak in contemporary Britain, see Richardson 2018).

So, if history can be as much a blessing as a curse in approaching the far right, and with the latter being a swiftly moving target, altering key elements of its core praxis in order to reach the mainstream (for example, swapping racism for identity, or revolutionary ultranationalism for illiberal populism), the question may then be asked 'Where are we now?' For one, things are speeding up. This entails more than just the effects of social media, where 280-character slogans and patchy digital literacy in Europe and the US means that far-right outpourings seemingly receive publicly polarized responses, ranging from 'fascist' to 'common sense'. The far right is neither of these—unless we let it be—but instead represents a well-co-ordinated revamp that has allowed far-right parties to be mainstreamed. This has had two significant political effects that are only now being felt.

The first point is that far-right parties continue to go from strength to strength. In 2016, the FPÖ's Norbert Hofer came within 350,000 votes of winning the Austrian presidency with 46 per cent of the vote—the highest result ever for either a fascist or a far-right candidate in Europe (for further discussion of the 'Austrian case', see Wodak 2018). There can scarcely be a blunter warning. Marginally less stark, since 1994—depending on how the term 'far-right party' is defined—as many as 24 government coalitions in 12 European countries have included far-right parties (Mudde 2017: 8). Still, others point to longer-term trends in Western and Central Europe, going as far back as the idiosyncratic Danish People's Party in 1973, but more specifically to the 1980s political breakthroughs for the Front National in France and the Vlaams Blok (VB) in Belgium.

Although the term, and political practice, of *cordon sanitaire* had first been applied to the Vlaams Blok following its 1988 result in Antwerp, when it garnered 17.7 per cent of the vote in the city, only three years later, on 'Black Sunday', Filip Dewinter's VB claimed nearly 7 per cent of the national vote, winning 5 Belgian senators and 12 delegates in the Chamber of Representatives. This familiar story in Europe was not just national, but regional and transnational as well. In 2004, the Vlaams Blok took 32 seats in the Flemish parliament, with nearly a quarter of the electorate's vote. That year, with nearly one million votes, it also took three seats in the European Parliament (Van Holsteyn 2018). Only a Belgian judicial ruling against Vlaams Blok for 'incitement to discrimination' stopped its rise in November 2004, when a new party emerged in its wake, Vlaams Belang (Erk 2005). The latter formed part of the short-lived European political party Identity, Sovereignty, Tradition between January and November 2007. Although I would not share Martin Schulz's definition of this group as 'fascist', his 2011 warning about the mainstreaming potential of far-right parties mirrors, in its way, the historian Aristotle Kallis's argument about the mainstreaming of the interwar 'fascist effect':

> The new fascist parliamentary grouping perpetrated permanent breaches of convention in a way that has become systematic. When no sanctions were imposed for racist, xenophobic or antisemitic statements, they were presented as permissible and therefore no longer subject to prosecution or sanction in the future. By deliberate breach of taboos, racist, xenophobic and antisemitic remarks were thrust into normal daily parliamentary affairs. In our opinion, this is an extremely dangerous development. (Schulz 2011: 28)

It is precisely these breaches of convention by what might be analogously called the 'far-right effect' that a leading political scientist on the subject, Cas Mudde, understands as 'pathological normalcy'—a breach of the civic *cordon sanitaire* as much as the political one:

> Establishing boundaries between populist radical right parties and mainstream right-wing parties has been significantly complicated by the rise of populist radical right politics in Europe, i.e. nativist, authoritarian, and populist discourses and policies from mostly mainstream parties. (Mudde 2016: 16)

Nor is Mudde alone in this concern. In fact, several books on the far right published in this decade alone employ the term 'mainstream' in the subtitle. In terms of voter appeal, Tjitske Akkerman summarizes this mainstream appeal effectively: 'Negative attitudes toward asylum seekers, legal and illegal immigration and multiculturalism prevail among radical-right voters and are the main reason why voters support these parties' (2012: 511).

To the question 'Where is the far right now?' the answer then must be 'Virtually mainstreamed'. That in itself is surely a challenge to liberal stability and legitimacy, and perhaps even a long-term threat to democratic security. This may be due to any number of factors: what has been dubbed a 'right turn' in Europe, away from inclusion and assimilation; the skilful use of pro-identity and nativist populism; or, again, propitious conditions in Europe (for example, historically low levels of political trust, shocking acts of jihadi Islamist terrorism and what is usually termed the refugee crisis). Nevertheless, a key concern should also be the new political terrain that the far right has opened this century. Like a vortex, anti-Muslim and broader nativist sentiment is sucking in new political players to the far right's (notionally) left and right. In terms of the latter, consider the development of the alt-right in the US, championed by no less than President Trump's sometime chief strategist Steve Bannon, ex-editor of 'the platform for the alt-right', Breitbart News (SPLC 2017). While there are many spokes to the alt-right wheel, its hub is the overt white supremacism pushed by the man who coined the term alt-right, Richard Spencer (Hawley 2017). Following Trump's election on 8 November 2016, footage appeared of celebrations at Spencer's National Policy Institute, in which he urged supporters to 'party like it was 1933', followed by fascist salutes and chants of 'Heil Trump!'[2]

Aided by a sophisticated use of social media and guaranteed funding from the conservative American political activist and donor William Regnery II, Spencer is now a familiar voice in the mainstream American media calling for, in his words, 'a racially based state'. That quotation was given to *Rolling Stone*, and its publication perhaps exacerbated the problem by giving Spencer high-profile media exposure in the same month as Trump won the election, without fundamentally challenging his racist views:

> 'We've been legitimized by this election,' he says. While the campaign itself was a huge boost to the movement, Trump's election, he says, has brought the Alt-Right to 'a new level.' 'Legitimacy is … an unmeasurable, intangible thing that is everything.' … 'We want to be radically mainstream—that is, we really want to enter the world, we want our ideas to be at the table, and people to listen to them,' says Spencer. (Posner 2016)

There is little that is backstage about what Spencer claims would be merely a case of 'peaceful ethnic cleansing', and his aim to rehabilitate historical fascism is unmistakable (Kentish 2017). This is revolutionary right-wing neo-fascism masquerading as a vision of reform. It is white paint over asbestos. Yet, in place of far-right parties that at one time were firmly beyond the *cordon sanitaire*, this is the new fringe, trying to find meme-friendly ways to advance biological racism back into the mainstream. From CasaPound in Italy to the transnational British Blood and Honour music scene, these would-be fashionable white supremacists are, of course, not the only neo-fascist game in town (Fielitz & Laloire 2016; Feldman & Jackson 2014). Yet what the alt-right and overt fascists share is the attempt to force neo-fascism back onto the public agenda. No doubt, this attempted rebranding owes much to the political space vacated by a far right that is moving towards the mainstream.

Finally, and perhaps most troublingly, in terms of the political tectonic plates moved by the mainstreaming of the far right, there is what I term the 'near right', sometimes also called 'right-wing populism'. One example of this trend is the Law and Justice Party in Poland (Prawo i Sprawiedliwość, PiS), described by Jean-Yves Camus and Nicolas Lebourg in cognate terms as an example of a 'radicalized conservative right' (2017: 241). Another instance is the 'illiberal democracy' now proudly touted by Victor Orbán's Fidesz Party in Hungary, exemplified above all by its disgraceful attack on the CEU, on gender studies programmes generally, and on liberal scholarship everywhere. It now holds a parliamentary supermajority and can change laws and liberal norms nearly at will.

Yet perhaps the leading exemplar of this near-right populism is Brexit. Few will forget the xenophobic fever leading up to the 23 June 2016 referendum, resulting in a 41 per cent increase in hate crimes in what might be termed a form of celebratory racism at the outcome. Indeed, of the nearly 6,000 reported hate crimes reported in the four weeks following the vote to leave the EU, more than half 'specifically referred to the referendum in the abuse' (Virdee & McGeever 2018: 1808). Needless to say, not all leave voters were xenophobic; however, it seems clear that all racist voters chose Brexit. Yet for this well-established spike in xenophobia, what responsibility might UKIP—the emboldened near-right Eurosceptic party—have for trafficking in rhetoric and images like the infamous 'Breaking Point' poster, unveiled a week before the vote? That the notorious image was actually of refugees in Slovenia trying to enter Croatia was surely of less import than that those depicted had dark skin.

Figure 1.2. The leave.eu 'Breaking Point' poster (https://www.theguardian.com/politics/2016/jun/16/nigel-farage-defends-ukip-breaking-point-pos-ter-queue-of-migrants, accessed 7 May 2019).

More recently, and once again in territory more redolent of the far right, both the one-time leader of UKIP, Nigel Farage, and the Prime Minister of Poland, Beata Szydło, quickly weighed in on the Westminster attack of 22 March 2017, which left four dead in a self-directed terrorist act by the 52-year-old Islamist convert, Khalid Masood, born and raised as Adrian Elms in southern England. They blamed 'immigration', but they were presumably not talking about Britain in the 1960s—when Masood was born in Britain's Home Counties. On 23 March 2017, they were trying to stigmatize rather more recent arrivals:

> We've made some terrible mistakes in this country, and it really started with the election of Tony Blair back in 1997, who said he wanted to build a multicultural Britain ... I'm sorry to say that we have now a fifth column living inside these European countries. (Nigel Farage, quoted in Warren 2017)
> I hear in Europe very often: 'Do not connect the migration policy with terrorism', but it is impossible not to connect them. (Beata Szydło, quoted in Montgomery 2017)

Figure 1.3. The *Daily Mail* front page on 10 April 2017.

Fanning the populist flames is a practice of an emboldened near-right media, from the Dutch Geenstijl ('No Style') blog to Breitbart News in the US. Nor have print newspapers been immune. For example, what is one to think of the cover of Britain's best-selling newspaper, the *Daily Mail*, declaring 'Crush the Saboteurs' (that is, 'Remainers' opposed to Brexit) the day after Theresa May's call for a snap election in Britain in 2017?

'Immune' is a word worth closing with, in the sense of Kenan Malik's apt phrase, 'Democracy is in rude health. It is liberalism that is in trouble' (2017). By eating away at the foundations of liberal democracy—tolerance, human rights, individual conscience—the risks to liberal democracy by the far right may, in years to come, be most palpably felt in the weakening of immunological defences, both political and civic. As this chapter argues, the risks are not posed by an assault on power like between the wars, nor even by a fundamental rupture with democracy, as the cases of Hungary and now Poland may suggest. But it is an ideological assault on the liberal status quo in Europe, nonetheless. Xenophobia acts like arsenic on the European body politic, administered not only by far-right parties, but increasingly by a populist near right, and by newly emboldened neo-fascists. That means extra susceptibility in a major crisis. And it also means the germs of a collective madness are again in the air, as in Albert Camus's novel of wartime occupation, *La Peste*: 'When you see the misery it brings, you'd need to be a madman, or a coward, or stone blind, to give in tamely to the plague' (1948: 115).

We need 'political immunologists' desperately today. For if liberalism fails over the next generation, it will be because we, its guardians, failed it. Let us demonstrate that liberal values include the protection of minority groups, equality of rights, and freedom from fear. This is the kernel of liberalism. Perhaps not of liberal democracy as such, the actual mechanics of governance in Europe, but certainly of liberal moderation, the petrol that makes it all work. It is that tank which in the end needs refilling with a bit more liberal horsepower: an evidence-based, even passionate, restatement of fundamental democratic values in the face of potential attacks from without and, especially in the years to come, from foreseeable attacks by what may be described as a fifth column (Feldman 2015) within liberal praxis.

Endnotes

[1] Aleksandr Dugin is a Russian 'neo-Eurasianist' with ties to the Kremlin; Dominique Venner was a long-time French radical right activist, who committed suicide at the altar of Notre-Dame in 2013; Guillaume Faye is a journalist and leading ideologue of the 'metapolitical' French New Right; and the writings of Pierre Krebs and Michael Walker were ideological offshoots in Belgium and Britain, respectively.

[2] For a video recording of this speech, with commentary on cited quotations, see *New Zealand Herald*'s 'The Big Read: Insight the alt-right world of Richard Spencer' (23 November 2016), www.nzherald.co.nz/world/news/article.cfm?c_id=2&objectid=11753791 (all websites last accessed 7 April 2019).

References

Akkerman, T. (2012), "Comparing radical right parties in government: Immigration and integration policies in nine countries (1996–2010)", *West European Politics*, 35/3: 511–29.

Bar-On, T. (2013), *Rethinking the French New Right: Alternatives to Modernity* (London).

Bastow, S. (2002), "A neo-fascist third way: the discourse of ethno-differentialist revolutionary nationalism", *Journal of Political Ideologies*, 7/3: 69–88, reprinted in R. Griffin & M. Feldman, *Fascism, Critical Concepts, v: Postwar Fascism* (London, 2004).

Betz, H. (1993), "The new politics of resentment: Radical right-wing populist parties in Western Europe", *Comparative Politics*, 25/4: 413–27.

Bauerkämper, A. (2010), "Transnational fascism: Cross-border relations between regimes and movements in Europe 1922–1939", *East Central Europe*, 37: 214–46.

Camus, A. 1948, *The Plague*, trans. Stuart Gilbert (London).

Camus, J.-Y. & N. Lebourg (2017), *Far-right politics in Europe*, trans. Jane Marie Todd (London).

Carioti, A. (1996), "From the ghetto to the Palazzo Chigi: The ascent of the National Alliance", *Italian Politics*, x. 91–110, reprinted in R. Griffin & M. Feldman, *Fascism, Critical Concepts, v: Postwar Fascism* (London, 2004).

Cowell, A. (1994), "Italy's neo-fascists: Have they shed their past?" *New York Times*, www.nytimes.com/1994/03/31/world/italy-s-neo-fascists-have-they-shed-their-past.html.

Eatwell, R. (2000), "The rebirth of the "Extreme right" in Western Europe", *Parliamentary Affairs*, 53/3: 410–14.

Eco, U. (1995), "Ur-Fascism", *New York Review of Books*, 405–416, reprinted in R. Griffin & M. Feldman, *Fascism, Critical Concepts, v: Postwar Fascism* (London, 2004)

Erk, J. (2005), "From Vlaams Blok to Vlaams Belang: The Belgian far right renames itself", *West European Politics*, 28/3: 493–502.

Fallend, F. (2004), "Are right-wing populism and government participation incompatible? The case of the freedom party of Austria", *Representation: Journal of Representative Democracy*, 40/2: 115–30.

Feldman, M. & P. Jackson (eds.) (2014), "Introduction" *Doublespeak: The Framing of the Far-Right since 1945* (Stuttgart).

—. (2015), "Hate-baiting: The radical-right and 'fifth column discourse' in European and American democracies today", *Journal of Political Criminology*, 1/1: 7–19.

Fielitz, M. & N. Laloire (eds.) (2016), "Trouble on the Far Right: Introductory Remarks", *Trouble on the Far Right: Contemporary Right-Wing Strategies and Practices in Europe*. Edited by Maik Fielitz and Laura Lotte Laloire. Bielefeld: transcript Verlag, 2016, pp. 13-26, https://www.transcript-publishing.com/media/pdf/a5/ab/f4/ts3720_1.pdf.

Gellately, R. (2001), *Backing Hitler: Consent and Coercion in Nazi Germany* (Oxford).

Griffin, R. (2008), "Exploding the continuum of history: A non-Marxist's Marxist model of fascism's revolutionary dynamics", in M. Feldman (ed.), *A Fascist Century: Essays by Roger Griffin* (Basingstoke).

Hawley, G. (2017), *Making sense of the alt-right* (London).

Kallis, A. (2013), "Breaking taboos and 'Mainstreaming the extreme': the debates on restricting Islamic symbols in contemporary Europe", in R. Wodak, M. KhosraviNik & B. Mral (eds.), *Right-Wing Populism in Europe: Politics and Discourse* (London), pp. 55-70, https://www.bloomsburycollections.com/book/right-wing-populism-in-europe-politics-and-discourse/ch4-breaking-taboos-and-mainstreaming-the-extreme.pdf.

—. (2015), "When fascism became mainstream: The challenge of extremism in times of crisis", *Fascism*, 4: 1–24.

Kentish, B. (2017), "White supremacist leader Richard Spencer forced to hold press conference in flat as hotels refuse to take him", *The Independent*, www.independent.co.uk/news/world/americas/richard-spencer-charlottesville-pro-tests-white-supremacist-press-conference-flat-hotels-refuse-a7894236.html.

Knox, M. (2000), *Common destiny: Dictatorship, foreign policy and war in fascist Italy and Nazi Germany* (Cambridge) (first pub. 1997).

Lee, M. (2000), *The beast reawakens* (London).

Lewis, S. (2017), *It can't happen here* (London) (first pub. 1935).

Lichfield, J. (2015), "Front national family feud? Marine Le Pen and her relatives clash over French far-right party's response to Paris terror attacks", *The Independent*: www.independent.co.uk/news/world/europe/front-national-family-feud-marine-le-pen-and-her-relatives-clash-over-french-far-right-partys-100 06562.html.

Linz, J. (2003), "Fascism and non-democratic regimes", in H. Maier (ed.), *Totalitarianism and political religions: Concepts for the comparison of dictatorships, iii: Theory and History of Interpretation*, trans. Jodi Bruhn (London).

Malik, K. (2017), "Liberalism is suffering but democracy is doing just fine", *The Guardian*: www.theguardian.com/commentisfree/2017/jan/01/liberalism-suffering-democracy-doing-just-fine.

Matthews, D. (2016), "I asked 5 fascism experts whether Donald Trump is a fascist. Here's what they said", Vox, www.vox.com/policy-and-pol-itics/2015/12/10/9886152/donald-trump-fascism.

Montgomery, J. (2017), "Polish prime minister: 'Impossible not to connect terrorism with migration policy'", Breitbart News, www.breitbart.com/london/2017/03/23/polish-prime-minister-impossible-not-connect-terrorism-migration-policy/#bbvb.

Mudde, C. (1996), "The war of words: Defining the extreme right party family", *West European Politics*, 19/2: 225–48.

—. (2016), "The study of populist radical right parties: Towards a fourth wave", C-Rex working paper 1, Centre for Research on Extremism, September, www.sv.uio.no/c-rex/english/publications/c-rex-working-paper-series/Cas%20Mudde:%20The%20Study%20of%20Populist%20Radical%20Right%20Parties.pdf.

—. (2017), *The populist radical right: A reader* (London).

Norocel, O. C. (2013), "Our people—A tight-knit family under the same protective roof: A critical study of gendered conceptual metaphors at work in radical right populism" (PhD diss., Helsinki), helda.helsinki.fi/bitstream/handle/10138/42162/ourpeopl.pdf?sequence=1&isAllowed=y.

Pirro, A. & S. van Kessel (2017), "United in opposition? The populist radical right's EU-pessimism in times of crisis", *Journal of European Integration*, 39/4: 405–20.

Posner, S. (2016), "'Radically Mainstream': Why the Alt-Right Is Celebrating Trump's Win", *Rolling Stone*, www.rollingstone.com/politics/politics-features/radically-mainstream-why-the-alt-right-is-celebrating-trumps-win-110791/.

Richardson, J. (2018), *British Fascism: A Discourse-Historical Analogy* (Stuttgart).

Rooduijn, M., B. Burgoon, E. J. van Elsas & H. G. van de Werfhorst (2017), "Radical distinction: Support for radical left and radical right parties in Europe", *European Union Politics*, 18/4: 536–59.

Saint-Martin, Elise (2013), "The front national: Model for the radical right?" University of Ottawa, ruor.uottawa.ca/bitstream/10393/26189/1/St-Martin_Élise_2013_mémoire.pdf.

Schulz, M. (2011), "Combatting right-wing extremism as a task for European policy-making", in *Is Europe on the 'Right' Path? Right-wing extremism and right-wing populism in Europe* (Berlin).

SPLC (Southern Poverty Law Center) (2017), "Breitbart exposé confirms: Far-right news site a platform for the 'alt-right'", Hatewatch Files, www.splcenter.org/hatewatch/2017/10/06/breitbart-exposé-confirms-far-right-news-site-platform-white-nationalist-alt-right.

Steigmann-Gall, R. (2017), "Star-spangled fascism: American interwar political extremism in comparative perspective", *Social History*, 42/1: 94–119.

Taguieff, P.-A. (1993), "Discussion or inquisition? The case of Alain de Benoist", *Telos* 98/9: 34–54.

—. (2001), *The Force of Prejudice: On Racism and Its Doubles*, trans. and ed. Hassan Melehy (London) (first pub. 1987).

van Holsteyn, J. J. M. (2018), "The radical right in Belgium and the Netherlands", in J. Rydgren (ed.), *The Oxford Handbook of the Radical Right* (Oxford).

Virdee, S. & B. McGeever (2018), "Racism, Crisis, Brexit", *Ethnic & Racial Studies*, 41/10: 1802–19.

Warren, J. (2017), "'Foul!' Labour MP accuses Farage of 'whipping up hate' in wake of Westminster attack", *Daily Express*, www.express.co.uk/news/uk/783421/Nigel-Farage-Labour-MP-accuses-whipping-hate-multicultur-alism-comment.

Wodak, R. & B. Forchtner (2014), "Embattled Vienna 1683/2010: Right-wing populism, collective memory and the fictionalisation of politics", *Visual Communication*, 13/2: 231–55.

—. (2018), "Driving on the right: The Austrian Case", Centre for Analysis of the Radical Right, Insight blog, www.radicalrightanalysis.com/2018/04/09/driving-on-the-right-the-austrian-case/.

13. On 'Lone Wolf' Terrorism

So-called "lone wolf terrorism" is on the rise by all accounts, and by every indicator, no matter how it is defined.[1] Unfortunately, for those determined to carry out premeditated acts of terrorism alone, there are unprecedented resources available, particularly online. Perhaps the most notorious examples date from the 2010s, ten years in which there have been scores of attacks, capped by the murder of 51 worshippers at two mosques in Christchurch, New Zealand, by a radical right extremist on 15 March 2019. At the other end of the decade, another anti-Muslim identitarian, Anders Behring Breivik, detonated a nail bomb in the heart of Oslo that killed eight people on 22 July 2011. He then went on a shooting spree that left 69 innocents—overwhelmingly teenagers, executed at close range—scattered dead around Utøya Island. His murder of 77 people, moreover, may well have been to draw attention to his first act of terrorism, the dissemination of his 1516-page tract, *2083: A Declaration of European Independence*, a terrorist do-it-yourself kit. These disasters are just the tip of the iceberg, not least as the phenomenon is much misunderstood.

It is clear that, given the increase in these solo actor terrorist attacks, both conceptual refining and a better understanding of this form of terrorism are urgently needed. If anything, this has become even more urgent with the maturation—if that is the right word—of new technologies—none more so than the internet. In attempting to flesh out the contours of this resurgent genre of terrorism, this chapter considers the rise of lone wolf terrorism over the last generation or so—roughly coterminous with the growing ubiquity of the web—by terrorists *going alone through the "terrorist cycle"* (target selection, operational planning, deployment, the attack, escape, and exploitation).[2] Sometimes called "leaderless resistance" or even, in the case of violent takfiri Islamism, "personal jihad", these diverse terms center on the key feature of this kind of terrorism: a single actor undertaking ideologically-motivated violence (especially political and/or religious, and typically against non-military targets) without external direction or coordination. But why has what is termed here "self-activating terrorism" spiked so massively this century; and just as pressingly, how does lone wolf terrorism relate to radical right extremism? The latter half of the chapter shall look more closely at Breivik's actions, including his manifesto, as the horrific template for this type of 21st century terrorism.

But first, why are we seeing this spike of lone wolf incidents now? Unfortunately, responses to this question are not helped by a slowly-corrected dearth of scholarship in this area.[3] To date, moreover, most of the information publicly available on lone wolf terrorism is to be found not in academic research but in reports by think tanks. One reason for this is that self-activated terrorism challenges some of our assumptions about terrorist violence itself. One early study of lone wolf terrorism, by the Dutch Crisis Management Team, or COT, in 2007, argued that terrorism is generally understood to be a communal act licensed by an outside agency—clearly a view having little room for individually planned and undertaken violence:

> The imbalance between the perceived threat of lone-wolf terrorism on the one hand and the almost exclusive scholarly focus on group-based terrorism on the other hand indicates the need for more conceptual and empirical analysis to enable a better understanding of lone-wolf terrorism.[4]

Just such a "better understanding" matters now more than ever. By attempting to contribute in this area, this chapter briefly recounts the history and development of lone wolf terrorism as well as some debates about the use of this term before formulating a new, and hopefully useful, definition of the nettlesome concept. To do so, a concise history of this phrase is called for. Strikingly, to date the term has been most effectively utilized in an impressive report from 2010 by The Hague's International Centre for Counter-Terrorism (ITTC). There, Edwin Bakker and Beatrice de Graaf suggest that the roots of lone wolf terrorism derive from nineteenth-century anarchism, specifically Mikhail Bakunin's "propaganda of the deed," first announced in his 1870 "Letters to a Frenchman on the Present Crisis" [*i.e.*, the Paris Commune]: "we must spread our principles, not with words but with deeds, for this is the most popular, the most potent, and the most irresistible form of propaganda."[5]

Over the next 60 years, anarchist bombings—poorlessly fictionalized in Joseph Conrad's 1907 *The Secret Agent*—were directed at royal, bourgeois, and economic targets. The most shocking of these include the assassination of King Umberto I of Italy in 1900, and a 1920 bombing on Wall Street in New York, killing 33 people and wounding more than 200. And in an earlier notorious case of lone wolf anarchism—in a case championed by John Merriman as one that "arguably ignited the modern age of terrorism"—Émile Henry bombed the Café Terminus adjacent to the Gare Saint-Lazare in France on February 12, 1894, killing one and wounding 20. At his widely-reported trial, the 21-year-old terrorist proclaimed:

> In the merciless war that we have declared on the bourgeoisie, we ask no mercy. We mete out death and we must face it. For that reason I await your verdict with indifference. I know that mine will not be the last head you will sever...You will add more names to the bloody roll call of our dead.[6]

Far more recently, this apologia for self-declared war was eerily echoed in Breivik's closing trial statement on June 22, 2012, which opened by similarly claiming that "what happened on July 22nd was an act of barbarism." This "merciless war," Breivik lengthily continued, was a "preventative" one against the multicultural "treason" of the Norwegian—and more broadly, European—postwar establishment of "cultural Marxists":

> The attacks of July 22nd were preventive attacks, serving the defense of the Norwegian indigenous people, ethnic Norwegians, our culture, and I cannot declare myself guilty before the law for conducting them. I was acting in defense of my people, my culture, my religion, my city, and my country. Therefore I demand to be acquitted of all charges.[7]

Put simply, David Rapoport describes "four waves" of terrorism: anarchist, anti-colonial, "new left" and religious terrorism; the fifth may simply be a more internet-friendly tactic, brought to life from a past age.[8] In practice, this means that the terrorist "propaganda by the deed" of anarchist infamy is quickly circulated internationally through the mass media—telegraphs, the penny press, and later, radio a century ago—and the internet, social media and encrypted communications today. In another similarity from the juxtaposed quotations above, with most cases of terrorism—both lone wolf and its more familiar group-based form—protagonists commonly seem to view their acts of terrorism less as justified crimes than as acts of asymmetrical warfare. As with group-based terrorism, likewise, targets of self-directed violence tend to be symbolic rather than strategic. With the waning of anarchism between the world wars, so too did the nigh-indiscriminate violence in this first phase of what might be considered "proto-lone wolf terrorism."

Yet the celebration of this tactic was emphatically revived by the radical right from the 1980s onward. Between 1980 and 1986 a long-term neo-Nazi ideologue named James Mason produced a monthly newsletter called *Siege*, which explicitly advocated this terrorist tactic. (*Siege* has been collected and reprinted in four editions between 1992 and 2018, in both print and .pdf editions that are currently widely read.) Mason had been a stalwart on the neo-Nazi scene since 1966, when at 14 he joined the American Nazi Party, then led by the notorious George Lincoln Rockwell.[9] In the years after Rockwell's murder, a disillusioned Mason gravitated to the terroristic California-based cell NSLF, or National Socialist Liberation Front, in which he came to reject political approaches as a legitimate avenue for fascist revolutionaries. In consequence, *Siege* is less engaged with theoretical discussions of fascist ideology or the history of National Socialism, and much more concerned with strategies to replace the 'mass movement' strategy of the American Nazi Party and others. Suggested tactics in *Siege* include survivalism and white separatism; withdrawal from the liberal-democratic 'System', which is allegedly controlled by Jews; and above all, political violence through lone actor or small cell terrorism. *Siege*'s 'direct action' tactics, moreover, were consistently formulated in support of National Socialist ideology. In James Mason's *Siege*, however, these standard neo-Nazi themes came with an ideological addition that very few fascists could endorse, either at the time or since. Shortly after the first instalment of *Siege* in summer 1980, according to Mason, he met the notorious American convict, Charles Manson, and changed the name of his organisation to Universal Order, with the following logo:

In *Siege*, a September 1981 text explained this change as simply a changed context for, or application of, National Socialism decades after Hitler's suicide in 1945: 'The One Truth came to be called National Socialism by Adolf Hitler in 1919. Today, under a different setting it might be called Universal Order, or something of the like'. In February 1983 another entry addresses these points more expansively—like that from September 1981, reprinted in all subsequent editions of the book—where the section 'Universal Order' is foregrounded over 35 entries and more than 60 pages' discussion in the following terms:

> Manson's Idea is the same as the NS Program only that it is, understandably, intended for THIS TIME and THIS PLACE. The vast differences in times and places fully account for the seemingly vast discrepancies between Manson and Hitler. Adolf Hitler was the LAST to offer the world workable, orderly and just solutions AND—most importantly—be in a position to actually deliver. The world's answer to Hitler was the Second World War. It was no fault of Manson's then that, though he wasn't in much of a position to deliver, he did still in all offer the Truth.[10]

In practice for individuals, moreover, this means either direct engagement with political violence or the withdrawal from the liberal-capitalist 'system' in the United States (and by implication elsewhere). In celebrating political violence, contemporary neo-Nazis see in James Mason's *Siege* an early advocacy of the doctrine of 'acceleration'; that is, direct attacks on the system (such as terrorist attacks on innocent people, national infrastructure or symbolic sites). That is to say, as a 'neo-Nazi accelerationist', Mason was the first to systematically advocate what are now understood as 'lone wolf', or self-activating terrorist, attacks by fascist revolutionaries. A key element in Mason's turn away from the mass strategy of the American Nazi Party and its successor groups is his championing of solo actors, first termed 'lone eagles' by NSLF leader Joseph Tommasi and later 'live wires' in Mason's *Siege*, in which all edited volumes present an entire section on "Lone Wolves and Live Wires". Isolated, contemporaneous instances of extreme right-wing extremist murderers are frequently singled out for praise in *Siege*, including the 1970s racist killers Fred Cowan and Joseph Paul Franklin, as well as the 1980s radical right murderers Gordon Kahl and Frank Spisak. This extensive discussion of self-directed terrorism provided in the pages of *Siege* represents the earliest systematic fascist or neo-Nazi engagement with this tactic for political violence. As the additional examples bear out still further, *Siege* may be considered highly significant for the then-unprecedented attention given to what Mason dubs a 'one-man army':

> Let us instead fully enjoin the concept of the One-Man Army and bring the struggle to the Enemy. Wherever you may be at this moment, let the revolution be there also. Spread a little revolution wherever you go! Never gripe about the System; project the Revolution! Get the people around you thinking in terms of TOTALITY, and not in terms of inches and degrees. Point out the real Enemy and not just the noisy, obnoxious symptoms—tell everyone it is the System itself that must go! Convey the feeling that it will be good to have all true White Men and Women as Comrades-in-Arms in the Revolution! Don't try to promulgate a "faith"- there's already too much of that. Be a spark for revolution.
>
> The lone wolf cannot be detected, cannot be prevented, and seldom can be traced. [...] For his choice of targets he needs little more than the daily newspaper for suggestions and tips galore. For his training the lone wolf needs only the U.S. military or any one of a hundred good manuals readily available through radical booksellers [....] His greatest concern must be to pick his target well so that his act may speak so clearly for itself that no member of White America can mistake its message.
>
> If I were asked by anyone of my opinion on what to look for (or hope for) next I would tell them a wave of killings, or "assassinations," of System bureaucrats by roving gun men who have their strategy well mapped-out in advance and well-nigh impossible to stop. [...] You must understand that this is something altogether NEW that they have never had to face.

> Let there only be talk of WAR! In the case of Gordon Kahl [Militant White tax protester who engaged in a shootout with Federal Marshals in which two of the pigs were killed and three wounded. Kahl was later killed in a second shootout.], this man took a toll against the Enemy. The only shame is that the toll couldn't have been much, much higher. With a relatively high degree of certainty, those of us who make up the high-profile segment of the Movement today may expect to one day face our own similar such test. It is criminal and cowardly to hope to avoid it. It is best to be ready to perform admirably when the time comes. No lambs to the slaughter.[11]

Given the way in which white supremacist literature circulated underground in the pre-Internet 1980s, it is likely Mason's individual call to arms was then popularised by two more recognised leaders drawing upon his inspiration: Louis Beam and 'Andrew Macdonald'. The latter was the pseudonymous author of the 1989 novel *Hunter*—penned by the notorious author of *The Turner Diaries*, the National Alliance ideologue William Pierce. The book itself is dedicated to Joseph Paul Franklin, a neo-Nazi serial killer who acted alone in trying to start a race war in the United States between 1977 and 1980. *Hunter* fictionalizes several of these episodes, before Oscar Yeager (based on Jäger; German for "hunter"), the novel's protagonist, moves on to targeting government officials. The book concludes with the following individual call to arms:

> By killing [FBI agent William] Ryan he had substantially increased the potential for flux. There certainly must be other men in key positions whose deaths also would influence the course of events. Both the worsening economy and the Black uprising would lead to a more unsettled climate in the country, the sort of climate which he ought to do everything in his power to exacerbate. Only in such a climate could the League hope to begin competing effectively with the Jews for the hearts and minds of the White public. He sighed. Well, he would be very busy during the next few days discharging responsibilities he already had incurred. But after that it would be time to do some more hunting.[12]

This method for political violence was given theoretical impetus by an influential 1992 (although first published in 1983[13]) essay by leading Ku Klux Klan activist Louis Beam, entitled "Leaderless Resistance":

> It is the duty of every patriot to make the tyrant's life miserable. When one fails to do so he not only fails himself, but his people. With this in mind, current methods of resistance to tyranny employed by those who love our race, culture, and heritage must pass a litmus test of soundness… participants in a program of Leaderless Resistance through phantom cell or individual action must know exactly what they are doing, and how to do it. It becomes the responsibility of the individual to acquire the necessary skills and information as to what is to be done. This is by no means as impractical as it appears, because it is certainly true that in any movement, all persons involved have the same general outlook, are acquainted with the same philosophy, and generally react to given situations in similar ways.[14]

Beam argues that pervasive state power made traditionally structured, pyramidal revolutionary movements too easy to penetrate and disrupt. "Leaderless resistance is a child of necessity," he therefore concluded:

> Utilizing the Leaderless Resistance concept, all individuals and groups operate independently of each other, and never report to a central headquarters or single leader for direction or instruction, as would those who belong to a typical pyramid organization.[15]

In the wake of FBI shootings at Ruby Ridge and Waco in the early 1990s—exercising the imagination of the far right in the United States around this time, with premonitions of a New World Order—in Jeffrey Kaplan's words, "suddenly the term leaderless resistance was on everyone's lips."[16] Particularly influential lips were those of American-based neo-Nazis Tom Metzger and Alex Curtis, leading proponents of lone wolf terrorism as a tactic—while the growth of the Internet has ensured its continued circulation among the far right in the US, Europe, and beyond.[17] In fact, populist right fears of a US government conspiracy to round up "patriots" at the end of the Cold War seems to have contributed to the spike in American militias and acts of terrorism in the 1990s —most horrifically, Timothy McVeigh's murder of 168 people at the FBI's Alfred P. Murrah building on April 19, 1995, of which more below. Exemplifying the way in which pre-Internet radicalization typically took place at this time, McVeigh had decided to turn some 50 tons of fertilizer into a truck bomb, in part, after coming into contact with William Pierce's earlier neo-Nazi "novel," *The Turner Diaries*, at American gun shows in the Midwest.

Characteristics of Self-Activating Terrorism

Although profiling is a profoundly risky business, recent scholars have observed that lone wolf terrorists tend to be overwhelmingly male, under 50, and principally operate in the US and Western Europe.[18] Furthermore, as Vic Artiga helpfully maintains, this taxonomy is applied to political and/or religious terrorism rather than actors who are emotionally disturbed, mentally ill, or reacting to violence experienced personally.[19] It is important to remember that mental illness or reactive spree killings should be distinguished from self-activating terrorism, which—despite being undertaken by an individual rather than by a terrorist movement or small cell—nevertheless must be plotted, prepared, and primed in a manner familiar to counterterrorism experts. Second, and correspondingly, unlike "emotional" mass murderers, or those driven by a specific personal grievance, these are actions undertaken by calculating, determined, "rational" individuals. Whatever the psychological world of lone wolf terrorists, consequently, it is both tautological and unhelpful to simply describe them as "crazy" following attacks that, seemingly, only a lunatic would envision, let alone undertake.[20] On this point, Fred Burton and Scott Stewart have separated an alleged prevalence of some form of severe psychological disorder—such as depression or lack of social skills—found in loner terrorists by usefully distinguishing between lone wolves and "lone nuts":

> A lone wolf ["a rare individual indeed"] is a person who acts on his or her own without orders from — or even connections to — an organization…A lone wolf is a standalone operative who by his very nature is embedded in the targeted society and is capable of self-activation at any time…We distinguish between lone wolves and "lone nuts" because, although many politically motivated attackers do have some degree of mental illness, rational and irrational individuals operate differently.[21]

Further diffusing these preexisting stereotypes of the far right has been the irresistible rise in digital technologies (especially the Internet and, more narrowly and pertinently here, social networking sites such as Facebook, Twitter, and others). Through often-anonymized websites and postings, the far right was an early adopter of this technology, stretching back to Don Black's Stormfront website, founded in 1995 and recently home to hundreds of thousands of radical right activists.[22] The technology was adopted, in turn, by groups ranging from the "new far-right" counter-jihad movement—whose prejudice against European Muslims is typically manifested culturally rather than racially—to more traditional neo-Nazi forums existing principally online (as "groupuscules" in the academic literature).[23] All of these groups may be considered radical right, in large measure, due to the illiberal stereotyping of all members in a given group (such as Muslims; the religion of roughly a billion persons around the world). The historically significant trope of anti-Semitism—that long-standing shibboleth of the far right—is often placed alongside biological and conspiratorial constructions of history and is still very powerful today. Broadly put, the white supremacism so characteristic of the "Fascist Epoch" before 1945 seems to be in the process of giving way to a more cultural intolerance that is less concerned about skin color than religious difference. Yet whatever the case, the authoritarian and illiberal far-right continues its enthusiastic embrace of the Web, spawning thousands of online radio stations, videogames, file-sharing sites, mailing groups, newsrooms and chatrooms, as well as websites containing all manner of extremist material. One compilation from 2010, aptly titled *The Hate Directory*, runs to fully 170 pages of listed Web addresses that are adjudged to "advocate violence against, separation from, defamation of, deception about, or hostility toward others based on race, religion, ethnicity, gender or sexual orientation."[24]

As Ramón Spaaij's superb academic study of this phenomenon since the 1970s emphasizes, the American radical right remains the most enthusiastic proponent of "leaderless resistance." If solo-actor ideological murders of pro-choice doctors are included as radical right actions, then roughly half of known lone wolf terrorist attacks have derived from far-right ideology since 1968. Spaaij places lone wolf terrorism at 1.8 percent of all terrorist attacks in the 15 Western countries included in the investigation, rising to five percent in the US during this time. Since the turn of this century, this previously little-used tactic has been measurably on the rise—and not just by American far-right extremists.[25] Yet at the same time, it is clear that the latter group in the latter geographical area remains the most likely one to produce "self-activating" terrorism. Rather more pressingly, in the words of the most recent study of lone wolf terrorism by Jeffrey D. Simon, the "cyber world has undoubtedly been a godsend for the individual terrorist," leading to "a proliferation of lone wolves around the world and allowed for anybody with a laptop to quickly become knowledgeable about terrorist tactics, targets, and weapons, including how to launch a terrorist attack."[26] To reiterate, far-right ideologues have been the most consistent champions of this embrace of both lone wolf terrorism and online extremism—the latter, at the aggressive end extending to what I have elsewhere understood, in the context of Breivik's and others' online progress through the terrorist attack cycle, as "broadband terrorism".[27] Short of the more overtly violent trade in terrorist manuals or weapons conversion kits, this far-right milieu daily traffics in a kind of online incitement to hatred that has been ignored for too long.

A comparatively mild example derives from the American Nazi Party website, White Revolution—proudly carrying the banners "EXTREME VIOLENT RACISM" and "WHITE REVOLUTION IS THE FINAL SOLUTION"—which claimed in 2009 that nearly half of informal poll respondents identified as lone wolves:

> Your Involvement in a Pro-White Organization:
> #1 – 47% said "Lone Wolf"
> #2 – 34% said "Looking to Join, But Not Sure Which Org is the Best for Me"[28]

That same year, a declassified *Intelligence and Analysis* report by the US Department of Homeland Security concluded: "lone wolves and small terrorist cells embracing violent rightwing extremist ideology are the most dangerous domestic terrorism threat in the United States."[29] A tripartite dynamic underwrites such far-right terrorism by lone wolf activists—and, more generally, use of the Internet is an indispensable feature of the terrorist attack cycle. The first condition is that of online incitement and prejudice—whether provided by the likes of Robert Spencer's Jihadwatch or the far more extreme Stormfront. Of course, only a few of those trafficking on aggressively racist forums and websites attempt violence; yet, conversely, online radicalization seems a *sine qua non* for far-right extremists turning into lone wolf terrorists. The second condition is that of the dissemination of materials for extremist violence online—particularly weapons, tactical and paramilitary manuals, bomb-making guides, and equipment (in terms of the latter, this may include the purchase of castor beans, the necessary ingredient for ricin, as in the case of neo-Nazi Ian Davison, or other materials for terrorism purchased online). Finally, the application and/or transmission of terrorist preparations online connects the virtual world underpinning broadband terrorism to allow them to carry out horrific acts.

Publicity and Radicalization

In the most recent, and indeed most destructive, case study of self-activating terrorism, the leading trends touched on already—radical right extremism, the use of new media over time, and self-defined acts of asymmetrical warfare against unsuspecting targets—are collectively exemplified by Andres Breivik's rampage on 22 July 2011. Even the date chosen was symbolic: on July 22, 1095, Jerusalem was sacked by the Ottoman Empire—an attack which prompted the Crusades and, for Breivik, represented the first of the three so-called Muslim invasions of Europe. (Never mind the geography!)[30] Yet most troublingly, Breivik's *2083* —posted online on the same date—is also more than a far-right manifesto. The final part, "A declaration of pre-emptive war", provides a step-by-step manual for lone wolf terrorism. This ranges from instructions for obtaining weapons, constructing explosives, securing materials, the use of Google Earth for logistical support and target acquisition, instructions for hiding IP addresses, and, crucially, summaries of many of the "bomb-making recipes, guides and other relevant instructions on the internet."[31] Under the section "How to disassemble an AK47", for instance, Breivik's answer is simply "See Youtube"; elsewhere, the use of "an internet cafe which facilitates multiplayer Modern Warfare 2 simulation" is recommended, while Breivik also claims that in the "first week of my 'explosive research phase' I googled for 200 hours over the course of 2 weeks." In other words, the Internet provided motive, means, and opportunity for Breivik's terrorist attacks.

Ultimately, the Internet also provided the platform for Breivik's statement to the world at large. As a perfect example of using the 21st century online virtual space to prepare and promote acts of terrorism, this was perhaps as devastating as the violent acts themselves: In keeping with *2083*'s instructions for "Sending announcements before an operation", Breivik concluded his manifesto: "I believe this will be my last entry. It is now Fri July 22nd, 12.51." The centrality of *2083* for Breivik is thus borne out not only by how long it took him to write—clearly it took years, long before planning and carrying out the attacks—but also, perhaps even more so, by the thousands of avowedly like-minded "European patriots" who received it seconds before the initiation of the operation. Amongst Breivik's actions, the dissemination of this terrorist DIY kit may yet have the worst and most far-reaching impact.

Chilling as it sounds, in a horrific inversion of the publicity sought as part of the normative terrorist cycle—exemplified, for instance, in the Unabomber's 35,000-word anti-technology rant published near the end of his 16-year bombing campaign—Breivik's acts are best understood as a kind of "terrorist PR."[32] Beyond his own (largely online) community of support, who else would have read Breivik's approximately 775,000-word conspiratorial analysis about the Islamification of Europe, had the document been released a year, or even a month, beforehand? Put another way, unlike terrorists seeking an ex post facto justification of their violent actions—seen, for instance, in the behavior of the 1970s Baader-Meinhof Gang (or "Red Army Faction") terrorist organization—Breivik's Norwegian attacks were intended, on the contrary, to create a readership for his manifesto as well as viewers for his 12-minute, summative online video. This was less "propaganda of the deed" than murderous deeds intended to draw attention to radical right propaganda—and tactics:

Table 1: Labor required vs. risk of apprehension for individuals who are not already on any watch list.

Labor	Time required to complete	Risk of apprehension
1 person	30 days	30%
2 people	20 days	60%
3 people	16 days	85%
4 people	13 days	90%
5 people	12 days	90-95%

Following this table, the final sentence in Breivik's *2083: A Declaration of European Independence* makes plain that his last acts before launching his mass murders were the completion of this mammoth work and sending it to hundreds of European "patriots" in the minutes before undertaking his terrorist attacks. Just as revealing—frightening, even—is Breivik's conclusion that self-activating terrorism is both the least complicated to logistically undertake while also holding the greatest prospect of success for terrorist actions:

> The old saying; "if you want something done, then do it yourself" is as relevant now as it was then. More than one "chef" does not mean that you will do tasks twice as fast. In many cases; you could do it all yourself, it will just take a little more time. AND, without taking unacceptable risks. The conclusion is undeniable.
> I believe this will be my last entry. It is now Fri July 22nd, 12.51.
> Sincere regards,
> Andrew Berwick
> Justiciar Knight Commander
> Knights Templar Europe
> Knights Templar Norway

It bears noting that these are not the writings of a crazy man: however much Breivik's actions smacked of delusion, it takes rational thought to compose (and indeed, plagiarize!) more than 1,500 pages of text—let alone to successfully work through the terrorist cycle with such inhumane effectiveness. Although a vexed area perhaps best left to psychologists, individuals with severe mental illness are usually excluded from constructions of lone wolf terrorism.[33] In Breivik's case (he was found both sane and culpable on the final day of his trial in Norway), he displayed another recurrent feature of lone wolf terrorism: the extensive justification expounded in *2083*; which also acts as a self-contained terrorist DIY manual, easy for other right-wing extremists to follow. This is especially significant given its widespread availability on the Internet, where *2083* and other paramilitary manuals have created, in Raffaello Pantucci's excellent phrase, the potential for autodidactic extremists: "The loner leaning towards violence can now easily teach himself the extremist creed, and then define his global outlook along the same lines, using it as a justification when carrying out an act of violence."[34] These terrorist tutorials online are also evident in Breivik's case—for example, he claims to have started working on manufacturing explosives by spending a fortnight scouring the Internet[35]—and his lessons from the Web were meticulously compiled and simplified for use by other autodidactic extremists:

> If I had known then, what I know today, by following this guide, I would have managed to complete the operation within 30 days instead of using almost 80 days. By following my guide, anyone can create the foundation for a spectacular operation with only 1 person in less than a month even if adding 2 "resting" days!:-)

So, can a freely downloadable, easily accessible manifesto be considered as an act of terrorism? Without in any way intending to diminish Breivik's subsequent actions and especially their heart-breaking consequences, it needs to be acknowledged that these acts of terrorism were intended as a form of publicity for *2083*. Put another way, the initial bombing was followed by a shooting spree, promoting the awareness of his 700,000+ word manifesto directed to inciting a European civil war.

Using the Internet to radicalize, educate and create lone wolf terrorists raises a definitional conundrum with respect to self-activating terrorism—namely, whether this typology of lone wolves can be extended to include multiple individuals forming a "wolf pack" (essentially like leaderless "groupuscules" but in the physical rather than virtual world). Does inspiring others turn you into a group? In the words of one proponent of this view, this need not preclude "contact with operational extremists," but it does exclude "a formal connection" with "particular command and control features" vis-à-vis an established organization: "Instead, they appear to be a small group of similarly minded individuals who choose to engage together in an act of terrorism."[36] A good example would be the aforementioned Oklahoma City bombing in 1995, which was masterminded by Timothy McVeigh but logistically assisted by Terry Nichols, who was sentenced to life without parole in 1998. The most recent definition of solo-actor terrorism understands these packs as lone wolves given the lack of hierarchical organizational structure:

> Lone wolf terrorism is the use or threat of violence or nonviolent sabotage, including cyber attacks, against government, society, business, the military (when the military is not an occupying force or involved in a war, insurgency, or state of hostilities), or any other target, by an individual acting alone or with minimal support from one or two other people (but not including actions during popular uprisings, riots, or violent protests), to further a political, social, religious, financial, or other related goals, or, when not having such an object, nevertheless has the same effect, or potential effect, upon government, society, business, or the military in terms of creating fear and/or disrupting daily life and/or causing government, society, business, or the military to react with heightened security and/or other responses.[37]

Yet the objections to this taxonomy should be, prima facie, obvious: individuals and groups are not the same, even if questions of leadership and direction do not necessarily obtain regarding "wolf packs." Conversely, lone attackers can also be part of a terrorist group—even if (as is often intended) invisibly so. The case of would-be airline bombers Richard Reid (the "shoe bomber") and Umar Farouk Abdulmutallab (the "underwear bomber") are perfect examples of directed solo-actor terrorists, but not self-activating terrorists, because their instructions came from (increasingly decentralized) Al-Qaeda networks. This consideration is effectively addressed in Spaaij's *Understanding Lone Wolf Terrorism*, which is equally nuanced on the twin issues of lone vs. group terrorism and individual initiative vs. external directives. According to Spaaij, "lone wolves" (a) operate individually, (b) do not belong to an organized terrorist group or network, and (c) their modi operandi are conceived and directed by the individual without any direct outside command or hierarchy.[38]

Clearly, a larger and more important distinction in these approaches, then, is between types of logistical support and hierarchical direction that, for the self-activating terrorist, is physically non-existent, but for explicit members and/or supporters of existing terrorist organizations may well be operationally necessary (such as in the case of the IRA in Northern Ireland in the 1980s and 1990s). Although here is not the place for further discussion on this issue, the difficulty seems to be the somewhat grey area in the middle, whereby a degree of outside influence and assistance—if not control—is employed during the terrorist cycle. At the very least, for present purposes, this is categorically different from self-activating terrorism, even when a (typically online) "community of support" may be instrumental with respect to radicalization, but not the command and control or logistical aspects of the terrorist cycle, which are instead undertaken individually.

Conclusion: Defining Self-Activating Terrorism

Anders Behring Breivik did not operate in a vacuum, but drew on currents of populist racism against already-disadvantaged Muslims that has broken out like a rash in Europe and the US over the first two decades of the 21st century. This raises a crucial terminological point raised in Gerry Gable and Paul Jackson's recent report "Lone Wolves: Myth or Reality?" Gable argues, "far-right terrorists are not lone wolves but are connected with, influenced by and often helped by organizations whose beliefs they share."[39] This position is in stark contrast to most definitions of lone wolf terrorism, like that offered by the aforementioned Dutch Crisis Management Team:

> In the case of lone-wolf terrorism, such intentional acts are committed by persons:
> (a) who operate individually;
> (b) who do not belong to an organized terrorist group or network;
> (c) who act without the direct influence of a leader or hierarchy;
> (d) whose tactics and methods are conceived and directed by the individual without any direct outside command or direction…
> Their terrorist attack or campaign, however, results from their solitary action during which the direct influence, advice or support of others, even those sympathetic to the cause, is absent. [40]

This point merits stressing still further: competing definitions also emphasize the solitary nature of lone wolf attackers. Yet Gable and Jackson are surely right to point out that, in all but the most rare of cases—such as the notoriously reclusive Unabomber, Theodore Kaczynski, whose mail bombs between 1978 and 1995 killed three and wounded 23 others—earlier approaches to lone wolf terrorism quite simply fail "to understand both the particular context from which 'lone wolf' ideology comes, and the community of support that backs up such solo actor terrorism."[41] That this is true, however, should not disqualify the term lone wolf terrorism; instead, it should properly add nuance to constructions of this phenomenon, understood here as self-directed rather than solo-actor terrorism.

Thus far, several features of lone wolf terrorism have been identified for their heuristic use in approaching self-activating terrorism as a generic phenomenon. Whether targeting the bourgeoisie or multiculturalism in Europe and the United States, self-activating terrorists have tended to see their acts as symbolic strikes in a war against parts of their own society. This "self-directed terrorism" is personally constructed and undertaken in terms of motivation, targets, and justification—with the latter sometimes extending to lengthy texts, such as 2009 self-activating Holocaust Memorial Museum shooter James von Brunn's approximately 400-page manifesto, instructively subtitled "The Racialist Guide to the Preservation and Nurture of the White Gene Pool." (It also bears noting for profilers that he was in his late 80s at this time of his attack!) The Internet has facilitated the dissemination and organization of hateful guidance among like-minded individuals and movements. This easy access to lone wolf tactics, training, manuals, and not least, radicalization and endorsement ought not, however, to invalidate the term lone wolf terrorism: if complete and total isolation were a definitional feature, perhaps the only lone wolf terrorist since 1945 would be Theodore Kaczynski, the Unabomber. Surely, the definition has greater utility and applicability than this.

A final and perhaps obvious caveat bears mentioning here as well, despite the foregoing emphasis. Even if lone wolf terrorism's most enthusiastic supporters in the last few years have been extreme-right activists, they are not the only ones—there have also been activists who have committed individual acts of "eco-terrorism" against symbolic targets, "single issue"[42] animal rights or abortion activists, and even, with sad irony, anti-war campaigners. That is to say, lone wolf terrorism is a terrorist method, and racism is by no means the defining feature of all self-activating terrorism. This is underscored by a prescient intelligence analysis by the Canadian Integrated Threat Assessment Centre (ITAC) in 2007:

> For the purpose of this assessment, a "lone wolf" is an individual who is inspired by a terrorist ideology or organization to conduct independent attacks. They may receive support from friends, but plan and conduct the attack alone. Lone wolves in North America have traditionally taken their inspiration from right-wing groups, single-issue causes, or national liberation movements.
> Lone wolves motivated by Islamic extremism are a recent development. Islamist terrorist strategists are now advocating that Muslims take action at a grassroots level, without waiting for instructions.
> Non-ideological factors, such as personal revenge, greed or coercion, do not appear to be motivators.[43]

Raffaello Pantucci's typological approach offers the most extensive discussion of lone wolf Islamist terrorism to date; a recent phenomenon seemingly sparked by "influential ideologues" such as Anwar al-Awlaki and Abu Musab al-Suri—the latter a prominent jihadi Islamist and author of the Breivik-length call for self-activating terrorism, *The Global Islamic Resistance Call*. "Similarly," writes Pantucci, "Al Qaeda's American spokesman Adam Gadahn openly praised Nidal Hassan Malik (the man who opened fire at Fort Hood)."[44] Needless to say, like Breivik's shooting rampage on Utøya island, the murder of 13 American soldiers and wounding of 29 others at Fort Hood in November 2009 not only highlights the general dangers posed by lone wolf terrorism, but more specifically, could portend a frightening change in tactics among violent takfiri Islamism.[45]

It is thus possible to conclude that lone wolf terrorism is *a form of self-directed ideological violence undertaken through the "terrorist attack cycle" by individuals—typically perceived by its adherents to be an act of asymmetrical, propagandistic warfare—which derives from a variable amount of external influence and context (notably now online), rather than external command and control*. This definition is slanted consciously toward perpetrator motivation rather than ex post facto perception (as in Jeffrey D. Simon's definition, cited earlier). It also excludes impromptu acts of violence, even if they are politically or religiously motivated. This could, contentiously, for example, include individual sleeper agents, who might have trained or radicalized with a hierarchical group or movement, but whose attack is self-activated with respect to timing, targeting, and the terrorism cycle. By focusing more squarely on lone wolf terrorism motives and logistical capabilities (not least those powered by the Internet) rather than perceptions by governments or other targets, it is hoped that this definition of self-directed, individual, ideological terrorism will go some way toward comprehending new tactics and help formulate better prevention and responses to this kind of violence.

Endnotes

[1] For four widely differing approaches to lone wolf terrorism, see Peter J. Phillips, "Lone Wolf Terrorism," *Peace Economics, Peace Science and Public Policy* 17/1 (2011), pp. 1-29; Chris Dishman, "The Leaderless Nexus: When Crime and Terror Converge," *Studies in Conflict and Terrorism* 28/3 (2005), pp. 237-252; Steven M. Chermak, Joshua D. Freilich, and Joseph Simone, "Surveying American State Police Agencies About Lone Wolves, Far-Right Criminality, and Far-Right and Islamic *Jihadist* Criminal Collaboration," *Studies in Conflict and Terrorism* 33/11 (2010), pp. 1019-1041; and Dennis Pluchinsky, *The Global Jihad: Leaderless Terrorism?* (Washington, DC: Woodrow Wilson International Center, 2006). Since the appearance of this chapter a number of vital studies on this subject have appeared, most notably Mark S. Hamm and Ramón Spaaij's panoramic *The Age of Lone Wolf Terrorism* (London: Columbia University Press, 2017). In keeping with other chapters largely cosmetic changes and updates were made here with the exception of new writing on James Mason's centrality to radical right self-activating terrorism.

[2] See, for example, Stratfor, "Defining the Terrorist Attack Cycle", Stratfor Worldview, online at: https://worldview.stratfor.com/article/defining-terrorist-attack-cycle (all websites last accessed 19 February 2020).

[3] Despite the term "lone wolf" being coined in 1909, there was little written on the subject before 2007; indeed, as Ramón Spaaij noted: "Research into lone wolf terrorism remains extremely scarce"; in "The Enigma of Lone Wolf Terrorism: An Assessment," *Studies in Conflict & Terrorism* 33/9 (2010), p. 855; see also, amongst the earliest academic approaches to the phenomenon of lone wolf terrorism, Ze'ev Iviansky, "Individual Terror: Concept and Typology," *The Journal of Contemporary History* 12/43 (1977), pp. 10ff.

[4] See the report by the Dutch Instituut voor Veiligheids- en Crisismanagement "Lone Wolf Terrorism: COT Study" (July 2007), p. 5.

[5] Edwin Bakker and Beatrice de Graaf, "Lone Wolves: How to Prevent this Phenomenon?," *ICCT Expert Meeting Paper* (Nov. 2010), p. 3, http://www.icct.nl/download/file/ICCT-Bakker-deGraaf-EM-Paper-Lone-Wolves.pdf. See also the American government texts and legal amendment by CRS, "Intelligence Reform and Terrorism Prevention Act of 2004: 'Lone Wolf' Amendment to the Foreign Intelligence Surveillance Act" (Dec. 2004); and Patricia L. Bellia's assessment of this bill, "The 'Lone Wolf' Amendment and the Future of Foreign Intelligence Surveillance Law," *Villanova Law Review* 50 (2005), pp. 425-455, https://scholarship.law.nd.edu/cgi/viewcontent.cgi?article=1358&context=law_faculty_scholarship.

[6] See, for example, John Merriman, "Is This the First Terrorist of the Modern Age?," *BBC Magazine*, http://news.bbc.co.uk/1/hi/magazine/8263858.stm.

[7] Among many other documents pertaining to Breivik's trial, see "Anders Behring Breivik Court Statement 2012-06-22" on the (admiring) website *The Breivik Archive*, http://sites.google.com/site/breivikreport/documents/anders-breivikcourt-statement-2012-06-22. On the conspiratorial construction of "cultural Marxism" in Breivik's formulation, see Chip Berlet, "Breivik's Core Thesis is White Christian Nationalism v. Multiculturalism," *Talk to Action*, www.talk2action.org/story/2011/7/25/73510/6015.

[8] See David Rapoport, "The Four Waves of Modern Terrorism," in *Attacking Terrorism: Elements of a Grand Strategy*, eds. Audrey Kurth Cronin and James M. Ludes (Washington, DC: Georgetown University Press, 2004), pp. 46–73. See also the four-volume collection for the Critical Concepts in Political Science series, *Terrorism* (Vol. 1: *The First or Anarchist Wave*; Vol. 2: *The Second or Anti-colonial wave*; Vol. 3: *The Third or New Left Wave*; Vol.

4: *The Fourth or Religious Wave*), ed. David Rapoport (London: Routledge, 2006), revealingly containing only two essays dealing with lone wolf terrorism only in the final volume. See also Jeffrey Kaplan, "Terrorism's Fifth Wave: A Theory, a Conundrum and a Dilemma," in *Perspectives on Terrorism* 2/2 (2008), pp. 12-24, http://www.terrorismanalysts.com/pt/index.php/pot/article/view/26/html.

9 Details on James Mason's biography and neo-Nazi activism was provided on 6 Sept. 2019 by the Bridge Institute Team at George Washington University in Washington, D.C.: https://bridge.georgetown.edu/research/factsheet-james-mason/. Another overview of James Mason is provided in the SPLC's 'Extremist Files: James Mason', online at: https://www.splcenter.org/fighting-hate/extremist-files/individual/james-mason.

10 James Mason, *Siege*, Third Edition ([N.p.]: Ironmarch Publications, 2017), pp. 398, 449.

11 *Ibid.*, cited pp. 59, 91-92, 276 and 339. See also Jeffrey Kaplan, "The post-war paths of occult national socialism: from Rockwell and Madole to Manson", *Patterns of Prejudice* 35/3 (2001), pp. 41-67.

12 Andrew Macdonald [William Luther Pierce], *Hunter* (Privately Published: 1989), p. 178.

13 "Leaderless Resistance," *Inter Klan Newsletter & Survival Alert*, Hayden Lake, Ida., ed. Robert E. Miles, Louis R. Beam, Paul D. Scheppe (*ca.* Spring/Summer (prob. May) 1983), pp. 12–13, http://simson.net/ref/leaderless/1983.inter-klan_newsletter.pdf.

14 www.louisbeam.com/leaderless.htm (bold text in original). For more on Louis Beam see Kathleen Belew, *Bring the War Home: The White Power Movement and Paramilitary America* (London: Harvard University Press, 2018), Part II.

15 *Ibid.* For an important discussion of this far-right trope, see George Michael, "Leaderless Resistance and the Extreme Right," *Lone Wolf Terror and the Rise of Leaderless Resistance* (Nashville: University of Vanderbilt Press, 2012), ch. 2.

16 Jeffrey Kaplan, "Leaderless Resistance," *Terrorism & Political Violence* 9/3 (1997), p. 87, which continues: "With Beam's formulation, the theory of leaderless resistance was essentially complete. All that remained was to adapt and disseminate it to ever wider constituencies of the far right wing", p. 89.

17 See, for example, the groundbreaking monograph by Ramón Spaaij, *Understanding Lone Wolf Terrorism: Global Patterns, Motivations and Prevention* (London: Springer, 2012), p. 25.

18 Pan Pantziarka, *Lone Wolf: True Stories of Spree Killers* (London: Virgin Books, 2002), p. 214.

19 See the point made by Vic Artiga in "Lone Wolf Terrorism: What We Need to Know and What We Need to Do," which argues: "Many lone wolves have difficulty obtaining professional level training in using weapons or explosives, have difficulty translating their rhetoric into action, and often make some sort of key mistake. In addition, lone wolves are still constrained by the terrorist attack cycle and consequently must conduct target surveillance by themselves", online at: https://web.archive.org/web/20100712041106/http://www.takresponse.com/index/homeland-security/lone-wolf_terrorism.html.

20 For two recent studies approach to these psychological questions, see Roger Griffin, "Shattering Crystals: The Role of 'Dream Time' in Extreme Right-Wing Political Violence," *Terrorism & Political Violence* 15, no. 1 (2003): 57-95; and more recently, Sophia Moskalenko and Clark McCauley, "The Psychology of Lone-wolf Terrorism," in *Counselling Psychology Quarterly* 24, no. 12 (2011): 115-126.

21 Fred Burton and Scott Stewart, "The 'Lone Wolf' Disconnect," *Stratfor*, January 30, 2008, https://worldview.stratfor.com/article/lone-wolf-disconnect.

22 For an excellent update on Stormfront and its current "major storm" of financial and logistical difficulties, see Heidi Beirich, "Gathering Storm" in *Intelligence Report: The Year in Hate and Extremism*, Southern Poverty Law Center 149 (Spring 2013), 63–66.
23 For more on the term groupuscule, see the special issue of *Patterns of Prejudice 36*, no. 3 (2002); and on the far-right use of the Internet, see, for example, the recent report "Online Terror + Hate: The First Decade" (Los Angeles: Simon Wiesenthal Center, 2010), http://web.archive.org/web/20110108215026/http://www.wiesenthal.com/atf/cf/%7BDFD2AAC1-2A DE-428A-9263-35234229D8D8%7D/IREPORT.PDF. For a general approach to the distinction between the "new far-right" and more familiar manifestations of neo-fascism, see Paul Jackson et al., *The EDL: Britain's New Far-Right Social Movement* (Northampton: RNM Publications, 2011), https://web.archive.org/web/20111122214646/http://www.radicalism-new-media.org/wp-content/uploads/2011/09/The_EDL_Britains_New_Far_Right_Social_Movement.pdf.
24 See Raymond Franklin, *The Hate Directory*, April 1, 2010, https://web.archive.org/web/20100616115812/http://www.hatedirectory.com/hatedir.pdf.
25 Spaaij, *Understanding Lone Wolf Terrorism*, 31.
26 Jeffrey D. Simon, *Lone Wolf Terrorism: Understanding the Growing Threat* (New York: Prometheus Books, 2013), 21.
27 See Matthew Feldman, "Breivik's Three Acts of Terrorism," *Society and Space: Environment and Planning D* 30, no. 2 (2012), pp. 193-195, https://web.archive.org/web/20130318044637/www.envplan.com/openaccess/d303.pdf.
28 Contained on the American Nazi Party straw poll, "White Revolution" (2009). See also my "Hate Globally, Act Locally: A Case Study of Universal Nazism Online," in Christian Dietrich and Michael Schüßler, eds., *Jenseits der Epoche* (Münster: Unrast, 2011), 89-101; and "Broadband Terrorism: A New Face of Fascism?" (September 2009), *History & Policy*, http://www.historyandpolicy.org/opinion-articles/articles/broadband-terrorism-a-new-face-of-fascism.
29 DHS/I&S, "Rightwing Extremism: Current Economic and Political Climate Fueling Resurgence in Radicalization and Recruitment" (2009), p. 7. See also Johnston's account of this report and the substantial internal resistance to its findings on right-wing extremism in the American government, Daryl Johnston, *Right Wing Resurgence: How a Domestic Terrorism Threat is Being Ignored* (London: Rowman & Littlefield Publishers, 2012). This approach to revolutionary terrorism was expanded to include potential jihadi Islamist lone wolves by CIA Director Leon Panetta, who claimed in a 2010 "terror assessment to Congress": "It's the lone-wolf strategy that I think we have to pay attention to as the main threat to this country"; "Intel Chief: Al-Qaeda Planning Attacks," *USA Today*, online at: https://web.archive.org/web/20100206035340/www.usatoday.com/news/washington/2010-02-03-terror-threats-cia_N.htm.
30 The subsequent dates of invasion were 1683 (the year of the Battle of Vienna) and, for whatever reason, 1999. Hence the importance of the date 2083, the title of Breivik's manifesto: It would be both the 400th anniversary of the Battle of Vienna as well as the 200th anniversary of the death of Karl Marx.
31 As Breivik asserted, "the internet truly transformed the market for acquisition of any imaginable product which has resulted in a scenario where ANYONE now has quick and easy access to suppliers worldwide."
32 See Matthew Feldman, "Slaughter Was the Killer's Appetizer. It Is the Trial That Is His Main Course," *The Independent*, 26 July 2011, online at: https://www.independent.co.uk/voices/commentators/dr-matthew-feldman-slaughter-was-killers-appetiser-it-is-the-trial-that-is-his-main-course-2325910.html.

33 See Donald G. Dutton, "Individual Transitions to Extreme Violence," *The Psychology of Genocide, Massacres, and Extreme Violence* (London: Praeger, 2007), ch. 9.
34 Raffaello Pantucci, "A Typology of Lone Wolves: Preliminary Analysis of Lone Islamist Terrorists", *Developments in Radicalisation and Political Violence* (ICSR, March 2011), p. 11, https://icsr.info/wp-content/uploads/2011/04/1302002992ICSRPaper_ATypologyofLoneWolves_Pantucci.pdf.
35 As Breivik claimed in his manifesto *2083: A Declaration of European Independence*: "The first week of my 'explosive research phase' I googled for 200 hours over the course of 2 weeks. I was worried that I had to use obscure search engines if Google had banned many search phrases or sources, but to my surprise Google seemed to be fully functional in this regard. There are a lot of various explosives forums around (for example: roguesci.org/theforum) which will discuss in depth concerning hundreds of different recipes and methods of manufacture explosives. There are hundreds of various books out there about this subject."
36 Pantucci, "A Typology of Lone Wolves: Preliminary Analysis of Lone Islamist Terrorists", p. 25.
37 Simon, *Lone Wolf Terrorism: Understanding the Growing Threat*, p. 266.
38 Spaaij, *Understanding Lone Wolf Terrorism*, p. 16.
39 See Gerry Gable and Paul Jackson," Lone Wolves: Myth or Reality?", *Searchlight Educational Trust Report* (2011), p. 5; online at: http://nectar.northampton.ac.uk/6014/1/Gable20116014.pdf.
40 See the Dutch COT report, "Lone Wolf Terrorism", p. 6.
41 Gable and Jackson, p. 81. This view is endorsed in the fourth edition of a popular overview; see Frank Bolz, Kenneth J. Dudonis, and David P. Schulz, *The Counterterrorism Handbook: Tactics, Procedures and Techniques* (London: Routledge, 2011), which argues: "in reality there are whole networks of supporting enablers for these [apparently lone-wolf] operatives, including publicists, counselors, tacticians, and legal advisors who communicate via websites, publication, blogs and other media to encourage and advise," p. 197.
42 This is one of Jeffrey D. Simon's five categories of lone wolf terrorists, in *Lone Wolf Terrorism*, pp. 43-46; the others are religious, secular, criminal, and "idiosyncratic" (largely mentally ill).
43 Integrated Threat Assessment Centre, Unclassified Intelligence Report, "Lone Wolf Attacks: A Developing Islamist Extremist Strategy?" (June 2007), p. 2, https://web.archive.org/web/20120914215901/www.nefafoundation.org/miscellaneous/FeaturedDocs/ITAC_lonewolves_062007.pdf.
44 Pantucci, p. 6; the lone wolf "types" he identifies range from loner (wholly self-radicalizing), lone wolf, lone wolf pack to lone attackers ("with clear command and control links with actual Al Qaeda core or affiliated groups"), pp. 29-30.
45 See Gabriel Weimann, "Lone Wolves in Cyberspace," *Journal of Terrorism Research* 3/2 (Autumn 2012), p. 3, https://cvir.st-andrews.ac.uk/articles/10.15664/jtr.405/.

14. Terrorist 'Radicalising Networks': A Qualitative Case Study on Radical Right Lone-Wolf Terrorism

INTRODUCTION

Less than a decade ago, Marc Sageman decried the 'stagnation' of research on terrorism. Since that time there has been a surfeit of both terrorist atrocities and scholarly approaches to understanding this growing phenomenon—growing in terms of both prevalence and potential destructiveness (Sageman 2008). In early 2014, for example, it was reported that only a dozen religiously motivated terrorist attacks had occurred in Europe in the preceding six years (Obeidallah 2015). Similar to the definition at work in the UK's present counter-terrorism strategy, 'Prevent' (launched in 2005), what the phrase 'religiously motivated' usually refers to is *Islamist terrorism*—the subject of an inestimable amount of commentary and research in recent years. Yet it remains the case that this is far from the only form, ideology, or aims motivating contemporary acts of political violence and terrorism.

Thus, in Asia, there have been Buddhist suicide bombers in Sri Lanka and organised political violence by the far-right Hindutva movement in Modi's India. By contrast, in western Europe, 'Christianist' terrorism has been perpetrated by the murder of 77 Norwegians by Anders Breivik in Norway on 22 July 2011, adding to a string of attacks by so-called 'Christian Identity' groups in the USA like the Aryan Nations and Phineas Priesthood (Önnerfors 2017). It therefore seems that a key challenge in reliably adding to academic knowledge is avoiding the pitfalls of inductive distention or imbalance in the overwhelming focus upon Islamist-induced terror attacks, even when, as during and following the horrors of 9/11, some cases appear to re-write the rulebook. That is to say, despite a spate of 'spectacular', well-coordinated jihadi Islamist attacks in Europe and the USA—massively destructive in terms of terrorist capabilities and, above all, human life—there are other forms of radicalised political violence that merit scholarly attention.

Accordingly, this chapter will explore two cases of right-wing terrorism in analysing the role played by radicalising networks—oftentimes, today, provided by online spaces. I will also consider how, and the extent to which, this can lead to so-called 'lone-wolf' terrorism. In doing so, I will argue that it is more appropriate to shift focus towards a closer analysis of 'radicalising networks', in this case, via a qualitative analysis of far-right ideology. These 'radicalising networks' form the underpinning of two qualitative case studies (Lewington 2008; Davison 2010) deriving from the author's practitioner experience in the UK Crown Prosecution Service, applicable not only to self-directed terrorists but to the study of terrorism and radicalisation more generally. Thus, as outlined in the introduction to this volume, it is possible to reach a deeper understanding of the dynamics of cognitive and behavioural radicalisation, whereby supposedly individual action of self-directed terrorists can be seen, at the micro-level, to be indirectly supported by extremist communities. In turn, it is hoped that this will contribute to clearer understandings at the meso-level and overarching ideological positions on the macro-level, which all reinforce each other.

'Lone Wolves' versus 'Lone Nuts' and the Imaginary 'Pack'

The point is elementary, but bears briefly restating. At the time of writing (autumn 2016), a 'lone-wolf' shooter in Houston, Texas, wounded nine before being killed in a shootout by police. Initial reports suggest he had difficulties at work, was of South Asian heritage, and had Nazi 'emblems' and 'paraphernalia' in his possession at the time of the attack (Marcin 2016). Was this an act of terrorism, or a spree shooting? Ideological attacker or disgruntled worker? Whatever the existing stereotypes, this was clearly not a jihadi Islamist attack; indeed, many such cases can raise these and other conceptual and taxonomic challenges. In the case of Houston shooter Nathan DeSai, if anything, early reports seemed to indicate yet another solo act motivated by radical right ideology—explained in detail below.

Recently, for example, a New America Foundation report found that 48 people were killed by white terrorists, while 26 were killed by radical Islamists, since 9/11 in the USA. This figure excludes the 2016 mass shooting of 49 people in Orlando by Omar Mateen (Plucinska 2015). Furthermore, from 1990 to 2010, there were 145 acts of political violence committed by the American far right, resulting in 348 deaths (Werleman 2014). By comparison, 20 Americans were killed over the same period in acts of political violence carried out by Islamists in the USA. These statistics naturally exclude the horror of 9/11, and it bears mentioning that mass casualty attacks remain high on jihadi Islamist agendas—from Spain in 2004, to the UK in 2005, and of course the attacks in Paris and San Bernardino in 2015, Brussels or Nice in 2016. These are headline-dominating acts in a burgeoning age of terrorism. Accordingly, they raise all the hallmarks of challenges facing the study of terrorism, not least that of public fears and perceptions as opposed to highly theoretical scholarship.[1] For example, were the unprecedented attacks of 9/11 to be included in the final statistic cited above, murders by Islamist terrorists in the USA would be ten times more lethal than that by right-wing terrorist murders; if counting those in the USA since 9/10 rather than 9/11, the amount would be a hundredfold. Put another way, how statistics are gathered and framed—even before being analysed—can be as revealing as, at times, it can mislead.

Now, while here advocating the view that far-right extremism is under-researched when compared with jihadi Islamism, this too can be spun out of control—exemplified by a widely circulating online meme of James Eagan Holmes, who attacked a screening of *The Dark Knight Returns* in July 2012. The text accompanying Holmes's mug shot (although it must be noted that there are many variants) suggests that skin colour and/or religion are decisive when labelling acts of mass violence 'terrorism': 'If I were Arab, the shooting would be TERRORISM. If I were Black, I'd be a THUG. But I'm White, so it's MENTAL ILLNESS'. (Dado 2012).[2] Using multiple (and legally purchased) weapons, Holmes murdered 12 people and wounded 70 more in a spree shooting; afterwards, once in custody, he claimed to be the Batman villain the Joker. While acting alone, it seems that mental illness played a large, even decisive, part in that Aurora, Colorado, mass shooting; at least there seemed to be no clear socio-political motive that might bring this attack into general approaches to terrorism as a political act. But terrorism sells papers, and even recent reports claiming that such outrages, when splashed across front-page news, might even increase terrorist activity are very unlikely to change that (Doward 2015).

As this suggests, at the forefront of challenges is the question of terminology, whether in terms of defining terrorism or its component parts. Take, as a final example at the outset, mental illness—or what, to introduce the penultimate term here, was identified as the distinction between lone wolves and what have been called 'lone nuts' (Burton and Stewart 2008). Returning to the meme above, the seeming lack of political motive, reports of schizophrenia, and the post-attack behaviour of James Holmes might seem to make him a classic 'lone nut', in contrast to the actions of another (still alleged) American mass murderer, Dylann Roof, in the latter case, for the murder of nine black churchgoers in Charleston, South Carolina, on 17 June 2015. That the shooter acted alone in a pre-planned assault on unsuspecting victims seems beyond doubt, while a posted 'manifesto' linked to Dylann Roof betrays links to a number of racist, even politically revolutionary groups (one of which was the Council of Conservative Citizens, the successor of the White Citizens' Councils, essentially the non-hooded face of the KKK during the struggle for desegregation and Civil Rights in the 1950s and 1960s in the USA; see also Quarles, 1999). The following is a telling excerpt from this 2500-word text, uploaded online the day of the Charleston killings:

Europe is the homeland of White people, and in many ways the situation is even worse there. From here I found out about the Jewish problem and other issues facing our race, and I can say today that I am completely racially aware [....] I have no choice. I am not in the position to, alone, go into the ghetto and fight. I chose Charleston because it is most historic city in my state, and at one time had the highest ratio of blacks to Whites in the country. We have no skinheads, no real KKK, no one doing anything but talking on the internet. (O'Connor 2015)

Now, the apparent radicalisation of Dylann Roof raises a number of questions about its specific American context: race relations, gun culture, the heritage versus hate symbolism of the Confederate flag, and so on. But that is not the focus here. Yet there are three previously mentioned key elements present in the Charleston attack that do form the backdrop to the remainder of this chapter—namely, lone-wolf terrorism, far-right ideology, and what will be termed here 'radicalising networks'.

There is an assumption that, like Theodore Kaczynski, the so-called Unabomber—who carried out sixteen bomb attacks between 1978 and 1995—lone wolves are necessarily 'loners', even agoraphobic or autarkic individuals. But this is rarely the case, whether for group-based political violence or for *self-activating* terrorists—the preferred term employed here—as is evident from a long and bloody history that stretches back to anarchist 'propaganda of the deed' in the nineteenth century. Self-activating terrorism, there can be no doubt, is a pan-ideological tactic. It is promiscuous precisely because it is hard to detect, harder to interdict, and at times horrifically lethal—whether in the case of Mario Buda's anarchist car bomb on Wall Street in 1920 that claimed 38 lives, or John Gilbert Graham's similarly mid-air bombing that murdered 43 in 1955. Yet, as I have argued elsewhere, it remains the case that far-right extremists have historically been the most enthusiastic practitioners of this genre of terrorism (Feldman 2013a, b: 275). Valuable scholarship by Ramón Spaaij has also shown that violent extremists with white supremacist and nationalist ideological motivations were responsible for the majority of attacks by self-activating terrorists between January 1968 and May 2007 (Spaaij 2012; Spaaij and Hamm 2014).

At the same time, Spaaij warns against overly mono-causal approaches to breaking down 'lone-wolf' attacks, with case studies often revealing a variable combination of political and personal motives (Spaaij 2010: 861). This view has been extended in recent scholarship to incisive consideration of the challenges of defining self-activating terrorism more broadly.[3]

Commenting on the difficulty of defining self-activating terrorism, Bjørgo and Hemmingby in *The Dynamics of a Terrorist Targeting Process* (2016) have recently offered a helpful aside in their study of Breivik progression through the 'terrorist cycle' (usually understood as comprising target selection, planning, deployment, the attack, escape, and propaganda/exploitation). There, they note the 'lack of consensus' and 'limited amount of in-depth studies on the topic' and argue for a 'rather narrow definition' of what they prefer to call '"solo terrorist" actions' (Bjørgo and Hemmingby 2016: 88). A good and early example of this narrower approach was already provided by the Dutch agency for crisis management, COT, in 2007:

> In the case of lone-wolf terrorism, such intentional acts are committed by persons:
> (a) who operate individually;
> (b) who do not belong to an organized terrorist group or network;
> (c) who act without the direct influence of a leader or hierarchy;
> (d) whose tactics and methods are conceived and directed by the individual without any direct outside command or direction [...] Their terrorist attack or campaign, however, results from their solitary action during which the direct influence, advice or support of others, even those sympathetic to the cause, is absent. (COT 2007)

In keeping with these approaches, crucially, the self-activating terrorist needs to go through the terrorist cycle alone and unaided—a telling contrast between, for instance, Anders Breivik and the 1995 Oklahoma City Bomber, Timothy McVeigh (who was convicted alongside an accomplice, Terry Nichols). Acting alone is surely more psychologically and logistically demanding; it is therefore more difficult to undertake. In Breivik's case the financing, perseverance, and, perhaps, ability or luck—as in not killing himself when constructing his fertiliser bomb—were instrumental in his undertaking of history's deadliest self-activating terrorist attack (Feldman 2012).

In recent years, Britain faced the real possibility of similar onslaughts by two would-be Breiviks: Lewington (2008) and Davison (2010).[4] That the two individuals to be considered below failed to carry their plans to their deadly conclusion was not for want of trying. But before moving to those cases, it is important to build upon the operational distinction between truly self-directed terrorists and what Bjørgo and Hemmingby rightly term 'accomplices', who are 'practically assisting' an act of terrorism (Bjørgo and Hemmingby 2016: 89). Attackers like the Tsarnaev brothers who carried out the Boston bombings in April 2013, and the husband and wife Islamist pair in San Bernardino who killed 14 people on 2 December 2015, have sometimes been called 'lone-wolf packs' (Pantucci 2011). Most problematic in this term is that it neglects the motivational reinforcement offered by a co-conspirator involved in the 'terrorist cycle'; put simply, having two or more co-conspirators in the conspiracy fundamentally changes terrorist dynamics.

This is but one reason 'small cell' acts of terrorism, involving two or three terrorists—as in the case of the horrific May 2013 murder of Lee Rigby in Britain—should be carefully separated from the wholly self-directed process through the terrorist cycle by a lone individual. It also acts as a terminological caution against broader and even maximal definitions of lone-wolf terrorism.

In making this important distinction between self-directed terrorists and accomplices, Bjørgo and Hemmingby build upon Beatrice de Graaf's and Edwin Bakker's influential report for the International Centre for Counter-Terrorism in The Hague in 2010, which rightly stresses that lone wolves are people who may be 'inspired by a certain group but who are not under the command of any other person, group or network. They might be members of a network, but this network is not a hierarchical organisation in the classical sense of the word' (2). These 'radicalising networks', as considered presently, can be either *active* or *passive* and are often vital in the process of radicalisation.

Indeed, if total isolation and lack of contact with others were to form a definitional feature of self-activating terrorism, perhaps the only true 'lone wolf' since 1945 would be the Unabomber. To take this point further, an active support network can come in the form of friends or family, marches or demonstrations, and even online relationships (such as through social media or email). By contrast, a passive, or indirect, radicalising network may exist for someone who is not participating in such dialogue, but might be reading extremist material online, or simply being radicalised by events or mainstream media reportage. These contacts with the wider world are invariably present for lone wolves; again, with the caveat that the person or persons forming this 'network' have no operational role in the necessarily self-directed terrorist cycle or attacks (Gill 2015). My definition of self-activating terrorism reflects these external actors in defining so-called 'lone wolf terrorism':

> self-directed political or religious violence undertaken through the 'terrorist attack cycle' by individuals—typically perceived by its adherents to be an act of asymmetrical, propagandistic warfare—which derives from a variable amount of external influence and context (notably now online), rather than external command and control. (Feldman 2013a, b: 282)

Before moving on, I should clarify that this is emphatically not to embrace the so-called 'conveyor belt' theory of terrorism, whereby fundamentalism invariably leads to 'non-violent extremism' and, ultimately, religiously motivated terrorism. The vast majority of fundamentalists are neither political actors nor extremists; likewise, the majority of non-violent extremists do not take the final step towards engaging in terrorist violence. Even if the path can be a conveyor belt, it usually is not.

Fascist Ideology as Cognitive Macro-Framework of Radicalisation

In pursuing this idea of *active and passive* 'radicalising networks', I want to focus on one qualitative example of each, drawn from previous experience in acting as an Expert Witness for the Crown Prosecution Service in Britain. In both cases to be discussed, in 2009 and 2010, respectively, the would-be lone wolves were apprehended prior to attempting their attacks, and when their property was seized, their writings clearly indicated that they were neo-Nazis. My role was to inspect these writings and report on their relationship to fascist ideology. This academic definition gave way to a more general characterisation of neo-Nazism, a distinct form of fascism, which can be understood as an ideology seeking to unite mythically defined 'Aryans' through a programme closely derived from the motivations and policies of Hitler's Third Reich. A working definition was provided in an entry to the 2006 two-volume encyclopaedia *World Fascism* (459–60):

> Neo-Nazism is an ideology or political movement in the tradition of historic National Socialism. *Tradition* in that context refers mostly to ideological aspects, such as racism or anti-Semitism, as well as the use of well-known symbols such as the swastika. Neo-Nazism is often linked with the international movement of Holocaust denial. Its propaganda is aggressive. Neo-Nazistic [sic] activists tend to use violence against foreigners, colored people, Jews, or political opponents [....] it holds that the 'white or Aryan race' is destined to dominate the rest of mankind, but in the postwar world of mass immigration to Europe from her former colonies, it is blacks or Asians rather than Jews who are highlighted as having inferior status.

This is, then, literally *neo-Nazism*, insofar as it is an updating of Nazi doctrines to include contemporary society rather than attempting any substantial revisions of National Socialist ideology—essentially bar one. While the Third Reich tended to view its racial-purifying mission in comparably national terms (with the notable exception of the SS 'International Brigades' established in 1942), post-war neo-Nazis see Aryans as a racially threatened, intrinsically superior, but most importantly, *globally diffuse* ethnic group. This was the milieu from which these two middle-aged, working-class white British males emerged which will be treated subsequently. Yet one appeared to be connected to a 'radicalising network' only indirectly, while the other was more directly connected by way of a group he co-founded called the Aryan Strike Force (hereafter ASF).

Passive Links to 'Radicalising Networks': Neil Lewington (2008)

But first I want to turn to the case of Neil Lewington, arrested at Lowestoft on 30 October 2008 while changing trains on his way to a blind date that he had met online (CPS 2009). He was drunk and urinating in public at the time, shouting abuse at a female train conductor who called the police. Upon being detained and searched by the police, Lewington was found to be in possession of two viable explosive devices. Lewington was arrested and his home in Tilehurst, near Reading, was searched under Section 18 of the Police & Criminal Evidence Act (PACE) 1984. There, according to *The Daily Mail*, authorities found a 'bomb-making factory', including 'shrapnel bombs disguised in tennis balls which he planned to hurl into the homes of Asian families', alongside

> drawings of electronics and a cocktail of explosive ingredients including weedkiller, firelighters, firework powder, electrical timers and detonators. Lewington also kept video footage about bombings in Britain and America as well as fascist literature including a handbook for 'Waffen SS UK members' which he wrote himself. (Camber 2009)

Described by Guido Knopp as 'the political soldiers of National Socialism', the Waffen-SS was established in autumn 1939 and ultimately grew into a force of nearly a million members and 38 divisions by the end of World War II (2003: 231, 246, and 281). The Waffen-SS international brigades, above all, have given nostalgic rise in some right-wing extremist circles to forms of neo-Nazism. I was provided scans of this 18-page 'Waffen-SS handbook' which, perhaps surprisingly, contained no references besides its title to this World War II paramilitary force. I was also provided scans that fell into three groups: images taken from Lewington's phone; writings from his notebook also taken from his person upon arrest; and third, a black folder containing texts relating to bomb-making as well as newspaper clippings, taken from his bedside drawer. The latter derived largely from the weeks after 9/11, in what may well have been a radicalising event for this anti-Muslim extremist.

I was asked to analyse the first three types of material, that is, the 'Waffen-SS UK Members Handbook', phone images, and Lewington's notebook entries. The terms of reference centred upon whether or not this material is related to right-wing extremism and whether neo-Nazi activists would normally possess such texts and images. Correspondingly, fitting Neil Lewington into the 'extreme right wing' of neo-Nazism—rather than the 'radical' or 'far-right' of then-visible British National Party (BNP)—depended upon specific content analysis of the 100 or so pages of writings and the dozen images provided by anti-terrorist police. Of the written material, much was banal—shopping lists and train timetables—and irrelevant to neo-Nazism, including the pages of racist 'jokes' of the crude, one-liner variety. Many entries were anti-Semitic, with dozens identifiable as clearly anti-black or anti-Muslim in nature. I ultimately selected seven items that I linked to one of two postwar fascist movements: four to Combat 18/Blood and Honour and three to Christian Identity/KKK. The latter was initially formed in 1865 following the defeat of the Confederacy in the American Civil War and soon had off-shoots all across the Deep South. One of these was the White Camelia Knights of the KKK, first founded in 1867, said to have rivalled the KKK in membership figures in the past (Quarles 1999: 34). This racist group was explicitly referred to in Lewington's notes.

While this seemed unusual at first, when taken together with two phone images and a transcribed Bible verse from St Luke's Gospel also in Lewington's notes, it was clear that all three had derived from the webpage of the White Camelia Knights, a KKK offshoot reformed a generation ago and now based in Texas. It has been reincarnated as a 'Christian Identity' movement. The strange and complex history of this doctrine derives from late nineteenth-century British Israelism, but progressively established itself amongst post-war American racists after the landmark 1954 desegregation case, *Brown v. Board of Education*. Christian Identity, in a summation by Martin Durham, 'is an American creation. It appeals both to the religious identity of most American extreme rightists and to their belief that not only they or the white race but America is special' (2007: 82). This belief is predicated on an apocalyptic worldview holding that 'Jews not only are Satanic but also represent a separate genetic seedline from Aryans', with the latter representing the actual 'lost tribe' of Israel (Berlet 2006: 128). Put simply, Christian Identity is a racist bastardisation of Christianity that has spawned a host of extreme right-wing groups in the USA, from the birth of Aryan Nations in the 1970s—under the late Christian Identity pastor Richard Butler—to the larger Posse Comitatus and violent Phineas Priesthood groups. According to the specialist Michael Barkun: 'Christian Identity clearly believes that the Last Days are imminent, a characteristic shared with most millennialists in contemporary America. Unlike many of their fellow chiliasts [adherents of millennialism], however, a high proportion of Identity believers adopt an active rather than a passive stance' (Barkun 1997: 208). These views are readily apparent on the group's webpage, titled 'Who We Are':

> WHO—The White Camelia Knights of the Ku Klux Klan is a group of men and women (families) that share a common belief in religion and race. We are not the Knights of the White Kamellia, Ku Klux Klan. Neither do we have any affiliation to this organization.
>
> WHAT—An organization of White Christians dedicated to the truth and education in a world of lies and ignorance.
>
> WHERE—The White Camelia Knights of the Ku Klux Klan is based in Texas, but with membership spread throughout many other states.

WHEN—The original White Camelia was organized in 1867, two years after the original Ku Klux Klan was formed in Puluski [sic], Tennessee. It has been reported that the White Camelia became larger than the original Ku Klux Klan in membership and power.

WHY—The White Camelia Knights of the Ku Klux Klan believes that White Christian ideals are under attack by anti-white and anti-Christ forces. We believe our race, country and our Christian way of life is being systematically destroyed.

HOW TO JOIN—Requirements for membership are simple. You must be 100% White, have an open mind to learn Christian Identity and be willing to follow Klan rules and regulations. (White Camelia Knights of the Ku Klux Klan 2011)

In the last decade, the web has been the KKK's main recruiting ground, albeit not the only one. On 10 June 1999, the BBC carried a news story entitled 'KKK plans infiltration of the UK'; since that time, KKK activists in the UK have been unmasked or imprisoned (Hosken 1999; Parry 2011; Morris 2014). By recourse to what may be a more cell-based structure, the Klan has established 'churches' in Wales and the rest of Britain, amongst a number of countries in Europe. This naturally extends to a web presence as well, from the Imperial Klans of America International Headquarters to European groups such as the UK-based European White Knights of the Burning Cross based in Britain. It was this small band of online white supremacists that formed one strand of Lewington's indirect 'community of support' online.[5]

The other strand was not imported from the USA but was the domestic hate group Blood & Honour. With their name taken from the translated German-language inscription on Hitler Youth daggers, Blood & Honour was created in 1987 by the ex-National Front member Ian Stuart Donaldson, lead singer of the lionised neo-Nazi 'Oi!' band, Skrewdriver. A year after his death in 1993, the White Noise CD label, ISD Records, was created to disseminate White Power music, thereby gaining for neo-fascist skinheads 'a reputation as the most consistently violent element of the diverse right-wing extremist constellation' (Cotter 2004: 33). A well-circulated slogan from this movement was one of the images on Lewington's phone: '100% White/100% Proud'. During the 1990s this movement merged with, and indeed in the UK was virtually indistinguishable from, Combat 18. Formed in 1992 as the bodyguard for the BNP, Combat 18 progressively divorced itself from the electoral 'opportunism' of the BNP in favour of perpetuating paramilitary violence and 'advocated a policy of violent 'direct action', [and] instructed its readers on how to prepare bombs and openly incited racial hatred'. Members targeted Asian and other ethnic minorities in Britain, while openly identifying with Nazism and anti-Semitism, as revealed by the group's numerological code, referring to the first and eighth letters of the alphabet, with A H referring to Adolf Hitler. Reflecting on his time with Combat 18 during the 1990s, the journalist Nick Ryan claimed that the 'reality on the ground for Combat 18 was football violence and the far-right music scene' (Ryan 2004: 28).

Yet in Lewington's case, there was no evidence at all that he had direct contact with Combat 18 activists, no evidence that he had attended racist skinhead gigs or been a football hooligan, and no suggestion that he had any operational assistance in his terrorist radicalisation; a loner, he hadn't spoken to his father for ten years—despite living in the same house. Like Breivik's imagined 'Knights Templar', Lewington's Waffen-SS UK 'command council' was entirely fictitious, as was his claim to have 30 fellow members, split into two-man cells, who were trained and willing to bomb the UK indiscriminately until only British people as 'defined by blood' remained. This attempt to start a race war, then, was totally imagined. More to the point, it was wholly derived from an indirect 'radicalising network' online.

Underscoring this point is the following statement, provided in both Lewington's 'Waffen-SS UK Members Handbook' and his notebook (mistakes and capitalisation in original):

> NO LONGER WILL THE WEAKLINGS RULE THE WHITE MAN BY LIES AND DECIET, BUT, THE WARRIOR WILL MAKE HIS COMEBACK, AND, RULE BY STRENGTH, HONESTY AND LOVE FOR HIS RACE.

This statement actually originates with Ian Stuart Donaldson and is contained in the *Ian Stuart Song Book* from 2001. Yet the printed original is different from the above in one crucial respect: the added commas before and after 'but'. This variation, instead, comes from the Combat 18/Blood & Honour homepage.[6] In the case of Neil Lewington, then, his support network was wholly online. To this day, all the evidence suggests that he was a lone actor radicalised by websites and racist fantasies passively—meaning that there was no evidence presented at trial of dialogue amongst fellow right-wing extremists. Lewington was convicted in July 2009 on seven of eight terrorism-related charges and handed an indefinite sentence in September 2009 after being told by the judge:

> You were in the process of embarking upon terrorist activity [....] designed to intimidate non-white people and it was for the purpose of pursuing the ideological cause of white supremacy and neo-fascism. (BBC News 2009)

Active Links to 'Radicalising Networks': Ian Davison (2010)

Although clearly also pursuing the 'cause of white supremacy', Ian Davison was at the opposite end of the spectrum in terms of 'radicalising networks' (CPS 2010). Davison was a founding member of the ASF, which he launched in early 2008 with his son, Nicky, who was underage at the time, alongside two older neo-Nazis, Trevor Hannington, based in north Wales, and Michael Heaton, based in northern England. At its peak, the movement purportedly had up to 350 virtual activists worldwide, with perhaps two dozen activists allegedly carrying out paramilitary-style 'street ops' to earn membership. Using the avatar 'Sweaney88', Ian Davison was in charge of propaganda, in which he was assisted by his son, who posted under the name 'Thorburn'.

For a year, this quartet operated the ASF website—its server was located in Ohio to avoid hate crimes or incitement charges—before a falling out led to Heaton's departure from the group and his founding of the much smaller British Freedom Fighters, while the three remaining ASF committee members 'rebranded' their larger organisation as Legion88/The Wolfpack. A fair summary of their views is contained in the 'ASF Official Statement', posted by Davison in January 2009 (mistakes in original):

> We at the ASF are a young organization that are fully commited to the defence of our people by any and all means necessary. We do not fight against our people but for our people yet still The British security forces have chosen to attack us. Unfortunately for them what they have found is that the ASF are alot stronger than we led them to believe, we are also ahead in the security game. This has been the first true test of ASF grit as the security forces smashed down doors and came away with nothing. Still Zog [the alleged 'Zionist Occupation Government'] has taken things to the next level and the ASF stands ready to meet this challenge head on and smash our enemies and grind them into the dirt that spawned them. So we say this to the Zog agents that have wrecked our comrades home and imprisoned with-out trial. Release our freedom fighter, our brother, our family or suffer the consequences of your cowardly actions. The ASF will not shrink under the persecusion of Zog troops, instead we will take the fight to you at every turn. Our brothers and sisters now stand ready to strike, the coming blood will be on your hands.

Following a counter-terrorism investigation, Ian Davison was arrested in June 2009—shortly after The Wolfpack's YouTube site uploaded videos of two pipe-bombs being detonated. Concerning though this was, it was dwarfed by the findings at Davison's Burnopfield home: a jar of ricin, which contained up to ten lethal doses of the biotoxin. It seems Davison had purchased castor beans online and then used paramilitary manuals to auto-didactically turn them into castor oil, the precursor of one of the world's deadliest substances. To put this into perspective, when Davison was caught, the so-called coalition of the willing was still in Iraq trying to locate weapons of mass destruction (WMD) that we now know could be built (if not weaponised with a dispersal agent) by a self-directed terrorist—needing only an Internet connection and a credit card. This, then, was a brave new world, whereby a working-class milkman with self-taught computing knowledge and a belief in neo-Nazism could seem to single-handedly cross the threshold of WMDs.

I say 'seem to' since, like Lewington, Davison was unwilling to speak with the authorities upon arrest—a stark contrast with the narcissistic Breivik, or other lone wolves like the Unabomber, Ted Kaczynski, the so-called Laserman (John Ausonius), or Peter Mangs in Sweden, convicted for multiple racist murders. Yet there was no suggestion that Davison shared his bombing plans or preparations with other activists from the ASF or its successor organisations—including his son, who was later charged with possessing materials useful for acts of terror. To be sure, all members of the online ASF forum had access to paramilitary manuals, thanks to uploads by—amongst others—the head of the 'US division' of the neo-Nazi group (mistakes in original):

> I wanted to provide the latest tactical as well as military training manuals to the Wolfpack, but at the same time I wanted them to be able to be accessed safely and easily so that no one felt the need to have them on there person i.e. there home or elsewhere. I also believe that these should be in pdf so they are accessed and viewed easily and securely. Well I have found a safe and secure method to view these on line, and you may still download if you like; if and only if it is legal in each of your geopolitical regions. I have promised this week they would be provided; so here they are in a safe web format to view and do with what you may.

Not to be outdone, by the end of 2008, Davison had personally uploaded 21 book-length texts to the ASF website, including *Mein Kampf*, George Lincoln Rockwell's *White Power*, and several paramilitary manuals, such as *Silent Killing*, *The Dark Art Of Death*, *Converting Model Rockets Into Explosive Missiles*, *Homebuilt Claymore Mines*, and the *Arsenal of Improvised Weapons*.

This was a small portion of the material I was tasked to inspect from the ASF's and associated websites. Unlike the scans provided in the Lewington trial, this took the form of CD-ROMS containing films and images, online books and links, as well as public blogs and private messages. These were presented to me in October 2009 alongside a similar remit to that above: to consider the ideological make-up and motivations of the group, as well as any political and international aims.

Whereas Expert Witness testimony in the Lewington case had been made challenging by a dearth of material, an opposite challenge faced me in the Ian Davison case: an almost unmanageable volume of captured material. I was presented with thousands of posts that contained all manner of racist hatred, incitement to violence, and aggressive expressions of neo-Nazism. Yet in this context, the trials against the membership committee of the ASF offered a rare opportunity to see the workings of a neo-Nazi 'small cell'. To make the 52 discs' worth of captured material manageable, I broke the texts into four categories: (1) glorification of Nazism/'Aryanism'; (2) violently racist and anti-Semitic language; (3) propaganda dissemination and international links with right-wing extremists and paramilitary; and finally, (4) materials geared toward paramilitarism and physical attacks.

In stark contrast to Lewington—and indeed to Breivik and others more recently, perhaps including Dylann Roof—Ian Davison had a very active 'radicalising network': daily exchanges online, an organisation he helped to lead for some 18 months, and a son who appeared to share the same values. This, in turn, raises an unusual proposition: a would-be lone wolf who was passively collecting information on terrorist attacks online, while at the same time cultivating an active support network via the offline ASF cell.

There seem to be other important contrasts between active online posters like Davison, on the one hand, and those more passively drawing upon 'radicalising networks' like Lewington. First, as noted above, Davison was trafficking paramilitary manuals online, as well as related extreme right materials. Davison was also very clear on the ASF forum about his neo-Nazi views. This frequently extended to both general threats of violence—such as the relatively tame 'i'm out tonight and scum is on the menue and this Aryan is f*cking hungry' (sic)—to far more violent expressions (mistakes in original):

> Its worth noting that in an incendiary attack on scum housing sometimes the letter box can be a better point of attack than the window. The letter box usually leads to the stairs, usually carpeted lot the time coats and things are behind that door and stairs are made of wood and represent the heart of the house. The same can be said of large buildings like flats, bars, restaurants and mosques. A fire starting on the stairs usually quickly takes out the building and removes the stairs as a means of escape.

Comments were sometimes directed at individuals alongside, in one instance, circulating a female police officer's home address. Amongst a motley crew of online racists, in fact, Davison typically used the most extreme expressions and threats. His violent language doubtless would have drawn attention to himself by anyone monitoring the Aryan Strike Force (mistakes in original):

> OK most muzzies work in some sort of food trade this we know they pool the resources of there fellow pedo worshipers to drive out white traders and take up local businesses usually corner shops, take aways and finally cash and carry now you can buy cockroaches for live feed in the hundreds and under the right conditions cockroach colonies will about double in numbers in about a month, cockroaches will fit through a letterbox and are very good at not setting off the alarm.

Yet it was more than just talk in Davison's case as well. Reflecting on ASF 'training days' in Cumbria he helped to organise, Davison proudly declared: 'the

[Wolf]packs paramilitary are picking up the pace'. In another post, Davison asserted (mistakes in original):

> street lads should be able to concentrate on the job they are doing but remember we cant use these lads later for paramilitary action. i say that because there faces and names will become known. once there faces are know to the enemies i wouldn't want them working on assassinations or other strikes.

Were all this not ominous enough, finally and perhaps most chillingly, Davison announced shortly before his arrest that he had recently 'worked on some germ warfare plans in the past but as always lacking resources were the biggest obstacle'. Davison ultimately pled guilty to six terrorism-related charges and remains the only person in the UK convicted under the 1996 Chemical Weapons Act. His active engagement with neo-Nazi fora clearly contributed to his 2010 sentencing (Lynn 2010).

Indeed, several of the above and cognate postings constitute prosecutable offences in the UK. But so-called keyboard warriors and other fantasists make these kinds of offensive statements all the time online—and not just on neo-Nazi forums. Surely this has to be balanced against the cost of compromising surveillance that may have been on-going for months, or even years. It also poses a challenge when policing right-wing extremists actively engaging with their 'radicalising networks': how do investigators know who is 'all talk', and who is a legitimate security threat? How does one separate the rhetoric of many aggressive posters online from that of talkative actors who, like Davison, deserve to be tried in a court of law?

Finally, it also may be worth considering how direct and intimate—as opposed to, like Lewington, passive and indirect—interactions with self-activating terrorists' 'radicalising networks' might increase the risk factor for acts of political violence and the challenges this poses in a legal context. For example, if Davison's online texts did indeed lead to his arrest and trial, at what point was the threshold crossed? And which online postings crossed that threshold: those with incitement to hatred, those circulating paramilitary manuals useful to terrorists, or those making incriminating statements about hate crimes and violence? Perhaps a final question that is equally pertinent for academics working in this area is the following: can working with legal and policing practitioners help us in sharpening our conceptual and analytical approaches to extremism?

CONCLUSIONS

Radicalisation, obviously, is not simply a matter of Islamist extremism and terrorism. As this chapter makes plain, both in Europe and the USA, radical right-wing terrorist attacks are a prevalent and recurrent feature of the violence-prone environment of political activism. Furthermore, the term 'lone wolf' is, when disregarding the enabling meso-level of support communities, as misleading as the perception of 'lone nuts', which risks marginalising extreme right solo actor terrorism. As I have demonstrated with regard to the two high-profile cases above, Lewington (2008) and Davison (2010), it is possible to distinguish between two different forms of interaction with and support from what I have called 'radicalising networks', indirect (or passive) and direct (or active). In both cases, it is crucial to stress the dynamics between online and offline radicalisation. Whereas Lewington predominantly constructed a fictitious community of support in more or less an entirely virtual reality ('Waffen-SS UK'), Davison used the Internet as a tool to encourage radicalisation among his online and offline supporters, the ASF, while at the same time single-handedly constructing a chemical weapon in his home. These different uses of the Internet highlight that we need to refine our tools of analysis when it comes to digital radicalisation and, moreover, that relevant perspectives for research can be substantially aided through collaboration with practitioners and specific case studies.

Endnotes

[1] For more on this theme, see my review of Roger Griffin's *Terrorist's Creed* in *Modernism/modernity*, 20/3 (Nov. 2013), pp. 594-597.

[2] See, for instance, www.arabamericannews.com/2012/07/29/If-Colorado-shooter-was-an-Arab-or-Muslim-would-he-be-labeled-a-terrorist/?-_html.

[3] For example, see the useful introductory chapters to two recent, book-length studies: Paul Gill, *Lone Actor Terrorists: A Behavioural Analysis* (London and New York: Routledge, 2015), introduction online at https://content.taylorfrancis.com/books/download?dac=C2013-0-27778-3&isbn=9781317660163&format=googlePreviewPdf, and Ramón Spaaij, *Understanding Lone Wolf Terrorism: Global Patterns, Motivations and Prevention* (Dordrecht: Springer, 2012).

[4] The murder of Labour MP Jo Cox in June 2016 by Thomas Mair would certainly also be subsumed under this category, since the offender displayed clearly far-right sympathies. The investigation revealed that Mair was motivated by extreme right-wing beliefs.

[5] See, for example, the Southern Poverty Law Center, The Klan Overseas, online at: www.splcenter.org/fighting-hate/intelligence-report/1998/klan-overseas; and more recently, Liam Miller, "Return of the KKK", *The Sun*, 6 June 2014, updated: 6 April 2016, online at: www.thesun.co.uk/archives/news/877092/return-of-the-kkk/.

[6] See the Blood & Honour homepage, no date, online at: http://www.bloodandhonour.net.

References

Bakker, E., and B. de Graaf. 2010. *Lone Wolves: How to Prevent this Phenomenon?* ICCT Expert Meeting Paper, November, The International Centre for Counter-Terrorism, The Hague. Accessed 20 April 2017. https://www.icct.nl/download/file/ICCT-Bakker-deGraaf-EM-Paper-Lone-Wolves.pdf.

Barkun, M. 1997. *Religion and the Racist Right: The Origins of Christian Identity*. Chapel Hill, NC: University of North Carolina Press.

BBC News. 2009. *Neo-Nazi Jailed Over Terror Plot*, 8 September. Accessed 22 April 2017. http://news.bbc.co.uk/1/hi/england/8243204.stm.

Berlet, C. 2006. "Christian Identity." In *World Fascism: A Historical Encyclopedia*, ed. C. Blamires, vol. 2. Oxford: ABC-Clio.

Bjørgo, T., and C. Hemmingby. 2016. *The Dynamics of a Terrorist Targeting Process: Anders B. Breivik and the 22 July Attacks in Norway*. London: Palgrave.

Burton, F., and S. Stewart. 2008. The "Lone Wolf" Disconnect. Stratfor, 30 January. Accessed 24 April 2017. www.stratfor.com/weekly/lone_wolf_disconnect.

Camber, R. 2009. The Bomb-making Kit Which White Supremacist Planned to Use Against 'Non-British'. *Mail Online*, 16 July. Accessed 24 April 2017. www.dailymail.co.uk/news/article-1199874/White-supremacist-guilty-plot-launch-terror-campaign-minorities.html.

Combat 18/Blood & Honour Homepage. Undated Webpage. Accessed 24 April 2017. Accessed 20 April 2017. www.skrewdriver.net/index2.html.

COT, ed. 2007. Lone-Wolf Terrorism. Case Study for Work Package 3 'Citizens and Governance in a Knowledge-based Society'. *TTSRL*, July. http://www.transnationalterrorism.eu/tekst/publications/Lone-Wolf%20Terrorism.pdf.

Cotter, J. 2004. "Sounds of Hate." In *Fascism: Critical Concepts, vol. V Postwar Fascisms*, ed. R. Griffin and M. Feldman. London: Routledge.

Crown Prosecution Service on Ian and Nikki Davison. 2010. 14 May. Accessed 24 April 2017. https://web.archive.org/web/20100802034803/http://www.cps.gov.uk/news/press_releases/118_10/.

Crown Prosecution Service on Neil Lewington. 2009. 15 July. Accessed 24 April 2017. https://web.archive.org/web/20100926171342/http://cps.gov.uk/news/press_releases/132-09/.

Dado, N. 2012. If Colorado Shooter was an Arab or Muslim, Would He Be Labelled a Terrorist? *The Arab America News*, 29 July. Accessed 24 April 2017. http://www.arabamericannews.com/2012/07/29/If-Colorado-shooter-was-an-Arab-or-Muslim-would-he-be-labeled-a-terrorist/?-_html.

Doward, J. 2015. Media Coverage of Terrorism 'Leads to Further Violence'. *The Guardian*, 1 August. Accessed 24 April 2017. www.theguardian.com/media/2015/aug/01/media-coverage-terrorism-further-violence.

Durham, M. 2007. *White Rage: The Extreme Right and American Politics*. London: Routledge.

Feldman, M., ed. 2008. *A Fascist Century*. Basingstoke: Palgrave.

—. 2012. Breivik's Three Acts of Terrorism. *Environment and Planning D: Society and Space* 30 (2): 193-195. https://web.archive.org/web/20130318044637/www.envplan.com/openaccess/d303.pdf.

—. 2013a. Comparative Lone Wolf Terrorism: Toward a Heuristic Definition. *Democracy & Security* 9 (3): 270–286. https://www.academia.edu/14688383/Proofs_for_Comparative_Lone_Wolf_Terrorism_Toward_a_Heuristic_Definition.

—. 2013b. *Terrorist's Creed* by Roger Griffin (Review). *Modernism/modernity* 20 (3): 594–597.

Gill, P. 2015. *Lone Actor Terrorists: A Behavioural Analysis*. London: Routledge.

Guido, K. 2003. *The SS: A Warning from History*. Stroud: Sutton.

Hosken, A. 1999. UK Plans 'Infiltration' of the UK. *BBC News*, 10 June. Accessed 24 April 2017. http://news.bbc.co.uk/1/hi/uk/366114.stm.

Lynn, J. 2010. Ricin Proved Neo-Nazi Ian Davison 'was Serious'. *BBC News*, 14 May. Accessed 24 April 2017. http://news.bbc.co.uk/1/hi/england/wear/8680225.stm.

Marcin, T. 2016. "Nathan Desai Was A Nazi? Houston Shooting Suspect Wore Uniform With Swastikas, Nazi 'Paraphernalia' Found." *International Business Times*, 26 September. Accessed 24 April 2017. www.ibtimes.com/nathan-desai-was-nazi-houston-shooting-suspect-wore-uniform-swastikas-nazi-2422119

Morris, S. 2014. Jail for Man Who Wore Ku Klux Klan Outfit and Posed with Lynched Golliwog. *The Guardian*, 8 January. Accessed 24 April 2017. https://www.theguardian.com/uk-news/2014/jan/08/jail-klu-kluxs-klan-golliwog-christopher-philips

O'Connor, B. 2015. Here is What Appears to be Dylann Roof's Manifesto. *Gawker*, 20 June. Accessed 24 April 2017. http://gawker.com/here-is-what-appears-to-be-dylann-roofs-racist-manifest-1712767241.

Obeidallah, D. 2015. Are All Terrorists Muslims?' It's Not Even Close. *The Daily Beast*, 14 January. Accessed 24 April 2017. www.thedailybeast.com/articles/2015/01/14/are-all-terrorists-muslims-it-s-not-even-close.html.

Önnerfors, A. 2017. Between Breivik and PEGIDA: The Absence of Ideologues and Leaders in the Contemporary European Far-Right. *Patterns of Prejudice* 51 (2): 159–175.

Pantucci, R. 2011. *A Typology of Lone Wolves: Preliminary Analysis of Lone Islamist Terrorists. Developments in Radicalisation and Political Violence.* London: The International Centre for the Study of Radicalisation (March). Accessed 24 April 2017. http://icsr.info/wp-content/uploads/2012/10/1302002992ICSRPaper_ATypologyofLoneWolves_Pantucci.pdf.

Parry, R. 2011. We Expose Vile Racist Biker as British Leader of the Ku Klux Klan. *Mirror*, 9 October. Accessed 24 April 2017. http://www.mirror.co.uk/news/uk-news/we-expose-vile-racist-biker-as-british-86445.

Plucinska, J. 2015. Study Says White Extremists Have Killed More Americans in the U.S. Than Jihadists since 9/11. *Time*, 24 June. Accessed 24 April 2017. http://time.com/3934980/right-wing-extremists-white-terrorism-islamist-jihadi-dangerous/?iid=sr-link1.

Quarles, C.L. 1999. *The Ku Klux Klan and Related American Racialist and Antisemitic Organizations: A History and Analysis*. London: McFarland & Company.

Ryan, N. 2004. *Homeland: Into a World of Hate*. Edinburgh: Mainstream.

Sageman, M. 2008. "The Stagnation in Terrorism Research". *Journal of Terrorism and Political Violence* 26 (4): 565–580.

Simon, J.D. 2013. *Lone Wolf Terrorism: Understanding the Growing Threat*. New York: Prometheus Books.

Spaaij, R. 2010. The Enigma of Lone Wolf Terrorism: An Assessment. *Studies in Conflict and Terrorism* 33 (9): 854–870.

—. 2012. *Understanding Lone Wolf Terrorism: Global Patterns, Motivation and Prevention*. New York: Springer.

Spaaij, R., and M.S. Hamm. 2014. Key Issues and Research Agendas in Lone Wolf Terrorism. *Studies in Conflict & Terrorism* 38 (3): 167–178.

Werleman, C.J. 2014. Americans Are More Likely to be Killed by Right Wing Terrorists Than Muslims—But the Media's Afraid to Say It. *Peninsula Peace and Justice Center*, 21 May. Accessed 24 April 2017. www.peaceandjustice.org/americans-are-more-likely-to-be-killed-by-right-wing-terrorists-than-muslims-but-the-medias-afraid-to-say-it/.

White Camelia Knights of the Ku Klux Klan. 2011. 26 September. Accessed 20 April 2017. www.wckkkk.org/who.html.

15. Choose Definitively Between Hell and Reason

> ... am I to show that not even a year's trial has taught me anything? Am I to leave this world as a man who has no common sense? Are people to say of me after I am gone that at the beginning of my case I wanted to finish it, and at the end of it I wanted to begin it again? I don't want that to be said.[1]
>
> - Franz Kafka

I.

Discussing the nature of tactical air strikes against Afghan targets following the 11 September attacks on America's East Coast, an Army planner told *Time* magazine, 'It's like turning on the light in your first apartment. Lots of roaches start running'.[2] As this forcefully illustrates in a number of ways, it can be difficult to distinguish between roaches and human beings, though for the purposes of this paper a more universal taxonomy will be attempted. Mere roaches have our species in a corner, for two reasons closely related to the quotation above. The first concerns the parochial attitude to our justifications and certainties that have so wrought the history of humanity. The second is that in so doing the human species has recently developed a capability to commit the truest genocide, collective suicide. And primitive, harmonious roaches stand poised to inherit the earth in the aftermath of humanity's so-far obscured self-destructive urges. It is this melancholy, and it is hoped, hopeful theme of potential sustainability and possible apocalypse which the present article sets out to investigate.

Although most comments below will focus upon our inheritance of the astonishing century past, a few remarks are necessary concerning the more general historical paradigms that have formed the backbone—or more precisely, the hamstring—of human progress. Both of these will be informed by what Howard Zinn calls 'value-laden historiography' in his essay 'What is Radical History?'. In calling for a return to (and necessary extension of) the ideals of Enlightenment thought in a manner similar to that of Jürgen Habermas, he argues that all analyses of history are necessarily subjective:

> The closest we can come to that elusive 'objectivity' is to report accurately all the subjectivities in a situation. But we emphasise one or another of those subjective views in any case. I suggest we depart from our customary position as privileged observers. Unless we wrench free from being what we like to call 'objective', we are closer psychologically, whether we like to admit it or not, to the executioner than to the victim.[3]

For Zinn, radical history is the catalyst for change rather than mere reflection; compassion instead of indifference; and, most importantly, a view of history siding with the weak, the needy and the grieving. This sensitive rubric rests upon five suggested propositions: namely, a deeper understanding of victims in the current world through studies of historical oppression; the exposure of institutions as self-interested rather than altruistic; ideology as both pervasive in liberal democracy and a buttress for the status quo; the heroic aspect of reformers and progressives to show us that a better world is possible; and finally, that fighting for this better world as revolutionaries can be as dangerous as complacency if it breeds sanctified destruction.[4]

These propositions will be explored below by juxtaposing some recent examples of the explosive clannishness marking human history with the threat this behaviour poses to our global bunker. In an epoch where we have all potentially become the same weak, needy, grieving individual cowering from the apocalypse, it makes no sense to pursue self-congratulatory 'clash of civilisations' or 'end of history' arguments.[5] Simultaneously, this view insists that the existential dilemma of the fortunate is in no way comparable to the additional travails of humanity's majority, suffering appallingly—and worthy of handwringing only when famines, slave labour, poverty or wars exceed their normalised terrors. With roofs over and pillows under our heads, uncontaminated drinking water and aspirin on the bedstand to relieve painful thoughts of ominous global disaster or perpetual regional tragedies, it is essential to remember that we readers are truly of the 'Minority' World as regards relative population and the ability to take for granted basic necessities (water and sanitation, peace, leisure, human rights, etc.) lacked by billions, even within highly industrialised states. On this point, one statistic is telling:

> In the 1990s the average global citizen (an abstraction of limited utility) deployed about 20 'energy slaves', meaning 20 human equivalents working 24 hours a day, 365 days a year.... The average American in the 1990s used 50 to 100 times as much energy as the average Bangladeshi and directed upwards of 75 energy slaves while the Bangladeshi had less than one.[6]

And economic globalisation—what has been elsewhere termed 'neo-liberalism'—means the world gets worse daily for the majority: the West insists on favourable trade terms in exchange for international development loans; once conditions are right, multinational companies "race to the bottom" to exploit labour, wage and environmental laws that are intolerable here, even though their products are certainly tolerable. Incredibly, in the postwar era, this oppressed three-quarters of the world, rich with earthly treasures but poor in organised resistance to American-led acronymic organizations such as the IMF, WTO, G8, NATO and SAPs, have actually decreased in relative living standards, life expectancy, and security from state terror. This exploitation, so effectively documented by Susan George,

Naomi Klein and others, is often dressed up in "trickle down" redistribution theories of an exported and recycled Industrial Revolution by scholars like Harvard economist Jeffrey Sachs, who argues:

> My concern is not that there are too many sweatshops but that there are too few ... those are precisely the jobs that were the stepping stones for Singapore and Hong Kong and those are the jobs that have to come to Africa to get them out of backbreaking rural poverty.[7]

In keeping with such sentiments, we would do well to think of these smartly dressed proponents of globalisation, Structural Adjustment and "free trade" not as intellectuals but as warriors. For as Michael McKinley's meticulously researched paper demonstrates, economic strangulation need not be seen as separated from 'a revolution, or a military defeat and subsequent occupation ... neither metaphor, nor simile, of war, but war itself':

> If 100 million have been killed in the formal wars of the twentieth century, why are they to be privileged in comprehension over the annual toll of five million children from Structural Adjustment programmes since 1982? Put another way, short of nuclear holocaust, what destruction and death could war bring to sub-Saharan Africa that the World Bank and IMF have not already brought?[8]

Surely, black words on white paper effect little justice for these crimes, and the suffering of youths barely conscious of their surroundings before death. Moreover, in a climate where Sachs represents the "liberal" consensus and McKinley the "radical" heresy, we desperately need to draft another ally standing on the side of Life; a humane forum illustrating the impoverishments of regressive reason and the urgency of solidarity: art. It is this wizened detour not afforded to suave establishment-warriors. Art removes us from the cycle of regressive rationalism (for example, Nuclear Missile Defence against terrorism or Kissinger's 'justified pre-emption'), while offering both an important sense of historical milieu (such as Solzhenitsyn's *Gulag Archipelago* or the brilliant film *Threads*). Additionally, art offers both a cultural critique of social values and, in many cases, particularly astute political commentaries through parody, allusion or allegory (as in Orwell's *Animal Farm*).

Thus, by a simultaneous appeal to politics and culture—the latter acting not only as a refuge or a force inherently capable of shifting such threatening paradigms but as a fulcrum around which applied paradigms are developed—it becomes possible to discern the foundations of praxis in the interests of learning about human experience; its contorted beauty and very indefinability. And in many ways, artistic connections to politics are a necessary manner of conceptualisation. To extrapolate from our current situation, "rationally" is to quickly lead to "insane" conclusions: humanity is crazy to have recently come so close to its end, and we would naturally be "sane" to avoid this. But if we do not make deep-seated changes, we are "crazy" anyway and it does not matter, which is itself a rational conclusion. This paradox can best be expressed by Joseph Heller's *Catch-22*:

> ... which specified that a concern for one's own safety in the face of dangers that were real and immediate was the process of the rational mind.... Orr would be crazy to fly more missions and sane if he didn't, but if he was sane he had to fly them. If he flew them, he was crazy and didn't have to; but if he didn't want to he was sane and had to.[9]

Just as useful as applying Heller's satirical insights into war and individuals' reactions to it is Camus' calls for reconciliation amongst warring sides in Algeria:

> It is as if two insane people, crazed with wrath, had decided to turn into a fatal embrace the forced marriage from which they cannot free themselves. Forced to live together and incapable of uniting, they decide at least to die together. And because each of them by his motives and excesses strengthens the motives and excesses of the other, the storm of death that has struck our country can only increase to the point of general destruction.[10]

It is for this reason that, in teaching Nazism, I am uncertain whether Ian Kershaw's definitive *The Nazi Dictatorship* or Bertolt Brecht's *The Resistible Rise of Arturo Ui* is of greater value. Surely both are indispensable for understanding such a vast and unspeakably personal catastrophe. This is demonstrated by juxtaposing their respective endings, clarifying the different utility of these two genres:

> Knowledge is better than ignorance; history better than myth. These truisms are more than ever worth bearing in mind where ignorance and myth spawn racial intolerance and a revival of the illusions and idiocies of fascism.
> Therefore learn how to see and not to gape.
> To act instead of talking all day long.
> The world was almost won by such an ape!
> The nations put him where his kind belong.
> But don't rejoice too soon at your escape—
> The womb he crawled from still is going strong.[11]

While the former is concerned with setting forth truisms by contributing to political knowledge, the latter, by way of artistic rendering, weaves an intricate and vivid tapestry of human interactions. For all its own tremendous worth, political discourse alone cannot convey this. Hence, we feel obliged to invoke art in our search for a more complete tapestry of human verity and images against the 'storm of death' threatening 'general destruction'.

And those against such destruction in the wider sense (global unsustainability) or narrower sense (5000 Iraqi children dying monthly since the imposition of Western sanctions) must conclude that those standing with them—artistically or otherwise—are indeed 'enemies of the apocalypse'. This phrase, first used by Günther

Anders to describe the insanity of nuclear weapons, is at the heart of the humanistic postmodern condition: for is Anders not right to say that in our absurd situation we have become 'inverted utopians'? For 'utopians cannot create that which they envision, [while] we cannot envision that which we create'.[12] He delimits 'enemies' as those who understand that trying to avoid living in a plastic bubble or scurrying around like rats in the aftermath of a nuclear winter—if "privileged" to live—is neither idealistic nor inconceivable. And when thinking of CIA-trained death squads so adept at removing extremities and trafficking tonnes of cocaine, or the starvation of the helpless in a world fat with food, or couples jumping from century-high windows to escape the thousand-degree heat of rationalised violence—it becomes an easy task to construct a universal assumption that no human actively seeks such afflictions; to declare oneself an 'enemy of the apocalypse'.[13] So like Anders' pleas for sanity and Zinn's value-laden evaluation, I too will wear my heart on my sleeve in the interests of compassionately standing against the annihilation of civilisation, in both a wider and narrower sense. For unless we see humanity as one sprawling hydra-headed civilisation and ubiquitously extend the tenets of a consistently humane liberalism to every one of its members, we may well come to the end of History, only in a decidedly eschatological culmination. Finally, as this remit allows for appropriations from art in the interests of the two things greater than itself—human societies which birthed it from the void, and the void which threatens to bury it through human societies—we can say that as 'inverted utopians' we humans also carry the crimson 'A' first worn by Hester Prynne in Nathaniel Hawthorne's *The Scarlet Letter*. The only difference is that our letter stands for 'apocalypse', a nadir even more difficult to visualise than adultery in mid-seventeenth-century Salem.

II.

It is again helpful to turn to art for perhaps the most incisive commentary on this willing paradox. This is found throughout Orwell's *1984*, particularly in the neologism 'doublethink',[14] which summarises not only the deliberate muteness of the press and the benevolent intentions of autocracies; but also the gamut of general inconsistencies within institutionalised ideologies better than any political analysis:

> Doublethink means the power of holding two contradictory beliefs in one's mind simultaneously, and accepting both of them.... The process has to be conscious, or it would not be carried out with sufficient precision, but it also has to be unconscious, or it would bring with it a feeling of falsity and hence of guilt.... To tell deliberate lies while genuinely believing in them, to forget any fact that has become inconvenient, and then when it becomes necessary again, to draw it back from oblivion for just so long as it is needed, to deny the existence of objective reality and all the while to take account of reality which one denies—all this is indispensably necessary ... in our society, those who have the best knowledge of what is happening are also those who are furthest from seeing the world as it is. In general, the greater the understanding, the greater the delusion: the more intelligent, the less sane.[15]

Needless to say, art in the hands of individuals like Orwell is a valuable heuristic tool, one every bit the equivalent of sober analysis and empiricism. But there is a dual function here. Art and culture can also become universally Truthful despite their mimetic and temporal constraints, like the blind prophet Tiresias 'throbbing between two lives' in T. S. Eliot's *The Waste Land*, or the picturesque landscape of the painted canvas of a painted canvas in René Magritte's *The Human Condition I*.[16] In our surreal times, when countries are bombed for humanitarian reasons with weapons whose names sound like gardening aids while inflicting 'collateral damage' against defenceless people, an analysis of language is essential; if the most free to contemplate critically are the most reflectively restrained, reason must sometimes choose silence in favour of paradoxical renderings; and where we—who were enlightened by liberal ideals but now find its permutations the world's greatest threat—feel the contradictions of modernity thrusting upon us 'an art of living in times of catastrophe in order ... to fight openly against the instinct of death at work in our history'.[17] Here art is not only a guide and a refuge, but an oracle as well.

Absurdity, paradox, self-reflexivity, nonrepresentation; these are the tools Modern Art employs in this Kafkaesque time to photograph the speeding train of human consciousness. But surely the most important of all of these mirrors turned upon modern society by art is that timeless mirror, analogy. Could Joseph Conrad's prophetic *Heart of Darkness*—subversively written for a conservative *fin de siècle* readership in *Blackwood's Magazine*—have ended otherwise than in the revelation of a comforting lie? Perhaps at that time Marlow's truth, seen by Conrad himself on his voyage down the Congo River, 'would have been too dark—too dark altogether'. Yet times have changed, and those peering into 'the heart of an immense darkness' need to use such texts didactically. In this case, an understanding of contemporary socioeconomic imperialism is only bolstered by this marginally fictional account of the mindsets and legacies bequeathed by "direct" colonialism. Arduous as it may be to sail along a river revealing the consequences of long-imposed suffering upon indigenous peoples and the pillage of their historic riverbanks for wealth and prestige, we must tell the truth about societies like those represented by Kurtz today; drowning in scuttled principles both idealistic and civilised, zealous yet easily adapted to 'exterminate all the brutes'.

Indeed, it is this interplay of light and darkness that characterises both the modern Minority World and Kurtz, of whom, in each case, 'All Europe contributed to the making'. For the task we face today, the enormity of opportunities and totality of risk lend special meaning to such a tension of opposites residing in Conrad's antagonist—that 'cliff of crystal'—the archetype of today's neo-liberal who 'wanted no more than justice' but believed 'everything belonged to him'; who 'was a universal genius' despite the 'colossal scale of his vile desires, the meanness, the torment, the tempestuous anguish of his soul'.[18] For in a world where we indeed will have 'a choice of nightmares' unless we are willing as a species to see 'The horror! The horror!' of threats to our very continuance in the foreseeable future, art itself, in Conrad's definition, may become not only a mode of understanding but an encouragement to action:

> Art itself may be defined as a single-minded attempt to render the highest kind of justice to the visible universe, by bringing to light the truth, manifold and one, underlying its every aspect.[19]

Such a difficult quest for truth, therefore, is not divorced from notions of human justice and solidarity but, as Albert Camus again reminds us, is the very axis upon which art rests:

> It is a means of stirring the greatest number of people by offering them a privileged picture of common joys and sufferings. It obliges the artist not to keep himself apart; it subjects him to the most humble and the most universal truth. And often he who has chosen the fate of the artist because he felt himself to be different soon realises that he can maintain neither his art nor his difference unless he admits that he is like the others.[20]

Precisely this commonality is at the heart of artistic projects seeking to cast light upon the shared yet elusive "human condition". And precisely this commonality is denied to starving, diseased, bombed and oppressed victims by the Minority World. Rarely is this juxtaposition more clearly delineated than in Steven Berkoff's stage adaptation of *The Trial*, which admirably captures the absurd flavour of Kafka's hypocrisy of accusation, faceless bureaucracy, selective facts of the 'case' and inevitability of judgement comprising Joseph K's unrelenting trial. And rarely is this juxtaposition more clearly delineated than in the case of the "War on Terror" prosecuted (principally) by the "Land of the Free". As with K's crimes prior to his arrest (echoed by Washington's demand of Pakistan on September 16th for 'a cut-off of fuel supplies ... and the elimination of truck supplies that provide much of the food and other supplies to Afghanistan's civilian population'), surely the punishment for the crime—in K's case, his execution 'Like a dog!' at the hands of two shadowy agents of the Court (read the Northern Alliance) seeming to relish their duty—is greater than the original crime itself.[21] Indisputably, the murder of 3000 civilians by Egyptian and Saudi followers of Osama bin Laden—on account of American support for the repressive Israeli occupation; murderous Iraqi sanctions; military support for Saudi Arabia, profit from Muslim (principally), Middle East destitution specifically; and existence as a non-fundamentalist-Islamic state generally—is a crime of staggering magnitude. In *The Trial*, the known collusion with Court officials, derision of other lawyers, insistence upon defending K alone and wholly questionable motives made K's lawyer, Dr Huld, appear more guilty than K himself. Huld's congruence with America in these instances is striking, including: US collusion with the *mujahideen* until at least 1998 (the end of US-sponsored negotiations with the Taliban for an oil pipeline from the Caspian Sea through Afghanistan and Pakistan to the Arabian Sea); frequent threats of unilateral action if other nations are unwilling to support continuing military action in Afghanistan; and a stated motivation to 'defend liberty at all costs' rather than extracting vengeance or profit from an already suffering populace.[22]

Furthermore, like Joseph K, exposed to the underside of the law through his accusation by the authorities, Afghanistan's—and by extension, the entire world's—own trial conducted by America has revealed greater crimes than the original, horrifying incident. The facts speak for themselves. A recent scholarly analysis placed the civilian death toll in Afghanistan, up to 6 February 2002, at a minimum of 3000 civilians. Given that bombing has continued to the time of writing and roughly 14,000 unexploded bomblets released from cluster bombs remain in Afghanistan, it can be said with certainty that the death toll in the "War on Terror" has exceeded by far the original act of terrorism itself.[23] RAWA estimates that virtually all of Kabul has been destroyed, much of the surrounding countryside has been rendered unusable as arable land, and women still live in fear of removing their *burkhas*.[24] The much-touted food parcels dropped by US aircraft—unfortunately looking virtually identical to cluster bombs—if wholly recovered by the starving populace, can only feed 27% of those who need the food, for one day.[25] After nearly a year, 1.2 million hungry and largely unsheltered refugees are finally starting to return to their shattered homes; however, despite assurances from the establishment-warriors as of 19 July 2002, the UN complained of lack of funds to repatriate refugees.[26] In America, ubiquitous charges of anti-Americanism tar anyone disposed to criticise the recent campaign, which the propagandistic media have shown absolutely no willingness to do.[27] The Patriot Act has undercut many long-held civil liberties, and military tribunals have been rapidly introduced. More than 1000 ethnic minorities (evidently almost all of Asian appearance) have been detained without charge for many months. And finally, Camp X-Ray, perhaps the *pièce de résistance* of a self-proclaimed liberal democracy-cum-autocracy, still holds 'the most dangerous men on earth' in concentration camp conditions, whose guilt, like Joseph K's, is unconfirmed yet assumed in an extraordinary inversion of the 5th Amendment.

The greatest charges able to be levelled at America following September 11, therefore, are both shameful hypocrisy and callous disregard for the 'rule of law' so spitefully violated by the nineteen suicide bombers. There is no international coalition save those countries that were press-ganged ('Either you're with us, or you're with the terrorists'), bribed (Pakistan received $1 billion in US aid and had sanctions lifted for its cooperation), or that were pre-existing 'lap-dogs' (Britain, in Will Hutton's words).[28] Nor is there any basis in international agreement for the violent course America has taken: as an Amnesty International spokesman stated regarding Guantánamo Bay, 'We are dismayed…. This partial compliance with the Geneva convention is a half-measure and continues an arrogant policy of pick and choose with regard to the laws of war.'[29] And the details above are merely the tip of a dissolving iceberg, not only with regard to the hypocritical crimes which have come before now, but also with regard to the future: as Vice President Dick Cheney has warned, '40 to 50' countries may be targeted next.[30]

One of these targets presents the final parallel with *The Trial*. Another of Huld's clients encountered by Joseph K, the pathetic Block, whose case has dragged on inexorably without promise of conclusion, echoes the ongoing crisis of Iraq following the 1991 Gulf War. On top of the 100,000+ killed that year, 5000 children, as previously mentioned, die monthly of starvation. Cancer is at epidemic levels due to the suffusion of depleted uranium dropped on Iraq and carried on the desert winds, yet even aspirin is barred under the pestilent sanctions imposed by the West. Despite Western rhetoric about Saddam's Weapons of Mass Destruction, 'UN inspectors certified that 817 out of the 819 Iraqi long-range missiles were destroyed', while 'the International Atomic Energy Agency reported that Iraq's nuclear weapons programme had been eliminated "efficiently and effectively"'. This pitiful, pitiful situation can only be exacerbated by the imminently expected attack by the US, whereby the death of 10,000 civilians is the Pentagon's 'medium case scenario' which avoids the 'total war' targeting of water and electricity favoured by US hawks.[31] Adjectives for this genocidal perpetuation are superfluous. Again, an appropriation from art is most apposite: this time from the text of *The Trial*. In an exchange anticipating K's death, a priest stands at the pulpit, ostensibly preparing to deliver another sermon. As the time approaches midnight, the 'solitary' and 'forlorn' K wonders: 'Could K represent the congregation all by himself?' Indeed for us, K represents our congregation of suffering multitudes, blameless victims and impoverished innocents. Finally, the priest calls to Joseph K by name, and seeing K's reluctance to engage him 'pointed with sharply bent forefinger to a spot immediately before the pulpit'. Thereupon the priest reveals himself as the prison chaplain, responsible for summoning the surprised K to the Cathedral. The chaplain need not here represent only America, but sanctimonious power itself. And between the powerful and powerless, the following exchange ensues.

> 'Your guilt is supposed, for the present, at least, to have been proved.' 'But I am not guilty,' said K.; 'it's a mistake. And if it comes to that, how can any man be called guilty? We are all simply men here, one as much as the other.' 'That is true,' said the priest, 'but that's how all guilty men talk.' 'Are you prejudiced against me too?' asked K.[32]

III.

In the postwar world, we indeed all share some guilt for silence or acceptance of the numerous ways human beings have devised in which to end our species and let the roaches take over. This danger is principally due to ingenious products and technological tools we have constructed that now dominate, manipulate and threaten the entire globe. Despite its lurking in the background throughout this supplication, self-annihilation is our own central adversary and beckoning—the final historical moment; the only thing the world is as yet capable of uniting to achieve. Of this reality, little needs to be expressed. The harnessed atom, capable of powering the world or destroying it; hyper-industrialisation, facilitating so much but at the same time threatening total environmental unsustainability; scientific advances that can cure diseases or unleash ones capable of infecting all life on earth: each of these represents a new era in human history that is everyone's domain, for everyone is potentially affected. And those obliged to weigh nearly two million years of history against recent changes in warfare, climate, communications, beliefs and leisure since the watershed year 1945—a year of victory also carrying the atomic fungus of our potentially mushrooming defeat, when DIY extinction became consciously possible for the human species—find the balance distinctly unfavourable for human destiny.

Despite amazing advances in everything from genetics to mobile phones, for all our constructs humans nevertheless remain human. Still made of frail skin unable to withstand speeding metal or radiation, with lungs that need oxygen produced by trees and bodies needing filtered light from the sun and, of course, retaining the human clannishness that has marked all but the last page of our Book of

Life. Because of our advances, we are now forever condemned to this last page, forever cursed to fight the future and the closing of this book. Just like Malone's own narrative in Samuel Beckett's *Trilogy*, this final page can never be punctuated, because to do so would be to write our own collective ending. Indeed, the only scenario capable of dwarfing the misfortune of most of the world today would be the extermination of the whole world tomorrow.

And there is enough evidence for such an extermination amassed already, for those willing to look. The ancient islanders of Tuvalu are only the first facing displacement (to New Zealand) as the warming environment causes the Pacific Ocean to rise around them.[33] Given that fully 25% of global emissions emanate from the United States—which has rejected the Kyoto Protocol and initiated 'voluntary incentives' for domestic emissions reductions—it is highly doubtful they will be the last victims of environmental convulsion. Although this did not make "news", the apparently unprecedented break of a 500 billion tonne area of ice—roughly the size of Wales—'warning of the effects of global warming' certainly did.[34] The threat found in America's recent 'Nuclear Posture Review' is also new, evolving out of operational use of quasi-nuclear weapons bearing names of garden implements, such as Daisy Cutters in Afghanistan and the strategic consideration of employing the B61-11 Bunker Buster, a tactical nuclear penetration bomb, to fulfil George W. Bush's desire to 'use all the tools at our disposal' to enact regime change in Iraq.[35] Most recently, the principle of 'limited nuclear conflict' of the variety so threatening to South Asia, on account of India–Pakistan hostilities, has been taken even further by the forward-planning Bush gang, toward new strategies to combat terrorism that include the option of pre-emptive nuclear strikes in the interests of 'self-defence'. Yet for all the futuristic talk of these forward-planners, such as the 'son of Star Wars', the attacks of 11 September surely demonstrated in a terrifying way that willing groups do not need sophisticated weapons to cause agony; only a fanatical belief that some cause is a just one. Speaking of Star Wars, it is ironic that even the Death Star would have no defence against spores of anthrax, and even the citizens of Cloud City need oxygen.

Moving into the future with technologies capable of ending unnecessary suffering or magnifying it thousandfold, we need to dwell on our past and the shaky certainties it has given us. Some of the paradigms mentioned previously may not define humanity, but the greatest danger is surely that they could. This much is clear: as described above, despite the seeming 'unnature' of human nature, our historic tendency to divide into always-justified provincial camps, tribalism has been a consistent theme in human history. Needless to say, our globalised existence today means that the little holocausts previously wrought by discredited ideologies in Europe, or currently credible ideologies in Latin America or in the Middle East, are both tendencies and warnings for the big holocaust lurking around the corner. It is for this reason that American actions (and as I am myself American, I do not mean the actions of the populace!) have been centrally targeted here. It is merely an exemplar of what has gone on throughout history and that cannot continue. We are now in a position where continued consumption at current levels, an attack on Iraq or the justifications elites wrap themselves in could all spell 'general destruction'—nuclear, environmental, biological, and so on. And it is this we need to understand about the same old mentalities and new risks: risks to a particular region or group are today risks to our worldwide congregation. Let this point not be mistaken: the global threats created as a result of human factionalism simply cannot coexist with the parochialism which has thus far shaped so much of human history, and another sixty years similar to the last will assuredly realise the 'inverted utopia' we cannot imagine.

The time has come to take an intellectual Hippocratic Oath to unite those whom bravely, absurdly, stand against the void yet to be initiated. We may have come to the final page in the Book of Life, but it need not be written on A4, or even A4000 paper. That is entirely up to us, particularly us, who as intellectuals forge the ideas that will later come into cultural practice. Ideas were once the case with nuclear weapons, so can they be with disarmament; ideas were once the case with agribusiness, so can they be with sustainability; and ideas were even once the case with passports and 'spheres of influence', so can they be with social justice and globalisation that is not punitive and exclusive, but compassionate and inclusive. Our future is not one of terraced Heideggerian destiny, but a Borgesian 'garden of forking paths' depending on the multiplicity of choices lying before us.

Therefore it is not necessary to conclude with a message of fear but one of cautious hope. We are diverse writers associated with this journal; different ethnic backgrounds and nationalities, different colours of skin and of politics, different religions and sexualities, different wants and different needs. Yet we principally appear here as one in solidarity and encouragement of each other. It is this great chorus that can and must be carried toward the barrels of guns to prove 'that words are stronger than bullets', so those not yet born can know the dignity of being human; for 'if the man who places hope in the human condition is a fool, then he who gives up hope in the face of circumstances is a coward'.[36] These sentiments again belong to Camus, whose inspirational editorials for the Resistance newspaper *Combat* remain an example of the powerful effects created by the fusion of the lyrical and the political. But even more urgent—to us now—than his writings confronting the extreme historical moments of Nazi occupation, are his warnings of a final precipice reached by human divisiveness and human-made hazards, and pleas for solidarity by US 'enemies' to combat the final fall:

... our technical civilisation has just reached its greatest level of savagery. We will have to choose, in the more or less near future, between collective suicide and the intelligent use of our scientific conquests.... There can be no doubt that humanity is being offered its last chance ... we refuse to see anything in such grave news other than the need to argue more energetically in favour of a true international society, in which the great powers will not have superior rights over small and middle-sized nations, where such an ultimate weapon will be controlled by human intelligence rather than by the appetites and doctrines of various states.... Before the terrifying prospects now available to humanity, we see even more clearly that peace is the only goal worth struggling for. This is no longer a prayer but a demand to be made by all peoples to their governments—a demand to choose definitively between hell and reason.[37]

Endnotes

1. Franz Kafka, "The End", in *The Trial* (New York: Shocken Books, 1992), pp. 225–6.
2. Cited in Joshua Cooper Ramo, "'Inside The Hunt'", *Time* 158/16 (October 8, 2001), online at: https://web.archive.org/web/20011002133131/https://time.com/time/magazine/article/0,9171,1101011008-176921,00.html.
3. Howard Zinn, "What is Radical History?", in *The Politics of History* (Boston: Beacon Press, 1970), p. 35.
4. *Ibid.*, pp. 35–56.
5. See Samuel Huntington, *The Clash of Civilizations and the Remaking of World Order* (London: Touchstone, 1998), and Francis Fukuyama, *The End of History and the Last Man* (New York: Free Press, 1992).
6. John McNeill, *Something New Under the Sun: An Environmental History of the Twentieth Century* (London: Penguin, 2000), pp. 15–16.
7. For texts dealing with this issue see Susan George, *The Debt Boomerang* (London: Pluto Press, 1992), especially, pp 93-110, and Naomi Klein, *No Logo* (London: Flamingo, 2000), cited p. 228.
8. Michael McKinley, "Triage: A Survey of the 'New Inequality' as Combat Zone", originally presented at the 42nd Annual Convention of the International Studies Association, 23 February 2001, p. 53. For a copy of this text, please refer to the author at Michael.McKinley@anu.edu.au. Published, as amended, under the title "Triage: A survey of casualties in the neo-liberal combat zone," in Michael McKinley, *Economic Globalisation as Religious War: Tragic Convergence* (London and New York: Routledge, 2007), pp. 38-57, where the quotation appears on p. 56.
9. Joseph Heller, *Catch-22* (London: Vintage, 1994), pp. 62–3.
10. Albert Camus, "Letter to an Algerian Militant", in *Resistance, Rebellion, and Death* (New York: Vintage, 1988), p. 129.
11. Ian Kershaw, *The Nazi Dictatorship* (London: Arnold, 2000), p. 270, and Bertolt Brecht, "The Resistible Rise of Arturo Ui", in *Plays: Three* (London: Methuen Drama, 1992), p. 214.
12. Günther Anders, "The Nuclear Threat". Private translation from German.
13. For information on domestic terrorism cultivated in America, see George Monbiot's comment 'Backyard Terrorism', *Guardian*, 30 October 2001, and John Pilger's article in the *New Statesman*, 19 October 2001. For details of the enormous quantities of cocaine (not to mention heroin and other narcotics) distributed through CIA and US government contractors supporting the Contras in 1980s Latin America, see Peter Dale Scott and Jonathan Marshall, *Cocaine Politics: Drugs, Armies and the CIA in Central America* (London: University of California Press, 1998), especially pp. 23–124.
14. Artistic prescience is evident in Orwell's writing but is certainly not limited to him. For example, consider Frederic Manning's 1929 preface to his First World War novel, *The Middle Parts of Fortune*: 'War is waged by men; not by beasts, or by gods. It is a peculiarly human activity. To call it a crime is to miss at least half its significance; it is also a punishment of a crime. That raises a moral question, the kind of problem with which the present age is disinclined to deal. Perhaps some future attempt to provide a solution for it may prove more astonishing than the last.'
15. George Orwell, *1984* (Finland: Kustannusoakeyhtio Otava Keuruu, 1974), p. 220.

16 T S Eliot, "The Fire Sermon", in *The Waste Land* (New York: Harvest Books, 1962), p. 38. René Magritte's *The Human Condition I*, painted in 1933, is currently held in the Spaak Collection in France.
17 Albert Camus, "Banquet Speech", The Nobel Prize, 10 December 1957, online at: www.nobelprize.org/prizes/literature/1957/camus/speech/.
18 These quotations, taken from Conrad's *Heart of Darkness* (New York: Bantam Books, 1981), can be found on pp. 131, 132, 84, 83, 120, 125, 82, 122, and 125, respectively.
19 *Ibid.*, pp 105, 118, and vii, respectively.
20 Camus, "Banquet speech", *op cit.*
21 For further details of discontinued aid and Pakistan's sealing of its 1,400-mile border with Afghanistan (on 27 September) at US insistence, see Noam Chomsky, *9-11* (New York: Seven Stories Press, 2001), p. 94. In a 30 December lecture in New Delhi, Chomsky also cites international human rights activists' comments on Northern Alliance raping and pillaging of areas under their control as '"the worst time in Afghanistan's history", with vast destruction, mass rapes and other atrocities, and tens of thousands killed'. Buttressing his assessment that as US proxy forces fighting in Afghanistan, the primarily Tajik Northern Alliance were essentially indistinguishable from their primarily Pashtun Taliban and al-Qaida ethnic enemies, Chomsky cites the new Tajik Justice Minister as stating 'that the basic structures of sharia [sic] law as instituted by the Taliban would remain in force, though "there will be some changes from the time of the Taliban. For example, the Taliban used to hang the victim's body in public for four days. We will only hang the body for a short time, say 15 minutes"'. Also, 'Judge Ahamat Ullha Zarif added that some new location would be found for the regular public executions, not the Sports Stadium. Adulterers, both male and female, would still be stoned to death, Zarif said, "but we will use only small stones"', online at: https://chomsky.info/20020201/. Agents of Kafka's court indeed.
22 *Not in My Name*, produced by Platform Films in association with TV Choice, London.
23 "Long after the air raids, bomblets bring more death", *Guardian*, 28 January 2001; "Afghanistan littered with 14,000 unexploded bomblets, says UN", *The Guardian*, 23 March 2002. As of 6 February 2002, Professor Marc Herold of the University of New Hampshire 'conservatively' estimates that Afghan civilian deaths are between 3,000 and 3,600, Marc Herold, "Afghan Killing Fields," letter to *The Guardian*, 13 February 2002, https://www.theguardian.com/theguardian/2002/feb/13/guardianletters3.
24 For the most reliable details on the current state of Afghanistan, see www.rawa.org, especially 'Reports on Afghanistan'.
25 Paul Foot in *Not in My Name*, op cit.
26 For details on the continuing refugee crisis see the UNHCR website; figures taken from 'Afghanistan: returns high, funds low' in http://www.unhcr.ch.
27 For an example of the line taken by the US media on the war in Afghanistan, see the cover story "Why they hate us" in *Newsweek* (15 October 2001). A representative quotation from this article is as follows: 'We stand for freedom and they hate it. We are rich and they envy us. We are strong and they resent this. All of which is true', p. 22.
28 Will Hutton, "Time to stop being America's lap-dog", *Observer*, 17 February 2002.
29 "Amnesty dismisses new US line on captives", *Guardian*, 8 February 2002.
30 John Pilger, "The Real Story Behind America's War", *The Mirror*, 17 December 2001.
31 *Ibid.* For further details of the situation in Iraq a year after invasion, see John Keegan, *The Iraq War* (London: Hutchinson, 2004).
32 *The Trial, op. cit.*, pp. 208-10.

33 Andrew Simms, "Going Down In History," *New Internationalist* 342 (Jan./Feb. 2002), https://newint.org/features/2002/01/05/history.
34 John Vidal, "Antarctica sends 500 billion tonne warning of the effects of climate change", *The Guardian*, 20 March 2002, online at: www.theguardian.com/environment/2002/mar/20/globalwarming.physicalsciences.
35 For Bush's quoted position on Iraq, see www.msnbc.com/news/777661.asp. For a copy of Rumsfeld's "Nuclear Posture Review", see https://fas.org/sgp/news/2002/01/npr-foreword.pdf. This document ominously states the need for '[d]esired capabilities for nuclear weapons systems in flexible, adaptable strike plans [that] include options for variable and reduced yields, high accuracy, and timely employment. These capabilities would help deter enemy use of WMD or limit collateral damage, should the United States have to defeat enemy WMD capabilities', cited in David A. Koplow, *Death by Moderation: The U.S. Military's Quest for Usable Weapons* (Cambridge: Cambridge University Press, 2010), p. 116.
36 Albert Camus, *Between Hell and Reason: Essays from the Resistance Newspaper Combat 1944–1947* (Hanover: Wesleyan University Press, 1991), pp. 140.
37 From "On the bombing of Hiroshima", *ibid.*, pp. 110–11.

16. 'It became Necessary to Destroy the Town to Save it': The United States Between Liberalism and Warfare before Donald Trump

Part I: Year 90: Liberalism on Wars, Wars on Liberalism

> Let every nation know, whether it wishes us well or ill, that we shall pay any price, bear any burden, meet any hardship, support any friend, oppose any foe to assure the survival and success of liberty.
>
> - President John F. Kennedy, 1961 Inaugural Speech

> The Good Book says that in the millennium days, swords shall be turned into plowshares and spears into pruning hooks. We are helping to hasten the glad time by selling cannon balls to heal the sick.
>
> - First Private Arms Dealer, Bannerman & Sons

As an ideology, liberalism is under the greatest assault since its triumph in western Europe and the United States after World War Two. In every country, illiberal forces on the far right and far left seek to offer their solutions to contemporary problems—from immigration and internationalism to terrorism and armed conflict. In the United States, the brash TV star with no political experience, Donald J. Trump, was, astonishingly, elected the 45th president. How had it come to this? This article will address this question by taking the long view. It will argue that contesting these populist challenges by perpetuating myths about liberal democracy, or by subscribing to myths, is counter-productive. The hypocrisies of liberalism are well-known to its enemies but are less familiar to its friends. Nowhere is this 'double think' more apparent than in matters of liberalism and warfare.[1] It does no good to the latter to neglect these troubling aspects of liberalism's frequent recourse to force—as exemplified by the United States in what is sometimes called the 'American century'—as this article will argue. In particular, the subject covered will be the too-frequent misfire between liberal democratic theory and aggressive American practice in the 20th century.[2]

By way of example, 'Year 90' refers to this year's ninetieth anniversary of the Kellogg-Briand Pact (sometimes called the Pact of Paris), a treaty first signed on 27 August 1928 and brought into force just under a year later, on 24 July 1929. It was on account of the bold foray into international law with which his name is associated that Frank Kellogg received the Nobel Peace Prize later in 1929, the same year that the 'sense-making crisis' of the World Economic Crisis (or Great Depression) first broke in Wall Street. Ratified with one dissenting vote in the

American Senate (85-1), and still in force in the United States today, the Kellogg-Briand Pact explicitly mandated the resolution of inter-state conflicts by "pacific means". It was adopted by liberal democracies to outlaw war forever, or in the words of the treaty, to "condemn recourse to war for the solution of international controversies, and renounce it as an instrument of national policy in their relations with one another".[3] Fully 62 countries eventually signed the Kellogg-Briand Pact, including every principal combatant of the Second World War; indeed, the State Department still lists this as a treaty currently in force between Iraq, Afghanistan and the United States.[4] Yet what is so strikingly symbolic about this Pact—coming as it did a decade after the 'war to end all wars'—is not the politics causing its 'official' military disregard by the Japanese in 1931, the Italians in 1935, the Germans, British and French in 1939, and the United States in 1941, but rather the noble yet insincere attempt to formally renounce war forever. Writing of this interwar period in his classic study, *The Twenty Years Crisis*, E.H. Carr concluded: "The fact that the utopian dishes prepared during these years at Geneva proved unpalatable to most of the principal governments concerned was a symptom of the growing divorce between theory and practice".[5]

With the sometimes-vexed relationship between liberal theory and practice in mind, a closer look at that year bisecting the two world wars, 1928, is merited. In the very same year that French Foreign Minister Aristide Briand and American Secretary of State Frank Kellogg agreed upon this treaty, with early British compliance, the United States sent 2,000 Marines to Nicaragua in its continuing pursuit of literal 'gunboat democracy' in the Caribbean; Britain was assisting Nadir Shah in Afghanistan's misnamed 'civil war'; and French colonials forcefully re-established control of Syria following the 'Druze Rebellion', while simultaneously repressing Indochina to such a degree that the Vietnamese Nationalist Party (VNQDD, later to become Ho Chi Minh's Communists) was secretly formed, launching an uprising in 1930 ending with the beheading of 12 of its leaders by the French military.[6] Significantly, the principal initiators of the Pact—France and the United States—were responsible for the most bloodshed in the year that international conflict was supposedly relegated to a thing of the past.

Given that the conclusion of WWI found self-determination, justice and freedom to be an intrinsic right of peoples, the "utopian" dishes served up during this time appear strikingly unpalatable for those 'unpeople' not allowed to dine with elites.[7] Nevertheless, as Woodrow Wilson explained in an important speech in 1919 regarding the Versailles Treaty, those at the High Table assumed a degree of benevolence, and would be willing to throw some scraps to the colonies, if only rhetorically: "The men who sat around the table in Paris knew that the time had come when the people were no longer going to consent to live under masters, but were going to live the lives that they chose themselves, to live under such government as they chose themselves to erect."[8] In a century where more than 100 million people, mostly non-combatants, died from warfare, the nobility of Wilson's sentiments and that of the Kellogg-Briand Pact need no elaboration. But the aforementioned 'insincerity' needs further consideration: for only in a world of tragic irony and maddening paradox can conquerors talk of ending wars.

In the face of this evident contradiction, this Orwellian 'double think', an important question must be posed: how central are cold, warm (or 'low-intensity') and hot wars to the practices of liberalism since World War One—let alone their logistical troupe of armaments industries and training bases, government subsidies and export markets, and all their attendant ramifications? In short, what challenge does the 'manufacturing of warfare' by liberal democracies pose to Carr's distinction between theory and practice? Does it demonstrate his "growing divorce", or highlight liberalism's by-implication 'double thought'? Or does this challenge instead, more controversially, imply that there was never *any* "divorce" in the first place; that what we understand as theories of liberalism might be somehow inextricable from political violence? This in turn may suggest that theory is not, in the end, the stuff of academic conferences and the 'classics' of liberal political philosophy, but perhaps the backrooms of bureaucratic institutions, related think-tanks, and what Antonio Gramsci famously called 'cultural hegemony'. By viewing the United States as a paragon of liberal democracy and inflating a few examples of its bellicose policies to the perhaps unworthy status of paradigms, I want to explore whether the word 'insincere' best characterises not only liberalism's interwar attempts at both 'positive' and 'negative' pacification; but furthermore, whether something altogether more concerning than 'insincerity' in the postwar world might underlie the practice of war. For as one of the preeminent artists and pacifists emerging from the First World War reminds us in his Prefatory Note to *The Middle Parts of Fortune*, also penned in 1928:

> War is waged by men; not by beasts, or by gods. It is a peculiarly human activity. To call it a crime against mankind is to miss at least half its significance; it is also the punishment of a crime. That raises a moral question, the kind of problem with which the present age is disinclined to deal. Perhaps some future attempt to provide a solution for it may prove to be even more astonishing than the last.[9]

In the foregoing attempt to understand this apparent praxis, we surely must first clarify these two main terms. First, in speaking of liberalism, as noted, the USA's model will be viewed as hegemonic. While this takes into account contributing paradigms as seemingly unrelated as the Kellogg-Briand Pact; or the strikingly consistent Monroe Doctrine formulated a century earlier, and the American

Civil War fought partly over the retention of slavery by a liberal democratic country, the emphasis will centrally encompass the current ascendant model of American liberalism as it has developed after 1945. Indeed, with a military presence in a large number of UN states and a recently announced annual defense budget now nearing $1 trillion, the United States' understanding of *laissez-faire* liberalism is a model for the developed world. For the rest, 90 developing countries are in the throes of World Bank and IMF 'structural adjustment' with its attendant debt and privatization; the 'military-industrial' complex warned against by President Eisenhower in 1961 remains the economic backbone of industrialised world exports, technology and budgets; and the creeping dissolution of welfare programmes and public expenditure in favour of monopolistic free enterprise proceeds apace, whereby insatiable multinational companies exploit labour and environment while free-floating capital turns over incredible profits.[10] This means that a majority of the 100 largest Gross Domestic Profits reside with private companies, not nation-states; for example, 'the Ford Motor Company [is] now bigger than the economy of South Africa and General Motors [is] wealthier than Denmark'.[11] Of course, when speaking of liberalism, we must understand this term to be a *particular permutation* of 'classical' liberal ideology referred to alternatively as 'neo-liberalism', 'globalisation', or the French word for the latter, 'Americanisation'. However, unlike many strident voices asserting that this phenomenon has become notable only relatively recently, I here argue that Cold War planner George Kennan's view has been a remarkably consistent feature of American liberal praxis since he wrote these words for policy formulation in the late 1940s:

> We have 50% of the world's wealth, but only 6.3% of its population. In this situation, our real job in the coming period is to devise a pattern of relationships which permit us to maintain this position of disparity. To do so, we have to dispense with all sentimentality...we should cease thinking about human rights, the raising of living standards and democratisation.[12]

For the second term, war, we will adopt and marginally alter Clausewitz's tripartite understanding of warfare as: organised violence by the state against an adversary; the establishment and management of armies as militaristic expressions of a government's interests; and finally, people, both as necessary fodder—that is, soldiers—and as innocent parties to be spared wartime tribulations as much as possible. It is possible to update these three points through a sketch of the United States' army of 'Contras' fighting the Nicaraguan Sandinista government in the 1980s. In this case, violence was initiated by a third-party state directing a rebellion *against* the government—hence the name 'contras', Spanish for 'against'—thus the adversary *was* the state. This proxy US war against the whiff of socialism was fought not by an army as Clausewitz understood it, but by a recruited group of irregulars—similar in this respect to the *mujahideen* in Afghanistan at the same time, later to coalesce around Osama bin Laden and Al-Qaida—not through an agency of any state as such; but rather, a privately funded (in this case, through the illegal sale of arms and drugs by American citizens and empowered civil servants[13]) consortium of mercenaries and regional militants recruited to advance US interests—a Blackwater-type organisation with close links to government elites long before the invasion of Iraq in 2003.[14] Finally, as roughly 95% percent of casualties in modern war are now civilians, the easy distinction between soldiers and non-combatants can no longer be maintained. In Nicaragua, as with the bombing of al-Jazeera in Afghanistan, bridges in Serbia and the al-Shifa pharmaceutical factory in Sudan, civilian targets can be no longer profitably understood as separate from combat objectives. Thus, for instance, despite characterisation of minimized 'collateral damage' by 'precision weapons', in truth only 7% of armaments dropped on Iraq in 1991 had 'smart' guidance systems. Due to these considerations, warfare is understood here as *organised violence supported by an interested party with the intention of killing large numbers of people to achieve their political aims.* Naturally, this description embraces terrorism of all forms (excepting that of 'lone-wolf' individuals), as well as Clausewitz's more traditional understanding of uniformed armies facing off against each other on the battlefield. As a leading military scholar has argued: "The whole of late twentieth century strategic thought rests on the idea that war is an instrument of policy; and indeed Clausewitz's main claim to fame comes from his being the first to base the theory of war on that proposition."[15]

Throughout, a close focus will be maintained on the argument that liberalism must acknowledge and resist its baser instincts—with our astonishing century past providing the backdrop. Perhaps the most abiding of these hypocrisies, no less so than 90 years ago, is the 'utopian' notion that liberalism and militarism are incompatible. In contrast, I want to argue here that *the functioning of liberalism is predicated upon war and the institutions of war.* Consequently, war remains intrinsic to liberal democracy's practice in execution. So-called universal doctrines and ideologies, it seems, can feed upon perceived enemies in much the same frightful way as do the more exclusionary ideologies of class or nation. By this I mean that the praxis of liberalism is not only financially predicated upon war (40 cents of every tax dollar in contemporary America goes to the Pentagon),[16] but politically and culturally reliant upon warfare as well. Thus, it is these aspects of liberalism and war, particularly the latter, of central concern in the following overview. This emphasis will not assert that the near-camp conditions of people working for a subsistence living at Export Processing Zones in, say, Indonesia, are involved in war in the manner understood by Clausewitz. In fact, this economic argument has previously been advanced with conviction and eloquence by Michael McKinley's provocative paper, *Triage*, where he points out that economic strangulation need not be separated from

> a revolution, or a military defeat and subsequent occupation... neither metaphor, nor simile, of war, but war itself.... If 100 million have been killed in the formal wars of the twentieth century, why are they to be privileged in comprehension over the annual toll of five million children from Structural Adjustment programmes since 1982? Put another way, short of nuclear holocaust, what destruction and death could war bring to sub-Saharan Africa that the World Bank and IMF have not already brought?[17]

Further to this argument regarding the kinship of war and liberalism, consider the case of Indonesia, where it is possible to say with certainty that the liberal West supported the Suharto dictatorship in enforcing highly dystopian conditions and continuing domestic repression visited upon that blighted country after 1965. And 'supported' is meant in every sense of the word: from the 5,000 names of PKI (Indonesian Communists) given to the Indonesian military by the CIA in a manner anticipating Operation Phoenix in Vietnam, to naval support by British battleships and the fortune in Western armaments transferred to the junta for more than 3 decades, allowing Suharto to retire with literally billions in the bank.[18] Given the historical need for the existence of enemies in United States politics, from 'commies', 'international terrorists' and 'narcotraffickers' to 'rogue states' and 'axises of evil', little needs to be said about liberalism and war through the lens of politics. In this view, the world is merely witnessing an acceleration of this political pattern after the terrorist crimes of September 11th, with Vice President Dick Cheney initially warning that '40 to 50 countries' might be the targets of American attack, not to mention a new strategic willingness to use functional nuclear weapons. As this has been amply documented elsewhere, I will instead examine the cultural mores allowing such policies in America, which incredibly regarded Indonesia as a 'moderate' liberal democratic state, despite the murder of hundreds of thousands of civilians by death squads and government-sanctioned paramilitaries in 1965 and 1966.

Therefore, this argument attempts to go even further than Günther Anders' superb use of the Vietnam War and the corresponding destruction of four countries (North and South Vietnam, Laos and Cambodia) as a model in the necessary production of war itself:

> The belief that today's aggressors wish to crown their aggression with victories is naïve. To win wars is no longer the aim of those who are eager to wage wars—at least not for those who make the prosperity of their country depend upon their armament industry. What American industry demands, in order to guarantee the continuation of its arms production, and, thereby, the continuation of the nation's prosperity, is to *have* wars. Wars are the basis of the industrialist's power. If this basis collapsed—and it would collapse through the victorious conclusion of a war—this power would be defeated. In other words: In the present stage of capitalism, *wars as such are victories*. Victories in the old-fashioned sense of the word, would amount to defeats, since they would promote a situation in which the further production of weapons (the prerequisite of power and prosperity) would become superfluous. What the U.S. desires is the smooth continuity and escalation of the sale and consumption of armaments, a continuity and escalation just as regular and just as reliable as that of the sale and consumption of bread or gasoline. This means that what is desired is a war which will never end, which will survive and which cannot be killed. No wonder that those of our fellow men who criticize and try to subvert this situation are called and treated as subversives.[19]

More forcefully than his philosophical contemporaries, Anders finds war to be a central pillar buttressing that Athenian temple of liberal democratic praxis. And that includes the preparation and desensitization of combatants sent to war in places from Southeast Asia to Iraq. An excerpt from a US pilot's conversation with a journalist in 1966 contains all the features of this desensitized, bureaucratized hatred characterizing so much of war fighting over the last half century:

> We sure are pleased with those backroom boys at Dow [Chemical Company, the manufacturer of napalm]. The original product wasn't so hot—if the gooks were quick they could scrape it off. So the boys started adding polystyrene—now it sticks like shit to a blanket. But then if the gooks jumped under water it stopped burning, so they started adding Willie Peter [WP—white phosphorus] so's to make it burn better. It'll burn even under water now. And just one drop is enough, it'll keep on burning right down to the bone so they die anyway of phosphorus poisoning.[20]

Two years later, as this pilot continued to do his work, USAF Major Chester I. Brown commented on the Vietnamese provincial capital, Ben Tre, carpet-bombed on 7 February 1968, that 'it became necessary to destroy the town to save it'. As this now-paradigmatic phrase is used for my title, it is important to pause over this exemplary statement made by a pilot and his commander with falling dominoes in the crosshairs, not indigenous people deserving those liberal ideals: freedom, justice, and equality.

Revealingly, American acceptance of these conditions imposed by the many hundreds of thousands of troops fighting in Indochina has remained a feature of debate ever since, where fallout from this war is threefold: 50,000 US military fatal casualties were sustained perhaps needlessly, it altered the American political landscape toward cynicism and distrust of government, and 20 years of conflict changed 'nothing' in the region. Rarely in the United States will one see a reference to the 3 million plus indigenous dead, to children still killed today by undetonated mines, or to the very fact that a sovereign country was invaded after the US sabotage of the 1954 Geneva Peace Accords for the unification of Vietnam. Much of this has been detailed in the indispensable *Manufacturing Consent*, where Noam Chomsky and Ed Herman argue that these omissions are a conscious decision by ideological gatekeepers in the media, whose major purpose is to "to inculcate and defend the economic, social, and political agenda of privileged groups that dominate the domestic society and the state. The media serve this purpose in many ways: through selection of topics, distribution of concerns, framing of issues, filtering of information, emphasis and tone, and by keeping debate within the bounds of acceptable premises."[21] In this view, it is the consistency of liberalism over time that is so striking, not the nefarious changes wrought by 'neo-liberalism' in more recent decades.

Further illustrating the cultural impact upon the flow of information by groups with a vested interest in war is the fact that, as of 1980, the US Air Force's Orwellian 'public information outreach' included, amongst other channels, 140 newspapers producing 690,000 copies weekly and 615,000 hometown news releases.[22] Perhaps more startlingly is the Church Committee's investigation of the CIA in the early 1970s, which found:

> The Central Intelligence Agency is now using several hundred American academics [note in report: administrators, faculty members and graduate students engaged in teaching] who, in addition to providing leads and, on occasion, making introductions for intelligence purposes, occasionally write books and other material to be used for propaganda purposes abroad .... These academics are located in over 100 American colleges, universities, and related institutes. At the majority of institutions, no one other than the individual concerned is aware of the CIA link. At the others, at least one university official is aware of the operational use of academics on his campus .... The CIA considers these operational relationships with the United States academic community as perhaps its most sensitive domestic area and has strict controls governing these operations.[23]

Finally, as regards vested interests, "the boys at Dow" is a reference to Dow Chemicals, a private firm which specialized in napalm for the US during the Vietnamese campaign. Far from atypical, as of 1990 Dow was not even amongst the top 100 global arms manufacturers. The list from that year reads like a Who's Who of private enterprise: Siemens, General Electric, Texas Instruments, Rolls Royce, FIAT, AT&T, Mitsubishi, Motorola, Toshiba, and NEC are all included; with IBM leading that year's profits with over $6 billion, while General Motors was the largest employer with 761,400 people. Although the United States' defense budget nearly equals the rest of the world combined, the private manufacture of weapons is a cultural phenomenon within liberal democracy itself, providing not only weapons for domestic use and foreign export and the aforementioned 'military-industrial complex', but also millions of jobs and accompanying security for workers and their families. As Frederic Pearson explains, this is not limited to governments, on one hand, or individuals on the other, but entire towns:

> because of this production, trade unions and interest groups gain a stake in the defense industry. Towns and cities come to depend on the payrolls, and national and local political officials play a role in promoting the industry, especially in the United States, where the Pentagon has followed a traditional policy of awarding contracts and facilities to nearly every country and congressional district.[24]

To be sure, much has changed since the time of the Kellogg-Briand Pact, when war critics labeled arms producers 'merchants of death'. But as the ninetieth year outlawing war passes unnoticed, and the law itself stays on the books but collects dust, perhaps a larger thesis is tenable for the all-too-frequently dystopian practices of contemporary liberalism: taking part in wars helps keep liberalism solvent.

Part II: From Idealism to Dystopia. American Conflict in the 21st Century: a Snapshot

> But for simpler souls, the evil of the present age is characterized by its effects, not by its causes. It is called the state, whether police or bureaucratic. Its proliferation everywhere on a variety of ideological pretexts make it a moral danger for all that is best in each of us, as does the insulting security it derives from mechanical and psychological methods of repression. In this sense, contemporary political society is contemptible, regardless of its content.
>
> - Albert Camus

> And I submit that nothing will be done until people of good will put their bodies and souls in motion.
>
> - Martin Luther King

On 12 June 2006, the media covered the endgame of three inmates at Guantánamo Bay, Cuba. They had finally escaped from the inferno of Camp I by way of suicide. Despite religious injunctions against self-harm, these men killed themselves after having been imprisoned for nearly 5 years without charge, without access to the outside world, and most of all, without hope of a trial. What made these men kill themselves? The following describes one-third of an average day (in this case, for detainee 063) at Camp X-Ray, the hellhole where these men hung themselves with their own bedding:

0001: Interrogation team was briefed on condition of the detainee's mental and physical state. Detainee's hands were cuffed at his sides to prevent him from conducted his prayer ritual.

0025: Lead begins berating detainee as coward and liar. Lead taped picture of 3 year old victim over detainees heart. Detainee is told he will never leave Cuba. Lead states that if he does not tell the truth, the interrogator will keep talking to him everyday until he does. Control orders detainee to sit up and pay attention. Control dripped a few drops of water on detainees [sic] head to keep him awake. Detainee struggles when water is dropped on his head. Detainee attempts to talk, but both control and lead scream over the detainee until he stops.

0120: Interrogators take a break and detainee listens to white noise. Detainee goes to bathroom and is exercised while hooded. Detainee returns to booth and continues to listen to white noise.

0140: Interrogators enter the booth and play cards while conducting a p/e [pride and ego] down. Detainee is told that we get paid to mess with him so we might as well play cards, a leisure he cannot participate in. Detainee is told to shut up and stay awake. At times detainee began to fall asleep and water was dripped on his head as he was ridiculed. White noise was playing in the background.

0330: Detainee was exercised and taken to the bathroom. Corpsman checks vitals and offers detainee water and food. Vitals are within normal range and detainee refuses water and food detainee is returned to booth and p/e down is continued [....]

1500: Detainee taken to bathroom and walked 10 minutes.

1630: Corpsman checks vitals—gives three bags of IV. Detainee was confronted with verses in Koran that state adding prohibitions not mentioned in the Koran is a sin. Detainee broke down crying and asking God for forgiveness, stating that he was with strangers. He still said that music was forbidden and stated that he could do nothing about the music that was played in the booth.
Detainee was shown photo of Al Masri and did not recognize him. Detainee asked to pray and was denied by the interrogator. Interrogator stated that the detainee would have to regain his honor before he would be allowed to pray.

1700: Detainee taken to bathroom and walked 10 minutes.

1800: Interrogation began, 3rd IV began [sic] finished. Theme of being able to read card Used [sic], detainee stated that he did not believe in card readers but he paid close attention to the reading stating that all the innocent spirits will haunt him in this life and the next one.

Forced feeding, refusal of religious rites, the use of 'white noise'—alongside sleep deprivation, physical abuse, dehumanisation, systematic sensory deprivation, all prominent elsewhere in the Secret Orcon Interrogation Log from 23 November 2002 to 11 January 2003[25]—evidently none of these constitute 'cruel and inhumane treatment', the standard commonly regarded as torture in standard international law. Abuse maybe. But not torture; in American jurisprudence, at least. Even children are subject to this rapacious form of 'interrogation': "Mohammed El Gharani, our client at Reprieve", wrote his solicitor that same day, Zachary Katznelson, on behalf of only one of the 460 'unpeople' held in Cuba by the United States, "was only 14 when he was seized in a mosque in Pakistan. He was only 15 when he arrived in Guantánamo Bay. Already twice this year he has tried to kill himself, once by hanging, once by slitting his wrists.'[26] But when listening to the mouth of the United States' then-Vice-President, the notorious Dick Cheney, you might be forgiven for thinking that suicide and attempts at self-harm are gestures of ingratitude: "They're living in the tropics ... They're well fed. They've got everything they could possibly want."[27] No doubt, such Orwellian double-thinkers are almost certainly beyond convincing. But they have not been able to convince the rest of the US, let alone the rest of the world, that 'war is peace'; at least, not yet.

But does anyone actually believe that the methods of torture put to use by the United States since 9/11 came from out of the blue? Just briefly consider the US Army training manual entitled AR 30-15, now more than a quarter century old. This how-to guide advocates both psychological techniques for interrogation (such as humiliation), and physical techniques for torture like "intrusion into Bodily Orifices":

The urethra is the most private hole. Forcibly shoving something up the slit in his penis can seem more penetrating than shoving a hard object up his ass. Any object can be used that is unbreakable, smooth without any sharp edges or jagged points that can cut or tear the delicate urethral lining, and of appropriate size. Toothbrush handles are perfect.[28]

One wonders, though, if those directing the infamous concentration camp on Cuban soil have convinced themselves of anything other than the value of "double think". For the official response to those suicides of 11 June 2006 could have been written by an ironist. The commandant, Naval Rear-Admiral Harry Harris, for example, resorted to good old-fashioned colonial language: "They have no regard for life, either ours or their own. I believe this was not an act of desperation, but an act of asymmetrical warfare waged against us": like a kind of victimless suicide attack for the *really* impoverished, executed by a bunch of savages.[29] The importance of these suicides was thus not, apparently, for the benefit of the three men from the Arabian Peninsula, intoned US Deputy Assistant Secretary of State for Public Diplomacy, Colleen Graffney; they were *actually* "a good PR move to draw attention".[30] Although naturally chained and largely protected from public view (forget, again, those images of orange-clad human shapes, hermetically sealed, or strapped down to a gurney)—as well as their families, friends, lawyers, and Amnesty International, for that matter—the men were nonetheless media-savvy 'unpeople'. Graffney's boss at the Pentagon, Donald Rumsfeld, could at least concede that:

We know that torture is not occurring there. We know that for a fact. We have enormously responsible people who are managing that situation. Literally hundreds of Members of the United States House of Representatives, the United States Senate, their staff members, journalists by the hundreds have been down there and seen the place. The International Committee of the Red Cross was in residence there for a period of years. They visited continuously. We see nothing, absolutely nothing from all of those various people who visit Guantanamo that even begins to represent the kind of information that these two or three rapporteurs who have never visited the place put out [....] The reality is that the terrorists have media committees. They are getting very clever at manipulating the media in the United States and in the capitals of the world. They know for a fact they can't win a single battle on the battlefields in the Middle East. They know the only place they can win a battle is in the capitol in Washington, D.C. by having the United States lose its will, so they consciously manipulate the media here to achieve their ends, and they're very good at it.[31]

In keeping with this snapshot, a second news example from the same day is no less appalling: a massacre of twenty-four unarmed Iraqis at Haditha in November 2005, including five women and four children, which finally makes the cover of *Time Magazine* on 12 June 2006. It seems the magazine had been withholding footage of the marines' 'kinetic operations' in an unarmed village, and its euphemistic deception by the American military hierarchy since, at least, March 2006. The whole affair, is the result of Kilo Company having "committed their crime in the worst possible place: outside the front door of a budding Iraqi journalist and human rights activist".[32] Had Taher Thabet been an activist without film, let alone been visible during this shooting of fish in a terrorised barrel by the 'stressed' killers—only recently returned from razing Falluja in a 2004/5 operation called "Hell House"—he would most likely be ignored or dead. Either way, his tale would not have reached the reluctant editors at *Time* which, now that the story is out, can somberly conclude in the story just quoted, "Thabet says his thoughts are mostly with the 24 who died. 'Nobody cares about what happens to ordinary Iraqis,' he says. They do now."[33] That, surely, remains debatable.

In terms of torture, a rather unusual companion "in solidarity with the suffering people" is the late Christopher Hitchens, ex-leftwing firebrand turned cheerleader for the American imperium. Note that examples of torture raised above are taken from *before* the mainstream media debate broke out over whether or not 'waterboarding' is torture. At this point, Hitchens threw his hat into the ring, claiming that waterboarding was largely an "enhanced interrogation technique". After subjecting himself to the procedure, in a subsequent article for *Vanity Fair*, tersely titled "Believe me, it's torture", Hitchens concluded:

You may have read by now the official lie about this treatment, which is that it 'simulates' the feeling of drowning. This is not the case. You feel that you are drowning because you are drowning—or, rather, being drowned, albeit slowly and under controlled conditions and at the mercy (or otherwise) of those who are applying the pressure. The 'board' is the instrument, not the method. You are not being boarded. You are being watered .... if waterboarding does not constitute torture, then there is no such thing as torture.[34]

Part III: A Second 'American Century' versus "People of Good Will"?

'We don't seek empires,' he snapped. 'We're not imperialistic. We never have been. I can't imagine why you'd even ask the question.'

- Donald Rumsfeld, 29 April 2003 interview

If we could love even those who have attacked us, and seek to understand why they have done so, what then would be our response? Yet if we meet negativity with negativity, rage with rage, attack with attack, what then will be the outcome? There are the questions that are placed before the human race today. They are questions that we have failed to answer for thousands of years. Failure to answer them now could eliminate the need to answer them at all.

- The Dalai Lama on invading of Afghanistan

"And yet, despite the powerful reasons for pessimism given us by our experience in the first half of the twentieth century, events in its second half have been pointing in a very different and unexpected direction', writes Francis Fukuyama in the conclusion to his first chapter in *The End of History and the Last Man*: '[the world] has gotten better in certain distinct ways .... Authoritarian dictatorships of all kinds, both on the Right and the Left, have been collapsing .... [their core] weakness, so massive and unexpected, suggests that the pessimistic lessons about history that our century supposedly taught us need to be rethought from the beginning."[35] Fukuyama's book is remarkably dated after less than twenty-five years. A chart of Liberal Democracies Worldwide in 1990 claims that, for example, Nicaragua then had a liberal democracy, as did Indonesia. Given the postwar American covert involvement in these countries, it is precisely these hypocrisies that must be confronted in honest accountings of liberal praxis. Aside from the hubris of Fukuyama's arguments, smacking as it does of a Western self-congratulatory zeal in a world more authoritarian (depending upon definition) than ever before, the most notable aspects of the text are its omissions; namely virtually nothing on the origins of capitalism, neo/liberalism, environmentalism, international organisations, globalisation, Majority/Minority world dichotomies, and so on. Given that Fukuyama's triumphalist *The End of History and the Last Man* was produced under the auspices of RAND, a right-wing think tank established by the US Air Force after WWII, I see no reason to conclude that any of these trends have ended or even decreased, particularly after September 11th. As such, the United States is exempt from Fukuyama's considerations, except as an implicit paradigm to be followed, not as an authoritarian actor abroad, and increasingly at home.

A good example is provided by Philippe Sands' insightful *Lawless World*. For Sands, the invasion of Iraq was not only "a mistake of historic proportions"; it was much worse than that: "It is a war in which tens of thousands of people have died for an outcome which remains, to put it at its most generous, of uncertain consequence against a background of dubious intelligence and flawed legal reasoning". This leads Sands to conclude: "Those most closely associated with the initiation of recent events in Iraq may also want to avoid holidays in those countries that have criminalized the planning, preparation or conduct of aggressive war."[36] Fukuyama may have distanced himself from the Iraq War, but ideas are powerful things. And his set may be said to have kick-started 'neo-conservatism', which reached its apogee with the 1997 founding of the "Project for a New American Century", a think-tank catapulting most of the Bush Administration's ideologues into power: Perle, Libby, Khalizad, Rumsfeld, Wolfowitz, Cheney, Armitage, Cohen, Abrams, Fukuyama and John Bolton. Their six-year campaign to invade Iraq, of course, finally succeeded on 20 March 2003. Victorious in the battle of ideas, at least in the domestic, mainstream media, PNAC has turned these ideas into a bloodsoaked reality over the last fifteen years.

With American troops still stationed in Iraq, it is fashionable these days to claim that the Iraq War has been an unmitigated disaster. Clearly, those who never supported rubbishing international law for a needless war in the first place have been vindicated in virtually all of their predictions. But has it all really been so bad for the protagonists of this conflict? Put another way, the most disastrous thing that could have befallen the invaders was to actually be greeted with Iraqi flowers; to have occupied a peaceful country which, as the neo-conservatives never tired of predicting, helped liberalism to flourish across the Middle East. Naturally, more than 4,000 British and American soldiers would not have died, nor many more thousands critically wounded; an important political consideration for our rulers. And hundreds of thousands of Iraqis would not have died, nor millions displaced internally and abroad. But more importantly for the 'liberators', had peace really followed the three weeks' war, could Paul Bremer have single-handedly rewritten the Iraqi Constitution to allow for an unparallel neo/liberal fire-sale of nationalised Iraqi industries? Or similarly, consider the 2009 Status of Forces agreement, essentially allowing United States troops to be stationed in numerous, enormous bases indefinitely? With the publication of a book entitled *The Destruction of Cultural Heritage in Iraq* exactly five years after the invasion, it should surprise no one that oil may have had something to do with the Iraq War as well: as Baghdad burned and was looted of its priceless artifacts, US soldiers were hastily sent to guard two of Iraq's 57 ministries; namely, the Interior Ministry and the Oil Ministry. For the rest, Donald Rumsfeld phrased the Unites States government's position with lapidary precision: "Stuff happens".[37]

To press this case a little further, how about the no-bid 'reconstruction' and 'security' contracts given out to Bush Administration cronies, ranging from Halliburton and Bechtel to Blackwater and yes, even British Petroleum (BP)? The latter, the multinational corporation first opening up Iraqi oil in 1935 under a League of Nations mandated British-French 'condominium' in Iraq, also gained some spoils from the invasion, as officially announced on 30 June 2008.[38] For many, this demonstrated that an overriding impetus for the invasion of Iraq was over oil. Yet ex-Chairman of the Federal Reserve, Alan Greenspan, had already stated months earlier: "I am saddened that it is politically inconvenient to acknowledge what everyone knows: the Iraq war is largely about oil".[39] Indeed, fully three years and a half years before that, one of the central architects of the Iraq War, Paul Wolfowitz, had claimed that "for reasons that have a lot to do with the US government bureaucracy, we settled on the one issue that everyone could agree on: weapons of mass destruction". The reason a *casus belli* was needed of course, was helpfully articulated by Wolfowitz in terms of an alleged 'Axis of Evil': "Let's look at it simply. The most important difference between North Korea and Iraq is that economically, we just had no choice in Iraq. The country swims on a sea of oil."[40]

No less significant was the response by BP. Acutely aware of Iraq's "sea of oil', let alone their being frozen out of oil exploration by Saddam's nationalised cash-cow before the war, the then-head honcho at BP, Lord Browne, asserted: "We have let it be known that the thing we would like to make sure, if Iraq changes regime, is that there should be a level playing field for the selection of oil companies to go in there if they're needed to do the work there".[41] Fortunately for BP and its shareholders, record profits have followed the Iraq War—although still not a patch on Exxon Mobil's $11.68 billion profits after the Iraq War. The latter represented the largest quarterly profit by a US firm in history in the second quarter of 2008; working out to roughly $1,500 profit per second over May, June and July 2008.[42] Thus, at the very least, the war has not been a total disaster for everyone. Think of it this way: in a microcosm of the true cost of war—Joseph Stiglitz estimated the cost of the Iraq War at $3 trillion, or roughly the equivalent of 15 years of feeding, vaccinating, clothing, and educating the globe—the world has paid for this liberal warfare with impending recession, while every major oil company given 'no-bid contracts' in Iraq has, quite simply, never had it so good.

Ranged against these torturers, warmongers and merchants of death stand those "forces of goodwill" that Martin Luther King, Jr. called upon to encourage the United States to practice the liberalism toward its own black population that it regularly preached to the world:

> True nonviolent resistance is not unrealistic submission to evil power. It is rather a courageous confrontation of evil by the power of love, in the faith that it is better to be the recipient of violence than the inflictor of it, since the latter only multiplies the existence of violence and bitterness in the universe, while the former may develop a sense of shame in the opponent, and thereby bring about a transformation and change of heart.[43]

The time for a head count of "people of good will" is long past. It must be admitted that, in the opening years of the twenty-first century, the self-interested, the careless, and the powerful have never had it so good; have never had such control over humanity's past (propaganda), present (the 'corporatocracy'[44]), or future (resources, development, 'full spectrum dominance'… the list seems endless). In this age, unsurprisingly, intellectual depression or studied indifference, tell-all mysticism or postmodern relativism—in short, despair or disengagement—are popular political responses within the Minority World. I have argued elsewhere that our species' appropriation of functions historically borne by the inexplicable or supernatural is our greatest threat faced today. For me, these extend, but are not limited to, abilities to create forms of life from GM seeds to human life, as well as the ability to destroy all life through various forms of environmental, biological, or nuclear destruction.[45] This may sound a philosophical point, but as the renowned philosopher of history, R.G. Collingwood, had it: 'The chief business of twentieth century philosophy is to reckon with twentieth century history'.[46] For modernity has outgrown all but the most recent past, and consigned the rest to an antiquity only drawn upon as precursors. So we must ask: What good are liberal democratic systems to victims of basic persecution? What use is the 'end of history' for the 10,000 persons who cannot even get through the end of the day, every day, because of starvation and preventable diseases in an otherwise fat and healthy world? And finally, What use are the values and traditions accumulated throughout our liberal, Manichean past if the future holds the serious prospect of a comprehensive end?

Unfortunately, brevity has mandated only the barest inquiry into what Susan George has called "Manufacturing Ideology". Indeed, it is George's application of 'cultural hegemony' to postwar liberalism that was inspirational to the construction of my initial argument: that liberalism as we understand it today is inextricable from the 'massification of militarism' in the political, economic, and cultural spheres. Moreover, George is right to find that the latter has facilitated the former two, and although she emphasises the cornering of discourse by the "Rule of the Right" within liberalism, this is eminently transferable to the cultural manufacture of warfare and torture. In her paper "Winning the War of Ideas", George argues that the impetus toward cultural hegemony was initiated by a small clique of postwar 'neo-liberals' establishing think-tanks, publications and institutions which have increasingly come to dominate the boundaries of debate: "Neo-liberals understood, however, that to transform the economic, political and social landscape they first had to change the intellectual and psychological one."[47] And change it they have, bastardising Enlightenment notions of liberalism, replacing them with murderous concepts of justice for the already free; opening the greatest growth of inequality between strong and weak in history. But I must ask, how is this 'neo-liberalism' substantially different from Kennan's strategy? Is 'neo-liberalism', in fact, not just an intensification of a trend far reaching back far beyond our already astonishing postwar decades?

Endnotes

1. As a reminder: of the term itself: '*Doublethink* means the power of holding two contradictory beliefs in one's mind simultaneously, and accepting both of them. The Party intellectual knows in which direction his memories must be altered; he therefore knows that he is playing tricks with reality; but by the exercise of *doublethink* he also satisfies himself that reality is not violated. The process has to be conscious, or it would not be carried out with sufficient precision, but it also has to be unconscious, or it would bring with a feeling of falsity and hence of guilt. *Doublethink* lies at the very heart of Ingsoc, since the essential act of the Party is to use conscious deception while retaining the firmness of purpose that goes with complete honesty. To tell deliberate lies while genuinely believing in them, to forget any fact that has become inconvenient, and then when it becomes necessary again, to draw it back from oblivion for just so long as it is needed, to deny the existence of objective reality and all the while to take account of the reality which one denies—all this is indispensably necessary…in our society, those who have the best knowledge of what is happening are also those who are furthest from seeing the world as it is. In general, the greater the understanding, the greater the delusion: the more intelligent, the less sane.' George Orwell, *1984* (Finland: Kustannusoakeyhtio Otava Keuruu, 1974), p. 220.
2. For a good account on the development of liberalism in the 20th century United States domestically, H.W. Brands, *The Strange Death of American Liberalism* (London: Yale University Press, 2001).
3. The full text of the Kellogg-Briand Pact is available online at: http://wwi.lib.byu.edu/index.php/Treaty_Providing_for_the_Renunciation_of_War_as_an_Instrument_of_National_Policy (all websites last accessed 2 March 2020).
4. https://www.state.gov/wp-content/uploads/2020/02/249-Kellogg-Briand-Treaty.pdf.
5. E.H. Carr, *The Twenty Years' Crisis 1919-1939* (London: Papermac, 1995), p. 31.
6. George Childs Kohn, *Dictionary of Wars* (New York: Checkmark Books, 1999).
7. Mark Curtis, *Unpeople* (London: Verso, 2004).
8. Woodrow Wilson's 'Pueblo Speech' in 1919 in Richard D. Heffner, ed., *A Documentary History of the United States* (New York: Penguin, 1991), p. 251.
9. Frederic Manning, *The Middle Parts of Fortune* (London. Penguin Books, 1990), p. xvi
10. For a robust defence of this position, see Paul L. Atwood, *War and Empire: The American Way of Life* (New York: Pluto Press, 2010), pp. 168ff.
11. John Pilger, *The New Rulers of the World* (London: Verso, 2002), p. 5.
12. *Ibid.*, p. 98.
13. For details on US governmental drug-trafficking to fund the Contras, see the stunning revelations in Peter Dale Scott and Jonathan Marshall's archival study *Cocaine Politics: Drugs, Armies, and the CIA in Latin America* (London: University of California Press, 1998).
14. For the paradigmatic instance of this nexus in the postwar world, for instance, see Thomas Merton's contemporaneous account of the Vietnam War for 1968, "War and the Crisis of Language" and "The Vietnam War: An Overwhelming Atrocity" and "Note for *Ave Maria* ('Non-Violence Does Not . . . Cannot . . . Mean Passivity')" in Thomas Merton, *Passion for Peace: The Social Essays*, ed. William H. Shannon (New York: Crossroad, 1995), pp. 300ff.
15. Martin van Creveld, *The Transformation of War* (New York: The Free Press, 1991), pp. 36-42ff., quoted pp. 160-1.
16. Pilger, p. 130.

17   Michael McKinley, *"Triage:* A Survey of the 'New Inequality' as Combat Zone", originally presented at the 42nd Annual Convention of the International Studies Association, 23/02/2001 and published, as amended, under the title "Triage: A survey of casualties in the neo-liberal combat zone," in Michael McKinley, *Economic Globalisation as Religious War: Tragic Convergence* (London and New York: Routledge, 2007), pp. 38-57, where quotations appear on p. 56.
18   See, for example, Noam Chomsky on American involvement with Sukarno's overthrow in Indonesia, *Year 501: The Conquest Continues* (London: Black Rose Books, 1993), pp. 122ff.
19   Günther Anders, "Victims of Aggression" in Ken Coates, ed., *Essays on Socialist Humanism* (Nottingham: Spokesman Books, 1972), p. 159.
20   Noam Chomsky, *The Backroom Boys* (London: Fontana, 1973), p. 23. The quotation was taken from Philip Jones Griffiths, *Vietnam Inc.* (New York: Collier Books; London: Collier-Macmillan, 1971).
21   Noam Chomsky, and Edward Herman, *Manufacturing Consent* (London: Vintage Books, 1994), p. 298.
22   *Ibid.*, p. 20.
23   United States. Congress. Senate. Select Committee to Study Governmental Operations with Respect to Intelligence Activities. *Final Report of the Select Committee to Study Governmental Operations with Respect to Intelligence Activities, United States Senate: Together with Additional, Supplemental, and Separate Views* (Washington: U.S. Govt. Off., 1976), pp. 189-190, https://archive.org/download/finalreportofsel01unit/finalreportofsel01unit.pdf, cited in Howard Zinn, *A People's History of the United States* (London: Longman, 1996), p. 544.
24   Frederic S. Pearson, *The Global Spread of Arms* (Oxford: Westview Press, 1994), p. 33.
25   Secret Orcon Interrogation Log, Detainee 063, https://web.archive.org/web/20060315035935/http://www.time.com/time/2006/log/log.pdf.
26   Zachary Katznelson, "A Tunnel Without End", *The Guardian*, 12 June 2006, available at: www.guardian.co.uk/commentisfree/2006/jun/12/comment.guantanamo.
27   http://www.tomdispatch.com/index.mhtml?pid=65894.
28   Cited in John Sutherland, in *The Guardian, G2*, 21 January 2002.
29   http://news.bbc.co.uk/2/hi/americas/5068606.stm.
30   "Washington condemns first suicides by Guantánamo inmates as 'a PR exercise", *The Independent*, 12 June 2006, online at: www.independent.co.uk/news/world/americas/washington-condemns-first-suicides-by-guantanamo-inmates-as-a-pr-exercise-6098436.html.
31   Donald Rumsfeld, interview with Jeffrey Agar on 2 March 2006; online at: www.dod.mil/transcripts/2006/tr20060302-12599.html.
32   Jeffrey Kluger, "How Haditha Came to Light", *Time Magazine*, 12/06/06, p. 50, online at https://web.archive.org/web/20060612165517/http://www.time.com/time/archive/preview/0,10987,1200780,00.html.
33   *Ibid.*, p. 51.
34   See Christopher Hitchens, "Believe me, it's torture", *Vanity Fair* (August 2008), online at: www.vanityfair.com/politics/features/2008/08/hitchens200808.
35   Francis Fukuyama, *The End of History and the Last Man* (New York: The Free Press, 1992), p. 12.
36   Philippe Sands, *Lawless World* (London: Penguin Books, 2006), pp. 281-83.
37   Reported, for example, by CNN on 13 April 2003, online at: www.cnn.com/2003/US/04/11/sprj.irq.pentagon/.

[38] As reported on 19 June 2008; see, for example, the *International Herald Tribune* article, "Deals with Iraq are set to bring oil giants back", online at: www.iht.com/articles/2008/06/19/africa/19iraq.php.

[39] See *The Times* article from 16 September 2007 entitled "Alan Greenspan claims Iraq war was really for oil", online at: http://www.timesonline.co.uk/tol/news/world/article2461214.ece.

[40] See, for example, the story on News 24 of 05 June 2003, "Update: Iraq war 'was about oil', online at: www.news24.com/World/Archives/IraqiDossier/Update-Iraq-war-was-about-oil-20030605; and *The Guardian's* partial retraction a day later, online at: www.guardian.co.uk/theguardian/2003/jun/06/correctionsandclarifications.

[41] See Lord Browne, chief executive of BP, quoted in *The Guardian* on 30 October 2008, online at: www.guardian.co.uk/uk/2002/oct/30/oil.iraq.

[42] As reported by *The Times* on 29/7/08 and by CNN on 31/7/08, respectively available at: http://money.cnn.com/2008/07/31/news/companies/exxon_profits/?postversion=2008073110, and http://business.timesonline.co.uk/tol/business/industry_sectors/natural_resources/article4420895.ece.

[43] Martin Luther King, Jr., *A Testament of Hope: The Essential Writings and Speeches of Martin Luther King, Jr.*, ed. James M. Washington (New York: HarperCollins, 1986), p. 26.

[44] This is John Perkins' useful catch-all term in *Confessions of an Economic Hit Man* (San Francisco: Berrett-Koehler Publishers, Inc., 2004).

[45] Matthew Feldman, "'Choose Definitively Between Hell and Reason'", *Third Text*, 61/4 (December 2002), pp. 439-449.

[46] Jonathan Glover, *Humanity: A Moral History of the Twentieth Century* (New Haven: Yale University Press, 2001), p. xii.

[47] Susan George, "Winning the War of Ideas" in *Dissent*, Summer 1997, available online at: www.tni.org/en/archives/act/1447.

17. A Failed Just War in Iraq

For reflections upon the ongoing conflict in Iraq (started in 2003 and continuing in varying intensity since), a 1,500-year-old Christian doctrine is surprisingly timely. By "just war" I understand those ideas first systematically put forward by Augustine and then refined by Aquinas and many important thinkers since; namely, that a just war consists of just cause (*jus ad bellum*, including right authority, last resort, and just intent) and just conduct (*jus in bello*, including proportionality of means, following the norms of war, and ensuring the right outcome). The US-led invasion and occupation of Iraq failed spectacularly on the last count: ensuring a just outcome. It also sparked intense debates and political protests the world over about whether it had the right authority, and whether war was indeed the last resort, or had been decided on before the evidence was weighed.

J.T. Johnson, one of the best-known living just war theorists, sets the features of just war theory out as follows:

> Thus the two major aspects of just war tradition, that having to do with just resort to force and that having to do with the proper use and the limits of justified force, derive from essentially distinct cultural heritages that, in the context of medieval Christendom, merged into a single culture...If we think of a just war theory in the way that has become normative...composed of just cause, right authority, right intention, proportionality of ends, reasonable hope of success, last resort, and the aim of peace [... as well as] comprising a broad concept of non-combatant immunity and the requirement of proportionality to means, this cannot be found in any of the medieval sources identified earlier...Just war tradition coalesced into a cultural consensus during the Middle Ages; this consensus was then expressed in systematic theoretical fashion by writers of the early modern period, who also transformed this developing doctrine into the base for modern international law.[1]

To be sure, precious few scholars today would regard the 2003 invasion of Iraq as a just war, based on Johnson's fairly uncontentious outline above. In fact, most of the just war *apologia* for this military and political disaster—there is no other word for it—in Iraq had already petered out by 2004. That was before the rise in prominence of Islamist beheaders like Abu Zarqawi's Al-Qaida in the Arabian Peninsula (AQAP), followed by the even more violent so-called 'caliphate' led by Daesh.

Nigel Biggar was a rare voice in finding the *casus belli* "reasonable" and "honourable" by 2011—that is, before the rise of Daesh in Iraq and Syria. In an article of his written with David Fisher for *International Affairs*, Biggar argues that the traditional criteria of just cause, last resort and legitimate authority were met, as well as using violence as a last resort.[2] Those are dubious contentions, as I aim to show here. They are also virtually alone in arguing this today. As recently as 2015, a survey of 109 Anglophone academics found that, of 18 selected American military interventions since World War One, the 2003 Iraq invasion ranked as the "most unjust" of all.[3] (However, we should note that several controversial conflicts and military engagements were not included, such as the 1980s "dirty wars" in Latin America). The authors of the study report that their respondents claimed the most just war was the Second World War.[4] This raises an unusual question to consider: what would it take to *correct* a failed just war? What would such an undertaking look like in the benighted country of Iraq?

In terms of Iraq, it bears recalling some of the historical context: ruled by a secular tyranny under Saddam Hussein since 1968, and at war more or less continually since 1980: first against Iran in a conflict costing more than a million lives; then an illegal invasion of Kuwait that triggered the UN-backed Operation Desert Storm, led by the US in 1991. This was followed by the country's experiencing crippling sanctions that, by then-Secretary of State Madeleine Albright's own admission, killed more than 500,000 children, which she explicitly claimed had been nonetheless "worth it" to keep Saddam Hussein contained in the Middle East. All that was before a US-led 2003 invasion and subsequent occupation which gave the world Abu Ghraib, sectarian civil war, a death toll in the hundreds of thousands—perhaps even a million by *The Lancet*'s accounting—and millions more displaced amongst the burning cities. And again, that was before the rise of a movement whose fuel seemed to run on human blood: Daesh.

Long after the Christian foundations had been separated from just war theory by the rise of international law and then secular nationalism, the aforementioned J.T. Johnson put forward what I consider to be the best summary of just war theory:

> Historical and anthropological evidence suggests that every human culture has generated some analogue of just war tradition: a consensus of beliefs, attitudes and behaviours that defines the terms of justification for resort to violence and limits, if any, to be set on the use of violence by members of that culture. Such justifications and limitations typically include a) a sense of injustice by a warring group; b) a tacit set of rules for belligerents, and c) the discrimination of non-combatants (such as the sparing of women, children, and the elderly).[5]

These criteria may be therefore understood as more or less inextricable from the history of warfare. To simplify massively, in European culture, this was embodied in the centuries-long development of just war theory following Augustine.

This raises a second aspect of justified warfare that also predating the formation of just war doctrine; on the cultural context. In the case of St. Augustine, what were the circumstances in which he wrote *The City of God*? Fifth century

Rome was by no means a pacifist state, but was a Christian one. It continued to fight against pagan invaders like the Vandals, Huns, and Visigoths—the former reaching North Africa near Augustine's home of Hippo. The Visigoths sacked Rome in 410—during Augustine's lifetime. Thus, while the Church father was exhorting his congregation to take up arms against invaders and in order to stamp out heretics, he was setting out the parameters of the initial just war doctrine at the same time.

Fully 1,000 years later, the Spanish-born Francisco de Vitoria defended the righteous conquest of the Americas on grounds of territorial imperialism considered virtuous at the time. Vitoria, amongst the most insightful of just war theologians due to his application of Just War criteria to the fledgling politics of international relations at the start of the 16th century, put forward the concept of natural law, which he defined thus:

> Everything which in the light of natural reason appears to all men to be clearly just, being unjust that which is opposed to it, such as, for instance, not to steal, kill an innocent person or do to anyone that which we would not suffer others to do to us.[6]

Vitoria was plainly concerned with indigenous peoples encountered in the misnamed "new world"; people he considered lesser specimens of humanity. It is notable that throughout history leaders have deemed certain people to be worth counting as human, and others not. For example, no government has endeavored to count how many Iraqis have been killed since the invasion of March 2003, whether military or civilian. Civilian groups such as the Iraq Body Count have estimated deaths based on triangulated reports, and their figure at the time of writing is 288,000 violent deaths which have occurred since the invasion, but this does not include deaths from disease, displacement, and the lack of functioning hospitals and infrastructure in many places, such as clean water. The true figure is likely to never be known.[7] Vitoria was not troubled by the hierarchy. He only disputed the plunder, forcible conversion of natives, and rapacious behavior of the conquistadors; he never wrote against the assumed superiority of Spanish culture over the indigenous population, only the blatant disregard of "natural law" all too often shown by Spanish soldiers.

The importance of cultural differences should not be overlooked, pervading as it does the historical understanding of the "rule of law" in international relations—past and present. For instance, the "rule of law" in the modern world clearly denotes distinctions between combatants and non-combatants that have generally been a feature of warfare throughout history. But it can assume other features too, such as the value of signed treaties that may well have been viewed in the past with suspicion or incomprehension by First Nations groups like Native Americans or Aborigines in Australia; these treaties throughout history and even today can be used not for peace-making and a codification of relations, but as tools of continuing oppression. While the rule of law may bear some relation to a natural law, my point is that the perception of any natural law is culturally relative, and viewed through every society's own cultural prism.

Understanding the impact of culture is important when discussing just war theory, because of the way war is promoted and understood in Christian traditions. Growing out of the Old Testament, Judeo-Christian teachings have always accepted the principle of divinely-sanctioned bloodshed. Although the figure of Jesus Christ in the New Testament is rightly seen as a break with this tradition in favour of forgiveness, love and peace, it ought to be noted that even His disciples carried swords, as recounted in Luke's 22nd chapter at the Garden of Gethsemane. My wider point is that conceptions of 'natural law', the Roman Empire's socio-political order, and the increasingly enshrined doctrines of Christianity all came together in the initial formulation of the just war theory. These powered Augustine's conditions for a just war, mandating that "a just war of aggression, however, must be carried out by the authority of the prince, and must have both a just cause and right intention."[8] This is because "a war inspired by a wrong spirit is not really a war but brigandage".[9] Entailed here are precepts of submission to empowered authority for the initiation of war and avoidance of gratuitous cruelty in warfare, as set against the Christian duty to confront evil.

The lack of development on Augustinian guidelines until St Aquinas in the 12th century meant that starvation, castle sieges, holy wars declared by Popes and other forms of violence in the Middle Ages were at least indirectly related to Augustine's licensing of theoretically unlimited violence to correct injustice and evil. Given that holy wars have been considered by a number of critics to be the "ultimate just war", consider Pope Urban II's declaration of the First Crusade in 1095:

> Let robbers become soldiers of Christ. Let them fight barbarians, not brothers. Let those who will fight and kill for any low wage now labor instead for an eternal reward [....] To kill Christians is a matter of horror; but it is not wicked to flourish your sword against Saracens. That is righteous warfare.[10]

I will shortly return to the importance of refracting contemporaneous events—in this case, the conflict over rule of the Holy Land—through long-standing theoretical ideals. But for the moment, it ought to be noted that, at the same time as Augustine's fledgling doctrine on war was first projected outward in an organized way during the Crusades—that is, not in response to a specific threat but for an idea born of European cultural traditions—recognised limitations on warfare were simultaneously coalescing within Europe.

These rules for war fighting form the second half of what is commonly understood as just war theory, and a bare summary poorly reflects the significance of these developments. First to be promulgated was the Truce of God in the 11th century, which limited warfare from Monday morning to Wednesday night; then followed the idea of the Peace of God, which prohibited warfare against certain people and property, such as the poor, the clergy, church possessions, and so on. These practices grew directly out of Christian culture in the territories of modern-day Italy and France, respectively. Such constraints on the practice of warfare were buttressed though the transmission of the "customs, attitudes, and behavior associated with the knightly class, the direct historical inheritor of the Germanic warrior tradition."[11] These constraints included demarcation of non-combatants, and efforts to limit certain types of armaments such as, in their day, crossbows and siege weapons, and in ours, landmines and depleted uranium shells.

Before moving on to a whistle stop tour of the metamorphosis of just war theory into modern international law, let me make explicit a contentious proposition that has been lurking throughout: at the same time as Europeans were "settling" the world from behind gun-barrels and all that entails—establishment of trading posts, territorial expansion, diversion of colonial goods to Europe, signed treaties, and so on—a consensus of how these practices were to be justly achieved had formed in Europe, in no small measure through the aegis of just war theory. Put another way, as European states gradually became dominant powers around the world, the imposition of social and economic norms was consistently backed by force, tacit or otherwise; norms which of course drew upon that very just war doctrine ultimately to be expressed in the law of nations—represented today, above all, in the Hague treaties, Geneva Conventions, and the United Nations.

As mentioned previously, the best example of the just war doctrine in a colonial setting is found in the writings of Francisco de Vitoria, who stated with regard to the recently encountered peoples of the Americas: "The people in question […] were in peaceable possession of their goods, both publicly and privately. Therefore, unless the contrary is shown, they must be treated as owners and not be disturbed in their possession unless cause be shown".[12] Thus, while Vitoria was laying the rules for secular European conduct with newly encountered peoples—and here is my point—he was simultaneously defining native conceptions of goods and property in European terms. A century later, these rights had become like second nature to the lawyer and theorist, Hugo Grotius, who, unlike the theologian Vitoria, is considered the founder what is today considered the science of international relations by placing considerations of humanity, war conduct and military necessity—such as proportion and discrimination of combatants—under the scope of a "Law of Nations" following the 1648 Treaty of Westphalia.

International law was not fundamentally changed so much as expanded in reach between Victoria and Grotius. In the words of another leading scholar of just war theory, William O'Brien:

> By the time of the American Revolution there was a well-developed law of war that the American armies were eager to abide by as a demonstration of American responsibility.[13]

By this time, justice via God had been almost completely transposed to justice via the judgment dispensed by, and within, nations. Staying with the US for the moment, the secular, internationalist principles derived from just war doctrine had so unified into a single body of parameters consolidated into the 1863 field manual governing Martial Law produced for fighters serving in the American Civil War, *Instructions for the Government of Armies of the United States in the Field*:

> Military oppression is not Martial Law; it is the abuse of the power which that law confers. As Martial Law is executed by military force, it is incumbent upon those who administer it to be strictly guided by the principles of justice, honor, and humanity—virtues adorning a soldier even more than other men, for the very reason that he possesses the power of his arms against the unarmed.[14]

By my lights, the high-water mark for the evolution of just war theory into international law arrived shortly thereafter, at the 1899 and 1907 International Peace Conferences at the Hague. At this time, agreements were formed about the uniforms of soldiers, flags of truce, rights of non-combatants, principles of arbitration and other normative regulations on warfare—at least within western states, which had anyway long defined the rules and made them binding for all. And despite further attempts to renounce war through the international 1928 Kellogg-Briand Pact—outlawing war in a treaty signed by France, Germany, the UK, Japan and all the combatants in the Second World War—the idea of limits on warfare were not enforced. The tactics used in that war were unprecedented in their scope and barbarity. Included here were area bombing, increased unrestricted naval warfare, nuclear warfare, and of course, the horrors of the Nazi gas chambers, constructed for the extermination of millions of "undesirable" civilians, mostly Jews, but also Roma, homosexuals and disabled people, amongst many others.

With this view in mind, let us now return to Iraq. As a Second World War battlefield, this country has long understood the destructive potential of modern warfare. And as one of the first signatories of the UN Charter, it also pledged "to ensure, by the acceptance of principles and the institution of methods, that armed force shall not be used, save in the common interest," and "to establish conditions under which justice and respect for the obligations arising from treaties and other sources of international law can be maintained."[15] As we have explored, the concept of the Just War was initially centered upon the authority and intention of the war-maker. Added to this were ideas of proportionality and discrimination, which have come down to us today as particular regulations bounding the conduct of war as considered internationally acceptable through international bodies like the UN. Understood in this context, such considerations are precisely where the debate on Iraq has rested since the 2003 invasion.

Critical to the recent resurgence of both academic and wider interest in just war theory was the tense period following the September 11th attacks in the US—the most deadly terrorist attacks ever. The debates were sparked by the subsequent American-led conflicts in Afghanistan in 2001 and then Iraq, and the term "just war" seemed to be on everyone's lips, from popes to diplomats. Exclaimed so often that it quickly became a cliché, it can scarcely be doubted that the "world changed" after 9/11. An earlier thesis stemming from a *Foreign Affairs* article discussing the inevitability of conflict between religions, Samuel Huntington's *The Clash of Civilizations*, produced in book form in 1996, was resurrected to explain the inevitability of war in this day and age. There could be no more tolerance, we were repeatedly told by western leaders, for states that harbor terrorists, or those who might threaten western civilization.

Not for the first time, this was a case of 'do as I say and not as I do' for permanent members of the UN Security Council. Yet even in these politically charged years, this was a dubious charge to level against Baathist Iraq; a secular and—like many others then and since—tyrannical state that had, despite its periodic non-cooperation with weapons inspectors, failed to raise red flags with either the UN or the International Atomic Energy Agency (IAEA) regarding banned stockpiles of weapons. Nonetheless, as the scholar Brian Stiltner candidly maintained in his 2006 "Just War: Second Thoughts on Iraq", the "misuses of the just war argument" had "duped" many like him into believing that "a war with Iraq was increasingly necessary"—whether for humanitarian, national security or counter-terrorism justifications.[16]

In the UK, the 2004 Butler Review established that those hyperbolic claims of an imminent threat—for who could forget the "45-minute claim" and the 'sexed up' intelligence from this period?—were made in "good faith" in the run-up to the Iraq invasion (Partridge LS). Recent revelations appear to make a nonsense of that quite forgiving finding, with evidence emerging that, in March 2002, Tony Blair had assured US officials that "Britain's Labour government would support a US invasion of Iraq", despite continuing "to insist throughout 2002 that he had taken no decision on whether to support the invasion that eventually began in March 2003."[17] Fully a year before the invasion of Iraq, then, the policy had been set, even if the *casus belli* had not. This clearly jars with the long-established just war criteria of warfare as a last resort. In March 2003, surely, diplomacy had not yet been exhausted. Days before the 19 March invasion the UN Weapons Inspectors (UNSCOM), led by Hans Blix, were still visiting purported WMD sites in Iraq, finding nothing; and discussion was still ongoing over whether invading forces needed a new UN resolution—an impossible task given the position taken by France, China and Russia—or if President George W. Bush's "coalition of the willing" could "reactivate" UN Resolution 678 from November 1990, which used the key phrase "all necessary means" in reference to liberating Kuwait from Iraqi occupation.

For many observers at the time and since, disliking Saddam's awful regime was not enough to attack a sovereign country and split it apart—for there are many awful regimes in the world. More was needed to establish a just cause. To great skepticism, this is precisely what Colin Powell attempted in his infamous and now widely-discredited United Nations presentation in February 2003, where he asserted: links to Al-Qaida, the group deemed responsible for the attacks on 9/11; concealment of chemical and biological weapons; and non-compliance with the UN generally.[18] Even Powell no longer stands by those claims. Yet his reason for doing so at the UN at a critical juncture on the road to war underscores the ongoing importance of right authority, a key element of just war theory.

Few would dispute that such right authority ultimately rests with the United Nations, especially through its Security Council. Yet it bears recalling that there was famously much behind-the-scenes wrangling in the eventually unanimous UN vote on Resolution 1441 on November 8, 2002, holding Iraq in "material breach" of disarmament obligations from 1991. That was also the year of the so-called "Yemeni Example", where the US withdrew nearly $70 million in aid to Yemen within days of its Security Council veto on the first Gulf War—in what the then-US Ambassador to the UN called "the most expensive 'no' vote you would ever cast". Of the ten non-permanent members of the Security Council in the run-up to war on 20 March 2003, at least six—Mauritius, Cameroon, Guinea, Bulgaria, Colombia, Mexico, and Singapore—received substantial economic or military aid from the United States.

To take but one example, Mauritius joined the Security Council under US sponsorship with a clear understanding of its role: "The U.S. aid package to the impoverished country, authorized by the U.S. African Growth and Opportunity Act (AGOA)", demands that the aid recipient "does not engage in activities contrary to U.S. national security or foreign policy interests."' Emphasizing this point, Mauritius temporarily recalled its UN Ambassador to chastise him for his recorded reservations about the imminent war on Iraq. Or again, at $656 million in fiscal year

2002-2003, the US was the largest supplier of arms to Singapore, and had earmarked another $370 million dollars in aid for 2003-2004. Given these circumstances, one must ask, "Could any of these countries easily stand up to the United States or refuse to fall in line with their benefactor or military ally [in a UN vote]?"[19] Put another way, does this not cloud the issue of "right intention?"

For reasons like the above, just war theory was often explicitly invoked by those opposed to invading Iraq. For example, on 19 September 2002, the US conference of Catholic Bishops wrote a letter to President Bush, urging him "to step back from the brink of war" and "to fashion an effective global response to Iraq's threats that conforms with traditional moral limits on the use of military force":

> People of good will may apply ethical principles and come to different prudential judgments, depending upon their assessment of the facts at hand and other issues. We conclude, based on the facts that are known to us, that a preemptive, unilateral use of force is difficult to justify at this time. We fear that resort to force, under these circumstances, would not meet the strict conditions in Catholic teaching for overriding the strong presumption against the use of military force. Of particular concern are the traditional just war criteria of just cause, right authority, probability of success, proportionality and noncombatant immunity.[20]

In the UK, speaking to *Newsnight* almost exactly 13 years ago, Bishop Richard Harries of Oxford—a retired army officer—likewise maintained, "I am not a pacifist", but offered supporting evidence for sceptics: he had supported both the first Gulf War against Iraq as well as the October 2001 "Global War on Terror" centered on Afghanistan. In respect to the Iraq invasion, one whose preparations were being finalized as he spoke, Harries demurred in the following terms: "the traditional Just War criteria have not been met."[21] Ex-US President Jimmy Carter later echoed this view, arguing in the *New York Times*—which had done perhaps more than any other outlet to push the faulty intelligence about aluminum tubes from Niger and other questionable intelligence findings by the Iraqi National Congress, amongst others—only 10 days before the invasion, "that a substantially unilateral attack on Iraq does not meet these [just war] standards."[22] For Harries, Carter and many millions of others around the world, even if they didn't know its contours, their applied just war criteria typically extended to the need for there to be credible evidence of Weapons of Mass Destruction in Iraq; the need for a second UN resolution backing an invasion; or the need for independently-verified proof of Al-Qaida partnering with Saddam Hussein in Iraq. The World Council of Churches, representing some 400 million parishioners in more than 100 countries, reiterated this view in the run-up to March 2003. Indeed, most of these countries—totaling 54 at last count—have formally protested against the 2003 invasion of Iraq. They recognized a vital consideration that has been all-too-often absent in the British and American press: the most powerful country in the world was marshalling an invasion of one of the weakest.

It is this disparity of strength that is all too rarely taken into account in discussions of just war theory. I want to advance the view here that just war doctrine offers a framework for inquiring not only into the causes and consequences of the Iraq debacle, but also into something much larger: first, a significant aspect of the cultural development of the west itself, as well as a portion of the value-system projected onto the wider world in a centuries-long process of European-American hegemony. That imperial hegemony has typically been voiced, as it was in 2003, in the tenor of just and necessary conflicts.

Nevertheless, some here may recall George Bush's State of the Union Address in January 2003: 'If war is forced upon us, we will fight in a just cause and by just means, sparing, in any way we can, the innocent'.[23] He could not have been more wrong, I submit. Summarizing the most familiar counter-arguments in 2006, Walter Burghardt puts the case clearly: "The traditional Catholic conditions for declaring a war just—defensive necessity, the last resort, approval of a large number of nations, endorsement of the United Nations, high probability of success—were not met by the Bush administration in the 2003 pre-emptive attack on Iraq".[24]

The specter of a *failed just war* raises the extraordinary proposition that a just war might actually be more defensible in response to a botched just war. In terms of historical precedent, think of the mutilated peace of WWI, and the war—at least on the Allied side of the line—considered to be the paragon of the modern 'just war': World War Two. Might not the just war of the Second World War be a response to the failed just war of the first, and the failure of the peace at Versailles? In terms of just war theory today, my suggestion would be as follow: the unjustness of the 2003 invasion of Iraq was so great that it might actually be more just to re-occupy the country in order to restore the *status quo ante* (that is, an autocratic Iraq without Saddam). This is simply to say: there is a sliding scale to be applied to recognized just war criteria: perhaps no war can be completely just; particularly as there is no way to know the outcome at the onset of military action. Of course, this is certainly no endorsement of Saddam Hussein's murderous rule!

Such is the state of Iraq today that overthrowing a creeping caliphate brought into being by the chaos of a war with dubious aims, legality and methods, would be more justified than searching for al-Qaeda terrorists and weapons of mass destruction that were not there. Indeed, in one of the great ironies of our time, it might be that US and UK actions against the death-cult ISIS would now constitute a 'just war'. So bad is this illegitimate state-within-two-states—persecution of Christians, fanatical and warlike followers, and an apocalyptic political theology—that a war in 2020 in Iraq would almost certainly be more just than in 2003. As Tony Blair has admitted recently, the rise of ISIS owes much to the Iraqi invasion and occupation from March 2003. Remember that no less a person than the 'Caliph', Abu Bakr al-Baghdadi himself, was radicalized in a US camp in the middle of 2003.

Iraq sees a confluence of complex factors, in their own way, relating to the historical concept of the just war. First is the increasingly obvious subjectivity of what constitutes a right intention. For the US, right intention since 1945 has been defense of liberal capitalism against communism, or recourse to selectively championed 'humanitarian interventions'— which has led to the bombing of more than 20 countries since 1945. In turn, this sheds light on Augustine's second proposition: right authority. Whatever the rhetoric, right authority in the modern age has always rested with the power of principal nation states—as today represented by the UN. And in conclusion, whether government lawyers recognize it or not, they stand upon the shoulders of giants such as Augustine, Vitoria, Grotius, and Lieber for justifying war. For those theologians and theorists knew, as our leaders now seem to forget, that pursuit of justice can pave the way to the hell of injustice. Having broken Iraq, the question of how to fix it seems to me pressing; indeed, morally serious. I'm certainly not advocating another invasion to restore the *status quo ante* in Iraq—which I hope I've made clear was unpleasant before 2003, for various reasons. So what, then: apology? Reparations? Neither is particularly realistic as things stand. So declared Field Marshal Ferdinand Foch, Commander in Chief of Allied armies in France, upon boycotting the signing of the Versailles Treaty in June 1919: "This is not a treaty. It is an armistice for twenty years."[25] What responsibility do we have, in and as countries that took part in a failed just war?

Endnotes

1. James Turner Johnson, "Historical Roots and Sources of the Just War Tradition in Western Culture," *Just War and Jihad: Historical and Theoretical Perspectives on War and Peace in Western and Islamic Traditions*, edited by John Kelsay and James Turner Johnson (Westport, Connecticut: Greenwood Press, 1991), pp. 12, 16.
2. David Fisher and Nigel Biggar, "Was Iraq an unjust war? A debate on the Iraq war and reflections on Libya." *International Affairs* 87/3 (May 2011), pp. 696ff., online at: www.chathamhouse.org/publications/ia/archive/view/164421 (all websites last accessed 29 February 2020).
3. A. Walter Dorn, David R. Mandel, and Ryan W. Cross, "How Just Were America's Wars? A Survey of Experts Using a Just War Index," *International Studies Perspectives*, 16/3 (Aug. 2015), p. 275.
4. *Ibid.*
5. Johnson, "Historical Roots and Sources of the Just War Tradition in Western Culture," p. 3.
6. Francisco de Vitoria, *The Principles of Political and International Law in the Work of Francisco de Vitoria: Extracts, with an Introduction and Notes by Antonio Truyol Sera* (Madrid: Ediciones Cultura Hispánica, 1946), p. 31.
7. For further discussion see Iraq Body Count, an NGO established for this very purpose, online at: www.iraqbodycount.org/.
8. J. E. Cross, "The ethic of war in Old English," *England Before the Conquest: Studies in Primary Sources Presented to Dorothy Whitelock*, edited by Peter Clemoes and Kathleen Hughes (Cambridge and New York: Cambridge University Press, 2010 [1971]), p. 271.
9. Joan D. Tooke, *The Just War in Aquinas and Grotius* (London: S.P.C.K., 1965), p. 11.
10. Geoffrey Regan, *First Crusader: Byzantium's Holy Wars* (Stroud: Sutton, 2001), p. 236.
11. Johnson, "Historical Roots and Sources of the Just War Tradition in Western Culture," p. 11.
12. de Vitoria, p. 57.
13. William V. O'Brien, "The International Law of War as Related to the Western Just War Tradition," *Just War and Jihad*, p. 164.
14. Francis Lieber, *Instructions for the Government of Armies of the United States, in the Field* (New York: D. Van Nostrand, 1863), p. 4, online at: https://babel.hathitrust.org/cgi/pt?id=mdp.35112102309871&view=1up&seq=13.
15. UN Charter https://www.un.org/en/sections/un-charter/un-charter-full-text/
16. Brian Stiltner, "Just War: Second Thoughts on Iraq," *The Christian Century*, vol. 123, no. 25 (December 12, 2006), pp. 34-35.
17. Simon Tisdale, "There is no doubt about it: Tony Blair was on the warpath from early 2002", *The Guardian*, 18 October 2015, https://www.theguardian.com/uk-news/2015/oct/18/tony-blair-warpath-from-early-2002-colin-powell-memo-chilcot-inquiry-invasion-iraq
18. "Full text of Colin Powell's speech," *The Guardian*, 5 Feb 2003, online at: www.theguardian.com/world/2003/feb/05/iraq.usa. Only the last point is factually accurate, however US non-compliance with United Nations resolutions dwarfs that of Iraq. For discussion, see William Blum, *Rogue State* (London: Zed Books, 2000), ch. 20.
19. Thalif Deen, "US Dollars Yielded Unanimous UN Vote Against Iraq," Inter Press Service, November 9, 2002, online at: www.ipsnews.net/2002/11/politics-us-dollars-yielded-unanimous-un-vote-against-iraq/.

[20] Letter to George W. Bush from the US Conference of Catholic Bishops, 13 September 2002, available online at: www.usccb.org/issues-and-action/human-life-and-dignity/global-issues/middle-east/iraq/letter-to-president-bush-from-bishop-gregory-on-iraq-2002-09-13.cfm.

[21] See also Lord Harries of Pentregarth, "Military Intervention from a Christian Perspective," *Having Faith in Foreign Policy*, edited by Alex Bigham (London: The Foreign Policy Centre, 2007), pp. 70-73, available online at: www.constantinian.org.uk/wp-content/uploads/2015/01/Having-Faith-in-Foreign-Policy.pdf.

[22] Jimmy Carter, "Just War, or Just a War?" *The New York Times*, 9 March 2003, online at: https://www.nytimes.com/2003/03/09/opinion/just-war-or-a-just-war.html

[23] George W. Bush, "Address Before a Joint Session of the Congress on the State of the Union," January 28, 2003, The American Presidency Project, online at: www.presidency.ucsb.edu/documents/address-before-joint-session-the-congress-the-state-the-union-23.

[24] Walter J. Burghardt, "Nourishing Head and Heart", *America: The Jesuit Review*, vol. 194, no. 10 [no. 4726] (March 20, 2006), pp. 13-15, online at: www.americamagazine.org/issue/565/article/nourishing-head-and-heart.

[25] Spencer C. Tucker, ed., *The Encyclopedia of World War I: A Political, Social and Military History* (Santa Barbara: ABC-CLIO, 2005) 426.

Part 3
Ends and Odds

18. Between 'Geist' and 'Zeitgeist': Martin Heidegger as Ideologue of Metapolitical Fascism

During the particularly severe crises affecting Germany in the early 1930s, perhaps the most creative philosophical mind, on one hand, and the most destructive political body of the 20th century, on the other, entered a temporary symbiosis, one that has since raised difficult questions and resisted comprehensive answers. The major European thinker was Martin Heidegger, rector of Freiburg University and central proponent of German academia's *Gleichschaltung* (political co-ordination) with the Third Reich between 27 May 1933 and 14 April 1934. The apparent paradoxes and implications arising out of Heidegger's relationship with National Socialism have forcefully re-emerged in the public sphere since the 1987 publication of Victor Farías' controversial *Heidegger et le Nazisme*.[1] This is understandable, for at stake is the re-evaluation of Heidegger and the contextualisation of his thought against events shaping recent history.

It is the aim of this article to complement the vast output of material released in the past fifteen years and to simultaneously offer a new perspective attempting to move beyond stratified divisions and their often unconstructive polemics.[2] These two tasks will be achieved by applying an ideological approach, borrowed from the burgeoning consensus within 'fascist studies',[3] to Heidegger's cultural projects following the 1927 publication of *Being and Time*, in addition to sketching out the legacy that his pioneering brand of 'apoliticism' bequeathed to post-war 'metapolitical' ideologues like Pierre Krebs and Alain de Benoist. In short, this study will seek to demonstrate that it is heuristically[4] useful to view Heidegger, both man and philosopher, as a case-study in the attraction that many intellectuals[5] experienced (and some continue to experience) for the myth of socio-cultural decline and renewal arguably constituting the 'ineliminable core'[6] of fascism. This core, when viewed as the matrix of generic fascism,[7] can be seen to underlie ostensibly diffuse movements such as Nazism and the European New Right. The nucleus of this ideological core will progress from a characterisation of the emergent consensus on the 'fascist minimum', recently defined as

> a genus of modern politics which aspires to bring about a total revolution in the political and social culture of a particular national or ethnic community. While extremely heterogeneous in the specific ideology of its many permutations, in its social support, in the form of organisation it adopts as an anti-systemic movement, and in the type of political system, regime, or homeland it aims to create, generic fascism draws its internal cohesion and affective driving force from a core myth that a period of perceived decadence and degeneracy is imminently or eventually to give way to one of rebirth and rejuvenation in a post-liberal new order'.[8]

As a political ideology whose fortunes depend extensively upon the degree to which a contemporary society believes itself to be in a state of profound crisis, the meteoric rise of fascism during the collapse of the Weimar Republic after 1929 becomes easier to comprehend. Yet despite the rapid increase in supra-class support for Nazism as the Depression struck home,[9] it is essential to note that this was not the only strand of fascism prevalent in Germany at the time. A disparate assortment of intellectuals, grouped by Armin Mohler under the title 'Conservative Revolutionaries' [hereafter CR][10] due to their championing of traditional (and decidedly anti-Enlightenment) culture and longing for an extensive spiritual renewal in Germany, also embraced the same *Weltanschauung* as the National Socialism. Despite their highly diverse theories of the origins of Germany's infirmity, these figures were connected by their distaste for Nazism's use of political coercion to rehabilitate Germany. They also eschewed the NSDAP's institutionalised violence and 'vulgar' biological determinism in favour of persuasion through the force of cultural ideas, which they felt alone could reclaim Germanic hegemony in Europe. Furthermore, these bourgeois radicals generally resisted the populist shift of National Socialism following its political reorientation toward contesting elections after 1925. That the CR essentially felt Nazism to be gallant in theory but errant in practice can be summarised in Mohler's retrospective description of these thinkers as 'the Trotskyites of the German Revolution'. This suggests that the CR's more enlightened course would have avoided the travesty of Hitlerism while simultaneously managing to relativise the uniqueness of Nazi crimes by equating it to Stalinism.[11]

Against this backdrop of diverse and often isolated fascist intellectuals, proffering vague philosophical solutions to analogous social diagnoses, the 'Heidegger Case' loses much of its singularity. This is neither to deny Heidegger's contribution to philosophy nor to ignore the mountain of recent biographical and historiographical studies investigating his complex relations with National Socialism.[12] By incorporating these essential studies into a more panoramic view of the attraction many intellectuals felt toward German fascism (including both Nazism and the CR), Heidegger's vital connection with Nazism becomes demystified. It then becomes heuristically profitable to treat him not as unique and anachronistic, but as representative of his milieu and epoch in his rejection of progressive Enlightenment ideals in favour of a sweeping organic rejuvenation of Germany's social, political and moral culture. This involves a greater readiness to dwell on the ideological dynamics of generic fascism than has characterised the Heidegger debate so far.

A good example of this reluctance can be seen in Tom Rockmore's otherwise indispensable scholarship on Heidegger, which delineates six principal interpretations of his association with National Socialism: first, everything Heidegger said and did was thoroughly Nazi; second, a historical revision of Nazism's depraved reality and Heidegger's role in it; third, Heidegger was dissociated and not responsible for the unforeseen consequences of Nazism; fourth, a distinction between man and thinker, first forwarded by Heidegger himself, centring on the contention that his activism was an insignificant miscalculation borne of a political naivety completely unrelated to his philosophy; fifth, Heidegger's early thought led to Nazism but his later thought moved away from it; and sixth, Nazism was inextricably bound to his philosophical thought.[13] Although aiming to augment the first, third, fourth, and particularly sixth positions, it will be suggested here that all of these approaches focus on Heidegger's collusion with the NSDAP (or lack thereof) in a political or philosophical connection and assume an understanding of Nazism's constitution. Yet it is arguably this very assumption which is central to the Heidegger debate, but which has been neglected to the detriment of scholarship. Indeed, Rockmore's comment on this issue is revealing: 'it is unnecessary to consider the nature of Nazism in detail, which, as an amorphous collection of doctrines that never assumed canonical shape, is in any case notoriously difficult to define.'[14]

The new consensus in fascist studies challenges such an assumption by locating Nazism within part of a larger politico-cultural movement, one that includes permutations as varied as the CR, Italian Fascism, the Romanian Iron Guard, the British Union of Fascists (BUF), and so on. Each of these revolutionary clusters can be usefully viewed in terms of prevailing inter-war sentiments of decline and expected collapse. As part of a general response to this European malaise, fascism attempted to implement a transformation of the ailing nation into a new and robust totality, one capable of subduing undesirable aspects of modernity such as *anomie*, fragmentation, and decadence. Just as importantly, these dynamic movements relied heavily upon the prognosis of self-appointed 'guardians of culture' who inflated widespread *fin de siècle* concerns into assessments of a society in death throes. These intellectuals were therefore indispensable to fascism in the diagnosis of these convulsions, just as fascism was frequently the solution for disaffected thinkers in search of comprehensive remedies to their anxieties.

As this synergy between fascism and disillusioned intellectuals is rooted in their respective 'world views', offering an *a priori* ideological explanation for the pull fascism exerted on this intelligentsia as the response to their fears suggests that disputed and problematic thinkers like Martin Heidegger often become part of a recognisable syndrome. This is the consequence of a renewed emphasis upon the cultural basis of fascism,[15] which offers the possibility of advancing new arguments on thinkers like Heidegger that conventional approaches have often overlooked: instead of How is it possible that such a major intellectual became a Nazi? and For how long did the residue of Nazism impact the work of this person?, the questions become: How might an approach rooted in current studies of fascism provide a more encompassing explanation for many inter-war European intellectuals' collusion with these movements? and To what degree does the relationship of this individual's *oeuvre* to fascism become more comprehensible when viewed in the context of the intellectual and ideological conceptions of his/her day?

In short, this article explores the heuristic value of viewing Heidegger as a leading representative of modern intellectuals bent on reconciling 'eternal' aspects of the human mind (*Geist*) with a 'spirit of the age' (*Zeitgeist*) characterised by an acute sense of the breakdown of Western civilisation. It then becomes possible to advance the stagnated debate regarding Heidegger's writings and actions by attributing to him a 'philosophical' acceptance of fascism typical of the CR. Like most of the intellectuals in this group who entered a dangerous liaison with National Socialism at some point, this paradigm will clarify both his short period of activism and subsequent shift away from the Third Reich toward apoliticism following his disillusionment with the 'spiritless' course of its revolution. Finally, this basis of inquiry can cast fresh light on Heidegger's later philosophical projects by proposing that he remained faithful to the 'ineliminable core' of fascist ideology even after his break with the NSDAP, while also positing reasons why the ideologues of post-war mutations arising from 'classic' fascism continue to champion him as a chief proponent in what they see as the current 'interregnum'.

The Environment and Context of Metapolitical Fascism

To support the contention that Heidegger accepted the basis of fascism in a manner characteristic of major artists and thinkers throughout inter-war Europe, the first task will be to illustrate the manner in which the ideology central to this argument offers a framework capable of assembling diverse intellectuals. Fascism reached maturity in the immediate years after 1918, in an atmosphere of perceived 'alienation', 'decadence', 'degeneration' and 'chaos'—all favourite expressions of these intellectuals subsequent to the shared European events shaping these perceptions (millions of war casualties, territorial adjustments, Bolshevism, empowered women and demobilised soldiers, the Spanish flu, etc.). In the wake of the Great War, a deliverance from what was widely felt to be the drowning of the West itself often became both a theoretical challenge and a practical project. And as this sentiment was manifested through a parochial patriotism exacerbated by WWI, the buoys necessary to save each nation's idealised essence resided in their own particular traditions once they had been stripped of liberal-egalitarian perversions. In this way, longstanding mores and recent experiences individuated fascism in every European country and simultaneously elevated artists like D'Annunzio and thinkers like Moeller van den Bruck to an often mythic status in nationalist circles as resuscitators of their respective civilisations.

Though unlike Marxism insofar as it lacked a codified textual doctrine originating with a single source, the driving myth of fascism as understood by fascists themselves displays remarkable homogeneity.[16] A typical excerpt from a BUF publication reinforces this point: '[we] demand action, and immediate action, to arrest the threatened decay and to end our cultural decline. It is in the spirit of defiance that our youth has arisen—defiance of impending fate; defiance of decadence and soft decline; defiance of a self-seeking humanism which saps cultural vitality'.[17] Despite this, fascism is still occasionally seen in terms of a checklist definition generally focussing on aspects it reacts against,[18] rather than as a cogent ideology containing logical or cultural 'adjacencies'[19] similar to other ideologies like Marxism or democracy. For example, the splitting of the SPD and USPD in 1917 over support for Germany during WWI, Stalin's dispute with Trotsky over the direction of Bolshevism, and debates between delegates of the 1927 Third International over the subordination of international Communist parties to the mandates of Moscow—each of these has been commonly viewed as unproblematic and accepted as viable interpretations stemming from Marxist ideology. The argument advanced by the new consensus is that fascism should also be understood as a *Weltanschauung* specifically configured by time, place, culture and knowledge. Therefore, Italian Fascism's hostility to religion and the Croatian Ustasha's fervent Catholicism, Nazism's 'blood and soil' biologism and the Conservative Revolutionaries' elitism and emphasis on 'cultivation', even Jünger's glorification of warfare and Spengler's anthropological investigations; all can be seen as highlighting the protean nature of generic fascism, rather than indicating an inherent vacuity or incoherence.

Far from posing as a 'revolution of nihilism', inter-war fascism instead offered a revolutionary cultural ideology based on affirmative values appealing to an array of outstanding inter-war intellectuals that Mohler has dubbed 'German nihilists', namely those 'who consciously take action filled with a sense of moral responsibility and with positive faith in the possibility of breaking through....It is the belief in unconditional destruction which suddenly metamorphoses into its opposite [*umschlagen*]: unconditional creation'.[20] As early as 1965, George Mosse's groundbreaking article 'Fascism and the Intellectuals' identified the appeal of such a vision to thinkers often misleadingly categorised as 'cultural pessimists'. Instead, they 'regarded themselves as guardians of ultimate values in society and saw in fascism a means to realize these values [which were not those] of the bourgeois age of the last century, but of Greco-Roman or more genuine spiritual values'.[21] The value of 'non-rational' creativity was indispensable for any quest to restore the spiritual unity of the nation, seen to be on the verge of politico-economic collapse:

> The obvious attraction which fascism could exercise upon the creative intellectual is often overlooked. It gave him a place in the movement and made it possible for such men to combine their creativity with a desire to infuse society with their concept of ultimate values....Moreover, because of the development of liberal-bourgeois society, poetry (by which they meant all creativity) had died into a shallow materialism and sentimentality and this decline was part and parcel of the corruption of society as a whole.[22]

The 'poets' striving to deliver this 'German' or positive nihilism to their deteriorating nations not only included recognised fascists such as Pound, Marinetti, Benn, Rosenberg, Bäumler and Gentile, but also implicated thinkers who either did not collude with empowered regimes in Germany and Italy (Jünger, Spengler), or lived in countries where fascism never seized power (la Rochelle, L.F. Céline, D.H. Lawrence, Wyndham Lewis). For Mosse, then, fascism was not a narrowly defined concept solely reacting against negative aspects found in the nation and society at large, but an affirmative and 'open-ended' ideal attracting a highly articulate and variegated group of artists and thinkers intent upon establishing 'ultimate values'.[23] This reading thus locates the principal allure of fascism as a cultural phenomenon in 'the prospect it held out of putting an end to *anomie* and alienation by restoring a sense of belonging and rejuvenating the life of the spirit, thereby bringing about the moral rebirth of society'.[24] Like a dried-out swimming pool, the fascist undertaking therefore not only called upon disaffected intellectuals to fill it with a meaningful elixir for the country to bathe in, but also required these same bearers of national renewal to act as 'lifeguards' in order to train the masses to swim.

Two central characteristics emerge to account for the fascist intelligentsia's prevalent influence within the specific milieu of inter-war Germany: the nineteenth century's groundswell of resistance to Enlightenment thought within the European intelligentsia, and the severe nature of the objective socio-political crisis impregnating Europe after 1918. In Germany in particular, the 'revolt against positivism'[25] was configured in a way that predisposed major intellectuals to defect from the values of Enlightenment humanism. A longstanding rejection of shallow, rational, 'civilised' values in favour of romanticised '*Geist*' following the years of French occupation under Napoleon imparted a powerful legacy to many intellectuals, encouraging a pervasive sense of inhabiting an apolitical or metapolitical realm high above the vulgar concerns of mundane democratic politics.[26] After the failure of the 1848 revolutions to secure any degree of liberalism, whether through internationalism or democracy, the ascendancy of Bismarckian 'blood and iron' authoritarianism precipitated military expansions culminating in German Unification.[27] By the time of the Kaiser's rule in Imperial Germany, a *status quo* had emerged, championing a particularly exclusive and intolerant nationalism.[28] Significantly aided by *völkisch*[29] ideals as well as the indelible experience of anticipated victory and punitive defeat in the First World War, an intellectual German tradition stressing spiritual irrationalism over political pragmatism and German '*Kultur*' over European '*Zivilisation*' (seducing even Thomas Mann) proved invaluable for CRs to draw upon, and extremely difficult for Social Democracy in 1918 to supplant.

Nonetheless, the collapse of parliamentary socialism was in no way a foregone conclusion. Necessary to the defeat of fledgling democracy in Germany was the well-documented procession of crises plaguing Weimar from its inception: the humiliating Versailles peace settlement and reparations; removal and foreign supervision of German territories and citizens; sweeping limitations of German armed forces under the auspices of 'war-guilt'; occupation by French and Belgian troops in 1923 leading to 'passive resistance' and rampant inflation (stabilised only by international mandate and assistance); attempted *coups* by left and right; pariah status in international diplomacy and a welter of domestic political parties and coalition governments. All of these were associated with the progressive structure and administration of Germany during the socialist republic's formative years, leading to a near-unanimous rejection of the system of government by German intellectuals. Although more than five years of stability brought psychological and material benefits to Germany from 1924, the economic collapse and staggering unemployment in the wake of the 1929 World Economic Crisis seemed to implicate the un-German character of democratic liberalism and validate assertions of the imminent disintegration of society by virtue of its thorough weaknesses.[30]

Conventional erudition within the civil service, which extended to academia, reflected the 'growth of irrational thought and the weak attempts to counteract it....[within] whole currents of intellectual thought'.[31] Juxtaposing cultivated values found in German idealism with the materialist and utilitarian sentiments of their European counterparts, this conservative elite struggled almost without dissent against the forces of Enlightenment modernity represented to them by the bureaucratic politics and 'cabaret' decadence exemplifying Weimar Germany. In his indispensable study of the intellectual climate amongst university instructors, Ringer convincingly demonstrates how anxiety over the erosion of a special German culture became 'something like a single theory of decadence which transcended very important individual differences of opinion'.[32] Typically following the lead of lecturers in the social sciences, this apolitical group (insofar as they disdained the mundane aspects of practical politics) only increased their demand for a renewal of authentic German *Wissenschaft* (learnedness) after 1918 through an overcoming of specialised and positivistic[33] disciplines in favour of a 'pattern which allowed many of them to seek the ultimate solution of modern cultural problems in a spiritual revival' from a cultural crisis that 'existed, if only by virtue of the fact that almost every educated German believed in its reality'.[34]

Also included in this group were numerous essayists and artists outside academia with their own cultural despondency and obscure solutions invariably taking the form of a German revival. Seeing themselves as similarly apolitical while simultaneously attempting to mould politics around their concerns, this collection includes Benn, Spengler, Carl Schmitt, Ernst Niekisch, Ernst Jünger, and others. Jünger, an archetypal CR figure closely associated with Heidegger,[35] 'dreamed up his own anarcho-fascist state in which the spirit of steel-jawed, clear-eyed soldier-workers reigned'. Heavily influenced by his experiences in the First World War, Jünger's vision of a new type of humanity combined physical and mental supremacy to express the 'total character' of work. With a similar critique of bourgeois values and a desire for a thorough social renewal of Germany, Jünger was initially enchanted with Nazism's revolutionary thrust, until it 'began to court the masses for votes like any other political party and cut deals with the traditional conservatives' and emphasise biological racism rather than spiritual nationalism.[36] By 1930, he had moved away from the movement into an 'inner emigration' characteristic of other CRs prior to the Second World War on the grounds that the national revolution 'cannot be a continuation of the great process of secularisation but only its termination'. This caution, written by Edgar Jung two years before his execution in the 1934 Röhm purge, neatly summarised both the CRs' response to Nazism's brusque squandering of the national revolution and their own spiritual alternative, which he concisely defined as:

> the return to respect for all of those elementary laws and values without which the individual is alienated from nature and God and left incapable of establishing any true order. In the place of equality comes the inner value of the individual; in the place of socialist convictions, the just integration of people into their place in a society of rank; in place of mechanical selection, the organic growth of leadership; in place of bureaucratic compulsion, the inner responsibility of genuine self-governance; in place of mass happiness, the right of the personality formed by the nation.[37]

Martin Heidegger as Metapolitical Fascist

Like Jünger, Heidegger's worldview was decisively shaped by his personal experiences. Born into the rural town of Messkirch in Baden in 1889, an environment disdaining modern encroachments, young Heidegger's personal and educational influences were strongly conditioned by staunch nationalism and reactionary Catholicism. Despite turning away from the latter after nearly a decade of theological training, spiritual residues of Christianity were transposed into an obsessive concern with the realm of *Geist* and the pursuit of ultimate truths. These remained central to his thought even as a growing hostility to organised religion, particularly Catholicism, later helped facilitate his identification with central features of National Socialism. Written while he was a non-combatant serving at a weather station near Verdun in 1918, Heidegger's letters at this time demonstrate the degree to which this spiritualism was associated with metaphysical (rather than militaristic) nationalism and an outright condemnation of the existing order: 'Certain and unshakeable is the challenge to all truly spiritual persons not to weaken at this particular moment but to grasp resolute leadership and to educate the nation towards truthfulness and a genuine valuation of the genuine assets of existence'.[38] As the ostensible result of longstanding academic training, his views were increasingly expressed through a philosophical critique of modern frivolities, the collapsing old order and the decadent one supplanting it, in addition to the distinction between 'authentic' and 'inauthentic'. Countering this perceived decay was the value of German *Wissenschaft* and the ability of quasi-mystic thinkers to diagnose and cure a society simply viewed as diseased.[39]

This cultural insight is remarkably in keeping with the prevalent syndrome Ringer analyses in his study of Germany's 'Mandarin' academics and with the metapolitical orientation of the CR in general. Yet in 1927, the year *Being and Time* was published, Heidegger's investigations still centred upon his 'existential analytic', a phenomenological approach to the concrete structures of individual existence (*Dasein*) as understood through temporality. Crucially, however, the main themes propounded in this work—notably in/authenticity, destiny, resoluteness, and particularly historicity—were soon applied by the philosopher to Germany as a whole, which became an organic and communal *Dasein* capable of self-renewal through a spiritual revolution.

This shift might be best explained in terms of the particular brand of 'German nihilism' prevalent during Weimar's final years, especially marked amongst intellectuals looking for historical paradigms to explain a secular collapse seemingly eschatological in scope. By shattering the fragile Republic's 'years of stability', the October 1929 market crash quickly radicalised the German electorate into revolutionary groups on the left and right (demonstrated by the rise in NSDAP support from 2.8% in May 1928 to 37.3% by July 1932). That the subsequent Depression, most severely felt in Germany, also affected Heidegger is evident through numerous letters sent to Blochmann and Jaspers between 1929 and 1933. In these, he stresses the need for a 'new beginning' to deliver Germany from its perceived nadir: 'Everywhere there are disruptions, crises, catastrophes, needs—the contemporary social misery, political confusion, the powerlessness of science, the erosion of art, the groundlessness of philosophy, the impotence of religion. Certainly there are needs everywhere.'[40]

Given his academic background, Heidegger's decision to explain these needs and his solutions in philosophical terms is surely axiomatic. To be sure, the concerns voiced during this period are manifested in Heidegger's philosophy, which reveals an attempt to analyse the construction and nature of existence by examining metaphysical concepts such as the Nothing and Truth.[41] For example, the 1931 treatise 'Plato's Doctrine of Truth' understands Plato's allegory of the Cave as a spiritual exhortation to the insightful 'who have not been blinded' by their milieu to become a 'freed prisoner'. But unlike before 1929, he suggests here that this attainment of personal 'authenticity' is not an end in itself, but a means toward true emancipation: 'the telling of the story does not end, as is often supposed, with the description of the highest level attained in the ascent out of the cave. On the contrary, the 'allegory' includes the story of the descent of the freed person back into the cave, back to those who are still in chains'.[42] This is clearly a movement away from earlier endeavours centring on the primacy of the individual. What starts to emerge at this point is an ominous sense of mission to liberate an enslaved community through redemptive higher knowledge. Moreover, this form of revolutionary gnosis is one that assumes increasingly explicit and contemporaneous political content.

Within the context of Germany's socio-economic situation at this time and Heidegger's consequent rethinking of his own philosophy, described by the Heideggerian scholar Otto Pöggeler as a personal 'crisis',[43] it is difficult to understand how work from the years 1929-1933 is not more closely scrutinised for its political implications. The essays written during this period appear to provide a crucial link between *Being and Time* and Heidegger's affiliation with the NSDAP. At some pivotal moment during these years Heidegger's cultural criticisms underwent a metamorphosis into 'German nihilism' and he embraced Nazism's fascist core. Heidegger saw in the Party a revolutionary method to reverse historical decay in a Mohlerian *Umschlag*, a turning point in the 2,500 year concealment of Being (*Sein*) in which everything he saw as impure would be mystically cleansed.[44] Projecting this belief in a secular 'Second Coming' onto a movement claiming to have the same objectives allowed him to become actively involved in the struggle for renewal by transforming his 'existential analytic' into a national call to arms. On 1 May 1933, Heidegger officially entered history as Nazi Party member 3,125,894.

From that day until his resignation from the rectorship on 14 April 1934, he enthusiastically set about appropriating his earlier thought in service of combating the national paralysis of the 1930s, thereby using his own philosophy as the basis for actively 'entering history'.[45]

In turning to Heidegger's assumption of the Freiburg rectorship, three essential components emerge: firstly, Heidegger deliberately used his own philosophical language to express his support for the regime; secondly, despite his later falsifications to the contrary, he was intensely political and 'Nazified' during this period of activism; and thirdly, the only aspect of his Nazism not to be submitted to his particular brand of self-exonerating hermeneutics on the matter was his absolutely unchanging assertion that his allegiance to Nazism was predicated on a belief that it could offer a comprehensive regeneration from national decline. As each of these themes has been treated by Ott, Wolin, Sheehan, Safranski and others, a short recounting of events surrounding Heidegger's infamous public debut for the NSDAP to best exemplify all three will suffice to illustrate the philosopher's zeal.

With the outright ban on Baden civil servants joining the Party, Heidegger's discreet embrace of National Socialism by the end of 1931 becomes rather unsurprising, especially when considering the threat of dismissal involved for supporting the Party, his young family, and the uncertain future of the NSDAP at the time.[46] Following the lifting of this state ban in late 1932, Heidegger was regarded as the 'spokesman' for the NSDAP by 9 April 1933 in an internal Party report, asserting that the reason he was not already a Party member was because 'he thinks it would be more practical to remain so for the time being in order to preserve a freer hand vis-à-vis his other colleagues whose position is either unclear still or openly hostile'. Moving from spokesman to political agitator later that month, Heidegger was at the centre of intrigues forcing the removal of the previous rector, an 'avowed democrat' named von Mollendorf, after less than a fortnight in office.[47] This account sharply diverges from his account given in a 1945 retrospective, 'The Rectorate 1933/4: Facts and Thoughts', a text likely written with an eye to posterity. Amongst other disingenuous claims, he states here that the previous two incumbents had forced the position of rector at Freiburg upon him and that he had wanted to withdraw his candidacy 'as late as the morning of the election day'. Yet when considering recent evidence, it becomes much more feasible to suggest Heidegger's assumption of the Freiburg leadership was a model of enthusiastic participation in National Socialism's bid to integrate autonomous institutions with the new state.[48]

In a public revelation of allegiance for Nazism on 27 May 1933, Heidegger's rectoral oration was an event flanked by swastikas and uniformed members of the SA, and culminated in the chanting of Nazi slogans. The address itself exhorted both staff and students to embrace their 'spiritual mission' by shaping their shared culture in a manner similar to Presocratic Greek philosophers, whose proximity to Being had allowed them to initiate history, logic, science, metaphysics and art—in short, culture as understood by Western society. Galvanised by the possibility of re-enacting this nativity, Heidegger urged his audience to seize the opportunity extended under the aegis of National Socialism by forming a collective entity through German *Wissenschaft*. This would be achieved by combining the military, labour and knowledge service of every individual in higher education with the state in order to erect a bulwark against the rotting of civilisation which only Aryans could reverse: 'when the spiritual strength of the West fails and its joints crack, when this moribund semblance of a culture caves in and drags all forces into confusion and lets them suffocate into madness...depends solely on whether we, as a historical-spiritual people [*Volk*] will ourselves—or whether we no longer will ourselves'.[49]

Following this address, Heidegger set about his task with relish in the following ten months, doing everything in his power to inculcate this spirit by co-ordinating his university with Nazi Germany. This included, but was by no means limited to: infusing a martial spirit (replete with SA paramilitary exercises) within Freiburg; denouncing democratic and 'pacifist' colleagues; holding a 'Scholarship Camp' of spiritual Nazis 'to reflect on ways and means of fighting for the attainment of the university of the future for the German mind and spirit'; and enforcing the *Führerprinzip* [leadership principle] amongst staff and students.[50] The last of these aspects is also illustrative of Heidegger's rectorship as a whole. In the days prior to a national plebiscite on 12 November 1933 regarding Germany's withdrawal from the League of Nations, Heidegger decreed that economic aid would be given only to students belonging to military groups such as the SS and SA, and would henceforth be 'denied to Jewish or Marxist students or anyone who fit the description of a non-Aryan in Nazi law'.[51] Additionally, Heidegger gave a series of political speeches exhorting all Freiburg students to vote in favour of Hitler's decision because 'there are not separate foreign and domestic policies. There is only the one will to the full existence [*Dasein*] of the State.' Before literally marching all students to the polls to vote, *Führer*-rector Heidegger made one final appeal:

> The choice that the German people must now make is, *simply as an event in itself*, quite independently of the outcome, the strongest expression of the new German reality embodied in the National Socialist State. Our will to national [*völkisch*] self-responsibility desires that each people find and preserve the greatness and truth of its destiny...The *Führer* has awakened this will in the entire people and has welded it into *one* resolve. No one can remain away from the polls on the day when this will is manifested. Heil Hitler![52]

Despite a Nazi report in May 1938 claiming that he remained an 'exemplary Party member', plus his occasional affirmations of Nazism's 'unique historical status' through 1942 and continuing paid membership until the regime's collapse in 1945,[53] it is clear that at some point around 1935 Heidegger became disillusioned with the regime. In fact, one of the specific reasons given by Heidegger to the Freiburg denazification committee in December 1945 for this estrangement was that 'I accepted the social and national (not National-Socialist) component, but rejected its intellectual and metaphysical underpinnings in the biologism in Party doctrine, because the social and national component as I saw it, had no essential connection with the ideological doctrine of biological racialism'.[54] This statement is instructive not only because it contains the nucleus of an apologia modified and repeated in later decades; but more importantly, he here draws a distinction between the positive and negative aspects of National Socialism. In clarifying his relationship with the Party, two essential features in keeping with both the CR and the ideological core of fascism become visible.

Time and again, Heidegger's post-war defence centres on his allegiance to the 'social' and 'national' virtues he attributes to National Socialism. These 'national' virtues are repeatedly presented in philosophical terms, demonstrated by the 1935 *Introduction to Metaphysics* where Heidegger testifies to the 'inner greatness and strength of National Socialism' as a mode of overcoming American and Soviet materialism crushing German culture on both sides: 'As the people placed at the centre we experience the hardest pressure…and on top of this we are the most metaphysical people….If the great verdict on Europe is not to be reached on its road to annihilation, then it can only be reached because of the unfolding of new spiritual forces from the centre'.[55] Significantly, after the experiences of the Second World War and a teaching ban resulting from his political association, these phrases were only marginally diluted (rather than struck out) at the insistence of his publisher, who claims he was told by Heidegger that the explicit references to Nazism were what he 'really meant'. This claim is directly opposed by Heidegger's suggestion that the less damning alterations were originally included in 1935, demonstrating his divergence from the Party, though this cannot be verified because the original hand-written page is the only one inexplicably missing from the text in the Marburg archives.[56]

More importantly, the 'social' aspect referred to in the 1945 letter becomes the primary motive for his activism: the decision to partake in a comprehensive renewal of a society in marked decline was a unique opportunity which Heidegger not only refused to express regret over, but steadfastly continued to endorse until his death. In keeping with his appeals as rector to initiate a 'new reality' through German insight, the earliest justification asserts:

At the time, I saw in the movement that had come to power the possibility of an inner self-collection and of a renewal of the people, and a path toward the discovery of its historical-Western purpose. I believed that the university, renewing itself, might also be called to significantly participate in the inner self-collection of the people. For that reason, I saw the rectorate as a possibility to lead all capable forces—regardless of party membership and party doctrine—toward this process of reflection and renewal, and to strengthen and secure the influence of these forces.[57]

Less than three years later (but following revelations regarding the scope of Nazi atrocities leading a chief Party ideologue like Alfred Bäumler to lament his complicity and 'madness'[58]), former student Herbert Marcuse's request for clarification of Heidegger's relationship with the NSDAP prompted him to respond, 'I expected from National Socialism a spiritual renewal of life in its entirety, a reconciliation of social antagonisms and a deliverance of Western *Dasein* from the dangers of communism'; concluding his letter by equating crimes against the Jews with those committed by the Russians in East Germany.[59] And nearly twenty years later, a mistrust of democracy and modern society still explicitly evident, the philosopher's most exculpatory account of his connection with Nazism still rested upon on the conviction that a 'new dawn' had arrived in 1933: 'In the general confusion of opinions and of the political trends of thirty-two parties, it was necessary to find a national, and especially a social, point of view'.[60] As these statements were never modified nor retracted, but were if anything reinforced by careful wording, amendments and release prior to publication, there is no reason to believe the axis on which Heidegger's stated relationship with National Socialism revolved was anything other than genuine.[61] Predicated upon a belief in the imminent remaking of German society akin to that of Ancient Greece and the fervent desire to assist in this project, his repeatedly avowed basis for 'entering history' suggests a profound kinship with the ideological core of fascism.

With one significant exception, Heidegger's retreat from 'history'—that is, Nazi activism and politics in general—showed remarkable similarity with the misgivings felt by other fascist intellectuals toward the Third Reich. Besides the adherence to fascist ideology, perhaps the defining feature of the CR was the variety of proposals to accomplish the shared desire for a cultural renewal, opposed by the realisation that the NSDAP either could not or would not implement any of them. That Heidegger had his own philosophical agenda to rehabilitate Germany appears incontrovertible; however, his willingness to enter populist politics by joining forces with Nazism in the belief that he could 'lead the leaders' remains his only significant divergence with the CR.[62] This assertion is supported by the previously cited 1945 letter to Freiburg's denazification commission: 'I believed the movement could be channelled in a different intellectual direction, and I regarded such an attempt as consistent with the social and broader political tendencies of the movement....This belief was mistaken'.⁶³ Though emerging later than most of his peers, Heidegger's disillusionment with Nazism is in accordance with the CR disposition, which held that the Third Reich's crude demagogy would invariably contravene any cultural advances. By the mid 1930s, both Heidegger and other cultivated German fascists had located National Socialism's vulgarity in two principal manifestations.

One of these features was an aversion to National Socialism's emphasis on the 'blood and soil' foundation of German superiority. As already presented, Heidegger's letter of December 1945 eschewed Nazi biologism as a method to determine German superiority, instead favouring metaphysical interpretations exemplified by the passage quoted from *An Introduction to Metaphysics*. Moreover, his view that science and technology rashly neglect prior thinking in the shift toward quantification and certitude is consistently demonstrated in texts as temporally and thematically diverse as his 1933 Rectoral Address and 1969 television interview.⁶⁴ Undoubtedly, Heidegger viewed the findings of science as much more problematical than did National Socialism, and instead places more emphasis on the spiritual ascendancy of German culture. For him, this is founded upon a vague but intimate connection between Germany and Ancient Greece, extending to 'the special inner relationship between the German language and the language and thinking of the Greeks. This has been confirmed to me again and again today by the French. When they begin to think, they speak German. They insist that they could not get through with their own language'.⁶⁵ Given how highly Heidegger praises the Presocratics' understanding of Being, comments of this nature must surely be understood as reinforcing his concept of the philosophical basis underlying German greatness. Moreover, unlike the Nazi juxtaposition between the physical attributes of the swindling Jew and noble Aryan, his view toward Judaism is also spiritual: 'we are faced with the choice of either bringing genuine autochthonous forces and educators into our German spiritual life, or finally abandoning it to the growing Judaization in the wider and narrower sense'. Though his attitude vis-à-vis Jews from 1933 remains ambiguous, with examples of kindness toward Jews and instances of eager compliance with NSDAP proclamations like the April 1933 Law on the Reestablishment of a Permanent Civil Service, any anti-Semitism shown by Heidegger (and the CRs in general) typically refrained from biologism.⁶⁶ Yet as Berel Lang charges, a degree of 'metaphysical anti-Semitism' allowed Heidegger to compare the extermination of six million Jews with the agricultural 'mechanised food industry' in an exceptionally scarce reference to the Holocaust. Lang supports his accusation on further grounds: while 'revisionists' accept that the Holocaust, if it *had* occurred in the manner generally thought, would merit serious moral reflection, 'Heidegger does not deny that the Nazi genocide against the Jews did occur—only that having occurred, it does not warrant serious thinking (even *about*)'.[67]

The other central reason for Heidegger's drift away from Nazism lay in his growing disdain for party politics. Unlike other CRs like Jünger and van den Bruck, this attitude was fostered in Heidegger not chiefly as the result of pre-existing elitism but by personal frustration. This arose from an inability to successfully promote his own philosophical agenda for achieving a decisive cultural renewal within the Third Reich. To be sure, his progressively reduced influence and regard amongst the Nazi hierarchy—who were generally wary of Heidegger's 'eccentric, vague, schizoform, and in part already schizophrenic, thinking', to use Jänsch's description—played a role in his estrangement from the movement. Following the resistance of many Freiburg colleagues to his rectorship, subsequent proposals for a *Dozentenakademie* in Berlin, envisioned as an 'educational community' allowing intellectuals to philosophise in a quasi-monastic atmosphere, were abandoned in 1934 after several Nazi functionaries inveighed against the idea.[68] Despite continuing to wear the swastika emblem in his lapel until 1936, continued Party scepticism from Rosenberg's office and regional ministers in Baden led Heidegger to remark to his former Jewish pupil Karl Löwith: 'things would have been "much worse" if at least a few intelligent persons hadn't become involved…If these gentlemen [intellectuals within the CR] hadn't been too refined to get involved, then everything would be different; but, instead, now I'm entirely alone.'[69] Convinced the imperative national revolution had been betrayed by the politics of Nazism, Heidegger had ceased all activism for the NSDAP prior to the outbreak of war in 1939.

It cannot be overstated that divisions between the CRs and National Socialism, predicated upon the eugenic basis of German superiority and the importance of mass-party politics, was separate from their shared ideological core. As Heidegger's association with these groups illustrates, both wholeheartedly believed in the need for a desperate and comprehensive rescue operation to save Germany from the forces of cultural decadence. Yet as evidenced by the debate between Goebbels and Rosenberg over what constituted 'degenerate art'[70], even Nazi leaders were not in unanimous agreement over where this decadence rested. Similarly, the CRs and National Socialists fundamentally disagreed on what constituted the best method to rehabilitate German society; indeed, the CRs typically disagreed among themselves, despite agreeing that a more spiritual course needed to be charted. Yet as Michael Freeden demonstrates, this interpretative 'logical adjacency' is separate from the 'ineliminable core' forming an ideology, and can be viewed as the reason countless permutations of the same ideology flourish. Therefore, proponents of one ideology can invariably appear distinct due to differing backgrounds, occupations, experiences, practical intentions, time periods, and so on, especially if separate from an organised political movement like Nazism, which had a 'Twenty-five Point Programme' from 1920.[71] Nevertheless, an ideological synergy can be said to unite these infinitely interpretative 'adjacencies', linking diverse phenomena like the Nazi state, CR apoliticism and Alain de Benoist's essays.[72]

In this respect, Heidegger becomes an exemplary case study in the kaleidoscopic permutations of a maintained ideological core. That his formulation of fascism is 'merely' philosophical rather than soldierly like Jünger's or biological like Streicher's (it should also be noted that as a failed painter, Hitler often referred to the Nazis' project in artistic terms) seems an unconvincing defence for an educator likely imbuing thousands of young German minds with 'national destiny' and 'metaphysical superiority' preceding 1939. Opposing Heidegger's assertions that his cultural theories distanced him from the Party's crimes appears an equally cogent perspective arguing that his unrepentant metapolitical allegiance to 'German nihilism' helped to win the ideological struggle which placed Nazism in power. To be sure, in later years he remained convinced that the opportunity to regenerate Germany, and subsequently the West—to recreate the proximity and 'unconcealedness' of Being last understood by the Presocratic Greeks—had been narrowly missed in early 1930s Germany because the few gnostics like Heidegger had not been heard. The movement had quite simply misunderstood and was unable to carry out its putative mission, located in the spiritualism of the Scholarship Camp and the *Dozentenakademie* rather than in the biologism of laboratories and Aryan 'Strength through Joy' propaganda films. Although clearly sanctioning the totalitarian and anti-liberal means necessary to achieve either goal, Heidegger wanted to *illustrate* the metaphysical superiority of German minds through culture instead of *proving* it by scientific measurements and rhetorical indoctrination. But just as importantly, as a result of his failure to promote this, he chose to jettison activism while unashamedly retaining the 'private' and 'authentic' basis of fascism first leading him to view National Socialism as a cultural oasis rather than a political mirage. As perhaps the first intellectual to move consciously from politics to metapolitics in response to Nazism, Heidegger is understandably pivotal to sophisticated post-war advocates of fascist ideology seeking to win cultural supremacy over liberalism, in an era of decadence and postponed renewal characterising the 'flight of the Gods', or interregnum.

Metapolitical Fascism in the Shadow of National Socialism

In 1950, following public awareness of and widespread revulsion at Nazi endeavours to remodel society, Armin Mohler's *Die Konservative Revolution* provided the earliest attempt to revive intellectual fascism by separating the CR's cultural aspirations for the German Revolution from the NSDAP's political pillaging of it. Though both were responding to a longstanding deterioration metaphysical in cause and social in effect, the Third Reich had myopically insisted on papering over fissures that it had originally intended to repair. For Mohler, this spiritual abdication initially resulted in the suppression of CR blueprints for a more profound metaphysical renovation, and later produced Nazi barbarity responsible for suspending the complete enterprise. As the CR's building project remained predicated on comprehensive renewal from comprehensive decline, National Socialism's tactical compromises with religious (such as the 1933 Concordat with the Vatican), industrial (for example, Hitler's 1932 speech to prominent capitalists in Düsseldorf) and political (notably the DNVP in 1929, and strikes organised in conjunction with communists in 1932) groups to gain power were viewed as spiritual, not tactical, compromises in order to advance the Party rather than the objective. As such, the CR could be simultaneously distinguished from Nazism's treasonous methods and praised for its insight into the nature of the Western malaise.[73] Mohler's thesis, therefore, was clearly not intended as a detached investigation of analogous interwar figures but served instead as a 'manifesto' of intellectual forerunners who understood the cultural primacy of their mission. And in a spiritless age dominated by the 'ideas of 1789'—where belief in a post-liberal order had been all but extinguished in favour of egalitarianism, humanism, and materialism—the renewal looming so imminently during the revolutionary 1930s had been deferred until some future date when it would be supplanted by a new unifying force:

> The old structure of the West as a synthesis of classical culture, Christianity, and the impulses of peoples entering history for the first time has broken down. A new unity, however, has not yet emerged. We stand in this transitional period, this 'interregnum' which leaves its mark on every spiritual activity. The Conservative Revolution is conditioned by it, and at the same time sees itself as an attempt to overcome it.[74]

Besides locating Heidegger firmly within this tradition, the other pertinent feature to emerge from *Die Konservative Revolution* is the recognition that German fascism's positive ideals had been corrupted by Nazism, which in turn ensured an indefinite preponderance of liberal values and their monopoly over the post-war political spectrum. Mohler's answer to this dilemma lay with his CR case-studies: by polishing the tarnished image of metapolitical fascism while presenting its discourse as a unified and reasonable alternative to modernity, the struggle for a future renewal of the West by discerning Europeans could proceed from a purely cultural standpoint. In moving beyond decadent politics and condemning the excesses of National Socialism, Mohler bequeathed an essential legacy to the European *Nouvelle Droite* (New Right, hereafter ENR).

This movement, under the acknowledged leadership of Alain de Benoist since his rise to prominence during the 1968 student revolts, also recognised the need to overhaul the vilified legacy of inter-war fascism and its associations with totalitarianism, Aryanism, and racial extermination. As demonstrated by an 'appeal to vigilance' by 1500 French intellectuals, the work of Pierre-André Taguieff and Roger Griffin,[75] and the repeated claims of ENR functionaries regarding 'the sheer size of a crisis that demands a radical renewal of modes of thought, decision and action' in a 'pivotal period—a turning point or an "*interregnum*"',[76] their ideological relationship to salient features of fascist thought remains perceptible. But despite their extreme right-wing language and origins, the ENR has developed a programme intent upon securing ideological hegemony prior to initiating social change. This project, significantly called 'right-wing Gramscism',[77] illustrates the ingenuity of post-war fascism: by locating their right-wing objectives solely within the cultural sphere while appropriating an array of thinkers critical of the modern *status quo* (especially left-wing thinkers like Gramsci, Herbert Marcuse, and Noam Chomsky); the ENR appears to overcome divisive political distinctions and renounce its threatening inter-war legacy. Its sophisticated discourse—exemplified by its appearance in New Left journals such as *Telos* and effective 'Third Way' fusion of the historic Right/Left dichotomy—typically remains difficult to assess due to its cultural emphasis. But as Bar-On has shown in his recent study:

> ENR thinkers such as Alain de Benoist steadfastly believed that only a change in the dominant cultural apparatus and spirit of the age, especially opinions of key cultural elites, could pave the definitive road towards a new, durable, and long-lasting post-liberal order. For de Benoist, the climate of the post-World War II era meant that it was intellectually and politically suicidal for a right-wing force to attempt to seize political power without first controlling the dominant cultural apparatus of the period and gaining general support. De Benoist recognised that the metapolitical struggle to displace liberalism, socialism, and the Judeo-Christian heritage would be a difficult one, but remained true to his metapolitical vocation from 1968.[78]

This vocation centres upon a 'right to difference' critique of modernity's egalitarian, 'desacralizing', and materialist attempts to banish the richness of indigenous cultures in favour of American-style universalism. Emphasising the traditions of Indo-European 'pagan' culture (in a manner quite similar to Heidegger's prizing of Presocratic thought) over the humanising traditions of Judeo-Christianity and its expansion via Enlightenment liberalism allows de Benoist and other ENR thinkers to invert ideals typically seen as emancipatory. Thus, the spread of democracy, 'acting to the detriment of the common interest',[79] becomes totalitarian and the global mixing of peoples becomes racist: 'There is a racism which absolutises the Other to create a Totally Other with whom no one can have anything in common. There is another, more perverse racism which absolutises the Same and, in the name of the Same, challenges the very idea of difference.'[80] Similar to Mohler's phrase 'the Trotskyites of the German Revolution', the objective of de Benoist's and other ENR critiques of European culture arguably rests upon a deconstruction of Enlightenment thought and a reconstruction of intellectual fascism. As such, it perhaps comes as no surprise that the figures most heavily drawn upon by the 'New Right' are selected from the frontlines of the CR. By advancing the project commenced by Mohler, a deluge of refined ENR material on Jünger, Schmitt, Heidegger and others has sprouted throughout Europe,[81] all attempting to illustrate the value of non-Nazi fascism to a post-war audience.

Although his limited emphasis in Mohler's text might be explained by Heidegger's academic ban in Germany to 1950 (suggestive of an overly close association with the NSDAP) or his later philosophical investigations of the interregnum undertaken in the quarter century after the publication of *Die Konservative Revolution*, there can be no doubt about the influence of his thought upon the current vanguard of ENR thinkers. Numerous essays written by de Benoist contain both explicit references and allusions betraying a significant Heideggerian influence, and despite generally persisting resistance to his thought in Germany, de Benoist's counterpart Pierre Krebs' recent edited volume[82] contains no fewer than twenty-two references to the philosopher. Nor is this impact strictly limited to the European continent. Michael Walker's British New Right publication *The Scorpion* regularly pays homage to Heidegger,[83] while an internet document entitled 'Russia and the New World Order: The Geopolitical Project of Pax Eurasiatica' by Nikolaj von Kreitor concludes by stating: 'This is a good point of departure because it presupposes the concept of the political. And after all, to paraphrase Heidegger, the political is the house of Being.'[84] Although each of these forums certainly has diverse interests and 'adjacencies', they all champion Heidegger and other CR figures as promising cultural heralds for a European renewal. As this acknowledged legacy suggests, the ENR has constructed 'a cultural strategy attempting to capture what it views as the "real" power centres of civil society and the cultural apparatus', one metapolitical rather than apolitical in its dedication to overcoming the predominance of liberalism in the interregnum.[85]

Though Mohler introduced the concept of the interregnum and the European New Right popularised it, Heidegger's immense influence on these thinkers has much to do with his intimate connection with the interregnum. Needless to say, this was expressed in philosophical language, frequently as a reference to an absent god: 'Only a god can still save us. I think the only possibility of salvation left to us is to prepare readiness, through thinking and poetry, for the appearance of the god or for the absence of the god during the decline; so that we do not, simply put, die meaningless deaths, but that when we decline, we decline in the face of the absent god.'[86] As a function of Heidegger's growing divergence from the politics of the Third Reich, this quite similar response to the predominance of the *status quo* originated as early as 1935 and continued until his death in 1976. Like the initial shift toward fascism in the early 1930s, this modification in his thought was not so much a 'turning'[87] away from a now-unworkable position as a philosophical addition to his views in response to perceived developments. Just as a sense of imminent rebirth was annexed onto his intense cultural criticisms and projected onto Nazism following the 1929 national paralysis, Heidegger's practical experiences and disillusion with aspects of Party doctrine resulted in the annexation of his own version of the interregnum.

Significantly, in addition to his enduring dialogue with the Presocratic Greeks—whose understanding of Being is a disintegrating legacy hardly remembered at all today—at the start of 1935 Heidegger commenced an examination of Friedrich Hölderlin: 'My thinking has an essential connection with Hölderlin's poetry. I think Hölderlin is the poet who points toward the future, who expects the god, and who therefore cannot remain simply a subject for Hölderlin research in the literary historical imagination'.[88] By creating a prophet out of an artist who resisted the development of Enlightenment thought, the 'essential connection' with Hölderlin can easily be viewed as a manifestation of 'Heidegger's specific philosophical and political concerns'.[89] As the interregnum gnostic *par excellence*, Hölderlin's poetry laments an absence of holiness while longing for a return to 'authentic' culture in an impoverished age that can only aspire to meditating on a world yet to emerge. By appropriating Hölderlin, Heidegger thus reveals an unchanging disdain for the components of liberalism, in addition to the desire for the revolutionary creation of a culture predicated upon Germanic values of the past to inaugurate a new relationship with modernity in the future. That poetry, not swastikas, became the preferred vehicle with which to escape from the 'cave' of an indefinite spiritual interregnum reinforces the shift toward a metapolitical critique of society and an underlying ideological unity persisting long after Heidegger's break with National Socialism.

Although debated, the contention that a degree of continuity exists in Heidegger's thought is by no means original.[90] Yet this debate, as well as ongoing conflicts over the depth of the philosopher's commitment to National Socialism, reflects differing ideal typical constructions of Heidegger's philosophical agenda by scholars. If anything, stratified camps have developed, each with their own (usually) valid interpretations of how Nazism impacted the work of Heidegger and forced subsequent changes in his thought. By reversing these readings; that is, by inquiring into the relationship of German (and European) politics to Heidegger rather than his relationship to politics, an alternative heuristic explanation surfaces. This construction rests upon an ideological approach to fascism as a generic phenomenon, centring on the expectation of cultural rebirth within a nation chained to decadent Enlightenment ideals, equally appealing to intellectuals and wider swathes of a despondent public.

The application of this conceptual framework to the 'Heidegger Case' suggests two central conclusions. The first asserts that Heidegger's philosophical acceptance of this ideology caused both his brief Nazi activism and his later movement away from practical expressions of fascism on the grounds that the Third Reich was simply unable to initiate the desired renewal. What was in 1933 an expectation of an impending Greek dawn thus became merely another confirmation of the withdrawal of Being, the 'flight of the Gods', or the preponderance of planetary technology; in short, an indefinite deferment of the necessary regeneration of Germany (and by extension, the West). As National Socialism, offering the best opportunity to counter this decline, had failed Heidegger (rather than *vice versa*) by becoming tainted by power and spiritless compromises, 'politics as we know it today must be given up on, because it pervades a concept of the will that is most detrimental to the possibility of an authentic repetition of the Greek moment and of the freeing of a new beginning'.[91]

The second conclusion, following on from the first, argues for Heidegger's continued adherence to an ideological core of fascism—albeit one adopting a strictly metapolitical discourse necessary to post-war fascism— as indicated by the 'new consensus' within this field. Aimed at separating the commendable aspects of fascism (cultural regeneration) from its unfortunate past enactment (the elimination of those who were deemed unworthy or disagreed with fascism's good points), his project would undoubtedly endorse Hitler's stated ideals at his 1924 trial for treason, which preceded Nazism's subsequent shift toward party politics: 'If we founded the new movement, we did so in the hope that we would one day change the destiny of Germany, even if it was in the twelfth hour'.[92] Moreover, by pointing to an ideological synergy connecting National Socialism, the Conservative Revolution, and post-war variants of fascist metapolitics—principally the European New Right—this contention therefore locates Heidegger's philosophy within a far more representative and far less politically disinterested milieu than previously maintained. The deep implication of his thought with all three permutations of fascism challenges scholars to keep the 'Heidegger Case' open as fresh evidence of his collusion with anti-humanist forces comes to light. This is done in the interest of more thoroughly understanding the ramifications of Heidegger's *oeuvre*, as well as helping to more generally appreciate the subtle forms extremism can take when confronted with the entrenched liberal, and hence hostile, climate which has prevailed since 1945.

In this respect, Heidegger's attempts to 'prepare the ground' for a post-liberal awakening to end the present interregnum that is impeding the return of an authentic culture cease to be innocuous. Indeed, even his later 'non-Nazi' philosophy assumes a much more intense political undertone and carries a much more noxious legacy, a realisation perfectly understood by contemporary fascists themselves. Thus, for example, Heidegger's meditations on Hölderlin become political exhortations for a future that finally overcomes the baleful legacy of Socratic humanism. For this German poet takes centre stage in Heidegger's later work as (in his view) the first gnostic to mourn the loss of the spiritual in a constantly unfolding Greek tragedy about the withdrawal of Being. Although this play nearly reached a triumphant climax under National Socialism, what seemed a final curtain signalled only an interval. For Heidegger and later the ENR, Western history is being performed in two acts rather than one, with only those of true cultural insight willing to sit in the darkened theatre throughout a seemingly endless intermission before the long-awaited anagnoris heralds a dramatic dénouement. Meanwhile, we mere lesser mortals, progressing through linear time without the recourse to metapolitical climax and resolution, must simply wait for Godot.

Endnotes

[1] Though generally agreed that the text contained serious academic flaws regarding the presentation and interpretation of primary material, Farías nevertheless renewed fierce international debate amongst scholars, particularly in France, where Heidegger's intellectual legacy had been immensely influential and rather unproblematic after 1945. For a discussion of the salient features and ramifications of Farías' book, see the forward to the English translation, *Heidegger and Nazism* (Philadelphia: Temple University Press, 1989). Demonstrating the extended audience this issue has persistently attracted on both sides of the Atlantic since its eruption is Thomas Sheehan's excellent summary 'Heidegger and the Nazis' in the *New York Review of Books*, 35/10 (June 16, 1988), pp. 38-47, available online at: www.researchgate.net/publication/249209399_Heidegger_and_Nazism (all websites last accessed 24 February 2020).

[2] A heated exchange in the journal *Philosophy* by Sharon Janusz and Glenn Webster on one side ("In Defence of Heidegger"; 66/257 (June 1991), pp. 380-385) and Paul Edwards on the other ("A Reply to Crude and Reckless Distortions"; 67/260 (April 1992), pp. 381-385) following the latter's October 1989 article "Heidegger's Quest for Being" (64/250, pp. 437-470) testifies to the often personal nature of these arguments: "The authors…reveal themselves as bigoted fanatics and their bigotry is compounded by a staggering incompetence and ignorance bordering on illiteracy" (67/260, p. 381).

[3] This field of study, currently undergoing a scholastic renaissance since the 1990s, views fascism generically [hence the small 'f' as distinguished from Italian Fascism] as a political ideology. Yet it is certainly not without its own controversies: i.e., whether to include wartime regimes in France, Japan, Spain, and even Germany as 'fascist'; whether post-war fascism exists as such; and so on. For a review of these debates see Roger Griffin, "The Primacy of Culture: The Current Growth (or Manufacture) of Consensus within Fascist Studies," *Journal of Contemporary History* 37.1 (Jan. 2002), pp. 21-43, available online at https://www.researchgate.net/publication/249709813_The_Primacy_of_Culture_The_Current_Growth_Or_Manufacture_of_Consensus_within_Fascist_Studies.

[4] Far from attempting to locate the 'essential' nature of diverse fascist movements in the twentieth century (many of which reject the classification), this study will instead follow Rickert and Weber's reasoning that *any* taxonomy of specific phenomena is necessarily contrived for the purposes of signification: 'general concepts do not describe the elements…a class of phenomena have in common in the empirical world, but the elements which they have in common in an imaginary world, a utopia', Burger, *Max Weber's Theory of Concept Formation: History, Laws, and Ideal Types* (Durham, NC: Duke University Press, 1976).

[5] Not only fascists themselves, but also large swathes of artists and thinkers at this time also point to the unsatisfactory nature of this term due to its implications of shallow 'cleverness' rather than 'spiritual' insight. Wyndham Lewis argues that 'we are obliged to use such terms, if we are to make ourselves understood…. So let us—with shame—use the word "intellectual"', *British Union Quarterly*, 3/2 (1938), p. 25.

[6] Michael Freeden's influential article "Political Concepts and Ideological Morphology" (*Journal of Contemporary History*, 2/2 (1994), pp. 140-164) argues that ideologies can be profitably defined in terms of a central core, with logical and cultural adjacencies creating infinite permutations of an ideology. This methodology is particularly helpful in the study of fascism, the core of which centres upon a desire for comprehensive renewal, while logical

and cultural adjacencies might be as varied as (respectively): militarism and Teutonic myths for Nazism; or Futurism and a recovery of Roman heritage for Italian Fascism.

[7] Roger Griffin, the most notable proponent of this 'new consensus' and first to attempt a concise definition of generic fascism, first introduced this ideological approach in *The Nature of Fascism* (London: Pinter, 1991), one subsequently endorsed by Stanley Payne in his review article "Historical Fascism and the Radical Right" in *Journal of Contemporary History*, 35/1 (2000), p. 110.

[8] Roger Griffin, "The Primacy of Culture", *op. cit.*, ref. 15.

[9] The *Volkspartei* thesis, demonstrating the considerable support of fascism by all social classes, has reached near unanimous agreement following the publication of Detlef Mühlberger's *Hitler's Followers* (London: Routledge, 1991).

[10] Armin Mohler, *Die Konservative Revolution in Deutschland 1918-1932* (Darmstadt: Wissenschaftliche Buchgesellschaft, 1994). Other scholars have expounded on this theme, for example, Roger Woods, *The Conservative Revolution in the Weimar Republic* (London: Macmillan Press, 1996).

[11] *Ibid.* Mohler makes no secret that the objective in the writing of his 'handbook' is to demonstrate the value of the CR to post-war intellectuals searching for cultural rather than military ascendancy following the travesty of Germany's National Revolution under Nazism.

[12] For example, see Rüdiger Safranski, *Martin Heidegger: Between Good and Evil* (London: Harvard University Press, 1999) and Hugo Ott, *Martin Heidegger: A Political Life* (London: Harper Collins, 1993) for two important biographies on Heidegger and Nazism, the former philosophical in content, the latter political.

[13] Tom Rockmore, *On Heidegger's Nazism and Philosophy* (Hemel Hempstead: Harvester Wheatsheaf, 1992), pp. 282-5.

[14] *Ibid.*, p. 9.

[15] The work of Zeev Sternhell and particularly George Mosse in this area is now gaining deserved recognition, as both analyse the importance of intellectuals on the development of fascism. For further discussion, see Griffin's "The Primacy of Culture", *op. cit.*

[16] For a catalogue of fascist texts both before and after 1945, see Griffin, ed., *Fascism: A Reader's Guide* (Oxford: Oxford University Press, 1995).

[17] *The Fascist Week* #14, Feb.9th-15th (British Union of Fascists, 1934), p. 4.

[18] This is characteristic of most surveys of fascism, from general overviews such as provided by the *Fontana Dictionary of Modern Thought* (London: Harper Collins, 1999), pp. 310-311, to specific analyses such as Dave Renton's recent *Fascism: Theory and Practice* (London: Pluto Press, 1999).

[19] See Freeden, *op. cit.*, ref. 6.

[20] In contrast to Hermann Rauschning's premise in his *Revolution of Nihilism* (New York: Arno Press, 1972) and *Hitler Speaks* (London: Thornton Butterworth, 1939), the first of many studies to submit that Nazism could only be defined by virtue of what it reacted against, Mohler here significantly understands 'German nihilism' as also containing an antithetical longing for rebirth 'as two sides of the same entity', see Griffin, ed., *op. cit.*, quoted p. 352.

[21] Just as importantly, Mosse characterises fascism here as 'an ideology which promised to restore culture as well as…the totality of society…The totality was symbolized by the temper of cultural activity—if the arts were restored, then society as a whole would be able to transcend the present. Idealism formed the core of their outlook upon the world…', S.J. Woolf, ed., *The Nature of Fascism* (London: Weidenfeld and Nicolson, 1968), Ch. 12, quoted pp. 206, 207, available online at: http://archive.org/download/georgemosse00reel12/georgemos

se00reel12.pdf; and https://ia902604.us.archive.org/14/items/georgemosse00reel12/george mosse00reel12.pdf.

[22] *Ibid.*, p. 209.
[23] *Ibid.*, p. 216.
[24] Griffin, "The Primacy of Culture", *op. cit.*
[25] This theme is of central importance to the change in modern intellectual thought throughout Henry Stuart Hughes' groundbreaking study, *Consciousness and Society: The Reorientation of European Social Thought 1890-1930* (Brighton: Harvester Press, 1986).
[26] Gottlieb Fichte's *Addresses to the German Nation* (London: The Open Court Publishing Co., 1922) offers a good example of this mentality. See also Hermann Glaser's *The Cultural Roots of National Socialism* (London: Croom Helm, 1978) and Harold James' *A German Identity 1770-1990* (London: Weidenfeld and Nicolson, 1996).
[27] For an overview, see Charles Breunig, *The Age of Revolution and Reaction, 1789-1850* (London: W.W. Norton and Co., 1977), pp. 260-267; Fritz Stern, *The Politics of Cultural Despair: A Study in the Rise of the Germanic Ideology* (London: Cambridge University Press, 1961), pp. xi-xxx.
[28] Hans Kohn, *The Mind of Germany: The Education of a Nation* (New York: Charles Scribner's Sons, 1960).
[29] This movement, centring on racialist and nationalist superiority, was later essential to the culture of Nazism. For comprehensive documentation of this German phenomenon, see Stern's study (particularly of Langbehn), *op. cit.*, and George Mosse, *The Crisis of German Ideology* (London: Weidenfeld and Nicolson, 1966).
[30] For an exhaustive survey of the causes, events and consequences of this fourteen-year period, see Hans Mommsen, *The Rise and Fall of Weimar Democracy* (London: University of North Carolina Press, 1996).
[31] See Geoffrey J. Giles' "National Socialism and the Educated Elite in the Weimar Republic" in Peter D. Stachura, ed., *The Nazi Machtergreifung* (London: George Allen and Unwin, 1983), pp. 49-67, quoted p. 53.
[32] Fritz Ringer, *The Decline of the German Mandarins: The German Academic Community 1890-1933* (Cambridge, MA: Harvard University Press, 1969), p. 259.
[33] 'Particularly in the humanistic disciplines, the antithesis between idealist and positivist methods became a veritable obsession with German scholars', *ibid.*, p. 254.
[34] *Ibid.*, p. 268 and p. 245.
[35] Jünger's acknowledged influence (particularly his 1932 *The Worker*) on Heidegger's thinking on modern production and technology has led Michael Zimmerman to conclude after extensive analysis: '[Jünger] is the link which mediates between Heidegger's thought…and his engagement with National Socialism', *Heidegger's Confrontation with Modernity: Technology, Politics, Art* (Indianapolis: Indiana University Press, 1990), see Chs. 4-6, quoted p. xviii.
[36] Elliot Neaman, "Ernst Jünger's Millennium: Bad Citizens for the New Century" in Richard J. Golson, ed., *Fascism's Return: Scandal, Revision, and Ideology Since 1980* (London: University of Nebraska Press, 1995), p. 221.
[37] Edgar Jung, "Germany and the Conservative Revolution" in Anton Kaes, Martin Jay and Edward Dimendberg, eds., *The Weimar Republic Sourcebook* (London: University of California Press, 1994), pp. 352-354. This compendium contains a number of valuable excerpts from CR figures echoing Jung's declaration, notably found in sections 11, 13 and 14.
[38] Letter to Elisabeth Blochmann, quoted in Safranski, *op. cit.*, p. 86.
[39] These themes are further detailed in *ibid*, Chs. 1-8.

[40] Safranski, *op. cit.*, pp. 189-224, quoted p. 195.
[41] During this period, the four major essays are "What is Metaphysics" (1929), "On the Essence of Ground" (1929), "On the Essence of Truth" (1930), and "Plato's Doctrine of Truth" (1931/2); William McNeill, ed., *Martin Heidegger: Pathmarks* (Cambridge: Cambridge University Press, 1998).
[42] *Ibid.*, p. 171.
[43] Pöggeler, *Heidegger's Path of Thinking* (Atlantic Highlands: Humanities Press International, 1987), especially pp. 180-190. Also see Richard Wolin, *The Politics of Being: The Political Thought of Martin Heidegger* (Oxford: Columbia University Press, 1990), *op. cit.*, pp. 70-75.
[44] Mohler, *op. cit.*, see also ref. 20.
[45] Heidegger's concept of historicity, simplified as the understanding that *Dasein* constructs meaning through time by placing locating itself within historical events, was cited by him in an infamous conversation with one-time pupil Karl Löwith as 'the basis of his political 'engagement'. He also left no doubt about his belief in Hitler.... He was convinced now, as before, that National Socialism was the right course for Germany; one only had to 'hold out' long enough. The only aspect that troubled him was the ceaseless 'organisation' at the expense of 'vital forces'.' Löwith, *My Life in Germany 1914-1933*, p. 60.
[46] For Heidegger's acceptance of Nazism in 1931, see Otto Pöggeler, "Heidegger, Nietzsche, and Politics," *The Heidegger Case: On Philosophy and Politics*, eds. Tom Rockmore and Joseph Margolis (Philadelphia: Temple University Press, 1992), p. 133.
[47] Hugo Ott, *Martin Heidegger: A Political Life* (London: Harper Collins, 1993), quoted p. 144.
[48] For Heidegger's apologia, see Günther Neske and Emil Kettering, eds., *Martin Heidegger and National Socialism* (New York: Paragon House, 1990), pp. 15-32. The crux of this essay contends that he was in fact attempting to mitigate higher education's relationship with Nazism rather than advance it. Given the existence of a telegram to Hitler a week earlier pledging his support 'with the aims of the *Gleichschaltung*' at Freiburg and his assistance in the drafting and implementation of the 21 August 1933 Baden University Reform in accordance with the *Führerprinzip* establishing Baden as the first German *Land* (province) fully co-ordinated with the Nazi state, this is highly unlikely. For details, see Hugo Ott, *Martin Heidegger: A Political Life* (London: Harper Collins, 1993), pp. 190-215.
[49] See Heidegger's "Rectoral Address" in Neske and Kettering, eds., *op. cit.*, pp. 5-13.
[50] For treatment of all of these events, see Safranski, *op. cit.*, pp. 258-275, quoted from Heidegger, p. 262.
[51] Sheehan, *op. cit.*, p. 40
[52] Quoted in Richard Wolin, ed., *The Heidegger Controversy: A Critical Reader* (London: The MIT Press, 1993), pp. 50-52; for further examples of Heidegger's political statements as rector of Freiburg, see Ch 2.
[53] Ott, *op. cit.*, p. 374 and p. 304 respectively.
[54] *Ibid.*, p. 333.
[55] Griffin, ed., *op. cit.*, pp. 151-2.
[56] Sheehan, *op. cit.*, p. 43. For Heidegger's response to these allegations, see the 1966 *Der Spiegel* interview reprinted in Neske and Kettering, eds., *op. cit.*, pp. 53-4. Additionally, Ott's work casts serious doubt on the veracity of a number of other claims Heidegger makes in the interview, including his interactions with Edmund Husserl, his resignation from the rectorship, the wartime ban of his publications by the Party, and his impressment into the *Volkssturm* (people's army) in 1944.
[57] Ott, *op. cit.*, p. 333.

58 Hans Sluga, *Heidegger's Crisis: Philosophy and Politics in Nazi Germany* (London: Harvard University Press, 1993), p. 242.
59 Wolin, ed., *op. cit.*, p. 61.
60 Neske and Kettering, *op. cit.*, p. 44.
61 Heidegger insisted on revising the manuscript of the *Der Spiegel* interview, in addition to giving instructions to the journal's editors to only publish the text after his death. Similar circumstances dictated the 1983 release of 'The Rectorate 1933/34: Facts and Thoughts' by Heidegger's son Hermann. For details on both, see *ibid.*, pp. 3-4 and 233-236.
62 For an excellent survey of Heidegger's attempt to locate the *Seinsfrage* in the 'National Revolution' and the reaction of Party functionaries to his short-lived brand of philosophical Nazism, see John D. Caputo, "Heidegger's Revolution: An Introduction to *An Introduction to Metaphysics*" in James Risser, ed., *Heidegger Toward the Turn: Essays on the Work of the 1930s* (Albany: State University of New York Press, 1999), pp. 53-73. See also Wolin, "To Lead the Leader" in *op. cit.*, Ch 3, esp. pp. 85-95.
63 Ott, *op. cit.*, p. 333.
64 For examples in both texts, see Neske and Kettering, eds., *op. cit.*, pp. 5-7 and pp. 83-84.
65 *Der Spiegel* interview in *ibid.*, p. 63.
66 Safranski, *op. cit.*, pp. 248-263, quoted p. 255.
67 Berel Lang, *Heidegger's Silence* (London: Athlone Press, 1996), pp. 14-16.
68 Safranski, *op. cit.*, pp. 270-331, quoted p. 280.
69 Löwith, *op. cit.*, p. 60. See also ref. 50.
70 For more than a decade, the *völkisch* quality of, for example, German Expressionism had been debated by Nazi leaders prior to the opening of the 'Degenerate Art' exhibit on 19th July 1937, See Brandon Taylor's "Post-Modernism in the Third Reich" in Brandon Taylor and Wilfried van der Will, eds., *The Nazification of Art* (Winchester: Winchester Press, 1990), pp. 130-133.
71 Available in English translation at http://germanhistorydocs.ghi-dc.org/sub_document.cfm?document_id=4625&language=english.
72 An excellent example of this correspondence can be found in some of the earliest work on de Benoist's fascist pedigree by Thomas Sheehan, 'Myth and Violence: The Fascism of Julius Evola and Alain de Benoist', *Social Research*, Spring 1981, pp. 45-73. Though an antecedent of both Freeden's methodology and Griffin's ideological studies of fascism, Sheehan's article clearly perceives a similarity between inter-war fascist intellectuals like Evola (and, by extension, Heidegger) and proponents of the 'New Right' such as de Benoist. See ref. 6 for Freeden's methodological arguments and ref. 3 for Griffin's ideological studies.
73 Mohler, *Die Konservative Revolution in Deutschland 1918-1932*, *op. cit.*
74 Quoted in Roger Griffin, "Between metapolitics and *apoliteia*: the New Right's strategy for conserving the fascist vision in the 'interregnum'", *Contemporary French Studies*, 8/1 (2000), pp. 35-53, quoted p. 39.
75 Similar to Mohler, the *Nouvelle Droite's* conscious attempts to distance itself from the practice of fascism in Internal Bulletins and the like has not escaped scholars like Taguieff. For an extensive discussion of the *ND*'s fascist legacy, see Griffin, 'Plus ça Change! The Fascist Pedigree of the *Nouvelle Droite*' in *The Development of the Radical Right in France: From Boulanger to Le Pen* (New York: St. Martin's Press, 2000).
76 Within the paradigm of generic fascism set out earlier, the New Right's programme contains a number of vehement condemnations of Enlightenment progress while steadfastly maintaining its desire for a sweeping renewal. See Alain de Benoist and Charles Champetier, "Manifesto for 2000" in *Telos*, 115 (Spring 1999), pp. 117-144, quoted p. 118.

[77] Taken from Marxist thinker Antonio Gramsci, this idea centres upon winning the 'battle of ideas', and is applied to the theories of the Conservative Revolution in the European New Right publication *Éléments* 20 (février-avril 1977). This number contains an editorial by Robert de Herte (pseud. of Alain de Benoist), "La 'révolution conservatrice'", and a "Dossier: Révolution conservatrice," with contributions by de Benoist ("Pour un 'gramscisme de droite'", pp. 7-10) and others.

[78] Tamir Bar-On, unpublished PhD. Thesis, "The Ambiguities of the Intellectual European New Right, 1968-1999", McGill University, Montreal, November 2000.

[79] De Benoist, "What is Sovereignty", *Telos*, 116 (Summer 1999), pp. 99-118, quoted p. 117.

[80] Quoted in de Benoist, "What is Racism?", *Telos*, 114 (Winter 1999), pp. 11-48, quoted p. 48.

[81] For example, see the *Nouvelle Droite* publication *Nouvelle École* for extensive coverage on figures in the CR: number 44 is dedicated to Carl Schmitt, number 48 to Jünger, and number 37 is entitled 'Lectures de Heidegger'.

[82] Pierre Krebs, ed., *Mut zur Identität: Alternatives zum Prinzip der Gleichheit* (Struckum: Thule Bibliothek, 1988).

[83] Interestingly, Alain de Benoist wrote one of the texts available for viewing on *The Scorpion's* website on Jünger entitled 'Between the Gods and the Titans', with reference to Benn, Niekisch, and particularly Heidegger; see: https://web.archive.org/web/20000914062038/http://utenti.tripod.it/ArchivEurasia/kreitor_rnwo_eng.html; and https://web.archive.org/web/20010624152334/http://www.stormloader.com/thescorpion/17jueng.html.

[84] https://web.archive.org/web/20000914062038/http://utenti.tripod.it/ArchivEurasia/kreitor_rnwo_eng.html.

[85] Bar-On, *op. cit.*, p. 7.

[86] *Der Spiegel* interview in Neske and Kettering, eds., *op. cit.*, p. 57.

[87] The concept of a *Kehre*, or turning, in Heidegger's philosophy of the 1930s is frequently invoked to demonstrate Heidegger's allegiance or rejection of Nazism. For an account of this ongoing debate, see Risser, ed., *op. cit.*

[88] *Der Spiegel* interview in Neske and Kettering, eds., *op. cit.*, p. 62. Safranski understands Heidegger's relationship with Hölderlin as a method of persevering through the 'night of the gods', or 'interregnum'; *op. cit.*, pp. 282-288.

[89] Zimmerman, *op. cit.*, p. 114.

[90] For example, see Frederick A. Olafson, "The Unity of Heidegger's Thought" in Charles Guignon, ed., *The Cambridge Companion to Heidegger* (Cambridge: Cambridge University Press, 1996).

[91] Quoted from Heidegger in Miguel de Beistegui, *Heidegger and the Political: Dystopias* (London: Routledge, 1998), p. 34.

[92] Taken from Hitler's speech to the People's Court in Munich, 26 February 1924, in Griffin, ed., p. 117.

19. Hate Globally, Act Locally: A Case Study of Universal Nazism Online

In June 2010, two neo-Nazis went to trial on charges relating to their roles in the British far-right extremist group Aryan Strike Force (ASF). Although acquitted on the most serious charges, both Michael Heaton and Trevor Hannington were sentenced on 24 June for inciting racial hatred. Six weeks earlier, and also in the north of England, a third member of the ASF's 'leadership committee' was jailed for two years, although in the case of Nikki Davison, his conviction was for possessing material useful for acts of terror.[1] Nikki had been sentenced at the same time as his father Ian Davison, the fourth and final member of the Aryan Strike Force's initial leadership group. Although the usual extreme right-wing infighting was to see Heaton eventually leave and found an even more short-lived, rival group called 'The British Freedom Fighters', all four of the above men were the co-creators of the ASF at its launch at the start of 2008. Their own views can be fairly summarised by the ASF's 'Mission Statement' from December 2008, some six months before the first arrests of leadership in June 2009:

> Today we live under a Zionist Occupation Government. This is a government that has corrupted the white culture and aims to ultimately destroy the Aryan race. For centuries, the Aryan race has been built on the principles of honour, loyalty and duty. These principles of looking out for ones own kind are fast becoming a thing of the past with the emphasis placed on the self. What we have now is a race of people who legally cheat, steal and lie to serve their own purposes, to meet their own ends. This lifestyle has been indoctrinated into the people through the media and schooling by our own Zionist Occupation Government.
>
> As true National Socialists, we have a duty to fight against this. Whether it's in the boardroom or on the streets, we will resist, we will fight. Whether we are one or a million, we will stay loyal and continue the fight. We will never give up, we will never be beaten. But how do we fight?
>
> The purpose of this organisation is to pull all national socialist, nationalists, racists and fascists together. Many people who consider themselves national socialists, although meaning well, neither know or live by the principles of national socialism. Our aim, amongst others, is to educate them. Its only when a man truly knows what he's fighting for can he expect to be victorious. We may not win a war, indeed, we may not even fight a war, but we will restore a culture amongst the white population of the world. From there, at least we'll have built solid foundation for the next generation.
>
> As for now, we'll still fight. With the right response, we'll develop active street crew in every town to deal with the local insurgents. We'll protect political parties that share our aims. We'll form pressure groups to resist the corruption of our society. In fact, we'll look to deal with every threat that threatens what we stand for. The list is endless.

So where do you fit into all this? Providing you're white and share our aims, we'll find a place for you. If you feel you want to participate in direct action then you can. If you feel that you're more suited to propaganda or political action then there is a place for you. If you simply want to visit the forum, speak to like minded people and post on various subjects then you're welcome. The real emphasis here is community and togetherness. Lets get together and make things work for us. Let's behave like Aryan men and women.
We must secure the existence of our people and a future for white children.[2]

Underscoring the nature of the threat posed by these British neo-Nazis, Davison Sr. received 10 years for producing the chemical weapon ricin—the first such conviction in the UK under the 1996 Chemical Weapons Act. In the words of the Crown Prosecution Service lawyer for the Counter-Terrorism Division, Stuart Laidlaw, these 'Nazi zealots' cultivated and disseminated 'a hatred of anyone who they considered a threat to their race. It is clear that they wanted to take violent, direct action and to that end they both downloaded terror manuals from the internet.'[3] While fully agreeing with Laidlaw, it is this last word, the 'internet', that this chapter will argue has made international neo-Nazism less a dream for the contemporary extreme right-wing than a virtual reality, and in turn, a potential nightmare for liberal societies in the 21st century.

The danger posed by online neo-Nazism was, to some extent at least, recognised by the thicket of media scrutiny following the removal of reporting constraints on the Aryan Strike Force with the Heaton and Hannington convictions on 24 June 2010. One of these reports, in fact, pointed out that more than a dozen far-right convictions had taken place in Northern England over the previous two years.[4] Yet it is the international links, to a greater extent than even the group's domestic networks, which show the ASF to be such a representative case study in contemporary neo-Nazi activism. Given the ubiquity of the internet as a means of communication, organisation and dissemination for the contemporary extreme right-wing, it is worth paying special attention to the international context of neo-Nazism that was both practiced and disseminated during the group's brief existence. This was a classic case of neo-Nazism (sometimes called 'Universal Nazism').[5]

Needless to say, however, neo-Nazism is a doctrine also tainted by the ideological marginality of postwar fascism as a whole. That is to say, since the watershed date of 1945, when fascism's unparalleled crimes were revealed to the world upon the dismemberment of the Fascist and Nazi regimes—above all, the murder of six million European Jews by the Third Reich—the reservoir of support for overtly fascist, extreme right-wing groups has since all but dried up. More to the point, where fascist movements before 1945 commonly attached their allegiance to the nation-state—whether it was Mussolini's Italy, Hitler's Germany, or the failed British Union of Fascists under Oswald Mosley—the community perceived to need 'saving' since World War Two is often international in scope, and racial in motivation.[6] In a word, postwar fascism is just as often based upon ethnicity as geography. This is especially the case with the most violent and revolutionary manifestation of fascism today, neo-Nazism; literally a 'new' or 'updated' form of the National Socialist *Weltanschauung*. Perhaps the most significant postwar revision extends Nazi racism to immigrants, multi-cultural society and non-whites more generally. This is so much the case that ethnic minorities may now be considered the primary targets of contemporary neo-Nazi groups. Consequently, Universal Nazism can be understood as a racist version of 'think globally, act locally'. As Nikki Davison, one of the committee leaders of the ASF, stated in a weblog message on the group's online forum: 'nationalism will sur[e]ly raise awareness, people may become interested by its increase in popularity and maybe lead them to learn the truth'—the 'truth', of course, being the values and morality derived from the supposedly global superiority of so-called 'Aryans'.[7]

As a result of this uncompromising ideology, as well as the continual infighting by extreme right-wing factions, there have been very few overt neo-Nazi groups with any political strength or longevity. But if conditions for neo-Nazism have seen such groups politically relegated off-stage—and even outlawed—in the postwar world, this does not discount the danger such groups pose. Far from it. The fact that Ian Davison could procure, prepare and weaponise ricin all alone, with only the help of the internet and assorted terrorist manuals, offers sufficient proof of the threat posed by neo-Nazism on the web—a confluence that Michael Reynolds has dubbed "Virtual Reich".[8]

For scholars of the various forms of postwar fascism, this virtual structure may be best described by the term 'groupuscular'. Roger Griffin has defined this 'political genus' as 'a political formation that, *when fully developed*, has only a small, even minute active membership, a negligible following, and does not aspire to become a 'player' in mainstream political culture."[9] In Griffin's view, extreme right wing groupuscules have an

> ability to thrive under liberal democracy; it is extra-parliamentary in nature, small in number but with a collective force greater than the sum of its parts, leaderless, centreless, intimately connected with other radical-right groupuscules, revolutionary and blatantly extremist. It is also commonly based on a notion of palingenetic nationalism, it uses violence and, sporadically, entrism or infiltrationist approaches.[10]

In fleshing out this concept, four articles followed Griffin's introduction to the journal *Patterns of Prejudice*'s 2002 Special Issue on "The 'Groupuscular Right'".[11] Subsequent articles have also taken up this useful concept, as with Bonnie Burstow's 2003 account of the 'disproportionate impact' such groupuscules have, especially given how the internet maximizes the accomplishments of a small group' and 'facilitates manifold connections and fosters synergy'; nor is it 'as vulnerable to attack by anti-racists or by the state.' As Burstow rightly concludes, the embrace of the internet by groupuscular movements should not be surprising: the web is, as she says, 'uniquely suited' to the extreme right-wing, given its ease of accessibility, relative anonymity, and potential permanency:

> It is not only that the Internet maximizes the accomplishments of a small group, though clearly it does, and clearly this capacity is a groupuscular strength. And it is not only that the Internet facilitates manifold connections and fosters synergy, though it performs these groupuscular functions as well. It is also that the Internet is not as vulnerable to attack by anti-racists or by the state. As such, it is uniquely suited to neo-fascism today.[12]

For precisely the reasons enumerated above, the case of the ASF shows that groupuscules may well represent the must unabashed forms of neo-Nazism anywhere—whether online or offline.

This perfectly characterizes the Aryan Strike Force. With a maximum of 350 members scattered around the UK, theirs was a largely underground presence, nurturing a commitment to racism alongside nostalgia for Nazi Germany; one simply transposed to a contemporary British context. Over the 18 months of this groupuscule's existence (during which time the group spawned smaller, successor organisations due to a falling out between committee members), most energy appears to have been devoted to the ASF website, which propagated an extreme right-wing ideology through ready access to downloadable books, videos and Nazi symbols, as well as open access weblogs and a private members' forum.

In particular, the latter corpus of material offers a rare insight into the debates, views and intentions of a contemporary neo-Nazi groupuscule. As may be expected, these online forum blogs and private messages were strikingly consistent in tone, and quintessentially neo-Nazi in sentiment. Like the evidence submitted toward the two ASF trials themselves, a few examples of statements by 'Wigan Mike' Heaton; Trevor 'Lee88' Hannington; Ian 'Sweaney88' Davison; and Nikki 'Thorburn1488' Davison are structured below into three key, recurring neo-Nazi themes:

a) Glorification of Nazism and 'Aryan' Superiority:

- Trevor Hannington

'our Day WILL come & The 3rd Reich Will Rise again'.
'Our time has come, Is everyone ready to take the challenge, Risk loosing all your Possessions and fight to the last. I know I am.'

'IF The UK had Fought on the Side of Nazi Germany; IF Hitler had won ww2 what a Wonderful Land we will now Have.......................... IF'

'You Join LEGION88 as a Life time Commitment "TO DEATH" if your NOT willing to take this commitment; for yourselves; your family; your Nation, or your race; then Fuck offand spend your life in Zog slavery; I KNOW where IM Going'

- Nikki Davison

'happy birthday Mien Führer. And if I can just say, I'm only 18 years old, but I will continue on fighting the day that I become food, when ever that is, even if i am alone. Sieg hail 88'

'i hope everyone here would be willing to die for the race without question.'

- Michael Heaton

'I'm the same as any Aryan, or Celt.. Niggers are the same as any monkey Paki's smell and are similier looking to any piece of shit you can find.'

'were gonna have a our race war soon'

'ASF is about race, and those chosen few that wanna do something about it'

- Ian Davison

'If ever there was a Messiah it was our beloved Adolf Hitler, If ever you feel the task is too great That the struggle is just that a struggle If ever you feel like you just cant Think of Him In his example we find our strength In Him we find all we aspire to be In Him our hearts burst with pride He is now and forever more our fuhrer Sieg Heil my Fuhrer'

'we all throw sayings around like our race is our religion well if anyone really believes that is true then you will see the truth in "Blood above Self" in national socialism we put blood above self and when we understand that blood must be above self then we understand that the advancement and survival of your blood must come before anything else. to neglect this is to condemn our people to death'

'we are NS and believe in the rights and freedom's of the Aryan race above sub-human scum and given that nigger rappers can play there so called music on our radio stations and have there shit shown on the jew box sitting in the corner of our living rooms, singing/rapping songs about killing Aryans and raping white women, what's said here pales by comparison. if you don't like entertaining the fact that people may not like the black cunts and may wish to harm the curly haired freaks of nature at least here you can leave we aren't forcing our believes on anyone unlike the scum bastards try and do with us.'

b) Racist and Anti-Semitic Rhetoric:

- Trevor Hannington

'1st it was the niggers. Then the Asians. Now the muslims, it will never stop, unless we do something.'
'True BUT what we do have is far more Sinister, A group of People, A very large and powerful group of People, Who more or less control 'The Media & EntertainmentIndustry in this country, Who have been Brainwashing the British Public for over 100 Years. Our Biggest threat to OUR way of Life; Its Not Communists, Its Not Scuzlims, Its Not even Niggers; Its the JEW'

- Nikki Davison

'most governments are under control. but it would be nice to see an important nigger get shot'
'never seen a poor Jew before. and I'm sick of seeing all this shit on the t.v, it's always glorifying race mixing or its showing how bad Nazi's are and about how bad the Holohoax was. all because they want white men against there own race.'
'If they go back to Africa good but i would still want them all dead for what they have done. killing them all in Africa wouldn't be that hard, poison the water for one. although many animals would be die off it which is a bad point. you could as well work them to death. or we could develop a virus that only targets niggers, through there DNA, all though that may take some time. Killing them all is a possibility and I for one would work myself to death doing it.'

- Michael Heaton

'You can tell by looking at him, that he's SATANS SPAWN, just look at him, hooked nose, wierd eyes, nigger hair, sterio type YID'
'SHINDLERS LIST is a good one, the way the Jews are tortured, brilliant.'
'What I find offensive is.. NIGGERS/PAKIS COMING INTO OUR COUNTRY RACE MIXING FORIEN RELIGIONS COMING BEING FORCED INTO OUR THROATS OUR RACE AND COUBTRY DYING OUR GUTLESS ROYALS AND GOVERNMENT BOWING DOWN TO ZOG'
'Well I hate Jews more than any other race'

- Ian Davison

'never had a nigger as a mate closest i ever came to that was breaking ones nose when i was about 12 or 13 :D'
'jews and mud scum are no different dirty scum bastards'
'for coons cut off there eyelids with razor blades may not kill em quick but you'll get more cotton picked'
'ok question is how the fuck do people exist without fucking exploding when some stinking fuckin kike is breathing the same air within hitting distance ??'

c) Statements Endorsing Violence and/or Paramilitarism

- Trevor Hannington

'a little while ago while sorting out the Admin charter; word was said about Admin Traitors; Now we have one; So what action should we take ? I Dont know his Home addy; but via a post he made ref his local Beer/Pub im running a trace; IF I can find his local pub; Kidnap and ....What you say Mate?'

- Nikki Davison

'the best time is to come, we will rise out of the ashes of a burning society, the land will be flooded with fire and blood. people will lie dead in the streets, dead from fighting for the future and for survival. Nature will begin to take back the land, overgrown runes of once huge cities. forests will grow from sea to sea, the land will never again look the same as it was. Our greatest test is coming my brothers and sisters, we have never lost before and have always rose to be the victorious ones, will that change now? No it wont because we will fight'
'Lets gain more soldiers and make this revolution a reality brothers and sisters'

- Michael Heaton

'but we also need street action, people will not react to a few leaflets, and info, all that is important, people need to feel safe, and they will only feel safe when they see action, then they will come out, and fight.'
'There is a time for talk, (all though I think thats long over due) There is a time for propaganda.. And there is a time for street action.. We won't get anywhere with out it.'
'JEWS always lie, but they also get found our in due time, FETCH THE NOOSE'
'All though we know not everyone is fighters, I'm afraid fighters as well as the brain division is what we need.. We have the chance of creating a fucking army here, especially whenn we go for hi level ops. But starting somewhere to build our rep up is also needed, otherwise we become just another POWER, wE NEED TO GET PHYSICAL, AND PUT OUR fISTS were our mouth is, or if no one will take us serious, how do we expect our members to?? Its simple what I have planned.. STREET WAR.. RACE WAR WAR,, ZOG WAR.. End result? Get our country back, and spread the word to all White couuntries.'

- Ian Davison

'list of books in store up to now 21 Techniques of Silent Killing Black Medicine I - The Dark Art Of Death hitman Converting Model Rockets Into Explosive Missi explosives and demolitions manual Homebuilt Claymore Mines Anarchy Cookbook 2000 By Louis Helm Homemade Detonators Zips, Pipes, And Pens Arsenal of Improvised Weapons'

'How many have died and will die before we stand up and deal with the scum once and for all? how many will wash on Aryan soil and defile our land in the world of tomorrow? if we rise up today and send them all packing to the slime that spat them to us we will only succeed in packing off our problems to the world of our children and our children's children. No we must embrace the time of blood and purge this diseased world of all its ill's before this world is lost forever.'

'Its worth noting that in an incendiary attack on scum housing sometimes the letter box can be a better point of attack than the window. The letter box usually leads to the stairs, usually carpeted lot the time coats and things are behind that door and stairs are made of wood and represent the heart of the house. The same can be said of large buildings like flats, bars, restaurants and mosques. A fire starting on the stairs usually quickly takes out the building and removes the stairs as a means of escape'

Not that the leadership quartet of the Aryan Strike Force would have known it—as the thuggish statements above suggest—but two postwar traditions bore directly upon the launch of the ASF website on 9 January 2008. The first and most persistent of these postwar neo-Nazi traditions is what Leonard Weinberg has described as the 'cultural and political affinity between right-wing extremist groups on both sides of the Atlantic, together with an increasing exchange of ideas, perspectives, forms of organization and so on'.[13]

In fact, nearly 50 years ago, this 'Universal Nazism' was codified in the Britain through the 1962 "Cotswold Declaration".[14] At this meeting in the British midlands, the Briton Colin Jordan was elected as the neo-Nazis' 'Führer' by the participating seven countries, with his elected 'Deputy Führer' the head of the American Nazi Party, George Lincoln Rockwell. It was this global unification of the neo-Nazi movement which led Weinberg to discern the existence of a "'Euro-American' radical right", which "offers an interesting case of reciprocal influence".[15] Yet I would go one step further and suggest that Universal Nazism may be understood even more narrowly than as a continental convergence of the extreme right-wing: as the leadership established by the 1962 "Cotswold Declaration" suggests, this was predominately a collaboration by the extreme right wing in Britain and the USA—one that is now decades old.

It is also tenacious. Today, for example, the World Union of National Socialists, or W.U.N.S., continues to advocate global Nazi ideology, biological anti-Semitism, and paramilitary violence, as well as an unshakeable 'faith' in the existence and superiority of a worldwide 'Aryan' race—one that is nevertheless on the verge of collapse. Moreover, this overt neo-Nazism tends to be far more self-selecting than other forms of postwar fascism; thus, all that is needed to join the WUNS group, above, is a total adherence to the "Cotswold Declaration". An individual or small group need only therefore self-identify as a 'White-Aryan' dedicated to the cause of a revolutionary rebirth in order to join W.U.N.S.: no membership cards, political meetings or codes of conduct are needed. As borne out by the 'Participating Members' webpage of the recently-reformed National Socialist Movement—naturally headquartered in the United States since its September 2006 re-launch—affiliated countries range from Spain to Serbia in Europe to Mexico, Costa Rica and beyond; there is even, apparently, an affiliated group called the Naska Party in Iran![16]

In Britain, this updating of National Socialism—particularly with respect to racism toward non-whites—was fully evident by the early 1960s, with the founding of Colin Jordan's short-lived National Socialist Movement. Jordan's "Philosophical appraisal" of Nazism in the lead issue of *National Socialist World* from 1966 thus contains all the hallmarks of neo-Nazism in Britain, both at the time and since:

> National Socialism's belief in the folk as the basic value, and its totality of outlook, results, figuratively speaking, in thinking with the blood on all questions. This immediately and inevitably gives rise to the definition of citizenship as a matter of race: only those who are members of the folk are members of the nation, and only those who are members of the nation can be citizens of the state—to paraphrase the fourth of the Twenty-five Points of Adolf Hitler's NSDAP.[17]

This starry-eyed adherence to Nazism, racism, and paramilitarism set Universal Nazism apart from the rest of the extreme right-wing in Britain, as it did elsewhere. This happened in 1967, with the founding of the National Front by the expelled John Tyndall (who was later to form the British National Party in 1982, only to be expelled there, too, in 1999). This was a break that reveals the difference between the ultra-nationalism of 'classic fascism' in the party political movements, such as the British National Party, and the avowed 'pan-Aryanism' of neo-Nazism. In fact, in Nicholas Goodrick-Clarke's estimation, the "question of how openly one could afford to embrace Nazi iconography has remained a persistent faultline in the future development of the British far right."[18] Bearing this out, as Trevor Hannington noted:

> the BNP Nazi ? very far from it; maybe years ago, but today the BNP in my view are far more "Central Party" having sold out to gain a Wider membership and gain Votes; I say "BOOTS, NOT VOTES" Now that's NAZI.

A second, and far more recent tradition is fittingly represented by the American-based *Stormfront* website, cited above, which is now fully 15 years old. Universal Nazism may have been 50 years behind the times ideologically, but in 1995, it was one of the first to grasp the communicative and organisational potential of the internet. As perhaps the oldest and biggest of these 'virtual reichs', Don Black's *Stormfront* exemplifies the wide circulation of these online forums, in addition to revealing neo-Nazism's international dimension, their ideologically extreme content, and ease of access. Hosting dozens of websites with a variety of so-called 'white nationalist' texts and media, as well as internet radio and online videos, "Stormfront" was the subject of perhaps the most substantial analysis of online extremism to date; namely the Wiesenthal Center's document, shorthanded "Hate 2.0":

> A veteran of the KKK, where he was a colleague of David Duke, Black served three years in Federal prison for being part of an armed attempt to take over the island of Dominica. Black used his time in jail to hone computer skills, and in 1995 began Stormfront. The site quickly became the most important and largest white nationalist site online. Using the Celtic cross as its logo, Stormfront.org has a large library, an active forum, an Internet radio program and is currently available in ten languages. As of May 2008, Stormfront's Forum claimed over 131,000 members. Today, Black operates out of Palm Beach, Florida.[19]

Another American publication from the web fully bears out this embrace of new media by hate groups. Raymond Franklin's helpful list of racist, and frequently far-right, websites has reached fully 170 pages as of 1 November 2009, giving the webpages of literally thousands of easily-accessible extremist materials online—ranging from websites, forums, racist images, videos and even games, to more recent technologies like internet television and radio.[20] As with previous versions of Franklin's *The Hate Directory*, the most recent list of extreme right wing groups making use of the internet has grown rapidly since last year. Given that most of these websites are hosted in the United States, it should come as no surprise that a recent Department of Homeland Security estimate noted that 'lone wolves and small terrorist cells embracing violent rightwing extremist ideology are the most dangerous domestic terrorism threat in the United States.'[21]

With these two extreme right-wing traditions in mind—namely, a longstanding Euro-American neo-Nazi movement, and an embrace of the internet to communicate, organise and propagate the message of Universal Nazism—this chapter will conclude by looking at three of these specific, yet representative, links that were internationally cultivated and disseminated by Aryan Strike Force. First off, given the First Amendment's protection of free speech, it is only to be expected that the ASF website was hosted by an American server—evidently costing a mere £36 per month.[22] From this secure location, military manuals, racist books and extremist videos were uploaded. By way of example, between 18 and 26 December 2008, Ian Davison uploaded fully 21 book-length texts to the ASF website, with titles like *White Power* by George Lincoln Rockwell, *Stormfront's* 370-page anti-Semitic rant, *Quotes about Jews*, and of course, Hitler's *Mein Kampf*. Of these 21 e-books, more than half are readily accessible from the American neo-Nazi website, www.whitehonor.com—itself touting the telling banner 'EXTREME VIOLENT RACISM: WHITE REVOLUTION IS THE FINAL SOLUTION'.[23] The traffic of such material online between the United States and Britain continues largely unabated.

A second example of the ASF's adherence to a kind of neo-Nazi 'special relationship' between the US and UK is demonstrated by the founding of a US Division. As the following weblog message shows, a number of military training manuals for the British Army, American Marines and others were made available to the groupuscule by the leader of the American Division (mistakes in original):

> I wanted to provide the latest tactical as well as military training manuals to the Wolfpack, but at the same time I wanted them to be able to be accessed safely and easily so that no one felt the need to have them on there person i.e. there home or elsewhere. I also believe that these should be in pdf so they are accessed and viewed easily and securely. Well I have found a safe and secure method to view these on line, and you may still download if you like; if and only if it is legal in each of your geopolitical regions. I have promised this week they would be provided; so here they are in a safe web format to view and do with what you may.

Third and finally, if the sharing of information highlights a US-UK 'special relationship' at the core of Universal Nazism, this does not mean that only British and American audiences are targeted for propaganda. Quite the opposite. As the ASF flyers produced by Nikki Davison reveal, Universal Nazism was intended as much for Scotland as for Finland, and as much for Australia as for Ireland (see images 1 and 2). For, like so many neo-Nazi groups now joined together globally via the internet, was a groupuscule about blood, not borders.

In closing, however, the Aryan Strike Force's significant international links should not obscure the fact that this manifestation of Universal Nazism is also distinctly British, motivated by experiences and concerns derived from the contemporary UK—even if the ideology is one that is based primarily on race, not nation. The ASF thus represents a perfect example of the neo-Nazi groupuscule today, where hating globally leads to acting locally—with the ante now firmly upped to include potential terrorist actions involving so-called 'Weapons of Mass Destruction'. As the materials briefly analysed here regarding the committee leadership of this organisation make clear, this paramilitary, racist and revolutionary form of fascism is at the very violent end of even the extreme-right wing spectrum—perhaps so much so as to justify a new formulation for such neo-Nazi groupuscules: 'broadband terrorism'.

 **This our land**

SO;

Why do you let Immigrants take your jobs?

Why do you allow Immigrants to steal your money?

Why are you giving them the chance to rape your daughters and kill your sons?

Stop the flow of criminals. NOW!
Be White, be proud!

www.aryansf.com

Image

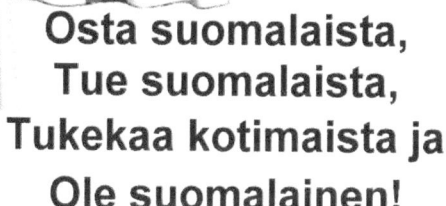

**Osta suomalaista,
Tue suomalaista,
Tukekaa kotimaista ja
Ole suomalainen!**

Älä anna niiden ottaa sisusi pois vaan

taistele vastaan ennen kuin on myöhäistä!

www.aryansf.com

Endnotes

1. Davison was convicted of three separate charges of possessing records useful in committing or preparing acts of terrorism. Three terror manuals—*The Anarchist Cookbook*, *The Kitchen Complete* and *Mujahadeen Explosive Handbook*—had been found on computers at his home. Gavin Engelbrecht, "Ian Davison and son, Nicky, 18 deny terrorism changes", *The Northern Echo*, 3 October 2009, https://www.thenorthernecho.co.uk/news/4663069.ian-davison-son-nicky-18-deny-terrorism-changes/; "County Durham teenager convicted of terror plot", BBC News, 30 April 2010, http://news.bbc.co.uk/2/hi/uk_news/england/wear/8653722.stm. Section 58 (Collection of information) of the Terrorism Act 2000 provides, in subsection (1), that "A person commits an offence if—(a) he collects or makes a record of information of a kind likely to be useful to a person committing or preparing an act of terrorism, or (b) he possesses a document or record containing information of that kind." Terrorism Act 2000 (as of 19/02/2001; superseded), http://www.legislation.gov.uk/ukpga/2000/11/section/58/2001-02-19.
2. The last sentence is actually David Lane's so called '14 words'. Lane remains an icon in the contemporary extreme right for his 190-year sentence for crimes committed as a member of 'The Order'. Created in 1983 under a name taken directly from William Pierce's infamous *The Turner Diaries*, 'The Order' was a direct action, paramilitary, extreme right-wing group responsible for a series of armed robberies, bombings and murders in the mid-1980s, including the execution of a Jewish talk-show host named Alan Berg outside the latter's Denver home.
3. See the Crown Prosecution Service website for details of the convictions of Heaton and Hannington on 24 June 2010, online at: https://web.archive.org/web/20100926144903/http://cps.gov.uk/news/press_releases/124_10/ (all websites last accessed 2 March 2020). The CPS press release for Davison father and son is online at:https://web.archive.org/web/20100802034803/http://www.cps.gov.uk/news/press_releases/118_10/.
4. See Simon Israel's 8-minute report for *Channel 4 News*, available online at: www.channel4.com/news/articles/politics/convictions%2Bpoint%2Bto%2Brise%2Bof%2Bfar%2Bright%2Bextremism/3690882.html. For a sample of the online reporting on the Aryan Strike Force, see the BBC coverage, online at: https://www.bbc.co.uk/news/10413611; and that by *The Telegraph* at: https://www.telegraph.co.uk/news/uknews/crime/7821034/Neo-Nazis-urged-eradication-of-all-ethnic-minorities-on-Aryan-Strike-Force-website.html. Also see coverage by the *Jewish Chronicle*, online at: www.thejc.com/news/uk-news/33689/aryan-strike-force-houses-horror-revealed.
5. See Roger Griffin, ed., *Fascism* (Oxford: Oxford University Press, 1995), pp. 325ff.
6. For a further discussion of this approach to fascist ideology, especially its postwar manifestations, see Matthew Feldman ed., *A Fascist Century* (Basingstoke: Palgrave, 2008), pp. xii-xxvii.
7. Mistakes in original hereafter. All primary materials taken from two summer 2010 trials of the Aryan Strike Force leadership. The author gave evidence in both trials, and all quotations are taken from those entered into evidence during late 2009 and early 2010.
8. Michael Reynolds, "Virtual Reich", reprinted in Roger Griffin with Matthew Feldman, *Fascism: Critical Concepts*, vol. 5 [*Postwar fascism*], pp. 339-51.
9. Roger Griffin, "The incredible shrinking ism: the survival of fascism in the post-fascist era", *Patterns of Prejudice*, vol. 36, no. 3 (July 2002), pp. 3-4.
10. Bonnie Burstow, "Surviving and Thriving by Becoming More 'Groupuscular': The Case of the Heritage Front," *Patterns of Prejudice*, vol. 37, no. 4 (Dec. 2003), cited p. 415.

[11] *Patterns of Prejudice*, vol. 36, no. 3 (July 2002).
[12] Burstow, *op. cit.*, pp. 415, 428.
[13] Leonard Weinberg, "Conclusion", in Peter Merkl and Leonard Weinberg (eds.), *The Revival of Right-Wing Extremism in the Nineties* (London: Routledge, 1997), p. 234.
[14] This agreement is fittingly reproduced by Stormfront, the leading radical right website, stormfront.org/forum/t331434/.
[15] See Weinberg, "Conclusion", pp. 236ff.
[16] The Naska Party's website, replete with songs, images and slogans from the Third Reich, is available here: naskaparty88.blogspot.com/.
[17] Colin Jordan, cited in Griffin, ed., *Fascism*, p. 326.
[18] Nicholas Goodrick-Clarke, *Black Sun: Aryan Cults, Esoteric Nazism and the Politics of Identity* (London: New York University Press, 2002), p. 38.
[19] See *Online Terror + Hate: The First Decade*, Simon Wiesenthal Center, iReport (May 2008), online at: www.csce.gov/sites/helsinkicommission.house.gov/files/Cooper%20Testimony.PDF.
[20] See the most recent edition of *The Hate Directory*, dating from 1 April 2010, online at https://web.archive.org/web/20110102071717/http://www.hatedirectory.com/hatedir.pdf. Over the past several years, Raymond Franklin has compiled several versions of this report. See also: www.oodaloop.com/documents/Legacy/asis/hatedir.pdf.
[21] Department of Homeland Security, Intelligence and Analysis Declassified Report, "Rightwing Extremism: Current Economic and Political Climate Fueling Resurgence in Radicalization and Recruitment", released 7 April 2009, and available online at: fas.org/irp/eprint/rightwing.pdf, cited p. 9.
[22] Details are provided by the *Daily Mail* website from 1 May 2010, online at: https://www.dailymail.co.uk/news/article-1271652/First-picture-The-neo-Nazi-terrorist-planning-poison-Jews-Muslims-deadly-ricin.html.
[23] "Online Books and Manuals Providing Information to Educate the More Militant Aryans in Our Movement", http://www.whitehonor.com/books2kill.htm.

20. A Case Study in Soviet Political Religion: Modernism and the Construction of a Stalinist Utopia

> Meditating on the infinite may be a religious activity, so may writing a cheque, eating corpses, copulating, listening to a thumping sermon on hell fire, examining one's conscience, painting a picture, growing a beard, licking leprous sores, tying the body into knots—a dogged faith in human rationality—there is no human activity which cannot assume religious significance.
>
> - Kenneth Burridge, *New Heaven, New Earth*[1]

Following Ezra Pound's imperative to 'make it new', a comradeship of artists—heavily influenced by Cubism, Dadaism, Pound's Imagists, and especially the Futurists in Italy—undertook an unprecedented, if too little known, synthesis of communist politics and high modernism. These were the Soviet Constructivists, who briefly flourished amidst the utopian expectations of the Russian Revolution. While in no way offering a cultural, let alone political, history of the period, this chapter considers several avant-garde artists active during Stalin's first Five Year Plan. Their artistic output reveals a striking interplay of politics, modernism and faith. Once more, the latter is understood here in terms of a "political religion". As formulated by Emilio Gentile,

> *Political religion* is a form of the sacralisation of politics of an exclusive and integralist character. It rejects coexistence with other political ideologies and movements, denies the autonomy of the individual with respect to the collective, prescribes the obligatory observance of its commandments and participation in its political cult, and sanctifies violence as a legitimate arm of the struggle against enemies, and as an instrument of regeneration. It adopts a hostile attitude toward traditional institutionalised religions, seeking to eliminate them, or seeking to establish with them a relationship of symbiotic coexistence, in the sense that the political religion seeks to incorporate traditional religion within its own system of beliefs and myths, assigning it a subordinate and auxiliary role.[2]

The establishment of virtually every modern political religion, interestingly, seems to have been forged in the fires of revolution or total war. Correspondingly, for one of Stalinism's most even-handed interpreters, Sheila Fitzpatrick, "in many ways the Soviet Union during the First Five-Year Plan did resemble a country at war". In Peter Kenez's influential view, this was also the onset of ossification of the world's first 'propaganda state'—what the excommunicated Leon Trotsky had famously described as "Soviet Thermidor" under Stalin's bureaucratic tyranny.[3]

Yet for all the Soviet terror, to cite Kenneth Burridge in the above epigraph, "there is no human activity which cannot assume religious significance." Recent research points to remarkable levels of voluntarism under Soviet totalitarianism—

and not just during 'The Great Terror' of the mid-1930s. One explanation is that a kind of ersatz faith underpinned much of Stalinism's transformative zeal in the 1930s:

> Stalin transformed the Leninist community of *virtuosi* into a church dispensing grace (*Anstaltsgnade*), which 'includes the righteous and the unrighteous and is especially concerned with subjecting the sinner to Divine law'. The organisational necessities of wartime communism and the revolutionary transformations of industrialisation and collectivisation in the 1930s transformed the Leninist community of *virtuosi* to (1) a bureaucratised and hierarchically organised institution of grace, with 'institutionalised salvation and an office of charisma'. This evolved into an administrative apparatus with obedient and disciplined cadres who substituted the pneumatic enthusiasm of the early *virtuosi*. The Stalinist church was also organised as (2) an office hierarchy that dispensed grace. The correct interpretation of the store of sacral scriptures, the supervision of canonical preaching, and the functioning of the missionary apparatus belonged to the duties of office holders. The vouchsafing of grace and absolution of sins are organised as a ritual which requires little 'personal ethical accomplishment'. The structural change from the Leninist political religion of *virtuosi* to the Stalinist church institution was accompanied by (3) a selective reformulation of the Leninist legacy of sacral scriptures, and ritual worship of the *numinous* leader of the October Revolution. The 'hierocracy' is forced to develop their own interpretations of the history and future of the revolutionary cause. 'The rise of a professional priesthood ... with salaries, promotions, professional duties, and a distinctive way of life', indicates that the ideological experts of propaganda and state security have noticed the heretical challenges. They are engaged with the task of rationalising 'dogma and rites [*Kultus*], [which were] recorded in holy scriptures, provided with commentaries, and turned into objects of systematic education, a distinct difference from mere training in technical skills'. The sacral experts of Stalinist orthodoxy worked out and invented the new sacral tradition of Marxism-Leninism, with the intention of legitimising the new monocratic office holder of the church. The deification of Stalin left the party unable to control his actions and justified in advance everything connected with his name ... The cult of Stalin, following the logic of any cult, tended to transform the Communist Party into an ecclesiastical organization, producing a sharp distinction between ordinary people and leader-priests headed by their infallible pope.
> The most important tenet of faith in this invented sacral tradition of Marxism-Leninism was that Stalin alone qualified as the only true disciple of Lenin; the consequence thus being his monopoly infallible interpretation of his holy scriptures.[4]

This extended quotation may well apply to totalitarian politics, but does it also capture the ethos of "totalitarian art"? Not in Golomstock's canonical *Totalitarian Art*, nor for much of the historiographical tradition seeing in Stalinist culture simply "Engineers of Human Souls" (in the words of "the Boss" to Maxim Gorki in 1932).[5]

Yet there was more to Stalinist culture than this. Take Alexander Rodchenko and El (Lazar Markovich) Lissitsky and their avant-garde artist-partners, Varvara

Stepanova and Sophie Lissitzky-Küppers.[6] Despite a Tate Modern permanent exhibition on these and other revolutionary modernists from the Soviet Union, there remains a paucity of Anglophone scholarship on perhaps their most influential undertaking: the *USSR in Construction*.[7] What little attention has been paid to this unmistakably modernist journal is usually relegated to general accounts in general surveys of Soviet art and propaganda, Victor Margolin's excellent 1997 monograph excepted.[8] Even catalogues of these luminaries of Modernism seem to marginalize the work undertaken on the *USSR in Construction*. It combined a groundbreaking aesthetic experimentalism—particularly the Russian Constructivists' (contested) invention of the photomontage—with the imperatives of external regime propaganda. All this was in a 1930s journal published simultaneously in five languages (German, French, English, Russian and, from 1938, Spanish), in an oversized (roughly the size of a broadsheet newspaper) colour monthly.

Before going into more detail about the Stalinist journal the *USSR in Construction*, a further word may be offered on what is understood here by "political religions", also referred to as "political faith" or "secular faith." It has sometimes been remarked that putting two such terms together is, quite simply, oxymoronic.[9] Yet recent books and articles, as well as a short-lived dedicated journal, *Totalitarian Movements and Political Religions*, helped to put this concept firmly back on the intellectual map.[10] As noted by perhaps its most perceptive advocate, the aforementioned Emilio Gentile, an intellectual heritage can be traced back to contemporaneous eye-witnesses of European totalitarian movements, including luminaries like Bertrand Russell, Raymond Aron, Uriel Tal and Eric Voegelin.[11] Yet one need not have been an intellectual luminary like them to have seen these movements of the revolutionary left and right at the time as something rather different from rational politics, Western secularization, modern decadence, and so on. Waldemar Gurian, for example—alongside Hannah Arendt, sometimes considered amongst the earliest to have systematically analyzed 20th century totalitarianism—had this to say about the religious "ideocracy" (or "dictatorship of a worldview"[12]) intrinsic to such movements:

> The totalitarian movements that have arisen since World War I are fundamentally religious movements. They aim not at changes of political and social institutions, but at the reshaping of the nature of man and society [...] The pretence of having the true doctrine gives to the totalitarian movements their basic character. They are intolerant. They aim at the extirpation of all other doctrines and philosophies. They cannot tolerate any limitation of their claims and their power.[13]

This spadework then led Gentile, at the turn of this century, to argue that political religions of both the revolutionary right (fascism) and left (communism) intended to shape the individual and the masses through an *anthropological revolution* in order to regenerate the human being and create the *new man*, who is dedicated in body and soul to the realisation of the revolutionary and imperialistic policies of the totalitarian party. The ultimate goal is to create a *new civilization*.

In another formulation, Juan Linz has posited that a political religion may be defined as "a system of beliefs about authority, society and history, providing a comprehensive worldview [...] that claims a truth-value incompatible with other views, including the existing religious tradition."[14]

Now, the hostility of fascism and communism to organized religions like Christianity is well-known and need not be repeated here, save for a basic point: by and large, the feeling was mutual. With relatively few exceptions—such as the "Nazified faith" of the notorious German Christians amongst other "clerical fascists"[15]—institutional faiths across Europe clearly recognized these ideologies as heresies. However, heresies, it should be pointed out, are not at all irreligious; they are simply anti-establishment. To take but one example, as early as 1934—the very year Socialist Realism was declared the favored artistic form for Soviet Communism—the exiled Russian philosopher Nikolai Berdyaev noted:

> Communism holds itself to be the only true religion and tolerates no other within its territory. It demands a religious worship of the proletariat as the chosen people of God; it deifies the social collectivity, which is called upon to replace god and the human being. Indeed, the social collective becomes the only subject of moral valuations and acts, the bearer and representative of truth itself. Communism preaches a new morality, one that is not Christian, but not humanitarian either. It has worked out an orthodox theology and a cult—the Lenin cult, for example—of its own, as well as its own symbolism; it has even introduced its own holidays, the red baptism and red burial. Communism possesses a generally binding dogmatism and a catechism; it exposes the heresies and damns the heretics.[16]

In turn, this has led Gentile and others to speak of a "metamorphosis", or "transfer of the sacred."[17] This raises a second introductory point, which is the source of no small confusion in the study of political religions. Is this phenomenon "like" a religion? Are political religions secular copies of existing monotheistic religions; or instead, are they proper religions in their own right? Here too the debates are complex and labyrinthine, and only a final, perhaps obvious, observation will be noted here: what matters is how one approaches religion.[18] That is to say, if one's definition of religion is conditioned by metaphysical belief in the supernatural, of course, political religion then becomes merely a form of atheism; but then again, so does both animism and Buddhism. In a word, metaphysics are no sure-footed way to distinguish between true and false faiths. Yet if one's definition of religion stems from a functionalist perspective, then political religions may hold a potentially similar power over people as other religions.

Nearly a century ago, two pioneers of Religious Studies, William James and Émile Durkheim, addressed this very problem. Coming from, respectively, the individual and social perspectives of "the sacred", both James and Durkheim recommended a rigorous analysis of religion based on how it presents itself through the actions of believing communities and individuals. Thus, James' groundbreaking *Varieties of Religious Experience* from 1902 defined religion not in terms of its content, but in terms of its functions; that is, as "the feelings, acts and experience of individual men in their solitude, so far as they apprehend themselves to stand in relation to whatever they may consider divine"; moreover, when "we speak of the individual's relation to "what he considers the divine," we must interpret the term "divine" very broadly, as denoting any object that is god*like*, whether it be a concrete deity or not."[19] Coming from the collective rather than the personal angle, Durkheim, for his part, understood religion as "society divinized."[20] By this, he meant a "system of beliefs and practices relative to sacred things, that is, things separated and forbidden, beliefs and practices that unite in a single moral community, called a Church, for all those who adhere to them."[21] Both of these views have impressively stood the test of time, and provide a good position to approach the matter of political religions as a modern, totalitarian expression of sacralized "ideocracy"—as it were, dictatorship "divinized"—with the propagators of these political faiths attempting to inspire acts of ideological devotion. Put another way, political religions are functionally and phenomenologically religious, and their propagators employ what may be considered religious behavior.

Irrespective of these theoretical ruminations, however, there is much to say about the overlooked history of the *USSR in Construction*, which lasted for roughly a dozen years beginning in 1930. Considering its international profile—being published in three and, for a time, four languages simultaneously—and given its publication by the Moscow State Publishing House, Izogiz, the role of international communist propaganda is necessarily a central theme here. But by using the term 'propaganda', this is not to subscribe to the tired, conventional view that describes propaganda essentially as synonymous with manipulation, deceit or brainwashing. This may be how it appears today, but for adherents to the competing political religions of fascism and communism, it seems, quite a different dynamic was at play.

Quite simply, this Soviet journal can be seen as an example of a certain type of 'devotional' propaganda, as it was informed by techniques and approaches to modernist art in the early twentieth century. In this reading, the *USSR in Construction* is both scarcely known and potentially paradigmatic: It presents a millenarian ideology, Stalinism, putting its best, utopian face to the world, on the one hand; while on the other, treating Soviet lives as so many disposable 'units'; working as slave labour constructing an industrial powerhouse, as with the Belomor Canal that cost—at the very least—tens of thousands of lives.[22]

There can be little doubt that, for European and North American readers of the journal, this was a type of devotional propaganda advocating that followers help build a kind of "heaven on earth"; a communist utopia, as it were, even if, in practice, this demanded millions of innocent lives, either executed or worked to death by Joseph Stalin's policies over the 1930s.[23]

In just such a jarring spirit, this chapter will now provide a snapshot of this monthly journal during the first Five Year Plan of Soviet breakneck industrialization from 1928. As suggested above, neither the broad churches of "art" nor those of "propaganda" alone characterize the *USSR in Construction*. Something else is also in the picture. Instead, the mixed-media presentation of *the USSR in Construction* may be more effectively described as a cultural sermon from devotees of a seductive political religion: one making use of idiosyncratically Russian pictorial traditions, as well as cutting-edge Modernist genres like photomontage; the publication also uses Bolshevik propaganda techniques and of course, Marxist-Leninist ideology.

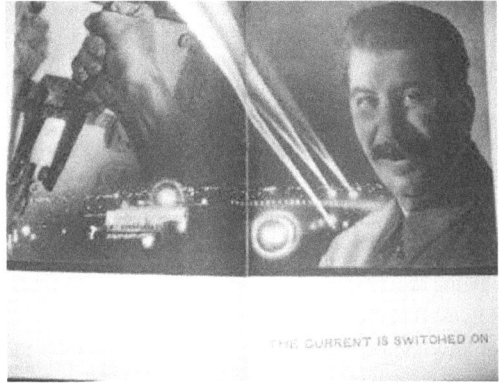

This triangulation of themes—political religion, Marxist-Leninism and propaganda as the modernist, ideological propagation of them both—may help to unpick some of the recurring features in this modernist journal.²⁴ Indeed, the movement of modern artists driving this journal, the Constructivists, made attempts at the "merging of art and life through mass production and industry" by means of a "radical reassessment of artistic activity."²⁵ According to Christiana Lodder, this revolutionary art

> was a direct response to the experience of the Russian Revolution of 1917 and the ensuing Civil War [... with the objective of advancing] an entirely new relationship between the artist, his work and society [... including] an approach to working with materials, within a certain conception of their potential as active participants in the process of social and political transformation.²⁶

These Constructivists were artists generally constructing "non-objective" (for them, anti-bourgeois) technocratic images and designs. Albeit far more politically, it might be said they were working on a kind of paradoxical "anti-art" akin to European Dadaism around the same time. After the formation of the Soviet Union, this loose-knit group of artistic revolutionaries—perhaps their defining feature—first exhibited internationally at the 1922 Berlin *Erste Russische Kunstausstellung* [*First Russian Art Exhibition*] at the Van Diemen Gallery alongside other Soviet modernists.²⁷ Later in the 1920s, they founded the Soviet journal *LEF* [*Zhurnal levogo fronta iskusstv*, or *Journal of the Left Front of the Arts*; later *Novyi LEF* or *New Left*, 1923-7]. They also founded the group *October* in 1928. From the signatories to the latter group's manifesto launching this group, the next decade or so found the Constructivists either working for *The USSR in Construction* (like El

Lissitsky and Aleksandr Rodchenko, of which more below), or dying in the gulag on the eve of World War Two (as was the fate of Aleksei Gan and Gustav Klutsis).

Here the Soviet system rears its Janus-faced head, as eloquently voiced by a specialist on Stalinism, Peter Holquist:

> the Soviets employed violence as technique to fashion society in their own image. And the Soviet state did so as an explicitly ideological regime. One can discern the Soviet state's constant devotion to the sculpting of its raw, human material...the Soviet regime's application of state violence is better understood as a fundamentally aesthetic project to sculpt an idealized image of the politico-social body.[28]

In this light, it is perhaps less surprising to find this duality evident not only in Stalinist repression but in Soviet Constructivism's aesthetics as well: images that resist simply being labelled as propagandistic—although these artists clearly perceived themselves to be Party Line adherents—yet neither are they constitutive of art as traditionally understood, even in the period of "high modernism" between the wars.

A commitment to totally reshaping society—one also no doubt demanding the breaking of millions of eggs in constructing this utopian omelet—is frequently evident in texts accompanying the Constructivists' modernist images. Indeed, the movement's own words mark them out as a sort of self-appointed modernist priesthood, creating what might be viewed as a transformative anti-art for the masses via the publishing pulpit of the Soviet state. In the light of this view of 'total art', consider some of the Constructivists' founding statement for the journal *October* in 1928:

> The ranks of the proletariat, progressive, active, and artistically concerned, are growing before our very eyes. Mass art summons the vast masses to artistic involvement. This involvement is linked to the class struggle, to the development of industry, and to the transformation of life. This work demands sincerity, high qualifications, cultural maturity, revolutionary awareness. We will dedicate all our strength to this work.[29]

Alongside the widespread dislocations caused by Stalinist collectivization, these artistic Marxist-Leninist "believers" were working in a specifically Russian, indeed Soviet, context, charging the "artist"—a word they often poured scorn upon—with the duty to act "as a citizen of the community who is clearing the field of its old rubbish in preparations for the new life."[30] This phrase, made by El Lissitsky more than a decade before he joined the *USSR in Construction*, in turn, reflects two broader points. The first relates to specifically modernist aesthetics: these were revolutionary artists concerned with representing the massification of modern life in a new, politically and culturally relevant way. Yet artists like El Lissitsky were also the standard bearers of Stalinist culture in the 1930s, and these collaborators cosmetically presented the outside world with a sanitized, heroic, and largely deceptive view of a regime at a time when it was inflicting unprecedented hardship upon the notoriously long-suffering peoples of Eurasia.[31]

Perhaps the most effective way to approach this astounding fusion—or compromise, or worse, sell-out—of artistic modernism with secular, millenarian politics, is to reappraise our use of the word 'propaganda'.

It bears remembering that, since Josef Goebbels' Ministry of Propaganda and Public Enlightenment in Nazi Germany (and, indeed, George Orwell's "Big Brother" from *1984*), we generally tend to think of "black propaganda" if we need to consider the term at all: brainwashing and cunning, cynicism and lies. But before the Holocaust happened—and here, it is clear, both word and world irrevocably changed in 1945—"propaganda" simply did not have the overwhelmingly pejorative meanings now given to the term. After all, in its original, Christian religious sense (and indeed its Latin epistemology), propaganda merely means "propagation of the faith", a heritage initiated by the Catholic counter-Reformation in early 17th century Europe to stop the hemorrhage of converts to the new, Protestant faith. In short, for many successive generations of Christians in modern Europe between then and now, propaganda had a distinctly sacral inflection.

This "sacralization of politics" can be seen across the pages of the *USSR in Construction*. In fact, Soviet Constructivism generally championed a number of aspects that are unmistakable right across this monthly journal. These include a dominating visual emphasis—at least partly due to Russia's still-feudal idiosyncrasies and persisting rates of illiteracy; the theme of "building socialism" in the multi-national Soviet Union (and attendant metaphors of progress, speed, the "path" and the "line", with their technological analogies to trains, aviation, and so on); and, unsurprisingly in a totalitarian state, submission to the "direct supervision" of the Communist Party Central Committee.[32] These elements sat uneasily alongside ever-more sophisticated avant-garde techniques in the journal's utopian portrayal of a paradise both physically and metaphorically "under construction." In fact, their own proximity to extremism was perfectly well understood by the Constructivists, whose motto was *"We declare implacable war on art."*

Theirs was a view most forcefully expressed by one of the early leaders of the movement, Aleksei Gan. Some 16 years before he was repressed during the Great Terror, Gan declared:

> MARXISTS MUST WORK IN ORDER TO ELUCIDATE [ART'S] DEATH SCIENTIFICALLY AND TO FORMULATE NEW PHENOMENA OF ARTISTIC LABOR WITHIN THE NEW HISTORIC ENVIRONMENT OF OUR TIME.
> In the specific situation of our day, a gravitation toward the technical acme and social interpretation can be observed in the work of the masters of revolutionary art.
>
> Constructivism is advancing—the slender child of an industrial culture.
> For a long time capitalism has let it rot underground.
> It has been liberated by—the Proletarian Revolution.
> A new chronology begins
>   with October 25, 1917[33]

Again, this seems to be directly relevant to some dynamic research being done of late on the interplay of propaganda and dictatorship on the one hand, and on comparative studies of totalitarianism on the other.[34] Given that *The USSR in Construction* was targeted at an international audience, it is surprising that virtually nothing has been written on the *USSR in Construction* in Anglophone scholarship, despite over 100 issues being produced in the English language. This is all the more unusual considering the journal's unique combination of groundbreaking aesthetic experimentalism in Soviet Russia—particularly the Russian Constructivists' early use of photomontage—with the imperatives of worldwide Soviet propaganda. That is to say, every month for a dozen years the *USSR in Construction* ran avant-garde propaganda, directed at the non-communist world, until the suspension of publication—and, indeed, redaction of editorial names on grounds of national security—following the Nazis' invasion of the Soviet Union on 22 June 1941.

Through the use of color, fold-outs, photojournalism, montage and fragmented layouts, contributors worked around a single theme per issue—covering subjects as diverse as the Soviet Press in Jan./Feb. 1931, Soviet Civil Aviation in June 1932, Soviet explorations of the Arctic in September 1933, Soviet Georgia in May 1936, the Soviet constitution in the next year[35], and more. During these years, moreover, the Constructivists' aesthetic ideas increasingly permeated the *USSR in Construction*, in contrast to its far less radical, black and white presentation in its 1930 launch year. In fact, increasingly avant-garde elements found their place in the *USSR in Construction* around the same time that Socialist Realism became the institutionalized artistic genre for the Soviet Union.

The *USSR in Construction* initially featured standard landscape and portrait images with limited text. Yet over the next two years, novel modern printed techniques extended to higher quality paper, the injection of color and sepia tones, larger images and fold-outs. Added to this were iconoclastic paeans to the 1930s "Cult of Stalin" that was such a key Soviet aesthetic at the time. This journal, in short, is nothing less than an attempted fusion of total art with total politics, one glued together by the Constructivists' devotion to Stalinist ideology.

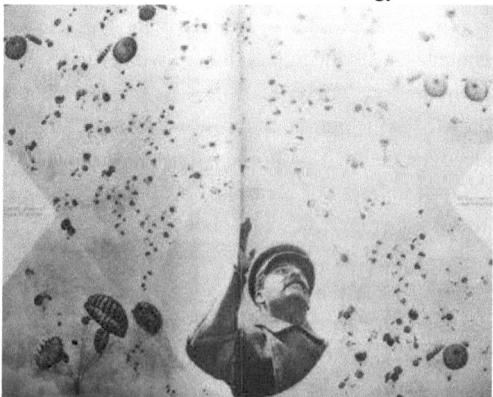

Put another way, as the *USSR in Construction* grew and evolved against the political background of arrests, starvation, terror and rising death-tolls in the USSR, the journal's own artistic radicalism seemed to connect with the radicalism of the regime itself. To take but one example, Nikolai Troshin's 1934 issue on "Physical Culture and Sports in the USSR" emphasizes the martial, youth, and collective health tropes across the issue. In the work of the comparatively conservative

Troshin—at least in comparison with Lissitsky and Rodchenko—the content attempts to merge with constructivist aesthetics; that is, artistic form. Perhaps only in this way can we understand how "walking with gas masks" and shooting can feature between images of gymnastics and cycling—as suggested by the text on the inside cover of this issue:

> We must rear a new generation of workers, healthy, cheerful, capable of increasing the power of the soviet land and defending it with their might and main against attacks from the enemy', Stalin; "It is difficult to imagine anything more beautiful, inspiring and rhythmical than the annual physical—culture parades on the squares of the Soviet cities. Frequently hundreds of thousands participate in these parades"; and "This is what the healthy young class, the victorious proletariat, the builder of socialism, looks like".

This example helps to show that, in the Constructivists' most avant-garde efforts on behalf of the *USSR in Construction*, a synthesis of art and politics, form and content, may be seen to emerge through this modern, technocratic form of propaganda, one perhaps only fully understood in the etymological, sacralizing sense of the word. At its height in the ideological warzone of the European 1930s, the *USSR in Construction* was doubtless one of the most adroit propaganda weapons available to international Communists who were seeking converts at the time. And moreover, from the Constructivists' point of view—or better, "system of belief"—the word propaganda would only make sense in terms of the total art proposed by these propagators of a political religion. By way of example, consider the words of the Constructivist Yakov Chernikhov around the time of the founding of the *USSR in Construction*:

the principles of simplification, acceleration, and purposefulness emerge as the constant attributes of a constructivist world view [...] which—for the first time in the history of man—has been able to unite the principle of mechanical production and the stimuli of artistic creation [....] A new conception of the beautiful, a new beauty, is being born—the aesthetics of industrial constructivism [....] It is not only destructive in relation to the old, but it is also creative in relation to the new [....] Constructivism can, and must, take into consideration all the concrete needs of contemporary life and must answer in full the needs of the mass consumer, the collective "customer"—the people.[36]

In bearing out the above quotation, a final example will be explored in conclusion to further highlight some aspects of political religion in Stalin's Russia. As revealed across the pages of the *USSR in Construction*, this form of "devotional modernism" intended to truly fuse the artistic and political. A good example is evinced by the work of the aforementioned Nikolai Troshin—the most prolific contributor to the journal between 1930 and 1936—whose themed issue from January 1932 is entitled "Magnetostroi: The Giant and the Builder". More than four years before the "bottom-up" Stakhanovite movement celebrated rewards for the over-production of industrial quotas, a "top-down" effort was consistently advanced by *The USSR In Construction*; in this case, through a representative "new man" named Kalmikov—one that is perfectly in keeping with this turn in historical approach—as asserted on the inside cover:

"Magnetostroi must become a training school"—said the party. In the process of socialistic construction a new man is being created,—a man of iron energy and socialistic habits, who embodies "Russian revolutionary enthusiasm and American efficiency".
In this issue of our magazine we show with what great speed the Soviet metallurgical giant is being erected, and also show the new type of man that the Magnetostroi has given.
This new man is Kalmikov—a worker, who within a period of eighteen months has risen from an illiterate village lad to a skilled workman, a member of the party and a carrier of the Order of the Red Banner. Kalmikov is not an exception. Kalmikov is one of the many thousands of new men that socialistic construction has re-moulded.

The entire issue, encapsulated by the "constructed" builder Kalmikov, is a propagandistic homage to a developing utopia in the USSR under Stalin, and the creation of a generation of new minds, bodies and souls—a recurring theme within *The USSR In Construction*.[37]

Ultimately the Constructivists' most avant-garde efforts on behalf of the *USSR in Construction* represented an explicitly modern technocratic form of propaganda; one, paradoxically, best understood in the traditional and religious sense of that word. As a replacement for traditional Judeo-Christian faith and morality, this form of political religion embraced avant-garde art as the vehicle for new men and women, and for a new communist world.

Can we say such brilliant and nefarious art represents—especially in those Janus-faced days of the 1930s—*revolutionary* offerings to the masses by modernist devotees of a fully-fledged Stalinist political religion? To connect this case study to wider themes in this volume, it bears concluding by pointing that, while Marxist-Leninism was always revolutionary in theory, Stalinism in practice constituted a fully-fledged political religion. Under a totalitarian regime, this was also manifested socio-culturally, as in the case of the Soviet Constructivists. The distinction corresponds to Gramsci's separation of dominion and cultural hegemony, extending even to the deployment of art as an ideological expression; or what is understood here as the kind of propaganda termed "devotional modernism." Put simply, not only are totalitarian dictatorships repressive and enormously barbaric, but they also have a utopian thrust and an overtly modernizing, even technocratic dimension. As the images presented in this chapter put beyond doubt, this was celebrated by the art, architecture and designs of Russian Constructivists after the 1917 October Revolution. It was, finally, part of a larger "high" modernist tendency—observable across the interwar European ideological spectrum, class background, and topography. Even if the *USSR in Construction* put its modernist aesthetic at the service of Stalinist totalitarianism, we are still left to reckon with the thought that this kind of technically gifted and ground-breaking art/propaganda also represents a *revolutionary* offering to the masses—by modernist devotees of a Stalinist political religion.

Endnotes

[1] Cited in Alberto Toscano, *Fanaticism: On the Uses of an Idea* (London: Verso, 2010), p. 203.
[2] Emilio Gentile, "Political Religion: A Concept and its Critics—A Critical Survey", *Totalitarian Movements and Political Religions* 6/1 (2005), p. 30.
[3] Sheila Fitzpatrick, *The Russian Revolution*, New Edition (Oxford: Oxford University Press, 2008), p. 120. See also Peter Kenez, *The Birth of the Propaganda State: Soviet Methods of Mass Mobilization, 1917-1929* (Cambridge: Cambridge University Press, 1985), pp. 251ff.
[4] Klaus-Georg Riegel, "Marxism-Leninism as a Political Religion", *Totalitarian Movements and Political Religions* 6/1 (2005), p. 111, online at https://www.researchgate.net/publication/333659317_Kopie_von_The_Confession_of_Sins_within_the_Communities_of_virtuosi.
[5] Stalin to Gorki on 26 October 1932, cited in Evan Mawdsley, *The Stalin Years: The Soviet Union, 1929-1953* (Manchester: Manchester University Press, 2003), p. 124. See also Igor Golomstock, *Totalitarian Art in the Soviet Union, the Third Reich, Fascist Italy and the People's Republic of China* (London: Gerald Duckworth & Co., 1990); and Hans Günther's edited *The Culture of the Stalin Period* (Basingstoke: Palgrave, 1990), esp. pp. 78ff.
[6] For useful overviews see, respectively, John Bowlt, ed., *Aleksandr Rodchenko, experiments for the future: diaries, essays, letters, and other writings* (New York: Museum of Modern Art, 2005); and Nancy Perloff and Bryan Reed, eds., *Situating El Lissitsky: Issues & Debates* (Los Angeles: Getty Research Institute, 2003).
[7] Hayley Card, "Special Report: The Tate Modern's *USSR in Construction*", *Totalitarian Movements and Political Religions* 8/1 (2007), pp. 149-52.
[8] Victor Margolin, "Representing the Regime: Lissitsky and Rodchenko, 1930-1941", *The Struggle for Utopia* (London: University of Chicago Press, 1997), ch. 7. See also Boris Groys, *The Total Art of Stalinism: Avant-garde, Aesthetic Dictatorship, and Beyond* (Princeton: Princeton University Press, 1992).
[9] For use of these synonyms of political religion, see, for example, Uriel Tal on political faith, *Politics and Ideology in the Third Reich: Selected Essays* (Abingdon: Routledge, 2005), pp. 16-54. For analysis more directly related to communism see for instance, Richard J. Arneson, "Marxism and Secular Faith", *The American Political Science Review* 79/3 (September 1985), pp. 627-640; and more recently, Leonid Luks, "Legitimation and repression in the Soviet State", in Uwe Backes and Steffen Kailitz, eds., *Ideocracies in Comparison: Legitimation—Cooptation—Repression* (London: Routledge, 2015), ch. 6.
[10] See, above all, Hans Maier's edited *Totalitarianism and Political Religions*, 3 vols., trans. Jodi Bruhn (Abingdon: Routledge, 2004 [vol. 1] and 2007 [vols. 2 and 3]). See also the fascinating contribution by John Gray's *Black Mass: Apocalyptic Religion and the Death of Utopia* (London: Allen Lane, 2007), which opens: "Modern politics is a chapter in the history of religion. The greatest of the revolutionary upheavals that have shaped so much of the history of the past two centuries were episodes in the history of faith—moments in the long dissolution of Christianity and the rise of modern political religion".
[11] See Emilio Gentile, *Politics as Religion* (Oxford: Princeton University Press, 2006), ch. 1.
[12] Waldemar Gurian, cited in Heinz Hürten, "Waldemar Gurian and the development of the concept of totalitarianism", *Totalitarianism and Political Religions*, vol. 1, ed. Hans Maier (Abingdon: Routledge, 2004), p. 41. See also Hannah Arendt, *The Origins of Totalitarianism* (New York: Harcourt Brace, 1951).
[13] Gurian, "Totalitarian Religions", in the *Review of Politics*, 14/1 (1952), pp. 3-4.

[14] Emilio Gentile, "The Sacralisation of Politics: Definitions, Interpretations and Reflections on the Question of Secular Religion and Totalitarianism", *Totalitarian Movements and Political Religions* 1/1 (2000), p. 19; and Juan Linz, cited in Richard Shorten, "The Status of Ideology in the Return Political Religion Theory", *Journal of Political Ideologies*, 12/2 (2007), p. 167.

[15] An excellent overview of this form of politicised religion can be found in Doris Bergen, *Twisted Cross: The German Christian Movement in the Third Reich* (London: University of North Carolina Press, 1996). See also the stimulating exchange in a special issue of the *Journal of Contemporary History* (42/1, 2007) on Richard Steigmann-Gall's ground-breaking *Holy Reich*. For more general surveys on fascism and Christianity, see Matthew Feldman and Marius Turda with Tudor Georgescu, eds., *'Clerical Fascism' in Interwar Europe* (London: Routledge, 2008).

[16] Nikolai Berdyaev, cited in *Totalitarianism and Political Religions*, Hans Maier, ed., vol. 2, pp. 84-5.

[17] Gentile (2000), pp. 11, 13.

[18] More extensive coverage of this issue is given in "'Political Religion'—a religion? Some remarks on the concept of religion", *Totalitarianism and Political Religions*, Hans Maier, ed., vol. 2, pp. 225-45.

[19] William James, *Varieties of Religious Experience: A Study in Human Nature* (London: Fontana Books, 1963), pp. 50, 53-4. For a far more recent account, largely in keeping with James' view, see Ann Taves, *Religious Experience Reconsidered* (Oxford: Princeton University Press, 2009), especially chs. 1 and 2.

[20] This is Stefan Malinowski's 1925 characterization, cited in Leslie Armour, "Knowledge, values and ideas: rethinking the notion of a social science", in the *International Journal of Social Economics* 30/1-2 (2003), p. 57.

[21] Durkheim, cited in Alexander Tristan Riley, *Godless Intellectuals?* (Oxford: Berghahn, 2010), p. 152. See also W.S.F. Pickering, ed., *Durkheim on Religion* (Atlanta: Scholars Press, 1994).

[22] See the contrast between, for instance, Cynthia Ruder, *Making History for Stalin: The Story of the Belomor Canal* (Gainesville, FL: University Press of Florida, 1998) and Maxim Gorki, ed., *Belomor: An Account of the Construction of the New Canal between the White Sea and the Baltic Sea* (Westport, CT: Hyperion Press, 1977 [1934]).

[23] To see a number of examples online for *SSSR na Stroika*, see the following (all websites last accessed 22 February 2020): www.drawingmatter.org/drawings/fantasy-reality/ussr-construction-no-9-1931/; https://library2.usask.ca/USSRConst/; and https://davidcampany.com/ussr-construction-no-12-baltic-white-sea-canal-1933-alexander-rodchenko/; and https://library2.usask.ca/USSRConst/about; www.flickr.com/photos/joeclark/sets/72157594320125220/. Other items from the Russian journal *Sovetskoe Foto* (Soviet Photography) also reveal the avant-garde and, more specifically, photomontage objects produced in the USSR; for example, see: www.moma.org/interactives/objectphoto/publications/785.html; https://petapixel.com/2017/03/21/can-browse-437-complete-issues-soviet-photo-magazine-online/; and www.openculture.com/2017/03/download-437-issues-of-soviet-photo.html.

[24] For some explorations of the term 'modernism', see insightful surveys by Susan Stanford Friedman, "Definitional Excursions: The Meanings of Modern/Modernity/Modernism", *Modernism/modernity* 8/3 (September 2001), pp. 493-513; and Peter Childs, *Modernism* (London: Routledge, 2000), pp. 1-25.

[25] Christina Lodder, *Russian Constructivism* (New Haven: Yale University Press, 1983), p. 3.

[26] *Ibid.*, p. 1.

[27] Miriam Hässler, "Moscow Merz and Russian Rhythm: Tracking Vestiges of the *Erste Russische Kunstausstellung*, Berlin, 1922", *Experiment: A Journal of Russian Culture* 23/1 (2017), pp. 117-126, available online at https://brill.com/view/journals/expt/23/1/article-p117_117.xml.

[28] Peter Holquist, "State Violence as Technique: The Logic in Violence in Soviet Totalitarianism", in David L. Hoffman ed., *Stalinism: The Essential Readings* (Oxford: Blackwell, 2003), pp. 134, 155.

[29] "October—Association of Artistic Labor Declaration, 1928", as cited in John E. Bowlt ed., *Russian Art of the Avant-Garde* (London: Thames and Hudson, 1988) p. 279.

[30] El Lissitsky, "Suprematism in World Reconstruction, 1920", cited in *ibid.*, p. 158.

[31] Amongst many works on the subject, see J. Arch Getty and Oleg Naumov, *The Road to Terror: Stalin and the Self-Destruction of the Bolsheviks* (London: Yale University Press, 1999).

[32] See Chonghoon Lee, 'Visual Stalinism from the Perspective of Heroisation: Posters, Paintings and Illustrations in the 1930s", *Totalitarian Movements and Political Religions* 8/3-4 (2007), pp. 503-521.

[33] Aleksei Gan, "Constructivism" in *Russian Art of the Avant-Garde*, ed. Bowlt, pp. 221-2. The Constructivist playwright Sergei Tret'iakov's appreciation of Futurism, written around the time of the launch of the *USSR in Construction*, is also relevant in terms of propaganda: "Propaganda about forging the new human being is essentially the only content of the works of the Futurists, who without this leading idea invariably turn into verbal acrobats ...what guided Futurism from the days of its infancy was not the creation of new paintings, verses and prose, but the production of a new human being through art, which is one of the tools of such production"; cited in Groys, *The Total Art of Stalinism*, p. 37.

[34] See, for example, Detlef Mühlberger, *Hitler's Voice: The Völkischer Beobachter 1920-1933*, 2 vols. (Bern: Peter Lang, 2005); Christoph Classen, "Thoughts on the Significance of Massmedia Communications in the Third Reich and the GDR", *Totalitarian Movements and Political Religions* 8/3-4 (2007), pp. 547-562; and Daniel Schönpflug, "*Histoires croisées:* François Furet, Ernst Nolte and a Comparative History of Totalitarian Movements", *European History Quarterly* 37/2 (2007), pp. 265-290.

[35] Issues 9, 10, 11, 12, September, October, November, December (combined) 1937.

[36] Yakov Chernikhov, "From "The Formations of Construction": Conclusion and Inferences' in Bowlt, ed., *Russian Art of the Avant-Garde*, pp. 260-1.

[37] For a brilliant synthesis on the totalitarian "new man", see Peter Fritzsche and Jochen Hellbeck, "The New Man in Stalinist Russia and Nazi Germany", in Sheila Fitzpatrick and Michael Geyer, eds., *Beyond Totalitarianism: Stalinism and Nazism Compared* (Cambridge: Cambridge University Press, 2008), ch. 8.

21. Samuel Beckett's Nominalist Politics and the Pitfalls of 'Presentism'

This chapter proposes to reappraise the subject of 'Beckett and Politics'. For this 'think piece', that much-contested term, politics will be viewed as 'high politics', to paint the canvas broadly (perhaps not broadly enough, some will object). 'High politics', or what's sometimes called 'geopolitics', are those big tectonic plates of international relations; of central types and objectives of domestic governance; and in the 20th century Europe to which Beckett was a traumatised witness: totalitarianism; total war; genocide; all unthinkable previously—and scarcely thinkable since. Considering Beckett's politics, in short, also means considering the revolutionary politics of Europe during his lifetime[1]—a historicist proposition, to be sure, and one that forms the backdrop to the ensuing points on Beckett, politics and finally, 'post-Holocaust art'.

First of all, this is emphatically *not* to simply dismiss *ex post facto* political engagements with Beckett's universalised message as apolitical or heuristically inferior. In the words of the 1969 Nobel Prize presentation speech: Beckett's art was often received at the time—and since—as a 'muffled minor key sounding liberation to the oppressed, and comfort to those in need.'[2] That claim entails surely more than just political liberation, narrowly understood. As Peter Boxall sagely puts it, this is due in no small amount to the 'nuanced political and critical difficulties posed by Beckett's writing'.[3] It is precisely the oft-cited openness of Beckett's work that has enabled cutting-edge inquiries via Queer Theory and Post-Colonialism, to take just two, or scholarship on Beckett and disability, mental health or the non-human. Representations of gender, ethnicity or the body—especially as they relate to Beckett's drama—and other forms of social identity are intensely political, it scarcely needs to be said. Indeed, some of the most fruitful theoretical work in Beckett Studies is taking place from just these perspectives. Admittedly, however, this is far removed from my focus in this short text.

In terms of 20th century 'high politics' I want to suggest that there are two main paradigms for approaching 'Beckett and politics', before attempting to sketch the outlines of a third. The first is probably the most common, which holds that Beckett is an 'apolitical' writer. In this view, his writing lacks overtly 'political' engagements; he's the quintessential 'absurdist', 'nihilist' or aloof artist; he wasn't a card-carrying anything; in short, Beckett is the antithesis of contemporary Laureates like Harold Pinter or Aleksandr Solzhenitsyn (the latter receiving the Nobel Prize in 1970, the year after Beckett). This broadside should be familiar to all, and likewise I will not engage much with it here. A better start, in contrast, is a revealing excerpt from the hand of the Socialist Worker's Party (SWP), which did a wide-ranging piece for Beckett's centenary in April 2006:

> Beckett is charged with the celebration of nihilism, despair and pessimism. His work is seen to represent the antithesis of any progressive political engagement.
> Georg Lukács, the Marxist literary critic and theorist, accused Beckett of portraying "the utmost pathological human degradation". The experimental writer Bertolt Brecht also despised Beckett's artistic vision, at one point planning to write a counterattack to the play Waiting for Godot.
> Sean O'Casey, the left wing Irish dramatist, wrote of Beckett's work, "there is no hazard of hope, no desire for it, nothing in it but a lust for despair"—and declared that he would have nothing to do with him.
> Another left wing writer, Dennis Potter, identified the instincts in Beckett's work with the moral deformities that created the concentration camps and gulags: "Is this the art which is the response to the despair and pity of our age, or is it made of the kind of futility which helped such desecrations of the spirit, such filth of ideologies come into being?"
> I want to argue that taking such a view is to profoundly misunderstand both Beckett the man and his work.[4]

This is an important break with the more familiar far left reduction; namely: Beckett equals wallowing in human degradation equals bourgeois apoliticism. This is exemplified by Jean-Paul Sartre's take during his years of political partisanship for Soviet communism:

> Beckett's work was "profoundly, essentially, bourgeois in content":
> Take Beckett. I like *Waiting for Godot* very much. I go so far as to regard it as the best thing that has been done in the theatre for thirty years. But all the themes in Godot are bourgeois—solitude, despair, the platitude, incommunicability. All of them are a product of the inner solitude of the bourgeoisie. And it matters little what Godot may be— God or the Revolution. [...] What counts is that Godot does not come because of the heroes' inner weakness; that he cannot come because of their "sin," because men are like that.[5]

Mistaken as I think this is, there is an instructive truism buried here: ideological types tend to know their own. And Beckett was certainly no Stalinist; in fact, the two characters in *Waiting for Godot* were initially presented as the 'Stalinist comedians'—sort of 'release valves' in the totalitarian USSR; a pseudo-couple who were able to publicly poke fun at Marshal Stalin. Four years earlier, in 'The End', an unmistakable caricature of communist fanaticism is presented in the figure of an orator 'perched on the roof of a car and haranguing the passers-by. That at least was my interpretation. He was bellowing so loud that snatches of his discourse reached my ears. Union ... brothers... Marx... capital...bread and butter...love. It was all Greek to me.' At the end of this paragraph, the narrator concludes: 'He must have been a religious fanatic, I could find no other explanation. Perhaps he was an escaped lunatic. He had a nice face, a little on the red side.'[6] That is hardly a sympathetic rendering of Marxism.

When it comes to recognising one's ideological confrères, moreover, Beckett has certainly never been claimed by the radical right. This is an unsurprising point for—unlike Sartre, Brecht and most far-left writers—Beckett got his hands dirty standing up to the Third Reich, risking life and limb in the French Resistance (for which Beckett later received the *Croix de Guerre*). Briefly, a good example of that radical right canon, underscoring my suggestion that ideological partisans recognise their comrades, comes from 2002; via a literary-minded neo-fascist from New Zealand named Kerry Bolton. Now, there are of course exceptions to ideological leopard-spotting—such as the astonishing left-wing literary-critical engagement with fascists like Heidegger or Carl Schmitt, to name just two—but whether you agree with my contention or not, there can be no doubt Beckett is not considered one of Bolton's (or others') *Thinkers of the Right*.[7]

The Marxist critic Terry Eagleton would have us believe that, '[u]nusually among modernist artists, this supposed purveyor of nihilism was a *militant of the left rather than the right*'; indeed, 'Beckett's is *an art born in the shadow of Auschwitz*'.[8] This article will return to the 'shadow of Auschwitz' assertion below conclusion, but for the moment I think it safer to posit that the *opposite* of Eagleton's view is closer to the mark: that Beckett's politics were un-militant, even anti-militant. That raises the second view, probably shared by most Beckett scholars: that Beckett was 'pink'; 'near left' rather than far-left, a reforming social democrat rather than a communist revolutionary. This political outlook might be characterised as a moderate, not Marxist leftism prioritising human liberation and equality. I suspect that most Beckett specialists hold this view, and with good reason (not least as it probably describes most of Beckett Studies politically).

Famously, his response to Nancy Cunard's *Authors Take Sides on the Spanish Civil War* was one word: UPTHEREPUBLIC!; two years later Beckett fell out with MacGreevy over the latter's nationalistic portrayal of Jack Yeats. He had seen enough nationalism visiting Fascist Italy in the 1920s and Nazi Germany in the 1930s, and about as far as he would go was an interwar notebook bearing the inscription on the cover: 'Irish Free State' (notwithstanding Beckett's Protestant, middle-class background). Forty years later to Mel Gussow he simply remarked 'Get the British out of Ireland', in reference to the 'Troubles' in Northern Ireland on 2 July 1985.[9]

In between these decades, we are given artistic portrayals that might today be characterised as 'progressive', such as what Peter Murphy calls the satirical rendering of Moran as a 'petty bourgeois tyrant' in *Molloy*,[10] or the lampooning of authority figures more generally, like Civic Guard in *Murphy* or moronic Garda encountered a decade later in *Mercier and Camier*. In a more allegorical hue, Pim Verhulst has made a compelling case that the backdrop of the bloody war in Algeria may have inspired the torture portrayed in *Rough for Theatre II*, concluding: 'Even though the play is not directly about the historical events, their influence proves that Beckett was not entirely aloof from the political issues of his time'.[11] Verhulst is right of course: Beckett kept up to date with the news, even on holiday, and preferred broadly left-wing sources of daily information (but not exclusively). His partner Suzanne was comfortably on the far-left—while his friends and contacts in Paris seem to have been largely drawn from the left rather than right. In this context of French use of torture during the Algerian War—which his publisher at Minuit, Jerome Lindon, was actively campaigning against (and whom Beckett helped by storing some censored books)—Verhulst cites a fascinating diary entry from 4 August 1958 by Robert Pinget:

> we talked about torture and the death penalty. At first Sam seemed to find it unacceptable that a person who kills someone in France would be let off with a brief imprisonment, thanks to all kinds of mitigating circumstances. So at first he seemed to be in favor of the death penalty. Violent reaction by Michel. Sam then seemed to side with him, with all of us, who were against it in principle—but very difficult to explain why. Sam then asked if torture could not be justified in some cases. Horrified reaction by Michel. Sam wondered if, for example, our mother or brother or some other dear one was being held captive, in danger of starving to death, would it not be justified to torture the captivator, if it were the only way to rescue our parent. I concurred at once. Michel still protested. *In the end we all agreed it was something one would do instinctively but which could never be justified in general.*[12]

I'll return to the significance this last sentence that I have italicised presently. But first, in this more familiar accounting, politics may be opaquely rendered in Beckett's work, but it is there, universalised and always applicable; a cantankerous humanitarianism. As usual, *Damned to Fame* captures this sense best in the chapter 'Politics and *Company*': 'Even though Beckett's attitudes were *basically left-wing and anti-establishment*', regarding

> the abuse of human rights, censorship, and attacks on individuals by a repressive political regime, his instinctive response was to ask what he could do to help. Mostly this involved making contributions (sometimes quite large ones) to fund-raising organisations and in giving regular support to Amnesty International) [....] It did not matter to him whether the regime perpetrating the oppression was left-wing (like the Communists in Eastern Europe) or right-wing (like the Fascists in Spain or the National Party in South Africa). It was enough that they were behaving with inhumanity, barbarity and injustice.[13]

This passage is provided in the context of Beckett's support for his Polish translator and pro-democracy campaigner, Antoni Libera. Still more famously,

Beckett's 1982 *Catastrophe* was dedicated to the Czech dissident leader of what became known as the 'Velvet Revolution' in 1989, Vaclav Havel (who became the President of Czechoslovakia on 29 December 1989, a week after Beckett's death).[14]

Yet the emergence of Beckett's moderate political stance was long in making, as Knowlson's biography makes clear. What might be called an 'anti-totalitarian left' attitude was traced, in *Damned to Fame*, back to a 'tolerance for religious difference' inculcated before university. This already extended to anti-racist views that were redoubled at Trinity College, Dublin—at that time, remarkably, still flying the Union Jack and not admitting Catholics—under his supervisor, Rudmose-Brown's, 'crucial' effect upon the young Beckett. Drawing from Thomas Rudmose-Brown's memoirs, Knowlson highlights the latter's vocal refusal to take a political side, and its effect upon the late-teenage Beckett: 'I accept no dogma and deny none [....] I am neither Fascist nor Communist, Imperialist nor Socialist'; and moreover, 'I cannot accept the interference of a Church in politics, social economy and ethics.'[15]

Conceived in this way, I think a third option might be discernible, between an apolitical Beckett and a 'soft left' Beckett: humanistic but not partisan, engaged specifically and individually rather than identified with an 'ism'. I want to therefore argue that, more than his contemporaries, Beckett's politics were shaped by the particular and the personal, and each political act or statement demands especial consideration in its own, socio-historical context. I'd like to call what Pinget identified as a politics that wants to ameliorate 'instinctively but which could never be justified in general' (albeit with a historicist caveat), as Beckett's political nominalism.

Let us approach this alternative framework by initially returning to 1936-37, when Beckett was travelling in Nazi Germany. He clearly rejected the racist norms and anti-Semitism there, as Mark Nixon and others have shown.[16] As a particularly insightful 'German Diary' entry from the time emphasises:

> I am not interested in the 'unification' of the historical chaos any more than I am in the 'clarification' of the individual chaos, & still less in the anthropomorphisation of the inhuman necessities that provoke the chaos. What I want is the straws, flotsam, etc., names, dates, births and deaths, because that is all I can know [....] Whereas the pure incoherence of times & men & places is at least amusing. Schicksal = Zufall, for all human purposes [e.g. fate equals coincidence ....] the expressions 'historical necessity' & 'Germanic destiny' start the vomit moving upwards.[17]

Before setting out what this might entail in terms of Beckett's wider politics, the caveat is that the term 'nominalism' is a freighted term. This is the case both philosophically and in Beckett studies. Already in 1983, Ruby Cohn's edited volume of Beckett's marginal writings, *Disjecta*, published the well-known 'German Letter of 1937', which sought 'to compare Nominalism (in the sense of the Scholastics) with Realism. On the way to this literature of the unword, which is so desirable to me, some form of Nominalist irony might be a necessary stage.'[18]

Understood philosophically, nominalism is the medieval doctrine that only individual things exist, not generic classes of things, no abstract entities (species, colours, ideologies, etc.). Nominalism allows only individual things rather than metaphysical concepts: it is countless grains of sand rather than a beach. The latter is associated with realism, or universalism. It seems Beckett was properly introduced to the scholastic debate between nominalism and realism through close note-taking from Wilhelm Windelband's *A History of Philosophy* in the middle 1930s— perhaps the most important text in Beckett's self-taught philosophical education— including a wonderfully Beckettian passage on the radical language scepticism of 'terministic nominalism':

> For this Terministic Nominalism, knowledge of the world refers to the inner states excited by phenomena. Nicolas Cusanus, who committed himself absolutely to this idealistic Nominalism, taught that human thought possesses only conjectures, modes of representation corresponding to its own nature. This awareness of relativity of all positive prediction, this knowledge of non-knowledge, is the docta ignorantia.[19]

As I have set out elsewhere, nominalism is also a discernible feature of Beckett's work long after the 1930s, drawn from his interwar "Philosophy Notes".[20]

Around the time of his 'German Letter of 1937' Beckett was also taking notes on nominalism from other sources. The following is a translation from Beckett's page-long Latin notes from the first of Joseph Gredt's two volume study *Elementa Philosophiae*. The first half, reproduced below, offers a much longer, albeit anachronistic, perspective on nominalism that included many of the figures he had learned about in his "Philosophy Notes":

2. Nominalists: Heraclitus (+475 BC), Cratylus, Heraclitus' disciple, Antisthenes (+369), the Epicureans like Roscellinus (XI century) who was St Anselmus' adversary. The Empiricists, the Sensualists and the Positivists of the most recent periods: Hobbes (1588–1679), Locke (1632–1704), Hume (1711–1776), Condillac (1715–1780), August Comte (1798–1857), Stuart Mill (1806–1873), Spencer (1820–1903), Wundt (1832–1921). They give to "universality" only a mere denominational meaning. In fact, they deny concepts and preach that the term "universal" does not correspond in one's mind to a universal concept, but to a group of individuals already established [....] Realists believe that universals have a correspondence with the individuals in the external reality. Nevertheless, once more we have two different positions: one which believes that the universal exists independently as such (exaggerated realism). The other instead, (i.e. Aristotle (384–322), Boethius (480–525), St Anselmus (1033–1109), St Thomas (1225–1274) and most Scholastics) teaches that we must distinguish two elements: the matter and what contains the universal concept, namely, nature and form. In fact, they teach that universality is present not only in the intellect but also in the singular object (moderate realism).[21]

After I presented some of my work on Beckett's archival engagements with nominalism at the 2011 *Samuel Beckett: Out of the Archive* conference, Shane Weller posed the question as to whether a 'politics of nominalism' could also apply to Beckett. Upon reflection, it might look something like Andrew Gibson's 'minimalist' intellectual study, especially the provocatively titled introduction, 'Fuck Life'. For Gibson, 'Beckett's art repeatedly turns towards *minima*', and any biographical approach needs to be 'respectful of that scepticism' so suffusing Beckett's temperament. It ought also to evince an awareness of the 'specificity of difficulty, suffering and waste' personified by his characters: the "life" with which they struggle or against which they set their face turns out to be, not a universal expressed in a particular form, but a particular form taken for a universal one'. Accordingly, Gibson's sensible biographical solution is to situate Beckett's life 'in relation to a succession of discrete contexts'.[22]

Gibson's minimalist approach fits well with Beckett's intellectual outlook, characterised by *Damned to Fame*, in part, as having a love of 'tiny verifiable details of individual human lives and [which] had no time for broad sweeping analyses of motives or movements.'[23] I think it also helps us to make a broader sense of Beckett's politics: a succession of isolated engagements rather than overarching 'sides' or 'ideologies' or organisational strategies. Put simply, if 'life is fucked' anyway, one response is to reject all labels and try to comfort our fellow galley-slaves as best we can—and not by taking some general position that is 'left' or 'right', 'radical' or 'moderate'. For Beckett, already by his late 20s this meant responding to specific needs and specific contexts.

Yet for any 'political nominalism' to be effective, that latter term, 'contexts', is all the more crucial. Attending to historical circumstances with care, above all, entails an awareness of the dangers of 'presentism'; that is, of projecting our current values and preferences onto the past.[24] For example, our objecting to the misogyny in some of Beckett's early writings—for instance, think of Celia the goddess-whore in *Murphy*—needs to be contextualised. To be more than simply patting ourselves on the back for being so 'right on' today, such a view must at least take into account just how prevalent those social attitudes were at the time. To take but one example, Beckett lived in France for several years before women received the right to vote there. Gender bias is unacceptable, but that was far from the case for most of the 20th century, in Europe and beyond.

On the other hand, avoiding 'presentism' also underscores just how ahead of its time, say, Beckett's 'poem to music' for Henry Crowder was in 1930, or how 'political' was Beckett's decision to translate some 63,000 words from 19 texts for Crowder's partner, Nancy Cunard's, *Negro Anthology* (the second most prolific contributor translated five)[25]. Rightly, it should be noted that the word 'negro' burns our ears; it's a slur today: but not 80 years ago. That's the key point and pitfall regarding 'presentism'.

Parenthetically, it must be restated, that is *not* to say that current concerns around, say, the politics of staging Beckett, the non-human, sexuality and so on are somehow invalid or less intellectually worthwhile—it is simply a different subject from that addressed here. When handled sensitively, political *contextualization* can be enormously productive. A good instance is the African-American cast of *Waiting for Godot* staged after Hurricane Katrina devastated parts of New Orleans. Or again, just to stick with *Waiting for Godot*, Susan Sontag's production in a Sarajevo under siege in 1993 was dubbed "Waiting for Clinton". She said simply: "Beckett's play, written over 40 years ago, seems written for, and about, Sarajevo".[26]

But 'presentism' becomes not just anachronistic but downright misleading in other sensitive contexts. Think of what has been all too loosely called Beckett's 'post-Holocaust' art. Since this is quite popular at present, I think addressing some of the underlying assumptions is necessary. Most of the works so concerned focus upon Beckett's breakthrough 'siege in the room' between roughly 1945 and 1953. To choose a forerunner here, the first chapter of David Houston Jones's 2008 *Samuel Beckett and Testimony* is taken with *The Unnamable* and *Texts for Nothing*; moreover, the very first page notes that 'Vladimir in *En attendant Godot* originally appears under the name Levy: the Jewish identity'. This, in turn, underscores the nature of 'Beckettian testimony, and equally pervades discussions of post-Holocaust art.'[27] Jackie Blackman goes still further in 'Beckett's Theatre: "After Auschwitz"', positing that 'the engagement with the Holocaust in Beckett's work figuratively recasts Beckett as a "survivor" and "witness" of "Auschwitz"'.[28]

Such a contention must be 'figurative', of course, since Beckett never visited Auschwitz—nor for that matter, did he ever visit Poland, where the Nazi death camps were all placed. Nor was he one of the 5% of Holocaust survivors who passed under the *Arbeit Macht Frei* gates and survived, unlike the 1.1 million other victims, overwhelmingly Jewish, at Auschwitz-Birkenau (that is, the name of the whole complex; Birkenau was where all but one of the gas chambers and crematoria were located).

Rhys Tranter published an excellent, even-handed review of the most recent and ambitious of these works, *Beckett's Creatures: Art of Failure after Holocaust*, which 'allows us to rethink the writer's complex negotiation with the Holocaust, and the failure of meaning that arose in its wake.'[29] Therein, like most scholarship on Beckett's 'post-Holocaust art', Joseph Anderton focusses 'upon *Molloy, Malone Dies, The Unnamable, Waiting for Godot* and *Endgame* since these texts are central to the Beckett canon, contemporaneous with the immediate post-Holocaust cultural milieu.' This is because 'Beckett's enduring texts are broadly recognized in relation to the author's wartime experiences and the Holocaust', especially those 'pertinent conditions or states made apparent by the catastrophe whilst having repercussions for the status of art and the human "after the Holocaust"'.

I think we need to be very careful in drawing these relations and repercussions—and not just for Beckett's (putative) 'nominalist politics', but for both 'historicizing' and theorizing more generally. During Beckett's aforementioned 'frenzy of writing', for one, only two transnational studies had appeared on the Shoah; the first appearing in French by Léon Poliakov in 1951 as *Bréviaire de la haine: Le IIIe Reich et les Juifs* (later translated as *Harvest of Hate*); and the second by Gerald Reitlinger in 1953, using the Third Reich's term for the 'Endlösung der Judenfrage', *The Final Solution: The Attempt to Exterminate the Jews of Europe, 1939-1945*. Even if most knew that Jews were singled out by Nazi racism, their genocidal plan for a 'judenfrei' Europe was simply not generally known at the time. Rather, the public impression was that the Nazi occupation was hell on earth for everyone—especially gays, leftists, Jews and other 'undesirables' targeted by the Third Reich, such as asylum patients—and not, as we now know, a parallel war against Jews and other civilians centered in central Eastern Europe (particularly the 'Bloodlands', in Timothy Snyder's memorable term, suffering double wartime occupation under Nazi and Soviet regimes).

This sense of a general inferno in 'les camps' rather than a specific, genocidal plan to murder Europe's estimated 11 million Jews was pervasive right through the 1950s, especially in postwar France: the evidence supporting our current explanations for the Holocaust simply was not there. In fact, the term 'Holocaust' itself, as it relates to the genocide of European Jewry—often these days expanded to include the millions of other civilians killed by the Third Reich during WWII—was only credited to Elie Wiesel in 1958; that is, a year after the opening of *Fin de Partie* at the Royal Court Theatre. A revealing example of this undifferentiated understanding is Alain Resnais's 1955 *Nuit et Brouillard* (*Night and Fog*; based on the 1941 Nazi decree *Nacht und Nebel*, licensing the Gestapo to arrest whoever they wanted in dead of night). In this celebrated 32-minute film, there is no recognition that 72,000 French Jews—more than all other targeted groups in France combined—were killed in (mostly) Auschwitz-Birkenau due, in part, to French collaboration; nor that the Nazi 'imaginary' viewed these groups as *more* marked for death than, say, socialists or Freemasons.[30]

In fact, historians really date the start of 'Holocaust studies' to the early 1960s, around the time of the Eichmann Trial in Jerusalem, and the publication of Raul Hilberg's widely-read masterpiece *The Destruction of the European Jews*. In the early 1960s, according to Deirdre Bair, Beckett 'replied to Kay Boyle, trying to remain noncommittal in response to her impassioned demand for his opinion of the Adolf Eichmann trial. As far as Beckett was concerned he had made his last political statement when he killed rats at St Lo'.[31] The latter was, of course, the context for Beckett's short piece on 'the time honored conception of humanity in ruins' for radio in 1946, 'The Capital of the Ruins', deriving from his postwar work with the Irish Red Cross Hospital in war-torn Normandy.[32]

Put simply, for nearly a generation after 1945, there was no 'Holocaust' as we conceive it today. To describe Beckett's work as engaging with the Holocaust mistakenly elides this point, and invests him and other contemporaries with a knowledge that simply was not available at the time. As late as 1984, tellingly, in thanking Gottfried Büttner for sending him a photographic text on the Warsaw Ghetto, Beckett merely remarked about 'that hellish place at that hellish time'.[33] Such a view, even into the 1980s, was standard fare across Europe, and only really started to deepen after Beckett's death, with the dissolution of the USSR and the opening of Soviet archives in the 1990s.[34]

By way of conclusion, I want to stress again that the temptation of eliding unprecedented genocide and Beckett's experiences of WWII into the mistitled container 'Holocaust experiences', is not the same as political recontextualization or appropriation. As it happens, starting with Adorno and other exiles (who had access to wartime information that occupied Europe did not) a number of writers on the historical Holocaust have championed Beckett's art in—to use the Pulitzer Prize winning Saul Friedländer's phrase—*Probing the Limits of Representation*. In a paradigm-shifting collection of that title, Friedländer characterizes the Holocaust as "an event which tests our traditional conceptual and representational categories, an "event at the limits" [....] there are limits to representation *which should not be but can easily be transgressed.* Intriguingly, Friedländer cites Paul Celan's poetry and Lanzmann's *Shoah* as instances where "the unsayable is almost directly presented", in a form of *"allusive or distanced realism"*, clearly his preference for artistically presenting the Final Solution: "Reality is there in its starkness, but perceived through a filter: that of memory (distance in time), that of spatial displacement, that of some sort of narrative margin which leaves the unsayable unsaid."[35]

To be clear, that is far removed from applying today's values and understandings to the past. The temptations of 'presentism', then, are incommensurate with the contextual, limited and specific nature of Beckett's—and most of the world's—immediate postwar knowledge about the Holocaust and the Second World War's aftermath. We are only properly learning about much of it now, and even then so much cannot be said. In any case, attending to these contexts, limits and specificities, it seems to me, is what the politics of nominalism might look like in Beckett Studies.

In closing, how might this be applied in terms of the above example of the Holocaust? For one, rather than projecting backwards our contemporaneous understandings of the Holocaust onto Beckett's attempt to turn what he called his 'dereliction, profoundly felt, into literature'—declared in 1937; not 1947 or 1957! —it might highlight his discrete experiences and relationships in their fixed and spectral historical milieu.[36] In this spirit, it bears noting that it was Beckett's friend and fellow Joycean assistant, the French Jew Alfred Péron, who brought Beckett into the Gloria French resistance group. Péron was later arrested under the aforementioned *Nacht und Nabel* decree on 14 August 1942, and sent from Paris to Mauthausen in German-annexed Austria—a concentration camp, that is, rather than an extermination camp (the latter all located in Poland). In Beckett *Remembering / Remembering Beckett*, he described the horrific aftermath as follows

> After the war, it was terrible! The forces just opened the extermination camps as they came through. They had nothing to eat, those of them who were left alive. So there was cannibalism. Alfred wouldn't do it. Amazingly he got as far as Switzerland and then he died of malnutrition and exhaustion [on 1 May 1945; the day Hitler's suicide was announced]. After the war we saw quite a bit of Mania, Alfred's widow.[37]

Rather than standing for 'Jews' as a whole, in an event poorly understood in the 1940s and 1950s, I think this affectionate, specific relationship is more likely the source for the early titling of Vladimir as 'Levy' in *Waiting for Godot*.

And as with that breakthrough play for Beckett, the message was universalized, but the creative impetus may well have come from personal experience; not owing as much to big terms like 'left' or 'anti-fascist'—or even French Resistor and Holocaust 'witness'—but as a sensitive individual driven to respond to the horror of specific lives and victims like Péron. I think attending to such searing moments across Beckett's *oeuvre* is, ultimately what a nominalist politics might look like. Rather than displacing apoliticism or 'pinko' sensitivities, characterizing Beckett's politics as nominalist, I hope, offers the possibility of bridging those very different approaches—through a historicizing spirit placing at the forefront those 'demented particulars' of which Beckett was so fond.

Endnotes

[1] A good overview from a left-wing perspective is Eric Hobsbawm's *The Age of Extremes: The Short Twentieth Century, 1914-1991* (London: Abacus, 1996). A more recent and neutral account is offered by Konrad Jarausch's Beckettian-entitled *Out of Ashes: A New History of Europe in the Twentieth Century* (Princeton: Princeton University Press, 2016); see also P.M.H. Bell, *Twentieth Century Europe: Unity and Division* (London: Hodder Arnold, 2006), and Eric Brose, *A History of Europe in the Twentieth Century* (Oxford: Oxford University Press, 2005).

[2] See the "1969 Award Ceremony Speech" delivered by Karl Ragnar Gierow of the Swedish Academy, online at: www.nobelprize.org/nobel_prizes/literature/laureates/1969/press.html (all websites last accessed 27 February 2020).

[3] See Peter Boxall, "Samuel Beckett: Toward a Political Reading", *Irish Studies Review* 10/2 (2002), p. 159.

[4] Sinead Kennedy, "Samuel Beckett: Poet of Pessimism or Herald of Resistance?", 8 August 2006, *Socialist Workers*, online at: https://socialistworker.co.uk/art/8440/Samuel+Beckett%3A+poet+of+pessimism+or+herald+of+resistance.

[5] Jean-Paul Sartre, "People's Theatre and Bourgeois Theater" in Michael Contat and Michel Rybalka, eds., *Sartre on Theater*, trans. F. Jellinek (London: Quartet Books, 1976), p. 51. Still later, in an interview with Kenneth Tynan of 1961 (published in *The Observer* in two parts, on 18 and 25 June 1961), Sartre continued: 'I have not liked Beckett's other plays, particularly *Endgame*, because I find the symbolism far too inflated, far too naked. And although that *Godot* is certainly not a right-wing play, it represents a sort of universal pessimism that appeals to right wing people. For that reason, although I admire it, I have reservations', *ibid.*, p. 128.

[6] Samuel Beckett, 'The End', in S.E. Gontaski ed., *Samuel Beckett: The Complete Short Prose 1929-1989* (New York: Grove Press, 1995), pp. 94-95.

[7] In this rather quixotic list are included Ezra Pound, Wyndham Lewis, Henry Williamson, D. H. Lawrence, H. P. Lovecraft, Gabriele D'Annunzio, Filippo Marinetti, W. B. Yeats, Knut Hamsun and Roy Campbell. See Kerry Bolton, *Artists of the Right: Challenging Materialism* (Luton, England: Luton Publications, 2003).

[8] Cited in Terry Eagleton, "Champion of Ambiguity", *The Guardian*, 20 March 2006, online at: www.theguardian.com/commentisfree/2006/mar/20/arts.theatre; see also Terry Eagleton, "Political Beckett", *The New Left Review* 40 (July-August 2006).

[9] Samuel Beckett, cited in Mel Gussow, *Conversations with and about Beckett* (New York: Grove Press, 1996), p. 52.

[10] Peter Murphy, *Beckett's Dedalus: Dialogical Engagements with Joyce in Beckett's Fiction* (London: University of Toronto Press, 2009), p. 191.

[11] Pim Verhulst, *The Making of Samuel Beckett's Radio Plays: Interpretative Implications of Reading and Writing Traces* (Doctoral Thesis: University of Antwerp, 2014), p. 124.

[12] Robert Pinget, cited in *ibid.*, p. 123; italics added.

[13] James Knowlson, *Damned to Fame* (London: Bloomsbury, 1996), p. 641; italics added.

[14] For further discussion of *Catastrophe*, see Paul Stewart, "The Politics of Form in Samuel Beckett's Late Theatre and Prose", *European Journal of English Studies* 20/3 (2016), pp. 264ff.

[15] Thomas Rudmose-Brown, cited in Knowlson, *Damned to Fame*, p. 50.

[16] See Mark Nixon, *Samuel Beckett's German Diaries 1936-37* (London: Continuum, 2011); see also James McNaughton, "Beckett, German fascism and history: The Futility of Protest", *Samuel Beckett Today / Aujourd'hui* 15 (2005), pp. 101-115.

[17] Samuel Beckett, 'German Diary' entry of 15 January 1937, cited in *Damned to Fame*, pp. 244-5.

[18] Samuel Beckett to Axel Kaun, 'Germany Letter of 1937', *Disjecta* ed. Ruby Cohn (New York: Grove Press, 1983), pp. 170-173.

[19] Samuel Beckett, Trinity College, Dublin mss 10967/170v-10967/171r, corresponding to Wilhelm Windelband, *A History of Philosophy* (New York: Harper, 1958 [1901]), pp. 342ff.

[20] See Matthew Feldman, *Falsifying Beckett: Essays on Archives, Philosophy and Methodology in Beckett Studies* (Stuttgart: ibidem/New York: Columbia University Press, 2015), ch. 10.

[21] Samuel Beckett, "Philosophy Notes", Trinity College Dublin MS 10971/6/37, corresponding to Joseph Gredt, *Elementa philosophiae Aristotelico-Thomisticae*, 2 vols. (Freiburg: Herder, 1926), pp. 96-97, cited in Matthew Feldman, "Samuel Beckett, Wilhelm Windelband and Nominalist Philosophy", *Falsifying Beckett*, pp. 225-226.

[22] Andrew Gibson, *Samuel Beckett* (London: Reaktion Books, 2010), 'Introduction: Fuck Life', pp. 11, 14ff.

[23] Knowlson, *Damned to Fame*, p. 244.

[24] See Dan Stone, "History and its Discontents", *The Holocaust, Fascism, and Memory: Essays in the History of Ideas* (Basingstoke: Palgrave, 2013), p. 3.

[25] Alan Warren Friedman, ed., *Beckett in Black and Red: The Translations for Nancy Cunard's Negro* (1934) (Lexington: The University Press of Kentucky, 2000), pp. 1-2.

[26] See, for instance, David Smith, "In Godot We Trust", *The Guardian*, 5 March 2009, online at: www.theguardian.com/culture/2009/mar/08/samuel-beckett-waiting-for-godot.

[27] David Houston Jones, *Samuel Beckett and Testimony* (Basingstoke: Palgrave, 2008), pp. 1-2.

[28] Jackie Blackman, "Beckett's Theatre 'After Auschwitz'", in Sean Kennedy and Katherine Weiss, *Samuel Beckett: History, Memory, Archive* (Basingstoke: Palgrave, 2009), p. 72.

[29] Rhys Tranter, review of *Beckett's Creatures: Art of Failure after the Holocaust*, by Joseph Anderton, *Studies in Theatre and Performance* 38 1 (Jan, 2018), pp. 97-98 (at 98).

[30] For further discussion, see Peter Hayes and John K. Roth, eds., *The Oxford Handbook of Holocaust Studies* (Oxford: Oxford University Press, 2011), and Matthew Feldman, "Debating Debates in Holocaust Studies", *Holocaust Studies* 6/3 (2011), pp. 156-174.

[31] Deirdre Bair, *Samuel Beckett: A Biography* (London: Picador, 1978), p. 456.

[32] See Samuel Beckett, "The Capital of the Ruins", in *Samuel Beckett: The Complete Short Prose*, p. 278.

[33] Samuel Beckett, cited in Lois More Overbeck, Dann Gunn, Martha Fehsenfeld and George Craig, eds., *The Letters of Samuel Beckett, vol. 4: 1967-1989* (Cambridge: Cambridge University Press, 2015), p. 639.

[34] Tom Lawson, *Debates on the Holocaust* (Manchester: Manchester University Press, 2010), ch. 1.

[35] Saul Friedländer continues, responding to Habermas' well-known position that "Auschwitz has changed the basis for continuity of the conditions of life within human history": "What turns the 'Final Solution' into an event at the limits is the very fact that it is the most radical form of genocide encountered in history: the wilful, systematic, industrially organized, largely successful attempt totally to exterminate an entire human group within twentieth-century Western society", *Probing the Limits of Representation: Nazism and the "Final Solution"* (London: Harvard University Press, 1992), quoted p. 3; italics in original.

[36] Samuel Beckett, German Diary" entry of 2 February 1937, cited in Mark Nixon, *Samuel Beckett's German Diaries*, p. 58.
[37] Samuel Beckett, in *Beckett Remembering / Remembering Beckett*, eds. James and Elizabeth Knowlson (London: Bloomsbury, 2006), p. 86.

Sources List

Chapter 1 (An ideologue's journey: Ezra Pound from tradition in Italian Fascism to the postwar fascist tradition) was originally written as a presentation for the Hebrew University of Jerusalem's workshop, "Tradition, Esoterism and Fascism: Then and Now" held on 29-30 December 2019. It is previously unpublished.

Chapter 2 (The 'Pound Case' in Historical Perspective: An Archival Overview) was originally published in *Journal of Modern Literature* 35.2 (Winter 2012): 83-97. It is available online at www.academia.edu/14687555/Proofs_for_The_Pound_Case_in_Historical_Perspective_An_Archival_Overview.

Chapter 3 (Ezra Pound and Ernst Kantorowicz: From medieval to modern autocracies) was originally published in *Book 2.0*, vol. 8, nos. 1-2 (September 2018), pp. 61-74. Reproduced with permission of The Licensor through PLSclear.

Chapter 4 (Make it crude: Ezra Pound's Antisemitic Propaganda for the BUF and PNF) was originally published in *Holocaust Studies*, vol. 15, nos. 1-2 (2009), pp. 59-77. Reproduced with permission of Taylor & Francis, https://www.tandfonline.com/.

Chapter 5 (Reappraising the 'Pound Case', 1940-45) was originally published as Chapter 4 of *Ezra Pound's Fascist Propaganda, 1935-45* (Basingstoke: Palgrave, 2013), pp. 65-79. Reproduced with permission of Palgrave Macmillan.

Chapter 6 (Ezra Pound's Political Faith From First to Second Generation; or, "It is 1956 Fascism") was originally published in *Modernism, Christianity and Apocalypse*. Eds. Erik Tonning, Matthew Feldman and David Addyman (Leiden: Brill, 2014), pp. 279-301. It is available online at https://www.academia.edu/14688207/Ezra_Pound_s_Political_Faith_from_First_to_Second_Generation_or_It_is_1956_Fascism. Used by permission of Brill.

Chapter 7 ('Penny-wise…': Ezra Pound's Posthumous Legacy to Fascism, by Andrea Rinaldi and Matthew Feldman), was originally published in *The Post-War Anglo-American Far Right: A Special Relationship of Hate*. Eds. Paul Jackson and Anton Shekhovtsov (Houndmills, Basingstoke, Hampshire: Palgrave Macmillan, 2014), pp. 39-66. Reproduced with permission of Palgrave Macmillan. A version printed in *Sanglap* 1.2 (2015): 1-41 is available online at https://sanglapjournal.files.wordpress.com/2015/01/vol1_no2_rinaldi-feldman.pdf.

Chapter 8 ("Fascism for the Third Millennium": An overview of language and ideology in Italy's CasaPound movement, by Anna Castriota and Matthew Feldman) was originally published in *Doublespeak: The Rhetoric of the Far Right since 1945*. Eds. Matthew Feldman and Paul Jackson (Stuttgart: ibidem-Verlag, 2014), pp. 223-246. It is available online at: www.academia.edu/14688010/_FASCISM_ FOR_THE_THIRD_MILLENNIUM_AN_OVERVIEW_OF_LANGUAGE_AND _IDEOLOGY_IN_ITALY_S_CASAPOUND_MOVEMENT. Reproduced with permission of ibidem-Verlag.

Chapter 9 (The Holocaust in the NDH: Genocide between Political Religion and Religious Politics) was originally published as "The Holocaust in The Independent State of Croatia: Genocide between Political Religion and Religious Politics," www.HolocaustResearchProject.org, ca. November 2008, available online at http://www.holocaustresearchproject.org/essays&editorials/croationholocaust.html. Also published in Croatian as the conclusion to *Nezavisna Drzava Hrvatska: 1941. – 1945.*, ed. and trans. Sabrina Ramet (Zagreb: Alinea, 2009), under the title 'Zaključak: Genocid između političke religije i religijske politike', pp. 215-234.

Chapter 10 (Showing the 'unshowable'?: A Generation of "mainstream" films on the Shoah) was originally published in *Ethics and Poetics: Ethical Recognitions and Social Reconfigurations in Modern Narratives*, edited by Margrét Gunnarsdóttir Champion and Irina Rasmussen Goloubeva (Newcastle upon Tyne: Cambridge Scholars Publishing, 2014), pp. 251-272. Published with the permission of Cambridge Scholars Publishing.

Chapter 11 ("Intellectual" Discourses on the Radical Right: from double-speak to Holocaust denial) was published in an earlier form in part as "Hate-baiting. The radical right and 'fifth column discourse' in European and American democracies today" in *The Journal of Political Criminology*, vol. 1, no. 1 (2015), available online at http://pops.uclan.ac.uk/index.php/JPolCrim/article/view/343/141. Licensed under CC BY 4.0 at https://creativecommons.org/licenses/by/4.0/. In part, as "Practice and Practitioners of Holocaust Denial," Fair Observer, May 14, 2015, available online at https://www.fairobserver.com/region/north_america/practice-practitioners-holocaust-denial-92241/.

Chapter 12 (On radical right mainstreaming in Europe and the US) was originally delivered as a lecture for the Council of Europe's Democracy & Security debates series on 28 April 2017. It was first published as "Far-Right, alt-right, near right: mainstreaming extremes" in the edited volume, *Safe and Free: Democratic Security and Human Rights: Democratic Security Debates at the Council of Europe,*

2015-2017 (Strasbourg: Council of Europe, 2018), pp. 115-124. © Council of Europe.

Chapter 13 (On 'Lone Wolf' Terrorism) appeared in two parts, the first of which appeared as "Breivik's Three Acts of Terrorism," *Society and Space: Environment and Planning D* 30(2) (2012), pp. 193–195, available online at https://journals.sagepub.com/doi/pdf/10.1068/d303. Licensed under CC BY-NC 3.0 at https://creativecommons.org/licenses/by-nc/3.0/. It was later expanded into a longer text as "Comparative Lone Wolf Terrorism" in the "Populist Racism and Lone-Wolf Terrorism in Democratic States" Special Issue of *Democracy & Security*, vol. 8, no. 3 (2013), pp. 270-286, available online at https://www.academia.edu/14688383/Proofs_for_Comparative_Lone_Wolf_Terrorism_Toward_a_Heuristic_Definition. Reproduced with permission of Taylor & Francis, https://www.tandfonline.com/.

Chapter 14 (Terrorist 'Radicalising Networks': A Qualitative Case Study on Radical Right Lone-Wolf Terrorism) was originally published in *Expressions of Radicalization: Global Politics, Processes and Practices*, edited by Kristian Steiner and Andreas Önnerfors (Cham: Palgrave Macmillan, 2018), pp. 39-60. Reproduced with permission of Palgrave Macmillan.

Chapter 15 (Choose Definitively Between Hell and Reason) was originally published in *Third Text*, 61/4 (December 2002), pp. 439-449. An extended version of the *Third Text* essay is available online at: www.academia.edu/14687526/Extended_Draft_text_of_Choose_Definitively_Between_Hell_and_Reason. copyright © Third Text reprinted by permission of Taylor & Francis Ltd, http://www.tandfonline.com on behalf of Third Text.

Chapter 16 (The United States Between Liberalism and Warfare before Donald Trump) has not previously been available in English. An Italian translation is available online as "Gli Stati Uniti tra liberalismo e guerra prima di Donald Trump," *Nazioni e Regioni. Studi e ricerche sulla comunità immaginata* 11 (2018), pp. 7-26, trans. Fabio De Leonardis, online at: www.nazionieregioni.it/wp-content/uploads/NR-11-2018.pdf. Licensed under CC BY-NC 4.0 at https://creativecommons.org/licenses/by-nc/4.0/.

Chapter 17 (A failed just war in Iraq) is previously unpublished. It was initially delivered as "Rethinking the Iraq War as a failed Just War" for the 'Religion and Culture' series at Regent's Park College, University of Oxford on 5 November 2015.

Chapter 18 (Between 'Geist' and 'Zeitgeist': Martin Heidegger as ideologue of metapolitical fascism) was originally published in *Totalitarian Movements and Political Religions*, vol. 6, no. 2 (Sept. 2005), pp. 175-198. It is available online at https://archief.socialhistory.org/sites/default/files/docs/feldman.doc. Reproduced with permission of Taylor & Francis, https://www.tandfonline.com/.

Chapter 19 (Hate globally, act locally: A Case Study of Universal Nazism online) was originally published in *Jenseits der Epoche: Zur Aktualität faschistischer Bewegungen in Europa*, eds. Christian Dietrich and Michael Schüßler (Münster: UNRAST, 2011), pp. 89-101. Reproduced with permission of UNRAST Verlag.

Chapter 20 (A Case study in Soviet Political Religion: Modernism and the construction of a Stalinist Utopia) was originally published as "A Case Study in Soviet Political Religion: Modernism, *The USSR in Construction*, and Stalin's Russia," *Religion Compass* vol. 5, no. 11 (November 2011), pp. 685-697. It is available online at https://www.academia.edu/14688697/A_Case_Study_in_Soviet_Politi cal_Religion_Modernism_The_USSR_in_Construction_and_Stalin_s_Russia. Reproduced with permission of John Wiley and Sons.

Chapter 21 (Samuel Beckett's nominalist politics and the pitfalls of 'presentism') is forthcoming in 2020 with Palgrave Macmillan, in a collection entitled *Beckett and Politics*, edited by William Davies and Helen Bailey. Reproduced with permission of Palgrave Macmillan.

***ibidem**.eu*